INTERNATIONAL COMMERCIAL SALES: THE SALE OF GOODS ON SHIPMENT TERMS

LLOYD'S COMMERCIAL LAW LIBRARY
Series Editors: Robert Merkin and Hakeem Seriki

Commercial Agents and the Law
Severine Saintier and Jeremy Scholes

Freezing and Search Orders
Fourth edition
Mark S.W Hoyle

The Practice and Procedure of the Commercial Court
Sixth edition
Anthony Colman, Victor Lyon and Philippa Hopkins

Financial Crisis Management and Bank Resolution
Edited by John Raymond LaBrosse, Rodrigo Olivares-Caminal and Dalvinder Singh

Deceit
The Lie of the Law
Peter MacDonald Eggers

EU Competition Law and the Financial Services Sector
Andrea Lista

Civil Jurisdiction and Judgments
Sixth edition
Adrian Briggs

Foreign Currency
Claims, Judgements and Damages
Michael Howard, John Knott and Howard Kimbell

Vitiation of Contractual Consent
Peter MacDonald Eggers

Conduct and Pay in the Financial Services Industry
The regulation of individuals
Thomas Ogg and Richard Leiper

Contractual Estoppel
Alexander Trukhtanov

For more information about this series, please visit:
www.routledge.com/Lloyds-Commercial-Law-Library/book-series/LCLL

INTERNATIONAL COMMERCIAL SALES: THE SALE OF GOODS ON SHIPMENT TERMS

BY

ANDREA LISTA

LL.D (Italy), LL.M (Soton) PhD (Lond)
Associate Professor in Commercial Law, University of Exeter
Legal Consultant SLIG Law LLP, London

Routledge
Taylor & Francis Group
LONDON AND NEW YORK

First published 2018 by Routledge

2 Park Square, Milton Park, Abingdon, Oxon, OX14 4RN

605 Third Avenue, New York, NY 10017

Routledge is an imprint of the Taylor & Francis Group, an informa business

First issued in paperback 2020

British Library Cataloguing-in-Publication Data
A catalogue record for this book is available from the British Library

Library of Congress Cataloging-in-Publication Data
A catalog record has been requested for this book

ISBN: 978-1-138-59302-2 (hbk)
ISBN: 978-0-367-73436-7 (pbk)

Typeset in Plantin
by Apex CoVantage, LLC

To Admiral Rocco Lista

CONTENTS

PREFACE

There would be no wealth without trade, and trade requires a clear and predictable legal framework for its paradigm transactions: the sales of goods on shipment terms.

This book endeavours to bring into sharp relief the challenging principles of international commercial law, and the harsh realities of the marketplace. Every day goods are globally traded between sellers and buyers placed in different countries and different jurisdictions. The long distance between the parties involved in such transactions, and the relative risks related to that, play a pivotal role in international commercial sales. Sales of goods carried by sea, thus, differ quite drastically from domestic sales; the goods will be normally shipped at a port very distant from the buyer, preventing his physical presence at the port of loading. Further, the goods will travel in the custody of a carrier, a party normally quite independent from either trader. Finally, transactions concluded on shipment terms are normally irreversible, in the sense that shipping the goods back to the seller represents an unlikely option for the buyer.

Issues related to the seller's risk of shipping the goods and not being paid, or the possibility that the goods will never reach the buyer (just to mention some), characterise this area of law rendering it very much *sui generis*, specific and rather complex.

Traders around the world very frequently choose English law to govern their contracts, with disputes to be resolved through London arbitration or litigation. The basis of that law is to be found in the English Sale of Goods Act (SOGA) 1979, and this book consequently includes an examination of the fundamental principles of that Act. The book shall also examine in detail and in a comprehensive fashion the entire legal process of international sales of goods, starting from the creation of the contract and continuing through to its fulfilment or termination.

The analysis will start from the creation of the contract and the incorporation of standard terms (Incoterms®, Fosfa, Gafta). Subsequently, the performance of contracts concluded on shipment terms will be object of scrutiny, with specific reference to physical and documentary duties of the seller, transfer of risk, transfer of property, bills of lading and their importance as trading documents, letters of credit as payment method, and remedies for breach of contract.

This book will also devote attention to the 1980 Vienna Convention on International Sales of Goods (CISG) with a view to outlining the differences with English law, together with the consequences for traders in choosing the Vienna Convention over English law as the governing law of the sale contract.

This book shall endeavour, inter alia, to answer the following questions: how does a statute like the SOGA 1979 devised for the sale of goods work where traders sell goods and also negotiate documents through banks; how do the various contracts involved in selling, transporting and financing the goods interrelate; what impact does the English SOGA 1979, originally devised for a domestic market, have upon international legal developments in international trade?

The analysis will start from the case law with the aim of identifying the principles underpinning the law of international sales of goods, so as to unfold the answers to what are very often intricate legal issues revolving around contracts concluded on shipment terms. The narrative of the book will guide the reader through the process of adaptation of domestic English law to international sales of goods. In other words, the reader will be made aware of the evolutionary process of English domestic law, i.e. how English domestic law has been adapted and moulded by the commercial awareness of English courts in order to meet the needs of the international trading community. The book will also provide legal advice for each scenario discussed through the use of practical examples; these will be translated into suggestions for traders on how to avoid unwelcome surprises when drafting contracts for the international sale of goods.

The book is devised for the fruition of legal practitioners, academics and students alike dealing with this area of law.

It is beyond conventional sincerity that I should like to express my gratitude to a numerous and heterogeneous cluster of people to whom I am greatly indebted.

First of all, I am extremely grateful and forever in debt to Ms Johanna Hjalmarsson, Associate Professor at the Law School, University of Southampton, for all her patience, invaluable intellectual and moral support.

Special thanks go to Rebecca Brennan and Caroline Church of Informa Law from Routledge, who respectively followed this book at the beginning and at the end of its process of fruition, for the rare blend of patience and courtesy they used to keep me to schedule.

Many thanks go to Mr Mateusz Beck, former Research Assistant at the Institute of Maritime Law, University of Southampton for assisting me with precious research in the preparation of the manuscript.

I must also extend my gratitude to Mr Charles Debattista, formerly Professor of Maritime Commercial Law at the Institute of Maritime Law, University of Southampton, for igniting in me the passion for this fascinating area of law.

My gratitude also goes to all my past students, at undergraduate and postgraduate level, from the Universities of Southampton and Exeter, for their many questions frequently fundamental for further reflection.

Last, but by no means least, my eternal gratitude goes to my father Admiral Rocco Lista, my mother Mimma Lista, and my brother Dr Ing. Antonello Lista. I have no words to express my gratitude to them; without them and their support, I simply would not be the person that I am today.

The law is stated as of 30 April 2016. The usual disclaimer applies.

Andrea Lista
1/06/2016

TABLE OF CASES

Austria

Germany

Italy

Russia

Singapore

Spain

Switzerland

International Chamber of Commerce

UNCITRAL Texts

TABLE OF LEGISLATION

National Legislation

UK Statutes

Italy

Netherlands

United States

EU Law

Directives

International Treaties and Conventions

International Chamber of Commerce

CHAPTER 1

The sources of contracts concluded on shipment terms

1.1 Introduction

This chapter will introduce the sources of international commercial sales. Emphasis will be placed on English law (case law and the Sale of Goods Act (SOGA) 1979, as amended), and on the Incoterms 2010® ("Incoterms®"), "cost, insurance and freight" (c.i.f.) and "free on board" (f.o.b.) contracts, standard contracts of trading associations (e.g. Fosfa, Gafta), and the Uniform Customs and Practice for Documentary Credits 600 (UCP 600).

The relationship between different sources (e.g. Incoterms® and standard contracts of trading associations) shall be under scrutiny, and the Convention for Contracts for the International Sale of Goods, known as the 1980 Vienna Convention or CISG, will be also introduced as a possible source governing the sale contract if invoked by it.

1.2 The need for a governing law: English law as the new *lex mercatoria*

International commercial sales entail by definition a legal exchange between parties placed in different countries and belonging to different jurisdictions. One of the very basic needs for such kind of transactions is the identification of the law governing the contractual exchange. The final choice on the governing law will depend on a heterogeneous cluster of factors, including the bargaining position of the parties involved; nevertheless, parties to international commercial sales would generally be unwilling to negotiate and discuss the law governing the contract on top of the other terms and conditions of the transaction at stake.

It is, thus, easy to understand the almost primordial need for the identification of a *lex mercatoria*, i.e. a body of laws governing international commercial sales as a consolidated system of common practice.

This need goes a long way back in time. Some authors suggest that the very first *lex mercatoria* is based on *ius gentium*, i.e. the body of Roman law that regulated economic relations between Roman citizens and foreigners.[1]

1 See F.K. Juenger, "The Lex Mercatoria and Private International Law", (2000) *La. L. Rev.* 60. See also N. Hatzimihail, "The Many Lives – And Faces – Of Lex Mercatoria: History as Genealogy in International Business Law", (2008) *Law & Contemp. Probs.* 71(3), 169–190, Duke University School

Other authors claim that the origins of *lex mercatoria* can be traced back even further, to before the Roman Empire, in Ancient Egypt, or even back to Greek and Phoenician trade.[2] This theory appears to be plausible since *lex mercatoria* is used by merchants in international trade, and commercial exchanges in antiquity are considered to have been governed by customary commercial rules.

Nevertheless, the majority of authors suggest that *lex mercatoria* has its origins in the merchant law of the Middle Ages.[3] Back then, the *lex mercatoria* was originally a body of rules and principles laid down by merchants to regulate their dealings.

In England, it was due to Lord Mansfield's genius that the "harmonisation of commercial custom and the common law was carried out with an almost complete understanding of the requirements of the commercial community, and the fundamental principles of the old law and that that marriage of idea proved acceptable to both merchants and lawyers."[4]

Often qualified as transnational law, *lex mercatoria* is considered to be "both a rebirth of medieval merchant law and a new understanding of the concept".[5]

The aforementioned hypothesis according to which *ius gentium* is the precursor to today's *lex mercatoria* has been severely criticised. Some authors question *ius gentium*'s independent status vis-à-vis Roman *ius civile* and state that, since *ius gentium*[6] was part of Roman law rather than an autonomous body of law, it cannot "be conceived as the precursor of today's *Lex mercatoria*".[7]

---

of Law, USA. It is accepted that Roman citizens entered into cross-border commercial relationships and that those transactions were governed by specific rules.

2 Z. Talgatovna Sairambaeva and Z. Mazhitovna Baimagambetova, "The Role of Lex Mercatoria in the Regulation of International Trade Relations", *Middle-East Journal of Scientific Research* 15(6) 790–793.

3 R. Michaels, The True Lex Mercatoria: Law Beyond the State, (2007) *Indiana Journal of Global Legal Studies* 14(2), 447. For a discussion on the use of history in debates about the current *lex mercatoria*, see Nikitas Hatzimihail, "The Many Lives – and Faces – of Lex Mercatoria: An Essay on the Genealogy of International Business Law" (2008) *Law & Contemp. Probs.* 71, 169; Harold J. Berman, *Law and Revolution: The Formation of the Western Legal Tradition* (Harvard University Press, 1983) 332–356 (discussing the rise of mercantile law); see also Mary Elizabeth Basile *et al.* (eds.) *Lex Mercatoria and Legal Pluralism: A Late Thirteenth-Century Treatise and Its Afterlife* (Ames Foundation, 1998) (providing an overview of the concept's history).

4 C.M. Schmitthoff, International Business Law: A New Law Merchant in *Current Law and Social Problems* 2 (1961) 137.

5 See generally L. Yves Fortier, The New, New Lex Mercatoria, or, Back to the Future, 17 *Arb. Int'l* 121 (2001) (describing the emergence of the new, new *lex mercatoria*). The Rt. Hon. Lord Justice Michael Mustill, The New Lex Mercatoria: The First Twenty-Five Years, 4 *Arb. Int'l* 86 (1988). See Andreas Fischer-Lescano and Gunther Teubner, Regime-Collisions: The Vain Search for Legal Unity in the Fragmentation of Global Law, 25 *Mich. J. Int'l L.* 999, 1009–1012 (discussing private legal regimes and their relation to the global legal system).

6 See P. Stein, *Roman Law in European History*, Cambridge University Press, 1999, p.72. In the great span of time during which the Roman Republic and Empire existed, there were many phases of legalistic development. During the period of the Republic (753–731 BC), the *jus civile* (civil law) developed. Based on custom or legislation, it applied exclusively to Roman citizens. By the middle of the third century BC, however, another type of law, *jus gentium* (law of nations), was developed by the Romans to be applied both to themselves and to foreigners. *Jus gentium* was not the result of legislation, but was, instead, a development of the magistrates and governors who were responsible for administering justice in cases in which foreigners were involved. The *jus gentium* became, to a large extent, part of the massive body of law that was applied by magistrates to citizens, as well as to foreigners, as a flexible alternative to *jus civile*.

7 For such a criticism directed at Teubner's concept, see Brigitta Lurger, Der Pluralismus der "lex mercatoria". Anmerkungen zu einem Aufsatz von Gunther Teubner, 16 *Rechtshistorisches J.* 705 (1997). For a political reconceptualisation under an approach closely related to that of systems theory, see

Even though the origins of *lex mercatoria* are vague, it is the opinion of this author that the concept of "*lex mercatoria*" transcends the idea of national or international law. Indeed, the definition of "*lex mercatoria*" could entail the concept of "universal" or "foremost" law governing international commercial sales.

From this perspective, *ius gentium* at the time of the Roman Empire could be defined as the *lex mercatoria* of that time, regardless of the fact that it was a body of laws belonging to Roman law.

Going above and beyond the nomenclature or abstract systems of categorisation, what is important to note is that the need to unify the law governing international private relations has existed since the first transnational commercial transactions.

Indeed, the need to identify the law governing contracts concluded by parties placed in different countries lies at the core of international commercial sales, and since the dawn of transnational commerce, only two possibilities appeared to represent the solution to this atavistic need: either the introduction of an international convention/set of rules devised to govern international commercial sales, or the adoption of a body of laws of a specific country.

This brings us to the next important question: what is the modern *lex mercatoria*? There are currently three bodies of laws competing for that title: English law, American law, and the 1980 Vienna Convention on the international sale of goods, with English law occupying the lion's share as the governing law of international commercial sale transactions.[8]

If it is not unusual for an international sale transaction to be governed by American law (if the bargaining position of American traders so allows), as we shall discover at a later stage in this book, the Vienna Convention on the international sale of goods failed to succeed in its scope of becoming the point of reference for the international sale of goods, and it seldom governs contracts concluded on shipment terms for important commodities such as oil, fats, and gasoil.

What caused English law to succeed in becoming the modern *lex mercatoria* (according to the definition proposed above), largely governing modern international trade as the default law of the standard terms of trading associations of the utmost international relevance such as Fosfa[9] and Gafta?[10]

Since the outset of modern international trade, the commercial awareness of English judges combined with the flexibility of the common law system allowed

---

Peer Zumbansen, Piercing the Legal Veil: Commercial Arbitration and Transnational Law, 8 *Eur. L.J.* 400, 418–421 (2002).

8 This is particularly true when it comes to contracts for the trade of oil, seeds, fats, and gasoil (see footnote below).

9 Formed in 1968, The Federation of Oils, Seeds and Fats Associations (Fosfa International) is the main trade association for the oil, seeds and fats industry. It regulates legal contracts in the industry.

10 The Grain and Feed Trade Association, or Gafta, is an international, London-headquartered trade association consisting of traders, brokers, superintendents, analysts, fumigators, arbitrators and other professionals in the international grain trade. Gafta can trace its origins back to 1878, when the London Corn Trade Association (LCTA) was established by members of the corn trade to protect their interests. The LCTA sought to achieve this through the adoption of standard forms of contract, drawn up by the association, with any disputes arising out of these contracts being settled by arbitration rather than legislation. Disputes were referred to London and conducted under English law.

English law to evolve in such a way as to meet the needs of the international trading community. What is important to emphasise is that, as will be readily appreciated, when it comes to international trade, we are not discussing quintessentially English contract law, but rather English contract law as adapted, moulded by English Courts, so as to become an efficient regulatory framework for these peculiar kinds of transactions.

1.3 The 1980 Vienna Convention on the sale of goods

The United Nations Convention on Contracts for the International Sale of Goods[11] (CISG; the Vienna Convention) is a treaty that is a uniform international sales law.

As of June 2014, it has been ratified by 81 countries that account for a significant proportion of world trade, allegedly making it one of the most successful international uniform laws.[12]

The CISG was developed by the United Nations Commission on International Trade Law (UNCITRAL) and was signed in Vienna in 1980, coming into force as a multilateral treaty on 1 January 1988, after being ratified by 11 countries.[13]

The CISG allows exporters to avoid choice of law issues, as the CISG offers "accepted substantive rules on which contracting parties, courts, and arbitrators may rely".[14]

Unless excluded by the express terms of a contract, the CISG is "deemed to be incorporated into (and to supplant) any otherwise applicable domestic law(s) with respect to a transaction in goods between parties from different contracting states".[15]

The CISG has been regarded as a success for UNCITRAL, as the Convention has been accepted by states from "every geographical region, every stage of economic development and every major legal, social and economic system".[16]

The CISG has been described as a great legislative achievement,[17] and the "most successful international document so far in unified international sales law in part due to its flexibility in allowing contracting states the option of taking exception to certain specified articles."[18]

This flexibility was instrumental in convincing states with disparate legal traditions to subscribe to an otherwise uniform code. A number of countries that have signed the CISG have made declarations and reservations as to the treaty's scope,[19]

---

11 *United Nations Convention on Contracts for the International Sale of Goods*, Vienna, 11 April 1980, S. Treaty Document Number 98–9 (1984), UN Document Number A/CONF 97/19, 1489 UNTS 3.

12 Congo was the most recent state to ratify the Convention, having acceded to it on 11 June 2014.

13 Argentina, China, Egypt, France, Hungary, Italy, Lesotho, Syria, the US, Yugoslavia, and Zambia.

14 US Department of Commerce, *United Nations Convention on Contracts for the International Sale of Goods.*

15 This statement is only applicable for the US, the Czech Republic, and China; See Article 1,1B/95 Verweyen, Foerster, Toufar Handbuch des Internationalen Warenkaufs UN-Kaufrecht (CISG) 2. Auflage, 2008 pt. 21.2, p. 248.

16 Peter Schlechtriem, Requirements of Application and Sphere of Applicability of the CISG (2005) 36 *Victoria University of Wellington Law Review* 781.

17 Bruno Zeller, *CISG and the Unification of International Trade Law* (1st Edition, Routledge, 2007) 94.

18 Joseph Lookofsky, Loose Ends and Contorts in International Sales: Problems in the Harmonization of Private Law Rules (1991) 39 *American Journal of Comparative Law* 403.

19 For a list of signatories and their declarations, see the UNCITRAL website.

though the vast majority – 56 out of the current 81 contracting states – have chosen to accede to the Convention without any reservations, including the US.

For obvious reasons, the Convention has not been ratified by the UK, with English law still being arguably the preferred governing law choice of international traders.

Indeed, despite the high number of ratifications, the Vienna Convention has failed, for reasons which will be fully unravelled at a later stage in this book, to assume a preponderant role as the governing law of contracts concluded on shipment terms.

1.4 Standard terms of common use in international sale transactions

As established above, in light of the US ratification of the Vienna Convention, English law and the Vienna Convention represent the main body of laws which nowadays govern the international sales of goods, with English law occupying the lion's share.

Alongside the need for the identification of a governing law, the complex nature of international commercial sales soon prompted the need for the creation of standard terms devised in order to accelerate the negotiation and ratification of contracts concluded on shipment terms.

We shall now consider the most relevant standard terms, i.e. the Incoterms®, the standard terms of international trading associations (e.g. Fosfa and Gafta terms), and finally the UCP 600, which is destined to play a crucial role in the analysis of documentary credits within the context of international trade.[20]

1.5 The Incoterms®

The International Commercial Terms or Incoterms® rules are a series of pre-defined commercial terms published by the International Chamber of Commerce (ICC) that are widely used in international commercial transactions or procurement processes.

The Incoterms® rules are "accepted by governments, legal authorities, and practitioners worldwide for the interpretation of most commonly used terms in international trade, and the purpose of the Incoterms® is to provide a set of international rules for the interpretation of the most commonly used trade terms in foreign trade, so as to avoid uncertainties which may arise on the basis of different interpretations of such terms in different countries".[21]

Indeed, more often than not, traders are not aware of the different international trading practices which may differ quite dramatically in different countries. This may give rise to misunderstandings, disputes and litigation, and ultimately hinder international commerce.

In order to remedy these problems, the ICC first published in 1936 a set of international rules for the interpretation of trade terms. These rules were known as "Incoterms® 1936". Amendments and additions were later made in various years in order

20 See chapter 11 below.
21 See the ICC website at: iccwbo.com.

to align the rules with modern international trade practices as they evolved in time, with the eighth version, Incoterms 2010®, having been published on 1 January 2011.

It should be emphasised that the sphere of application of the Incoterms® is confined to matters relating to the rights and obligations of the parties to the contract of sale with respect to the delivery of goods sold.

Nevertheless, as we shall discover in the following, the use of a specific Incoterm reverberates its legal consequences vis-à-vis the other contracts involved in that specific transaction. For instance, a seller who agreed to a c.i.f. contract is thereby compelled to a method of performance which invariably entails the carriage of goods by sea as the means of transportation. Indeed, under c.i.f. terms the seller is under the obligation to tender a bill of lading or other maritime document to the buyer which is simply not possible if other means of transportation are entailed.

More specifically, the Incoterms® deal only with a selective number of obligations, e.g. the seller's obligation to place the goods at the disposal of the buyer or hand them over for carriage, or deliver them at their destination. Further obligations, such as clearing the goods for export and import, obligations related to the packaging of the goods, alongside rules related to the transfer of risk between the seller and the buyer, are also enshrined in the Incoterms®.

Nevertheless, a great number of legal issues arising within the context of international commercial sale transactions, such as, inter alia, transfer of property, retention of title, and remedies for breach of contract, are not dealt with by the Incoterms® at all, and must be resolved by other stipulations in the contract of sale and on the basis of the applicable law. In this regard, it is worth noticing that the Incoterms® were not devised in order to cover all the legal aspects of international commercial sales, and attempting to do so would have been a utopian endeavour.

In terms of structure, in 1990, for ease of understanding, the Incoterms® were grouped into four basically different categories; namely, starting with the term whereby the seller only makes the goods available to the buyer at the seller's own premises ("Ex Works" term); followed by the second group, whereby the seller is called upon to deliver the goods to a carrier appointed by the buyer (the "F" terms: FCA, FAS and FOB); followed by the "C" terms where the seller has to contract for carriage, but without assuming the risk of loss of or damage to the goods, or additional costs due to events occurring after shipment and dispatch (CFR, CIF, CPT and CIP); and, finally, the "D" terms whereby the seller has to bear all costs and risks needed to bring the goods to the place of destination (DAF, DES, DEO, DDU and DDP).[22]

The latest version of the Incoterms® outlines 11 rules, and introduced for the first time two brand new rules, "delivered at terminal" (DAT) and "delivered at place" (DAP).

The Incoterms 2010® abandoned the four category partition of the rules, and are now subdivided into two categories only based solely on method of delivery.

---

22 See the ICC official rules for the interpretation of trade terms. Incoterms® 2010. ISBN 92 842 1199 9.

The current classification of the trade terms[23] is outlined in the following:

EXW – ex works (named place of delivery)
Under Ex Works stipulations, the seller makes the goods available at his premises. This term places the maximum obligation on the buyer and minimum obligations on the seller. The Ex Works term is often used when making an initial quotation for the sale of goods without any costs included. EXW means that a buyer incurs the risks for bringing the goods to their final destination.

The seller does not load the goods on collecting vehicles and does not clear them for export. If the seller does load the goods, he does so at the buyer's risk and cost. If parties wish the seller to be responsible for the loading of the goods on departure and to bear the risk and all costs of such loading, this must be made clear by adding explicit wording to this effect in the contract of sale.

The buyer arranges the pick up of the freight from the supplier's designated ship site, owns the in-transit freight, and is responsible for clearing the goods through customs. The buyer is responsible for completing all the export documentation. The cost of goods sold transfers from the seller to the buyer.

FCA – free carrier (named place of delivery)
Under FCA terms, the seller delivers the goods, cleared for export, to the carrier nominated by the buyer at the named place. It should be noted that the chosen place of delivery has an impact on the obligations of loading and unloading the goods at that place.

If delivery occurs at the seller's premises, the seller is responsible for loading, or if delivery occurs at any other place, the seller is not responsible for loading. In case the buyer nominates a person other than a carrier to receive the goods, the seller is deemed to have fulfilled his obligation to deliver the goods when they are delivered to that person.

CPT – carriage paid to (named place of destination)
CPT terms entail that the seller pays for carriage. Risk transfers to the buyer upon handing goods over to the first carrier at the place of shipment in the country of export.

The shipper is responsible for origin costs including export clearance and freight costs for carriage to the named place (usually destination port or airport). The shipper is not responsible for buying insurance and for delivery to the final destination (buyer's facilities).

This term is used for all kind of shipments.

CIP – carriage and insurance paid to (named place of destination)
This is the containerised transport/multimodal equivalent of CIF. The seller pays for carriage and insurance to the named destination point, but the risk passes

23 International Chamber of Commerce, Incoterm® 2010: ICC Rules for the Use of Domestic and International Trade Terms (ICC Publications 2010) 87, Page 122.

when the goods are handed over to the first carrier. CIP is used for intermodal deliveries and CIF is used for sea.

DAT – delivered at terminal (named terminal at port or place of destination)

This term means that the seller covers all the costs of transport (export fees, carriage, insurance, unloading from main carrier at destination port and destination port charges) and assumes all risk until the destination port, the import duty/taxes/customs costs to be borne by the buyer.

DAP – delivered at place (named place of destination)

DAP terms can be used for any transport mode, or where there is more than one transport mode. The seller is responsible for arranging carriage and for delivering the goods, ready for unloading from the arriving conveyance, at the named place. Duties are not paid by the seller under this term (an important difference from DAT, where the buyer is responsible for unloading).

DDP – delivered duty paid (named place of destination)

Under DDP terms, the seller is responsible for delivering the goods to the named place in the country of the buyer, and pays all costs in bringing the goods to the destination including import duties and taxes. The seller is not responsible for unloading. This term is often used in place of the non-Incoterm "free in store (FIS). This term places the maximum obligations on the seller and minimum obligations on the buyer. With the delivery at the named place of destination all the risks and responsibilities are transferred to the buyer and it is considered that the seller has completed his obligations.

FAS – free alongside ship (named port of shipment)

Under these terms, the seller is required to deliver goods to a named port alongside a vessel designated by the buyer. "Alongside" means that the goods are within reach of a ship's lifting tackle. This means that the buyer has to bear all costs and risks of loss of or damage to the goods from that moment. The FAS term requires the seller to clear the goods for export, which is a reversal from previous Incoterms® versions that required the buyer to arrange for export clearance. However, if the parties wish the buyer to clear the goods for export, this should be made clear by adding explicit wording to this effect in the contract of sale. This term can be used only for sea or inland waterway transport.

FOB – free on board (named port of shipment)

F.o.b terms are one of the most commonly used Incoterms®. If a contract is concluded on f.o.b. terms, the seller must advance government tax in the country of origin to load the goods on board a vessel designated by the buyer.

Cost and risk are divided when the goods are transported by sea in containers, and the seller must instruct the buyer of the details of the vessel and the port where the goods are to be loaded, and there is no reference to, or provision for, the use of a carrier or forwarder.

This term has been greatly misused over the last three decades ever since the Incoterms® 1980 explained that FCA should be used for container shipments. It means that the seller pays for transportation of goods to the port of shipment, and loading costs. The buyer pays the cost of marine freight transportation, insurance, unloading, and transportation costs from the arrival port to the destination.

The passing of risk occurs when the goods are in the buyer's account. The buyer arranges for the vessel and the shipper has to load the goods onto the named vessel at the named port of shipment with the dates stipulated in the contract of sale as informed by the buyer.

CFR – cost and freight (named port of destination)
Under CFR terms, the seller must pay the costs and freight to bring the goods to the port of destination. However, risk is transferred to the buyer once the goods are loaded on the vessel. Insurance for the goods is not included, and this term is formally known as CNF (c.&f., c.+f. or c.f.).

CIF – cost, insurance and freight (named port of destination)
Together with f.o.b. terms, this is arguably the most commonly used term in contracts concluded on shipment terms. Exactly as with CFR, the seller must pay the costs and freight to bring the goods to the port of destination; in addition, (and contrary to CFR terms), the seller must in addition procure and pay for the insurance.

1.6 The Fosfa and Gafta standard terms

As established in above, the Federation of Oils, Seeds and Fats Associations (Fosfa) is a "professional international contract issuing and arbitral body concerned exclusively with the world trade in oilseeds, oils and fats, with over 1,000 members in 84 countries. These members include producers and processors, shippers and dealers, traders, brokers and agents, superintendents, analysts, shipowners, tank storage companies, and others providing services to traders. Fosfa has an extensive range of standard forms of contracts covering goods shipped either c.i.f., c.&f. or f.o.b. for soya beans, sunflower seed, rapeseed, and other seeds, vegetable and marine oils and fats, and refined oils and fats, from all origins worldwide, for different methods of transportation and different terms of trade".[24]

The federation's contracts incorporate a dispute procedure involving arbitration by experienced individuals from within the trade.

The Grain and Feed Trade Association (or Gafta) is a London based trade organisation consisting of professionals, operators, traders, and transporters in the international grain trade.[25]

24 Internationally, 85% of the global trade in oils and fats is traded under Fosfa contracts. See Fosfa website for a breakdown of the specific statistics.

25 See Gafta website. "Gafta can trace its origins back to 1878, when the London Corn Trade Association (LCTA) was established by members of the corn trade in order to protect their interests. the LCTA sought to achieve this through the adoption of standard forms of contract, drawn up by the

Gafta protects its members' interests through standard forms of contract, alongside an internationally respected dispute resolution service offering both arbitration and mediation to parties using Gafta standard contracts.

Like Fosfa, Gafta has an extensive range of standard forms of contracts covering goods shipped either c.i.f., c.&f. or f.o.b.

Both Fosfa and Gafta standard contracts can be defined as a more detailed version of the Incoterms® which deal with specific lines of international trade.

The Fosfa and Gafta standard contracts are drawn on CIF as well as FOB terms; nevertheless, compared to the Incoterms®, they are much more comprehensive and encompass all the terms and clauses relevant to an international sale of goods transaction, starting from the basic obligations in terms of quality standard and transport arrangements.

For traders operating within the Fosfa and Gafta commodities trade, the standard contracts of the aforementioned trading associations represent a very appealing and effective alternative, although blind incorporation of standard contracts may lead to unwelcome surprises, as will be readily appreciated in the following chapters.

1.7 Letters of credit and the UCP 600

Importing and exporting involves risks.

Indeed, one way of reducing the risks is to use a letter of credit – sometimes known as "documentary credit". This can "offer a guarantee to the seller that they will be paid, and the buyer can be sure that no payment will be made until they receive the goods. A letter of credit is basically a guarantee from a bank that a particular seller will receive a payment due from a particular buyer. The bank guarantees that the seller will receive a specified amount of money within a specified time. In return for guaranteeing the payment, the bank will require that strict terms are met, i.e. the tender of specific documents by the seller".[26]

The Uniform Customs and Practice for Documentary Credits (UCP) is a set of rules on the issuance and use of letters of credit. The UCP is utilised by bankers and commercial parties in more than 175 countries in trade finance.[27]

---

association, with any disputes arising out of these contracts being settled by arbitration rather than by legislation. Disputes were referred to London and conducted under English law.

In 1906, a group of traders broke away from the LCTA and formed a new more specialised association, the London Cattle Food Trade Association (LCFTA), for those trading in vegetable proteins used as animal feeding stuffs. In 1965, the LCFTA dropped 'London' from its title, reflecting growing internationalisation.

In 1969, merger talks commenced between the LCTA and CFTA. the outcome of these talks was the formation of a new joint association, the Grain and Feed Trade Association in 1971."

26 See the guidance on letters of credit at: www.gov.uk.

27 Some 11–15% of international trade utilises letters of credit, totalling over a trillion dollars (US) each year.

1.8 C.i.f and f.o.b. contracts: The heart and soul of international commerce

This book will primarily focus on the two most common Incoterms®, i.e. c.i.f. and f.o.b. contracts, although reference to other Incoterms® will be occasionally made where applicable or necessary.

In legal terms, it is of crucial importance to emphasise that the Incoterms® do not have the force of law; rather, they represent a self-regulatory framework devised by merchants in order to aid international commercial sale transactions.

This means that the mere use of the letters c.i.f. or f.o.b. would not suffice to ignite the incorporation of the Incoterms®, which will need to be clearly referred to by the sale contract. Incorporation should also explicitly refer to a particular Incoterm and to the latest version (Incoterms 2010®), unless a previous version is preferred.

Although they do not possess force of law, the Incoterms® will be legally binding if invoked by a sale contract, regulating the legal obligations and rights of the parties involved in the transaction. In their apparent simplicity, the Incoterms® are very successful in delineating the basic obligations and rights of seller and buyer within the context of contracts concluded on shipment terms.

By way of example, if a contract is concluded on c.i.f. terms and the Incoterms® are referred to by it, it will be self-evident in legal terms that the seller is placed with the obligations to cater for transport and insurance arrangements for the goods sold.

In the next chapter, we shall consider the legal nature of c.i.f. and f.o.b. contracts more in detail. Nevertheless, many of the intricate legal issues which revolve around c.i.f. and f.o.b. contracts are going to be thoroughly unravelled throughout the manuscript in relation to the relevant phases of the sale contract considered by the individual chapters to follow.

CHAPTER 2

The legal nature of c.i.f and f.o.b. contracts

2.1 The legal nature of c.i.f. contracts

The commercial structure and relevance of c.i.f. and f.o.b. contracts has been unfolded in the previous chapter. Our attention shall now focus on the legal nature of these two types of contracts for the international sale of goods, starting with contracts concluded on c.i.f. terms.

As we shall appreciate in this manuscript, the legal essence of contracts concluded on shipment terms does not rest on shipment alone; indeed, it revolves around the obligation of the seller to ship the goods and tender documents to the buyer as per what was originally established in the sale contract.

A c.i.f. contract is no different in that regard, with the aforementioned additional obligation of the seller to make the necessary transport arrangements.

As pointed out by Lord Wright in *Ross T. Smyth & Co. Ltd. v T.D. Bailey, Son & Co.*,[1] c.i.f. is one of the most popular trade terms used in international sale contracts where sea carriage is involved:

> It is a type of contract which is more widely and more frequently in use than any other contract used for the purposes of seaborne commerce.
>
> An enormous number of transactions, in value amounting to untold sums, are carried out every year under c.i.f. contracts.[2]

In commercial terms, a c.i.f. contract entails that the price paid by the buyer encompasses the cost of the goods alongside insurance and transport costs. The commercial nature of a c.i.f. contract translates into two subordinate contracts the seller is obliged to enter into: the contract of carriage, also referred to as the contract of affreightment, and the contract of insurance.

C.i.f. contracts are generally considered appealing to both sellers and buyers. Indeed, considered from a vendor's perspective, the seller is in the position to charge a higher price which will take into account the additional obligations to provide for freight and insurance.[3] Moreover, the seller is usually paid for the goods before their arrival at the destination, that is, upon the tendering of the documents to the buyer or to the bank in the case of a documentary credit arrangement.

1 *Ross T. Smyth & Co. Ltd. v T.D. Bailey, Son & Co.* (1940) 3 All ER 60.

2 *Ibid.*, at 69.

3 The margin of profit for the c.i.f. seller could be substantially higher than in the case of an f.o.b. contract due to the fact that he is normally likely to obtain reasonable rates for insurance and carriage.

A c.i.f. contract is equally gainful for a buyer, as the buyer does not have to undertake transport or insurance arrangements and, as will be readily appreciated in the following, is in the position to trade the goods whilst the goods are in transit.

Further, under a c.i.f. contract, the risk of any increases and fluctuations in terms of transport and insurance costs also rests with the seller.[4]

The essential feature of the c.i.f. contract is that a seller fulfils his obligations by shipping goods and tendering shipping documents as per originally established in the sale contract. On presentation of compliant shipping documents, the buyer is bound to pay for the goods, and this obligation transcends the actual arrival of the goods.

The buyer cannot decline the documents demanding the actual goods instead, nor can the vendor withhold the documents and tender the goods they represent.

The legal traits of contracts concluded on c.i.f. terms have been eloquently described by the court in *Comptoir d'Achat et de Vente du Boerenbond Belge S.A. v Luis de Ridder Limitada (The Julia)*.[5] As pointed out by Porter LJ:

> The obligations imposed upon a seller under a c.i.f. contract are well known, and in the ordinary case include the tender of a bill of lading[6] covering the goods contracted to be sold and no others, coupled with an insurance policy in the normal form and accompanied by an invoice which shows the price and, as in this case, usually contains a deduction of the freight which the buyer pays before delivery at the port of discharge. Against tender of these documents the purchaser must pay the price. In such a case the property may pass either on shipment or on tender, the risk generally passes on shipment or as from shipment, but possession does not pass until the documents which represent the goods are handed over in exchange for the price. In the result the buyer after receipt of the documents can claim against the ship for breach of the contract of carriage and against the underwriter for any loss covered by the policy. The strict form of c.i.f. contract may, however, be modified: a provision that a delivery order may be substituted for a bill of lading or a certificate of insurance for a policy would not, I think, make the contract concluded upon something other than c.i.f. terms, but in deciding whether it comes within that category or not all the permutations and combinations of provision and circumstance must be taken into consideration. Not every contract which is expressed to be a c.i.f. contract is such. Sometimes, as in *The Parchim* [1918] A.C. 157, terms are introduced into contracts so described which conflict with c.i.f. provisions . . . the object and the result of a c.i.f. contract is to enable sellers and buyers to deal with cargoes or parcels afloat and to transfer them freely from hand to hand by giving constructive possession of the goods which are being dealt with.[7]

4 The use of c.i.f. contracts has been linked to the economic climate of a country, see I. Carr, *Principles of International Trade Law*, 2nd Edition, Cavendish Publishing Limited, 1999, p. 3. Carr points out that developing countries whose foreign currency reserves are healthy usually see importing traders operating on c.i.f. terms rather than f.o.b. Nevertheless, the opposite is also true, and certain countries such as Colombia, Algeria, Pakistan and Iran actually proscribe imports on c.i.f. terms. This is due to the fact that f.o.b. agreements circumvent the necessity to pay for insurance and freight in hard currency such as the US dollar and German mark.

5 *Comptoir d'Achat et de Vente du Boerenbond Belge S.A. v Luis de Ridder Limitada (The Julia)* (1949) AC 293.

6 A bill of lading (sometimes abbreviated as B/L or BoL) is a document issued by a carrier which details a shipment of merchandise and gives title of that shipment to a specified party. Bills of lading are one of three important documents used in international trade to help guarantee that exporters receive payment and importers receive the goods. See Levi, Maurice D. (2005). *International Finance*, 4th Edition. New York, NY: Routledge.

7 *Ibid.*, p. 312.

Within this context, the bill of lading plays a prominent role conferring upon the buyer the possibility to dispose and trade the goods whilst the cargo is in transit.[8] In legal teleological terms, the tender of the bill of lading substitutes the delivery of the goods. As put by Hatherly LC in *Barber v Meyerstein*:[9]

> In the case of goods which are at sea being transmitted from one country to another, you cannot deliver actual possession of them, therefore the bill of lading is considered to be a symbol of the goods, and its delivery to be a delivery of them.

The holder of the bill is thus in the same commercial position as if he were in physical possession of the goods. The bill of lading is, accordingly, recognised as a "symbol" of the goods, and the transfer of the bill is regarded as a form of "symbolic delivery". Consequently, the transfer of the bill of lading would symbolically represent delivery of possession of the maize to the buyer, the seller simultaneously divesting himself of control and relinquishing his *animus possidendi*.

The concept of "symbolic" delivery of the goods through the endorsement of the bill of lading was elegantly described in *Sanders Bros v Maclean & Co*[10] by Bowen LJ, as follows:

> A cargo at sea while in the hands of the carrier is necessarily incapable of physical delivery. During [the] period of transit and voyage, the bill of lading by the law merchant is universally recognised as its symbol, and the indorsement and delivery of the bill of lading operates as a symbolical delivery of the cargo. Property in the goods passes by such indorsement and delivery of the bill of lading, whenever it is the intention of the parties that the property should pass, just as under similar circumstances the property would pass by an actual delivery of the goods. And for the purpose of passing such property in the goods and completing the title of the indorsee to full possession thereof, the bill of lading, until complete delivery of the cargo has been made on shore to someone rightfully claiming under it, remains in force as a symbol, and carries with it not only the full ownership of the goods, but also all rights created by the contract of carriage between the shipper and the shipowner. It is a key which in the hands of a rightful owner is intended to unlock the door of the warehouse, floating or fixed, in which the goods may chance to be.[11]

The specific obligations of a c.i.f. seller have been further elaborated in *Johnson v Taylor Brothers*,[12] where Atkinson LJ noted that:

> when a vendor and purchaser of goods . . . enter into a c.i.f. contract . . . the vendor in the absence of any special provision to the contrary is bound by his contract to do [the following]. First, to make out an invoice of the goods sold. Secondly, to ship at the port of shipment goods of the description contained in the contract. Thirdly, to procure a contract of affreightment under which the goods will be delivered at the destination contemplated by the contract. Fourthly, to arrange for an insurance upon the terms current in the trade which will be available for the benefit of the buyer. Fifthly, with all reasonable despatch to send forward and tender to the buyer these shipping documents, namely, the invoice, the bill of lading and policy of insurance, delivery of

8 See *Benjamin's Sale of Goods* (8th edition, Sweet & Maxwell, 2010) p. 137.
9 *Barber v Meyerstein* (1870) L.R. 4 HL 317 at 329, 330.
10 *Sanders Bros v Maclean & Co* (1883) 11 QBD 327, 341.
11 *Ibid.*, at 332, 333.
12 *Johnson v Taylor Brothers* (1920) LT 130.

which to the buyer is symbolic delivery of the goods purchased, placing the same at the buyer's risk and entitling the seller to payment of their price.[13]

Due to the nature of the performance of a c.i.f. contract, and to the emphasis posed by the judiciary on tender of documents, much debate arose in the past on whether c.i.f. sales are sales of goods, or effectively sales of documents.

Part of the doctrine maintains that c.i.f. sales are, in effect, sales of documents rather than goods. Indeed, in *Arnold Karberg & Co. v Blythe, Greene, Jourdain & Co*,[14] Scrutton J pointed out that:

> The key to many of the difficulties arising in c.i.f. contracts is to keep firmly in mind the cardinal distinction that a c.i.f. sale is not a sale of goods, but a sale of documents relating to goods. It is not a contract that goods shall arrive, but a contract to ship goods complying with the contract of sale, to obtain, unless the contract otherwise provides, the ordinary contract of carriage to the place of destination, and the ordinary contract of insurance of the goods on that voyage, and to tender these documents against payment of the contract price. The buyer then has the right to claim the fulfillment of the contract of carriage, or, if the goods are lost or damaged, such indemnity for the loss as he can claim under the contract of insurance. He buys the documents, not the goods, and it may be that under the terms of the contracts of insurance and affreightment he buys no indemnity for the damage that has happened to the goods. This depends on what documents he is entitled to under the contract of sale. In my view, therefore, the relevant question will generally be not "what at the time of declaration or tender of the documents is the condition of the goods?" . . . but "what, at the time of tender of documents was the condition of those documents as to compliance with the contract of sale?"[15]

The claim that c.i.f. sales are, in effect, sales of documents is based on the fact that in c.i.f. contracts the seller performs his obligations by shipping the goods and tendering the documents. From this standpoint, the buyer would merely buy the rights of action against the carrier and the underwriter contained in the shipping documents, rather than the goods.

Part of the doctrine emphasised that, if this were the case, c.i.f. contracts would not be governed by the SOGA in the United Kingdom, as documents per se can hardly qualify as goods.[16] This conclusion is nevertheless not as startling as it might seem at first sight, as the SOGA provisions are excluded by contrary agreement more often than not.

The literature has also pointed out that from a commercial perspective the essence of c.i.f. contracts revolves not around the sale of the goods themselves, but rather on a sale of the documents which relates to the goods.[17] Rather than obtaining the goods per se, the aim of the buyer would be to acquire, in the shortest time possible, the possibility to trade in the goods. This can only be achieved through the possession of the documents.

---

13 *Ibid.*, at 139.

14 *Arnold Karberg & Co. v Blythe, Greene, Jourdain & Co* (1915) 2 KB 379, 388.

15 *Ibid.*, at 415.

16 See A.G. Guest, *Benjamin's Sale of Goods*, 5th Edition, Sweet & Maxwell, 1997, p. 1252.

17 See L. D'Arcy, *Schmitthoff's Export Trade – The Law and Practice of International Trade*, 10th Edition, Sweet & Maxwell, 2000, p. 30.

In *Ross T. Smyth & Co. Ltd. v T.D. Bailey, Son & Co.*[18] an interesting parallel between goods and documents was drawn by Wright LJ:

> The essential characteristics of this [c.i.f.] contract have often been described. The seller has to ship or acquire after that shipment the contract goods, as to which if unascertained he is generally required to give a notice of appropriation. On or after shipment he has to obtain proper bills of lading and proper policies of insurance. He fulfils his contract by transferring the bills of lading and the policies to the buyer. As a general rule he does so only against payment of the price, less the freight, which the buyer has to pay. In the invoice which accompanies the tender of the documents on the "prompt," that is, the date fixed for payment, the freight is deducted for this reason.[19]

From a commercial point of view, the delivery of shipping documents is, thus, the equivalent of the goods.

According to a different view, c.i.f. contracts are nothing but ordinary sale contracts, with the only difference being that the seller undertakes no obligation as to physical delivery and remains free to tender the shipping documents even if the goods have been lost after the making of the contract of sale and before the tender.[20] This represents the only possible deviation from the normal duties of the seller under an ordinary sale contract. Since the seller does not actually promise the delivery of the goods, but only shipment, what is crucial under a c.i.f. contract is that the goods must be shipped in conformity with what was originally established in the sale contract in terms of description, quality and fitness, and that the seller must pass a good "title" to the buyer.

2.2 C.i.f. contracts: Contracts for the sale of goods or documents?

A number of early common law judgments seem to point towards the presumption that c.i.f. contracts constitute a sale of documents.[21] The strongest argument supporting this view is that when goods are lost at sea the documents remain valid and can be tendered just the same in exchange for the full purchase price. The performance of the contract is therefore fulfilled by the delivery of the documents and not by the actual delivery of the goods by the vendor.

In *Arnold Karberg & Co. v Blythe Green Jourdain & Co.*,[22] by way of *obiter dictum* Scrutton J stated that:

> A CIF sale is not a sale of goods, but a sale of documents relating to goods. It is not a contract that goods shall arrive, but a contract to ship goods complying with the contract of sale, to obtain, unless the contract otherwise provides, the ordinary contract of

18 *Ross T. Smyth & Co. Ltd. v T.D. Bailey, Son & Co.* (1940) 3 All ER 60.

19 *Ibid.*, at 72.

20 See R. Goode, *Commercial Law*, 2nd Edition, Penguin Books, 1995, p. 948.

21 See, inter alia, *Holland Colombo Trading Society Ltd. v Segu Mohamed Khaja Alawdeen* (1954) 2 Lloyd's Rep. 45 (PC); *Continental Imes Ltd. v Dibble (HE)* (1952) 1 Lloyd's Rep. 220; *Toepfer v Lenersan-Poortman NV* (1980) 1 Lloyd's Rep. 143 (CA); *Biddell Brothers v Clements (E) Horst Co.* (1911) 1 KB 214, 220.

22 *Arnold Karberg & Co. v Blythe Green Jourdain & Co.* [1915] 2 KB 379.

carriage to the place of destination and the ordinary contract of insurance of the goods on that voyage, and to tender these documents against payment of the contract price.[23]

There are, however, dissenting arguments to this rule. As we shall discover in the following,[24] one important objection lies with the fact that even if a c.i.f. seller has tendered valid documents, the buyer would still be in the position to reject the actual goods if they do not conform to the requirements of the contract. Moreover, the aforementioned dictum of Scrutton J was expressly dissented from by the Court of Appeal,[25] where Bankes LJ held:

I am not able to agree with that view of the contract, that it is a sale of documents relating to goods. I prefer to look upon it as "a contract for the sale of goods to be performed by the delivery of documents".[26]

In this case, the emphasis on the documents was primarily related to the terms of the contract and the manner of its performance rather than its essence.

The view that documents are in essence vital only in respect of them representing the goods was portrayed in *Manbre Saccharine Co, Ltd v Corn Products Co, Ltd*[27] by McCardie J:

If the vendor fulfils his contract by shipping the appropriate goods in the appropriate manner under a proper contract of carriage, and if he also obtains the proper documents for tender to the purchaser, I am unable to see how the rights or duties of either party are affected by the loss of ship or goods, or by knowledge of such loss by the vendor prior to actual tender of the documents. If the ship be lost prior to tender, but without the knowledge of the seller, it was, I assume, always clear that he could make an effective proffer of the documents to the buyers. In my opinion, it is also clear that he can make an effective tender even though he possessed at the time of tender actual knowledge of the loss of the ship or goods. For the purchaser in case of loss will get the document he bargained for, and if the policy be that required by the contract and if the loss be covered thereby, he will secure the insurance moneys. The contingency of loss is within and not outside the contemplation of the parties to a cif contract.[28]

This apparent conflict between goods and documents may be portrayed merely as a question of semantics. Whether this is the correct view or not, it is undeniable that in a c.i.f. contract there exist two distinctly separate sets of rights and obligations: the right to reject documents and the right to reject the goods if, after examination, they are found not to be in conformity with the sale contract. This was pointed out by Devlin J in *Kwei Tek Chao (Trading as Zung Fu Co) v British Traders and Shippers*:[29]

Now, in this case, as I have said, I think there is a right to reject documents and a right to reject goods, and the two things are quite distinct. A c.i.f. contract puts a number of obligations upon the seller, and for the purpose of this case one may say that they

23 *Ibid.*, at 379.
24 See chapter 12.
25 *Arnold G Karberg v Blythe* [1916] 1 KB 495 (CA).
26 *Ibid.*, at 510.
27 *Manbre Saccharine Co, Ltd v Corn Products Co, Ltd* [1918–19] All ER Rep 980.
28 *Ibid.*, at 984.
29 *Kwei Tek Chao (Trading as Zung Fu Co) v British Traders and Shippers* [1954] 1 Lloyd's Rep. 16.

are obligations some of which are in relation to the goods and some of which are in relation to the documents. So far as the goods are concerned, he must put on board at the port of shipment goods that are in conformity with the contract description, and in so far as the goods are concerned, that finishes his obligations if the goods are in conformity with the contract description. But he must also send forward documents, and those documents must also comply with the contract. If he commits a breach, of course the breaches may in one sense overlap, in that they flow from the same act. If there is a late shipment, as there was in this case, the date of the shipment being part of the description of the goods, he has not put on board goods that conform to the contract description, and therefore he has broken that obligation. He may or may not break the obligation to send forward a correct bill of lading. I should think it follows that in that particular case a man knows that he cannot send forward a bill of lading which at once conforms with the contract and describes accurately the date of shipment, and so in that sense it is true to say that the same act necessarily causes the breach of two independent obligations.

There may, however, of course, be cases where the two breaches are not necessarily reflected both in the documents and in the goods. However that may be, there are distinct obligations, and the right to reject the documents arises when the documents are tendered, and the right to reject, or the moment for rejecting, the goods arises when the goods are landed and after examination they are found not to be in conformity with the contract. There are very many cases, of course, where the documents are accepted and then the goods are subsequently rejected.[30]

Although the right to reject the goods and the right to reject the documents are quite distinct from one another, it appears in this judgment that the value of the documents and the goods cannot be distinguished.

Another interesting case where the view of the court is uncluttered from any sort of dichotomy between goods and documents is *Hindley & Co v East Indian Produce & Co*.[31]

Here, the sellers sold to the buyers 50 tons of Siamese jute, grade A, c.&f. When the vessel arrived at Bremen, no jute of the contract description was found to be on board because it had never been shipped.

A dispute arose, and the sellers contended, inter alia, that they were not liable because a contract of sale on c.&f. terms was one for the sale of documents or one to be performed by the delivery of documents, and in the present case the bill of lading was in all respects proper on its face.

The claim was rebutted by Kerr J, who stated that:

It [. . .]is indeed a matter of elementary law – that a c.&f. or c.i.f. contract is to be performed by the tender of documents covering goods which have been shipped either by the seller or by someone else in accordance with the terms of the contract. If no goods have in fact been shipped the sellers have not performed their obligation. I cannot see any basis for the distinction which the sellers here seek to draw between a seller who is also the shipper and a seller who is not the shipper. At the date of the contract it may well be unknown which means of performance the particular seller will employ, and in an ordinary c.i.f. or c.&f. contract, as in the present case, there will be nothing in the contract which restricts his choice between the two alternative methods of performance.

30 *Ibid.*, at 36, 37.

31 *Hindley & Co v East Indian Produce & Co* [1973] 2 Lloyd's Rep. 515.

> Since there was no shipment of any goods in the present case, either by these sellers or by anyone else, this is in my judgment sufficient to enable the buyers to succeed in recovering damages for breach of that part of the sellers' obligations.
>
> But I also consider that exactly the same result follows if the sellers' obligations under this form of contract are considered in relation to the bill of lading which was tendered, this being merely another aspect of the same point. It is an implied term of a contract of this nature that the bill of lading shall not only appear to be true and accurate in the material statements which it contains, but that such statements shall in fact be true and accurate.[32]

It is therefore clear that whenever under a c.i.f. contract the seller has never shipped the goods and the bill of lading is a nullity,[33] the seller has not performed his obligations and cannot claim payment on the ground that the contract was performed through the tender of conforming documents.

The judgment in *Hindley & Co v East Indian Produce & Co* indeed casts grave doubts re the possibility to qualify c.i.f contracts in legal teleological terms as contracts for the sale of documents.

2.3 The legal and commercial nature of f.o.b. contracts

In the past, the earliest types of international sales contracts were structured on the basis of what are now known as free on board (f.o.b.) and the free aside ship (f.a.s) contracts. These contracts started to be developed in the eighteenth century, predating regular shipping lines and modern communication networks.[34]

At that time, more than a venture, international trade was an adventure in its true sense; the only way a buyer could import goods internationally was either to travel to the country of origin of the goods himself, or to send a vessel or an agent to various ports in order to buy goods. The buyer would accordingly take care of all the transport arrangements and buy goods alongside the ship.

It has been pointed out that in traditional f.o.b. contracts the buyer was usually the shipper.[35] Even today, as we are about to discover, under specific types of f.o.b. arrangements (f.o.b. with additional services), the seller ships the goods as the agent of the buyer, under a separate agency contract, which is quite distinct from the sales contract. Under those circumstances, the seller "becomes the alter ego of the buyer for the purposes of the contract of affreightment".[36]

The general rule is nevertheless that under f.o.b. terms the buyer arranges for the freight and marine insurance, and the seller ships the goods at the port of origin on board a vessel nominated by the buyer.

32 *Ibid.*, at 518.

33 On this point see Sassoon D. *FOB and CIF Contracts*, (5th Edition) Sweet & Maxwell 2012, p. 53. See also P. Todd, *Non-Genuine Shipping Documents and Nullities* [2008] LMCLQ 547. See *United City Merchants (Investments) Ltd v Royal Bank of Canada (The American Accord)* [1983] 1 AC 168; *Motis Exports Ltd v Dampskibsselskabet AF* 1912 A/S (No.1) [2000] 1 Lloyd's Rep. 211.

34 Sassoon D. The Origin of Fob and Cif Terms and the Factors Influencing their Choice [1967] *JBL* 32.

35 See C.H. Spurin, *The Law of International Trade and Carriage of Goods*, 2004, UK National Academy for Dispute Resolution, chapter 5.

36 See C.H. Spurin, *The Law of International Trade and Carriage of Goods*, 2004, UK National Academy for Dispute Resolution, Chapter 5.

As a consequence, the buyer retains control over the shipping transport arrangements and the relative documentation, and the seller is not saddled with the burden of arranging for the contract of carriage or making insurance arrangements for the goods. Equally, the seller does not bear the risk of the freight and insurance market fluctuations.

An early judicial definition of f.o.b terms can be found in *Stock v Inglis*,[37] where Brett MR held that:

> it is not denied but that the words "free on board," according to the general understanding of merchants, would mean more than merely that the shipper was to put them on board at his expense; they would mean that he was to put them on board at his expense on account of the person for whom they were shipped; and in that case the goods so put on board under such a contract would be at the risk of the buyer whether they were lost or not on the voyage.[38]

Subsequently, the relationships between the parties to a contract concluded on f.o.b. terms were considered in *J. & J. Cunningham, Ltd. v Robert A. Munro & Co., Ltd*,[39] where Lord Hewart CJ described the obligations of f.o.b. sellers and buyers as follows:

> The contract under consideration was for 200 tons of Dutch bran for shipment during October, 1920, price £13 per ton f.o.b. Rotterdam, buyers finding freight room. Under such an agreement it was the duty of the purchasers to provide a vessel at the appointed place, Rotterdam, at such a time as would enable the vendors to bring the goods alongside the ship and put them over the ship's rail, so as to enable the purchasers to receive them within the appointed time – in this case October. It would not, for example, be sufficient for the vendors to bring them to a warehouse in Rotterdam or bring them alongside the vessel at five minutes before midnight on Oct. 31. The usual practice under such a contract is for the buyer to nominate the vessel and to send notice of her arrival to the vendor in order that the vendor may be in a position to fulfil his part of the contract. When the vendors tender the goods in question to the purchasers theoretically by placing them on the ship's rail, it is open to the purchasers to reject if the goods are not in accordance with the contract.
>
> This being the relationship between the parties the liability on either side may be varied
>
> (1) by express contract altering the place or date of loading
> (2) by the conduct of the parties.
>
> For example, there may be circumstances which disentitle the purchaser to reject the goods when they are being placed on the ship's rail, as for instance where he has by his conduct already accepted them before their arrival there; there may also be circumstances where, although the purchaser may be entitled to reject when the goods are being placed over the ship's rail, yet the vendor may be entitled to recover damages in respect of the deterioration of the goods. Assuming the sale of a perishable cargo, say of fresh vegetables for October shipment, suppose the purchasers nominate their vessel and write to the vendors saying "she will be at the quayside in three days time." The vendors gather their vegetables and send them to the quayside; but the nominated ship does not arrive for a fortnight, during which time the vegetables go bad. It may be

37 *Stock v Inglis* (1884) 12 QBD 564.
38 *Ibid.*, at 573.
39 *J. & J. Cunningham, Ltd. v Robert A. Munro & Co., Ltd.* (1922) 13 Lloyds Rep. 216.

> that the purchasers are entitled to reject the vegetables which have so deteriorated, but the vendors are then entitled to rely upon and bring into play another legal principle. It is not exactly an estoppel which prevents the purchasers from rejecting, but it is the doctrine that where one person makes a statement to another meaning that statement to be relied upon and acted upon by that other, if the other suffers damage by so relying and acting upon it he is entitled to recover such damage from the person making the statement. In the case put forward the damage would be the loss of price which the vendors would otherwise have obtained from the purchasers. This legal doctrine might be put in ordinary language as it is put in the case stated by the arbitrator, viz., that under such circumstances after the vendor has brought the goods to the quay at the invitation of the purchaser the goods remained at the purchaser's risk.[40]

On a general level, f.o.b. contracts are considered as flexible legal instruments, and it is rather difficult to provide a single definition capable of encompassing the nature of the various forms of f.o.b. contracts.[41] A famous attempt to legally qualify the various forms of f.o.b. terms was made in *Pyrene v Scindia*,[42] where Devlin J pointed out that:

> The f.o.b. contract has become a flexible instrument, so much so that no really satisfactory definition of such a contract is possible. It embraces (a) cases where the buyer arranges and nominates the ship, but the seller ships and takes the bill of lading in his own name as consignor, (b) cases where the seller arranges shipment and takes the bill in his own name as consignor and (c) cases where the buyer arranges and nominates the ship, and the seller ships but the buyer is named in the bill as consignor.[43]

2.4 Classification of f.o.b. contracts

The judicial recognition of at least three distinct forms of f.o.b. contracts made by Devlin J in *Pyrene v Scindia* inspired the doctrine to construct further qualifications. Sassoon defined the three types of variation of f.o.b. contracts theorised by Devlin J as: "classic f.o.b. contracts", "f.o.b. contracts with additional services", and "straight f.o.b. contracts".[44]

The classification of f.o.b. contracts provided by Devlin J in *Pyrene & Co. v Scindia* was subsequently endorsed in *The El Amria and El Minia*,[45] where Donaldson LJ specified that:

> In the first, or classic type, the buyer nominates the ship and the seller puts the goods on board for account of the buyer, procuring a bill of lading. The seller is then a party to the contract of carriage and if he has taken the bill of lading to his order, the only contract of carriage to which the buyer can become a party is that contained in or evidenced by the bill of lading which is endorsed to him by the seller. The second is a variant of the first, in that the seller arranges for the ship to come on the berth, but

40 *Ibid.*, at 216, 217.

41 Gbenga Odutan, "C.I.F. Gatwick" and Other Such Nonsense Upon Stilts: Incoterms and the Law, Jargon and Practice of International Business Transactions (2010) 6 *ICCLR*, 214

42 *Pyrene v Scindia Navigation* [1954] 2 QB 402.

43 *Ibid.*, at 424.

44 See D. Sassoon, *CIF and FOB Contracts* (4th Edition), Sweet & Maxwell, 1995, pp. 355–357.

45 *The El Amria and El Minia* [1982] 2 Lloyd's Rep. 28. See also *Agricultores Federados Argentinos Sociedad Cooperativa Ltda. v Ampro S.A. Commerciale Industriere et Financere* [1965] 2 Lloyd's Rep 157.

> the legal incidents are the same. The third is where the seller puts the goods on board, takes a mate's receipt and gives this to the buyer or his agent who then takes a bill of lading. In this latter type the buyer is a party to the contract of carriage *ab initio*.[46]

Under "classic" f.o.b. contracts, the seller places the goods on board on a ship nominated by the buyer. In this case, the seller is said to become a party to the contract of carriage until he takes out the bill of lading in the name of the buyer.

A classic type of f.o.b contract where provision of the ship was an obligation of the buyer was considered in *Scandinavian Trading Co. A/B v Zodiac Petroleum S.A. and William Hudson Ltd. (The Al Hofuf)*.[47] Here the f.o.b. contract provided that the buyer was under the obligation to give, in succession, notices of expected time of arrival of the vessel at the refinery or lifting port in question, 72, 48 and 24 hours in advance of the anticipated date of arrival. It was held by the court that provision was to be a condition of the contract and of its essence, and that timely notices of expected time of arrival of the vessel in accordance with the custom of the trade was also a condition and of the essence of the contract.

Under "f.o.b. contracts with additional services", the situation is radically different as the seller makes the necessary transport arrangements for shipping the goods acting as agent of the buyer; this means that the seller will sign the charter party or other contract of carriage in his own name, but the buyer will be bound by its terms as his principal. Under those circumstances, the seller is not at any rate party to the contract of carriage, which will reverberate its legal consequences only vis-à-vis the buyer and the carrier.

In its delineated features, an "f.o.b. contract with additional services" appears to be remarkably similar to a c.i.f. contract. The main difference between these two terms lies with the discrepant commercial nature of these two terms; indeed, under a c.i.f contract, the seller will receive only one sum of money which will cover the price of the goods, the cost of freight and of insurance arrangements, bearing the risk of market fluctuations for insurance and freight costs. On the contrary, under an "f.o.b. contract with additional services", the seller will be paid separately and fully reimbursed of the transport arrangements and insurance costs, where applicable.[48]

Finally, under the third type of f.o.b. contracts, i.e. "straight" f.o.b., the buyer will stipulate the contract of carriage by sea directly or through an agent with the carrier. The seller will ship the goods on board the vessel nominated by the buyer, and the bill of lading will reach the buyer directly, usually through his agent. Under those circumstances, the seller will not play any part in the contract of carriage.

---

46 *Ibid.*, at 32.

47 *Scandinavian Trading Co. A/B v Zodiac Petroleum S.A. and William Hudson Ltd. (The Al Hofuf)* [1981] 1 Lloyd's Rep. 81. See also *Av Pound & Co v Hardy & Co Inc* [1956] 1 AC 588; *Brandt & Co v Morris & Co Ltd* [1917] 2 KB 784; *Bunge Corporation New York v Tradax Export SA Panama* [1981] 2 All ER 513; *Cargill UK Ltd v Continental UK Ltd* [1989] 2 Lloyd's Rep. 290; *Colley v Overseas Exporters* [1921] 3 KB 302 *Cunningham (J.J.) Ltd v Robert A. Munro & Co. Ltd.* (1922) 28 Com Cas 42; *ERG Raffinerie Mediterranee SpA v Chevron USA Inc.* [2007] 1 CLC. 807; *Harlow & Jones Ltd v Panex (International) Ltd* [1967] 2 Lloyds's Rep. 509.

48 As an example of this type of f.o.b. contract see *The El Amria and El Minia* [1982] 2 Lloyd's Rep. 28.

An example of a "straight" f.o.b. contract can be found in *President of India v Metcalfe Shipping Co*,[49] where a sale contract concluded on f.o.b. terms listed the following terms:

> **16. Shipping**
> The stores shall be delivered by the sellers free on board stowed on such vessels as may be nominated by the purchaser . . . Inspection certificates, advice notes, packing accounts and invoices in such manner as may be required by the Director-General, India Store Department, shall be furnished by and at the cost of the sellers . . .
> The term "FOB vessel port of loading" means:
>
> (a) Loaded and stowed or trimmed on board overseas vessel at named port of loading, free of expense to purchaser.
> (b) That it shall be the responsibility of the sellers to do the following:
> (i) provide for and pay and bear all charges incurred in placing goods actually on board the vessel designated and provided by purchaser on the date or within the period fixed;
> (ii) provide clean on board ocean bill of lading;
> (iii) be responsible for any loss or damage or both until goods have been placed actually on board the vessel on the date or within the period fixed and clean on board ocean bill of lading is delivered to the purchasers or the agent nominated by purchasers;
> (iv) render purchaser or his authorised agents assistance in obtaining the documents issued in the country of origin or of shipment, or of both, which may be required for purpose of exportation.

The flexibility of f.o.b. contracts is further accentuated by the fact that, on the basis of the principle of freedom of contract, parties are at liberty to alter the terms of an f.o.b. contract.

If a sale contract is governed by English law, "classic", "additional services", and "straight" f.o.b. terms are ultimately defined in accordance with English law, but traders from other countries may wish to apply exclusive national definitions. Nevertheless, such terms may be beneficial to one party at the expense of the other, therefore parties are best advised to investigate limitations that may derive from adopting the interpretation of a particular nation.

Indeed, stipulating contractual agreements to be governed by transnational definitions can ultimately avert disputes which often arise due to the variety of interpretations between different jurisdictions.[50]

It is worth mentioning that English law, in line with the Incoterms® themselves, has always referred to f.o.b. terms as vehicles for seaborne commerce only.[51]

---

49 *President of India v Metcalfe Shipping Co* [1970] 1 QB 289.

50 Incoterms 2010®, alongside the Revised American Foreign Trade Definitions (RAFTD), and the Uniform Commercial Code (UCC) are some examples of sources of interpretation that parties deliberately choose in drafting f.o.b. contracts. The RAFTD and the UCC are an attempt made by the US to standardise international trade terms. Although no longer predominant within the context of international trade practices, they have offered a significant contribution for the creation of a framework for the analysis of shipping terms and their implications.

51 However, some jurisdictions, namely the US and Canada, have adopted FOB terms with reference to both transport by water and transport by land; therefore "FOB Los Angeles" could refer to a delivery at a harbour as well as at a truck terminal.

This unusual opportunity for parties to agree to different terms and conditions as they see fit for their needs is the element that renders f.o.b. contracts one of the most flexible and popular instruments in the international sale of goods.[52]

Such flexibility has been recognised by courts from the outset. In *Ian Stach Ltd v Baker Bosley Ltd*,[53] the buyers had stipulated a "classic f.o.b. contract" in that the buyers were entitled to call for shipment at any time within the shipping period and up to the end of the shipping period. The buyers did make the relevant shipping arrangements, but they did not open the documentary credit, neither after the shipment period had started nor after the sellers had called for it. Although it was recognised by the court that there are probably as many exceptions to f.o.b. contracts as there are examples of them, it was held that documentary credit was to be opened before the start of the shipment period in order to ensure certainty.

The flexibility of f.o.b. contracts was further evidenced in *ERG Raffinerie Mediterranee SpA v Chevron Usa Inc*,[54] where it was acknowledged by the court that traders are constantly adapting and even changing traditional f.o.b. contracts in the course of their business.

Nevertheless, the elasticity of f.o.b. contracts can be also seen as a double-edged sword becoming a source of legal confusion and disadvantage among parties. When legal complexities arise, courts will ultimately resort to the identification of the will of the parties involved in order to qualify additional conditions agreed in addition to customary forms of f.o.b. contracts.[55]

Nevertheless, with so many f.o.b. variations and combinations, determining the exact f.o.b. terms and conditions agreed by the party could become a daunting exercise even for a court of law.[56]

The flexibility offered by f.o.b. terms, in conjunction with a wide and heterogeneous cluster of factors pertaining to the individual nature of international commercial transactions very often render formalistic legal definitions of difficult execution.

Indeed, it has been correctly pointed out that ultimately "any rigid and inflexible interpretation of the f.o.b. term which failed to take into account the various factors surrounding a particular transaction would be doing violence to reality".[57]

52 Frecon Alain, Practical Considerations in Drafting F.O.B. Terms in International Sales (1986) 3 *Int'l Tax & Bus Law* 346.

53 *Ian Stach Ltd v Baker Bosley Ltd* [1958] 2 QB 130; *Mitsui & Co Ltd v Flota Mercante Grancolombiana SA (Ciudad de Neiva Ciuda de Pasto)* [1988] 2 Lloyd's Rep. 208; *NV Handel NY J Smits Import-Export v English Exporters (London) Ltd* [1957] Lloyd's Rep. 517; *Olearia Tirrena SpA v NV Algermeene Oliehandel (Osterbeck)* [1973] 2 Lloyd's Rep. 86.

54 *ERG Raffinerie Mediterranee SpA v Chevron USA Inc.* [2007] 1 CLC 807.

55 Williamson John, FOB Contracts: An Examination of Their Principles and Practical Application in Internal Trade (1984–1987) 5 *Auckland U. L. Rev.* 476.

56 On this point see Chuah, *Law of International Trade: Cross-Border Commercial Transactions*, 5th Edition, Sweet & Maxwell, 2013, p. 59.

57 See D. Sassoon, *CIF and FOB Contracts*, (5th Edition), above, at p. 350.

CHAPTER 3

The creation of a contract concluded on shipment terms

3.1 Introduction

A very common source of legal controversy is usually generated by a situation of conflict between terms stipulated in the sale contract and clauses enshrined into standard contracts and invoked by the original sale agreement.

Disputes frequently arise because of something which happens in the performance of a contract; however, their resolution frequently depends on what is said in the contract itself and on the formation of the contract.

3.2 When was the contract concluded and what were its terms?

It is difficult at times to ascertain when a contract has been concluded. The moment of formation of a contract is of the utmost importance, as it represents a necessary prerequisite for the identification of the terms of the contract itself, and the relative obligations of its signatories.

Indeed, disputes very often arise in practice in relation to the exact determination of the terms and conditions of contractual arrangements, and parties will endeavour to deny the validity of terms having an adverse effect to their legal position.[1]

In *Jayar Impex Ltd v Toaken Group Ltd*,[2] an agreement for the sale of the 47 tonnes of Nigerian gum had originally been reached in telephone conversations between the sellers and buyers, followed by a written contract, on which the sellers relied, which provided, inter alia, that International General Produce Association Ltd (IGPA) spot terms and conditions were to apply, and further stated that any dispute arising out of the contract was to be settled by arbitration in accordance with "the above rules and conditions".

1 See Morris J in *Société Cooperative Suisse des Céréales et Matières Fourragères v La Plata Cereal Company SA* (1947) 80 Lloyds Rep. 530, 538: "The problems of construction of contractual documents are not easy of solution and I doubt whether the parties gave to the compilation of these documents one hundredth part of the thought which has been devoted to their explanation". See also *The Antaios* [1985] A.C. 191.

For a detailed overview of issues of interpretation of contracts, see H.G. Beale, *Chitty on Contracts*, 30th Edition (Sweet & Maxwell, 2008), Vol. 1 para 12–061 *et seq.* See also K. Lewison, *The Interpretation of Contracts*, 5th Edition (Sweet & Maxwell, 2001).

2 *Jayar Impex Ltd v Toaken Group Ltd* [1996] 2 Lloyd's Rep. 437.

It was common ground that the only reference to IGPA terms as between the parties was to be found in the written contract. Rule 124 of the IGPA rules provided that: "No claim shall lie in respect of the quality, condition brand or description of the goods after the Prompt Day or after the removal from wharf warehouse or store if removed prior to the Prompt Day".

The sellers contract form stated at the bottom "Important – Please sign date and return this document". The buyers never did so.

The buyers alleged that the goods were of an unsatisfactory specific optical rotation (SOR), the SOR value of gum arabic being a critical factor in its quality, and that there was a proportion of caked bags and that the goods were underweight. Further, the buyers stated that they did not consider themselves bound by the sellers' contract form nor therefore by the IGPA terms.

The sellers replied that they would credit the buyers on proof of shortage but not for any complaint regarding quality, and that if payment was not promptly received they would seek arbitration under the contract terms.

The court held that the submissions by the sellers that either the telephone agreements were binding including the reference in them to the sellers' contract form whatever that turned out to be, or there never was any contract until the buyers' acceptance of the sellers' contract form since the parties' telephone conversation had contemplated a written contract, would be rejected. It would have been, indeed, unbusinesslike to infer that the buyers intended to accept the terms of the sellers' contract form whatever it should turn out to be; and the written contract was never executed by the buyers.

As stated by Rix J:

> In my judgment, even assuming some reference in the telephone conversations to a written contract form to come from the sellers in due course, I cannot accept the first and last of those three alternatives. The first assumes that the parties' contract was made there and then on the telephone but already incorporated the sellers' contract form. That would be acceptable if the sellers' contract form was known in advance to be identical to the oral contract (in which case it would be unnecessary), or if there was a course of dealing between the parties from which one could infer that the parties intended to contract on the basis of some standard form of the sellers, including standard terms and conditions. But Mr. Hamblen, quite properly, told me that he did not rely on a course of dealing. In such circumstances it is most unbusinesslike to infer that the buyers intended to accept the terms of the sellers' contract form whatever it should turn out to be. There was no attempt by the sellers to prove that their contract form was in some normal and accepted form. That is to buy a pig in the poke. I reject that alternative. The third alternative on the other hand assumes no agreement save by reference to the written contract. In that case the parties' agreement is subject to contract, yet the written contract was never executed by the buyers, and the sellers moreover recognize contract terms which were never incorporated within it. The sellers' written submissions to Mr. Bostelmann themselves stated that agreement was reached by telephone. I reject that third alternative too.[3]

The buyers' acceptance of the seller's standard form and conditions was also questioned by Rix J, who pointed out that:

3 *Jayar Impex Ltd v Toaken Group Ltd* [1996] 2 Lloyd's Rep. 444, 445.

It seems to me that if the sellers' contract form is to bind the buyers it can only be because it was accepted by the buyers as a variation of an existing contract: see *Pagnan S.p.A. v Feed Products Ltd.* [1987] 2 Lloyd's Rep. 601 at pp. 611, 614, 619–620. That is the second of Mr. Hamblen's three alternatives. He seeks to support it by relying on the absence of any objection to the contract form upon its receipt, on the collection of goods without objection to the contract form, and on the reference to a contract number in the fax of Nov. 11, 1994. The absence of objection is not, he submits, reliance on acceptance by silence, because the context is such as to create an expectation of objection, if any there be, especially where the parties had contemplated the reduction of their oral contract to written form. It is, he says, like a charter of a vessel, where the fixture is made orally or in fixture telexes, the parties contemplate that that binding contract will be ultimately contained in a charter, and that the charter may well add to or otherwise vary the original terms of the fixture: if in such a context one party sends out a signed charter for signature by the other party, and that other party commences performance of the charter without objecting to the terms of the charter, he will be bound by the terms of the charter. First, the incorporation of the IGPA terms is undoubtedly a proposed amendment of the existing contract by way of addition. Secondly, because of the stringent nature of the spot terms, that addition would involve a cutting back on the buyers' normal and statutory rights and remedies. Such a variation is not to be lightly inferred. Thirdly, the contract does not contain admitted terms of the contract, such as the warranted SOR values and the arrangement for deblocking the Bow goods at the sellers' expense. In such a case there is still less reason to think that the contract form has to be given some special status, requiring objection to prevent it supplanting the parties' existing contract. Fourthly, the contract form would have changed the sellers' role from that of seller to that of agent, buying on behalf of the buyers. That would have been a fundamental change to the existing contract, one that did not fit the facts, and something that could I think be achieved only by the plainest evidence of assent on the part of the buyers. Fifthly, the contract form itself contemplated that it would take effect on signature and return of the addressee: it was neither signed nor returned. Sixthly, the buyers' collection of goods was not something only referable to acceptance of the terms set out in the sellers' contract form. The sellers were perfectly willing, and bound, sellers on the terms of their oral contract. They may have wanted to improve their contractual position, but they could not do so unilaterally. If without more the buyers collect goods, that collection is as referable to the existing oral contract concluded between the parties as it is to some new contract to be found in an unexecuted written contract form. If it were otherwise, the sellers would be imposing on the buyers the obligation to negate the sellers' offer to vary fundamentally the parties' contract; whereas in principle the sellers, if in doubt about whether their offer to amend had been accepted in the absence of a signed and returned document, should have been querying the matter with the buyers expressly rather than relying on silence. Seventhly, the heading to the buyers' fax of Nov. 11 can provide the sellers with no assistance. That heading refers to the sellers' invoices, not to the contract form. Mr. Hamblen suggests that the reference to any contract number is an acceptance of there being some governing document. That is simply not so. Any party may choose to put its own reference upon a transaction. If that reference is included in an invoice, and the invoiced party responds by quoting the reference, that signifies nothing concerning written contracts; and that is a fortiori the case where the reference on the invoice is, as here, different from the reference on the contract form.[4]

The court found no authority to support the sellers' claim that the buyers implicitly accepted the sellers' standard form. As held by Rix J:

4 *Jayar Impex Ltd v Toaken Group Ltd* [1996] 2 Lloyd's Rep. 447.

I would be unwilling to infer that the parties had agreed to amend their contract so as to adopt the terms of the sellers' contract form, unless authority compelled me to. I would be surprised if in such circumstances authority would compel me to; and I do not think that the only two authorities relied on by Mr. Hamblen do compel me. He referred me, as did Mr. Phillips on behalf of the buyers, to *Brogden v The Metropolitan Railway Co.* (1877) 2 App. Cas. 666. In that case Brogden had been supplying the railway company with coals for years. There came a time when it was suggested that their relations should be formalized by a contract. An agreement was negotiated and the railway company drew up a contract and sent it to Brogden for signature. Brogden made some minor changes, filled in some gaps, wrote "approved" and signed and returned it. The railway company's agent put it in the drawer of his desk, but did not sign it. The contract was thereupon acted upon for almost two years; it was referred to in most of the letters passing between the parties during that period. In the absence of that contract, the parties had no contract between them. When Brogden then ceased to supply coals, was sued, and denied the existence of the contract, the stage was set for one of the leading cases on the formation of contract. In the House of Lords, Lord Cairns L.C. said (at p. 680):

My Lords, those are the grounds which lead me to think that, there having been clearly a consensus between these parties, arrived at and expressed by the document signed by Mr. Brogden, subject only to approbation, on the part of the company, of the additional term which he had introduced with regard to an arbitrator, that approbation was clearly given when the company commenced a course of dealing which is referable in my mind only to the contract, and when that course of dealing was accepted and acted upon by Messrs. Brogden & Co. in the supply of coals.

At p. 686 Lord Hatherley said: If you ask me, when in my judgment the agreement was complete, I answer that the agreement was complete when the first coals, the 300 tons of coal supplied in January, were invoiced at the differing price, and when that differing price was accepted and paid. I think that did bring the case up to what Mr. Herschell very fairly admitted, as he was bound to admit it, would be a sufficient case to make out on the part of the Plaintiffs. It does establish a course of action on the part of the Plaintiffs of such a character as necessarily to lead to the inference on the part of the Defendants that the agreement had been accepted on the part of the Plaintiffs, and was to be acted upon by them; and they did act upon it accordingly.

Lord Blackburn was dubious about the result, but not prepared to dissent. He stressed, however, that where conduct is said to fulfil the role of a signature as evidence of consent, the onus of proof lies upon him who asserts the making of a contract (at p. 693).

In that case, however, the evidence of acceptance by conduct was overwhelming: moreover, that conduct was only referable to the contract document, since there was no other contract between the parties. In the present case, the buyers were entitled to performance of their oral contract and their own performance was referable to it. Both Lord Cairns ("referable in my mind only to the contract") and Lord Hatherley ("as necessarily to lead to the inference") stressed the importance of such factors. In my judgment the Brogden case does not assist the sellers; if anything it assists the buyers.

In *Pagnan S.p.A. v Feed Products Ltd.*, the parties had made a contract, but were continuing to negotiate to sort out its details. In that context one party made a compromise proposal, and the other party responded by "noting" it without objection. Mr. Justice Bingham and the Court of Appeal held that this amounted to acceptance in the circumstances (at pp. 614, 620). That, however, is not this case. Here the parties were not continuing negotiations about details, but the sellers were attempting, whether consciously or not, to present a fundamentally different contract for acceptance from the one that had been concluded.

In conclusion, the parties' contract was not to be found in the sellers' contract form. It did not incorporate IGPA's spot terms. It did not incorporate IGPA arbitration.[5]

5 *Jayar Impex Ltd v Toaken Group Ltd* [1996] 2 Lloyd's Rep. 446.

In other words, if the sellers' contract form was to bind the buyers it could only be because it was accepted by the buyers as a variation of an existing contract. On the facts and the evidence, the court was unwilling to infer that the parties had agreed to amend their contract so as to adopt the sellers' contract form.

The buyers were entitled to performance of their oral contract and their own performance was referable to it; the parties were not continuing negotiations about details, rather the sellers were attempting (whether consciously or not) to present a fundamentally different contract for acceptance from one that had been concluded.

Here the nature of the exchanges between the parties and the behaviour of the buyers represented the two standout factors in determining the moment of formation of the contract and the identification of its terms. Clearly, the first telephone exchange between the parties was considered exhaustive in terms of formation of the contract.

The subsequent exchange with the attempts of the sellers to "impose" their own standard terms was held to be, in legal teleological terms, a variation of the existing contract; a variation to which the buyers did not subscribe, as they never signed, acknowledged or returned the seller's standard form in any way.

3.3 Traders' standard terms and conditions

Disputes often arise in practice in relation to standard conditions and terms. In *Albright & Wilson UK Ltd v Biachem Ltd*,[6] the claimants ordered two different chemicals from two different suppliers who instructed the same company to deliver them. The driver of one consignment, by some mistake, presented the delivery note relating to the other. As a result, his cargo was discharged into tanks containing the other product and a large explosion occurred. One of the issues was whether, in relation to one of the contracts, the standard terms of either party was incorporated.

The order in question was the fifth in a series, with the first order having been preceded by a quotation which was subject to the supplier's terms and conditions of sale. After that the purchaser faxed a "blanket" order which stipulated that supply should be subject to the purchaser's conditions. The order was confirmed by telephone. Delivery took place.

The supplier then sent an invoice with his terms on the back. There were then four telephone orders which were followed by a standard form purchase order which called for supply on the purchaser's terms and conditions. In each case an invoice with the supplier's terms was sent after delivery.

Similarly, in *Continental Tyre & Rubber Co Ltd v Trunk Trailer Ltd*,[7] manufacturers of trailers ordered a quantity of tyres from a tyre supplier on their printed purchase order which purported to incorporate their conditions of purchase.

The sellers claimed that their terms applied because when the first batch of tyres was delivered one of the purchasers' employees signed a delivery note with the words "All offers and sales are subject to the [seller's] current terms and conditions, a copy of which will be supplied on request". The Inner House of the Court

6 *Albright & Wilson UK Ltd v Biachem Ltd* [2001] 2 All ER 537.
7 *Continental Tyre & Rubber Co Ltd v Trunk Trailer Ltd* 1987 SLT 58.

of Session rejected this contention on the basis that the contract was complete as soon as the first batch of tyres was delivered.

The signature of the purchaser's employee on the delivery note had no contractual effect; it was not a contractual document and was only required for the purpose of confirming the quantity and description of the goods delivered.

The aforementioned cases emphasise two important aspects in relation to the incorporation of terms: first, at any rate where parties have dealt with each other more than once or twice, it may not be critical to the incorporation of standard terms that those terms be set out in a contractual document, i.e. one that itself constitutes an offer or its acceptance, or even in a purported record of the contract, nor that the document containing the terms relied on has preceded the making of every contract.

Second, the sequence of events is also important. An invoice following a concluded contract effected by a clear offer on standard terms which are accepted, even if only by delivery, will or may be too late. But, if there has been no reference to rival terms, the appearance of terms on the back of every invoice and the acceptance of delivery of goods without objection may indicate acceptance of the terms.

In *Balmoral Group Ltd. v Borealis UK Ltd, Borealis AS, Borealis A/S*,[8] a dispute arose as to the validity of the incorporation of the sellers' standard terms and conditions into a sale contract. Initially, Borealis UK faxed a quote to Balmoral for the supply of polyethylene. The quote stated that it was "subject to normal terms and to current conditions of sale".

Those conditions excluded the statutory implied terms of satisfactory quality and fitness for purpose. Invoices were sent to Balmoral with Borealis' conditions on the back; the managing director of Balmoral reviewed the invoices without studying them, initialling them for payment. Balmoral duly made payment without comment, query or objection.

Subsequently, Balmoral faxed another order which contained a stamped reference to its own terms and conditions: those terms provided that Borealis was to "warrant that the Goods . . . will be of satisfactory quality and fit for the purpose held out by the Seller or made known to the Seller in Writing at the time the purchase order is placed".

The court held that Borealis' standard terms applied throughout. In the words of Christopher Clarke J:

> I am not persuaded that when Balmoral first contracted to purchase polyethylene from Borealis in December 1994 the common understanding between them was that the purchase was on Borealis' terms and conditions. In British Crane Hire both parties were crane hirers. They each hired out cranes on similar conditions. The defendants had signed and sent back the plaintiff's conditions twice before; and would have done so again if the accident had not happened. In December 2004 Balmoral had not purchased material from Borealis before; nor had they ever signed or sent back Borealis' conditions; nor, so far as the evidence shows, had they received a copy of those conditions when they sent their purchase order or took delivery. In those circumstances I do not think that Borealis was entitled to conclude that Balmoral had agreed to their terms.

8 *Balmoral Group Ltd. v Borealis UK Ltd, Borealis AS, Borealis* A/S [2006] 2 Lloyd's Rep. 629.

> But by the fax of 18 January 1995 Borealis made it plain that its prices were quoted "subject to normal terms and to current conditions of sale" and Balmoral had received an invoice with Borealis' terms on the back. By putting its terms on the back of their invoices Borealis indicated to Balmoral that, so far as Borealis were concerned, they intended the contract to be on those terms: see clause 2 cited at para 30 above. Those invoices were seen and initialled by Mr Joyce, the Managing Director of Balmoral's rotomoulding division. He realised that there were terms on the back of the invoices. He reviewed them but did not study them. Balmoral thereafter purchased material at the quoted prices with knowledge of Borealis' conditions without ever suggesting that they were not applicable. Borealis did not know that each invoice in respect of borecene was initialled by Mr Joyce before payment. But they did know that they were received and paid without demur. A reasonable person in their position would be entitled to assume, as was the fact, that someone at Balmoral had considered whether or not to pay the invoice and had seen the conditions on the back.
>
> In those circumstances Borealis was, in my judgment, reasonably entitled to assume that Balmoral accepted the applicability of the conditions subject to which the price had been quoted. If Balmoral wanted to pay the price quoted without accepting the terms, it was incumbent on it to say so.[9]

It was held that when Balmoral first contracted to purchase polyethylene from Borealis, there was no common understanding between them that the purchase was on Borealis' terms and conditions. Balmoral had not purchased material from Borealis before; nor had they ever signed or sent back Borealis' conditions; nor, so far as the evidence showed, had they received a copy of those conditions when they sent their purchase order or took delivery.

In the circumstances, Borealis was not entitled to conclude that Balmoral had agreed to their terms.[10] Nevertheless, by the fax of 18 January 1995 Borealis made it plain that its prices were quoted "subject to normal terms and to current conditions of sale" and Balmoral had received an invoice with Borealis' terms on the back. By putting its terms on the back of their invoices Borealis indicated to Balmoral that, so far as Borealis were concerned, they intended the contract to be on those terms.

Those invoices were seen and initialled on behalf of Balmoral, but they were not studied. Balmoral thereafter purchased material at the quoted prices with knowledge of Borealis' conditions without ever suggesting that they were not applicable. A reasonable person in Borealis' position would be entitled to assume, as was the fact, that someone at Balmoral had considered whether or not to pay the invoice and had seen the conditions on the back.

In other words, the stamp on Balmoral's order of 6 December 1995 referring to Balmoral's own conditions was insufficient to reverse the previous position and to signify (much less to secure agreement) that Balmoral's terms were now to apply instead. Balmoral said nothing about any change in terms. It did not say

---

9 *Balmoral Group Ltd. v Borealis UK Ltd, Borealis AS, Borealis A/S* [2006] 2 Lloyd's Rep. 629, 691, 692.

10 See also *McCutcheon v David Macbrayne Ltd* [1964] 1 Lloyd's Rep. 16; *Kendall & Sons v Lillico & Sons* [1969] 2 AC 31; *Hollier v Rambler Motors (AMC Ltd)* [1972] 2 QB 71; *SIAT v Tradax Overseas SA* [1978] 2 Lloyd's Rep. 470; *Continental Tyre & Rubber Co Ltd v Trunk Trailer Ltd* 1987 SLT 58; *Circle Freight International Ltd v Medeast Gulf Exports Ltd* [1988] 2 Lloyd's Rep. 427; *Albright & Wilson UK Ltd v Biachem Ltd* [2001] 2 All ER 537, considered; *British Crane Hire Corporation Ltd v Ipswich Plant Hire Ltd* [1975] QB 303, distinguished.

that Balmoral was going to treat Borealis' quotes as no longer linked to Borealis' conditions. Balmoral did not provide a copy of its conditions then or thereafter, nor, apart from the stamp on the order form, make any reference thereto. In those circumstances, a supplier in Borealis' position would be entitled to expect that, if Balmoral was seeking to reverse the previous position, it would make explicit reference to the fact that it was proposing a change.

A buyer in Balmoral's position would not be entitled reasonably to assume that Balmoral had agreed to its conditions because of the stamp that now appeared on its purchase order or because Borealis did not comment on it.

3.4 The battle of the forms

Legal disputes often arise where both parties accept that a legally binding contract exists, but disagree about whose standard terms apply.

Such disputes may be resolved by reference to the "last document rule", i.e. whichever business/trader sent the last document.

In *Sterling Hydraulics Ltd v Dichtomatik Ltd*,[11] the claimant purchaser (SHL) asked the defendant seller (DL) to quote for a quantity of O-ring seals. DL faxed its quotation to SHL, which subsequently sent a purchase order to DL stating: "Please supply the following subject to the terms and conditions as set out below and overleaf." The terms and conditions were set out on the second page of the fax. They provided, inter alia, that payment should be made on the last day of the calendar month, two months following the month in which the goods were received.

At a later stage, DL faxed an acknowledgement of order to SHL. The acknowledgement was printed by computer onto two blank sheets of paper bearing DL's printed letterhead. The first page contained the words "Terms of Payment: by the end of the month of delivery plus two months". The second page was a continuation of the first which, after repeating the heading on the previous page, stated "With best regards, Dichtomatik Limited". Most of the rest of the second page was blank save, at the foot of the page, the words: "Delivery based on our General Terms of Sale".

The seals were eventually delivered to SHL in batches, in each case accompanied by a delivery order which stated "Delivery based on our General Terms of Sale". DL subsequently issued invoices containing the words "Delivery based on our General Terms of Sale". A number of terms were printed on the reverse of the page under the heading "Sales and Delivery Conditions", which were the standard terms used by DL at the material time.

In the event a large number of seals failed in operation, causing the manifold blocks to malfunction. SHL claimed damages from DL for the costs incurred in replacing the seals in the manifold blocks and for the costs of compensating its purchaser. SHL contended that the seals were ineffective because the wrong material had been used, that it was an express term of the contract that the seals should

11 *Sterling Hydraulics Ltd v Dichtomatic Ltd* [2007] 1 Lloyd's Rep. 7.

be made of EPDM rubber of a specified hardness, and that DL was in breach of contract by supplying seals made of nitrile rubber.

DL's case was that the contract incorporated DL's standard terms and conditions rather than those of SHL. DL contended that by virtue of its standard terms, it was under no liability to SHL.

The court held, on the evidence, that DL's sales and delivery conditions had not been incorporated into the contract, as DL's faxed acknowledgment of order was not a counter offer.

In the words of HHJ Havelock-Allan:

> DL's primary case is that the contract was concluded upon delivery. The premise is that the acknowledgement of order was a counter-offer rather than an acceptance. The counter-offer was accepted by SHL taking delivery. The contract incorporated DL's standard terms because delivery was proffered on those terms and the goods were physically accepted. In sum DL relies on the last shot doctrine [. . .]
>
> First, the payment terms were not that different, if different at all. The offer made in clause 7 of SHL's conditions of purchase was for payment "on the last day of the calendar month, two months following the month in which the goods are received by us". DL's acknowledgement of order contained the following statement: "Terms of Payment. By the end of the month of delivery plus two months." Some attempt was made by Mr Beresford to argue that the credit conferred by clause 7 of SHL's terms was more generous because the clause went on to say: "Invoices received after the third working day of the month following that in which the goods were received, will be considered to be dated in the month in which they are received." Whatever that sentence means, I do not think it has the effect of extending the time for payment beyond two months after the month in which the goods are delivered.
>
> Second, the words "Delivery based on our General Terms of Sale" at the foot of the first page of the acknowledgement of order were not sufficient, in my judgment, to convert the acknowledgement into a counter-offer. It is DL's case that its Sales and Delivery Conditions were printed on the reverse of the acknowledgement of order and on the reverse of the delivery orders. Whilst I am prepared to accept that that was the case (albeit that the original documents were not in evidence), the practice of DL was to send acknowledgements of orders by fax without faxing the reverse of the page. It follows that SHL did not receive a copy of DL's standard terms when it received the acknowledgement on this, or any previous, occasion. That is not in itself an end of the matter because the words of purported incorporation on the face of the acknowledgement did not refer to terms "on the reverse" or "overleaf". They simply referred to DL's "General Terms of Sale". There can be no argument that in appropriate cases words of reference of this kind are capable of incorporating standard terms which are to be found elsewhere. It is also true that they are more likely to do so in a commercial or business context, where the parties to the transaction might be expected to have trading terms which they want to govern their transactions. Nevertheless, even in this context, adequate notice of the terms must be given if they are to prevent the acknowledgement of an offer made on different terms from resulting in a binding contract.
>
> I do not think that the words of incorporation used here, without an accompanying copy of the terms in question, provided adequate notice that the acknowledgement of order was not an acceptance of the order but a counter-offer.[12]

In *Sterling Hydraulics Ltd v Dichtomatik Ltd*, the battle of the forms took an unusual twist.

---

12 *Sterling Hydraulics Ltd v Dichtomatik Ltd* [2007] 1 Lloyd's Rep. 7, 14.

Indeed, the court held that insufficient notice of DL's standard conditions had been given to SHL to make them a term of the contract. DL's acknowledgment of order was an acceptance of the offer to purchase contained in SHL's purchase order. The contract was therefore held to be concluded on SHL's standard terms.

3.5 Recent developments regarding the battle of the forms

Two decisions of the courts in recent years have focused on the question of what is to happen when parties' standard terms of contract conflict and there is a dispute as to which set of terms should prevail.

3.5.1 Specialist Insulation Ltd v Pro-Duct (Fife) Ltd

The first decision is a judgment of Lord Malcolm in the Outer House of the Court of Session in *Specialist Insulation Ltd v Pro-Duct (Fife) Ltd.*[13]

The parties' contract had been preceded by two written communications between them: (i) on 29 October 2010 the pursuer sent a quotation for the supply of ductwork in the sum of £216,819.40. This had stated that the supply was "subject to our standard terms and conditions of trading (available on request)".

Along with this, although not referred to in it, the defender forwarded a document headed "Pro-Duct (Fife) Ltd – Material Supply only Sub-contract Agreement".

This document, though its heading referred to "material supply only", narrated that the defender wished to engage the "sub-contractor" (i.e. the pursuer) to carry out certain work ("the sub-contract works") on a "labour only basis". There was thus an internal inconsistency as to the nature of the contract envisaged, between its being either "material supply only" or "labour only". The price of works was stated as £211,469.12 (note the difference to the price stated by the pursuer).

This document was executed on behalf of the defender. Immediately below the defender's signature was the heading "Executed on behalf of the sub-contractor", and then space for the name, signature and date of signature on behalf of the sub-contractor. This document was never executed on behalf of the pursuer.

One of the terms in this document was a clause stating that "Either party may refer such disputes as may arise under this contract to adjudication at any time". It was this clause on which the pursuer sought to rely.

Lord Malcolm disposed of an initial question – was there a contract at all? – by stating: "It would be unrealistic to hold that the parties had not reached an agreement that the ductwork should be supplied at the specified price".

The defender, in accepting the goods, had therefore accepted the pursuer's terms, and the contract was concluded on that basis, i.e. without the incorporation of any adjudication clause. Lord Malcolm therefore found for the defender, held the decision of the adjudicator to be invalid, and granted a decree of absolvitor.

Lord Malcolm might conceivably have held there to be no contract at all: the pursuer had proposed a contract for the supply of goods; the defender bizarrely

13 *Specialist Insulation Ltd v Pro-Duct (Fife) Ltd* [2012] CSOH 79.

appeared either to have proposed a "labour only" contract, i.e. one for the provision of services, or no contract at all (arguably its terms were inconsistent as to whether the contract was one of supply or of labour, and therefore void for uncertainty).

The court could therefore have taken a similar approach to that adopted in *Gee (Ayrshire) Ltd v Quigley*,[14] where one party had proposed a contract of hire of goods, the other of hire and the provision of labour: in that case there was held to be no contract, there being dissensus between the parties as to the nature of the contract.

While the same result might have prevailed in this case, a more realistic view is that both parties knew that what was envisaged was the simple supply of goods for an agreed price, the defender's inclusion of the language of a labour only contract apparently the result of infelicitous language used because of the attachment of a not wholly appropriate set of standard terms.

Nevertheless, if that is right, and there was a contract, there was an evident problem: if the defender's standard terms used inappropriate or inconsistent language to describe the contract, could those terms be held to govern the contract in any so called battle of the forms?

The traditional approach to solving such a battle of the forms is to apply a "last shot" analysis: whoever's terms are stated last are treated as the contractual offer, accepted either by an unqualified agreement to those terms or by performance by the offeree.

On that approach, Lord Malcolm's decision might appear suspect: it was the defender's terms which were the "last shot" (if one assumes, as Lord Malcolm does, that the document accompanying the purchase order was correctly seen as a proposal of contractual terms), and on that basis the conduct of the pursuer in supplying the goods without any demur as to those terms would, one might have expected, have been seen as an unqualified acceptance of those terms.

Moreover, the defender's reply being a counter offer, the pursuer's original offer should have been seen as having been "killed off", and should not have been open for acceptance by the defender; yet Lord Malcolm holds that it was. Is there anything that can be said in favour of Lord Malcolm's seemingly unorthodox approach, of using the first shot rather than the last shot, and of seeing the original offer as not having been killed off?

Lord Malcolm highlights two matters as being important in his decision: (1) the absence of any signature of the pursuer agreeing to the defender's terms; and (2) the fact that the terms proposed by the defender envisaged a contract of a type (the provision of labour) which was patently inappropriate to what both parties knew was a contract for the supply of goods.

On the first point, Lord Malcolm's view is that, because the defender's offer envisaged that it had to be accepted in writing before a contract was concluded, the supply of goods by the pursuer without such a written acceptance ought not to be seen as referable to the defender's offer, but rather to its own proposed terms.

14 *Gee (Ayrshire) Ltd v Quigley* [1952] UKHL 2.

3.5.2 Grafton Merchandising Gb Ltd t/a Buildbase v Sundial Properties (Gilmerton) Ltd

This second decision is an unreported decision of the Edinburgh Sheriff Court, in *Grafton Merchandising Gb Ltd t/a Buildbase v Sundial Properties (Gilmerton) Ltd.*[15]

In this case, the defender applied to the pursuer for a trade credit account. The application form which the defender completed and returned contained the pursuer's terms and conditions. Condition 1 of the pursuer's conditions provided:

> All orders are accepted by the Company solely on these Terms and Conditions, which override any terms and conditions stipulated, incorporated or referred to by the Customer whether in its order or any negotiations. No variation or addition to these Terms and Conditions shall be incorporated into the Contract unless such variation or additions and the Company's agreement thereto are both expressly agreed in writing.

The defender submitted a purchase order being subject to the defender's terms and conditions (which it averred were printed on the back of the purchase order).

Unsurprisingly, given the apparent non-application of the orthodox approach to the battle of the forms in the earlier decision of Lord Malcolm in *Specialist Insulation Ltd v Pro-Duct (Fife) Ltd*, "that earlier case was relied upon by the pursuer in an attempt to argue that it had ring fenced its terms through its 'first shot'."[16]

The Sheriff however "distinguished this earlier case on the basis that the outcome of *Specialist Insulation* had been dependent upon the judicial view expressed in it that the defender's terms envisaged signature as a prerequisite to their being accepted (which had not occurred): it was that factor (in the Sheriff's view), rather than an attempted ring fencing of the pursuer's terms in the 'first shot', which had determined that the defender's terms had not applied."[17]

Grafton Merchandising Gb Ltd t/a Buildbase v Sundial Properties (Gilmerton) Ltd is more in line with the orthodox approach to the battle of the forms.

15 *Grafton Merchandising Gb Ltd t/a Buildbase v Sundial Properties (Gilmerton) Ltd*, unreported.

16 See Hogg, M. "Two recent decisions on the battle of the forms (i.e. conflicting standard conditions of contract)", OLB, 2013.

17 Ibid.

CHAPTER 4

Incorporation of standard terms

4.1 Validity of incorporation of standard terms

The existence of standard terms and contracts devised to aid traders is very appealing and of great use within the international trading communities.

Nevertheless, incorporation of standard clauses and contracts can give rise to serious legal complexities which will be the object of scrutiny in this chapter. If, in the previous chapter, our attention focused primarily on when a contract comes into existence, we shall now turn to the intricate legal issue of validity of incorporation of standard terms, such as Incoterms® or Fosfa and Gafta terms, and on issues of conflicts between terms of sale contracts and standard terms incorporated therein.

One of the first legal issues which may arise in the case of a dispute relates to the effectiveness of incorporation of standard terms (likely to be raised by a party in breach of those terms); when do we have an effective legal incorporation of standard clauses?

Apart from validity of incorporation issues, disputes may arise because of something which happens in the performance of a contract; however, as we shall discover in the following, their resolution frequently depends on what is said in the contract itself and on the exchanges between parties prior to the formation of the contract.

4.2 Incorporation of standard clauses: Legal problems and solutions

The practice of incorporation has made it increasingly common for deals to be closed on the barest of terms on the basis that "other terms" are incorporated into the contract. Indeed, it is not unusual to see two-pages long contracts for extremely valuable international commercial sales.

The rationale for this lies with the extreme efficiency of incorporating standard terms and contracts which enables traders to save valuable contracting time.

In legal terms, the legal complexities arising from incorporation are, as will be readily appreciated, many. This is due to the fact that the incorporation of terms may stem from a variety of sources, e.g. earlier exchanges, tender terms, in-house standard terms and conditions, trade association terms and conditions, earlier contracts between the parties, or even other contracts entirely.

In the course of the years, courts have established various criteria for incorporation of standard terms into contracts,[1] but we shall focus here on the ones applicable within the context of international commercial sales.

On a general level, in order for effective incorporation to take place, it is necessary to prove that parties had reasonable notice of the standard terms/forms to be incorporated into the sale contract. Nevertheless, it has been noticed that this generic criterion is subject to a series of exemptions:[2] first of all, in the case that the standard form has been signed by the parties, no requirement of notice arises.

This is what happened in *L'Estrange v F Graucob Ltd*,[3] where the court held that in principle parties are bound by their own signature. As put by Scrutton LJ:

> The parties may, however, reduce their agreement into writing, so that the writing constitutes the sole evidence of the agreement, without signing it; but in that case there must be evidence independently of the agreement itself to prove that the defendant has assented to it. In that case, also, if it is proved that the defendant has assented to the writing constituting the agreement between the parties, it is, in the absence of fraud, immaterial that the defendant had not read the agreement and did not know its contents.[4]

Similarly, the requirement of notice does not arise whenever the standard form is incorporated within the context of a course of dealing, provided that the form is of common use and not exceedingly onerous. This was held in *Circle Freight International Ltd v Medeast Gulf Export Ltd*,[5] where a dispute arose around the incorporation into a sale contract of the standard trading conditions of the Institute of Freight Forwarders. On appeal, it was held that the conditions were effectively incorporated into the contract, due to the fact that the parties were commercial companies, there had been a long course of dealing between them, and the standard terms were of common use and not particularly onerous.

Indeed, Taylor LJ held that:

> it is not necessary to the incorporation of trading terms into a contract that they should be specifically set out provided that they are conditions in common form or usual terms in the relevant business. It is sufficient if adequate notice is given identifying and relying upon the conditions and they are available on request. Other considerations apply if the conditions or any of them are particularly onerous or unusual. Again, it is not necessary that notice of the conditions should be contained in a contractual document where there has been a course of dealing. Here, the parties were commercial companies. There had been a course of dealing in which at least 11 invoices had been sent giving notice that business was conducted on the IFF terms at a place on the document where it was plain to be seen [. . .] The IFF conditions are not particularly onerous or unusual and, indeed, are in common use.[6]

---

1 For a detailed analysis see *Chitty on Contracts*, 31st Edition, 2013, Sweet & Maxwell, London, chapter 2.

2 On this point, see C. Debattista, *Bills of Lading in Export Trade*, Tottel, 2008, p. 18.

3 *L'Estrange v F Graucob Ltd* [1934] 2 KB 394.

4 *Ibid.*, at 421.

5 *Circle Freight International Ltd v Medeast Gulf Export Ltd* [1988] 2 Lloyd's Rep. 427.

6 *Ibid.*, at 434.

Finally, whenever notice is indeed required, the extent of it will be dependent on the nature and complexity of the standard form/terms to be incorporated: the higher the complexity of the terms, the greater is the degree of notice required. This can be evinced in *Interfoto Picture Library Ltd. v Stiletto Visual Programmes Ltd*,[7] where the court held that clear and reasonable efforts must be made to bring any particularly onerous and unusual conditions to the attention of the other party if they are to form part of a contract.

As eloquently put by Bingham LJ:

> In many civil law systems, and perhaps in most legal systems outside the common law world, the law of obligations recognises and enforces an overriding principle that in making and carrying out contracts parties should act in good faith. This does not simply mean that they should not deceive each other, a principle which any legal system must recognise; its effect is perhaps most aptly conveyed by such metaphorical colloquialisms as "playing fair," "coming clean" or "putting one's cards face upwards on the table." It is in essence a principle of fair and open dealing. In such a forum it might, I think, be held on the facts of this case that the plaintiffs were under a duty in all fairness to draw the defendants' attention specifically to the high price payable if the transparencies were not returned in time and, when the 14 days had expired, to point out to the defendants the high cost of continued failure to return them.

English law has, characteristically, committed itself to no such overriding principle but has developed piecemeal solutions in response to demonstrated problems of unfairness. Many examples could be given. Thus equity has intervened to strike down unconscionable bargains. Parliament has stepped in to regulate the imposition of exemption clauses and the form of certain hire purchase agreements. The common law also has made its contribution, by holding that certain classes of contract require the utmost good faith, by treating as irrecoverable what purport to be agreed estimates of damage but are in truth a disguised penalty for breach, and in many other ways.

The well-known cases on sufficiency of notice are in my view properly to be read in this context. At one level they are concerned with a question of pure contractual analysis, whether one party has done enough to give the other notice of the incorporation of a term in the contract. At another level they are concerned with a somewhat different question, whether it would in all the circumstances be fair (or reasonable) to hold a party bound by any conditions or by a particular condition of an unusual and stringent nature.[8]

The position of the Court in *Interfoto* was endorsed by the Court of Appeal in *AEG (U.K.) Ltd. v Logic Resource Ltd.*[9] Here, a majority of the Court of Appeal found that insufficient steps had been taken to draw attention to an onerous clause. As held by the court, although the party receiving the document knows it contains conditions, if the particular condition relied on is one which is a particularly onerous or unusual term, or is one which involves the abrogation of a right given

7 *Interfoto Picture Library Ltd. v Stiletto Visual Programmes Ltd.* (C.A.) [1988] 2 WLR 615.
8 *Ibid.*, at 622.
9 *AEG (U.K.) Ltd. v Logic Resource Ltd.* [1996] CLC 265.

by statute, the party tendering the document must show that it has been brought fairly and reasonably to the other's attention.[10]

Aside from the aforementioned legal criteria of effective incorporation, when it comes to international commercial sales, four separate main issues may give rise to problematic scenarios: blind incorporation, incorporation of unusual or unreasonable clauses, incorporation of clauses from contracts not yet drawn, and possible conflicts between a term of the incorporating contract and an incorporated clause. These issues shall be considered in the following.

4.3 Incorporation of standard terms: Blind incorporation, incorporation of alien, unreasonable and yet to be drawn clauses

Let us assume that two parties have negotiated and concluded a contract for the purchase of soya bean oil, incorporating Fosfa 54 standard terms. The buyers are located in the UK, whereas the sellers are based in Australia. If the cargo took a very long time to reach the buyers, this should not come as a surprise to them.

Indeed, an attentive scrutiny of Fosfa 54 will show that clause 4, lines 33 and 34, allows sellers to "load the oil in one or more origin ports, aboard of a ship which will proceed directly or indirectly on a geographically normal route from the port/s of shipment to the port/s of destination".[11]

In the absence of a detailed knowledge of the terms due to be incorporated, blind incorporation of standard terms may indeed lead to unwelcome surprises.

Provided that parties do have complete knowledge of the terms they are willing to incorporate, how far can the process of incorporation of standard terms be stretched? Shrewd incorporation of sharp, invisible clauses has given rise to a certain degree of hostility from UK courts.

For instance, clauses which are not germane to the nature of a sale contract will not be seen positively by the scrutiny of English courts. In *OK Petroleum A.B. v Vitol Energy S.A*,[12] the court was asked whether a time bar applicable in case of demurrage under the charter party was incorporated from a charter party (yet to be drawn up at the moment in which the sale contract was stipulated) into the sale contract.

Since the incorporated charter party was yet to be drawn up when the incorporating contract was entered into and could not be presumed by the parties to the latter to

10 *Ibid.*, at 269. Nevertheless, see Hobhouse LJ's dissenting speech: "In my judgment, it is desirable as a matter of principle to keep what was said in the *Interfoto* case within its proper bounds. A wide range of clauses are commonly incorporated into contracts by general words. If it is to be the policy of English law that in every case those clauses are to be gone through with, in effect, a toothcomb to see whether they were entirely usual and entirely desirable in the particular contract, then one is completely distorting the contractual relationship between the parties and the ordinary mechanisms of making contracts. It will introduce uncertainty into the law of contract."

11 See Fosfa 54, clause 4, lines 33–34.

12 *OK Petroleum A.B. v Vitol Energy S.A.* [1995] 2 Lloyd's Rep. 160.

contain any specific wording or terms, the established approach to construction was that general words of incorporation would not normally suffice for incorporation.

As eloquently put by Coleman J:

> In my judgment the correct analysis of the authorities is that in a case, such as the present, where the incorporated contract does not exist when the incorporating contract is entered into and cannot be presumed by the parties to the latter to contain any specific wording or terms, the established approach to construction is that general words of incorporation will not normally be construed as wide enough to incorporate any provision from the other contract unless that provision is part of the subject-matter of that contract and not merely ancillary to it, such, for example, as an arbitration clause or a jurisdiction clause. Such ancillary provisions will not generally be treated as relevant or germane to the rights and obligations of the parties under the incorporating contract. I do not suggest that this is an invariable rule of construction and that there can never be a case where general words will be construed as incorporating such ancillary provisions. That would depend upon the surrounding circumstances and the relationship between the parties to the incorporating contract. That such cases are likely to be extremely uncommon must be the consequence of what on analysis is, in my view, the rationale for the approach to construction which I have sought to identify, namely that the Courts impute to the parties to the incorporating contract a mutual intention by their use of general words of incorporation to be bound only by the relevant subject-matter of the incorporated contract because the parties are taken to treat those matters which are merely collateral or ancillary to the subject-matter as, for that reason, intrinsically personal to the parties to the incorporated contract and therefore not self-evidently germane to be incorporated into their own contract.
>
> In the present case cl. 10 – the time bar provision – although exclusively applicable to claims for demurrage under the charter-party, is essentially ancillary to the substantive or subject-matter provisions of that contract relating to demurrage. Its ancillary nature is conclusively demonstrated by the fact that its contractual function is confined to the enforcement of already-accrued contractual rights. It is exclusively concerned with recovery of such demurrage as has already fallen due. The words of incorporation in the sale contracts, being in general terms, do not, in my judgment, clearly express a mutual intention to incorporate into those contracts any provision of the charter-party which is not part of the demurrage subject-matter of that contract but is merely ancillary to it.[13]

It is therefore clear on authority that incorporation of ancillary clauses whose content is alien to the nature of the incorporating contract would not generally be treated by English courts as relevant or germane to the rights and obligations of the parties under the incorporating contract.

By the same token, incorporation of unreasonable clauses in sale contracts will be also struck down by judicial intervention. That was the scenario which arose in *The Northern Progress*,[14] where a c.&f. contract for the sale of Brazilian solvent extracted soya bean meal pellets purported to incorporate a charter party clause

13 *Ibid.*

14 *The Northern Progress* [1996] 2 Lloyd's Rep. 319.

allowing the seller-charterers to have the goods discharged at a place other than the c.&f. destination in the sale contract.[15]

In assessing the nature of the deviation clause enshrined into the charter party and incorporated by the sale contract, Rix J held that:

> Clause 55 [the charterparty deviation clause] was an unreasonable and unusual term in the trade. It may be that this factor by itself would be enough to exclude its incorporation. After all, the parties can hardly have contemplated that the sellers would procure a contract of affreightment which, because it was not in a form reasonable and customary in the trade, rendered the sellers in breach of their duty as c.&f. sellers. But even if that factor does not entirely by itself go to override or exclude what might otherwise be a prima facie incorporation, it is highly relevant in the overall consideration of what the parties must be regarded as intending by their incorporation clause.
>
> There is then the element of rationality or commercial commonsense. [. . .] indeed, it seems to me that the doctrine of the exclusion of terms which do not make sense (and the doctrine of manipulation which is designed to save an appropriate term for incorporation which would otherwise have to be excluded) as well as the doctrine of inconsistency are but aspects of the overall process of arriving at the true intention of the parties in which the concept of rationality and commercial commonsense must play their appropriate and fundamental roles.
>
> In my judgment the incorporation of cl. 55 into the sale contract, and a fortiori the sale contract as amended, in the absence of specific negotiation between the parties, lacks rationality and flies in the face of commercial commonsense.[16]

Interestingly, the court was not prepared to "manipulate" the unreasonable deviation clause so as to make it effective in the sale contract.[17] Parties may of course agree to unreasonable terms or terms which fly in the face of commercial reality (and all the more readily of course where the commercial difficulty is not manifest).

If, however, a court is to conclude that, by means of something as imprecise as an incorporation clause, the parties have intended to agree what is manifestly unreasonable, then the parties must make that intention clear. As the doctrine points out, "where the intention of the party is doubtful, the court will not hold that a term is incorporated".[18]

The last issue to unravel in this section revolves around the possibility of incorporating clauses from contracts which have not yet been drafted, e.g. a sales contract incorporating clauses from a charter party not yet concluded. It is indeed common practice for international commercial sales contracts to incorporate terms from a contract of carriage like a charter party, especially when under the sales contract

15 According to the sales contract, delivery was to be one safe port out of Rijeka/Koper at the buyers' option to be declared when the vessel was passing Gibraltar. Clause 55 of the charter party concluded by the sellers provided that:

> In the event that Yugoslavian ports are closed to merchant shipping or the area is subject to an insurance premium due to war-like conditions then Owners to declare this to Charterers and Charterers to nominate alternative port within Italian Adriatic. Extra insurance premium for this to be for Charterers' account. Any deviation incurred to be compensated to the Owners by the Charterers at cost duly substantiated.

16 *The Northern Progress* [1996] 2 Lloyd's Rep. 319, 330.

17 *Ibid.*, at 331.

18 See *Scrutton on Charterparties and Bills of Lading*, Sweet & Maxwell, 22nd Revised Edition, 2011, p. 64.

the seller is to make the transport arrangements. Can a sales contract incorporate terms of a charter party yet to be drawn up?

In regard to this matter, the case law is oscillatory. In the aforementioned *OK Petroleum v Vitol Energy*,[19] a time bar enshrined into a charter party was not deemed to be validly incorporated into a sales contract partly, it appears, because the charter party had not yet been drawn up at the time when the sales contract was agreed. The rationale for this lies with the impossibility of ascertaining with precision the content of the incorporating terms, as Coleman J held:

> In the case of these sale contracts, as would normally be the case with such contracts, the charter-parties whose terms as to demurrage are said to have been incorporated had not been brought into existence at the time when the sale contracts were entered into. Nothing in the terms of the sale contracts specified the precise terms of the charter-party which the seller might enter into. He had complete freedom to contract on any terms provided that he procured delivery of the goods in accordance with the terms of the sale contract and tendered a bill of lading in terms consonant with his obligations as a c.i.f. seller.[20]

A different view was taken in *Gill & Duffus v Rionda*,[21] where it was held that a sales contract could incorporate a clause from a charter party which had not yet been drawn up, so long as the charter had been fixed on clear terms. The dispute here arose in relation to the validity of incorporation of a demurrage clause of a charter party which was on the standard Cubasugar form, but yet to be drawn up. As put by Clarke J:

> In my opinion the expression "as per charter-party" refers to the charter-party pursuant to which this cargo was being carried or was to be carried from Cuba to Libya under the bills of lading referred to in the contract. Provided that the charter-party concerned was a genuine commercial arrangement I do not think that it matters that the charter-party had not been drawn up at the time when the contract of sale was made.[22]

A discerning element in *Gill & Duffus v Rionda* appears to be the fact that although the terms of the incorporated charter party were yet to be drawn up, they were nonetheless ascertainable by the parties as the charter party was a standard Cubasugar form. Under these circumstances, it may be indeed possible to incorporate clauses of contracts not yet concluded, although parties are best advised to draw up terms prior their incorporation.

Above all, in light of the above, parties incorporating standard terms need always to be aware of the nature of those terms, their compatibility with the sale contract, and their overall reasonableness.

A further problematic issue which relates to the incorporation of standard terms lies with inconsistencies and discrepancies between incorporated standard terms and the clauses of the incorporating sale contract. This issue shall be unravelled in the following.

19 *OK Petroleum v Vitol Energy*, above.
20 *Ibid.*, at 164.
21 *Gill & Duffus v Rionda* [1994] 2 Lloyd's Rep. 67
22 *Ibid.*, at 73.

4.4 Incorporation of standard terms: Inconsistencies and discrepancies

Far from being free from any deficiency, the process of incorporation of standard terms into a sales contract may ultimately lead to inconsistencies and discrepancies between the clauses enshrined in the sales contract originally agreed by the parties, and the terms printed in standard forms invoked by the original sale contract.

In case these inconsistencies arise, judges and arbitrators will usually endeavour to ascertain what the intention of the parties was at the time the contract was drawn up. The outcome of this endeavour will be dictated by the presence or not in the contract of a clear hierarchy clause devised to deal with conflicts between the original contract and the standard terms incorporated therein.

If a hierarchy clause is present in the contract, arbitrators and judges will usually ordain it. This is what happened in *Pagnan S.p.A. v Tradax Ocean Transportation S.A.*,[23] where an FOB sale contract for Thailand tapioca pellets incorporated the provisions of Gafta 119 which provided, inter alia, a prohibition clause (clause 19) whereby the contract was deemed to be cancelled in the event of a prohibition of export enacted by the government of the country of origin of the goods.

The sales contract provided for a special obligation for the sellers to provide for an export certificate enabling buyers to obtain an import licence into the EEC with a 6 per cent import levy.

The contract further provided for a hierarchy clause whereby, in case of inconsistencies between them, the clauses of the sale contract were destined to prevail vis-à-vis the standard terms of Gafta.

By a co-operation agreement between the EEC and Thailand which came into force in July 1982, Thailand, inter alia, undertook to limit, by a system of export certificates, its export of tapioca pellets to the EEC. An exporter had to be registered and had first to obtain, inter alia, an export licence before he could obtain an export certificate. As a result, it was not possible for the sellers to obtain export certificates to enable the goods to be imported into the EEC at a 6 per cent levy. The buyers declared the sellers in default and claimed damages on the basis of the fact that the prohibition clause contained in clause 19 of Gafta 119 was overruled by the special obligation of the seller to obtain export certificates on the basis of the hierarchy clause enshrined in the sale contract.

The Court of Appeal held that the natural construction of this contract was that the sellers were to provide for the export certificate but in the case of prohibition of export, or in the case of any executive or legislative act done by or on behalf of the government of Thailand restricting export, the unfulfilled portion of the contract was to be cancelled; that construction did not deprive the special condition of effect; the obligation to provide for the export certificate remained on the sellers; if the sellers were unable to provide for the certificate because of any impediment falling within the carefully defined ambit of clause 19 they were relieved of their contractual obligations, and there was no indication that clause 19 was not to apply to this as to all other contractual obligations.

23 *Pagnan S.p.A. v Tradax Ocean Transportation S.A.* [1987] 2 Lloyd's Rep. 342.

Ultimately, there was no inconsistency between the special condition of the sale contract and clause 19 of Gafta 119; there was a prohibition of export or an executive or legislative act done by or on behalf of the government of Thailand restricting export, with the result that the contract was cancelled.

As eloquently put by Woolf LJ:

> In any contract in which there are standard terms and special terms, it is desirable to have a provision to avoid conflict between the standard and special terms [. . .] if the parties do make express provision, the Court has to give effect to that express provision.[24]

If, on the contrary, no hierarchy clause is present in the sales contract, special terms of the sale contract prevail on the basis of the old Roman law principle *lex specialis derogat lex generalis.*

In *Indian Oil Corporation v Vanol Inc.*,[25] a conflict arose between the sales contract which provided for an English courts jurisdiction clause, and the standard terms incorporated therein, which quite on the contrary indicated arbitration in India as a dispute resolution mechanism.

The court held that, in the absence of any hierarchy clause, where an incorporated document contained provisions which conflicted with provisions of the written document, the terms of the written document in the ordinary way prevailed over the terms incorporated by the reference. As stated by Webster J:

> The principles of construction that are to be implied can be shortly stated: the purpose of construction is to give effect to the intention of the parties at the time the contract was made, which is to be objectively determined as far as possible from the words actually used. Where an incorporated document contains provisions which conflict with provisions of the written document, the terms of the written document in the ordinary way prevail over the terms incorporated by reference.[26]

The established legal principle whereby, in the absence of a hierarchy clause, special terms are destined to prevail vis-à-vis generic standard terms has been, nevertheless, somewhat called into question in *The Leonidas*,[27] where it was held that, although tailor-made clauses would normally prevail over typed clauses, the courts would however seek to construe a contract as a whole. If a reasonable commercial construction of the whole could reconcile two provisions (whether typed or printed) then such a construction could and should be adopted.[28]

In light of *The Leonidas*, under English law a construction of the contract could therefore be necessary at times, in order to solve a conflict between special and standard terms.

The construction of the contract under the common law differs radically from the one conducted by judges in civil law jurisdictions. Indeed, under civil law, the construction of the contract will very often see the application of articles of the

24 *Ibid.*, at 352.

25 *Indian Oil Corporation v Vanol Inc.* [1991] 2 Lloyd's Rep. 634, revsd. on other grounds at [1992] 2 Lloyd's Rep. 163.

26 *Ibid.*, at 636.

27 *The Leonidas* [2001] 1 Lloyd's Rep. 533.

28 *Ibid.*, at 536.

civil code which will be often superimposed against the will of the parties. On the contrary, in common law, the construction of a contract is entirely focused on establishing what the original will of the parties was, also according to what are considered to be reasonable commercial practices and customs.

In the case of discrepancies between standard and special terms, the construction of the contract based on the exchanges between the parties involved and standard business practice may well lead to a reconciliation between the conflicting clauses at stake, or to an enactment of standard terms against conflicting special clauses.

The principle of freedom of contract will ultimately lead the way and prevail against any formalistic nomenclature or pre-fixed legal principles.

A recent example can be found in *Nidera BV v Venus International Free Zone for Trading and Marine Services SAE*.[29] Here, the court construed a contract for the sale and shipment of corn and determined that the buyer had validly extended the delivery period. Under the extension of delivery clause contained in the Gafta 49 standard form of contract on f.o.b. terms for the delivery of goods from Central and Eastern Europe in bulk or bags, the buyer had an unqualified right to extend the delivery period.

The right could not be exercised by a buyer who feared that the nominated vessel might not be presented in readiness to load within the stipulated period.

In the words of Walker J:

> Accordingly I conclude that sellers' arguments provide no sound basis for departing from what sentence [8.1] of clause 8 appears to say on its face: where a timely notice is served, there is an unqualified right of extension under clause 8. I reach that conclusion without needing to place reliance on the general aspects and particular matters identified by Ms Cockerill QC. In that regard I observe only that Ms Cockerill QC was plainly right to stress that the clause 8 construction issue concerned an unmodified provision in a standard form contract used, and intended for use, all over the world from day to day.
>
> I consider that where there are clear and unqualified words in such a contract, if it would not be obvious to a trader that they have a limited meaning, then there would have to be a most compelling case before the court could properly read down the words in question. Had it been necessary, I would have decided against sellers on this basis.[30]

The purpose of this particular standard form contract was to enable traders to make contracts speedily. Where there were clear and unqualified words in such a contract, if it would not be obvious to a trader that they had a limited meaning, then there would have to be a most compelling case before a court could properly read down the words in question.[31]

The construction of the contract under English law would entail an attentive scrutiny of its wording. Indeed, it would almost never be possible to determine

29 *Nidera BV v Venus International Free Zone for Trading and Marine Services SAE* [2014] EWHC 2013 (Comm); [2014] 2 Lloyd's Rep. 425.

30 *Ibid.*

31 R. Thomas, "International Sales: FOB contract – delivery period – extension claimed." *J.I.M.L.* 2014, 20(4), 239–241; A. Arkpin, "Sale of goods – FOB sale of Ukrainian corn – delay." *L.M.L.N.* 2014, 903, 1–2; and R. Veal, "Let the seller beware – extension clauses in Gafta standard terms." *S.T.L.* 2014 (Sep), 3–5.

the meaning of a contract without looking very closely at the words themselves. In that regard, Lord Hoffmann in *Bank of Credit and Commerce International SA v Ali*[32] stressed that the primary source for understanding what the parties meant is their language interpreted in accordance with conventional usage.[33]

This entails that, when construing a standard form, the view of a trade tribunal with significant familiarity with the standard form's use and function is to be given considerable weight.[34]

Although the interpretation of the wording in a contract is of the utmost importance, the principles of modern contract interpretation, summarised in *Investors Compensation Scheme Ltd v West Bromwich Building Society*,[35] place great weight on the commercial purpose of the agreement, which may even take priority over the literal meaning of the words used. In the words of Lord Hoffmann:

> In the Court of Appeal, Leggatt L.J. said, on the authority of *Alice Through the Looking Glass*, that the judge's interpretation was "not an available meaning of the words." "Any claim (whether sounding in rescission for undue influence or otherwise)" could not mean "Any claim sounding in rescission (whether for undue influence or otherwise)" and that was that. He was unimpressed by the alleged commercial nonsense of the alternative construction.
>
> My Lords, I will say at once that I prefer the approach of the learned judge. But I think I should preface my explanation of my reasons with some general remarks about the principles by which contractual documents are nowadays construed. I do not think that the fundamental change which has overtaken this branch of the law, particularly as a result of the speeches of Lord Wilberforce in *Prenn v Simmonds* [1971] 1 WLR 1381, 1384–1386 and *Reardon Smith Line Ltd v Yngvar Hansen-Tangen* [1976] 1 WLR 989, is always sufficiently appreciated. The result has been, subject to one important exception, to assimilate the way in which such documents are interpreted by judges to the common sense principles by which any serious utterance would be interpreted in ordinary life. Almost all the old intellectual baggage of "legal" interpretation has been discarded. The principles may be summarised as follows:
>
> (1) Interpretation is the ascertainment of the meaning which the document would convey to a reasonable person having all the background knowledge which would reasonably have been available to the parties in the situation in which they were at the time of the contract.
> (2) The background was famously referred to by Lord Wilberforce as the "matrix of fact," but this phrase is, if anything, an understated description of what the background may include. Subject to the requirement that it should have been reasonably available to the parties and to the exception to be mentioned next, it includes absolutely anything which would have affected the way in which the language of the document would have been understood by a reasonable man.
> (3) The law excludes from the admissible background the previous negotiations of the parties and their declarations of subjective intent. They are admissible only in an action for rectification. The law makes this distinction for reasons of practical policy and, in this respect only, legal interpretation differs from

32 *Bank of Credit and Commerce International SA v Ali* [2002] 1 AC 251.

33 *Ibid.*, 269.

34 See *Novasen SA v Alimenta SA* [2013] 1 Lloyd's Rep. 648, paras. 24–26, quoting *André et Cie v Cook Industries Inc* [1986] 2 Lloyd's Rep. 200 and *Kershaw Mechanical Services Ltd v Kendrick Construction Ltd* [2006] 4 All ER 79. See also *Chitty on Contracts,* 31st Edition, Sweet & Maxwell 2013, chapter 2.

35 *Investors Compensation Scheme Ltd v West Bromwich Building Society* [1997] UKHL 28.

the way we would interpret utterances in ordinary life. The boundaries of this exception are in some respects unclear. But this is not the occasion on which to explore them.

(4) The meaning which a document (or any other utterance) would convey to a reasonable man is not the same thing as the meaning of its words. The meaning of words is a matter of dictionaries and grammars; the meaning of the document is what the parties using those words against the relevant background would reasonably have been understood to mean. The background may not merely enable the reasonable man to choose between the possible meanings of words which are ambiguous but even (as occasionally happens in ordinary life) to conclude that the parties must, for whatever reason, have used the wrong words or syntax. (See *Mannai Investments Co Ltd v Eagle Star Life Assurance Co Ltd* [1997] 2 WLR 945.)

(5) The "rule" that words should be given their "natural and ordinary meaning" reflects the common sense proposition that we do not easily accept that people have made linguistic mistakes, particularly in formal documents. On the other hand, if one would nevertheless conclude from the background that something must have gone wrong with the language, the law does not require judges to attribute to the parties an intention which they plainly could not have had. Lord Diplock made this point more vigorously when he said in *The Antaios Compania Neviera SA v Salen Rederierna AB* [1985] 1 AC 191, 201:

> . . . if detailed semantic and syntactical analysis of words in a commercial contract is going to lead to a conclusion that flouts business commonsense, it must be made to yield to business commonsense.

If one applies these principles, it seems to me that the judge must be right and, as we are dealing with one badly drafted clause which is happily no longer in use, there is little advantage in my repeating his reasons at greater length. The only remark of his which I would respectfully question is when he said that he was "doing violence" to the natural meaning of the words. This is an over-energetic way to describe the process of interpretation.

[. . .] Finally, on this part of the case, I must make some comments upon the judgment of the Court of Appeal. Leggatt L.J. said that his construction was "the natural and ordinary meaning of the words used." I do not think that the concept of natural and ordinary meaning is very helpful when, on any view, the words have not been used in a natural and ordinary way. In a case like this, the court is inevitably engaged in choosing between competing unnatural meanings. Secondly, Leggatt L.J. said that the judge's construction was not an "available meaning" of the words. If this means that judges cannot, short of rectification, decide that the parties must have made mistakes of meaning or syntax, I respectfully think he was wrong. The proposition is not, I would suggest, borne out by his citation from *Alice Through the Looking Glass*. Alice and Humpty Dumpty were agreed that the word "glory" did not mean "a nice knock-down argument." Anyone with a dictionary could see that. Humpty Dumpty's point was that "a nice knock-down argument" was what he meant by using the word "glory." He very fairly acknowledged that Alice, as a reasonable young woman, could not have realised this until he told her, but once he had told her, or if, without being expressly told, she could have inferred it from the background, she would have had no difficulty in understanding what he meant.[36]

In *Investors Compensation Scheme Ltd v West Bromwich Building Society*, Lord Hoffmann, thus, set out five principles, so that a contract should be construed according

36 *Investors Compensation Scheme Ltd v West Bromwich Building* Society [1997] UKHL 28, 911–913.

to: a) what a reasonable person having all the background knowledge would have understood; b) where the background includes anything in the "matrix of fact" that could affect the language's meaning; c) but excluding prior negotiations; d) for the policy of reducing litigation where the meaning of words is not to be deduced literally; and e) but contextually on the presumption that people do not easily make linguistic mistakes.

Indeed, at common law, the commercial purpose of the contract has been exceedingly weighed by courts of law,[37] and occupies a predominant role also in

---

37 See *Burges v Wickham* (1863) EngR 314, where at 686 Cockburn J stated that: "I cannot but think that where some rule of law does not stand in the way, we shall be best consulting the interest of the commercial world by giving effect to the intention of the parties to a contract where we can sufficiently collect it, rather than by insisting rigidly on a distinct enumeration of every particular." See also Lord Steyn in *Society of Lloyd's v Robinson* [1999] 1 All ER (Comm) 545, at p.551: "Loyalty to the text of a commercial contract, instrument, or document read in its contextual setting is the paramount principle of interpretation. But in the process of interpreting the meaning of the language of a commercial document the court ought generally to favour a commercially sensible construction. The reason for this approach is that a commercial construction is likely to give effect to the intention of the parties. Words ought therefore to be interpreted in the way in which a reasonable commercial person would construe them. And the reasonable commercial person can safely be assumed to be unimpressed with technical interpretations and undue emphasis on niceties of language."

More recently, see Longmore LJ in *Barclays Bank plc v HHY Luxembourg SARL* [2010] EWCA Civ 1248; [2011] 1 BCLC 336, at paras 25 and 26: "The matter does not of course rest there because when alternative constructions are available one has to consider which is the more commercially sensible . . . The judge said that it did not flout common sense to say that the clause provided for a very limited level of release, but that, with respect, is not quite the way to look at the matter. If a clause is capable of two meanings, as on any view this clause is, it is quite possible that neither meaning will flout common sense. In such circumstances, it is much more appropriate to adopt the more, rather than the less, commercial construction."

See also as per Lord Clarke in *Rainy Sky S.A. and others (Appellants) v Kookmin Bank (Respondent)* [2011] UKSC 50 at para 21: "exercise of construction is essentially one unitary exercise in which the court must consider the language used and ascertain what a reasonable person, that is a person who has all the background knowledge which would reasonably have been available to the parties in the situation in which they were at the time of the contract, would have understood the parties to have meant. In doing so, the court must have regard to all the relevant surrounding circumstances. If there are two possible constructions, the court is entitled to prefer the construction which is consistent with business common sense and to reject the other."

Finally, see as per Lord Neuberger in *Arnold v Britton & Ors* [2015] UKSC 36 at paras 17–23:

> First, the reliance placed in some cases on commercial common sense and surrounding circumstances (eg in Chartbrook, paras 16–26) should not be invoked to undervalue the importance of the language of the provision which is to be construed. The exercise of interpreting a provision involves identifying what the parties meant through the eyes of a reasonable reader, and, save perhaps in a very unusual case, that meaning is most obviously to be gleaned from the language of the provision. Unlike commercial common sense and the surrounding circumstances, the parties have control over the language they use in a contract. And, again save perhaps in a very unusual case, the parties must have been specifically focussing on the issue covered by the provision when agreeing the wording of that provision.
>
> Secondly, when it comes to considering the centrally relevant words to be interpreted, I accept that the less clear they are, or, to put it another way, the worse their drafting, the more ready the court can properly be to depart from their natural meaning. That is simply the obverse of the sensible proposition that the clearer the natural meaning the more difficult it is to justify departing from it. However, that does not justify the court embarking on an exercise of searching for, let alone constructing, drafting infelicities in order to facilitate a departure from the natural meaning. If there is a specific error in the drafting, it may often have no relevance to the issue of interpretation which the court has to resolve.
>
> The third point I should mention is that commercial common sense is not to be invoked retrospectively. The mere fact that a contractual arrangement, if interpreted according to its natural

the judicial interpretation of the commercial nature of a contract concluded on shipment terms.[38]

---

language, has worked out badly, or even disastrously, for one of the parties is not a reason for departing from the natural language. Commercial common sense is only relevant to the extent of how matters would or could have been perceived by the parties, or by reasonable people in the position of the parties, as at the date that the contract was made. Judicial observations such as those of Lord Reid in *Wickman Machine Tools Sales Ltd v L Schuler AG* [1974] AC 235, 251 and Lord Diplock in *Antaios Cia Naviera SA v Salen Rederierna AB (The Antaios)* [1985] AC 191, 201, quoted by Lord Carnwath at para 110, have to be read and applied bearing that important point in mind.

Fourthly, while commercial common sense is a very important factor to take into account when interpreting a contract, a court should be very slow to reject the natural meaning of a provision as correct simply because it appears to be a very imprudent term for one of the parties to have agreed, even ignoring the benefit of wisdom of hindsight. The purpose of interpretation is to identify what the parties have agreed, not what the court thinks that they should have agreed. Experience shows that it is by no means unknown for people to enter into arrangements which are ill-advised, even ignoring the benefit of wisdom of hindsight, and it is not the function of a court when interpreting an agreement to relieve a party from the consequences of his imprudence or poor advice. Accordingly, when interpreting a contract a judge should avoid re-writing it in an attempt to assist an unwise party or to penalise an astute party.

The fifth point concerns the facts known to the parties. When interpreting a contractual provision, one can only take into account facts or circumstances which existed at the time that the contract was made, and which were known or reasonably available to both parties. Given that a contract is a bilateral, or synallagmatic, arrangement involving both parties, it cannot be right, when interpreting a contractual provision, to take into account a fact or circumstance known only to one of the parties.

Sixthly, in some cases, an event subsequently occurs which was plainly not intended or contemplated by the parties, judging from the language of their contract. In such a case, if it is clear what the parties would have intended, the court will give effect to that intention. An example of such a case is *Aberdeen City Council v Stewart Milne Group Ltd* [2011] UKSC 56, 2012 SCLR 114, where the court concluded that "any . . . approach" other than that which was adopted "would defeat the parties' clear objectives", but the conclusion was based on what the parties "had in mind when they entered into" the contract (see paras 17 and 22).

Seventhly, reference was made in argument to service charge clauses being construed "restrictively". I am unconvinced by the notion that service charge clauses are to be subject to any special rule of interpretation. Even if (which it is unnecessary to decide) a landlord may have simpler remedies than a tenant to enforce service charge provisions, that is not relevant to the issue of how one interprets the contractual machinery for assessing the tenant's contribution. The origin of the adverb was in a judgment of Rix LJ in *McHale v Earl Cadogan* [2010] EWCA Civ 14, [2010] 1 EGLR 51, para 17. What he was saying, quite correctly, was that the court should not "bring within the general words of a service charge clause anything which does not clearly belong there". However, that does not help resolve the sort of issue of interpretation raised in this case.

38 By way of example, see *Soufflet Negoce SA v Fedcominvest Europe Sarl* [2014] EWHC 2405 (Comm); [2014] 2 Lloyd's Rep. 537. In that case, the court held that in clause 19 of Gafta 64 the words "any notice received after 1600 hours on a business day shall be deemed to have been received on the business day following" did not apply to all contracts but only to "resales/repurchases" (see also: Notification under GAFTA terms. Edward Yang Liu. S.T.L. 2014, Oct). See *Bunge SA v Nidera* BV (formerly *Nidera Handelscompagnie BV*) [2013] EWCA Civ 1628; [2014] 1 Lloyd's Rep. 404, where it was decided by the court that the GAFTA prohibition clause required a causal link between the event in question, usually but not necessarily a total or partial prohibition of the shipment of goods, and the seller's inability to perform the contract.

See also *Seagrain LLC v Glencore Grain BV* [2013] EWCA Civ 1627; [2014] 1 All ER (Comm) 540; [2014] 1 Lloyd's Rep. 598, where it was held that the prohibition clause in the GAFTA 48 contract form could not be construed so that the reference to an "executive act . . . restricting exports" extended to every action by an official body which had the effect of restricting exports. However, depending on the particular facts of a case, an act which implicitly restricted export might fall within the prohibition clause.

This chapter has explored possible legal problems arising from the creation of the sale contract, and the incorporation of standard terms. Another important aspect of the creation of a contract concluded on shipment terms lies with the definition of the transport obligations.

As it will be readily appreciated in the following, this aspect can give rise to problematic scenarios especially within the context of c.i.f. sales, where the seller is tasked with the duty of making all the necessary transport arrangements for the goods.

Finally, see also *RG Grain Trade LLP (UK) v Feed Factors International Ltd* [2011] EWHC 1889 (Comm); [2011] 2 Lloyd's Rep. 433; the case revolved on the true construction of a GAFTA contract; certificates of quality and condition issued by an inspector appointed by the sellers of an animal feed supplement were not final and binding. However, the GAFTA Board of Appeal had erred in concluding that the buyers were entitled to reject the goods as it had failed to consider whether the relevant provision should properly be regarded as a condition as opposed to a warranty or an innominate term.

CHAPTER 5

The sales contract and the transport obligations of the seller

5.1 The making of a contract of carriage within the context of international commercial sales: Preliminary issues

Any international commercial sales contract is directly or indirectly linked by default to a contract of carriage. Indeed, contracts concluded on shipment terms provide for the obligation of the seller to ship the goods for transport in accordance with what was originally established in the sales contract.

The analysis of contracts of carriage and charter parties falls outside the subject matter of this manuscript. Nevertheless, when it comes to c.i.f. contracts (but also some forms of f.o.b. contracts), the seller's transport obligations are of the utmost importance; they are usually embedded into the sales contract, and should be carefully crafted so as to avoid unwelcome surprises.

A preliminary issue to be unravelled revolves around the identification of the transport obligations when it comes to contracts concluded on shipment terms.

C.i.f. contracts will see the obligation of the seller to make the necessary transport arrangements for the goods, whereas in sale contracts concluded on f.o.b. terms, usually the transport arrangements will be executed by the buyer.

Nevertheless, certain forms of f.o.b. contracts will see the transport obligations pending on the sellers' shoulders.

Indeed, as established in the above, in *Pyrene v Scindia*,[1] Devlin J identified three varieties of f.o.b. contract: a) "straight" f.o.b. contracts whereby the buyer nominates the vessel and makes the contract of carriage (probably the most common variety today); b) f.o.b. contracts "with additional duties", which provide for the seller nominating the vessel and making the contract of carriage as an agent of the buyer (probably the rarest variety); and c) "classic" f.o.b. contracts, whereby the seller makes the contract of carriage, but the buyer nominates the vessel.[2]

1 *Pyrene v Scindia* [1954] 2 QB 402.

2 As put by Devlin J:

> What counsel called the classic type as described, for example, in *Wimble, Sons & Co v Rosenberg & Sons* [1913] 2 KB 743, the buyer's duty is to nominate the ship and the seller's to put the goods on board for account of the buyer and procure a bill of lading in terms usual in the trade. In such a case the seller is directly a party to the contract of carriage, at least until he takes out the bill of lading in the buyer's name. Probably the classic type is based on the assumption that the ship nominated will be willing to load any goods brought down to the berth or at least of which she is notified. Under present conditions, when space often has to be booked well in advance, the contract of carriage comes into existence at an earlier point of time. Sometimes the seller is asked to make the necessary arrangements,

These variations translate into different legal scenarios in terms of the possible impact of transport obligations on sellers rather than buyers.

In case of straight f.o.b contracts, the buyer enters into a contract of carriage with the carrier and acquires the right to sue the carrier under this contract. This means that the signatories of the charter party[3] are, and will remain, the carrier and the buyer.

After the goods are shipped on board by the seller, the carrier will issue a bill of lading which is then destined to reach the buyer and will allow him to claim the goods from the seller as a document of title.[4]

Notably, this situation does not entail the extension of the legal effects of a sale contract vis-à-vis the contract of carriage, as the sale contract will not contain any obligation in terms of transport arrangements; these will be made directly by the buyer with a carrier. The same does not apply to f.o.b. contracts with additional duties, whereby the seller makes the contract of carriage acting as an agent of the buyer, who will thus be bound by the terms enshrined in the charter party as a principal. Here, in making the contract of carriage with the carrier, the seller will be bound by the transport obligations enshrined in the sales contract.

The scenario is the same with classic f.o.b. contracts, which see the seller as the stipulating party of the contract of carriage.

Whenever the seller makes the transport arrangements, e.g. in c.i.f., c.&f., f.o.b. contracts with additional services and classic f.o.b. contracts, the sale contract will contain specific transport obligations pending on the sellers' shoulders to be translated into the contract of carriage which the seller will stipulate with the carrier.

Thereafter, a bill of lading[5] issued by the carrier after the goods are shipped on board, incorporating the conditions of carriage enshrined in the charter party (including the arbitration clause), will be endorsed by the seller to the buyer.[6]

---

and the contract may then provide for his taking the bill of lading in his own name and obtaining payment against the transfer, as in a cif contract. Sometimes the buyer engages his own forwarding agent at the port of loading to book space and to procure the bill of lading; if freight has to be paid in advance this method may be the most convenient. In such a case the seller discharges his duty by putting the goods on board, getting the mate's receipt and handing it to the forwarding agent to enable him to obtain the bill of lading.

3 A charter party is the contract between the owner of a vessel and the charterer for the use of a vessel. The charterer takes over the vessel for either a certain amount of time (a time charter) or for a certain point-to-point voyage (a voyage charter), giving rise to these two main types of charter agreement.

4 See chapter 6.

5 A bill of lading (sometimes abbreviated as B/L or BoL) is a "document issued by a carrier which details a shipment of merchandise and gives title of that shipment to a specified party. The bill of lading also serves as a receipt of shipment when the good is delivered to the predetermined destination. This document must accompany the shipped goods, no matter the form of transportation, and must be signed by an authorised representative from the carrier, shipper and receiver". See businessdefinitions.org.

6 Sometimes the B/L does not identify the charter party, the terms of which are to be incorporated into the B/L, and there might be a string of charter parties.

Although it is a question to be determined on a case-by-case basis, the general rule is that the head charter, to which the shipowner is party, is incorporated. *The San Nicholas* [1976] 1 Lloyd's Rep. 8.

Where the head charter party is a time charter party, the position can be different due to the unlikelihood of the will of the parties to incorporate the terms of a time charter party which are different in nature. *The Kallanag* [2008] EWHC 2761.

5.2 Identification of transport obligations and legal repercussions for the sales contract

Whenever the seller makes the transport arrangements, the terms of his contract with the carrier are evidenced in any agreement which he stipulates with the carrier. Evidence of that agreement may be found in a booking note, rather than in a charter party or bill of lading, or in nothing at all.

In *The Ardennes*,[7] in breach of his verbal promise, the shipowner deviated from the route to London and called first at Antwerp but later, in reply to the shipper's claim for damages, contended that on the terms of the bill of lading, evidence of any other bargain or promise was not admissible. As stated by Lord Goddard CJ:

> The contract has come into existence before the bill of lading is signed; the latter is signed by one party only, and handed by him to the shipper usually after the goods have been put on board. No doubt if the shipper finds that the bill contains terms with which he is not content, or does not contain some term for which he has stipulated, he might, if there were time, demand his goods back; but he is not, in my opinion, for that reason, prevented from giving evidence that there was in fact a contract entered into before the bill of lading was signed different from that which is found in the bill of lading or containing some additional term. He is no party to the preparation of the bill of lading [not always the case, remark is mine]; nor does he sign it. It is unnecessary to cite authority further than the two cases already mentioned for the proposition that the bill of lading is not itself the contract; therefore in my opinion evidence as to the true contract is admissible.[8]

Whenever the seller is to make the transport arrangements, the only transport document which the buyer gets sight of is the bill of lading, at any rate where the buyer is not already a party to a charter party.

The nature of a bill of lading within these kind of transactions was discussed by Esher MR LJ in *Leduc v Ward*,[9] as follows:

> It is true that, where there is a charterparty, as between the shipowner and the charterer the bill of lading may be merely in the nature of a receipt for goods, because all the other terms of the contract of carriage between them are contained in the charterparty; and the bill of lading is merely given as between them to enable the charterer to deal with the goods while in the course of transit; but, where the bill of lading indorsed over, as between the shipowner and the indorsee, the bill of lading must be considered to contain the contract, because the former has given it for the purpose of enabling the charterer to pass it on as the contract of carriage in respect of the goods. When there is no charterparty, as between the grantee of the bill of lading and the shipowner, the bill of lading is no doubt a receipt for the goods, and as such, like any other receipt, it is not conclusive, for it may be controverted by evidence shewing that the goods were not received. But the question whether it will be more than a receipt as between the shipper and shipowner depends on whether the captain has received the goods, for he has no authority to make a contract of carriage to bind the shipowner, except in respect of goods received by him. If the goods have not been received, the bill of lading cannot contain the terms of a contract of carriage with respect to them as against

7 *The Ardennes* [1951] 1 KB 55.
8 *Ibid.*, at 58.
9 *Leduc v Ward* (1888) 20 QBD 475.

> the shipowner. But, if the goods have been received by the captain, it is the evidence in writing of what the contract of carriage between the parties is.[10]

It is of the utmost importance to note at this stage that, whenever the seller is to procure the contract of carriage, there is no obligation under the common law for him to tender the original charter party stipulated with the carrier alongside the bill of lading, unless otherwise agreed by the parties in the sales contract.

In *Finska Cellulosaforeiningen v Westfield Paper Co Ltd.*,[11] the buyer in a c.i.f. sale rejected the documents tendered by the seller due to the fact that only the bill of lading was consigned and the charter party was missing. Indeed, buyers in this case only received a bill of lading containing the following clause: "All conditions and exceptions as per charter-party dated [blank]."

The buyers claimed that in all cases of c.i.f. contracts, the charter party must be tendered alongside the bill of lading where it is a relevant document. As authority for that proposition, reference was made to a passage from the well-known opinion of Mr Justice Blackburn in *Ireland v Livingston*,[12] where it was stated that:

> for the balance a draft is drawn on the consignee which he is bound to accept (if the shipment be in conformity with his contract) on having handed to him the charter-party, bill of lading, and policy of insurance.[13]

It is, nevertheless, to be observed that in *Ireland v Livingston* there is no mention of the charter party as one of the necessary documents to complete delivery in accordance with the agreement. The same can be said in *Johnson v Taylor Brothers*,[14] where Lord Atkinson canvassed on the sellers' duties under a c.i.f. contract. He concluded that there was no mention of the charter party as a necessary document to be produced by the seller together with the invoices, bill of lading and policy of insurance in order to entitle him to receive payment.[15]

Dismissing the aforementioned claim put forward by the buyers in *Finska Cellulosaforeiningen v Westfield Paper Co Ltd*, Viscount Caldecote LCJ stated that:

> In the circumstances of this case, at any rate, the tender of the bill of lading duly endorsed was in my opinion a sufficient compliance with the contract of sale to entitle the sellers to payment of the price of the goods.[16]

We shall discover in the following how this may entail serious legal consequences for a buyer in possession of a short delivered or damaged cargo.

For the moment, a very important qualification needs to be delineated: is the question of who must make the transport contract altogether a completely different matter to the question of who is or becomes a party to that contract?

---

10 *Ibid.*, at 479.

11 *Finska Cellulosaforeiningen v Westfield Paper Co Ltd* [1940] Lloyd's Rep. Vol 68, at 75.

12 *Ireland v Livingston*, L.R. 5 HL 395.

13 *Ibid.*, at 425.

14 *Johnson v Taylor Brothers* [1920] AC 144.

15 *Ibid.*, at 156. See also judgment of Mr Justice Hamilton *in Biddell Bros. v E. Clemens Horst Company, Ltd.* [1911] 1 KB 214, 221, and judgment of Lord Justice Kennedy in the Court of Appeal.

16 *Finska Cellulosaforeiningen v Westfield Paper Co Ltd*, above, 80.

As established in the above, under c.i.f. and c.& f. contracts, the seller is initially party to the contract of carriage which he stipulates with the carrier.

Once the goods are shipped on board, the carrier will issue a bill of lading, which on its back incorporates the conditions of carriage as per that originally established in the charter party. Thereafter, the bill of lading incorporating the conditions of carriage enshrined into the charter party (including the arbitration clause) is endorsed by the seller onto the buyer.[17]

Within the context of a c.i.f. transaction, the bill of lading could represent evidence of the contract of carriage stipulated by the seller and the shipowner.[18] When the bill of lading is endorsed to a third party buyer, it will become conclusive evidence of the contract of carriage as far as the endorsee/consignee is concerned.[19]

Under f.o.b. contracts, the variations theorised by the court in *Pyrene v Scindia* translate into and reflect different legal scenarios in terms of performance of transport obligations.

In the case of straight f.o.b. contracts, the buyer enters into a contract of carriage and acquires the right to sue the carrier under this contract. This means that the signatories of the charter party and of the arbitration clause enshrined therein are and will remain the carrier and the buyer.

After the goods are shipped on board by the seller, the carrier will issue a bill of lading which is then destined to reach the buyer and will allow him to claim the goods from the seller as a document of title.

---

17 Sometimes the B/L does not identify the charter party, the terms of which are to be incorporated into the B/L, and there might be a string of charter parties.

Although it is a question to be determined on a case-by-case basis, the general rule is that the head charter, to which the shipowner is party, is incorporated. *The San Nicholas* [1976] 1 Lloyd's Rep. 8.

Where the head charter party is a time charter party, the position can be different due to the unlikelihood of the will of the parties to incorporate the terms of a time charter party which are different in nature. *The Kallanag* [2008] EWHC 2761.

18 The rationale for considering a bill of lading as evidence of the contract of carriage lies primarily with two basic propositions of contract law; first, bilateral contracts can only be concluded on the basis of an exchange of mutual promises. Second, the validity of a contract does not rest on written records. Indeed, a contract of carriage might be concluded orally before a bill of lading is issued after the goods have been shipped on board, and its existence might be inferred by booking notes, mate's receipts, freight tariffs, negotiations with agents and brokers, along with the bill of lading itself (on this point see C. Debattista, *Bills of Lading in Export Trade*, Butterworths, 2008, p. 135). Within the context of a c.i.f. sale, when a bill of lading is issued under a charter party and there is a conflict between the clauses enshrined in the two documents, the bill of lading might not even be considered evidence of the contract of carriage, whose terms needs to be found exclusively in the charter party (see *Radocanachi Sons & Co v Milburn Bros* (1886) 18 QBD 67, 479; *Swell v Burdick* (1884) 10 App Ca 74, 105; *President of India v Metcalfe Shipping Co Ltd (the Dunelmia)* [1970] 1 QB 289, 305; *Trade Star Line Corp. v Mitsui & Co Ltd (The Arctic TraderI)* [1996] 2 Lloyd's Rep. 449, 455). In *Ardennes SS (Cargo Owners) v SS Ardennes* (Owners) [1951] 1 KB 55, a delay caused by an intermediate stop in Antwerp of a vessel which was supposed to sail from Spain directly to London caused loss to the cargo owner. In defence against the claim brought by the cargo owner, the carrier endeavoured to rely upon a clause enshrined into the bill of lading which allowed for an intermediate step in Antwerp. It was held by the court that the bill of lading might not even be evidence of the contract of carriage, whose exhaustive terms need to be found in the charter party. This view was re-emphasised by the Court of Appeal in *Cho Yang Shipping Co Ltd v Coral (UK) Ltd* [1997], 2 Lloyd's Rep. 641.

19 See *Trade Star Line Corp. v Mitsui & Co Ltd (The Arctic Trader)I* [1996] 2 Lloyd's Rep. at 455. See also *Camapania Commercial Naviera San Martin S.A. v China National Foreign Trade Transportation Corp. (The Constanza)* [1981] 2 Lloyd's Rep. 148, 150.

Any cargo action destined to arise between the buyer and the carrier will be subject to arbitration (if so established by the charter party), and the arbitral proceedings are going to involve the carrier and the buyer as original signatories of the arbitration agreement enshrined in the charter party. Noticeably, this situation does not entail the extension of the legal effects of an arbitration agreement to a third party non-signatory.

The same applies to f.o.b. contracts with additional duties, whereby the seller makes the contract of carriage acting as an agent of the buyer, who will thus be bound by the arbitration agreement enshrined in the charter party (if any) as a principal. Here, the classic principles of agency law set aside any issues of extension of the legal effects of arbitration agreements to third parties.

The situation is radically different with classic f.o.b. contracts, as in this case the buyer only becomes party to any contract of carriage and is able to sue on it when the bills of lading were endorsed to him, and the only contract of which he could avail himself is that contained in or evidenced by the bill of lading.

Although issues related to contracts of carriage fall outside the scope and the aims of this manuscript, it is nonetheless crucial to emphasise that, whenever on the basis of the terms enshrined in the sales contract the seller is to arrange for the necessary transport obligations, this scenario can have serious legal consequences vis-à-vis the sale contract itself, and its performance by the seller.

Therefore, if refrigeration of the goods at a particular temperature is crucial to the buyer, the best guarantee that the goods will be carried at that temperature – and, more importantly, that there will be effective remedies against the carrier if they are not – is for the contract of sale expressly to stipulate that the seller will procure a contract of carriage stipulating for such refrigeration.

Moreover, for the seller to have performed his duty under the contract of sale, it is not enough for him to have agreed with the carrier that the goods would be carried at a certain level of refrigeration: he must also have procured and tendered a bill of lading binding the carrier to carry the goods at that level.[20]

This is because the buyer's contract of carriage with the carrier is not that agreed between the carrier and the shipper, but that contained in the bill of lading. Indeed, whenever within the context of international commercial sales the seller stipulates the contract of carriage with the carrier, the buyer has no control over that scenario, and he is, thus, best advised to delineate meticulously the seller's transport obligations in the sale contract itself.

For instance, let us reconsider the scenario which arose in *Finska Cellulosaforeiningen v Westfield Paper Co Ltd*. As established above, in that case, the c.i.f. buyer received a bill of lading simply stating on its back that all conditions and exceptions are as per charter party (stipulated by the seller and the carrier).

Under those circumstances, a c.i.f. buyer who required specific transport arrangements to be made by the seller, e.g. in terms of a specific vessel to be used, rather than a requirement for specific needs such as refrigeration of the cargo and so on,

20 See C. Debattista, *Bills of Lading in Export Trade*, above, p. 96.

will not be in the position to ascertain whether the responsibility lies with the seller or the carrier.

Indeed, a bill of lading simply referring to the conditions of carriage enshrined in the original charter party will be of no use in order to ascertain those terms and conditions without the original charter party itself.

Nevertheless, we have just established that, under the common law, no implied obligation to tender a charter party alongside a bill of lading pends on the sellers' shoulders.

The line of reasoning in a case like *Finska Cellulosaforeiningen v Westfield Paper Co Ltd* can be evinced on the basis of an extremely important characteristic of English judges: commercial awareness. As will be readily appreciated, what rendered the process of adaptation of English law to international commerce a successful endeavour was indeed the commercial awareness of English judges, who were capable of moulding domestic English law and adapting it to the needs of the international trading community.

Seen from this perspective, *Finska Cellulosaforeiningen v Westfield Paper Co Ltd* makes perfect commercial sense; the law needs to aid international commerce by embracing its natural connotations and circumventing all its atavistic elements of risk and problematic issues.

Within the context of a c.i.f. transaction, much can be gained in terms of efficiency and simplicity by reducing the amount of documentation the seller is to tender to the buyer, hence the rationale for the unnecessary obligation to tender a charter party alongside a bill of lading, considering that the latter document is deemed to contain the terms of the former.

The commercial awareness of English judges needs to be coupled to a very important principle, the principle of freedom of contract,[21] and its pervasive

---

21 For a detailed analysis of the historical evolution of the principle of freedom of contract, see Atiyah, P.S. *The Rise and Fall of Freedom of Contract*, OUP; New Edition, 1985); Trebilcock, Michael J *The Limits of Freedom of Contract* (Harvard University Press, 2008). Freedom of contract is the freedom of private or public individuals and groups (of any legal entity) to form contracts without government restrictions. This is opposed to government restrictions such as minimum wages, competition law, or price fixing. The freedom to contract is the underpinning of laissez-faire economics and is a cornerstone of free-market libertarianism. Through freedom of contract, individuals possess a general freedom to choose with whom to contract, whether to contract or not, and on which terms to contract. In the late nineteenth century, the English judiciary espoused "freedom of contract" as a generally applicable feature of public policy, best expressed in *Printing and Numerical Registering Co v Sampson* (1875) 19 Eq 462, 465 (regarding freedom of contract and patents) by Sir George Jessel MR. In the later twentieth century, the view of the common law had changed completely. *In George Mitchell (Chesterhall) Ltd v Finney Lock Seeds Ltd*, [1982] EWCA Civ 5 and [1983] 2 AC 803, Lord Denning MR compared "freedom of contract" with oppression of the weak, as he outlined the development the law had undergone. In his words:

> None of you nowadays will remember the trouble we had – when I was called to the Bar – with exemption clauses. They were printed in small print on the back of tickets and order forms and invoices. They were contained in catalogues or timetables. They were held to be binding on any person who took them without objection. No one ever did object. He never read them or knew what was in them. No matter how unreasonable they were, he was bound. All this was done in the name of "freedom of contract." But the freedom was all on the side of the big concern which had the use of the printing press. No freedom for the little man who took the ticket or order form or invoice. The big concern said, "Take it or leave it." The little man had no option but to take it. The big concern could and did exempt itself from liability in its own interest without regard to the little man. It got away with it time

consequences under the common law. Indeed, the common law dictates a linear framework of rules uncluttered by unnecessary obligations; it is then up to the parties operating within this kind of context to generate further obligations if they so wish, by virtue of the principle of freedom of contract.

A *Finska Cellulosaforeiningen v Westfield Paper Co Ltd* scenario, where the buyer receives from the seller a bill of lading simply referring to the charter party, can be easily circumvented with the insertion in the sales contract of an obligation on the seller to tender a bill of lading listing in detail all the conditions of the charter party or, alternatively, the obligation to tender the charter party itself alongside the bill of lading.

As we shall discover in the following, whenever the seller is to make the transport arrangements, the sales contract holds the key for the solution of possible disputes arising from shipping complications.

---

after time. When the courts said to the big concern, "You must put it in clear words," the big concern had no hesitation in doing so. It knew well that the little man would never read the exemption clauses or understand them.

It was a bleak winter for our law of contract. It is illustrated by two cases, *Thompson v London, Midland and Scottish Railway Co.* [1930] 1 K.B. 41 (in which there was exemption from liability, not on the ticket, but only in small print at the back of the timetable, and the company were held not liable) and *L'Estrange v F. Graucob Ltd.* [1934] 2 K.B. 394 (in which there was complete exemption in small print at the bottom of the order form, and the company were held not liable).

Faced with this abuse of power – by the strong against the weak – by the use of the small print of the conditions – the judges did what they could to put a curb upon it. They still had before them the idol, "freedom of contract." They still knelt down and worshipped it, but they concealed under their cloaks a secret weapon. They used it to stab the idol in the back. This weapon was called "the true construction of the contract." They used it with great skill and ingenuity. They used it so as to depart from the natural meaning of the words of the exemption clause and to put upon them a strained and unnatural construction. In case after case, they said that the words were not strong enough to give the big concern exemption from liability; or that in the circumstances the big concern was not entitled to rely on the exemption clause. If a ship deviated from the contractual voyage, the owner could not rely on the exemption clause. If a warehouseman stored the goods in the wrong warehouse, he could not pray in aid the limitation clause. If the seller supplied goods different in kind from those contracted for, he could not rely on any exemption from liability. If a shipowner delivered goods to a person without production of the bill of lading, he could not escape responsibility by reference to an exemption clause. In short, whenever the wide words – in their natural meaning – would give rise to an unreasonable result, the judges either rejected them as repugnant to the main purpose of the contract, or else cut them down to size in order to produce a reasonable result. This is illustrated by these cases in the House of Lords: *Glynn v Margetson & Co.* [1893] A.C. 351; *London and North Western Railway Co. v Neilson* [1922] 2 A.C. 263; *Cunard Steamship Co. Ltd. v Buerger* [1927] A.C. 1; and by *Canada Steamship Lines Ltd v The King* [1952] A.C. 192; and *Sze Hai Tong Bank Ltd. v Rambler Cycle Co. Ltd.* [1959] A.C. 576 in the Privy Council; and innumerable cases in the Court of Appeal, culminating in *Levison v Patent Steam Carpet Cleaning Co. Ltd.* [1978] Q.B. 69. But when the clause was itself reasonable and gave rise to a reasonable result, the judges upheld it; at any rate, when the clause did not exclude liability entirely but only limited it to a reasonable amount. So where goods were deposited in a cloakroom or sent to a laundry for cleaning, it was quite reasonable for the company to limit their liability to a reasonable amount, having regard to the small charge made for the service. These are illustrated *by Gibaud v Great Eastern Railway Co.* [1921] 2 K.B. 426; *Alderslade v Hendon Laundry Ltd* [1945] K.B. 189; and *Gillespie Bros. & Co. Ltd. v Roy Bowles Transport Ltd.* [1973] Q.B. 400.

5.3 The sales contract and the performance of the seller's transport obligations

In terms of performance of transport obligations, the buyer is in the first place entitled to the contract of carriage stipulated for in the sales contract.

This means that if a c.i.f. buyer wishes the cargo to be subject to specific arrangements whilst in transit, or for a specific vessel to be engaged for transport, he is best advised to turn those requirements into specific obligations to be enshrined in the sales contract itself.

Translating transport arrangements into contractual obligations will see the seller in breach of contract as a consequence in the case that those obligations are not fulfilled.

In *The Intan 6*,[22] two sales contracts for a cargo of Muntok white pepper incorporated IGPA contract form N.5 Clause 6 (shipment and classification) of the IGPA contract form N.5, provided shipment by first class ship, classed not lower than 100 A1 in The Lloyd's Register, or an equivalent classification in any register a member of the International Association of Classification Societies.

The goods of the contract description were to be shipped on ships which would proceed directly or indirectly on a geographically normal commercially acceptable route from the port of shipment to the port/s of destination: "'Overseas ship'; 'ocean-going ship', or similar words, shall mean a ship employed in carrying the contract goods on a sea-voyage from the port, place or country of shipment to the destination named in the contract direct or indirect with liberty to call and/or tranship at other ports . . . Where in any contract for goods sold for shipment it is expressly stipulated that shipment must be made on an ocean-going ship or ships, as defined above, a shipment shall be deemed not to have been made unless and until the contract goods are shipped on board the overseas ship."

The buyers refused to accept the shipping documents tendered by the sellers because of the characteristics of the vessel deployed by the sellers, i.e. the *Intan 6*. The *Intan 6* was an unpowered barge and the goods were lost while the containers were being towed on the *Intan 6* from Indonesia to Singapore. The buyers considered that the *Intan 6* was not a first class ship within the meaning of clause 6 of the IGPA contract. As held by Havelock-Allan J:

> Aside from cases of fraud, the buyer under a c.i.f. or c.&f. sale can only reject the shipping documents in two circumstances: (1) where, by their express terms, they do not conform to the requirements of the contract in a respect which is more than minimal, and (2) where, even if they appear to conform to the requirements of the contract, they are not genuine in the sense that they contain false information about an aspect of the performance of the contract which would normally be disclosed in the documents and which is of more than minimal importance e.g. the date of shipment.[23]

22 *The Intan 6* [2003] 2 Lloyd's Rep. 700.

23 *Ibid.*, at 709. See also *Benjamin's Sale of Goods*, 8th Edition, paras. 19–074 to 19–075, and 19–142. In general, the buyer is bound to pay for documents if, on their face, they conform to the terms of the contract. Lord Diplock so held in *Gill & Duffus S.A. v Berger & Co. Inc.* [1984] 1 Lloyd's Rep. 227; [1984] AC 382.

At any rate, the seller must give the buyer a bill of lading which complies with the contract of sale.

In *SIAT di dal Ferro v Tradax*,[24] there was a grave and unexplained failure by the sellers to provide documents containing or evidencing a contract or contracts of carriage of the contractual goods from the contractual port of loading to the contractual destination. It was held by the court that it is not enough for the seller to come to arrangements with the carrier outside the bill of lading.

The function of the bill of lading within the context of a c.i.f. transaction was enunciated by Megaw LJ as follows:

> The principle of law applicable to c.i.f. contracts is clear [. . .] the bill of lading must provide for the carriage of the goods to the agreed destination: if the bill of lading does not satisfy this requirement, the seller is in breach even though the actual contract of carriage made by him did provide for carriage to the destination stipulated in the contract of sale.
>
> The buyer is not under any obligation to speculate or to investigate, or to accept assurances outside the bill of lading. The bill of lading is the document to which he is entitled to look as being definitive of the contract of carriage binding on the shipowner, as being a contract entered into or in existence at the time of the shipment of the goods, so as to cover the whole of the carriage from the port of loading to the port of discharge provided for by the contract of sale. Thus, if there should be non-delivery of, or damage to, the goods (the existence of which may not become known until after the documents have been taken up and paid for) the buyer, if he has taken a proper bill of lading, in conformity with the rights which he obtains under the Bills of Lading Act, 1855, can look to the carrier for a remedy in so far as the loss or damage is his responsibility under the contract of carriage. But not so, or not necessarily so, if the bill of lading, on the face of it, is defective or contrary to the contract of sale.[25]

The importance of the compliance of shipping documents as a testament to the fulfilment of the contractual transport obligations under a c.i.f sale was further emphasised in *Bergerco U.S.A. v Vegoil Ltd.*[26]

The case concerned a c.&f. sale under which, in return for the buyers agreeing an extension of shipment, it was expressly stipulated that the ship should sail directly from the port of loading to the port of discharge. In fact, she deviated to other ports in the course of the voyage. By the time the buyers found out, their bank had already paid for the shipping documents. But the vessel was delayed in berthing at the discharge port and, before she berthed, the buyers rejected the goods. Mr Justice Hobhouse upheld their right to do so. He said this of the agreement that the ship should be a direct ship:

> the term is more correctly described as a stipulation than a promise. The promise is to ship the goods. The term restricts the ways in which the seller can contractually perform that promise. It is in an all or nothing situation. Either the ship is a contractual ship, in which case the shipment discharges the promise, or the ship is non-contractual, in which case the shipment is nugatory unless and until the buyer with knowledge of the relevant facts chooses to accept it.[27]

24 *SIAT di dal Ferro v Tradax* [1980] 1 Lloyd's Rep. 53.
25 *Ibid.*, at 63.
26 *Bergerco U.S.A. v Vegoil Ltd.* [1984] 1 Lloyd's Rep. 440.
27 *Ibid.*, at 442.

The test is whether the documents contain a statement or statements which, without further investigation, demonstrate that the transport obligations enshrined in the sales contract have not been honoured in one or more respects.

In *Ashmore & Son v CS Cox & Co*[28] the sales contract provided for the goods to be shipped from a port or ports in the Philippine Islands, by sailor or sailors, directly or indirectly to London, between 1 May and 31 July, 1898, both inclusive. In that case, the declaration of shipment made by the seller did not tally with what was originally established in the sales contract in terms of transport obligations, as it expressly identified the vessel on board of which goods were shipped as being a steamship rather than a sailer.

In order for the buyer to reject the shipping documents, the shortfalls of the seller's transport obligations must be apparent from the terms of the documents themselves, without inquiry into the physical performance of the contract.

In *Marshall, Knott & Barker Ltd. v Arcos Ltd.*,[29] the sale was a c.i.f. sale for shipment to "Grimsby, Alexandra Dock, buyers' quay". Nevertheless, the charter party did not oblige the vessel to reach the buyers' quay; she was obliged only to deliver at that quay "or as near thereunto as she may safely get". The shipping documents were, thus, held not to be of contractual specification, because the bills of lading expressly incorporated the charter party and the terms of the charter party qualified the delivery obligation in the contract of sale.

Similarly, in *Soon Hua Seng Co. Ltd. v Glencore Grain Ltd.*,[30] a sale was concluded on c.&f. liner terms Rotterdam. That meant that the goods were to be landed at Rotterdam, free of expense to the buyers. The bills of lading did not comply with the contract because they expressly incorporated the voyage charter party which was for the carriage of the cargo on Free in out and trimmed (f.i.o.t.) terms.

Whenever in light of the terms of the sales contract the seller is to arrange for transport, it is therefore crucial to specify the seller's transport obligations in the sale contract itself. Nevertheless, that will not suffice, as the buyer needs to be in the position to assess the compliance of the seller's transport obligations.

To this end, it may well be in the buyer's interests, therefore, to translate the seller's transport obligations into documentary duties, imposing upon the seller the duty to tender shipping documents which reflect and testify the fulfilment of the transport obligations as per that originally established in the sales contract.

In the absence of specific documentary duties, if a seller failed to comply with a "non-documentary term" in the sales contract, he would still be in breach; nevertheless, the buyer would only learn of the breach after he had paid the price against the documents and it would be then up to him to recover damages for breach from a foreign seller, possibly in a foreign land.

Terms in the trading contract regarding the shipping arrangements come in many different forms, and might be enshrined in standard contract forms invoked by the sale contract itself.

28 *Ashmore & Son v CS Cox & Co* [1899] 1 QB 436, 441.
29 *Marshall, Knott & Barker Ltd. v Arcos Ltd.* (1932) 44 Ll L Rep. 384.
30 *Soon Hua Seng Co. Ltd. v Glencore Grain Ltd.* [1996] 1 Lloyd's Rep. 398.

For instance, if a sale contract were to incorporate Fosfa 54, clause 4 (shipment and classification), that would entail shipment in ship/s which comply with the Fosfa qualifications and which, after loading in one or more ports of origin, will proceed directly or indirectly on a geographically normal route from the port/s of shipment to the port/s of destination.

For the purposes of Fosfa 54, the words "ship" or "ships" means any full-powered engine-driven ship, and transhipment shall only be allowed under a through bill of lading and shall be restricted to the area of origin and/or customary transhipment ports in the area of destination for the goods specified in the contract, provided that transhipment at origin is completed within the original contract shipment period and/or agreed extension period.

In the case of transhipment at origin, according to Fosfa 54 clause 4, shipping documents shall include the Fosfa certificate of compliance, cleanliness and suitability of ship's tank and a Fosfa combined masters certificate in respect of the ocean carrier. Further, in the event of such transhipment at origin the declaration of shipment shall include the name of the ocean carrier and transhipment location.

Fosfa 54 clause 4 is quite specific in terms of shipment obligations, and translates those obligations into documentary duties pending on the sellers' shoulders. Nevertheless, specific provisions allowing for shipment in more than one port of origin, indirect transit and transhipment may not be particularly appealing for certain buyers and, as established above,[31] might be contracted out on the basis of an agreement with the seller.

Apart from contractual transport obligations explicitly agreed by the parties, whenever the seller makes the transport arrangements, he is compelled to tender a "reasonable contract of carriage".

5.4 The seller's obligation to tender a reasonable contract of carriage

Any other features of the contract of carriage tendered by the seller must be "reasonable". This obligation is an implied duty enshrined in section 32(2) of SOGA 1979, whereby the contract of carriage tendered must be "reasonable having regard to the nature of the goods and other circumstances of the case".

Whenever the Incoterms® are invoked by the sales contract, the duty becomes to procure a "contract for the carriage of the goods from the agreed point of delivery, if any, at the place of delivery to the named port of destination or, if agreed, any point at that port. The contract must be made on usual terms at the seller's expense and provide for carriage by the usual route in a vessel of the type normally used for the transport of the type of goods sold."[32]

This obligation for a reasonable/usual contract of carriage in the first place denotes factual connotations to be ascertained on a case by case basis, depending on the nature of the cargo/transport, and this transcends from any legal principle.[33]

31 See chapter 2.
32 See Incoterms 2010® rule c.i.f. A3(a).
33 Bradgate, R., *Commercial Law*, Third Edition, Butterworths, Lexis Nexis, 2003, p.79.

In *Burstall v Grimsdale*,[34] a sales contract was stipulated on c.i.f. terms, London from America, for the sale of meal. The bill of lading tendered by the seller conferred upon the carrier the liberty to deviate, and as a result was rejected by the buyers as inconsistent with what was originally established in the sales contract. The court was asked, inter alia, to assess whether under that specific line of transit, the liberty to deviate was a usual contract of carriage term. Kennedy J found that the shipping documents were not inconsistent with the sale contract:

> If the effect of the clause in the bill of lading is to make the calling at another port [. . .] out of the direct line to London, permissible, the question then is, was the adoption by the shippers under the through bill of lading of such a method of carriage by the Leyland Line, a well known line of steamers, necessarily inconsistent with the terms of the sale contract and the American germ meal contract which it embodies? That appears to me to be eminently a question of fact or commercial usage, and upon the findings in the case it seems to me that there was no inconsistency. If I were trying this case as an action before a jury, the question I should have to ask the jury would be whether it is or not in accordance with the usage and practice in the trade to accept this method of carriage to London under a contract such as this, and is such custom or practice or usage well known and acted upon? I feel no doubt, in fact, it is found for me in the case that that question would be answered, as it has been in this case, in the affirmative.[35]

On the contrary to *Burstall v Grimsdale*, a bill of lading containing an extensive liberty to deviate would not, under normal circumstances, be considered to be "reasonable" or "usual". Indeed, in *Shipton, Anderson & Co v Weston & Co*,[36] the dispute revolved around a c.i.f. contract for the sale of American malting barley, which was to be shipped from any Atlantic or Canadian port to Bristol or Avonmouth. A condition of the contract was that the ship might call at one other port in the United Kingdom, but in fact it called first at Glasgow and then at Belfast, with the carrier allowed to do so on the basis of a wide deviation clause enshrined into the bill of lading. It was held by Greer J that the bill of lading was unusual and ergo not a good tender:

> On the c.i.f. contract, the applicants, the sellers are either to ship the goods in accordance with the contract, or to allocate goods which have been shipped in accordance with the contract, to this contract. I think it is clear that they may allocate goods which have been shipped by somebody else. But, having shipped or allocated goods which have been shipped, or are in accordance with the contract, they have to do something more. They have to procure the usual and proper shipping documents called for by their contract of sale. When they have done that and handed over delivery to the purchasers upon those documents, then their obligations under the contract as sellers have been complied with. The purchasers at the time the documents are delivered to them are not in a position to say whether goods of the contract description have or have not been put on board at the port of shipment; and they are entitled, when they see the goods, if the goods by their condition show that they cannot have been of contract condition or contract quality when shipped, to reject, notwithstanding that they have taken up the documents. As far as the voyage is concerned, the sellers have nothing whatever to

34 *Burstall v Grimsdale* (1906) 11 Comm Cas 280.
35 *Ibid.*, at 290.
36 *Shipton, Anderson & Co v Weston & Co* (1922) 10 Ll L R 762.

> do with what happened on the voyage. Their obligations are to secure a proper fulfilment of the contract; and I therefore read the words of this contract as meaning that the sellers are to procure a carrying contract which contains an option of calling at a port in the United Kingdom; and that is a description of the kind of bill of lading which he is to obtain and has nothing whatever to do with the condition of the goods.
>
> The first question which arises is whether or not the documents which were in fact tendered were in accordance with the contract. The contract is, according to my judgment, a contract or bill of lading that goods are to be shipped on a ship which has the option of calling at another port in the United Kingdom. If it had remained there I am clear that the tender of a bill of lading which gave the shipowner the wide option described in condition No. 1 on the bill of lading dated Baltimore, Aug. 13, 1921, would not be compliance with the obligations under the section. The words are so wide that the ship might have called anywhere she liked and almost have gone round the world before she came to the port of discharge. That would not in my judgment be a compliance with the obligations of the sellers under this c.i.f. contract; and the buyers would be entitled, when they got the bills of lading, to say "the documents which I stipulated to have from you as representing the goods are quite different from the documents you have delivered to me, and I will not take them".[37]

Bills of lading containing wide discretionary liberties are, nevertheless, not always considered unusual or unreasonable. In *Finska Cellulosaforeiningen v Westfield Paper Co Ltd*,[38] a widely discretionary war risk clause did not affect the validity of a bill of lading tendered within the context of a c.i.f sale of sulphite pulp from Finland. As held by Viscount Caldecote CJ:

> The argument was pressed upon me that a bill of lading under a c.i.f. contract must be in a form which is reasonable and usual in the trade, and that this clause was neither one nor the other. It was said on behalf of the defendants that the wide discretion given to the master to discharge the cargo at any convenient port or place in the conditions of war stated in the clause had the effect of making the bill of lading no longer one for the carriage of goods to Leith. I do not accept this contention. It is every day practice to deal in bills of lading with war conditions or with the interference with a contract of carriage by blockade or similar action by inserting a clause not different in essence from the clause to which the defendants take exception. The insertion of a clause in a bill of lading giving a discretion to the master, in the case of war or hostilities rendering the prosecution of the voyage unsafe, to land the goods at any port he may consider safe at shippers' risk and expense, does not, in my opinion, prevent the bill of lading from being for the carriage of goods to a named port. Evidence, moreover, was given to show that in this trade this identical clause, or one very like it, has been widely used since the outbreak of war in September, 1939. A number of the bills of lading issued by the Finnish Steamship Company produced before me contained the clause, and except in the present case, and in the case of one other shipment, no question has been raised concerning the clause. It is true that it has not been the practice to pay the price of the goods before their arrival, but I should have expected some objection to have been taken to the clause, if it was so unusual or unreasonable as to make a bill of lading containing it defective as a shipping document, under a c.i.f. contract.
>
> [. . .] a bill of lading tendered under a c.i.f. contract must be, as in the case of the policy of insurance, in a form usual or current in the trade. In *Burstall v Grimsdale & Sons*, 11 Com. Cas. 280, Mr. Justice Kennedy considered a question whether clauses introduced into a bill of lading were usual and proper in performance of a c.i.f. contract,

37 *Ibid.*, at 763.
38 *Finska Cellulosaforeiningen v Westfield Paper Co Ltd*, above.

> and treated it as a question of fact. Here, the fact that other shipments have been made on the terms of a bill of lading containing the clause in question is relied on as evidence not to show that there was waiver but that the clause is well known and, to use the epithet insisted on by Sir Robert Aske on behalf of the defendants, "usual."[39]

Procuring a "usual" or "reasonable" contract of carriage also depends on freight market availability.

In the Australian case *Plaimar Ltd v Waters Trading Co Ltd*,[40] the bills of lading reflecting the shipment of a cargo of Zanzibar clove oil contained limitation liability clauses in favour of the shipowner exempting him from liability for loss or damage for transhipment of the goods. Those clauses did not preclude a valid tender as the seller succeeded in proving he had no other option available in the freight market, having concluded a carriage of goods by sea contract with the only carrier available at that time for shipment from Zanzibar.

Aside from the factual connotation to be assessed on a case by case basis, the duty of a c.i.f. seller to procure a "reasonable"/"usual" contract of carriage also entails the obligation to provide "continuous documentary cover".

5.4.1 Continuous documentary cover

This duty is exceedingly important for the buyer and, as we shall discover in the following, it is particularly crucial within the context of the transfer of risk.[41]

The duty means above all that the seller must provide the buyer with "continuous documentary cover" against the carrier, i.e. a continuous cause of action against the carrier taking the buyer from the port of loading to the port of discharge.

In *Hansson v Hamel & Horley*,[42] 46 tons of cod guano c.i.f. Kobe/Yokohama were shipped from Norway, and transshipped from Kiev to Atlas Maru in Hamburg. The bill of lading endorsed by the seller did not impose contractual obligations on the carrier in relation to the first leg of the transit, and therefore it was considered as an invalid tender. As stated by Lord Sumner:

> As there were not, I suppose, to be two contracts for carriage as far as Hamburg, this is strong evidence to show that the appellant never intended the ocean bill of lading to be a contract of carriage from Braatvag to Hamburg. When documents are to be taken up the buyer is entitled to documents which substantially confer protective rights throughout. He is not buying a litigation, as Lord Trevethin (then Mr. Justice A.T. Lawrence) says in the General Trading Company's case (16 Com. Cas. at p. 101). These documents have to be handled by banks, they have to be taken up or rejected promptly and without any opportunity for prolonged inquiry, they have to be such as can be re-tendered to sub-purchasers, and it is essential that they should so conform to the accustomed shipping documents as to be reasonably and readily fit to pass current

39 *Ibid.*, at 83.

40 *Plaimar Ltd v Waters Trading Co Ltd* [1945] HCA 34; 72 CLR 304.

41 As will be discovered, the obligation of the seller to tender shipping documents which cover all the transit is also crucial in terms of transfer of risk. Indeed, in most international sales, the risk passes to the buyer on or as from shipment and the only basis on which it makes sense for the buyer to purchase on these terms is that the buyer takes from the seller a contract of transport which entitles him to sue the carrier for breach of contract if anything happens to the goods in transit.

42 *Hansson v Hamel & Horley* [1922] 2 AC 46.

> in commerce. I am quite sure that, under the circumstances of this case, this ocean bill of lading does not satisfy these conditions. It bears notice of its insufficiency and ambiguity on its face, for, though called a through bill of lading, it is not really so. It is the contract of the subsequent carrier only, without any complementary promises to bind the prior carriers in the through transit. The appellant's contract with Mr. Lind was not transferable by indorsement and delivery, nor was it tendered; the Kiev bill of lading he kept to himself, and endorsed to Mr. Lind under his own contract with him. I do not suggest that tender of either document would have carried matters any further, but, as things stood, the buyer was plainly left with a considerable lacuna in the documentary cover to which the contract entitled him.[43]

In *Fishel & Co v Spencer*,[44] the court was asked whether the bill of lading tendered by the c.i.f. sellers for 500 tons of Manila copra cakes in bags was such as the sellers were entitled to tender. The particular document upon which the controversy arose was a bill of lading which called for shipment of goods by steamer or steamers from the Philippine Islands to Rotterdam.

The bill of lading was in the usual form adopted by the four shipping companies which carried the bulk of the trade from those islands. It provided for transhipment from steamer to steamer, sailing vessels or lighters, and the goods were shipped under the bill of lading to Rotterdam with this liberty of transhipment.

Arriving in London, the goods were discharged into lighters and put on a vessel for Amsterdam, where they were again put on board lighters and conveyed to Rotterdam, their port of destination. Now the question which arose as between the buyers and sellers was whether the bill of lading was good tender having regard to the transhipment and, in particular, whether it provided the buyers with continuous documentary cover.

The bill of lading was not considered a valid tender, as it did not cover all the transit of the goods. Whenever transhipment is permitted, the buyer is indeed entitled to reject a bill of lading which leaves the cargo exposed without documentary cover until it is received by a subsequent carrier within the context of transhipment.[45]

Similarly, in *Holland Colombo Trading Society Ltd v Segu Mohamed Khaja Alawdeen*,[46] the bill of lading was held to be quite inoperative in terms of allowing the respondents to get the goods from the port of origin, and it did not give them the protection they were entitled to – namely, a right against the shipowner should the goods be damaged.

As put by Lord Asquith of Bishopstone:

> A bill of lading with a transhipment clause is not necessarily a bad tender under a c.i.f. contract: but it must in some way give "continuous documentary cover" in respect of the goods over the whole transit (*Hansson v Hamel & Horley, Ltd.* [1922] 2 A.C. 36; (1922) 10 Ll.L.Rep. 507); and a bill of lading issued by a shipowner who by the transhipment terms in it disclaims all liability in respect of the goods in the event and as from the time of transhipment, gives no such "continuous" cover. It was

43 *Ibid.*, at 49.
44 *Fishel & Co v Spencer* (1922) 12, Ll L Rep 36.
45 See D. Sassoon, *FOB and CIF Contracts* (5th Edition, Sweet & Maxwell 2012) p. 239.
46 *Holland Colombo Trading Society Ltd v Segu Mohamed Khaja Alawdeen* [1954] 2 Lloyd's Rep. 45.

> argued for the appellants that the defect was cured by Clause 2 (a) of the bill of lading, which incorporates the Hague Rules; and that the effect of their incorporation is to override, and impliedly delete from the bill of lading, the peccant transhipment provisions. But the Hague Rules are only incorporated "unless otherwise provided in the bill of lading"; hence the provisions of the bill of lading prevail in case of conflict. It is true that Clause 2 (b) makes all "compulsory provisions" of the law to which the carriage might be subject prevail over contrary stipulations in the bill of lading. The only relevant "compulsory provisions" in this case are the Hague Rules themselves, and these are not in the present case "compulsory." For although by 1948 they had been incorporated in the English Carriage of Goods by Sea Act, 1924, that Act only applies to transit from United Kingdom ports, not to a transit from, e.g., Rotterdam; and (if Netherlands law be relevant) at the time in question the "Hague Rules" would appear not to have been incorporated into the statute law of the Netherlands (Scrutton on Charter-parties, 15th ed., pp. 440–441). Hence their Lordships are of opinion that the bill of lading is not so affected by the Hague Rules as to become part of a good documentary tender under a c.i.f. contract.[47]

Continuous documentary cover entails the obligation of the seller to provide for a bill of lading which covers all the transit of the goods, from the port of origin to the destination. In *SIAT di Del Ferro v Tradax Overseas SA*,[48] the sellers or their associate companies agreed to sell to the buyers nearly 5000 tonnes of Brazilian soya bean meal c.i.f. free out Venice. The contract incorporated the terms of Gafta 100, and the bills of lading tendered by the sellers showed destination "As Per Charter Party" in the case of two groups, and destination "Ancona/Ravenna" in the remaining two groups. The tender was considered invalid, as the destination shown by the bills of lading did not comply with what was originally established in the sales contract. Indeed, in the absence of a contrary stipulation by the parties, the bill of lading needs to indicate the destination stipulated in the sales contract, and clauses indicating destination "As Per Charter Party" will not be considered valid.

As held by Megaw LJ:

> The principle of law applicable to c.i.f. contracts is clear. It is stated as follows in *Benjamin's Sale of Goods*, par. 1514:
>
> The bill of lading must provide for the carriage of the goods to the agreed destination: if the bill of lading does not satisfy this requirement, the seller is in breach even though the actual contract of carriage made by him did provide for carriage to the destination stipulated in the contract of sale.
>
> In the group 4 documents, the bills of lading, on first presentation, evidenced a contract of carriage to Ancona or Ravenna. I find it impossible to think that it could be seriously argued that a buyer whose contract was c.i.f. Venice was not entitled to reject those documents as they then stood. To my mind, it is inconceivable that he should be required by law to accept them and pay for them and take his chance of what might befall, with a remedy merely of a potential claim for damages against the seller. I would reject out of hand the suggestion that a buyer who refused to accept such a bill of lading under such a contract would himself be liable for a breach of contract towards the seller.
>
> The bills of lading tendered among the group 2 and group 3 documents were, in my opinion, also fatally defective: they failed to comply with a requirement of the contract which can properly be described as fundamental to a c.i.f. contract. It

47 *Ibid.*, at 54.

48 *SIAT di Del Ferro v Tradax Overseas SA* [1980] 1 Lloyd's Rep. 53.

may be not necessary to decide that a tender of documents would not be invalid if the bill of lading, showing the port of discharge "As Per Charter Party", were to be accompanied by the charter-party, or an acceptable copy of it, which showed that the contract of carriage unequivocally required delivery of the bill of lading cargo at the port of discharge named in the contract of sale. But in the absence of such inclusion among the documents, the buyer does not get that which he is entitled to require: a document which evidences a contract of carriage to the port of discharge specified in the contract of sale.

Even if the charter-party had been tendered in this case, it would not have filled the gap: for by its terms it did not show a contract of carriage with discharge of the goods at Venice. Venice was, in the charter-party, merely one of two ports to which the charterer could, under his contract with the shipowners, order the vessel to go "on signing bills of lading". The very fact that the bills of lading, when signed, merely said "port of discharge as per charter party", would cause the prudent buyer, not only to realise that he did not have the assurance to which he was entitled, but, affirmatively, to suppose that orders as to the port of discharge had not been given when the bill of lading was signed, as required by the charter-party contract. For if they had been given, they would presumably have been shown in the bill of lading.[49]

5.5 Limits of the seller's obligation to provide a reasonable contract of carriage

The obligation of the seller to provide for a reasonable contract of carriage entails that the seller must make a contract of carriage which conforms to the contract of sale, or which is reasonable (or which is usual). This does not mean that the seller guarantees to the buyer that litigation on such a cause of action will be successful.

In *The Galatia*,[50] it was specified by the court that the shipping documents tendered by the seller ought simply to be "enforceable against the carrier", not successful in the enforcement. As held by Donaldson J:

> At first sight, it may seem obvious that the bill of lading should evidence an effective contract of carriage. But this is not necessarily true. Thus a bill of lading relating to the carriage of goods which have been lost on the voyage is a good tender. And this is so even if the ship has also been lost. In such cases the contract is clearly ineffective. In *Arnhold Karberg & Co. v Blythe, Green, Jourdain & Co.* [1916] 1 K.B. 495, the expression used by Lord Justice Bankes at p. 509 was a "subsisting" contract of carriage. There the further performance of the contract had become illegal as a result of the war. But I am not sure that even "subsisting" is always the right word, because the loss of the ship and goods might be said to put an end to the contract. "Enforceable" might be a better term, because although the further performance of the contract may be at an end, the holder of the bill of lading will have rights against the shipowner. In the Arnhold Karberg case, the contract was unenforceable for reasons of public policy. This bill undoubtedly evidences an enforceable contract, whether or not the shipowners had a complete defence on the facts.[51]

By the same token, the obligation of the seller to provide for a reasonable contract of carriage does not mean that the seller undertakes to top up the buyer for

49 *Ibid.*, at 63, 64.
50 *The Galatia* [1979] 2 Lloyd's Rep. 450.
51 *Ibid.*, at 456, per Donaldson J, approved at [1980] 1 Lloyd's Rep. 453.

any loss beyond the limitation of the carrier's liability provided for in the contract of carriage.

As established above, the failure to provide a reasonable contract of carriage will see the seller in breach of contract and exposed to liabilities vis-à-vis the buyer.

Moreover, if the contract of carriage made by the seller is not reasonable, another serious legal consequence which will arise is that the seller will retain the risk for the goods whilst in transit, with the seller ultimately responsible for transit loss and damage to the goods.

CHAPTER 6

Bills of lading and their role in contracts concluded on shipment terms

6.1 The role of bills of lading in contracts concluded on shipment terms

A bill of lading is a document of crucial importance within the context of contracts concluded on shipment terms. The bill of lading is a document issued by a carrier which details a shipment of merchandise and gives title of that shipment to a specified party.

Etymologically, the origin of the bill of lading can be traced to the word "lading" which means "loading", both words being derived from the Old English word "hladan",[1] with the word "lading" specifically referring to the loading of cargo aboard a ship.

While there is evidence of the existence of receipts for goods loaded aboard merchant vessels stretching back as far as Egyptian and pre-Roman times,[2] and the practice of recording cargo aboard ship in the ship's log is almost as long lived as shipping itself, the modern bill of lading only came into use with the growth of international trade in the medieval world.

Although it is not possible to "establish with any degree of precision when the bill of lading was used for the first time, its origins can be traced to Italy at the beginning of the second millennium. The 'Ordonnance Maritime de Triani' (an Italian town) of 1063 laid down that every master was obliged to have a clerk (in fact a writer) on board. It also made mention of a log book or register. This is the first indication that goods which were shipped were registered".[3]

1 Old English hladan (past tense hlod, past participle gehladen) "to load, heap" (the general Germanic sense). See the online etymology dictionary at: http://www.etymonline.com.

2 See Sanborn, F.R. *Origins of the Early English Maritime and Commercial Law* (1930; reprinted by Professional Books Ltd), particularly chapters I, II and IV; Gilmore and Black, *The Law of Admiralty*, (Foundation Press, 1975) pp. 3–11; *Gold Maritime Transport* (1981) 4f. Indeed, in Purchase, H.G. *The Law Relating to Documents of Title to Goods* (Sweet & Maxwell 1931), p. 208 one finds the following in an appendix: "In an address to the Humber District Association of Chartered Shipbrokers, December 9, 1924, on the Carriage of Goods by Sea Act, 1924, Colonel Jackson, DL, refers to a form of bill of lading before the Christian era which was discovered in Egypt. The lecturer stated that it was not materially different from any bill of lading in use up to about 1850. It was for a cargo of wheat to be carried from the Fayoum by the Nile to a town in Lower Egypt. There was a full provision for lay-days, measuring out the cargo, payment of freight and advances, and even for a gratuity to the master consisting of certain measures of wine." Purchase provided no further details of this document. Bennett, W.P. in *The History and Present Position of the Bill of Lading as a Document of Title to Goods* (University Press, 1914) also remarked that "it is quite possible that documents corresponding to the 'Registers' of the Customs of the Sea . . . may have been also known to the Ancient World but of this there is no evidence".

3 This historical analysis of the origin of the bill of lading is based on *Bills of Lading: An Historical Introduction*, available at www.maritimeknowhow.com.

The ordinances of the Mediterranean towns and the "Consulat de la Mer", made reference to a "scribanus" or writer. The writer had to "enter all the goods that were loaded on board in a log book and keep it up to date. In accordance with the "Consulat de la Mer", the master or the crew were not allowed to load or discharge the goods without the writer being informed."[4]

When goods which were entered in the log book by the writer were lost, the master was obliged to refund them. If he could not refund them, his ship could be sold. All entries in the log book had force of law.

Entry of the goods in the log book thus served as "evidence that the goods had been shipped on board. Shippers could receive an excerpt of the log book that could be presented in case the log book was lost. These excerpts can be considered as the precursors of the bill of lading".[5]

The bill of lading, "just like the insurance policy and the bill of exchange, originated in Italy. It was found for the first time in 1526, in a decree of the town of Florence under the name of 'polizza di carico' or 'police de chargement'".[6]

In the sixteenth century, the use of the bill of lading was "extended to Western europe and the ordinances around that time contained several provisions which were related to the bill of lading".[7]

A vital step towards the shaping of the bill of lading as a crucial document within the context of commercial sales was made in France at the beginning of the nineteenth century, under the Napoleonic regime. For the first time, the bill of lading could be issued to a named person, to bearer, or to order, thus becoming a negotiable document of crucial importance for every maritime trade transaction.[8]

The growth of mercantilism, which produced "other financial innovations such as the charter party (once *carta partita*), the bill of exchange, and the insurance policy, ignited a requirement for a title document that could be traded in much the same way as the goods themselves. It was the modern way of trading that effectively moulded the bill of lading in much the same form as we know today".[9]

---

4 See Murray A., "History and development of the bill of lading 1982–1983", *University of Miami LR* 1, 689, 690.

5 See De Roover, R. The organization of trade in Postan, Rich & Miller (Eds) *III The Cambridge Economic History of Europe* (1963), p. 48.

6 See *Bills of Lading: an Historical Introduction*, above, p. 39.

7 *Ibid.*, p. 4, where it is stated that the "Ordonnance de Philippe II" of 1563 regarding maritime commerce, the "Ordonnance d'Anvers" of 1570, the "Ordonnance d'Amsterdam" of 1598 and the "Ordonnance des villes Hanséatiques" promulgated at Lübeck in 1591. In those days, the bill of lading was merely a receipt, delivered by the master which was defined in the "Guidon de la Mer" as follows: "Le connoissement est la promesse particulie`re que fait le maistre du navire de la réception de telle et telle sorte de marchandise appartenant a` tel marchand, et faut tant de connoissements comme il y a de diversité de personne a` qui elles appartiennent".

Later, with the "Ordonnance de la Marine" from 1681 from Colbert, the bill of lading, amongst others, received a more definite form.

8 See *Bills of Lading: an Historical Introduction*, above, p. 5.

9 Codified provisions on bills of lading may be found in the 1924 Hague Rules, the 1968 and 1979 Hague-Visby Rules, and the Hamburg Rules. For a more detailed analysis, see Gaskell N., *Bills of Lading: Law and Contracts*, LLP Publishing, 2000, pp. 1–10.

In its apparent simplicity, a bill of lading performs functions of immense relevance for contracts concluded on shipment terms. Its main functions are, in essence, three: a) as a snapshot of the conditions of the goods after the cargo is shipped on board; b) as evidence of the contract of carriage within the context of a c.i.f. transaction; c) a bill of lading.

These three main functions shall be now considered in turn below.

6.2 Bills of lading as evidence of the conditions of the goods shipped on board

The essence of contracts concluded on shipment terms revolves around the obligation of the seller to ship the goods on board a designated vessel in conformity with the specifications originally agreed in the sales contract.

The main issue arising from this all too familiar scenario is that the buyer will not be in the position to witness the shipment of the goods, or their condition.

Therefore, what the bill of lading says about the goods represents a crucial testament for the buyer in relation to the fulfilment of the seller's obligation to ship the goods in conformity with what was originally established in the sale contract. Moreover, the statements appearing on the bill of lading in relation to the goods are of the utmost importance for a buyer in possession of damaged or short delivered goods, in terms of deciding the appropriate legal course of action.[10]

Indeed, if a bill of lading testifies that the seller shipped the goods in "apparent good order and condition" and according to the contractual weight/quantity, that entails that the seller fulfilled his obligations arising from the sales contract, and the liability for a short delivered or damaged cargo will rest with the carrier.

The bill of lading therefore plays a crucial role as evidence of the condition of the goods shipped on board. Before considering this aspect in more detail, one question needs to be unravelled in the first place: is there any obligation at all under common law for a carrier to issue a bill of lading if so requested by the seller qua shipper?

6.2.1 The obligation of the carrier to issue a bill of lading

A sales contract concluded on shipment terms will usually require the seller to tender a bill of lading alongside other documents after the goods are shipped on board. As we shall discover in this chapter, indeed, the bill of lading is a document of the utmost importance within the context of international commercial sales.

Therefore, the very first question to be unfolded relates to the identification of a right of a seller qua shipper to obtain a bill of lading from the carrier after goods are shipped on board.

10 See Debattista, C. *Bills of Lading in Export Trade*, above, p. 131. See also A. Lloyd, The Bill of Lading: do we really need it? (1989) *LMCLQ* 47; Goode, R. *Commercial Law*, 3rd Edition, LexisNexis, 2004; Bridge, M. *The International Sale of Goods Law and Practice*, OUP, 1999.

Surprisingly, under the common law there does not seem to be any authority providing for an obligation for the carrier to provide the shipper with a bill of lading.[11] Equally, the Carriage of Goods by Sea Act 1971 (hereafter, COGSA 1971) does not contain any such duty either.

Nevertheless, it is this time not a surprise that the incorporation of the Hague-Visby Rules into English law as a schedule to COGSA 1971 altered the position in the shipper's favour where the Act applies (and, being an integral part of the common law, the Act will apply by default whenever English law governs a sale contract).[12]

The Hague-Visby Rules are a set of international rules for the international carriage of goods by sea. They are an updated version of the original Hague Rules which were drafted in Brussels in 1924, and contain the following provision (Article III, rule. 3):

The Hague-Visby Rules, Article III, rule. 3

> After receiving the goods into his charge the carrier or the master or agent of the carrier shall, on demand of the shipper, issue to the shipper a bill of lading showing among other things:
>
> (a) The leading marks necessary for identification of the goods as the same are furnished in writing by the shipper before the loading of such goods starts, provided such marks are stamped or otherwise shown clearly upon the goods if uncovered, or on the cases or coverings in which such goods are contained, in such a manner as should ordinarily remain legible until the end of the voyage.
> (b) Either the number of packages or pieces, or the quantity, or weight, as the case may be, as furnished in writing by the shipper.
> (c) The apparent order and condition of the goods.
>
> Provided that no carrier, master or agent of the carrier shall be bound to state or show in the bill of lading any marks, number, quantity or weight which he has reasonable ground for suspecting not accurately to represent the goods actually received, or which he has had no reasonable means of checking.[13]

The content of Article III, rule. 3 of the Hague-Visby Rules is relatively unblemished: the carrier is indeed under an obligation to issue, on demand of the shipper, a bill of lading which is capable of identifying the goods shipped in terms of quantity, weight, and condition.

Nevertheless, what Article III, rule. 3 fails to address is how far a carrier can go in qualifying the aforementioned aspects of the goods. This is, as it will be readily appreciated, of crucial importance as the bill of lading that the seller wishes to obtain is a so called "clean" bill of lading, i.e. a bill of lading which states that goods have been shipped in apparent good order and condition, as opposed to

11 See Debattista, *Bills of Lading in Export Trade*, above, p. 131.

12 For a doctrinal discussion related to the applicability of COGSA 1971, please see *Carver on Bills of Lading*, (Sweet & Maxwell, 2012) paras 9.072–9.098; Aikens, *Bills of Lading* (2nd Edition, Informa London, 2015) 10.20–10.61; and A. Diamond QC, The Hague-Visby Rules, 1978 *LMCLQ* 225, 256–263.

13 See Article III, rule. 3 of the Hague-Visby Rules. Before these, the Hague Rules, incorporated as an annex to the Carriage of Goods by Sea Act 1924, provided for a similar provision in relation to the obligation of the carrier to issue a bill of lading.

a claused bill of lading. As we shall discover in more detail in the following,[14] a claused bill of lading is a bill of lading which contains statements to the effect of conflicting with the idea of the goods being in apparent good order and condition.

That bill of lading will be a testament to the fact that the seller fulfilled his obligation in accordance with the sale contract, entitling him to payment.[15]

The content of the obligation of the carrier to release a bill of lading according to Article III, rule. 3 of the Hague-Visby Rules was further specified in *The David Agshamenebeli.*[16] The dispute revolved around a sale of urea in bulk initially on f.o.b. terms, which then turned into a c.i.f. sale down a string involving three other buyers.[17]

Initially, the master refused to issue a bill of lading, which was eventually released at a later stage when the vessel *David Agshamenebeli* was about to approach its final destination. The bill of lading eventually issued was claused as it annotated the presence of discoloration in the cargo of urea, and that ultimately frustrated all the sales of the cargo concluded down the string.

The question the court was asked to address was, inter alia, whether the actual apparent order and condition of the goods at the time of loading was such as to justify the description of the goods which the master inserted in the bills of lading.

It was held by the court that the duty enshrined into Article III, rule. 3 of the Hague-Visby Rules requires that the master should make up his mind whether in all the circumstances the cargo, insofar as he could see it in the course and circumstances of loading, appeared to satisfy the description of its apparent order and conditions in the bills of lading tendered for signature; he will be entitled to form his own opinion from his own observations and the failure to ask for expert advice was unlikely to be a matter of criticism; for this purpose the law did not cast on the master the role of an expert surveyor and he need not possess any greater knowledge or experience of the cargo in question than any other reasonably careful master; what he was required to do was to exercise his own judgement on the appearance of the cargo loaded; and if he took the view that the cargo was not or not all in apparent good order and condition he was entitled to qualify the bill of lading.

Indeed, it was held that the shipowners' duty was to issue a bill of lading which recorded the apparent order and condition of the goods according to the reasonable assessment of the master; there was not any contractual guarantee of absolute accuracy as to the order and condition of the cargo or its apparent order and condition; and there was no basis for the implication of any such term; the shipper was taken to know the actual apparent order and condition of his own cargo.

---

14 See chapter 6.

15 See chapter 6.

16 *The David Agshamenebeli* [2003] 1 Lloyd's Rep. 92.

17 Indeed, an f.o.b. sale can naturally evolve into a c.i.f sale. This is due to the fact that the first f.o.b. buyer is already in possession of all the necessary transport and insurance documents which can then be passed on to a subsequent buyer on c.i.f. terms.

As put by Colman J:

> It seems to me that the contract is to deliver the goods in the same condition as that in which they are shipped, coupled with an acknowledgment that the condition at the time of shipment, was good. The words "shipped in good order and condition" are not words of contract in the sense of a promise or undertaking. The words are an affirmation of fact, or perhaps rather in the nature of an assent by the captain to an affirmation of fact which the shipper may be supposed to make as to his own goods.
>
> [. . .] It is necessary to keep in mind two areas of distinction which underlie the analysis of this issue.
>
> First, a bill of lading has two distinct functions: (i) as evidence of the contract of carriage; and (ii) as a receipt and document of title to the goods laden on board.
>
> Secondly, whether the carrier's duty in respect of the statement in the bill of lading as to the apparent order and condition is of a contractual nature is a distinct issue from the question what scope that duty has and in particular it is duty of care or analogous to a duty of care or whether it is merely a duty honestly to state the apparent order and condition of the goods.
>
> The starting point in this analysis is to identify the function of the statement of the order and condition of the goods in a bill of lading. For this purpose it is necessary to go back to the issue of the bill. It is the shipper or the shipper's agent who in the ordinary way tenders the bill to the carrier or the carrier's agent, usually the master, for signature. In so doing, the shipper invites the carrier to acknowledge the truth of the statement in the tendered bill as to the order and condition of the goods which the shipper has delivered into the possession of the carrier pursuant to the contract of affreightment. In determining whether the carrier by the master's or other agent's signature accepts contractual responsibility for the accuracy of the statement as to the condition of the goods it is relevant to take account of the fact that it is the shipper or his agent who is delivering the goods and that accordingly any such statement would be as to facts of which he must already have actual or imputed knowledge. Further, because the shipper already has that knowledge he cannot be said to rely on the accuracy of the statement. His requirement goes no further than the need to obtain from the carrier a receipt for the goods in appropriate form. The tender for signature of a bill which states the order and condition of the goods is thus an invitation to the carrier to express his acknowledgment of the truth of the statements in the bill. As such it is an invitation to make a representation of fact as distinct from a binding promise as to the accuracy of the represented facts. The purpose of making that representation is to record the carrier's evidence as to his receipt of the goods and as to their apparent condition when he did receive them for carriage. Given that bills of lading are negotiable instruments, the specific function of recording that evidence is to inform subsequent holders of the facts represented, for those facts are likely to be relevant to their exercise of contractual rights against sellers of the goods or, indeed, the carriers themselves.
>
> Against this background, it is not difficult to see why it has been said in many of the authorities on the Harter Act, the Hague Rules and the Hague-Visby Rules that those codes stop short of imposing on the carrier any contractual obligation as to the accuracy of that which is stated in the bill as to the order and condition of the goods.
>
> Moreover, the wording of art. III, rr. 3, 4 and 5 of the Hague Rules and their successor, the Hague-Visby Rules, is clearly consistent with this analysis. It imposes a contractual duty to issue a bill of lading containing the information specified but by r. 4 provides only that such statements are to be prima facie evidence of the facts stated. That is to say, it is always open to the carrier to adduce evidence displacing what would otherwise be concluded from the statements in the bill of lading. Where, however, the bill has been transferred to a third party acting in good faith there is an estoppel as to the accuracy of the statements: the carrier is precluded from proving the contrary. Whereas at common law the rules of estoppel may in certain circumstances preclude the carrier as against the lawful holder of the bill from the opportunity to displace such conclusion.

[. . .] The duty owed to shippers under art. III, r. 3(3) of the Hague Rules is to issue, on demand, a bill of lading which states "(c) the apparent order and condition of the goods". This requires an accurate statement of fact. (We would reject Mr. Hamblen's somewhat extreme submission that the duty can be discharged by making any such statements, whether accurate or not.) It is moreover, in our judgment, an unqualified or "absolute" contractual undertaking, not merely one which the shipowner, or the master, must take reasonable care to perform. However, since making an accurate statement as to the apparent order and condition of goods may involve some degree of skill and expertise, though it does not necessarily do so, then in such cases the distinction between a duty to exercise reasonable skill and care in making an accurate statement, on the one hand, and a contractual duty to base the statement on the exercise of reasonable skill and care, is of no practical relevance. But one should not, in our judgment, lose sight of the fact that the duty is to make an accurate statement in the circumstances of the case.

It is common ground that this observation was obiter. That the effect of art. III, r. 3 is to impose some contractual duty on the carrier is beyond argument. The master or carrier's agent must at least issue to the shipper on demand a bill of lading showing the specified information. Refusal to issue any bill of lading accurate or not in respect of the goods received on board would thus be a breach of the contract of carriage in respect of which the shipowner would be liable to the shipper. But that duty is more specifically defined in as much as r. 3(a), (b) and (c) specifies those matters which the bill of lading is required to show, including "the apparent order and condition of the goods".

A refusal to issue a bill which made any statement as to the apparent order and condition of the goods would thus be a failure to comply with the contractual obligation imposed by the rule.

[. . .] If there is a contractual obligation to the shipper that the bill of lading should state the apparent order and condition of the goods, how is that duty to be performed? In my judgment, the general effect of the authorities is that the duty requires that the master should make up his mind whether in all the circumstances the cargo, in so far as he can see it in the course and circumstances of loading, appears to satisfy the description of its apparent order and condition in the bills of lading tendered for signature. If in doubt, a master may well consider it appropriate to ask his owners to provide him with expert advice, but that is a matter for his judgment. In the normal case, however, he will be entitled to form his own opinion from his own observations and the failure to ask for expert advice is unlikely to be a matter of criticism. For this purpose the law does not cast upon the master the role of an expert surveyor. He need not possess any greater knowledge or experience of the cargo in question than any other reasonably careful master. What he is required to do is to exercise his own judgment on the appearance of the cargo being loaded. If he honestly takes the view that it is not or not all in apparent good order and condition and that is a view that could properly be held by a reasonably observant master, then, even if not all or even most such masters would necessarily agree with him, he is entitled to qualify to that effect the statement in the bill of lading. This imposes on the master a duty of a relatively low order but capable of objective evaluation.[18]

In light of the *David Agshamenebeli*, the duty enshrined into Article III, rule. 3 of the Hague-Visby Rules requires that the master should exercise his reasonable judgement in annotating statements on bills of lading. This clarification was necessary in order to unfold the important legal issues revolving around bills of lading subject to scrutiny in the following.

18 *Ibid.*, at 103, 104, 105.

6.3 Bills of lading as evidential devices

The bill of lading represents a crucial document for a buyer in possession of damaged or short delivered goods.

Indeed, the buyer is well placed in relation to the assessment of the condition of the cargo once the cargo is delivered to him, but the same cannot be said about the moment of shipment, which under normal circumstances will remain outside any possibility of inspection by a buyer placed in a different country altogether.[19]

The importance of the bill of lading in cargo claims is therefore of crucial importance, as the statements carried by the bill of lading in relation to description, quantity, and condition will represent the evidence on the basis of which the buyer can evaluate possible legal courses of action in deciding to claim against the seller or the carrier.

Nevertheless, it is of the utmost importance to clarify what is the legal value of a bill of lading as a form of evidence; are the statements annotated on the bill of lading describing the connotations of the cargo shipped on board conclusive evidence of the conditions of the goods after they have been shipped on board? Can those statements be retracted and modified by the carrier at a later stage?

COGSA 1971 introduced an absolute ban on evidence contradicting statements on the bill as to the identity, quantity, and apparent condition of the goods on shipment, where the bill has been transferred to a third party acting in good faith.[20]

A similar ban was introduced by COGSA 1992, section 4,[21] which made the bill of lading in the hands of the lawful holder conclusive as to the shipment or receipt for shipment of the goods. Is that always the case? The controversial decision *Grant v Norway*[22] saw an action upon the case by the endorsees of a bill of lading against the owners of a vessel, to recover the amount of advances made by the former upon the bills of lading, the goods never having in fact been shipped.[23] The court held that the master has neither actual nor apparent authority to sign a bill of lading for goods not received.[24]

---

19 See Debattista, *Bills of Lading in Export Trade*, above, p. 126.

20 The requirement of good faith appears to be fulfilled insofar as the consignee did not have "any actual notice at the time of receiving the bill that the goods shipped did not correspond with the bill of lading statements". See A. Diamond QC, "The Hague-Visby Rules", 1978 *LMCLQ* 225, 253. See also Debattista, *Bills of Lading in Export Trade*, above, p. 126.

21 Section 4 of COGSA 1992 recites as follows:

Representations in bills of lading.
A bill of lading which –

(a) represents goods to have been shipped on board a vessel or to have been received for shipment on board a vessel; and
(b) has been signed by the master of the vessel or by a person who was not the master but had the express, implied or apparent authority of the carrier to sign bills of lading, shall, in favour of a person who has become the lawful holder of the bill, be conclusive evidence against the carrier of the shipment of the goods or, as the case may be, of their receipt for shipment.

22 *Grant v Norway* (1851) 10 CB 665.

23 Heiko Giermann, *The Evidentiary Value of Bills of Lading and Estoppel*, Verlag, 2004, p. 93.

24 *Ibid.*, pp. 688–689.

As a consequence, it would be theoretically possible for a shipowner whose master issued a bill of lading to prove that no goods had been shipped,[25] and this would pose some serious doubts as to the effectiveness of the bill of lading as an evidential device.

It has been noted that section 4 of SOGA 1992 was primarily conceived as a means to deal with a *Grant v Norway* scenario where the rights of a buyer, the third party consignee of the bill of lading, would be severely curtailed.[26]

Despite section 4 of SOGA 1992, according to part of the doctrine, a buyer may still be facing a *Grant v Norway* situation.[27] Nevertheless, considering the overall judicial distaste for *Grant v Norway*, it is submitted that that is unlikely to happen.[28]

In light of the above, and the introduction of section 4 SOGA 1992, one may claim that the buyer is well protected by the statements appearing on a bill of lading which should serve him as a *prima facie* indication of potential liabilities.

Indeed, according to section 4 SOGA 1992, the statements made by the carrier on the bill of lading should be deemed to be conclusive evidence of the conditions of the goods after the cargo is shipped on board, with the consequence of the carrier being estopped from altering the original annotations or making further qualifications.[29]

Nevertheless, it has been correctly pointed out by the doctrine that COGSA 1992, section 4 needs to be read in conjunction with the common law rules governing representational estoppel.[30]

6.3.1 Bills of lading as evidence and the common law doctrine of representational estoppel

Estoppel in English law is a "doctrine that may be used in certain situations to prevent a person from relying upon certain rights, or upon a set of facts (e.g. words said or actions performed), which are different from an earlier set of facts".[31]

---

25 See Debattista, *Bills of Lading in Export Trade*, above, p. 127. See also N. Gaskell, *Bills of Lading: Law and Contracts*, above, p. 211.

26 See Debattista, *Bills of Lading in Export Trade*, above, p. 127. See also N. Gaskell, *Bills of Lading: Law and Contracts*, above, p. 211.

27 See *Benjamin's Sale of Goods*, above, paras. 18.030, 18.036, 18.037. Benjamin argues that the possibility for a buyer to face a *Grant v Norway* scenario is still plausible, unless section 4 SOGA 1992 "were treated as an exception to the normal rule that estoppel does not give rise to a course of action". See also Debattista, *Bills of Lading in Export Trade*, above, p. 127. See also N. Gaskell, *Bills of Lading: Law and Contracts*, above, p. 211.

28 See *The Nea Tyhi* [1982] 1 Lloyd's Rep. 606 and *The Saudi Crown* [1986] Lloyd's Rep. 261, as quoted in Debattista, *Bills of Lading in Export Trade*, above, p. 127.

29 Section 4 of COGSA 1992 deals with representations in bills of lading, and states as follows:

> A bill of lading which (a) represents goods to have been shipped on board a vessel or to have been received for shipment on board a vessel; and (b) has been signed by the master of the vessel or by a person who was not the master but had the express, implied or apparent authority of the carrier to sign bills of lading, shall, in favour of a person who has become the lawful holder of the bill, be conclusive evidence against the carrier of the shipment of the goods or, as the case may be, of their receipt for shipment.

30 See Debattista, *Bills of Lading in Export Trade*, above, p. 127.

31 See the definition of estoppel given by E.Peel, *Treitel on contracts*, Sweet & Maxwell 14th ed. (2015) at 3–090. Under English law, estoppel, promissory estoppel, and proprietary estoppel are regarded as "reliance-based estoppels" by *Halsbury's Laws of England*, Vol 16(2), 2003. Both *Halsbury's*

Under such rules, the prerequisite for estoppel are:[32] a) the representor must have intended (actual or presumed) the representee, or have been reasonably understood by the representee as having intended him, to act on the relevant representation (or promise), a statement of the existence of a fact; b) the form of reliance must have been reasonable or intended; and c) the representation must have caused the representee to act in such a way that it would be "unconscionable" for the representor to resile. Detriment is measured at the time when the promisor proposes to withdraw his promise, not at the time when the promise is made.[33]

If we read section 4 of SOGA 1992 in conjunction with the common law rules of representational estoppel, the consequences which will arise are that, in order to ground an estoppel preventing the carrier from retracting the statements appearing on the bill of lading, the statements appearing on the bill of lading must in the first instance be clear and unambiguous.[34]

---

and Spencer Bower in *The Law Relating to Estoppel Representation*, 4th Edition, Bloomsbury, 2004, para. I.2.2 (see below) describe all three estoppels collectively as estoppels by representation. These estoppels can be invoked when a promisee/representee wishes to enforce a promise/representation when no consideration was provided by him. The court will only enforce this lack-of-consideration promise if and only if it would be "unconscionable" for the promisor/representor to rescind from his promise/representation. Estoppel by representation of fact is a term coined by Spencer Bower. This species of estoppel is also referred to as "common law estoppel by representation" in *Halsbury's Laws of England*, Vol 16(2), 2003 re-issue.

In *The Law Relating to Estoppel Representation*, 4th Edition, 2004, para. I.2.2, Spencer Bower defines estoppel by representation of fact as follows:

> where one person ("the representor") has made a representation of fact to another person ("the representee") in words or by acts or conduct, or (being under a duty to the representee to speak or act) by silence or inaction, with the intention (actual or presumptive) and with the result of inducing the representee on the faith of such representation to alter his position to his detriment, the representor, in any litigation which may afterwards take place between him and the representee, is estopped, as against the representee, from making, or attempting to establish by evidence, any averment substantially at variance with his former representation, if the representee at the proper time, and in proper manner, objects thereto.

A second definition can be found in Wilken and Villiers, *The Law of Waiver, Variation and Estoppel*, 2nd Edition, OUP, 2003, para. 9.02:

> An estoppel by representation [of fact] will arise between A and B if the following elements are made out. First, A makes a false representation of fact to B or to a group of which B was a member. [It is not necessary to demonstrate A knew that the representation was untrue.] Second, in making the representation, A intended or [in the alternative] knew that it was likely to be acted upon. Third, B, believing the representation, acts to its detriment in reliance on the representation. [It must have been reasonable to rely on the representation.] Fourth, A subsequently seeks to deny the truth of the representation. Fifth, no defence to the estoppel can be raised by A.
>
> A representation can be made by statement or conduct. Although the representation must be clear and unambiguous, a representation can be inferred from silence where there is a duty to speak or from negligence where a duty of care arises. Under English law, estoppel by representation of fact is not a cause of action, though it may be a defence or acts in support of a cause of action.

32 These are based on *Halsbury's Laws of England*, Vol 16(2), 2003.

33 See *Nippon Menkwa Kabushiki Kaisha v Dawson's Bank Ltd.* (1935) 51 Ll L R. 147. At 155, Russel LJ stated that: "Estoppel is not a cause of action. It may (if established) assist a plaintiff in enforcing a cause of action by preventing a defendant from denying the existence of some facts essential to establish the cause of action or (to put it) in another way by preventing a defendant from asserting the existence of that which would destroy the cause of action."

34 See Debattista, *Bills of Lading in Export Trade*, above, p. 128. As we shall discover in the following, the annotation of ambiguous or conflicting statements indeed has the effect of "clausing" the bill of lading, indicating a *prima facie* sign of liability pointing towards the seller.

Indeed, within the context of contracts concluded on shipment terms, the buyer's acceptance of the bill of lading tendered by the seller relies entirely on the good faith of the statements made by the carrier and contained therein.[35]

However, at common law a shipowner is estopped, as against a transferee for value who acts to his detriment on a statement in a bill of lading that the goods were shipped in "apparent good order and condition", from alleging that the goods were not in good condition when shipped.

That is what happened in *Silver v Ocean Steamship co Ltd*,[36] where a cargo of cans of frozen eggs were "shipped in apparent good order and condition for delivery subject to conditions" in London. On arrival at the discharge port, a large number of the cans containing the eggs were dented or perforated; some had large gashes, whilst others merely had pin hole perforations.

The shipowners tried to avoid liability for damage and loss by alleging some of the damage had occurred prior to shipment.

It was held on appeal that while the shipowners were estopped from contending either the cargo was insufficiently well packed or that the tins were gashed on shipment, they were not estopped from alleging that pinhole perforations in the tins were present on shipment, since the latter would not necessarily be apparent on reasonable inspection.

In this case, the bill of lading was used as a receipt for goods shipped. It even described the condition of the goods (apparent good order and condition). Consequently, the shipowner could not blame the shipper prior to shipment, because the bill of lading acted as evidence for the good condition of the shipment.

It has been noted that the buyer transferee of the bill of lading is in an even stronger position than he would be at common law.[37] Indeed, in *Peter Cremer GmbH v General Carriers SA (The Dona Mari)*,[38] it was held by the court that the carriers were estopped by the statement that the goods were "shipped in good order and condition", for it had been shown that the plaintiffs would have rejected the documents if the bills of lading had been claused, and they had relied on the statements enshrined therein.

As put by Kerr J:

> The only ingredient of this estoppel which is in issue is whether or not the plaintiffs relied on the representation in the clean bills of lading in the sense of having acted upon it to their detriment. The defendants conceded that on the basis of *Silver v Ocean* there was prima facie reliance by the plaintiffs when they took up the clean documents without objection. The defendants however contended that this prima facie reliance was displaced by the fact that the plaintiffs were in any event bound to take up the documents by reason of the terms of the contracts of sale.
>
> [. . .] On the question of estoppel, Mr. Justice Langton first referred at some length to *Silver v Ocean Steamship Co.* and said that the presumption that the plaintiffs relied

35 See Debattista, *Bills of Lading in Export Trade*, above, p. 128.

36 *Silver v Ocean Steamship Co* [1930] 1 KB 416 (CA).

37 See *Scrutton on Bills of Lading*, (Sweet & Maxwell) p. 191. See also Debattista, *Bills of Lading in Export Trade*, above, p. 128. On the same lines, see *Carver on Bills of Lading*, (Sweet & Maxwell, 2012) paras. 2.031–2.034.

38 *Peter Cremer v General Carriers; Peter Cremer GmbH v General Carriers SA (The Dona Mari)* [1973] 2, Lloyd's Rep. 366.

on the clean bill of lading certainly assisted them in the absence of any evidence to the contrary. He then turned to the evidence of reliance and said that this was "meagre". There appear to have been a number of plaintiffs, and he said that the evidence was confined to that of a cashier of one of them who claimed that if the bill of lading had notified him that the goods were shipped in bad condition his principals would have claimed total rejection. The Judge said that he had no reason to doubt the bona fides of the cashier in making this statement, but it is clear from the judgment as a whole that he did not accept it as evidence of what the plaintiffs would in fact have done. He then discussed the contract of sale and held that its terms were admissible in evidence against the plaintiffs on the question of reliance. Up to this point he was therefore merely saying that, in deciding whether or not the plaintiffs relied on the clean bills of lading and would have rejected claused bills of lading, regard must be had to the presumption of reliance in the plaintiffs' favour and the "meagre" evidence of the cashier on the one hand, and on the other hand to the clear terms of the contract of sale which in that case barred the right of rejection in the widest terms. With this analysis I respectfully agree. He then referred to certain authorities cited on behalf of the plaintiffs which he found of no assistance, but he noted that they supported the view "that Courts would not be astute to suppose that any merchant would be eager to break his contract". This again suggests that he was considering the probabilities of what the plaintiffs would in fact have done if the bills of lading had been claused and that he was not purporting to lay down any principle to the effect that the terms of the contract of sale were conclusive one way or the other about the plaintiffs' rights.

Taking the judgment as a whole, I therefore consider that the case decides no more for present purposes than that a person in the position of the plaintiffs in the present case cannot rely on the presumption in his favour laid down in *Silver v Ocean Steamship Co.* (viz. that he must be assumed to have relied and acted to his detriment in taking up clean bills of lading which should have been claused) if he was bound to do so in any event under the terms of his contract of purchase. [. . .] Looking at the matter broadly, it seems to me contrary to all principle that an issue should be tried, as in the present case, between a carrier and a cargo-owner in which the carrier seeks to say that by operation of law he can avoid liability under the contract of carriage because, on the true construction of a contract sale to which he was not a party and of which he knew nothing, the holder of a clean bill of lading (which should have been claused by the carrier) would have been in breach and liable to pay damages to his supplier if he had rejected the claused bill, notwithstanding the fact that the Court may be wholly satisfied that this would indeed have happened, as in this case. I therefore reject the defendants' submissions that the plaintiffs are not entitled to rely on the estoppel created by the clean bills of lading and delivery orders.[39]

Apart from clear and unambiguous statements, in order to ignite the doctrine of representational estoppel, statements enshrined in a bill of lading must be made with authority; under the common law, alongside the shipowner himself or his agent, a master clearly has the authority required to prevent the shipowner from circumventing the estoppel.

Indeed, the shipowner is usually bound by the master's signature to a bill of lading, unless the master, in signing the bill of lading, exceeds his authority. As Esher LJ stated in *Leduc & Co v Ward*:[40]

[A master] . . . has no authority to make a contract of carriage to bind the shipowner, except in respect of goods received by him. If the goods have not been received, the

---

39 *Ibid.*, at 372–375.

40 *Leduc & Co v Ward* (1888) 20 QBD 475.

> bill of lading cannot contain the terms of a contract of carriage with respect to them as against the shipowner. But, if the goods have been received by the captain, it is the evidence in writing of what the contract of carriage between the parties is . . .
>
> The following statements acknowledged by master's signature in the bill of lading will bind the shipowner: 1) statements relating to the amount of freight to be paid by the consignee; 2) statements relating to the shipment or receipt of the goods; 3) statements relating to the condition of the goods.[41]

Therefore, when the goods are shipped "in good order and condition", the master is expected to be able to assert whether the goods were actually shipped in good condition, if unwanted liabilities on the shipowner's part are to be set aside.

Conversely, the estoppel is grounded if the statements contained in the bill of lading are weighed down with qualifications. For instance, "weight unknown" clauses and other qualifying statements very often pre-printed on the face of bills of lading are a testament to the fact that the carrier had no reasonable means of accurately establishing the quantity of cargo effectively shipped on board. In *New Chinese Antimony Co Ltd v Ocean Steamship Co Ltd*,[42] Viscount Reading, CJ held that;

> Where the statement of the amount or quantity of the goods in the bill of lading is qualified by such words as "weight or quantity unknown," the bill of lading is not even prima facie evidence against the shipowner of the amount or quantity shipped, and the onus is on the cargo owner of proving what in fact was shipped.[43]

And by way of further explanation, Reading, CJ added further that:

> Where in a bill of lading, which is prepared by the shippers for acceptance by the defendants' agent, the agent accepts in the margin a quantity "said to be 937 tons," and in the body of the bill of lading there is a clause "weight, &c., unknown," there is no prima facie evidence that 937 tons have been shipped.[44]

However, the *New Chinese Antimony* case was decided before the Hague-Visby Rules were drafted. Article III Rule 4 states that a bill of lading issued in accordance with Article III Rule 3 shall be *prima facie* evidence of the receipt by the carrier of the goods therein described in terms of identification, quantity, weight, and condition of the goods.[45]

---

41 *Ibid.*, at 479.

42 *New Chinese Antimony Co Ltd v Ocean Steamship Co Ltd* [1917] 2 KB 664.

43 *Ibid.*, at 670.

44 *Ibid.*, at 671.

45 See Article III, rules 3 and 4 of Hague-Visby Rules, which state as follows:

> 3. After receiving the goods into his charge, the carrier, or the master or agent of the carrier, shall, on demand of the shipper, issue to the shipper a bill of lading showing among other things
>
> (a) the leading marks necessary for identification of the goods as the same are furnished in writing by the shipper before the loading of such goods starts, provided such marks are stamped or otherwise shown clearly upon the goods if uncovered, or on the cases or coverings in which such goods are contained, in such a manner as should ordinarily remain legible until the end of the voyage;
>
> (b) either the number of packages or pieces, or the quantity, or weight, as the case may be, as furnished in writing by the shipper;
>
> (c) the apparent order and condition of the goods:
>
> Provided that no carrier, master or agent of the carrier shall be bound to state or show in the bill of lading any marks, number, quantity, or weight which he has reasonable ground for suspecting not accurately to represent the goods actually received or which he has had no reasonable means of checking.

Whether a bill of lading with a "weight unknown" clause is *prima facie* evidence of the weight of the cargo shipped was subject to scrutiny in *The Mata K.*[46] Here the shippers and charterers of the vessel argued that the "weight unknown" clause offended against Article III Rule 8 of the Hague-Visby Rules as well as section 4 of the UK Carriage of Goods by Sea Act 1992.[47]

Nevertheless, because of the circumstances in which the bill of lading was issued, the court held that there was no evidence that the shipper had in accordance with Article III Rule 3 "demanded" a bill of lading that showed the weight of the cargo without the "weight unknown" qualification. As such, the bill of lading in the hands of the holder was deemed not to be conclusive evidence of the quantity shipped in accordance with section 4 of COGSA 1992.

As put by Clarke J (as he then was):

> It seems to me that it would make little sense to hold that a bill of lading in this form "shows" the quantity of cargo shipped within the meaning of art. III, r. 3 but that it does not "represent" the quantity of cargo shipped within the meaning of s. 4 of the Carriage of Goods by Sea Act, 1992. That view is I think reinforced by the sentence added to art. III, r. 4 in the Hague-Visby Rules. That addition has the effect that, where the bill of lading shows the quantity within the meaning of art. III, r. 3, proof to the contrary shall not be admissible against the lawful holder of the bill. If the reasoning in The Atlas were rejected, the result would be that the bill of lading did not "represent" the quantity of cargo within the meaning of s. 4 of the Carriage of Goods by Sea Act, 1992 so that it would not be conclusive evidence against the carrier under that section but that it did "show" the quantity shipped within the meaning of art. III, r. 3 and in effect be conclusive evidence against him under art. III, r. 4. In my judgment it is likely that s. 4 of the Carriage of Goods by Sea Act, 1992 was intended to lead to the same result as art. III, r. 4 of the Hague-Visby Rules.[48]

Apart from issues related to the common law doctrine of representational estoppel, qualifying statements annotated by carriers on bills of lading produce the effect of "clausing" the bills, exposing the seller to liabilities under the sales contract. This shall be the object of scrutiny in the following.

---

4. Such a bill of lading shall be prima facie evidence of the receipt by the carrier of the goods as therein described in accordance with paragraphs 3(a), (b) and (c).

However, proof to the contrary shall not be admissible when the bill of lading has been transferred to a third party acting in good faith.

46 *Agrosin Pte. Ltd. v Highway Shipping Co. Ltd. (The "Mata K")* [1998] 2 Lloyd's Rep. 614.

47 Section 4 COGSA 1992 (Representations in bills of lading) states as follows:

A bill of lading which –

(a) represents goods to have been shipped on board a vessel or to have been received for shipment on board a vessel; and
(b) has been signed by the master of the vessel or by a person who was not the master but had the express, implied or apparent authority of the carrier to sign bills of lading, shall, in favour of a person who has become the lawful holder of the bill, be conclusive evidence against the carrier of the shipment of the goods or, as the case may be, of their receipt for shipment.

48 See *Agrosin Pte. Ltd. v Highway Shipping Co. Ltd. (The "Mata K")*, above, at 621.

6.3.2 "Clean on board" and "claused" bills of lading: Meaning and legal issues

A sales contract concluded on shipment terms will invariably encompass the obligation of the seller to tender, inter alia, a "clean" on board bill of lading.

A bill of lading is clean if it testifies that the goods were shipped on board in "apparent good order and condition". As established above, provided that it has been signed with authority, a clean bill will give rise to representational estoppel preventing the carrier from retracting the statements made on the bill, representing at the same time conclusive evidence of the conditions of the goods shipped on board.

Needless to say, both the seller and the buyer desire a clean on board bill of lading; the buyer wishes to receive the document clean as per contractual specification, and if the seller does not tender a clean bill, he is not going to be paid by the buyer and will be considered in breach of contract.

The carrier on the other hand will be keen to "clause" the bill of lading by weighing it down with qualifying statements, such as "weight and quantity unknown", rather than "condition unknown", etc. The more he does so, the more he is going to prevent future liabilities pending on his shoulders. Indeed, one should always bear in mind that, as established above, what the bill of lading says about the goods will determine the course of action of a buyer in possession of short delivered/damaged cargo.

In the case that the bill of lading received by the buyer is clean, that will entail the seller fulfilling his obligations according to what was originally established in the sales contract by shipping goods in good order and condition. If the cargo which thereafter reaches the buyer is short delivered or damaged, the liability will therefore rest on the carrier's shoulders.

The legal scenario pictured obviously raises a conflict of interest and a dichotomy between the seller and the carrier, with the seller clearly adamant that he should obtain a clean receipt from the carrier, who, on his part, is keen on clausing the bill so as to set aside future liability vis-à-vis the buyer.

We have established that the carrier's clausing statements, such as weight unknown clauses, are very common in practice, and often pre-printed on the face of bills of lading. What now remains to be assessed is their legal impact on the position of the seller vis-à-vis the buyer.

Since, as it will promptly be evident, the case law in relation to statements regarding weight and quantity, rather than statements revolving around the condition of the goods shipped on board, differs considerably; these two categories shall be now considered individually.

6.3.3 Clean bills of lading: Carrier's statements related to quantity and weight

It has been noted that, at common law, a c.i.f. seller is under the implied obligation to tender a bill of lading for the contract quantity.[49]

49 See Debattista, *Bills of Lading in Export Trade*, above, p. 137. The same considerations are equally valid for c.&f. contracts, f.o.b. classic contracts or with additional services, or any other term which entails the obligation of the seller to arrange for the transport of the goods.

In *Re Keighley, Maxted & Co and Bryan, Durant & Co*,[50] although the c.i.f. seller of a cargo of wheat expressly reserved the right to ship goods aboard in excess of the quantity originally established in the sale contract (3,000 tonnes, 10 per cent more or less), he was nonetheless held by the court to be bound to tender a bill of lading for the contract quantity.

The rationale for this decision is to be found in the very essence of this area of law, i.e. the possibility of trading the goods. Indeed, a bill of lading showing the wrong contract quantity (even in excess), would thwart the possibility of the buyer trading on the cargo and selling the goods over whilst on transit.

By the same token, the quantity/weight indicated in the bill of lading must correspond to the quantity/weight of the commercial invoice. This was held in *Libau Wood & Co v H Smith and Sons Ltd*[51] where Macnaghten J pointed out that:

> Is such a document a bill of lading which the buyer under a c.i.f. contract is bound to accept? No authority precisely covering the point has been cited to me. I have come to the conclusion that it is not a proper bill of lading which a buyer under a c.i.f. contract is bound to accept as a sufficient bill of lading under the contract. It was pointed out by Sir Robert Aske on behalf of the sellers that this bill of lading contains what I suppose almost all bills of lading contain, a statement that although there is an acknowledgment of the shipment of a specified quantity of goods there is a qualification by the master of the ship that he does not know the quantity or condition or quality of the goods in question. And if I followed him aright every bill of lading is nothing more than an acknowledgment of the shipment of an unknown quantity of goods, the description of which may or may not be in accordance with the statement in the document. [. . .] A bill of lading which the buyer is bound to accept must be a document acknowledging the shipment of a quantity of goods according with the quantity specified in the invoice and for which the seller demands payment. And if there is an invoice for a specified quantity and the bill of lading is for either an unknown quantity of goods or a quantity of goods substantially different from that in the invoice, the bill of lading would not be a proper bill of lading which the buyer would be compelled to accept.[52]

Be that as it may, a bill of lading qualified by the wording "weight and quantity unknown" in its statements related to quantity/weight of the goods shipped on board hardly represents a good tender.

In *The Galatia*,[53] the sellers sold to the buyers 12,000/13,200 tonnes of omnibus white and/or refined sugar in jute bags c.&f. free out of Bandar Shahpour, Iran. A bill of lading issued, inter alia, on the "Congenbill" form was annotated as follows: "said to be 200 tonnes of sugar, shipped in apparent good order and condition . . . weight, measure quantity condition contents and value unknown".

On a preliminary level a distinction between a clean and a claused bill of lading was made by Donaldson J, who stated that:

> A clean shipping document is one which bears no superimposed clause or notation which expressly declares a defective condition of the goods and/or the packaging.

50 *Re Keighley, Maxted & Co & Bryan, Durant & Co* (No 2) (1894) 70 LT 155.
51 *Libau Wood & Co v H Smith and Sons Ltd* (1930) 37 Ll L Rep 296.
52 *Ibid.*, at 300. On this point see also Debattista, *Bills of Lading in Export Trade*, above, p. 137.
53 *The Galatia* [1979] 2 Lloyd's Rep. 450.

> Banks will refuse shipping documents bearing such clauses or notations unless the credit expressly states clauses or notations which may be accepted.
>
> This definition fails to specify the time with respect to which the notation speaks. The bill of lading and any notations speak at the date of issue, but they may speak about a state of affairs which then exists or about an earlier state of affairs or both. If the rule refers to notations about the state of affairs at the time of the issue of the bill of lading or, indeed, at any time after shipment of the 200 tonnes was completed, the bill of lading is not "clean" within the meaning of that word in the rule for the notation clearly draws attention to the cargo being damaged. If, however, it refers to notations about the state of affairs upon completion of shipment, the bill of lading is equally clearly clean for it shows that the goods were in apparent good order and condition on shipment and suggests only that they were damaged after shipment.
>
> [. . .] I, therefore, proceed to apply the legal test. As Mr. Justice Salmon remarked in *British Imex Industries Ltd. v Midland Bank Ltd.* [1957] 2 Lloyd's Rep. 591; [1958] 1 Q.B. 542, a "clean bill of lading" has never been exhaustively defined. I have been referred to a number of text books and authorities which support the proposition that a "clean" bill of lading is one in which there is nothing to qualify the admission that the goods were in apparent good order and condition and that the seller has no claim against the goods except in relation to freight. Some clearly regard the relevant time as being that of shipment. Some are silent as to what is the relevant time. None refers expressly to any time subsequent to shipment.
>
> As between the shipowner and the shipper (including those claiming through the shipper as holders of the bill of lading) the crucial time is shipment. The shipowners' prime obligation is to deliver the goods at the contractual destination in the like good order and condition as when shipped. The cleanliness of the bill of lading may give rise to an estoppel and the terms of the bill of lading contract may exempt the shipowner from a breach of this obligation, but everything stems from the state of the goods as shipped.[54]

Thereafter, the legal analysis shifted on the assessment of "weight and quantity unknown" annotations made on bills of lading preceded by the qualification "said to weigh" made by the carrier.

In the words of Donaldson J:

> In these circumstances, it is not surprising that there appears to be no case in which the Courts or the text-book writers have had to consider a bill of lading which records the fate of the goods subsequent to shipment and, indeed, I have never seen or heard of a bill of lading like that in the present case. Nor is it surprising that some of the judgments and text-books do not in terms say that when reference is made to the condition of the goods what is meant is their condition on shipment.
>
> However, I have no doubt that this is the position. The bill of lading with which I am concerned casts no doubt whatsoever on the condition of the goods at that time and does not assert that at that time the shipowner had any claim whatsoever against the goods. It follows that in my judgment this bill of lading, unusual though it is, passes the legal test of cleanliness.[55]

More specifically, Donaldson J analysed the statements as they appeared on the bill of lading, i.e. "said to weigh" 200.8 tonnes and "weight unknown", in order to determine whether a conflict arose between the two assertions. In his words:

54 *Ibid.*, at 454, 455.
55 *Ibid.*, at 457.

> What is acknowledged is goods "said to weigh" 200.8 tonnes. "Weight unknown" does not qualify this acknowledgment. Nor is any conflict produced by the other words in the phrase. "Measure" and "quantity" must both, I think, relate to the sugar itself rather than to the number of bags and there is no acknowledgment as to the measure or quantity of sugar shipped. "Condition unknown" does not qualify an acknowledgment of apparent condition and there is no acknowledgment of value.
>
> Accordingly, I do not think that this common printed clause contains any qualification of the acknowledgment contained in the bill of lading rendering it otherwise than "clean". I am not unhappy to reach this conclusion since "weight unknown" provisions occur in most printed forms of bill of lading, but are not objected to. Indeed, the buyers themselves did not demur at these words in the bill of lading for the bulk of the shipment for which they paid or in this bill of lading. Their objections were limited to the typewritten clause. This objection seems to be something in the nature of a Temple afterthought.[56]

Thus, weight or quantity unknown qualifications do not "clause" a bill of lading if preceded by the wording "said to be" or "said to weigh". The rationale for this is to be found in Donaldson J' s analysis of the statements appearing on the face of the bill of lading, with the starting point of his analysis being that a bill of lading comes to be "claused" if the statements contained therein are in conflict with one another.

The aspect which becomes crucial is, thus, to attempt to perceive any idiosyncrasies arising from the bill of lading statements related to quantity/weight. In *The Galatia*, the bill of lading carried both the statements "said to be" (followed by a specific indication of weight, i.e. 200.8 tonnes of sugar), and "weight and quantity unknown".

Prima facie, the latter statements appear to "clause" the bill of lading, creating a conflict with the specific indication of quantity given by the carrier.

Nevertheless, Donaldson J's considerations "save" the bill of lading, as the conflict is merely apparent. Indeed, there is no real conflict between the statements "said to be" and "weight and quantity unknown"; the statement "said to be" is to be interpreted as the seller qua shipper saying that what was shipped on board were 200.8 tonnes of sugar, whereas the wording "weight and quantity unknown" can be attributed to the carrier as a statement relating to the impossibility of him weighing the cargo shipped on board, and to corroborate the statement made by the seller qua shipper of the goods.

Far from being far-fetched, this interpretation has its own value and solid foundations; indeed, one should not forget that a carrier is seldom placed in a position to assess the weight of the cargo shipped on board, and in any case will be reluctant to make specific indications in terms of weight and quantity of the cargo shipped on board.

The interpretation of weight and quantity statements appearing in bills of lading in *The Galatia* case should, nevertheless, not be overextended so as to cover all scenarios.

---

56 *Ibid.*

Indeed, it has been noted that Donaldson J's decision revolving around the consistency of the statements related to quantity contained in a bill of lading is based on a wide interpretation of the concept of "clean" bill of lading.[57]

Two approaches may be in contention here: a narrow interpretation of the concept of "clean" bill of lading, which would see a bill of lading clean only insofar as it contains no further qualifications other than that the "goods have been shipped on board in good order and condition";[58] and a wider interpretation which qualifies a bill of lading as "clean" if no inconsistency arises between the statements concerning the representation of the goods contained therein.[59]

As we shall discover in the following, a wider interpretation of the concept of "clean" bill of lading is not only preferable, but also much more consistent with the customs of commerce.

A different scenario compared to the one in *The Galatia* arose in *Libau Wood & Co v H Smith and Sons Ltd*,[60] where the sale contract provided that payment should be made on presentation of, among other things, a bill of lading, and it is not disputed that it meant a proper bill of lading. The bill of lading in this case was a bill of lading stating that 854.48 fathoms of pit props had been shipped, followed by the annotation that part of the cargo had been lost during loading and a statement "weight and quantity unknown".

Such a bill of lading was not considered "clean" by Macnaghten J, who held as follows:

> Is such a document a bill of lading which the buyer under a c.i.f. contract is bound to accept? No authority precisely covering the point has been cited to me. I have come to the conclusion that it is not a proper bill of lading which a buyer under a c.i.f. contract is bound to accept as a sufficient bill of lading under the contract. It was pointed out by Sir Robert Aske on behalf of the sellers that this bill of lading contains what I suppose almost all bills of lading contain, a statement that although there is an acknowledgment of the shipment of a specified quantity of goods there is a qualification by the master of the ship that he does not know the quantity or condition or quality of the goods in question. And if I followed him aright every bill of lading is nothing more than an acknowledgment of the shipment of an unknown quantity of goods, the description of which may or may not be in accordance with the statement

---

57 See Debattista, *Bills of Lading in Export Trade*, above, p. 137. See also, *Benjamin's Sale of Goods*, (Sweet & Maxwell) para. 19.038.

58 See *British Imex v Midland Bank* [1957] 2 Lloyd's Rep. 591. Here goods were shipped under a bill of lading stating: "Shipped at Antwerp in apparent good order and condition, weight, measure, marks, numbers, quality, contents and value unknown". It meant clean bills of lading, that the bills of lading in this case were clean bills of lading in that they contained no reservation by way of endorsement, clausing, or otherwise, to suggest that the goods were or might be defective in any respect. In the words of Salmon J (at 597): "I think that, in normal circumstances, the ordinary business man who undertakes to pay against the presentation of bills of lading means clean bills of lading; and he would probably consider that that was so obvious to any other business man that it was hardly necessary to state it. [. . .] A 'clean bill of lading' has never been exhaustively defined, and I certainly do not propose to attempt that task now. I incline to the view, however, that a clean bill of lading is one that does not contain any reservation as to the apparent good order or condition of the goods or the packing. In my judgment, the bills of lading in this case are plainly clean bills of lading. They contain no reservation by way of indorsement, clausing or otherwise, to suggest that the goods or the packing are or may be defective in any respect."

59 *Ibid.*

60 *Libau Wood & Co v H Smith and Sons Ltd*, above.

> in the document. I think the argument of Mr. Willink on that point is right. A bill of lading which the buyer is bound to accept must be a document acknowledging the shipment of a quantity of goods according with the quantity specified in the invoice and for which the seller demands payment. And if there is an invoice for a specified quantity and the bill of lading is for either an unknown quantity of goods or a quantity of goods substantially different from that in the invoice, the bill of lading would not be a proper bill of lading which the buyer would be compelled to accept.[61]

The line of reasoning in *Libau Wood* is perfectly consistent with the rationale of *The Galatia*. Indeed, if one interprets the statements appearing on the bill of lading in *Libau Wood*, one cannot help but notice a clear conflict between a statement indicating that a specific amount of goods was shipped aboard, and the annotation which pointed out the loss of part of the cargo during shipment along with a "weight and quantity unknown" clause.

Weight and quantity unknown clauses need, thus, to be assessed in conjunction with the presence of "said to be" or "said to weigh" preceding statements; the latter statements are likely to "save" the bill of lading, whereas in the absence of "said to be" or "said to weigh" wording, a bill of lading simply indicating a specific weight or quantity of the goods will be weighed down by a "weight and quantity unknown" clause, and thus be considered "claused".[62]

In *Noble Resources Ltd. v Cavalier Shipping Corporation (The Atlas)*,[63] Longmore J rejected an argument that the same approach should not be adopted where the bill of lading contained no equivalent of "said to be" but only "weight unknown". He said:

> it is impossible to imagine that the New Chinese Antimony case would have been decided differently if the bill in that case had said merely "weight unknown"; one has to construe the bill of lading to determine whether it is an unqualified assertion or representation of the shipment of a particular quantity of goods. If the bill of lading provides that the weight is unknown it cannot be an assertion or representation of the weight in fact shipped. Mr Jacobs said that the typed figures should prevail over printed "weight unknown" but, if Russian bills are construed as a whole, they must be held to mean that the shipowners are not committing themselves, one way or the other, as to the weight of the cargo shipped.[64]

Clean bills of lading: statements related to condition of the goods

Apart from statements related to quantity/weight, bills of lading contain statements concerning the quality and condition of the goods.

---

61 *Ibid.*, at 300.

62 In a series of cases, *The "Herroe" and "Askoe"* [1986] 2 Lloyd's Rep. 281, *The "Atlas"* [1996] 1 Lloyd's Rep. 642, and *The "Mata K"* [1998] 2 Lloyd's Rep. 614, each involving bills of lading on the Congen form, bills of lading containing "weight and quantity unknown" clauses have been considered clean. *The "Herroe" and "Askoe"* was a case where the number of bags of cargo was in dispute. Since the bills of lading stated "quantity unknown" they did not make any statement of the number of bags actually shipped. They merely recorded that the shipper had informed the carrier that this number had been shipped. The same applied to both weight and number of bundles in *The "Atlas"* and to weight in *The "Mata K"*.

63 *Noble Resources Ltd. v Cavalier Shipping Corporation (The Atlas)* [1996] 1 Lloyd's Rep. 642.

64 *Ibid.*, 664. See also to the same effect *River Gurara (Cargo Owners) v Nigerian National Shipping Line Ltd.* [1998] 1 Lloyd's Rep. 225, 234; [1997] 3 WLR 1128, 1141 per Lord Justice Phil.

As with "weight and quantity unknown" clauses, bills of lading very often contain "quality and condition unknown" statements pre-printed on their face, which usually read as follows: "shipped in apparent good order and condition . . . condition, quality and value unknown".[65]

Do those qualifications have the effect of weighing down the bill of lading, consequently clausing the bill?

In *Compania Naviera Vasconzada v Churchill and Sim, Compania Naviera Vasconzada v Burton & Co*,[66] the court distinguished qualifications as to the quality of goods ("quality unknown") from a statement related to condition ("in good order and condition"). In the words of Channell J:

> The words "shipped in good order and condition" are not words of contract in the sense of a promise or undertaking. The words are an affirmation of fact, or perhaps rather in the nature of an assent by the captain to an affirmation of fact which the shipper may be supposed to make as to his own goods. [. . .] It seems to me that with reference to some things and to some defects in them "condition" and "quality" may mean the same thing, yet that they do not either necessarily or even usually do so. I think that "condition" refers to external and apparent condition, and "quality" to something which is usually not apparent, at all events to an unskilled person. I think a captain is expected to notice the condition of the goods, though not the quality.[67]

As we established above, a master is not required to be an expert on the condition of the cargo loaded, so he may ask for professional advice from a surveyor but ultimately it will be a matter of his own judgement on the appearance of the cargo being loaded.

Moreover, a master is seldom in the position to assess the effective condition of the cargo. That is the rationale of *Compania Naviera Vasconzada v Churchill*, where Channell J made a distinction between the bill of lading's statement that the cargo was "shipped in apparent good order and condition", which was held to refer to the "external condition" of the goods, and the words "quality and measure unknown", deemed to indicate the "internal" condition of the goods.

In other words, no conflict was found between the aforementioned statements, which were interpreted as an indication by the carrier that, as far as he could see, the "external" condition of the cargo was apparently in good order, whereas he did not have the possibility of checking the "internal" condition of the cargo, hence the subsequent statement, "quality and measure unknown".

A similar scenario arose in *The Tromp*,[68] where a cargo of bags of potatoes was held by the bill of lading to have been "shipped in good order and condition . . . quality, condition unknown".

The judge held that, having stated in the bill that the cargo was in "good order", the carrier was fixed with that description, which referred to the external condition of the cargo. The qualifying words meant that there was no representation of the

65 See Congenbill form 1978.

66 *Compania Naviera Vasconzada v Churchill and Sim; Compania Naviera Vasconzada v Burton & Co* [1906] 1 KB 237, 10 Asp MLC 177.

67 *Ibid.*, at 245.

68 *The "Tromp"* [1921] P 337; (1921) 8 Ll L Rep 28.

"internal" condition and quality of the potatoes themselves but did not affect the statement that the bags were in good order.

It will be noted that the word "condition" appears twice in the Congenbill. The bill records that the cargo was shipped "in apparent good . . . condition" but then goes on to state "condition . . . unknown". It seems that the intention is that the bill of lading records that the apparent condition of the cargo was good but makes no statement as to the actual condition, which is something other than its appearance, and beyond any possibility of assessment by the carrier.

Similarly, in *The Skarp*,[69] a cargo of timber was described by the bills of lading tendered by the seller as shipped in: "Apparent good order and condition . . . Condition quality description and measurement unknown". As Langton J said:

> The controversy then centred upon this main question of estoppel. The books, again, do not show any case in which a shipowner has attempted to clause his bill of lading by the introduction of the word "condition" in these circumstances. For, be it observed, you are dealing here with timber goods, and there is no question that there are many cases of goods as to which there may be a distinction when one is speaking of their apparent condition and of their real condition. Potatoes in sacks may be in apparent good order and condition because the outside of the sacks is dry and in good condition, although in fact the condition of the potatoes inside the sacks may be deplorable. But we are here dealing with goods as to which the condition must refer to apparent condition, and the bill of lading as it stands makes the two diametrically contradictory statements (1) "shipped in good order and condition." and; (2) "condition unknown." Mr. Davies on behalf of the defendants, in an adroit argument, said that this is the way in which a shipowner ought to deal with a matter of this kind. If he wants to say that he has not measured the goods, he says "measurement unknown." If he wants to say that he has not weighed them, he says "weight unknown"; and if he wants to say that he makes no representation as to condition, he puts in "condition unknown."
>
> [. . .] The master was confronted with the fact that the goods were certainly damaged. What was the straightforward thing to do? I suppose one must not rule out of all possibility - even in commercial documents - the chance that people might want to do the straightforward thing. The straightforward thing to do was surely to put upon the bill of lading, in the very ample margin which is apparently provided for that purpose, a clause which would clearly advertise to any buyer of that bill of lading that the goods he was going to receive were not in good order and condition. It would not have been beyond the master's power to take the entry from his own log and to put upon the bills of lading "very black, wet and partly musty." If he could see it for the purposes of his log he could surely, with the same eye, have seen it for the purposes of the bill of lading. But in truth and in fact, of course, he was much worried about his own employers' interests, and it was for that reason that he took this circuitous route of putting the word "condition" in what is, to my mind, a most obscure place. That is just the business of the matter.
>
> [. . .] One must look at it from the legal point of view. What would those words in a bill of lading convey to anybody who read them? What, first of all, would "shipped in good order and condition" and then "condition unknown" convey, among other things? Speaking for myself, they would have conveyed nothing at all to me. The only witness who was called (I cannot place much dependence upon him here, although I think he was an entirely honest man, because he was the cashier and did not appear to have any long experience of the business side of this class of transaction) said that he had regarded the bill of lading as "clean." To my mind, having regard to the very well-known method

69 *The "Skarp"*, [1935] 2 Lloyd's Rep. 152.

> which is always at the disposal of the masters of steamships to describe damaged goods, this is a wholly unsuitable method - a most ambiguous method - and to my mind does not convey at all that the goods are damaged or even may be damaged.
>
> [. . .] I had to speculate as to what was the most probable effect on the mind of anybody who read a bill of lading so phrased, I should say that the most probable effect would be that the person reading it would say, "Oh, this master has got some idea that he is responsible for the condition of the wood, whether it is ripe, or over-ripe, or whatever it may be"; but I cannot imagine that it would bring to the mind of the reader the fact that a man who had been at no pains to clause the bill of lading in the natural way, saying what he did see and what was there for him to see, meant to convey in fact that the goods were or might be damaged.
>
> Another and perhaps clearer way of putting it is this, that it is difficult to understand why the affirmation, or acceptance, of one untruth should be cured by a deliberate statement of another untruth. It is true that the words "shipped in good order and condition," as Mr. Justice Channell pointed out, are not words of contract, but they are an affirmation - or assent to an affirmation - of fact, and in this case they were an affirmation of an untruth. They were words which to the plain knowledge of the master in this case were totally untrue; the goods were not shipped in good order and condition, and well he knew it.
>
> It is argued that he escapes from any difficulties occasioned by this assent or affirmation of an untruth by making of his own free will another statement which he knows quite well to be untrue, namely, that "the condition was unknown." The condition was not unknown. The condition was stated clearly, forcibly, and lucidly in the master's log; and, therefore, even on the ground of public policy, I should have thought that it was possible to argue that it would be deplorable that a person should be allowed to escape from the penalties, if any attached to the first assent to an untruth, by a deliberate statement of another.
>
> But, primarily, of course, this is a matter of construction, and I hold, as a matter of construction, that the insertion of the word "condition" in the way it was inserted here, is not such a qualification of the original statement "shipped in good order and condition" as to bring to the mind of anybody reading that document that the goods were, or even might be apparently, and to the knowledge of anyone who had seen them, damaged goods.[70]

It is therefore clear on authority that "condition, quality and value unknown" clauses do not weigh down bills of lading and therefore do not have the effect of clausing them.

The rationale for the aforementioned case law is consistent with the approach adopted by the court in *The Galatia* in relation to "weight and quantity unknown clauses", and the approach adopted by the court aims at interpreting statements appearing on the face of bills of lading so as to identify discrepancies or idiosyncrasies; only under those circumstances will bills of lading be considered "claused" from a trade perspective.

Indeed, one should not forget that the master's signature on the bill confirms conformity of the quantity and quality of the cargo loaded with the description represented in the bill of lading. If the master signs the bill knowing that the statement as to apparent quality and quantity of the goods or the date of shipment is incorrect, he makes the owners vicariously liable in fraud to anyone who suffers loss by relying on the presentation.

70 *Ibid.*, at 156, 157.

Therefore, the importance of taking great care on the part of a ship's master when signing the bill of lading can hardly be exaggerated – a master or his representative who signs a bill of lading that inaccurately describes the cargo is making a misrepresentation of fact, which can have considerable legal consequences.

The basic idea of the importance of the master's obligation to provide a correct description of the cargo in the bill of lading is that the final holder of the bill will have to rely completely on the master's statement when he pays for the cargo.

Since a bill of lading defines mutual liabilities between the shipowner and the holder of the bill of lading (the cargo owner), the industry promptly developed bills of lading carrying pre-printed statements along the lines of: "shipped in apparent good order and condition, quantity, condition, value unknown". Such statements on bills attempt to constrain the liability of the carrier in relation to the cargo shipped on board.[71]

Courts were soon called to assess the "cleanness" of those bills of lading from the perspective of a sales contract, and it is hardly surprising that a way of compromise had to be found in order not to frustrate contracts concluded on shipment terms, which by default require the seller, inter alia, to tender a "clean on board" bill of lading alongside other documents of contract specification.[72]

If bearing this perspective in mind, the interpretation of statements appearing on bills of lading conducted in the aforementioned case law – which may *prima facie* appear to some quite convoluted or far-fetched – make, on the contrary, a great deal of sense; indeed, a legal compromise had to be found between the growing tendency of carriers to annotate weight/condition unknown statements on bills of lading so as to minimise possible future liabilities, and the position of sellers in need of "clean on board" bills.

The interpretation given by the courts in the case law ultimately reaches that aim, striking a balance between the need of the carrier not to expose himself to unwanted and unnecessary liabilities and the necessity of the seller to obtain a clean bill of lading.

This scenario does not see the buyer paying the price for the compromise reached by the courts: as will be appreciated from the following, far from being deprived of any protection, the buyer is still in a position to reject the cargo or rely on the insurance policy for the goods.

It is worth noting that this is one of the numerous examples of the judicial creativity characterising common law judges, which has allowed English law to be swiftly moulded so as to meet the needs of the international trading community.

6.4 Bills of lading as evidence of the contract of carriage

Although this book is primarily concerned with issues revolving around contracts concluded on shipment terms and not contracts for the carriage of goods by sea, the function of a bill of lading as evidence of the contract of carriage retains a

71 *Compania Naviera Vasconzada v Churchill and Sim, Compania Naviera Vasconzada v Burton & Co* [1906] 1 KB 237, 10 Asp MLC 177.

72 *The "Skarp"*, [1935] 2 Lloyd's Rep. 152.

prominent role for the purposes of ascertaining whether the seller has fulfilled his contractual transport obligations, at any rate, when the nature of the contract obliges the seller to make transport arrangements (e.g. c.i.f.).

Whenever that happens, unless otherwise agreed by the parties, the buyer will only receive a bill of lading incorporating the conditions of carriage of the charter party stipulated by the seller with the carrier.

Once endorsed onto the buyer, the bill of lading under those circumstances becomes evidence of the contract of carriage. The authority most frequently cited for this proposition is *obiter dictum* by Lord Bramwell in *Sewell v Burdick*.[73] Speaking about the Bills of Lading Act 1855, Lord Bramwell held as follows:

> There is, I think, another inaccuracy in the statute . . . It speaks of the contract contained in the bill of lading. To my mind, there is no contract in it. It is a receipt for the goods, stating the terms on which they were delivered to and received by the ship, and therefore excellent evidence of those terms, but it is not a contract.[74]

This statement was further explained in *S.S. Ardennes (Cargo Owners) v S.S. Ardennes (Owners) (The Ardennes)*.[75] Here, a delay caused by an intermediate stop in Antwerp of a vessel which was supposed to sail from Spain directly to London caused loss to the cargo owner. In defence against the claim brought by the cargo owner, the carrier endeavoured to rely upon a clause enshrined in the bill of lading which allowed for an intermediate step in Antwerp.

It was held by the court that the bill of lading might not even be evidence of the contract of carriage, the exhaustive terms of which needed to be found in the charter party. In breach of his verbal promise, the shipowner deviated from the route to London and called first at Antwerp but later, in reply to the shipper's claim for damages, contended that on the terms of the bill of lading, evidence of any other bargain or promise was not admissible. Lord Goddard CJ in his judgment said that:

> It is, I think, well settled that a bill of lading is not in itself the contract between the shipowner and the shipper of goods though it has been said to be excellent evidence of its terms (*Sewell v Burdick*, 10 App. Cas. 74, at p. 105, per Lord Bramwell; *Crooks & Co. and Another v Allan and Another*, 5 Q.B.D. 38). The contract has come into existence before the bill of lading is signed; it is signed by one party only and handed by him to the shipper usually after the goods have been put on board. No doubt if the shipper finds it contains terms with which he is not content or does not contain some term for which he has stipulated, he might if there were time demand his goods back; but he is not in my opinion for that reason prevented from giving evidence that there was in fact a contract entered into before the bill of lading was signed different from that which is found in the document or containing some additional term. He is no party to the preparation of the bill of lading, nor does he sign it. It is unnecessary to cite authority further than the two cases already mentioned for the proposition that the bill of lading is not itself the contract; therefore in my opinion evidence as to the true contract is admissible.[76]

73 *Sewell v Burdick* [1875] 10 AC 74.
74 *Ibid.*, at 105.
75 *S.S. Ardennes (Cargo Owners) v S.S. Ardennes (Owners) (The Ardennes)* [1951] 1 KB 55.
76 *Ibid.*, at 73.

This view was re-emphasised by the Court of Appeal in *Cho Yang Shipping Co Ltd v Coral (UK) Ltd*,[77] where it was held that a bill of lading was only evidence of the contract between the shipper and the carrier which had been made before the goods were shipped, not of any terms and agreement that were to be inferred from what had happened prior to shipment. In the words of Hobhouse LJ:

> In English law the bill of lading is not the contract between the original parties but is simply evidence of it. (e.g. *The Ardennes* (1950) 84 Ll.L.Rep. 340; [1951] 1 K.B. 55.) Indeed, though contractual in form, it may in the hands of a person already in contractual relations with the carrier (e.g. a charterer) be no more than a receipt. (*Rodocanachi v Milburn* (1886) 18 Q.B.D. 67.) Therefore, as between shipper and carrier, it may be necessary to inquire what the actual contract between them was; merely to look at the bill of lading may not in all cases suffice. It remains necessary to look at and take into account the other evidence bearing upon the relationship between the shipper and the carrier and the terms of the contract between them. (Scrutton, art. 33). The terms upon which the goods have been shipped may not be in all respects the same as those actually set out in the bill of lading. It does not necessarily follow in any given case that the named shipper is to be under a personal liability for the payment of the freight.[78]

The rationale for considering a bill of lading as evidence of the contract of carriage lies primarily with two basic propositions of contract law: first, bilateral contracts can only be concluded on the basis of an exchange of mutual promises, and second, the validity of a contract does not rest on written records.

A contract of carriage might be concluded orally before a bill of lading is issued after the goods have been shipped on board, and its existence might be inferred by booking notes, mate's receipts, freight tariffs, negotiations with agents and brokers, along with the bill of lading itself.[79]

Indeed, contracts of carriage may, like most other contracts, be made without any writing at all[80] and "the issue of the bill of lading does not necessarily mark any stage in the development of the contract."[81]

Thus, the issue of a bill of lading does not of itself indicate the conclusion of a contract of carriage,[82] and the identification of the terms of the contract of carriage on the basis of the bill of lading used as its "evidence" may sometimes result in a problematic endeavour.[83]

---

77 *Cho Yang Shipping Co Ltd v Coral (UK) Ltd* [1997] 2 Lloyd's Rep. 641.

78 *Ibid.*, at 643.

79 On this point see C. Debattista, *Bills of Lading in Export Trade*, Butterworths, 2008, p. 135. See also C. Debattista, The bill of lading as a contract of carriage, a reassessment of *Leduc v Ward*, *The Modern Law Review*, 45, 1980, 652.

80 *Harland & Wolf v Burns & Laird Lines*, 1931 S.C. 122, 729, per Lord President Clyde.

81 *Pyrene Co. Ltd. v Scindia Navigation Co. Ltd.* [1954] 2 QB 402, 419, per Devlin J. On this point see also Debattista, The bill of lading as a contract of carriage, a reassessment of *Leduc v Ward*, above, p. 653.

82 See *Geskell v Continento1 Express Ltd.* [1950] 1 All ER 1033, 1041, per Devlin J who stated that: "The bill of lading which had been issued could never have been more than a bit of paper purporting to record a bargain that had never been made."

83 Indeed, at common law, express terms have contractual force only if they are notified to either party before or at the time of the conclusion of the contract, see *Olley v Marlborough Court* [1949] 1 K.B. 532. On this point see also Debattista, The bill of lading as a contract of carriage, a reassessment of *Leduc v Ward*, above, p. 653.

In *Pyrene Co. Ltd. v Scindia Navigation Co. Ltd.*,[84] Devlin J recognised that rigid principles must be interpreted somewhat flexibly in the context of everyday commercial dealings. In his words:

> When parties enter into a contract of carriage in the expectation that a bill of lading will be issued to cover it, they enter into it upon those terms which they know or expect the bill of lading to contain. Those terms must be in force from the inception of the contract; if it were otherwise the bill of lading would not evidence the contract but would be a variation of it. Moreover, it would be absurd to suppose that the parties intend the terms of the contract to be changed when the bill of lading is issued.[85]

The legal nature of the bill of lading as evidence of the contract of carriage was also discussed in *Leduc v Ward*,[86] where Lord Esher MR held that:

> It is true that, where there is a charterparty, as between the shipowner and the charterer the bill of lading may be merely in the nature of a receipt for the goods, because all the other terms of the contract of carriage between them are contained in the charterparty; and the bill of lading is merely given as between them to enable the charterer to deal with the goods while in the course of transit; but, where the bill of lading is indorsed over, as between the shipowner and the indorsee the bill of lading must be considered to contain the contract, because the former has given it for the purpose of enabling the charterer to pass it on as the contract of carriage in respect of the goods. Where there is no charterparty, as between the grantee of the bill of lading and the shipowner, the bill of lading is no doubt a receipt for the goods, and as such, like any other receipt, it is not conclusive, for it may be controverted by evidence shewing that the goods were not received; the question whether it will be more than a receipt as between the shipper and shipowner depends on whether the captain has received the goods, for he has no authority to make a contract of carriage to bind the shipowner, except in respect of goods received by him. If the goods have not been received, the bill of lading cannot contain the terms of a contract of carriage with respect to them as against the shipowner. But, if the goods have been received by the captain, it is the evidence in writing of what the contract of carriage between the parties is; it may be true that the contract of carriage is made before it is given, because it would generally be made before the goods are sent down to the ship: but when the goods are put on board the captain has authority to reduce that contract into writing: and then the general doctrine of law is applicable, by which, where the contract has been reduced into a writing which is intended to constitute the contract, parol evidence to alter or qualify the effect of such writing is not admissible, and the writing is the only evidence of the contract, except where there is some usage so well established and generally known that it must be taken to be incorporated with the contract.[87]

Part of the doctrine considers *Leduc v Ward* to be authority for the view that, since the Bills of Lading Act 1855, the contract of carriage is to be found exclusively in the bill of lading; no extraneous evidence is admissible which may either vary or contradict the terms contained in the bill of lading.[88]

84 *Pyrene Co. Ltd. v Scindia Navigation Co. Ltd.* [1954] 2 QB 402, 419.
85 See *Pyrene Co. Ltd. v Scindia Navigation Co. Ltd.* C19541 2 QB 402, at 419,
86 *Leduc & Co v Ward* (1888) 20 QBD 475.
87 *Ibid.*, at 475, 479, 480.
88 See C. Debattista, The bill of lading as a contract of carriage, a reassessment of *Leduc v Ward*, *The Modern Law Review*, 45, 1980, 660.

Be that as it may, within the context of a c.i.f. sale, when a bill of lading is issued under a charter party and there is a conflict between the clauses enshrined in the two documents, the bill of lading might not even be considered evidence of the contract of carriage, the terms of which need to be found exclusively in the charter party.[89]

6.5 Bills of lading as document of title

The last function performed by a bill of lading is that of a document of title.

As a document of title, the bill of lading is unique among transport documents, enabling merchants to trade the goods, by trading the document.[90]

Despite the importance of bills of lading in international sale transactions, there is surprisingly little agreement in relation to the concept of "title" and its legal implications.[91]

It is the word "title" which causes difficulty: what does exactly title mean? That the lawful holder of the bill of lading *owns* the goods or, rather, that he is entitled to the delivery of the goods. Does the word title entail "the possibility of giving to the carrier instructions as to the delivery of the goods, or the possibility of transferring one or all of those rights to others by endorsing the document?"[92]

Further, does the concept of document of title "infer that the lawful holder is entitled to sue the carrier if the cargo is damaged in transit, or that his rights, whatever they may be, survive a defect in the rights of the seller?"[93]

In *Sanders Brothers v Maclean & Co*,[94] Bowen LJ described a bill of lading in the following terms:

> A cargo at sea while in the hands of the carrier is necessarily in-capable of physical delivery. During this period of transit and voyage, the bill of lading by the law merchant is universally recognized as its symbol, and the endorsement and delivery of the bill of lading operates as a symbolical delivery of cargo. Property in the goods passes by endorsement and delivery of the bill of lading, whenever it is the intention of the parties that the property should pass just as under similar circumstances the property would pass by an actual delivery of the goods. And for the purpose of passing such property in the goods and complete the title of the endorse to full possession thereof, the bill of lading until complete delivery of the cargo has been made on shore to some one rightfully claiming under it, remains in force as a symbol, and carries with

89 See *Radocanachi Sons & Co v Milburn Bros* (1886) 18 QBD. 67, 479; *Swell v Burdick* (1884) 10 App Ca 74,105; *President of India v Metclafe Shipping Co Ltd (the Dunelmia)* [1970] 1 QB 289, 305; *Trade Star Line Corp. v Mitsui & Co Ltd (The Artic Trader) I* [1996] 2 Lloyd's Rep, 449, 455.

90 Bills of lading are usually issued in sets of three originals. This practice is very ancient and was explained in *Malynes's Lex Mercatoria* (1686), p. 97: "Of the Bills of Lading there is commonly Three Bills of one tenor. One of them is enclosed in the letters written by the same Ship; another Bill is sent overland to the Factor or Party to whom the goods are consigned; the third remaineth with the Merchant, for his testimony against the Master, if there were any occasion of loose dealing." It is noticeable, however, that there are only very few cases reported (*Scrutton on Charterparties*, 18th Edition, Sweet & Maxwell 1974 mentioned only two) on the fraud related to Bills of Lading where existence of more than one bill was justified.

91 See C. Debattista, *Bills of Lading in Export Trade*, 3rd Edition, Tottel Publishing, 2009, p. 26.

92 ibid.

93 ibid.

94 *Sanders Bros v Maclean & Co (1883)* 11 QBD 327, 341. 2.

it not only the full ownership of the goods, but also all rights created by the contract of carriage between the shipper and the shipowner. It is a key which in the hands of a rightful owner is intended to unlock the door of the warehouse, floating or fixed, in which the goods may chance to be.[95]

Bowen LJ famously described the bill of lading as "a key which in the hands of a rightful owner is intended to unlock the door of the warehouse, floating or fixed, in which the goods may chance to be".[96]

Indeed, this is essentially no more than a description of its role as a document of title. If this means anything, it must be that the holder of the bill is entitled to take delivery of the goods from the vessel when they arrive at their destination, or to sue the carrier in the event of their non-delivery or misdelivery.

Nevertheless, it would not be entirely accurate to interpret the word "symbolise" in Bowen LJ's aforementioned passage as the epitome of the description of the bill of lading as a document of title.

In *Scottish & Newcastle International Limited v Othon Ghalanos Ltd*,[97] a case which revolved, inter alia, around goods shipped under non-negotiable bills of lading, i.e. straight consigned to the buyers, Lord Mance opined that bills of lading symbolise the goods and possession of the goods. Any inference that bills of lading were, in this case, to be intended as documents of title just because they "symbolised" the goods would be rebuttable on the basis of the fact they have been made "non-negotiable".

Any generic reference to bills of lading as being symbolic of the goods should, thus, not be interpreted so as to consider them as documents of title to such goods.

In light of the above, it appears to be necessary to take a closer look at the origin of the expression "document of title" under English law.

Under English law, the expression "document of title" has been characterised by a twofold connotation: a traditionally narrow common law conceptual interpretation, and a broader statutory construction considered in the following.

6.5.1 The narrow common law interpretation of the concept of document of title

There is no authoritative definition of "document of title" at common law, but its original concept refers to a document the transfer of which is capable of transferring constructive possession of the goods covered by it.

We have seen that in *Sanders Bros v Maclean & Co*,[98] Bowmen LJ stated that during the period of transit and voyage, the bill of lading by the law of merchants is universally recognised as its symbol, and the endorsement and delivery of the bill of lading operates as a symbolic delivery of the cargo.

Nevertheless, as put by Lord Roger in *The Rafaela S*,[99] whether or not the transfer of the bill of lading transfers the property of the goods is always a question of

---

95 *Ibid.*

96 See P. Todd, The Bill of Lading and Delivery: The Common Law Actions, *LMCLQ*, 2006, 539.

97 *Scottish & Newcastle International Limited v Othon Ghalanos Ltd* [2008] UKHL 11.

98 *Sanders Bros v Maclean & Co (1883)* 11 QBD 327, 341. 2.

99 *JI MacWilliam Co Inc v Mediterranean Shipping Company SA* [2005] UKHL 11 ("*The Rafaela S*").

fact, with the answer depending on the nature of the agreement under which the transfer takes place.[100]

In order to trace the origins of the concept of "document of title" it is necessary to go back in time to the case *Lickbarrow v Manson*,[101] where the custom of merchants to negotiate and endorse the delivery of goods by endorsing the bill of lading was acknowledged for the first time by a court of law. Indeed, the possibility of transfering a bill of lading by endorsement lies at the very heart of the traditional common law concept of a document of title.

Nevertheless, *Lickbarrow v Manson* represents only the first embryonic stage of the development of the bill of lading as a document of title, as in that case the transfer of the bill of lading was only intended to be capable of generating a presumption of an intention to transfer the property of the goods.

The ability of a bill of lading to give its holder symbolic possession of the goods was only developed at a later stage, with the House of Lords decision in *Barber v Meyerstein*,[102] where Lord Hatherley stated that:

> There has been adopted, for the convenience of the mankind a mode of dealing with property the possession of which cannot be immediately delivered, namely that of dealing with the symbols of the property. In the case of goods which are at sea being transmitted from one country to another, you cannot deliver actual possession of them, therefore the bill of lading is considered to be a symbol of the goods, and delivery to be a delivery of them.[103]

At common law, the bill of lading soon assumed the form of "symbol of possession", and of a document which "represents the goods".[104] The bill of lading in law and fact represents the goods, and its possession places the goods at the disposal of the purchaser.[105]

Delivery of the bill of lading, thus, operates as a "symbolic delivery" of the goods referred to in it. This strict linkage between the bill of lading and the goods led Bowen LJ in the aforementioned case *Sanders v Maclean & Co* to describe the bill of lading as "the key to the warehouse, floating or fixed".

It needs to be emphasised that, although the endorsement of a bill of lading (like the endorsement of a key to a warehouse) is capable of transferring symbolic possession of the goods, not all transfers of bills of lading necessarily transfer possession of the goods. Ultimately, the legal presumptions raised by the transfer of a bill of lading are indeed capable of being rebutted by evidence of a contrary intention.

Traditionally, the narrow interpretation of the expression "document of title" refers to a document which is "negotiable and transferable". The distinctive feature of such a document is represented by its ability to perform a sort of "conveyancing

---

100 *Ibid.*, at 36.

101 *Lickbarrow v Mason* (1793) 4 Bro PC 57, 2 ER 39.

102 *Barber v Meyerstein (1869–70)* LR 4 HL 317.

103 *Ibid.*, at 321.

104 On this point see Sasson, D., *Fob and CIF Contracts*, 5th Edition, Sweet & Maxwell, 2012, p. 230. See also P. Todd, Non-Genuine Shipping Documents and Nullities [2008] *LMCLQ*, 547.

105 See A. Lloyd, The Bill of Lading: do we really need it? (1989) *LMCLQ* 47. Roy Goode, *Commercial Law*, 3rd Edition,. LexisNexis, 2004; Michael Bridge, *The International Sale of Goods Law and Practice,* OUP, 1999.

function", in that its transfer can indeed operate as a transfer of the constructive possession of the goods and, depending on the facts, of the property in them.

As we shall soon discover, a somewhat "broader" definition of bills of lading as documents of title is given by the statutory definition enshrined into the Factors Act 1889.

6.5.2 Bills of lading as documents of title: A broader statutory definition

According to section 1(4) of the Factors Act 1889, "the expression 'document of title' shall include any bill of lading, dock warrant, warehouse-keeper's certificate, and warrant or order for the delivery of goods, and any other document used in the ordinary course of business as proof of the possession or control of goods, or authorising or purporting to authorise, either by endorsement or by delivery, the possessor of the document to transfer or receive goods thereby represented".[106]

When a document falls within the aforementioned statutory definition, but not within the traditional common law connotation analysed above, its endorsement does not appear at common law to transfer constructive possession to the transferee, subject to the statutory exceptions to the general principle *nemo dat quod non habet.*[107]

Apart from the Factors Act 1889, another statute which deals extensively with bills of lading is the Carriage of Goods by Sea Act 1992 (COGSA 1992).

Nevertheless, since COGSA 1992 only deals with contractual rights and liabilities, consequently any possessory or proprietary connotations of bills of lading fall outside its scope of application, leaving us with no further legal definitions.

This interpretation of COGSA 1992 has been fully endorsed by Lord Hobhouse in *The Berge Sisar*,[108] where he stated that:

> But it must be observed that all these statements in the report, like the terminology used in the Act, are expressed in terms which refer explicitly to "the contract of carriage" and not to the right of the holder of the endorsed bill of lading to the possession of the goods as the bailor as against the bailee. It is thus categorizing the delivery up of the goods in this context as the performance of a contractual obligation not a bailment obligation. This is not objectionable since where there is a contract of carriage the contract certainly includes a contractual obligation to deliver the goods. A bill of lading invariably includes words evidencing the carrier's agreement to deliver the goods at destination to "or order or assigns" or words to that effect; the bailment is a contractual bailment. The relationship of the original parties to the contract of carriage is a contractually mutual relationship, each having contractual rights against the other. The important point which is demonstrated by this part of the report, and

106 Section 1(4) of the Factors Act 1889.

107 The original owner can obtain protection against the former owner through the doctrine of estoppel (see also section 21(1) of SOGA 1979 "unless the owner of the goods is by his conduct precluded from denying the seller's authority to sell"). Methods of the estoppel can be by words, by conduct, or by negligence. Estoppel by words, or representation by the original owner through words that he is the true owner or has the owner's authority to sell (see *Henderson & Co v Williams* [1895] 1 QB 521; *Shaw v Commissioner of Metropolitan Police* [1987] 1 WLR 1332).

For examples of estoppel by conduct see *Farquharson Bros v C King & Co Ltd* [1902] AC 325; *Mercantile Bank of India Ltd v Central Bank of India* [1938] AC 287, upholding *Farquharson*; and *Central Newbury Car Auctions Ltd v Unity Finance Ltd* [1957] 1 QB 371.

108 *Stargas Ltd. and Bergesen D.Y. A/S "Berge Sisar"* [2001] 1 All ER (Comm) 673.

> carried through into the Act is that it is the contractual rights, not the proprietary rights (be they general or special), that are to be relevant. The relevant consideration is the mutuality of the contractual relationship transferred to the endorsee and the reciprocal contractual rights and obligations which arise from that relationship.[109]

Our digression on the concept of document of title has, thus far, suggested that this concept entails a strict linkage between the bill of lading and the goods.

Nevertheless, it is also very important to emphasise the existence of a connotation which relates to the relationship between the bill of lading and its lawful holder. This shall be object of scrutiny in the following.

6.5.3 The concept of lawful holder of a bill of lading

The concept of lawful holder of a bill of lading has been the object of much debate. The starting point of our analysis is section 2 of COGSA 1992

Carriage of Goods by Sea Act 1992, section 2

Rights under shipping documents

(1) Subject to the following provisions of this section, a person who becomes –
  (a) the lawful holder of a bill of lading;
  (b) the person who (without being an original party to the contract of carriage) is the person to whom delivery of the goods to which a sea waybill relates is to be made by the carrier in accordance with that contract; or
  (c) the person to whom delivery of the goods to which a ship's delivery order relates is to be made in accordance with the undertaking contained in the order, shall (by virtue of becoming the holder of the bill or, as the case may be, the person to whom delivery is to be made) have transferred to and vested in him all rights of suit under the contract of carriage as if he had been a party to that contract.

(2) Where, when a person becomes the lawful holder of a bill of lading, possession of the bill no longer gives a right (as against the carrier) to possession of the goods to which the bill relates, that person shall not have any rights transferred to him by virtue of subsection (1) above unless he becomes the holder of the bill –
  (a) by virtue of a transaction effected in pursuance of any contractual or other arrangements made before the time when such a right to possession ceased to attach to possession of the bill; or
  (b) as a result of the rejection to that person by another person of goods or documents delivered to the other person in pursuance of any such arrangements.

(3) The rights vested in any person by virtue of the operation of subsection (1) above in relation to a ship's delivery order –

109 *Ibid.*, at 681.

(a) shall be so vested subject to the terms of the order; and
(b) where the goods to which the order relates form a part only of the goods to which the contract of carriage relates, shall be confined to rights in respect of the goods to which the order relates.

According to COGSA 1992, section 2(1)(a), the lawful holder of a bill of lading shall (by virtue of becoming the holder of the bill or, as the case may be, the person to whom delivery is to be made) have transferred to and vested in him all rights of suit under the contract of carriage as if he had been a party to that contract.

In order to acquire the above rights, a person must have become the lawful holder of the bill of lading. Nevertheless, the Act does not provide a definition of who is to be considered as the "lawful holder of a bill of lading", apart from linking that concept with someone who in good faith has the possession of it and: a) is the consignee of the goods to which the bill relates; b) a person with possession of the bill as a result of the completion, by delivery of the bill, of any endorsement of the bill or, in the case of a bearer bill, of any other transfer of the bill; or c) acquires the possession of a bill after it has become "spent" or after the goods covered by it have been destroyed.

The concept of delivery/endorsment of the bill of lading has been the subject of judicial investigation on a number of occasions. In *The Aegean Sea*,[110] an interesting passage of Thomas J's judgment reads as follows:

> I do not consider that a person satisfies the requirements under s. 5(2)(b) and becomes the holder of a bill of lading if that person obtains the bill of lading merely in consequence of someone endorsing it and sending it to him. The section requires him to have possession as a result of the completion of an endorsement by delivery. Although the sending and receipt of a document through the post often constitutes service of a document, the sending of a bill of lading through the post does not without more constitute delivery; the person receiving it has to receive it into his possession and accept the delivery before he becomes the holder.
>
> The provisions of COGSA, 1992 do not depend on the passing of property; it would be impermissible, in my view, to re-introduce the link between the passing of property and rights under the bill of lading that existed under the Bills of Lading Act, 1855 by interpreting the word endorsement in such a way as to link it with the passing of property.
>
> The Act does not define good faith in contradistinction, for example to s. 62(2) of the Sale of Goods Act, 1979 which provides that "a thing is deemed to be done in good faith . . . when it is done honestly, whether it be done negligently or not" or the Uniform Commercial Code (Section 1–201 (19)) where good faith is defined as "honesty in fact or in the conduct of the transaction".
>
> Although it could be argued that in view of lack of definition in COGSA, 1992, a broad meaning should be attributed to "good faith", I do not consider that would be the correct interpretation. In the commercial context of bills of lading, the meaning of the term good faith should be clear, capable of unambiguous application and be consistent with the usage in other contexts and countries. In my view, it therefore connotes honest conduct and not a broader concept of good faith such as "the observance of reasonable commercial standards of fair dealing in the conclusion and performance of the transaction concerned".[111]

110 *The "Aegean Sea"* [1998] 2 Lloyds Rep. 39.
111 *The "Aegean Sea"* [1998] 2 Lloyds Rep. 39, 45.

The combination of the two elements of endorsement and possession deserves some consideration: when goods are shipped by a seller and the bill of lading is made to the buyer's order, the mere delivery of the bill of lading to the buyer should make the buyer the lawful holder of the bill of lading under section 5(2) of COGSA 1992,[112] as in this case the endorsement of the bill is enshrined in the document itself.

Nevertheless, if under the same circumstances the buyer was to re-deliver the bill of lading to the seller, the act of re-delivery would not suffice to qualify the seller as a lawful holder, as the bill must be also re-endorsed.[113]

By the same token, if goods are shipped and the bill of lading representing them is made to the seller's order, and the seller endorses the bill to the order of a first buyer, and the first buyer in turn delivers the bill to a second buyer without further endorsement, the second buyer would not be qualified as a lawful holder within the meaning of COGSA 1992.[114]

Conversely, in the case of a blank endorsed bill, its mere delivery would see its holder fulfilling the requirements of COGSA 1992 on the grounds that such an act of delivery amounts to the completion of the original endorsement as the bill of lading is in this case a bearer bill.[115]

According to Aikens J in *The Ithan*,[116] the possession of the bill of lading under any of the circumstances specified in section 5(2) of COGSA 1992 would not suffice, per se, to qualify the possessor as the "holder" of the bill. Indeed, the buyer in that case did not become the "holder" of the bills of lading on their transfer to the buyer's insurance agent, as that transfer "had nothing to do with the normal course of trading a bearer bill of lading". The sole purpose of the transaction in that case was to enable the buyer to collect from the underwriter once the insurance settlement had been made.[117]

The relevance of the connotation of the context within which a subject becomes the holder of the bill of lading for the purpose of application of section 5(2) of COGSA 1992 has been rebutted by the Singaporean Court of Appeal in *UCO*

112 Section 5(2) COGSA 1992 recites as follows: "References in this Act to the holder of a bill of lading are references to any of the following persons, that is to say –

(a) a person with possession of the bill who, by virtue of being the person identified in the bill, is the consignee of the goods to which the bill relates;
(b) a person with possession of the bill as a result of the completion, by delivery of the bill, of any indorsement of the bill or, in the case of a bearer bill, of any other transfer of the bill;
(c) a person with possession of the bill as a result of any transaction by virtue of which he would have become a holder falling within paragraph (a) or (b) above had not the transaction been effected at a time when possession of the bill no longer gave a right (as against the carrier) to possession of the goods to which the bill relates; and a person shall be regarded for the purposes of this Act as having become the lawful holder of a bill of lading wherever he has become the holder of the bill in good faith."

113 See Thomas J in *East West Corp v DKBS* 1912; [2003] EWCA Civ. 83, 96.

114 *The Captain Gregos (No2)* [1990] 2 Lloyd's Rep. 395.

115 See *Primetrade AG v Ythan Ltd (The Ythan)* [2006] 1 Lloyd's Rep. 457.

116 *Ibid.*, at 465.

117 *Ibid.*

Bank v Golden Shore Transportation Pte Ltd,[118] and has been equally subject to academic criticism.

Indeed, it has been noted that there is no direct support in the wording of COGSA 1992 for the further requirement of the transfer having been made "in the normal course of trading". If there were such a requirement, one might still be entitled to wonder what is "abnormal" in the underwriters transferring the bill of lading in order to make a claim vis-à-vis the carrier.

With respect, the reasoning of the court in *The Ithan* is unconvincing: the judgment itself accepts the view that a "transaction" within the meaning of section 5(2) of COGSA 1992 refers only to the transfer of the bill of lading as opposed to the reason or cause for the transfer.[119]

The view that there is no transaction of the bill since the transfer did not amount to the "normal course of trading" is hard to reconcile with the aforementioned position, as it entails an enquiry into the purpose of the transfer.

This digression into the concept of lawful holder of a bill of lading is of the utmost importance, as a person who has become the "holder" of a bill of lading can acquire the rights under section 2(1)(a) of COGSA 1992 only if he is the "lawful" holder, with the latter requirement satisfied "whenever he has become the holder of the bill in good faith".[120]

6.5.4 The notion of good faith

Let us turn our attention to the concept of good faith. In *The Aegean Sea*,[121] the court held that COGSA 1992 does not define good faith.

This is in contrast, for example to section 62(2) of SOGA 1979, which provides that "a thing is deemed to be done in good faith . . . when it is done honestly, whether it be done negligently or not",[122] or the Uniform Commercial Code, where good faith is defined as "honesty in fact or in the conduct of the transaction".[123]

Although it could be argued that in view of the lack of definition in COGSA1992, a broad meaning should be attributed to "good faith", it is the opinion of this author that this would not be the correct interpretation.

118 *Bank v Golden Shore Transportation Pte Ltd* [2005] SGCA 42. Here, the court held that the original bills were "to order" bills, i.e. transferable and therefore governed by the Act. The court found that the nature of a bill of lading is determined as at the date of issue and does not change by subsequent events. Once the named consignee comes into possession of the bill of lading, the consignee will, pursuant to section 5(2)(a) of the Act, become the lawful holder, even without any endorsement by the shipper. This is not limited to a direct transfer by the shipper to the consignee. A person becomes a lawful holder if he has become the holder in good faith. "Good faith" connotes honest conduct. How and from whom the named consignee obtained the bill of lading is not relevant provided that it was obtained in good faith. That was the case here. The object behind the Act is to transfer the right to sue from the shipper to the specified categories of persons, in order to promote international trade and to facilitate the enforcement of rights by third parties against the carrier.

119 *Ibid.*, at 84.

120 Section 5(2) COGSA 1992.

121 "*The Aegean Sea*" [1998] 2 Lloyds Rep. 39.

122 Section 62(2) of the SOGA 1979.

123 UCC (sections 1–201(19)). See "*The Aegean Sea*" [1998] 2 Lloyds Rep. 39, 59.

In the commercial context of bills of lading, the meaning of the term "good faith" should be clear, capable of unambiguous application, and be consistent with the usage in other contexts and countries.

This concept should, therefore, connote honest conduct and not a broader concept of good faith such as "the observance of reasonable commercial standards of fair dealing in the conclusion and performance of the transaction concerned".[124]

The concept of "good faith" has been also linked to the meaning of the "delivery" of the bill of lading. The meaning of delivery within the context of COGSA 1992 was also the subject of scrutiny by Thomas J in *The Aegean Sea*, where he held that the simple endorsement and transmission of a bill of lading to a person does not suffice for his qualification as "holder" under the requirements expressed in section 5(2) of COGSA 1992.

According to Thomas J, the section requires a person to have possession as a result of the completion of an endorsement by delivery. As a consequence, sending a bill of lading through the post does not without more constitute delivery, as the person receiving the bill of lading has to receive it into his possession and accept the delivery before being qualified as a holder.

It follows from this statement of principle that, rather than a unilateral action, the delivery of a bill of lading can be defined as a bilateral act requiring the recipient's acceptance as the endorsee or transferee. Nevertheless, *The Aegean Sea* does not define precisely what is sufficient to constitute acceptance, and the judge had to determine what amounted to acceptance in that present case.

Apart from acquiring possession of a bill of lading through fraudulent behaviour or theft,[125] it is submitted that a buyer would also have not acted in good faith where he had acquired possession of the bill from the seller without fulfilling the requirements and conditions necessary under the sale contract in order for him to be entitled to such possession.

In the absence of clear authority, where a bill of lading names several persons as consignee in succession,[126] it appears that any one of them can be qualified as the lawful holder, if in possession of the bill.

In *The Aramis*,[127] the bills of lading were endorsed by the shippers and by forwarding agents appointed by the buyers to obtain delivery of the goods and, in the case of one consignment, to arrange for their onward carriage.

The scope of the endorsement of the bills by the agents in this case was quite unusual in that the bills were not further endorsed, but just presented to the carrier for delivery, and it was unclear whether this satisfied the requirements of the normal course of business.

This is an important point as in practice, even when a bill of lading is transferred to a buyer, that buyer may take delivery of the goods as an agent acting on behalf of the seller. This was the position of the buyer in *The Aliakmon*,[128] where a

124 See *The "Aegean Sea"* [1998] 2 Lloyds Rep. 39, 60.
125 See Debattista C. *"Bills of Lading in Export Trade"*, above, at p. 213.
126 See *K/S A/S Seateam Co v Iraq National Oil co (The Sevonia Team)* [1983] 2 Lloyd's Rep. 641.
127 *The Aramis* [1989] 1 Lloyd's Rep. 213.
128 *Leigh & Sillivan Ltd v Aliakmon Shipping Co Ltd (The Aliakmon)* [1986] AC 785.

c.&f. seller originally endorsed a bill of lading to the buyer who in the meantime became insolvent and no longer capable of fulfilling payment.

The buyer in that case agreed to take delivery of the cargo acting as agent of the seller. The court held that the buyer was not in this case the lawful holder of the bill of lading, and consequently had no course of action vis-à-vis the carrier either in contract or tort in respect to the damage done to the goods by the carrier (who was found to be in breach of the contract of carriage). This was the finding, even though the resulting loss in that case fell on the buyer's shoulders due to the risk having passed to him as from shipment.

6.6 Document of title and lawful holder: Two faces of the same coin?

In legal teleological terms, the concept of document of title is the prerequisite for the legal definition of the lawful holder of a bill of lading. The two concepts indeed go *pari passu* with one another, as the definition of lawful holder of a bill of lading stems directly from the concept of document of title.

In other words, it is necessary to legally identify the subject who can exercise the rights arising from the lawful possession of the bill of lading.

We have seen that there is no comprehensive definition of document of title under English law; this creates uncertainty which invariably reverts onto the concept of lawful holder.

As established above, a holder of a bill of lading is defined in section 5(2) of COGSA 1992 as essentially a person with possession of the bill of lading, either by being identified in the bill as the consignee, or by endorsement. Traditionally, the debate surrounding section 5(2) and the identification of the holder of a bill of lading involves two main issues: the material possession of the bill, and its endorsement.

In the past it was suggested, although without a specific decision of merit, that the holder of a bill of lading did not actually have to have the bill of lading in his material possession in order to fulfil the criteria of section 5(2): the mere transmission and endorsement of the bill of lading by a courier was enough for the identification of the "holder".[129]

On the other hand, *The Aegean Sea* subsequently postulated that the person receiving the bill of lading has to receive it into his possession and accept the delivery before being qualified as a holder. *The Aegean Sea*, arguably, created a new legal connotation for the identification of a holder under section 5(2) of COGSA 1992; rather than a unilateral action, the delivery of a bill of lading was implicitly defined as a bilateral act requiring the recipient's acceptance as the endorsee or transferee.

Still, acceptance was as yet an undefined concept to be defined on a case by case basis, and this scenario led to a certain degree of uncertainty especially in relation to the position of banks receiving bills of lading within the context of documentary credit.

129 See *The Giovanna* [1999] 1 Lloyd's Rep. 867, 874.

Here, when a bank to whom a presentation of documents had been made by the seller's agent at the counters of the bank then dishonoured the presentation, the seller's agent would take the documents away with him. If for some reason the documents were left with the bank, for example, pending possible waiver of the discrepancies by the buyer, the documents would be held to the order of the seller.

Consistent with this is the reference by Aikens J in *The Ythan* to the position where "a bank receives bills of lading as part of shipping documents for which payment is to be made pursuant to sale contract (say f.o.b. or c.i.f.). So long as payment is not made, the bank will normally hold the shipping documents to the order of the seller."[130]

In *Credit Industriel et Commercial v China Merchants Bank*,[131] reference was made to an ICC report which stated that "once documents are presented to the bank, those documents belong to the presenter until the documents are taken up".[132] Does this mean that a bank receiving a bill of lading cannot be considered as a holder within the meaning of section 5(2) of COGSA 1992?

Herein lies the importance of the recent case, *The Erin Schulte*:[133] here, the Court of Appeal unfolded a number of points of general importance to the operation of bills of lading and letters of credit. The facts of the case revolve around a sale of cargoes of gasoil down a string. Gunvor was the original seller of two cargoes of gasoil to UIDC, who was in turn on selling them to Cirrus. Cirrus opened a letter of credit in favour of UIDC, which was confirmed by Standard Chartered Bank ("SCB"), and in due course, at UIDC's request, transferred to Gunvor.

There were issues between the parties to the sales contracts as to the quality of the gasoil, with the result that, as between UIDC and Cirrus, Cirrus accepted the first cargo only. An amendment to the letter of credit was requested by Cirrus' bank, reducing the value and the quantity of the cargo covered by the letter of credit to that on board the first vessel.

Having obtained the consent of UIDC, but before obtaining the consent of Gunvor, SCB consented to that amendment. The cargo on the second vessel, the *Erin Schulte*, was in due course on sold by UIDC to new sub-purchasers. Gunvor rejected the requested amendment to the transfer letter of credit, and presented documents, including endorsed bills of lading, to SCB under the transfer letter of credit in respect of the cargo on the *Erin Schulte*.

By virtue of its error in accepting the amendment without confirmation from both beneficiaries, SCB remained liable to Gunvor under the transfer letter of credit, but had no right of recourse in respect of that liability. SCB wrongfully rejected what was (and was subsequently agreed to be) a compliant presentation, and stated that it held the documents to the order of Gunvor. Gunvor continued over the following month to insist on the validity of its original presentation, but was met by intransigence on the part of the bank. During this period, the cargo

130 See *Primetrade AG v Ythan Ltd (The Ythan)* [2006] 1 Lloyd's Rep. 457, 465.

131 *Credit Industriel et Commercial v China Merchants Bank* [2002] EWHC 973.

132 *Ibid.*

133 *Standard Chartered Bank v Dorchester LNG (2) Limited ("The Erin Schulte")* [2014] EWCA Civ 1382.

was discharged against a letter of indemnity issued by Gunvor to the carrier, Dorchester LNG (2) Limited ("Dorchester").

After Gunvor had issued Commercial Court proceedings against SCB, the bank paid up, settling the claim by making payment in full of the amount due under the letter of credit, along with interest and costs (by now over a month after the original presentation and three weeks after the expiry of the letter of credit).

Having paid Gunvor, SCB then sued Dorchester for misdelivery, since the carrier had delivered the cargo other than upon presentation of the bills of lading (which at all times were sitting at SCB's counters).

The issue between the parties was whether SCB had at any time become the holder of the bills of lading under the COGSA 1992, such that it had acquired rights of suit against Dorchester.

Teare J decided at first instance[134] that SCB had become the holder of the bill of lading, either on 4 June 2010 (upon and by virtue of the original presentation, notwithstanding the rejection of that presentation) or alternatively on 7 July 2010, when SCB settled Gunvor's claim in full.

Moore-Bick LJ, giving the judgment of the court, ultimately dismissed the appeal, overturning the finding that SCB had become the holder of the bills on 4 June 2010, but affirming the conclusion that it became the holder on 7 July 2010.

The court of first instance judgment ruled on a number of points of general importance in the field of international trade. In particular, issues arose in the appeal as to the true meaning and effect of section 5(2)(b) of COGSA 1992 (prescribing when and how an endorsee becomes the holder of a bill of lading), and of the true meaning and effect of section 2(2)(a) of COGSA 1992 (dealing with the transfer of spent bills of lading, and whether and when such a transfer confers rights of suit).

The Court of Appeal ruled that the judge had erred in holding the endorsement had been completed by delivery on 4 June 2010. It was held that mere receipt by the bank of the endorsed bills of lading was sufficient to complete the endorsement and render the bank the holder of the bills (i.e. the bank became holder upon presentation, regardless of whether it accepted or rejected the presentation).

The Court of Appeal further stated that the endorsement was not completed until the bank accepted the presentation and took up the bills, as "completion of an indorsement by delivery requires the voluntary and unconditional transfer of possession by the holder to the indorsee and an unconditional acceptance by the indorsee".[135]

As to the test in section 2(2)(a) of COGSA 1992, which had been the subject of a string of first instance decisions, the Court of Appeal concluded that it was not "helpful to seek to identify the 'real and effective cause of the transfer'", but

134 *Standard Chartered Bank v Dorchester LNG (2) Limited ("The Erin Schulte")* [2013] EWHC 808 (Comm).

135 *Standard Chartered Bank v Dorchester LNG (2) Limited ("The Erin Schulte")* [2014] EWCA Civ 1382, para. 28. This conclusion has important ramifications for the everyday operation of letters of credit and bills of lading – for example, it is apparent from this that, following rejection of a presentation, bills of lading need only be returned to the presenter, not re-endorsed back to him by the bank.

rather that the court should "simply. . . identify the arrangement, if any, pursuant to which the transfer was made".[136]

The Court of Appeal clearly emphasised that, although until the documents are "taken up" following a compliant presentation, the documents are held to the order of the presenter by the bank acting as an agent, this does not lead to the conclusion that the bank has not accepted delivery of the endorsed bill of lading for the purposes of COGSA 1992. A bank which receives and retains the possession of the bills of lading within the context of a documentary credit for the purpose of establishing compliant presentation can therefore be identified as a holder within the meaning of section 5(2) of COGSA 1992.

It appears from *The Erin Schulte* that it is the contractual rights, not the proprietary rights (be they general or special), that are to be relevant for the identification of the lawful holder of a bill of lading. The relevant consideration is the mutuality of the contractual relationship transferred to the endorsee and the reciprocal contractual rights and obligations which arise from that relationship.

Despite these aforementioned considerations, it is submitted that the roots of the concept of document of title lie with the concept of property and possession.

In property law, a title is a bundle of rights in a piece of property in which a party may own either a legal interest or equitable interest. The rights in the bundle may be separated and held by different parties. It may also refer to a formal document such as a deed that serves as evidence of ownership.

That deed could be identified as a document of title. This dichotomy between property and possession was codified for the first time in the legal institute of "dominium" under Roman law, and it appears to be the very foundation of the concept of document of title.[137]

---

136 *Standard Chartered Bank v Dorchester LNG (2) Limited ("The Erin Schulte")* [2014] EWCA Civ 1382, para. 56.

137 See Max Radin, Fundamental Concepts of the Roman Law, 13 *Cal L Rev* 207 (1925). "The special characteristic of *dominium* as a complex of privileges rather than of claims may be inferred from a sentence of the Roman jurist Ulpian, when he compares *dominium* with possession. *Differentia inter dominium et possessionem haec est quod dominium nihilo minus cius manet qui dominus esse non vult, possessio autem recedit ut quisque constituit nolle possidere*. "Dominium remains even when he who has it does not wish to be *dominus*; possession however disappears as soon as the possessor has determined not to possess." In *dominium*, however, there was another class of possible activities that seemed as characteristicas the privileges already mentioned. This was the capacity of abandoning the privileges involved altogether, or of abandoning some of them while retaining others, or of transferring all or part of them. These powers, especially the power of transfer, are legally and popularly associated with the idea of *dominium* as fundamental parts of it. It has been pointed out that the term "transfer" is a figure of speech, and that the process of transferring is really the process of creating in the transferee hitherto non-existing rights, which bear only a general resemblance to those rights in the transferor which are simultaneously extinguished However, figure of speech or not, it is a very old one and it dominated both expert and lay imagination. The easiest way to conceive of a person becoming *dominus* was to fancy the various groups of rights and powers inherent in the term as though they formed a concrete object which was capable of being physically carried from the grantor's hand to the grantee. How was the transfer made? The oldest form demanded a series of ritual acts, the "*mancipatio*". The later law had a general and much cited rule to the effect that ownership was changed not by mere consent but by delivery or by adverse possession of the goods.

Nevertheless, under Roman law it was also possible to transfer the title of the goods, without their delivery to the transferee. An agreement to that effect was called the *constitutum possessorium*, which produced the result of a change of title without delivery physical delivery of the goods. It is opinion of this author, that, just like with the endorsement of a bill of lading, the title conferred onto the endorsee

6.7 Other types of bills: Straight consigned bills of lading and sea waybill

Straight consigned bills of lading

Traditionally, bills of lading have been classified as "negotiable" or "non-negotiable" according to whether they might act as documents of title, transferring to the endorsee the right to claim the goods from the carrier as previously mentioned.

It is clear on the authorities that only "order" bills of lading are capable of being "transferable" to third parties. Such "transferability" is evidenced by the designation of the consignee on the bill of lading as "Buyer or Order", or simply "Order",[138] in the absence of which the bill of lading ceases to be a transferable document.

Indeed, bills to "order" or "bearer" are transferable by endorsement and delivery and entitle the holder to possession of the goods upon production of the bill. They will not necessarily transfer title to the goods and are not negotiable in the strict sense of that word either, although colloquially such bills are described as documents of title, which are negotiable.

The wording "Buyer or Order", or simply "Order", usually appears in the consignee box on the front page of the bill of lading, but could also appear elsewhere.[139]

Conversely, bills of lading lacking the wording "Buyer or Order", or simply "Order", or which are explicitly described as "non transferable" are not considered documents of title at common law, and are sometimes defined as "straight" bills or sea waybills.

A "straight" bill has no English law definition but the term derives, it appears, from earlier US legislation referring to a "straight" bill as one in which the goods are consigned to a specific person as opposed to an "order" bill where the goods are consigned to the order of anyone named in the bill, or bearer.[140]

A straight bill of lading is a non-negotiable bill of lading. It is used where the goods have been paid for or do not require payment, such as donations or gifts, with the bill stating that the goods are consigned to a specified person and it is not negotiable. The straight bill of lading details the type, quality, and quantity of the goods but, because it is assigned to a specific party, it is not negotiable and may not be re-assigned to another party.

---

was the "entitlement" to the delivery of the goods (from a carrier or a seller). This is because under Roman law possession and property used to be quite distinct. More interestingly, just like with the transfer of a bill of lading which requires its holder to be "lawful", we are expressly warned that a mere delivery, a *nuda tradito*, was not enough. A *iusta causa* must accompany delivery (like the lawful holder of a bill of lading), that is, a situation of which the natural incident is that the transferee is to be put in the position of the transferor. The rationale for the additional legal element of *iusta causa* lies with the fact that the delivery (documentary or of goods) per se is ambiguous and needs an explanation. The *iusta causa* is the required explanation. The *iusta causa* under Roman law was in legal teleological terms the situation that preceded the delivery that might show that the parties had entered into a contract of sale, or that a stipulation had been entered into or the object was a legacy owing to the transferee".

138 See C. Debattista, *Bills of Lading in Export Trade*, 3rd Edition, Tottel Publishing, 2009, p. 67. See also *Benjamin's, Sale of Goods*, paras. 18.010 and 18.018. See also H. Bennet, *The History and Present Position of the Bill of Lading as a Document of Title to Goods*, University Press, 1914, p.17.

139 See *The Happy Ranger* [2002] 2 Lloyd's Rep. 357. In this case, the consignee box in the bill of lading did not contain the word "order", which nonetheless appeared elsewhere on the bill, effectively classifying the bill of lading as a document of title capable of being transferred to a third party.

140 *Ibid.*, at 363 per Tuckey LJ.

Under this kind of bill, the shipping company will deliver the shipment to its consignee on presentation of identification.

This *prima facie* easily identifiable distinction between fully endorsable bills of lading and straight consigned bills may at times be problematic in practice.

In *The Chitral*,[141] the box in which the consignee of the bill was named said "If order state notify party" and no such notify party was stated. The judge construed the bill as one which enabled the form to be used both as a "straight" consigned bill and as a negotiable bill with delivery to the consignee or his assigns "if applicable" and so (because no notify party had been stated it had been shown that the printed words were not applicable).

A similar conclusion was reached by Mr Justice Langley in *The Rafaela S*.[142] Here, the consignee box of a bill of lading said "Consignee (B/L not negotiable unless 'order of')" and only the consignee's name was inserted in the box.

As put by Mr Justice Langley:

> There is no definition of a "bill of lading" in COGSA, 1971. But plainly the sub-section is referring to a bill of lading as a document of title. Indeed, Article III Rule 7 . . . the bill of lading to be issued by the carrier . . . to the shipper shall, if the shipper so demands, be a "shipped" bill of lading, provided that if the shipper shall have previously taken up any document of title to such goods, he shall render the same against the issue of the "shipped" bill of lading.
>
> [. . .] I think, the antithesis of a document which can evidence the title of only one person. It is general not specific to one person. It is a document by which goods can be transferred by endorsement and delivery of the document itself. A straight consigned bill of lading is not such a document. Indeed the parties to this bill have a choice, exercisable by inclusion in Box (2) of the words "Order of" before naming the consignee, whether or not to constitute the bill a document of title in the sense to which I have referred.
>
> While in terms of strict analysis Mr. Schaff is right that no binding authority has determined the question, the consistent and overwhelming burden of judicial and other legal sources is against his submission.
>
> The established definition of a bill of lading includes the characteristics of "transferability" of title to the goods: Scrutton on Charterparties 20th ed., art. 2, pp. 1–2; *Benjamin's Sale of Goods*, 5th ed. par. 18–007; Carver on Bills of Lading, 1st ed. pars. 6–007 and 6–014. The Law Commission Report (Law Com No 196) which led to the Carriage of Goods by Sea Act, 1992 noted, at par. 2.50, that a straight consigned bill of lading was not a document of title at common law. The terms of the 1992 Act itself reflect that in s. 1(2).
>
> In *Hugh Mack & Co. v Burns & Laird Lines* (1944) Ll.L. Rep. 377 at p. 383 Lord Chief Justice Andrews held that "above all" the reason why a receipt for goods marked "non-negotiable" was not "similar to" a bill of lading was precisely because it was not "a negotiable instrument, the endorsement and delivery of which may affect the property in the goods shipped".
>
> [. . .] that in any event I do not think the printed words in the bill of lading requiring surrender of the bill against delivery of the goods can bear even the weight which Mr. Schaff seeks to put on them. MSC were obliged to deliver the cargo to and only to the consignees. That obligation and the concomitant entitlement of the consignees is not affected by whether or not the consignee has or surrenders the bill of lading. It is a consequence of the agreement between MSC and the shipper to be found in the

141 *The Chitral* [2000] 1 Lloyd's Rep. 529.
142 *The Rafaela S* [2002] 2 Lloyd's Rep. 403.

> fact that the bill of lading names the consignee without the words "Order of". Nor does MSC need the protection of delivering only in exchange for the bill of lading as it would with a transferable bill. While the point is one of some nicety, I also agree with the arbitrators that delivery against the bill of lading was not necessary. The printed words appear in a document which can be used either as a straight consigned bill of lading or as a transferable bill of lading. The language used is indicative ("duly endorsed") of the latter. The proper construction and application of the words may properly be influenced by the chosen use.[143]

In *The Rafaela S*, the bill contained a clause expressly requiring presentation, and hence was to be presented to the carrier alongside proof of identity of the consignee for the release of the goods.

By way of *obiter dictum*, Bingham LJ concluded that at any rate, and even where there is no express provision to that effect, the production of a straight bill of lading is a pre-condition of delivery.[144] In his words:

> I would, if it were necessary to do so, hold that production of the bill is a necessary pre-condition of requiring delivery even where there is no express provision to that effect. The most recent decisions on this subject, as I understand them, support these conclusions. In The Duke of Yare (ARR-RechtB Rotterdam, 10 April 1997) the Dutch court considered a straight bill of lading, and observed in para 4.1 of its judgment, as translated:
>
> "First of all, the question needs to be answered as to whether the documents . . . can be considered as bills of lading or as 'similar documents'". As stated before under 3.1, the documents contain the wording "Bill of Lading" in the top right hand corner and are in the name of the addressee. According to Dutch Law – in which the Hague-Visby Rules are incorporated [references omitted] – the straight bill of lading, also called "rektacognossement", exists alongside the bearer or order bill of lading. The fact that a straight bill of lading cannot be treated in the same way as a bearer or order bill of lading does not detract from the fact that the present straight bill of lading meets the legal requirements to be considered as such.
>
> As opposed to a non-negotiable seaway bill – said document not normally considered "a similar document" in English and Dutch literature – the holder of a straight bill of lading has the exclusive right to delivery of the goods, therefore delivery of the bill of lading is a requirement for obtaining the load.[145]

The Court of Appeal of Singapore also considered a straight bill, although not in the context of the Hague or Hague-Visby Rules, in *Voss v APL Co Pte Limited.*[146] The issue at stake here was whether a straight bill had to be produced by the consignee to obtain delivery, and it was held that it did.

The main characteristics of a bill of lading were its negotiability and its recognition as a document of title, requiring presentation to obtain delivery of the cargo. While a straight bill lacked the first of these characteristics, there was no reason to infer that the parties intended to do away with the other also.

This conclusion was, in the court's opinion, supported by considerations of commercial efficacy and convenience. The decision of the 2nd Division of the Court

143 See *The Rafaela S*, above, at 422–23.
144 *Ibid.*, at 436.
145 *Ibid.*, at 439.
146 *Voss v APL Co Pte Limited* [2002] 2 Lloyd's Rep. 707.

of Appeal of Rennes on appeal from the Commercial Court of Le Havre in *The MSC Magallanes* also concerned straight bills of lading. The court observed (as translated):

> These documents bear the comment "on board" proving that the merchandise had been loaded; by making this comment the common carrier acknowledged that the merchandise was loaded on board the vessel and guaranteed the delivery of the cargo to the bearer of the original bills of lading. It is of little relevance [therefore] that, following the example of the sea waybill, this bill of lading is nominative and non-negotiable.[147]

The court continued:

> It follows that these documents constitute bills of lading, it is the responsibility of MSC [as carrier] to hand over the merchandise to the consignee Delta Shipping, as stipulated in the bills of lading.
>
> [. . .] In effect, having given the original bills of lading and documents of title of the merchandise to Delta Shipping, MSC could only follow the instructions given by the legitimate bearer of the bills of lading, these documents giving rights.
>
> [. . .] Calberson [the shipper's agent] cannot therefore reproach MSC for having committed a fault in executing the contract of carriage, in accordance with particulars of the bill of lading. Far from contravening its obligations the carrier has ensured the respect owed to the documents of title to the merchandise.
>
> [. . .] Calberson could not be unaware of the fact that MSC could only deliver the merchandise to the bearer of the original bills of lading. It is plain, as Rix LJ accepted in para 94 of his judgment, that a straight bill of lading is not a bill of lading for the purposes of the Carriage of Goods by Sea Act 1992. It is also correct, as appears from para 2.50 of their report "Rights of Suit in respect of Carriage of Goods by Sea" (HC 250, March 1991), quoted by Rix LJ in para 88 of his judgment, that the Law Commission and the Scottish Law Commission did not consider a straight bill of lading to be a document of title at common law. The conclusion of such bodies, following wide consultation, must command respect. But a 1991 report and a 1992 statute cannot govern the meaning of Rules given statutory force in 1924 and 1971, and the question before the House is not whether a straight bill of lading is a document of title at common law but whether it is "a bill of lading or any similar document of title" for purposes of the Hague and Hague-Visby Rules. It is noteworthy that, by section 5(5) of the 1992 Act, the provisions of the Act are to have effect without prejudice to the application, in relation to any case, of the rules (the Hague-Visby Rules) having the force of law by virtue of the 1971 Act.[148]

These remarks are *obiter* and not of binding effect but are an indication of the way that the courts might address this issue in the future.

With respect, Bingham LJ's *obiter* comments are difficult to reconcile with the classification of straight bills of lading enshrined in COGSA 1992. That Act expressly states that the transfer of rights and liabilities for straight bills is the same as for sea waybills.[149] In other words, exactly as with sea waybills, a presentation of a straight bill is not required for delivery as no transfer of the document is envisaged, and a consignee acquires rights simply by being named as the consignee.

147 *Ibid.*, at 716.
148 *Ibid.*, at 718.
149 See COGSA 1992, section 2.

If COGSA 1992 envisages the named consignee of a straight bill as the only party to whom the cargo is to be delivered, it is hard to appreciate why should there be an obligation to present a straight bill of lading to trigger delivery of the goods, unless that obligation is otherwise specified by terms in the bill.[150]

In practice carriers can, and often do, expressly require delivery against presentation of a straight bill of lading, and there is no legal barrier to the contrary.

Nevertheless, although this is common practice, it does not necessarily translate into a legal obligation to be applied by default, especially considering the aforementioned difficulties in reconciling such an obligation with COGSA 1992.

By the same token, traders or carriers who wish to benefit from the security of a presentation prerequisite are always in the position and best advised to use traditional negotiable bills of lading, particularly if goods are destined to be sold whilst in transit.

6.8 Mate's receipts

A mate's receipt is a "document signed by an officer of a vessel evidencing receipt of a shipment onboard the vessel. It is not a document of title, and it is usually issued as an interim measure until a proper bill of lading can be issued."[151]

Production of mate's receipt is if not "a completely archaic practice then rather outdated nowadays, although apparently still existing in some places. It belonged to the pre-containerised shipping era when general goods, so called break-bulk cargoes, were shipped packed in bags, barrels, pallets, etc".[152]

Each item of such merchandise when delivered on board a sea carrier, i.e. "shipped", would be inspected for defects, tallied up and registered by the ship's officer (mate) in agreement with the shipper representative (tally clerk or tallyman). Nowadays such goods are usually delivered for shipment in containers, therefore, there is no longer the need to check and record every item or pallet.

Thus, a mate's receipt is a document originally issued by the first mate of the ship, who is in charge of cargo operation. The mate's receipt or receipts are "collected by the shipper or his representative and later exchanged for a bill of lading, which should incorporate any qualifications or conditions inserted into the mate's receipt.

In modern practice, the mate's receipt, when it exists, is usually signed by the representative of the shipping company or its agents, who are responsible for loading, and not by the ship's officer." [153]

The case law analysed in the following shows ways of dealing with mate's receipts and associated legal issues and liabilities.

In *Schuster v M'Kellar*,[154] London merchants Schuster & Co., by order of another London merchants, Coles Brothers, and on their account, purchased on their own credit and in their own names a large quantity of spelter. They accepted drafts

---

150 Such a requirement would also create a fracture between English law and US law, which does not require presentation of straight bills for the delivery of the cargo.

151 See the business definition of a Mate's Receipt provided at businessdictionary.com.

152 See N. Gaskell, *Bills of Lading: Law and Contracts*, LLP London, 2000, p. 139.

153 See the business definition of a Mate's Receipt provided at businessdictionary.com.

154 *Schuster v M'Kellar*, 1857, 26 LJQB 28.

for the price, and debited Coles, Brothers with the amount of those drafts and a commission of 1 per cent, for purchasing.

The greater part of this spelter was shipped from Hamburg for New York in the name of Schuster & Co. and the bills of lading were made deliverable to their order. The remainder, which consisted of two parcels forming together a little more than 100 tons, was, by order of Coles, Brothers, shipped from Hamburg for London. This was also shipped in the name of Schuster & Co. and on its arrival was warehoused in the wharf, in the name of Schuster & Co.

There was a custom between Coles, Brothers and Schuster & Co. (such a course of business was general in London) that when Coles, Brothers wished to ship any goods so pledged, the course of business was for Schuster & Co. to give to the lightermen employed by Coles, Brothers an order on the warehousemen for the delivery of the goods, taking at the same time the lighterman's undertaking to give the mate's receipt to Schuster & Co.

The lighterman then shipped the goods as directed by Coles, Brothers, taking the mate's receipt which he delivered to Schuster & Co.

Coles, Brothers procured from Schuster & Co. the mate's receipt by paying off the advance upon the goods; it was then attached to the bills of lading, which were delivered to the ship's broker; the bills of lading were signed immediately thereafter.

In this particular transaction, Coles, Brothers informed Schuster & Co. that they intended to ship the spelter in question, part to Bombay and part to Calcutta; and Schuster & Co., at their request, gave to a lighterman who ordinarily acted for Coles, Brothers a delivery order for 100 tons split in two parcels, one for Bombay and one for Calcutta to be delivered on board of *The Emperor*. The mate's receipt for Calcutta's parcel was blank, i.e. without the name of the shipper from whom the goods were received.

The shipowner, and the master, of *The Emperor*, admitted that the goods were delivered and the mate's receipt was signed by the mate of that ship.

Coles, Brothers sent to the shipowner's broker for signature bills of lading bearing for 3268 plates spelter, fraudulently expressing that they were shipped by Coles, Brothers, deliverable at Calcutta to order.

Ultimately a memorandum "eight pieces in dispute, if on board, will be delivered" was added to the bills of lading; and, with this addition, they were signed and delivered to Coles, Brothers, without a request for a mate's receipt, who endorsed the bills of lading to The Oriental Bank as security for an advance.

After receiving the mate's receipt, Schuster & Co. repeatedly applied to Coles, Brothers to redeem it, and were informed they would do so presently. Schuster & Co. made no application to the ship brokers, and made no further enquiries until, on 24 June, Coles, Brothers failed. Schuster & Co. then learned for the first time that *The Emperor* had sailed on 16 June.

On arrival at Calcutta, the master delivered the goods to the holder of the bill of lading. Schuster & Co. sued the owner for conversion.

Evidence provided by the merchant witnesses in the court was to the effect that bills of lading ought to be given to the holder of the mate's receipt and that, although sometimes they were signed without requiring its production, if it was known that the mate's receipt existed, that was irregular practice.

A mate's receipt is always given when goods are shipped from a lighter, but not when they are shipped from the quay; consequently, a mate's receipt does not necessarily accompany all bills of lading.

The court held that Schuster & Co. purchased the spelter from the merchant at Hamburg, with the view of transferring it to Coles, Brothers. They paid for it with their own money, and received it under a bill of lading making it deliverable to their own order.

The court further held that the intention of the parties was that the goods should remain the property of the shipowner until, according to the usual course of dealing, the sellers received the price of it from Coles, Brothers, by the redemption of the mate's receipt.

Accordingly, the property therefore remained in Schuster & Co. when the spelter was delivered at Calcutta.

The master was held to be responsible for conversion because he, being employed to superintend the loading of the ship, must have known that there was a mate's receipt, as it would have been his duty to have required its production, and to have attached it to the bill of lading.

Mate's receipts continued in existence as a mere receipt for goods tallied up for shipment in the twentieth century. In *Nippon Yusen Kaisha v Ramjiban Serowgee*[155] a clear distinction was made by the court in terms of the function of a mate's receipt compared with that of a bill of lading. More specifically, it was held that a mate's receipt is not a document of title to the goods shipped, and its transfer does not pass property in the goods, nor is its possession equivalent to possession of the goods.

In that case, Ramjiban Serowgee, brokers and merchants of Calcutta, entered into three identical contracts on 4 May 1926 with three mills for the purchase of 250 bales of gunnies. On the same day the respondents sold the same quantity of 250 bales and on the same terms to the International Export Company, Limited (hereinafter called the "Export Company").

Clause 3 of the terms and conditions provided that "Payments to be made in cash in exchange for . . . mates' receipts (which . . . are [to] be handed . . . to the seller's representatives)"; and by clause 4: "The buyers hereby acknowledge that so long as such . . . mates' receipts (whether in sellers' or buyers' name) are in possession of the sellers, the lien of the sellers as unpaid vendors subsists both on such mates' receipts and the goods they represent until payment in full."

The contracts stipulated for delivery free alongside export vessel in the port of Calcutta. The Export Company booked freight space with the shipowners, Nippon Yusen Kaisha, and stipulated in the shipping order that the mate's receipts must be exchanged for bills of lading.

On 4 May 1926, the Export Company gave shipping instructions to the brokers Ramjiban Serowgee, which they passed on in the same terms to the three mills, and in due course the goods were sent on board two of the owners' vessels for

155 *Nippon Yusen Kaisha v Ramjiban Serowgee* [1938] AC 429.

delivery to Kobe, Japan, and mates' receipts, in which the Export Company was identified as shippers, were delivered to the mills on 17, 18, 24 and 25 May.

The shipowners issued bills of lading forthwith to the Export Company without the mates' receipts being given in exchange, but in exchange for a letter of guarantee or indemnity from the Export Company by the appellants. The brokers Ramjiban Serowgee paid for the goods and obtained the mates' receipts, and then tendered the mates' receipts to the Export Company, who defaulted in payment.

Thereupon the brokers Ramjiban Serowgee, on 27 May 1926, notified the shipowners in writing that they had an unsatisfied lien or claim for the price of the goods as unpaid vendor, and that bills of lading must not be issued by the master until the mates' receipts had been surrendered to them.

By that time, however, the Export Company, having the bills of lading in their possession, had resold the goods to purchasers in Japan, and had drawn bills of exchange for the price on the purchasers, which bills they had discounted with the International Banking Corporation and it endorsed the bills of lading to that Bank by way of security.

The brokers Ramjiban Serowgee, as they could get no satisfaction from the Export Company, and as the shipowners replied that they had passed bills of lading on the shipper's (that is, the Export Company's) own letter of guarantee. Immediately thereafter, they referred the respondents to the shippers, issued their writ, claiming payment of the price from the Export Company and damages from the brokers. In due course the vessels, the *Moji Maru* having sailed on 19 May and the *Hakata Maru* on 4 June 1926, proceeded to their destination, and the goods were delivered at Kobe on presentation of the bills of lading. The brokers claimed from the shipowners the value of these three consignments of jute gunny bags.

The House of Lords held that the brokers never had delivered the goods to the ship in their own name as shippers, because the mate's receipts were in the name of the Export Company. Thus, they never had title in the goods and property never passed from them, therefore the brokers never had a right in the nature of property and would not be able to support an action in conversion or trespass. Lord Wright gave the following characteristics to a mate's receipt:

> The mate's receipt is not a document of title to the goods shipped. Its transfer does not pass property in the goods, nor is its possession equivalent to possession of the goods. It is conclusive, and its statements do not bind the shipowner as do the statements in a bill of lading signed within the master's authority. It is, however, prima facie evidence of the quantity and condition of the goods received, and prima facie it is the recipient or possessor who is entitled to have the bill of lading issued to him. But if the mate's receipt acknowledges receipt from a shipper other than the person who actually receives the mate's receipt, and, in particular, if the property is in that shipper, and the shipper has contracted for the freight, the shipowner will prima facie be entitled, and indeed bound, to deliver the bill of lading to that person.[156]

Both cases above were concerned with situations where an unpaid vendor was trying, in one case successfully and in another not, to recover damages that resulted partly

156 *Nippon Yusen Kaisha v Ramjiban Serowgee* [1938] AC 429, at 445.

from the fact that the shipowner had signed the bill of lading without exchanging it for the mate's receipt(s).

The unpaid vendor succeeded in the case when, although the mate's receipt was in blank, on the weight of the evidence provided to the court, it was found that the regular practice of London merchants required that bills of lading ought to be given to the holder of the mate's receipt.

Nevertheless, the main tenor was that property was not intended to pass and actually always remained with the vendor, i.e. delivering the goods to the holder of the bill of lading constituted conversion.

On the other hand, when a vendor delivers the goods as being shipped by another company who books freight from the owner, and also takes a mate's receipt which expressly states the name of this other company as shippers, then such an unpaid vendor has no course of action against the shipowner, because the former has never had possession of the goods; these were always with the shippers and the owners were entitled therefore, and indeed bound, to deliver the bill of lading to the holder.

A further case, *The Nogar Marin*,[157] postulates another side of the operation of a mate's receipt.

On 4 January 1980, the *Nogar Marin* sailed from Caen to Tampa laden with a cargo of wire rods in coils. The charterers were manufacturers of the goods, who conveyed them to the quay at Caen, and shipped them for their own account. Although some of the coils were rusty when shipped, the ship's agents signed clean bills of lading.

Upon arrival at Tampa, the damage was discovered. The receivers of the cargo arrested the vessel and made a claim to which the shipowners had no answer except on quantum, since the bills had not been claused. The owners settled this claim under the bill of lading contract and proceeded with a claim against the charterers alleging that the charterers were obliged to indemnify them to the extent that the bill of lading imposed greater obligations on them than did the charter party.

In particular, the owners contended that the charterers could not seek to defeat the owners' claims on the grounds of the master's negligence in signing clean bills of lading because, since they knew about the true condition of the cargo and the discrepancy between its true condition and its description on the mate's receipt and bill of lading, it could not be said that the master was in breach of a duty owed to the charterers.

The Court of Appeal disagreed with the owners, holding that the fact that the charterers might have actual or constructive knowledge of the condition of the cargo does not mean that a master owes them no duty of care when signing documentation which will be negotiated for value to third parties. In the words of Mustill LJ:

> A mate's receipt is in a quite different category from a bill of lading. No doubt the parties foresee that some such document will be signed. But the mate's receipt is what its name indicates: an acknowledgment to the shippers that the ship has taken delivery of the goods.

---

157 *Naviera Mogor S.A. v Société Metallurgique de Normandie (The Nogar Marin)* [1988] 1 Lloyd's Rep. 412.

> [. . .] Nor does it share the prime characteristic of a bill of lading, of being a document which can be negotiated to third parties, thereby putting the shipowners into a new contractual relationship over which they have no control. It is a simple receipt. True it is, that if the mate or master signs it without qualification, it may put his owners into difficulties with the shipper who bails the goods into the custody of the ship, because it is prima facie evidence of receipt in good order and condition. But this creates no new liability, and no new party is involved. The master must choose for himself how to act, and the notion that if the charterer happens also to be the shipper he is in breach of duty under the charter-party by offering the master a document which, if carelessly signed by the master without proper enquiry, will constitute evidence in favour of the person who tenders it, is not a concept which we can grasp.[158]

The function of the mate's receipt under a charter party is therefore to delimit the authority which the master or the charterers have to issue bills of lading. There is an implied requirement that a bill of lading should relate to the goods actually shipped and it should not contain a description of the goods which is known to be incorrect.

Neglect in the recording of cargo quantities in mate's receipts will make owners liable for cargo-related claims such as, for example, as deadfreight.[159]

158 *Ibid.*, at 420.

159 See *The Boukadora* [1989] 1 Lloyd's Rep. 393. The case involved a voyage charter party on the STB Voy Form. Clause 20(a) of the STB Voy Form, which is similar to clause 20(a) of the STB Time Form, provided that "Bills of Lading shall be signed by the Master as presented . . . and the Charterer shall indemnify the Owner against all consequences . . . which may arise from . . . an irregularity in papers supplied by the Charterer or its Agents."

CHAPTER 7

The transfer of risk

7.1 The meaning of transfer of risk in international commercial sales

Within the context of contracts concluded on shipment terms, the risk related to the distance between the parties and the many uncertainties revolving around international business govern these kinds of transactions.

Needless to say, the risk for the goods whilst they are in transit is one of the key elements of international commercial sales, and a precise legal identification of the party bearing the risk for the goods is of the utmost importance for the success of contracts concluded on shipment terms.

The starting point of our analysis lies with the nature of international transactions, which can be divided into *shipment* contracts (the object of scrutiny of this monograph) and *arrival* contracts. As will be readily appreciated, the distinction between these two different types of international transactions goes to the heart of how a seller performs his duty to deliver under the contract of sale, and ultimately shapes the legal issues related to the transfer of risk.

The crucial question here becomes what exactly does a seller of goods on c.i.f., c.&f., or f.o.b. terms promise to the buyer; does he promise that the goods will be shipped on a vessel bound for a particular destination (in c.i.f. or c.&f.) or on a particular vessel at a particular loading port (in f.o.b.)? Or rather does he actually promise, in either case, that the goods will reach the buyer at the port where the goods are unloaded?[1]

Whenever the sale is concluded on shipment terms, the seller actually promises only to ship goods in conformity with what was originally established in the sales contract, not to deliver them to the port/s of destination, or that the goods will reach the buyer.

This basic principle entails a number of important consequences: first, as we shall discover in the following, the seller does not bear the risk of loss of or damage to the goods during transit.

Second, the risk is generally transferred from the seller onto the buyer at an early stage, i.e. the point of shipment, with the main consequence being that the

1 See Debattista, *Bills of Lading in Export Trade*, above, p.138. See also *Benjamin's Sale of Goods*, 8th Edition, Sweet & Maxwell, 2010, paras. 18–032 *et seq.*

buyer's remedies for the loss of or damage to the goods during transit do not lie against the seller, but rather they lie vis-à-vis the carrier or the insurer.

Far from being free of legal complexities, the rule whereby in international commercial sales the risk is transferred from the seller to the buyer on or as from shipment along with its legal consequences is, as we shall soon discover, the outcome of a complex judicial process of adaptation of English domestic law to the needs of the international trading community.

7.2 The transfer of risk in shipment sales

The starting point under SOGA 1979 is that in domestic sales the transfer of risk and property is joined and goes *pari passu*. Indeed, section 20(2) of SOGA 1979 starts with the assumption that risk passes with property:

> Unless otherwise agreed, the goods remain at the seller's risk until the property in them is transferred to the buyer.[2]

This linkage between the transfer of risk and the transfer of property hardly comes as a surprise as the rule is very old and finds its roots in the principle of Roman law, *res perit domino*. The meaning of the rule is that 'the thing is lost to the owner'. This phrase is used to postulate that when a thing is lost or destroyed it is lost to the person who was the owner of it at the time.[3] The transfer of the title and ownership thus entails the transfer of the risk for the goods, and that would usually happen with the *datio rei*, i.e. the delivery of the goods to the buyer.

For instance, if the goods are sold by the seller and the transfer of title is perfected, in the case that the goods are destroyed or lost, the buyer will bear their loss. On the other hand, if the title to the goods is yet to be vested in the buyer, the loss will be on the seller.

As a consequence, when a person is bound to bear the accidental loss of or damage to the goods, they are said to be at his risk. The legal meaning of the rule is that if the non-performance is due to the seller, the resolution of the dispute due to the parties lies in contractual liability whereas, if the non-performance is not due to an act or fact of the seller, the rule *res perit domino* entails that the buyer still has the duty to pay the price and nothing can be held against the seller.

This rule holds its value within the context of domestic sales; however, where goods are sold across international boundaries and carried across the ocean the physical risks of loss in transit are very much greater than they are within a domestic market.[4]

---

2 See SOGA 1979, section 20(2).

3 For a detailed analysis of the development of the rule under Roman Law, see Barry Nicholas, *An Introduction to Roman Law* (Clarendon, 1962) 171, and Andrew Borkowski and Paul du Plessis, *Textbook on Roman Law* (3rd Edition, OUP, 2005) 261. See also F. de Zulueta, *The Roman Law of Sale: Introduction and Selected Texts* (OUP, 1945) 1; J.A.C. Thomas, *Textbook of Roman Law* (North-Holland, 1976) 289.

4 See Debattista, *Bills of Lading in Export Trade*, above, p. 145. See also *Benjamin's Sale of Goods*, above, paras 18.286 *et seq.*

To these natural risks, one needs to add other commercial risks, such as the difference in commercial cultures and the difficulties of payment which very often characterise such kinds of transactions.

If we were to apply section 20(2) of SOGA 1979 and the rule *res perit domino* to international commercial sales transactions, the legal implications arising from this scenario would be devastating for both sellers and buyers.

Indeed, one should not forget that if the rule *res perit domino* were to apply, the seller is to retain the risk whilst the goods are in transit, with the main consequence being that, in the case that the cargo is lost, the seller will be considered in breach of contract.

This carries unwelcome consequences both for the seller and for the buyer; the seller, who shipped the goods fulfilling his primary obligation under the sales contract, will be forced to retain the risk for the goods shipped whilst in transit, and, most importantly, completely outside his control.

The buyer, on his part, is also not at all well served by this scenario: indeed, in the case that the cargo is lost, the buyer will have to sue the seller for breach of contract with the burden of proving when the cargo was lost (in any case, not the easiest burden of proof). The situation becomes even more intricate in the case that the goods are sold down a string whilst in transit (which is very often the case with c.i.f. contracts), as each of the buyers will have to sue their respective sellers with the same burden of proving exactly when the cargo was lost.

This will ignite a chain of international litigation between different buyers and sellers placed in different jurisdictions, with all the consequent legal complexities that a situation like that would entail.

That is the reason why since the dawn of modern international commercial sales, English courts and the commercial community have found a way out of this impasse by casting asunder two things traditionally treated as indissoluble, namely risk and property.

The transfer of risk rule within the context of contracts concluded on shipment terms was eventually consolidated into the concept that the risk for the goods is shifted over from the seller onto the buyer "on or as from shipment", as elaborated by the House of Lords in *The Julia*.[5] Here, Lord Porter elegantly postulates the legal rationale for the transfer of risk in contracts concluded on shipment terms:

> My Lords, the obligations imposed upon a seller under a c.i.f. contract are well known, and in the ordinary case include the tender of a bill of lading covering the goods contracted to be sold and no others, coupled with an insurance policy in the normal form and accompanied by an invoice which shows the price, and, as in this case, usually contains a deduction of the freight which the buyer pays before delivery at the port of discharge. Against tender of these documents the purchaser must pay the price. In such a case the property may pass either on shipment or on tender, the risk generally passes on shipment or as from shipment, but possession does not pass until the documents which represent the goods are handed over in exchange for the price. In the result, the buyer, after receipt of the documents, can claim against the

5 *The Julia* [1949] AC 293.

ship for breach of the contract of carriage and against the underwriter for any loss covered by the policy.[6]

The legal rationale for the rule that within international commercial sales transactions the transfer of risk happens "on or as from shipment" is quite simple to discern: one should never forget that we are dealing with contracts concluded on shipment terms. The legal nature of such contracts entails that the seller's obligations need to be assessed in terms of shipment rather than delivery. Indeed, what the seller is promising under a contract concluded on shipment terms, is to ship the goods, not to deliver them. In legal teleological terms, the main consequence in terms of transfer of risk is that the risk is transferred from the seller onto the buyer with the shipment of the goods.

Saddling the seller with the risk for the goods whilst on transit would not, thus, be on any basis germane to the legal nature of contracts concluded on shipment terms.

Moreover, one should also consider the legal consequences of the rule that the transfer of risk happens with shipment both from the seller's and buyer's perspective. We have just established that the rule retains valid foundations in legal teleological terms for the position of the seller due to the nature of contracts concluded on shipment terms.

The rule equally carries significant and logical implications for the buyer. A buyer will bear the risk for the goods whilst the cargo is in transit, and, in the case that the cargo is lost, he will not be in a position to initiate legal action vis-à-vis the seller.

Far from being in a weak position or deprived of any remedy, on the contrary, the buyer will retain the bill of lading, with the consequence of being in the position to claim on the insurance policy and sue the carrier.

In other words, instead of suing a seller located in a different jurisdiction and being saddled with a very onerous burden of proof (i.e. to prove the ship sank on a specific date), the buyer will hold in his hands the remedy which makes the most sense, i.e. suing the carrier (the likely cause for the loss of the goods) and claiming on the insurance policy for the cargo on the basis of the right of action deriving from the bill of lading.[7]

7.3 Transfer of risk "on or as from shipment"

After having explored the rationale for the rule whereby the transfer of risk happens from shipment, we shall now proceed with the analysis of the meaning of "on" or "as from" shipment.

The idea of the transfer of risk "on" shipment arises whenever the cargo has only one buyer, with consequently no need for any retroactive shift of the risk.

It has been noted that the concept of the risk passing "on" shipment could give rise to uncertainty in relation to what phase of the shipment process the rule

6 *The Julia* [1949] AC 293, 309.

7 In practice, a buyer whose cargo was lost at sea will do the two things simultaneously, i.e. he will claim on the insurance policy and initiate legal action vis-à-vis the carrier, with the insurer most likely to replace him in the latter legal action.

actually refers to, and this is especially relevant in the case that the goods are damaged whilst shipped on board.[8] Traditionally, the identification of the exact point of time of the transfer of risk has been linked with the moment where goods are put across the "ship's rail".

This concept was defined in *Pyrene & Co v Scindia Steam Navigation Co.*[9] Here, the carrier was found to be negligent in loading the goods which caused damage prior to the goods crossing the "ship's rail". *Pyrene* raises questions of liability if the damage occurs at any point other than after crossing the "ship's rail". Devlin J stated that if the goods are damaged during loading, whether that damage occurs on either side of the "ship's rail", then the carrier's liability for negligence would have to extend to cover the damages. In his words: "goods are loaded on the ship as soon as they are put cross the ship's rail". Nevertheless, Devlin J subsequently added that:

> Only the most enthusiastic lawyer could watch with satisfaction the spectacle of liabilities shifting uneasily as the cargo sways at the end of the derrick across a notional perpendicular projecting from the ship's rail.

The problem that emerged from the early "ship's rail" cases and the judgment in *Pyrene* is: who bears the responsibility if the goods sway back over the "ship's rail" and fall onto the wharf? However, it still stands that, in general, f.o.b. holds the seller/exporter responsible for delivering the export-cleared goods to a named port and loading them onto a vessel. As the goods pass over the "ship's rail" the risk of loss or damage to the goods is transferred from the seller to the buyer.

In sum, the buyer assumes all peril of loss or damage after the goods have passed the "ship's rail". If, as the goods are being loaded, they fall onto the wharf or into the water, then the seller bears the loss. If, however, the goods fall on the deck or any point over the "ship's rail", the buyer bears the loss.

The concept of the "ship's rail" has been stylishly described in the doctrine by Professor Schmitthoff, who described the "ship's rail" as:

> the dividing line to which lawyers and businessmen attach equal importance. The ship's rail determines not only the charges which have to be borne by the seller or buyer respectively, but it is also the legal test adopted for the performance of the contract, the passing of property, the delivery of the goods, and the passing of risk, except where a different intention of the parties is evident. The ship's rail is, thus, the legal frontier between the seller's and buyer's lands.[10]

Although, as we shall discover, the Incoterms® seem to depart from it, the concept of the ship's rail is very commonly used in contracts concluded on shipment terms as the discerning moment for the identification of the transfer of risk.[11]

The concept of the transfer of risk happening "as from shipment" entails the retroactive shift of the risk from the seller onto the last buyer in the case that the

8 See D. Sassoon, *CIF and FOB. Contracts*, above, p. 16.

9 *Pyrene & Co v Scindia Steam Navigation Co* [1954] 2 QB 402.

10 See Schmitthoff, *Legal Aspects of Export Sales*, Institute of Export 1953, p. 43.

11 See *Primetrade AG v Ythan Ltd (The Ythan)* [2005] EWCH 2399 (Comm), and *The Red Sea* [1999] 1 Lloyd's Rep. 28.

goods are traded down a string. In practice, goods can be traded down a string and sold multiple times to different buyers even before they are shipped on board,[12] or subsequently.

Be that as it may, the rule of the transfer of risk provides that the risk is retroactively shifted from the seller onto the last buyer from the moment of shipment, and this entails that the last buyer will bear the risk for the goods whilst they are in transit. Yet again, it is worth noting that this leads to a very efficient scenario in legal terms, as it allows the avoidance of a string of international litigation between different buyers and their respective sellers; and the last buyer, in possession of the bill of lading, will be in a position to sue the carrier and claim on the insurance policy.

The retroactivity of the transfer of risk is ultimately the enabling factor of string sales; after all, one should always consider that the "object and the result of a c.i.f. contract is to enable sellers and buyers to deal with cargoes or parcels afloat and to transfer them freely from hand to hand by giving constructive possession of the goods which are being dealt with."[13]

Nonetheless, it has been correctly pointed out that the retroactivity of the transfer of risk has encountered some resistance in the doctrine. Indeed, an element of academic doctrine claims that a c.i.f. seller who tenders documents testifying the shipment of goods which are subsequently lost in transit, is far from being discharged of his legal duties under the sale contract.[14]

On the other hand, other authors point out that the established rule is that arising as from shipment even if this has to be accomplished retroactively.[15]

The latter interpretation is more preferable and, in particular, it appears to be more in line with the judicial interpretation given by English courts. The retroactivity of the transfer of risk has been stretched, in fact, as far as governing scenarios where the cargo has been lost in transit and the seller has knowledge of the loss of the cargo before concluding the contract and endorsing over the relative documentation.

This was evident in *Manbre Saccharine Co, Ltd v Corn Products Co, Ltd*[16] McCardie J holding that:

> I conceive that the essential feature of an ordinary c.i.f. contract as compared with an ordinary contract for the sale of goods rests in the fact that performance of the bargain is to be fulfilled by delivery of documents and not by the actual physical delivery of goods by the vendor. All that the buyer can call for is delivery of the customary documents. This represents the measure of the buyer's right and the extent of the vendor's duty. The buyer cannot refuse the documents and ask for the actual goods, nor can the vendor withhold the documents and tender the goods they represent. The position is stated with weight and clearness in the treatise on charter-parties by Scrutton

12 See *The David Agmashenebeli* [2002] EWHC 104 (Admlty).

13 *The Julia* [1949] AC 293, 309.

14 See *Benjamin's, Sale of Goods* (Sweet & Maxwell, 2010) para. 19–083 and Goode, R. *Commercial Law*, 3rd Edition, (Penguin, 2004) pp. 941–943.

15 See Debattista, C. *Bills of Lading in Export Trade*, above, p. 145. See also *Benjamin's Sale of Goods*, above, paras. 18.290 et seq.; *Halsbury's Laws of England*, Vol 41, p. 346, and Bridge, M. *The International Sale of Goods: Law and Practice*, 2nd Edition (OUP, 2007), para. 8.53.

16 *Manbre Saccharine Co, Ltd v Corn Products Co, Ltd* [1918–19] All ER 980.

> L.J., 8th ed., p. 167, in the notes to article 59 as follows: "The best way of approaching the consideration of all questions on c.i.f. sales is to realise that this form of the sale of goods is one to be performed by the delivery of documents representing the goods – i.e., of documents giving the right to have the goods delivered or the possible right, if they are lost or damaged, of recovering their value from the shipowner or from underwriters". It results from this that various rules in the Sale of Goods Act, 1893, which is primarily drafted in relation to the sale and delivery of goods on land, can only be applied to c.i.f. sales *mutatis mutandis*. And there may be cases in which the buyer must pay the full price for delivery of the documents, though he can get nothing out of them, and though in any intelligible sense no property in the goods can ever pass to him – i.e., if the goods have been lost by a peril excepted by the bill of lading, and by a peril not insured by the policy, the bill of lading and the policy yet being in the proper commercial form called for by the contract. In *Arnhold Karberg & Co. v Blythe, Green, Jourdain & Co.*, Scrutton L.J., when a judge of first instance, described a c.i.f. contract as being a sale of documents relating to goods and not a sale of goods. But when the Court of Appeal considered that case commented on the language of Scrutton J. and indicated their view that a c.i.f. contract is a contract for the sale of goods to be performed by the delivery of documents. But I respectfully venture to think that the difference is one of phrase only. For in reality, as I have said, the obligation of the vendor is to deliver documents rather than goods – to transfer symbols rather than the physical property represented thereby.
>
> If the vendor fulfils his contract by shipping the appropriate goods in the appropriate manner under a proper contract of carriage, and if he also obtains the proper documents for tender to the purchaser, I am unable to see how the rights or duties of either party are affected by the loss of ship or goods, or by knowledge of such loss by the vendor prior to actual tender of the documents. If the ship be lost prior to tender, but without the knowledge of the seller, it was, I assume, always clear that he could make an effective proffer of the documents to the buyers. In my opinion, it is also clear that he can make an effective tender even though he possessed at the time of tender actual knowledge of the loss of the ship or goods. For the purchaser in case of loss will get the document he bargained for, and if the policy be that required by the contract and if the loss be covered thereby, he will secure the insurance moneys. The contingency of loss is within and not outside the contemplation of the parties to a c.i.f. contract.[17]

Similar in fashion is *C Groom Ltd v Barber*[18], where it was held by Atkin J:

> In my opinion the result is that the contract of the seller is performed by delivering to the buyer within a reasonable time from the agreed date of shipment the documents, ordinarily the bill of lading, the invoice, and the policy of insurance, which will entitle the buyer to obtain on arrival of the ship delivery of goods shipped in accordance with the contract, or in case of loss will entitle him to recover on the policy the value of the goods if lost by a peril agreed in the contract to be covered, and in any case will give him any rightful claim against the ship in respect of any misdelivery or wrongful treatment of the goods. It therefore becomes immaterial whether before the date of the tender of the documents the property in the goods was the seller's or buyer's or some third person's. The seller must be in a position to pass the property in the goods by the bill of lading if the goods are in existence, but he need not have appropriated the particular goods in the particular bill of lading to the particular buyer until the moment of tender, nor need he have obtained any right to deal with the bill of lading until the moment of tender. If it were otherwise the shipper of goods in bulk, or of goods intended for several contracts, or the intermediate seller who may be the last of

17 *Ibid.*, at 984.
18 *C Groom Ltd v Barber* [1915] 1 KB 316, 321.

> a chain of purchasers from an original shipper, might find it impossible to enforce a contract on c.i.f. terms. The seller's obligation cannot depend upon whether the goods are lost or not, and if when there is no loss the property has to pass to the buyer before delivery of the documents, at what stage of the transaction must it pass? Unless it be at the time of shipment I can see no reason for fixing upon any other time than on delivery of the documents, and if it be the law that a tender of documents is ineffectual unless in fact at the moment of shipment the property actually passed to the ultimate buyer, it appears to me that business operations would be very seriously embarrassed.[19]

The key obstacle to the possibility of a seller transferring the risk to a buyer having the knowledge that the cargo is lost, revolves around the concept of "appropriation" of the goods to a contract. "Under a contract for sale of chattels not specific the property does not pass to the purchaser unless there is afterwards an appropriation of the specific chattels to pass under the contract, that is, unless both parties agree to the specific chattels in which the property is to pass, and nothing remains to be done in order to pass it."[20]

It is indeed sometimes necessary to find some evidence of the intention of the parties as to the time at which the property is to pass.[21]

Nevertheless, the concept of appropriation of the goods to a contract relates to the transfer of property which, within the context of contracts concluded on shipment terms, is (as established above) quite distinct from the transfer of risk.

Furthermore, one should not forget that, although goods can be (and often are) sold down a string to different buyers, materially there is one shipment, and that shipment usually appropriates the cargo to the documents.

In *Re an Arbitration between Olympia Oil and Cake Co Ltd and Produce Brokers Co Ltd*,[22] a cargo of soya beans was lost at sea, with the buyers of the cargo taking the view that the sellers could not declare a cargo which they knew to be lost at the time it was declared, as it was not possible to appropriate the goods which were lost to the sale contract.

The court of first instance upheld the buyers' claim. In the words of Rowlatt J:

> In my opinion, clauses 3 and 10 of this contract both contemplate a declaration and appropriation of a ship and goods then in existence by the seller to the buyer under the particular contract which is in question; that a valid appropriation cannot be made

---

19 *Ibid.*

20 *Halsbury's Laws of England*, p. 169, citing Blackburn, *Contract of Sale*, 1st Edition, p. 128, 3rd Edition, p. 138; *Fragano v Long*, 1825, 4 B&C 219 (insuring and despatch of goods by seller upon buyer's instructions).

Section 18(e), rule 5 of SOGA 1979 states that: (i) Where there is a contract for the sale of unascertained or future goods by description, and goods of that description and in a deliverable state, are unconditionally appropriated to the contract, either by the seller with the assent of the buyer, or by the buyer with the assent of the seller, the property in the goods thereupon passes to the buyer. Such assent may be expressed or implied. and may be given either before or after the appropriation is made; (ii) Where, in pursuance of the contract, the seller delivers the goods to the buyer or to a carrier or other bailee (whether named by the buyer or not), for the purpose of transmission to the buyer, and does not reserve the right of disposal, he is deemed to have unconditionally appropriated the goods to contract.

21 *Mirabita v Imperial Ottoman Bank*, 1878, 3 Ex D 164, 172; cf. *Pignataro v Gilroy* [1919] 1 KB 459 (assent of buyer implied from failure to reply to notice); *Mason & Risch v Christner*, 1918 44 OLR 146, 46 DLR 710 (no appropriation by seller with consent of buyer), SC, 1920, 48 O.L.R. 8, 54 D.L.R. 653; *Sells v Thomson*, 1914, 19 BCR 400, 17 DLR 737.

22 *Re an Arbitration between Olympia Oil and Cake Co Ltd and Produce Brokers Co Ltd* [1915] 1 KB 213.

under this contract of goods which for the purpose of the contract are at the time no longer in existence, even though there may have been a prior valid appropriation of the same goods by the original seller; and that clause 10 does not come into operation in a case where there has been no valid declaration and appropriation as between the seller and the buyer under the particular contract in question. Further, this construction involves what to my mind is the absurdity of supposing that a contract like this, which contemplates the handing on of rights acquired by the seller from a third party, can be fulfilled by handing on a right which has ex hypothesi become void. In the hands of the Produce Brokers Company their contract with the Asiatic Company had become, or was bound to become, void under clause 10. Yet the contention is that they can hand on this avoided contract in fulfilment of their own with the Olympia Company. I think that the plain object of this contract is to secure the appropriation of a cargo shipped, and at any rate believed to be afloat, and then expected to be duly delivered; and that when a cargo is known to be lost it becomes, for the purpose of any tender, as if it had never been shipped. For these reasons I agree with the answers read out by my brother Avory, though I prefer to limit myself to the case of a ship known to be lost, the case of a ship lost but not known to have been lost not, in my judgment, arising.[23]

Rowlatt J's position was fully endorsed by Shearman J who, on his part, stated that:

Here the parties have agreed in their written form of contract a number of terms, which deal with these retransfers and with the string of transactions; but the framer of the contract did not have in his mind the particular event that has occurred, and consequently we have to try to spell a meaning out of it in applying it to that event. It is argued that, as this is a string contract, the moment one gets a cargo which could be tendered, the appropriation must be deemed to be good through all the transfers of people who are on this chain or string. I think that argument rests on an entire fallacy. In those cases, when all the string has been gone through, one can treat it as they do here. They talk about resale, which, to my mind, means a second sale, or a sale in sequence or a string. I think that is the meaning of the word "resale," though different interpretations were put upon it in the argument. But in dealing with that point, one must not forget that one is looking at the entire series of transactions in which the original seller is supposed to sell to somebody else, who passes it on to a third party, and then that third party passes it on to a fourth; that is the way the transaction grows, though they are not in that exact sequence. As often as not, as, indeed, in this case, after the sale has been made the seller buys for the purpose of delivering the same. In my judgment the transaction between two parties in this chain does not come into the line at all until a valid appropriation has been made. When that is borne in mind there is not much difficulty in solving this question. The sellers in this case did not have a cargo to appropriate, and at the time they purported to make their formal appropriation the ship was at the bottom of the sea and the goods were not in a deliverable state. Under those circumstances this was not a good tender.[24]

The court of first instance's judgment was eventually reversed by the Court of Appeal in *Produce Brokers Co Ltd v Olympia Oil and Cake Co Ltd*,[25] which held that the risk for the goods was transferred on to the buyer regardless of the knowledge of the seller that the cargo was lost at sea. In the words of Scrutton LJ:

The custom is not inconsistent with the contract. In applying the law under the Sale of Goods Act to the sale of goods over the sea it is necessary to be careful lest the

23 *Ibid.*, at 239.
24 *Ibid.*, at 245.
25 *Produce Brokers Co Ltd v Olympia Oil and Cake Co Ltd* [1917] 1 KB 320.

application be too literal. This is not a contract to deliver goods in a deliverable state. It does not put the whole risk of the voyage upon the seller. The meaning of the contract is that when a seller has received a good declaration he may hand it on to the buyer, and if the ship is lost, whether before or after the declaration, the seller is to be held to have fulfilled his obligation. In *Humfrey v Dale* (3) evidence of a custom was held admissible as not contradicting the written instrument but explaining its terms, or adding a tacitly implied incident. "To fall within the exception of repugnancy, the incident must be such as if expressed in the written contract would make it insensible or inconsistent": per Lord Campbell C.J. That applies here, for if the customary provision had been written into this contract there would have been no inconsistency but they found that there was a custom of trade that buyers should accept the original shipper's appropriation if passed on without delay, at the time of being made by the original shipper to his buyer, and then that their sellers should be under no obligation to make any appropriation other than that of passing on a copy of the original shipper's appropriation without delay, even though the said appropriation at the time of being passed on might, apart from such custom and implied agreement, be invalid and not in order. Having recited these facts, Scrutton L.J. again respectfully agreed with Lord Loreburn's remark that to decide a dispute in this way by a combination of commercial men and the High Court is about the very worst way that you could do it. But we have to do it. Now the question which we have to consider is whether the custom as found by the arbitrators contradicts the written contract. The point that the award is bad because certain alleged facts in the special case show it is bad has been practically abandoned by Mr. Dunlop on the production of a document which shows that he cannot rely on the alleged facts. Therefore it comes simply to the question, Is the custom alleged one which contradicts the written contract and which, therefore, cannot be relied upon or given in evidence? I think it is first of all necessary to try and understand on this point what the original contract means in order to see whether the custom contradicts it. Mr. Leslie Scott has not argued that the custom contradicts any particular clause of the contract, so that if the two were read together they would appear to be inconsistent, but, as I understand him, he says that the custom is inconsistent with the scheme or the tenor of the contract. Now the contract itself is this. A cargo of beans is to pass from seller to buyer at an English port, payment on delivery, but if you ask what cargo perils involving total loss of the cargo, involving partial loss of the cargo, involving damage to part of the cargo, and involving loss of profits on cargo. The mere shipment of the cargo does not appropriate it to the contract; that is to say, a man who has sold a cargo, supposing that the original seller to him had shipped a cargo at the Oriental port during the named period, would not by that fact alone be bound to deliver it under this contract, and you would consequently expect, if you were familiar with commercial transactions, that there might be some provisions by which the seller was either bound to or might during the voyage or at the time of shipment appropriate the cargo to the contract, not in the sense of passing the property in the cargo, but in the sense of binding himself to deliver that cargo against that contract. You find in the contract a provision that particulars of shipment with date of bills of lading be declared by original sellers not later than forty days from the date of the last bill of lading. Now where the party to this contract, the seller, is himself the shipper, he would absolutely be bound under that clause to make the declaration within forty days from the date of the last bill of lading, and the effect of that clause in this contract appears to be that where the seller is not the original seller or the shipper, if he is bound to declare, or if he is under any duty to declare, he must declare a cargo which fulfils the description given that the original seller has declared it within forty days of the date of the bill of lading. This contract does not in terms say anything about a seller declaring who is not the original seller, but it assumes that such a declaration will be made, for it says "The buyer shall have at least three clear days after appropriation," which can only be appropriation by declaration under the contract, "to give the necessary orders for the port of destination at the port of call." Then it goes on

> "in case of resales" – that is to say, where there is a sale of something which has been already sold; that is to say, where the seller under this contract is selling something which he has already bought – "a copy of the original appropriation shall be accepted by buyers if passed on without delay." Now it is not necessary in this case to decide what I am about to say; but my own strong impression is that on the true meaning of this contract without any custom, where a seller under the contract has received an appropriation from an original buyer [. . .] There is therefore a period between the time when the cargo is shipped and the time when it is delivered, during which it will be at the risk of sea perils, and you will consequently expect that there should be some provisions showing who is to bear the risk of sea perils involving total loss of the cargo, involving partial loss of the cargo, involving damage to part of the cargo, and involving loss of profits on cargo. Now it is not necessary in this case to decide what I am about to say; but my own strong impression is that on the true meaning of this contract without any custom, where a seller under the contract has received an appropriation from an original buyer, this clause binds the buyer under that contract to accept that declaration, whether the cargo is lost or not.[26]

The rationale for the Court of Appeal's judgment lies with the aforementioned observations made in relation to the transfer of risk: especially when goods are traded in a string, making an exemption to the retroactive shift of the transfer of risk from the seller onto the buyer as from shipment would entail particularly unwelcome commercial and legal consequences.

Indeed, the legal position of each buyer would be quite unwieldy, as each would be saddled with the task of initiating legal action vis-à-vis their respective sellers in a different jurisdiction with the usual difficult burden of proof that the vessel sank on a specific date, coupled this time with the additional and even more cumbersome burden of proving that the seller had the actual knowledge that goods were lost, which is an extremely difficult task to accomplish.

On the other hand, the re-instatement of the rule that the risk has been shifted on to the last buyer as from shipment despite a seller having the knowledge that the cargo was lost, produces the all too familiar consequence that the last buyer in possession of the bill of lading is in a position to initiate legal action against the carrier and recover losses from the insurance policy. The result is, yet again, blindingly efficient.

7.4 The exceptions to the transfer of risk: When risk does not pass to the buyer

The rule whereby the risk is transferred from the seller to the buyer "on or as from shipment" is subject to a series of exceptions which can be divided into two categories: a) statutory exemptions and b) contractual exemptions. Each of them shall be now considered in turn.

7.4.1 Statutory exemptions to the transfer of risk

SOGA 1979 provides for a series of rules which derogate from the general principle of the risk passing from the seller to the buyer "on or as from shipment".

26 *Ibid.*, at 329–331.

Delay caused by the seller

According to section 20(2), "where delivery has been delayed through the fault of either buyer or seller the goods are at the risk of the party at fault as regards any loss which might not have occurred but for such fault".

In light of section 20(2) it is clear that in the case of delayed delivery imputable to the seller, the seller will retain the risk. Nevertheless, the doctrine has questioned the possibility of applying section 20(2) to c.i.f. contracts, as this type of contract does not provide for the obligation to deliver the goods,[27] rather, just to ship them. Section 20(2) should therefore apply to contracts concluded on shipment terms in case the seller delays the shipment of the goods.

The confirmation of the possibility of a "full" application of section 20(2) to c.i.f. contracts can be found in *Gatoil International Inc v Tradax Petroleum Ltd (The Rio Sun)*.[28] Indeed, here the scope of application of section 20(2) was overextended to possible delays in terms of the delivery of the goods if this was caused by the seller. As stated by Bingham J:

> It was submitted, as an alternative way of putting the claim for damage to the cargo by the formation of R.O.B., that having delayed delivery of the cargo to Gatoil Tradax were liable for any damage which might not have occurred but for the delay. That submission was based on s. 20 (2) of the 1979 Act, which provides:
>
> But where delivery has been delayed through the fault of either buyer or seller the goods are at the risk of the party at fault as regards any loss which might not have occurred but for such fault.
>
> In resisting this contention Mr. Merriman adopted the argument in par. 1695 at p. 908 of *Benjamin's Sale of Goods*, 2nd ed. This argument is that s. 20 (2) is not directly applicable to c.i.f. contracts because the "delivery" referred to is delivery of the goods and the c.i.f. seller is not under any obligation to deliver the goods at the agreed destination. Were the point crucial to the outcome of this case it would be necessary to consider it in some detail. It is not. I shall, therefore, confine myself to a tentative expression of opinion. Despite the peculiar features of a c.i.f. contract, what the buyer wants at the end of the day is actual delivery of the goods, and he wants them in good condition. The seller need do nothing after tendering the shipping documents against payment. But if the seller does wrongfully delay actual delivery of the goods, whatever other breach of contract may be involved, I see no reason why the sub-section should not have the effect of putting upon him the risk of any loss which might not have occurred but for the delay which he caused.[29]

Reasonable/usual contract of carriage, SOGA 1979, s 32(2)

Another statutory exception to the transfer of risk is to be found in the aforementioned obligation of the seller to provide the buyer with a reasonable contract of carriage as per section 32(2) SOGA 1979.[30]

---

27 See *Benjamin's Sale of Goods*, 2nd Edition, 908, para 1695.

28 *Gatoil International Inc v Tradax Petroleum Ltd (The Rio Sun)* [1985] 1 Lloyd's Rep. 350.

29 *Ibid.*, at 362. If the application of section 20(2) SOGA 1979 to contracts concluded on shipment terms has ignited some doctrinal debate, the same cannot be said about section 20(3), which states "Nothing in this section affects the duties or liabilities of either seller or buyer as a bailee or custodier of the goods of the other party". This rule has not attracted much attention in relation to contracts concluded on shipment terms as in that case the bailee or custodier of the goods whilst they are in transit is the carrier, not the seller (on this point see Debattista, C., *Bills of Lading in Export Trade*, above, paras. 4.15 *et seq.*).

30 See chapter 13.

As established above, according to section 32(2), "Unless otherwise authorised by the buyer, the seller must make such contract with the carrier on behalf of the buyer as may be reasonable having regard to the nature of the goods and the other circumstances of the case; and if the seller omits to do so, and the goods are lost or damaged in course of transit, the buyer may decline to treat the delivery to the carrier as a delivery to himself or may hold the seller responsible in damages."[31]

We have seen that the seller's obligation to provide a reasonable contract of carriage entails a factual element (i.e. the duty of the seller to ship the goods in an adequate manner, and this will depend on the nature of the goods and is assessed on a case by case basis); and a "legal" element, namely the obligation of the seller to provide the buyer with continuous documentary cover, i.e. a bill of lading which covers all the transit.

Failure to do so would result in the seller retaining the risk for the goods whilst in transit. In *Hansson v Hamel & Horley*,[32] a cargo of cod guano was to be shipped c.i.f. Kobe or Yokohama from Norway. There were however no ships sailing directly from Norway to Japan, therefore transhipment had to be made, and the goods were placed on a local ship to be carried to Hamburg before being transhipped to Japan. The bill of lading issued at the port of Hamburg made no reference to the transit leg between Norway and Hamburg, thus not covering all the transit of the goods.

The Court of Appeal held that the bill of lading in this case afforded the buyer no protection with regard to the first voyage. Although labelled a "through bill of lading", it was not really so, as the buyer was left with a considerable lacuna in the documentary cover to which the contract entitled him. Therefore, he was entitled to repudiate the contract.

In the words of Benks LJ:

> A seller under a contract of sale containing such terms has firstly to ship at the port of shipment goods of the description contained in the contract; secondly, to procure a contract of affreightment, under which the goods will be delivered at the destination contemplated by the contract.
>
> Then Mr. Justice Scrutton goes on: "I should myself add to the first requisite the words 'within the time named in the contract,' and to the second that such a contract must be procured on shipment." Now, these goods were shipped at the port of shipment within the contract time, but the question is whether, in respect of these goods the seller did procure a contract of affreightment on shipment. What is meant by the expression, "contract of affreightment"? In my opinion, to satisfy the requirements in reference to a contract of affreightment, the seller must bring into existence a contract embodied in a form capable of being transferred to the buyer, and which, when transferred, will give the buyer two rights: (1) a right to receive the goods, and (2) a right against the shipowners who carry the goods should the goods be damaged or not delivered. If that is the correct view of what is meant in this case and other cases by a contract of affreightment, no such contract ever came into existence on shipment, or within the period fired by the c.i.f. contract for shipment.[33]

31 Section 32(2) SOGA 1979.
32 *Hansson v Hamel & Horley* [1922] 2 AC 36.
33 *Ibid.*, at 433.

Although the Court of Appeal does not make any specific reference to issues related to the transfer of risk, the rationale of *Hansson v Hamel & Horley* is perfectly consistent with its underlying line of reasoning.

Indeed, we have established that the main reason why the rule whereby the retroactive shift of the risk from the seller onto the buyer on or as from shipment is efficient and creates a balanced legal proposition within the context of international commercial sales is that the buyer risk bearer, far from being deprived of any remedy, is on the contrary in a position to exercise legal rights vis-à-vis the carrier and the insurer.[34]

Nevertheless, one should bear in mind that this is only possible insofar as the bill of lading the buyer receives offers him continuous documentary cover; if, on the contrary, the bill of lading covers only part of the transit, the buyer will no longer be in the position to exercise those rights which lie at the core of the rationale for the transfer of risk.

The obligation to provide information necessary to insure goods, SOGA 1979, section 32(3)

According to section 32(3), "unless otherwise agreed, where goods are sent by the seller to the buyer by a route involving sea transit, under circumstances in which it is usual to insure, the seller must give such notice to the buyer as may enable him to insure them during their sea transit, and if the seller fails to do so, the goods are at his risk during such sea transit."[35]

Section 32(3) will find application within the context of c.&f. contracts, where the seller is under the obligation to make all the necessary transport arrangements rather than providing for the insurance coverage for the goods. In this case, failure to provide the buyer with vital information re the insurance policy (e.g. the name of the vessel on board which the goods are destined to be shipped) will result in the seller bearing the risk whilst the goods are in transit.

Yet again, this is in line with the *raison d'être* of the transfer of risk, as the buyer will not be in a position to claim on the insurance policy for the goods, i.e. the remedy which, alongside the possibility of suing the carrier, counterbalances in legal terms the position of the buyer vis-à-vis the seller providing for an effectual scenario.

Some debate surrounds the possibility of application of section 32(3) to f.o.b. contracts. In *Wimble, Sons & Co v Rosenberg & Sons*,[36] the court held that the section indeed finds application to f.o.b. contracts.[37] Here the plaintiffs sold to the defendants goods f.o.b. Antwerp, to be shipped as required by the buyers, cash against bills of lading. Subsequently, the defendants sent instructions to the

---

34 See Debattista, C. *Bills of Lading in Export Trade*, above, p. 154. See also *Benjamin's Sale of Goods*, above, paras. 18.301 *et seq*.

35 Section 32(3) SOGA 1979.

36 *Wimble & Sons v Rosenberg and Sons* [1913] 3 KB 743.

37 As it was then, section 32(3) of the Sale of Goods Act 1893 (which is exactly the same as section 32(3) of SOGA 1979) stated that "Unless otherwise agreed, where goods are sent by the seller to the buyer by a route involving sea transit, under circumstances in which it is usual to insure, the seller must give such notice to the buyer as may enable him to insure them during their sea transit, and, if the seller fails to do so, the goods shall be deemed to be at his risk during such sea transit."

plaintiffs to ship the goods to Odessa and to pay freight on their account, leaving it to the plaintiffs to select the ship.

The goods were shipped to Antwerp on a steamer which became, with the goods, a total loss. The defendants received no information as to the shipment until the bills of lading were presented for payment. The defendants had not insured, and they refused to pay for the goods on the grounds that the plaintiffs had not given them such notice as was required by sub-section 3 of section 32 of SOGA 1893.

It was held by a majority of the Court of Appeal (Hamilton LJ dissenting) that the relevant subsection does find application to f.o.b. contracts. Bailhache J stated that:

> This case turns to my mind on construction. No facts are in dispute. I am of opinion that sub-s. 3 of s. 32 of the Sale of Goods Act covers an f.o.b. contract. To say generally that sub-s. 3 does not cover an f.o.b. contract seems to me to be a conspicuous illustration of departure from Lord Herschell's canon of construction which I have already quoted. The natural meaning of the words of sub-s. 3 does not exclude an f.o.b. contract. The real ground for the suggested exclusion is that the sub-section, construed according to its natural meaning, is hard to reconcile with some of the previous law laid down in the cases relating to the carriage of goods under an f.o.b. contract, and that it is highly improbable that the Legislature intended to alter or modify law which is the result of a series of decisions laid down by great commercial lawyers.
>
> Mr. Leck, in his excellent argument on behalf of the plaintiffs, to my mind was evidently pressed by a strong desire to avoid a breach of Lord Herschell's canon of construction of codifying statutes and argued that sub-s. 3, read in the light of sub-s. 1, has no application to a case where, in pursuance of a contract of sale, the seller is "authorized or required" to send goods to the buyer, and says that under an f.o.b. contract the seller is never authorized nor required to send the goods to the buyer, but completely performs his duty when he puts the goods on board the steamer. Bailhache J. based his judgment on this contention of Mr. Leck and, as I understand his judgment, in effect held that an f.o.b. contract is excluded unless it includes some words whereby the vendor undertook to send the goods by some ship selected by himself, and that in this case the shipping instructions ought not to be regarded as part of the contract, in which case Bailhache J. thought sub-s. 3 would have applied.
>
> I construe the word "send," both in sub-s. 1 and in sub-s. 3, in the sense of "forward" or "despatch," and in my opinion the word "send" covers every obligation of the seller in reference to effecting or securing the arrival of the goods the subject of sale at the destination intended. It is not true in fact to say that the purchased goods are being sent to the ship on which they are placed for the purpose of delivery at the port of destination. The purchased goods are not the less being sent to the buyer at the port of destination because delivery f.o.b. is prima facie delivery to the buyer, or because the property has passed to the buyer. Sub-s. 3, in my opinion, casts a duty on the seller forwarding the goods to the buyer by a route involving sea transit, under circumstances in which it is usual to insure, to give such notice as may enable the buyer (to whom be it observed the property in the purchased goods has passed), to insure them during their sea transit. The penalty for not performing this duty is that goods, though the goods of the buyer, shall be at the risk of the seller during such sea transit. Moreover the same result is arrived at if the words "where goods are sent by the seller to the buyer," at the beginning of sub-s. 3, are construed as describing the whole transaction.
>
> I have already said that I cannot agree with the argument of Mr. Theobald Mathew that the contract of sale itself was notice within the meaning of sub-s. 3, and I have arrived at this conclusion not only on the ground that the contract did not afford sufficient information to enable the buyer to insure the purchased goods during their

sea transit, but also on the ground that knowledge of the buyer, actual, inferred, or assumed, which would enable the buyer to insure, does not dispense with the statutory obligation of the seller, where the route involves sea transit under circumstances in which it is usual to insure, to give such notice to the buyer as may enable him to insure the goods during their sea transit. The obligation, unless dispensed with by the agreement, – and in this case there was no dispensing agreement – on the seller is to give such notice, with such details, to the buyer as may be necessary to effect insurance of the goods during sea transit. It is to my mind impossible to construe the words as meaning that the obligation to insure does not arise in case the buyer happens to have sufficient information from some other source than the statutory notice to enable him to insure the goods.

I have only to add that, whichever of the suggested constructions relieving the seller from obligation to give the statutory notice in the case of an f.o.b. contract is adopted, the practical utility and application of sub-s. 3 of s. 32 are reduced to nil.[38]

---

38 See *Wimble & Sons v Rosenberg and Sons* [1913] 3 KB 743, 749. Hamilton LJ dissented by stating that:

The question in this case is whether the contract is or is not within s. 32, sub-s. 3, of the Sale of Goods Act.

The action is brought for the price of goods sold and delivered. The plaintiffs were not the sellers, who were foreign millers, but were the brokers between the parties. In the events which happened they conceived themselves liable to pay the sellers and have done so, and the case here and below has proceeded on the footing that, as regards the contract in dispute, they have the rights and are subject to the liabilities of the sellers. This is worth noting, because for this reason the case is unaffected by any prior course of business between the defendants and the actual sellers. What was done in regard to contracts, which the plaintiffs did not put in suit, would now be material only to reasonableness in performing this contract, but there is no such question. Further, there was no contention and no finding below as to general custom or particular practice, such as would add any implied term to the present contract. Hence the case as between the present parties rests barely on the written contract of sale itself. As the goods clearly were sold and delivered, subject to the question which is raised by the alleged failure to give notice, as provided by sub-s. 3 of s. 32 of the Sale of Goods Act, the burden of proof is on the defendants. They further alleged against the plaintiffs in the alternative that the latter were not sellers to but agents of the defendants, and that they were negligent in the performance of their duty to their principals. These defences were mutually exclusive. If the plaintiffs were not sellers to but agents of the defendants, s. 32 of the Sale of Goods Act had nothing to do with them. In my opinion this was the real defence, if there was one, but Bailhache J. decided against this alternative contention, not, be it said, on the ground that the plaintiffs were not in fact agents or not in law open to any defence arising out of a contract of employment, but solely on the ground that no damage resulted from any breach of such contract. No point has been made before us that the decision should have been for the defendants for nominal damages on a counter-claim, if they chose to amend. In fact the learned judge's decision on this part of the case is not appealed against. Bailhache J. decided that s. 32, sub-s. 3, of the Sale of Goods Act did not apply to this case. This is the subject of the appeal. The question is whether he was right. I think he was.

(1) The "sending" of the goods in sub-ss. 1 and 3 of s. 32 is the same thing in each case, an actual forwarding or transmission. The use of the same word "send" in s. 29 shews this. But in sub-s. 1 the case is, "where the seller is authorised or required to send the goods" and that too "in pursuance of a contract of sale"; in sub-s. 3 the case is, "where the goods are sent by the seller to the buyer" simply. In the former, which is a provision in favour of the seller limiting his responsibility, the questions are, Was he authorized or required to send the goods, that is, to transmit or forward them, to start them on their journey? Has he done so? When and where does his responsibility cease? A further question was raised, which we need not decide, namely, does "in pursuance of a contract of sale" mean "in performance of" or "as required under the terms of"? On the other hand the latter sub-s. 3 is one in favour of the buyer and makes his responsibility in certain circumstances conditional on the seller's giving a certain notice. Here the question is not merely have the goods been "sent" in the above sense, but have they been so sent by the seller to the buyer, that is, by the sender as seller to the receiver as buyer, or, in the language of sub-s. 1, sent "in pursuance of a contract of sale." Hence, in spite of the use of the same verb "to send," it does not necessarily follow that a contract involving sending, if

within sub-s. 1, must therefore also be within sub-s. 3. It is well settled that, on an ordinary f.o.b. contract, when "free on board" does not merely condition the constituent elements in the price but expresses the seller's obligations additional to the bare bargain of purchase and sale, the seller does not "in pursuance of the contract of sale" or as seller send forward or start the goods to the buyer at all except in the sense that he puts the goods safely on board, pays the charge of doing so, and, for the buyer's protection but not under a mandate to send, gives up possession of them to the ship only upon the terms of a reasonable and ordinary bill of lading or other contract of carriage. There his contractual liability as seller ceases, and delivery to the buyer is complete as far as he is concerned. In such a case the goods are not "sent by the seller to the buyer," though they then begin a journey which will end in the buyer's hands. In law, as between buyer and seller, they are then and there delivered by the seller to the buyer, and thereafter it is by the buyer and his agent, the carrier, and not by the seller, that the goods are "sent" to their destination. It is in this sense that I understand the words of Bailhache J., "what one generally understands by an f.o.b. contract is that the goods are not sent by sea by the vendor but are delivered by him at the rail of the ship and are then taken over by the shipowner nominated by the buyer and conveyed by him across the sea." So understood, I agree with them.

(2) The sub-section obliges the seller, "under circumstances in which it is usual to insure," to give a notice, and that notice such "as may enable the buyer to insure the goods." The sub-section does not say how or by whom it is usual to insure, or that the buyer is to be enabled to insure at any particular time or in any particular way. Nor, again, does it say such notice as would be reasonably sufficient to enable him to insure, but such as may enable, that is, in fact and under the circumstances actually enable, him to insure. If the seller fails to fulfil this obligation, then, in addition to or in substitution for (I know not which) any provable damages for the breach, he loses both the goods and the price in case the goods are lost at sea. It is a heavy responsibility. Without his fault and perhaps without his knowledge, without negligence and perhaps in spite of his diligence, the notice may miscarry or fail to convey sufficient information to the particular buyer, or be such as in his particular case may not enable him to insure, though in other circumstances it might suffice well enough.

In the present case the buyer was in London buying to sell, or at any rate to send abroad. The contract only named the port of loading. Ordinarily it would have been an implied obligation upon the buyer to declare the port of discharge within a reasonable time; here it is an express obligation that this should be done within three months. Till the buyer performs this, the seller cannot deliver. Delay in declaring is a breach, for which the seller may recover damages if he can prove them, and under certain circumstances such delay might give the seller the right to treat the contract as repudiated by the buyer.

When the buyer declared the port of discharge, Odessa, he did not name any ship or even any line by which the goods were to be sent. He might have done either or both, provided they were such as would enable the seller to get the goods delivered on board within a reasonable time and gave him a reasonable time within which to do so. No new promise or obligation can be implied from the sending or acceptance of such instructions. They are sent and complied with under and in performance of the contract of sale. In the present case the buyer's instructions were accompanied by a request to the brokers to prepay the freight and they did so. They were not bound to do so, but they were accommodating. Beyond the obligation of the buyer to indemnify them, no new obligation arose. The transaction is not, "send the goods to Odessa; choose your own ship; but let me know her name." It is, "I nominate, as the ship on which you are to put the goods free of charge, any reasonable Odessabound ship from Antwerp in the ordinary course of trade." There is no new transaction, separate from the contract of sale – no mandate to send nor a new contract to forward. In choosing a ship and in shipping the goods the seller is acting solely in performance of the contract of sale and the parties are governed by its terms, especially by the term "free on board." If then the seller at this stage does send the buyer notice of the ship's name, he is giving him "such notice as may enable him to insure the goods." If he does not, does he "fail" to give him such notice as may enable him to insure them? I think the answer to both questions is no. If the buyer chose, he could, as far as the practice of insurance is concerned, cover the goods himself by ship or ships, or by steamer to be declared, or in other forms. If, owing to circumstances affecting himself, he cannot do so, or does not know the name of a suitable ship, the seller, being a stranger to them, is not affected and cannot have his obligations increased thereby. Independently of the seller, the buyer has information enough to enable him to insure, and if the seller sends none, he does not thereby fail to send was further re-emphasised in *Northern Steel and Hardware Co Ltd v John Batt & Co (London) Ltd*.[39]

Here, the plaintiffs sold to the defendants a quantity of nails to be delivered f.o.b. New York, for shipment to the destination specified by the defendants on receipt of shipping instructions from the defendants, for cash against shipping documents.

In June 1916, the defendants sent an order under the contract and specified the shipping marks. On 16 August, the plaintiffs gave notice to the defendants that the goods would shortly be made. The goods were shipped on a vessel which sailed from New York on 24 August. On 26 August, the shipowners notified the defendants that the ship had sailed and, by 6 September, the defendants knew that the goods had been shipped.

---

an enabling notice; he merely omits to make a superfluous communication. I do not think the sub-section is meant to bind men of business to write immaterial letters, and to penalize the omission in the price of the goods if they should afterwards be lost at sea, uninsured.

(3) It has been argued that, in signing and sending to the buyer the contract note itself, the seller, to the benefit of whose acts the plaintiffs succeed, did give to the buyer such notice as might enable him to insure the goods. Literally this is undeniably true. The appellants say that this is a paradox, which would make every f.o.b. contract its own enabling notice and so, also, so far nullify the sub-section. I think this is true too, but my conclusion is that the paradox helps to shew that f.o.b. contracts are not within the sub-section. It is a *reductio ad absurdum*.

Whether, on giving instructions, the buyer waived any further information as to the ship's name is a question of fact not answered or, I think, raised in the Court below, on which I prefer to express no opinion.

(4) The whole sub-section is prefaced by the words "unless otherwise agreed." The mercantile meaning of f.o.b., of the words "free on board," has long been known and is stated by the high authority of Brett M.R. in *Stock v Inglis*:

> "If the goods dealt with by the contract were specific goods, it is not denied but that the words 'free on board,' according to the general understanding of merchants, would mean more than merely that the shipper was to put them on board at his expense; they would mean that he was to put them on board at his expense on account of the person for whom they were shipped; and in that case the goods so put on board under such a contract would be at the risk of the buyer whether they were lost or not on the voyage. Now that is the meaning of those words 'free on board' in a contract with regard to specific goods, and in that case the goods are at the purchaser's risk, even though the payment is not to be made on the delivery of the goods on board, but at some other time, and although the bill of lading is sent forward by the seller with documents attached in order that the goods shall not be finally delivered to the purchaser until he has either accepted bills or paid cash."

This passage is adopted, not in terms but in substance, by Lord Blackburn in the same case in the House of Lords, where he too says that the seller's obligations were at an end when the goods were put on board. The important point is to observe that Brett MR states it as part of the mercantile meaning of f.o.b. that the buyer should do the things he mentions and no more. True the contract does not in terms say anything about giving notice, but in saying that all the seller need do is to ship, it says, in the understanding of merchants, that he need not go on to give a notice. If, instead of the letters f.o.b., their meaning were written out at length in the contract, in the words of Lord Esher, it would be plain that there was no liability upon the seller to be at the risk of the loss of the goods at sea, if he has failed to give a notice, because the parties had otherwise agreed, namely, had agreed that "the goods so put on board (without any notice called for or given) would be at the risk of the buyer, whether they were lost or not on the voyage." It is not that the common law annexes, as an incident to such a contract, that the seller should deliver on board and be liable no further. If that were so, the statute of 1893 might have altered and increased his obligations. It is that by agreement between buyer and seller in these words the contract means that only certain obligations are incumbent on the seller, and giving notice is not one of them. If so, "unless otherwise agreed" ousts the application of sub-s. 3 to an f.o.b. contract.

39 *Northern Steel and Hardware Co Ltd v John Batt & Co (London) Ltd* (1917) 33 TLR 516.

On 18 September, the ship was torpedoed and the goods were lost. The defendants had not insured the goods. In an action for the purchase money there was evidence that the defendants could have effected an insurance before they knew of the loss.

The court held that SOGA, section 32(3), did apply to a contract for the sale of goods f.o.b., but as the defendants had sufficient knowledge of the facts to enable them to insure, the plaintiffs were entitled to recover.

Mash & Murrel[40] and the implied obligation of shipping goods capable of withstanding transit

In addition to the aforementioned statutory exceptions to the transfer of risk, another very important implied seller's obligation created by the courts of law in the case *Mash & Murrel* translates into a further exception.

In *Mash & Murrel*, the dispute arose from a sale by the defendant vegetable importers to the plaintiff vegetable dealers of 50 tons of Cyprus potatoes, c.&f. Liverpool. The potatoes were found to be rotten upon arrival at the port of destination. The buyers alleged that the sellers were in breach of implied warranty in c.i.f. and c.&f. contracts that goods should be fit to stand a normal voyage and should arrive sound and fit for sale for human consumption.

It was held by the court that the sellers were in breach of warranty to ship the goods in such a condition as to be capable of standing a normal voyage and to be of merchantable quality on arrival.[41]

In the words of Diplock J:

> On those findings of fact, a question of law, which has been hotly debated, arises. I have so far travelled through my legal life under the impression, shared by a number of other Judges who have sat in this Court, that when goods are sold under a contract such as a c.i.f. contract, or f.o.b. contract, which involves transit before use, there is an implied warranty not merely that they shall be merchantable at the time they are put on the vessel, but that they shall be in such a state that they can endure the normal journey and be in a merchantable condition upon arrival.
>
> [. . .] The implied term which is based upon a passage in the judgment of Mr. Justice McCardie in *Evanghelinos v Leslie & Anderson* (1920) 4 Ll.L.Rep. 17. The passage is a very short one. Mr. Justice McCardie was dealing with a special case stated by Mr. Chance, of Messrs. Coward, Chance & Co., the well-known solicitors, and I need do no more than read what he says on p. 18. He says:
>
> [. . .] There may be a point as to the obligations of the sellers [This was a c.i.f. contract]. If there is, that point of law has been correctly stated by Mr. Chance among his findings of fact, where he says that the sellers were under an obligation to ship the goods in such a condition as would enable the goods to arrive at their destination on a normal voyage, and under normal conditions, in merchantable condition.
>
> [. . .] It follows, therefore, applying that view of the law to the present case, that, these goods being bought c.&f. Liverpool, the warranty as to merchantability was a warranty that they should remain merchantable for a reasonable time, the time reasonable in all the circumstances, which means a time for the normal transit to the destination, Liverpool, and for disposal after. That warranty was, in my view, broken.[42]

40 *Mash & Murrell v Joseph I Emanuel* [1961] 1 Lloyd's Rep. 46.

41 The judgment was reversed by the Court of Appeal but with no impact on the rule established re the implied obligation of a c.i.f. seller to ship goods in a condition capable of withstanding transit.

42 *Mash & Murrell v Joseph I Emanuel* [1961] 1 Lloyd's Rep. 46, 50, 53.

The judgment in *Mash & Murrel* translates into an exception to the rule whereby the transfer of risk is shifted from the seller onto the last buyer "on or as from shipment". Indeed, if the seller does not ship goods capable of withstanding transit on board the designated vessel, he shall bear the risk for the goods whilst in transit.

The *Mash & Murrel*'s exception was the object of scrutiny in the relatively recent case *The Mercini Lady*.[43] In this case, the defendant sellers sold to the claimant buyers 38,500 million tonnes of gasoil to be shipped on board the vessel *Mercini Lady* f.o.b. Antwerp. Clause 4 of the contract set out various specifications that the gasoil had to meet at the time of shipment, including as to total sediment.

The oil discharged at the port of destination was not of the same specification as that certified on shipment, and it was claimed by the buyers that it was, thus, not "capable of remaining" of satisfactory quality.

In discussing the *Mash & Murrel*'s rule, Diplock LJ stated that:

> In *Mash & Murrell Ltd v Joseph I Emmanuel Ltd* [1961] 1 WLR 862 Diplock J held that in a cif or c&f contract for the international sale of perishable goods, such statutory conditions required the goods "to be capable of standing a normal voyage to Liverpool and to be of merchantable quality at the time of arrival" (at page 872). So expressed, the warranty plainly attached at the time of shipment (there from Limassol): the warranty related to the goods' then capability (in the terms of the modern statute, durability).
>
> There has been some controversy as to whether Diplock J was speaking of a continuing warranty, and it is true that some formulations in his judgment are potentially ambiguous, as for instance at page 870: "these goods being bought c&f Liverpool, the warranty as to merchantability was a warranty that they should remain merchantable for a reasonable time, the time reasonable in the circumstances, which means a time for the normal transit to the destination, and for disposal after". Similarly, in *Ollett v Jordan* [1918] 2 KB 41, cited by Diplock J at page 868, Atkin J had said at page 47:
>
> > "the condition that the goods must be merchantable means that they must be in that condition when appropriated to the contract and that they will continue so for a reasonable time."
>
> In the present case, it is agreed by both parties that the implied condition of satisfactory quality applies only at the time of delivery, and is a fixed point or prospective warranty only, and not a continuing one, and that that is how Mash & Murrell is to be understood.[44]

In order to avoid complication, traders are best advised to indicate in the sale contract possible margins for deterioration of goods whilst in transit, whenever that is applicable or necessary in relation to the nature of the goods shipped on board.

7.4.2 Contractual exemptions to the transfer of risk

Two types of clauses are commonly used by buyers in order to attempt to limit the risk they bear whilst goods are in transit: outturn quantity clauses, and arrival date. Since these clauses deviate from the legal nature of contracts concluded on shipment terms, as we shall discover in the following, they have unsurprisingly been subject to restrictive interpretations by courts of law.

43 *The Mercini Lady* [2011] 1 Lloyd's Rep. 442.
44 *Ibid.*, at 445, 446.

Outturn quantity clauses

With these clauses, the price of the goods will be adjusted by reference to the quantity of goods actually discharged.[45]

This entails that the buyer will originally pay for the contractual quantity of the goods, but that price is subject to being discounted according to the quantity of the goods which are effectively delivered at the port of destination.

Such kinds of clauses translate into an exception to the transfer of risk, as the risk for the goods whilst in transit is in practice borne by the seller.

What happens in the case that a sales contract contains an outturn quantity clause and no goods are discharged, or the goods are damaged?

The contract itself can sometimes provide a solution to that question.[46] Conversely, if the contract is silent in that regard, it is clear on authority that the courts are likely to interpret outturn quantity clauses *contra preferentem*, and that the buyer is under the duty to pay the full price without any adjustments.[47]

In *Soon Hua Seng Co Ltd v Glencore Grain Ltd*,[48] the sellers entered into two rice contracts for the sale of Thai white broken rice in bulk to the buyers. Each contract was headed "C.&F. full outturn weight" and, except for the quantity shipped and price per tonne, were on similar terms. The goods were to be shipped c.&f. liner terms Rotterdam. En route the vessel met first with technical problems and storm damage and later ran aground on the Somalian coast on 6 June 1992, becoming a total loss.

As to the buyers' notice, the contracts had to be viewed as essentially c.&f. in their nature with the simple proviso that, if and when the goods did arrive and outturn, they would be weighed and the price would in that event be adjusted by reference to the outturn weight; if the goods covered by the shipping documents and invoice were lost in transit and did not arrive at all, the risk of loss remained on the buyer and no question of any adjustment of the payment due against the commercial invoice could arise.

In the words of Mace J:

> The only point left concerned the nature of the contract as "C.&F. full outturn weight" and the provision for the price to be based on "full outturn weight at port of destination". Buyers submitted that, since there was never any outturn, no price could ever have become due. No damages could therefore be payable for rejection of the shipping documents and/or non-acceptance of the goods, since the sellers had lost nothing.
>
> This submission depends upon a conclusion that in circumstances of loss as distinct from damage the contracts operate not as true c.&f. contracts but as delivered contracts. The buyers cited *Produce Brokers New Co. (1924) Ltd. v Wray Sanderson & Co. Ltd.* (1931) 39 Ll.L.Rep. 257, where, under a contract for sale at a price c.i.f Hull, buyers agreed to pay 98 per cent. of provisional invoice amount against shipping documents on arrival of the vessel in Hull, with the balance to be paid or refunded as soon as

45 See, for instance, Fosfa 54, lines 170–172.

46 See the contract of the Sugar Association of London CIFFO rule 117 whereby the buyer under those circumstances shall be invoiced for the full price for the shipped weight. See Debattista, C. *Bills of Lading in Export Trade*, above, p. 159. See also *Benjamin's Sale of Goods*, above, paras. 18.286 *et seq.*

47 See Sassoon, *CIF and FOB Contracts*, above, p. 20. See also *Schmitthoff's Export Trade* (9th Edition, Sweet & Maxwell, 1990), p. 54 in relation to "net landed" or "delivered" or "outturn" weight c.i.f. contracts generally.

48 *Soon Hua Seng Co Ltd v Glencore Grain Ltd* [1996] 1 Lloyd's Rep. 398.

> possible after delivered weight was ascertained. Part of the oil was spilled during discharge at Hull and the sellers were held to have no right to receive or retain payment in respect of that part, which was regarded as being at their risk. The contract in that case was "full of reference to delivery, the actual delivery at Hull"; it contained for example obligations regarding discharging, pumping, strikes and quality and condition, all relating to the position at Hull and pointing towards it being in reality a contract for delivery ex ship at Hull. The conclusion was that the risk remained on the buyers.
>
> Here the position appears to me different. The contract has the hallmarks of a true c.&f. contract. The focus of sellers' obligations is upon shipment to be followed by tender of appropriate shipping documents, including certificates of quality, condition and fumigation at time of shipment and a commercial invoice. By condition 4, the risk is expressly provided to pass from warehouse in Thailand, and the insurance policies are to be held at sellers' disposal "until documents are retired". This is a printed clause, but it is consistent with the typed provisions contemplating payment against documents "on arrival of the vessel at destination, but not later than forty-five days after Bills of lading".
>
> In context this means in my view full and unrestricted payment against a commercial invoice, to be based on the weight appearing in the shipping documents. Unless all these provisions are to be undermined, the contracts must be viewed as essentially c.&f. in their nature, with the simple proviso that, if and when the goods do arrive and outturn, they will be weighed and the price will in that event be adjusted by reference to the outturn weight. If the goods covered by the shipping documents and invoice are lost in transit and do not arrive at all, the risk of loss remains on the buyers and no question of any adjustment to the payment due against the commercial invoice can arise.[49]

The rationale for a *contra preferentem* interpretation of outturn quantity clauses by courts of law lies with the underlying difficulties of reconciling in legal teleological terms such provisions with the essence of contracts concluded on shipment terms; indeed, one should not forget that we are dealing with contracts concluded on shipment terms, rather than on delivery terms.

Consequently, if the parties to a contract concluded on shipment terms preferred to stipulate a contract on delivery terms, they would have done so. By virtue of the fact that the contract had instead been negotiated and concluded on shipment terms, the obligations of the seller are to be ascertained in legal terms in relation to what the seller effectively promised the buyer, i.e. to ship the goods.[50]

The introduction of clauses such as outturn quantity clauses or, as will readily be appreciated, arrival date clauses (i.e. terms which are not germane to the legal nature of contracts concluded on shipment terms), will entail that courts asked to interpret them will do so restrictively.

Here lies the rationale of *Soon Hua Seng Co Ltd v Glencore Grain Ltd*: in the case that the cargo is lost in transit, to extend the effect of an outturn quantity clause to such an extreme consequence as the buyer receiving all the money back from the seller would entail, in practice, a violation of the very nature of a contract which had originally been concluded on shipment terms; this would render the contract in effect a contract on delivery terms, leaving the seller to bear the risk whilst the goods are on transit.

49 *Ibid.*, at 404, 405.

50 See Debattista, C. *Bills of Lading in Export Trade*, above, p. 145. See also *Benjamin's Sale of Goods*, above, paras. 18.286 *et seq.*

It is clear on authority that the English courts will not be prepared to do this, and it is submitted that the court's approach is, in legal teleological terms, resoundingly fitting.

The same considerations are equally applicable to arrival date clauses.

Arrival date clauses

Another type of stipulation capable of violating the legal nature of contracts concluded on shipment terms are arrival date clauses.

Arrival date clauses stipulate the date by which goods must reach the port of destination, so as to leave the risk of delay with the seller. What is the effect of arrival date clauses? Do they change the nature of a contract concluded on shipment terms into one on destination terms?

The answer to this question was provided by the court in *The Wise*.[51] Here a c.&f. contract, Hobart and Melbourne for the sale of premium motor spirit provided for arrival of the vessel at the ports of destination, 15–30 March 1986. The cargo was not delivered by 30 March and the buyers felt entitled to reject it due to the breach of the arrival date clause.

It was held by the court that the natural construction of the delivery clause (i.e. clause 9) was that the nominated vessel would be expected to arrive within the period mentioned; it was not designed to procure the guarantee of delivery within the period stipulated; and the sellers' submission that on a true construction of the contract their obligation was to load a contractual cargo on board a nominated vessel within a time which in the ordinary course of events would enable the cargo to arrive at both discharge ports within the stipulated period, would be accepted.

As held by Leggatt J:

> It seems to me that since the parties have chosen to designate the contract as a c.&f. contract, I should approach the construction of it in the expectation that that is what it is. When I look at the delivery clause, I find that it is to be performed by a vessel to be nominated followed by the words "Arrival: March 15–30, 1986". It seems to me that the natural construction of the clause is that the nominated vessel shall be such as is expected to arrive within the period mentioned. It does not wear the air of a contract designed to procure the guarantee of delivery within the period stipulated. I decline so to construe it, especially since to do so would be inconsistent with a c.&f. contract in classic form. I accept the plaintiffs' submission that on a true construction of the contract their obligation was to load a contractual cargo on board a nominated vessel within a time which in the ordinary course of events would enable the cargo to arrive at both discharge ports within the stipulated period.[52]

The arrival date clause was therefore restrictively interpreted so as to mean that the vessel is simply expected to reach the port of destination by a certain date, rather than meaning that the seller actually guarantees the arrival by that date.

Indeed, the arrival date clause, a term alien to the nature of contracts concluded on shipment terms is likely to be interpreted by the courts of law as an obligation

51 *The Wise* [1989] 1 Lloyd's Rep. 96.

52 *Ibid.*, at 101.

on the seller to ship the goods with no delay so as to render possible the arrival of the vessel by the date specified in the sales contract.

Such interpretation is indeed germane to the nature of contracts concluded on shipment terms, and translates the arrival date term into an obligation on the seller to be ascertained at the moment of shipment rather than on arrival of the vessel.

Interpreting arrival date terms otherwise would entail a violation of the essence of a contract concluded on shipment terms, turning it into a contract concluded on delivery terms.[53]

7.5 The transfer of risk under the Incoterms 2010®

As we have established above, the Incoterms 2010® not only describe the seller's and buyer's obligations and specify the point at which the responsibilities for the transportation costs shift from the seller to the buyer, but also specify the point when the risk associated with transportation transfers from the seller to the buyer. Foreseeing the transfer of risk is a key aspect of preparing the contract. Through the use of the Incoterms®, the risk of loss and damage can be shifted in different ways between the supplier and the buyer.

When products that are "at the seller's risk" are damaged or lost, the seller may be prevented from completing his obligation to deliver according to the terms of the sales contract. In this situation, the buyer will not have to pay the purchase price and may appeal to legal remedies available to recover any losses incurred because of the default.

On the contrary, when damage or destruction occurs to products "at the buyer's risk", the buyer will have to bear the loss. The buyer must still fulfill his obligations to pay the seller. It will be up to the buyer to claim for damages with insurance companies or transport operators, as appropriate. Such claims may involve both contracts for sale and carriage as well as mandatory international legal conventions.

More specifically, the Incoterms® deal with the transfer of risk differently in relation to different terms as follows:[54]

F.o.b. terms: as established in the above, "Free On Board" means that the seller delivers when the goods have been loaded on board of the ship[55] at

53 The same happened in *"The Ballenita"* [1992] 2 Lloyd's Rep. 455. Here, the buyers agreed to purchase from the sellers 25,000–30,000 tonnes EEC qualified gasoil meeting Italian winter guaranteed specifications, c.i.f. Genoa. The contract provided, inter alia, for an arrival date clause, which was interpreted restrictively by the court. See also *Cargill U.K. Ltd. v Continental U.K. Ltd.* (C.A.) [1989] 2 Lloyd's Rep. 290; *Gill & Duffus S.A. v Societe Pour L'Exportation des Sucres S.A.* (C.A.) [1986] 1 Lloyd's Rep. 323; *Kawasaki Kisen Kabushiki Kaisya v Belships Co. Ltd.* (1939) 63 Ll L Rep 175; (1939) 55 T.L.R. 520; *Moel Tryvan Ship Co. v Andrew Weir & Co.* [1910] 2 KB 844; *Vitol S.A. v Phibro Energy A.G. (The Mathraki)* [1990] 2 Lloyd's Rep. 84.

54 Note that the transfer of risk under the Incoterms 2010® is mainly governed by sections A5 and B5, which equate the time of passing of risk to the time of delivery. Sections A4 and B4 define the moment of delivery in each and regulate the time of handing over of the goods by the seller and the taking over by the buyer. However, the passing of risk before delivery is the default position also according to the Incoterms 2010® when it comes to the terms of customary use for contracts concluded on shipment terms. The below definitions are extracts from the ICC website, iccwab.org.

55 Previous versions of the Incoterms® used to link the transfer of risk to the moment goods passed the "ship's rail", i.e. some imaginary line that extends perpendicularly from the ship's rail into the

the named port of shipment. This means that the buyer has to bear all cost and risk of loss of or damage to the goods from that point.

F.a.s. terms: "Free Alongside Ship" means that the seller delivers when the goods are placed alongside the vessel at the named port of shipment. This means that the buyer has to bear all the cost and risk of damage to the goods from that moment.

C.f.r. terms: "Cost and Freight" means that the seller delivers when the goods pass the ship's rail in the port of shipment. The seller must pay the costs and freight necessary to bring the goods to the named port of destination, but the risk of loss or damage to the goods as well as any additional costs due to events occurring after the time of delivery are transferred from the seller to the buyer.

C.i.f. terms: "Cost, Insurance, and Freight" means that the seller delivers when the goods are loaded on the vessel in the port of shipment. The seller must pay the cost and freight necessary to bring the goods to the named port of destination but the risk of loss or damage to the goods, as well as any additional costs due to events arising after the time of delivery, are transferred from the seller to the buyer.

The Incoterms® cover any physical loss or damage to the goods that is accidental and for which none of the parties is responsible. The terms cover only the "price risk"[56] in effect, determining whether the buyer is liable to pay the price or whether the seller is entitled to claim the price in case of accidental loss or damage to the goods.

It follows that the Incoterms® do not regulate the risk of non-performance or of breach of contract.[57]

---

stratosphere. The Incoterms 2010® abolished the concept of the "ship's rail", and endorsed a different notion, that is, the risk passing when the goods are on board the vessel. This means the whole consignment has been loaded. Should half a consignment be loaded and the ship sinks, then complete loading presumably won't have occurred and the risk won't have transferred to the buyer. This has caused buyers to want to insist on shipped onboard notations on maritime transport documents. Where receipts for shipment bills are issued, this is prudent in any case; nevertheless, when shipped onboard bills are issued, there should be no need for the additional notation.

56 See Valioti, Z., Passing of Risk in International Sale Contracts: A Comparative Examination of the Rules on Risk under the United Nations Convention on Contracts for the International Sale of Goods (Vienna 1980) and INCOTERMS 2000, 2 *NJCL* 7, (2004) available at http://www.njcl.fi/2_2004/article3.pdf (last visited on 24 April 2007). The notion of risk may encompass the "insurance risk", "commercial risk" and "political risk" as well.

57 As we shall discover in the following, in the case that the Vienna Convention applies, this raises some uncertainty in transactions regarding the international sale of goods, since the transfer of the risk of non-performance is actually linked with delivery of the goods as well and with the implication that in appropriate instances, the seller will have to provide substitute goods.

Thus, if the Vienna Convention applies to the sale contract, this may lead to a scenario whereby the seller finds his obligations to care, to repair and eventually to re-deliver, all reborn, with no clear time limit and under vague standards.

CHAPTER 8

The transfer of property in contracts concluded on shipment terms

8.1 Introduction

A contract of sale of goods is defined by SOGA 1979 as a contract by which the seller transfers or agrees to transfer the property in goods to the buyer for a money consideration, called the price.[1]

The transfer of property in international trade is of the utmost importance in case the seller or the buyer becomes insolvent after the contract on shipment terms is concluded.

In such circumstances, it is indeed crucial to establish who has property in the goods, as this will determine the possibility for actions aimed at clawing back the goods for the benefit of creditors.[2]

The general rule for the transfer of property is enshrined in SOGA 1979, section 16, which provides that:

> **SOGA 1979, section 16**
>
> Subject to section 20A below where there is a contract for the sale of unascertained goods no property in the goods is transferred to the buyer unless and until the goods are ascertained.[3]

Section 16 appears to subject the transfer of property to the ascertainment of goods. If goods need to be ascertained (i.e. separated from a bulk) for the property to pass, this would leave the question of the transfer of property unresolved whenever goods are shipped in bulk.

We shall discover in the following how this question was solved by the introduction of section 20A. For the moment, our attention will focus on ascertained goods.

---

1 SOGA, section 2(1).

2 See R. Goode, *Proprietary Rights and Insolvency in Sale Transactions*, Sweet & Maxwell, 2009, pp. 3, 16. See also, *Benjamin's Sale of Goods*, above, para. 5.005. Under those circumstances, the liquidator or curator in charge of the winding up procedure will endeavour to recapture transactions made by the insolvent entity which proceedings they are in charge of. They shall be able to do so only insofar as the property has not yet passed, as transactions which have already transferred the property of the goods are beyond recuperation.

3 See SOGA 1979, section 16.

8.2 The transfer of property of ascertained goods

When it comes to ascertained goods, according to section 18, the property is transferred to the buyer when goods are "unconditionally appropriated to the contract".[4] When contracts are concluded on shipment terms, this happens at the moment of shipment as per SOGA, section 18, rule 5, which states the following:

SOGA, section 18, rule 5

(1) Where there is a contract for the sale of unascertained or future goods by description, and goods of that description and in a deliverable state are unconditionally appropriated to the contract, either by the seller with the assent of the buyer or by the buyer with the assent of the seller, the property in the goods then passes to the buyer; and the assent may be express or implied, and may be given either before or after the appropriation is made.

(2) Where, in pursuance of the contract, the seller delivers the goods to the buyer or to a carrier or other bailee or custodier (whether named by the buyer or not) for the purpose of transmission to the buyer, and does not reserve the right of disposal, he is to be taken to have unconditionally appropriated the goods to the contract.

(3) Where there is a contract for the sale of a specified quantity of unascertained goods in a deliverable state forming part of a bulk which is identified either in the contract or by subsequent agreement between the parties and the bulk is reduced to (or to less than) that quantity, then, if the buyer under that contract is the only buyer to whom goods are then due out of the bulk –

(a) the remaining goods are to be taken as appropriated to that contract at the time when the bulk is so reduced; and

(b) the property in those goods then passes to that buyer.[5]

Thus, whenever goods are ascertained, according to section 18, rule 5(2), the property will pass from seller to buyer at the moment of shipment unless it is otherwise specified in the sales contract.[6]

8.3 The transfer of property of unascertained goods

Section 20A was introduced into SOGA 1979 in 1995 in order to deal with the concept of a shared ownership in commingled goods in an identified bulk. It states as follows:

Section 20A SOGA 1979

(1) This section applies to a contract for the sale of a specified quantity of unascertained goods if the following conditions are met:

(a) the goods or some of them form part of a bulk which is identified either in the contract or by subsequent agreement between the parties; and

(b) the buyer has paid the price for some or all of the goods which are the subject of the contract and which form part of the bulk.

4 See SOGA 1979, section 18(1).
5 See SOGA 1979, section 18 rule 5(2).
6 For expressed and implied reservations of title see chapter 8.

(2) Where this section applies, then (unless the parties agree otherwise), as soon as the conditions specified in paragraphs (a) and (b) of subsection (1) above are met or at such later time as the parties may agree –
   (a) property in an undivided share in the bulk is transferred to the buyer, and
   (b) the buyer becomes an owner in common of the bulk.

(3) Subject to subsection (4) below, for the purposes of this section, the undivided share of a buyer in a bulk at any time shall be such share as the quantity of goods paid for and due to the buyer out of the bulk bears to the quantity of goods in the bulk at that time.

(4) Where the aggregate of the undivided shares of buyers in a bulk determined under subsection (3) above would at any time exceed the whole of the bulk at that time, the undivided share in the bulk of each buyer shall be reduced proportionately so that the aggregate of the undivided shares is equal to the whole bulk.

(5) Where a buyer has paid the price for only some of the goods due to him out of a bulk, any delivery to the buyer out of the bulk shall, for the purposes of this section, be ascribed in the first place to the goods in respect of which payment has been made.

(6) For the purposes of this section payment of part of the price for any goods shall be treated as payment for a corresponding part of the goods.[7]

Thus, two conditions need to be satisfied in order for the property of unascertained goods to pass from the seller to the buyer: a) the bulk has been identified and b) the price has been paid.

The problem with section 20A lies in the way in which goods forming part of a bulk need to be identified, namely, "in the contract or by subsequent agreement". Unfortunately, this would appear not to cover a classic scenario where a c.i.f. seller notifies the buyer that goods have been shipped on a nominated vessel. This declaration of shipment would in fact identify the goods in the contract, or by a subsequent agreement if it happens after the contract has been concluded, and it is the outcome of a unilateral action by the seller.[8]

Another section of SOGA of utmost importance for unascertained goods is section 20B:

Section 20B SOGA 1979

A person who has become an owner in common of a bulk by virtue of section 20A above shall be deemed to have consented to:

(a) any delivery of goods out of the bulk to any other owner in common of the bulk, being goods which are due to him under his contract;

(b) any dealing with or removal, delivery or disposal of goods in the bulk by any other person who is an owner in common of the bulk in so far as the goods fall within that co-owner's undivided share in the bulk at the time of the dealing, removal, delivery or disposal.[9]

---

7 See SOGA 1979, section 20A.

8 This point has been smartly made by Debattista, C. *Bills of Lading in Export Trade*, above, p. 145. See also *Benjamin's Sale of Goods*, above, paras. 18.286 *et seq.*

9 SOGA 1979, section 20B.

By legally presuming the consent of each of the co-proprietors of a cargo shipped in bulk to discharge or disposal operations, section 20B, thus, allows the normal and necessary operations of discharge of goods shipped in bulk avoiding possible legal complications arising from co-ownership issues.

8.4 Contractual derogations to the transfer of property

Sections 16 and 20A of SOGA 1979 are subject to express or implied reservations of title, which shall be considered in the following.

Express reservations of title

The seller may retain the property of the goods by virtue of explicit contractual stipulations which are devised to specify the conditions which must be fulfilled in order for the property to pass.

This is possible according to section 19 of SOGA 1979, according to which:

Section 19 SOGA 1979

(1) Where there is a contract for the sale of specific goods or where goods are subsequently appropriated to the contract, the seller may, by the terms of the contract or appropriation, reserve the right of disposal of the goods until certain conditions are fulfilled; and in such a case, notwithstanding the delivery of the goods to the buyer, or to a carrier or other bailee or custodier for the purpose of transmission to the buyer, the property in the goods does not pass to the buyer until the conditions imposed by the seller are fulfilled.

(2) Where goods are shipped, and by the bill of lading the goods are deliverable to the order of the seller or his agent, the seller is prima facie to be taken to reserve the right of disposal.

(3) Where the seller of goods draws on the buyer for the price, and transmits the bill of exchange and bill of lading to the buyer together to secure acceptance or payment of the bill of exchange, the buyer is bound to return the bill of lading if he does not honour the bill of exchange, and if he wrongfully retains the bill of lading the property in the goods does not pass to him.

An example of such clauses can be found in the *Antares III*,[10] where a clause enshrined in the sales contract provided for the property to pass to the buyer at the moment of payment.

A further example of expressed reservation of title clauses characterised the case of *Armour v Thyssen*.[11] Here, contracts for the sale of steel strip were subject to an expressed reservation of title whereby the title of the goods was to be retained by the sellers until payment was made. More specifically, the clause stated as follows:

> All goods delivered by us remain our property (goods remaining in our ownership) until all debts owed to us including any balances existing at relevant times – due to us on any legal grounds – are settled. This also holds good if payments are made for the purpose of settlement of specially designated claims. Debts owed to companies, being members of our combine, are deemed to be such debts.[12]

10 *Antares III* [1987] 1 Lloyd's Rep. 424.

11 *Armour v Thyssen Edelstahlwerke A.G.* [1991] 1 Lloyd's Rep. 95.

12 *Ibid.*, at 95.

A dispute arose as to whether 67,423 kilograms of steel strip remained the property of the sellers by reason of the aforementioned clause reserving title, or whether it formed part of the assets of the buyer available to its preferred or other creditors.

It was held by the court that, by entering into the contract of sale, Carron agreed that they should receive possession of the goods on delivery but should not acquire the property until all debts due to the appellants had been paid, and thus agreed that the appellants would in effect have security over the goods after they came into Carron's possession.

Indeed, the parties to the contract of sale clearly expressed their intention that the property in the steel strip should pass to Carron only when all debts due by them to the appellants had been paid; there were no grounds for not giving effect to that intention.[13]

The appellants, by the terms of the contract of sale, had in effect reserved the right of disposal of the steel strip until fulfilment of the condition that all debts due to them by Carron had been paid; by virtue of section 19(1) of SOGA 1979 the effect was that the property in the goods did not pass to Carron until that condition had been fulfilled; clause I.3.(1) could not be regarded as amounting to the creation by the buyer of a right of security in favour of the seller and, although it did in a sense give the seller security for the unpaid debts of the buyer, it did so by way of a legitimate retention of title.

As stated by Keith LJ:

> In the present case the appellants, the owners of the steel strip, transferred possession of it to Carron under what was unquestionably a contract of sale. There was no question of the appellants creating a right of security. They were not in the position of debtors seeking to give a right of security to a creditor. They were themselves creditors of Carron for the price of the steel strip and it may be for other debts also. Carron obtained possession of the steel strip upon delivery, subject to a condition that it should not obtain the property until it had paid all debts due to the appellants. Can it be said that Carron somehow attempted to create a security over the goods in favour of the appellants? In order that it might do so it would require to have both the ownership and the possession, actual or constructive, of the goods. The essence of a right in security is that the debtor retains at least what Gloag & Irvine call the ultimate right to the goods. Can it be said that Carron obtained anything which gave it the capacity to retain an ultimate right to the goods? That could be so only if the contract of sale gave it the property in the goods, but the contract of sale said that the property in the goods was not to pass until all debts due to the appellants had been paid. We are here very far removed from the situation where a party in possession of corporeal moveables is seeking to create a subordinate right in favour of a creditor while retaining the ultimate right to himself. It is true that by entering into the contract of sale Carron agreed that it should receive possession of the goods on delivery but should not acquire the property until all debts due to the appellants had been paid, and thus agreed that the appellants would in effect have security over the goods after they had come into Carron's possession.
>
> [. . .] Further, s. 19(1) of the same Act (SOGA 1979) provides: "Where there is a contract for the sale of specific goods or where the goods are subsequently appropriated to the contract, the seller may, by the terms of the contract or appropriation, reserve the right of disposal of the goods until certain conditions are fulfilled; and in such a

13 See p. 98, col. 2; p. 100, col. 1.

> case, notwithstanding the delivery of the goods to the buyer, or to a carrier or other bailee or custodier for the purpose of transmission to the buyer, the property in the goods does not pass to the buyer until the conditions imposed by the seller are fulfilled".
>
> Here the appellants, by the terms of the contract of sale, have in effect reserved the right of disposal of the steel strip until fulfilment of the condition that all debts due to them by Carron have been paid. By virtue of this enactment, that has the effect that the property in the goods did not pass to Carron until that condition had been fulfilled. Counsel for Carron argued that the word "conditions" in s. 19(1) must be read as excluding any condition which has the effect of creating a right of security over the goods. I am, however, unable to regard a provision reserving title to the seller until payment of all debts due to him by the buyer as amounting to the creation by the buyer of a right of security in favour of the seller. Such a provision does in a sense give the seller security for the unpaid debts of the buyer. But it does so by way of a legitimate retention of title, not by virtue of any right over his own property conferred by the buyer.
>
> In all cases where a right of security is conferred the debtor retains an ultimate right over the subject matter in question. The creditor, having realised out of that subject matter a sufficient sum to meet the debt, is obliged to account to the debtor for any surplus. Where, however, the seller of goods retains title until some condition has been satisfied, and on failure of such satisfaction repossesses them, then he is not obliged to account to the buyer for any part of the value of the goods. Where the condition is to the effect that the price of the goods shall have been paid and it has not been paid, then in the situation where the market price of the goods has risen, so that they are worth more than the contract price, the extra value belongs to the unpaid seller. That is clearly the position where the condition relates to payment of the price of the actual goods, and goes to show that the retention of title provision is not one creating a right of security forming an exception to the general rule requiring possession by the creditor. The same is true, in my opinion, where the provision covers not only the price of the very goods which are the subject of the particular contract of sale, but also debts due to the seller under other contracts.[14]

Contractual provisions expressly reserving the title until payment is made are known as "*Romalpa*" clauses. In *Aluminium Industrie Vaassen B.V. v Romalpa Aluminium Ltd*,[15] a sale of aluminium foil was accompanied by the stipulation that the general selling terms and conditions applied to the transactions between the plaintiffs and the defendants and in particular clause 13 which stated:

> The ownership of the material to be delivered by Aluminium Industrie Vaassen (A.I.V.) [the plaintiffs] will only be transferred to purchaser when he has met all that is owing to A.I.V. no matter on what grounds. Until the date of payment, purchaser, if A.I.V. so desires, is required to store this material in such a way that it is clearly the property of A.I.V.[16]

Nevertheless, the buyers were entitled to sell these objects to a third party within the framework of the normal carrying on of business and to deliver them on condition that – if A.I.V. so requires – the purchaser, as long as he has not fully

---

14 *Ibid.*, at 98, 99, 100.

15 *Aluminium Industrie Vaassen B.V. v Romalpa Aluminium Ltd* [1976] 1 Lloyd's Rep. 443. See Debattista, C. *Bills of Lading in Export Trade*, above, p. 175. See also *Benjamin's Sale of Goods*, above, paras. 19.200 *et seq.*

16 *Ibid.*, at 443.

discharged his debt to A.I.V., shall hand over to A.I.V. the claims he has against his buyer emanating from this transaction.

Mocatta J held that the retention of title clause was effective; *Aluminium Industrie Vaasen* was still the owner of the aluminium foil, and could trace the price due to them into the proceeds of sale of the finished goods, ahead of *Romalpa*'s unsecured and secured creditors.

In his words:

> The preservation of ownership clause contains unusual and fairly elaborate provisions departing substantially from the debtor/creditor relationship and shows, in my view, the intention to create a fiduciary relationship to which the principle stated in In re Hallett's Estate, [2] applies. A further point made by Mr Pickering was that if the plaintiffs were to succeed in their tracing claim this would, in effect, be a method available against a liquidator to a creditor of avoiding the provisions establishing the need to register charges on book debts: see section 95(1)(2)(e) of the Companies Act 1948 [now Companies Act 2006, section 860(7)(g)]. He used this only as an argument against the effect of clause 13 contended for by Mr Lincoln. As to this, I think Mr Lincoln's answer was well founded, namely, that if property in the foil never passed to the defendants with the result that the proceeds of sub-sales belonged in equity to the plaintiffs, section 95(1) [now Companies Act 2006, section 860] had no application.[17]

The scope of retention of title clauses was described by Roskill LJ in *Aluminium Industrie Vaassen B.V. v Romalpa Aluminium Ltd* as:

> The respondents as sellers were to retain the property in the goods until all, and I underline "all", that was owing to them had been paid.
>
> [. . .] It is obvious, to my mind, that the business purpose of the whole of this clause, read in its context in these general conditions, was to secure the respondents, so far as possible, against the risks of non-payment after they had parted with possession of the goods delivered, whether or not those goods retained their identity after delivery.[18]

Security for sellers vis-à-vis non-payment by buyers lies at the core of the "*Romalpa*" clauses, allowing the seller to repossess the goods in the case that the buyer subsequently goes into bankruptcy.

'*Romalpa*' clauses are often seen as a "natural extension of the credit economy; where suppliers are expected to sell goods on credit, there is a reasonable expectation that if they are not paid they should be able to repossess the goods. Nonetheless, in a number of jurisdictions, insolvency regimes or credit arrangement regimes prevent title retention clauses from being enforced where doing so would upset administration of the regime".[19]

Although title retention clauses are conceptually very simple, they have become increasingly widely drafted, which has resulted in the courts in a number of countries striking down the clauses, or recharacterising them as the grant of a "security interest".[20] It has consequentially been noted that "the practical outcome

---

17 *Ibid.*, at 454.

18 *Ibid.*, at 455.

19 Rolf B. Johnson (1994). A Uniform Solution to Common Law Confusion: Retention of Title under English and U.S. Law. *Berkeley Journal of International Law* 12 (1): 99–129.

20 Retention of title clauses are mandated in the EU by Article 9 of the Late Payments Directive (Directive 2011/7/EU of 16 February 2011 on combating late payment in commercial transactions

of a series of later cases has put it beyond doubt that "extended" title reservation clauses will not work."[21]

Although in line with legal principle under section 19 of SOGA 1979 (which expanded upon the aforementioned judgment of the Court of Appeal in *Aluminium Industrie Vaassen BV v Romalpa Aluminium Ltd*), "*Romalpa*" clauses are not always recognised by the English courts.[22]

In practice, "*Romalpa*" clauses can assume a myriad of different forms or variety, and their complexity has been acknowledged in *Hendy Lennox Ltd v Grahame Puttik*

(recast), replacing Article 4 of Directive 2000/35/EC of 29 June 2000 on combating late payment in commercial transactions), and sellers' ROT rights are recognised by Article 7 of the Insolvency Regulation (Regulation (EU) No 1346/2000 of 29 May 2000 on insolvency proceedings).

Especially prevalent in Germany (see William Davies (2006) Romalpa thirty years on – still an enigma? *Hertfordshire Law Journal* (University of Hertfordshire) 4 (2): 2–23), these clauses are permitted in the UK by section 19 of the SOGA 1979, which expanded upon the 1976 judgment of the Court of Appeal of England and Wales in *Aluminium Industrie Vaassen BV v Romalpa Aluminium Ltd.* In contrast to English law (see M.G. Bridge, R.A. Macdonald, R.L. Simmonds, and C. Walsh (1999) Formalism, Functionalism, and Understanding the Law of Secured Transactions, *McGill Law Journal* 44 (2): 567–664), the common law jurisdictions in Australia, Canada, New Zealand, and the US have instituted the concept of "security interest", under which ROT clauses may need to be registered in order to have effect. The US states have adopted Article 9 of the UCC, which limits the clause's effectiveness (see William Davies (2006) Romalpa thirty years on – still an enigma?, above, pp. 15–18). Similar to the US, the common law provinces in Canada have adopted their Personal Property Security Acts, according to which, there is no "presumption of hypothec", and therefore an ROT clause is not considered to be a security interest (Article 1497 of the Civil Code of Quebec provides that "An obligation is conditional where it is made to depend upon a future and uncertain event", which gives legal authority to such clauses; Australia and New Zealand have also adopted their own versions of the Personal Property Security Act).

21 See M.G. Bridge, R.A. Macdonald, R.L. Simmonds, and C. Walsh (1999) Formalism, Functionalism, and Understanding the Law of Secured Transactions, above, p.639. Several particular problems have been identified: if, for example, the clause reserves only part of the title to the seller (instead of reserving title to the whole thing) then in many jurisdictions this is recharacterised as an equitable charge, and is often void if certain registration requirements are not complied with (for instance, in *Re Bond Worth Ltd* [1980] Ch 228 such a clause was held to be void as it had not been registered within 21 days as required by section 395 of the 1985 Companies Act). Problems can also arise where the goods sold are mixed with other goods of a similar nature, so that they are no longer identifiable, e.g. a quantity of oil, or grain (in most common law jurisdictions, so long as the clause prohibited mixing in this manner, the rule is that the buyer and the seller jointly own the whole mixture as tenants in common, see *Indian Oil v Greenstone Shipping* [1987] 3 WLR 869). Many jurisdictions allow the buyer to resell the goods before title has passed to him (often this is the only way that he can pay the seller). In many jurisdictions such an onward sale passes good title to the subsequent purchaser, and the original seller loses title despite the clause (for instance, in England this is the effect of section 25(1) of the Sale of Goods Act 1979, and section 2(1) of the Factors Act 1889). Where the seller tries to have a clause which provides that, if the buyer resells the goods, then the proceeds of sale of the goods shall be held on trust for the seller, this can be recharacterised as a registrable charge, which may also be void for non-registration (see *E Pfeiffer v Arbuthnot Factors* [1988] 1 WLR 150, although a differently worded clause was distinguished and upheld in *Compaq Computer v Abercorn* [1991] BCC 484).

Another frequently litigated problem occurs where the goods which are subject to the clause are then either improved (e.g. raw thread is worked into cloth) or mixed with other raw materials to form a new product (e.g. silica is used to make glass). (Generally speaking, in England, the law has been consistently applied that if the retention of title clause purports to apply to the new substance which has been made, then it takes effect as a charge and would be void if not registered. See, for example, *Re Peachdart* [1984] Ch 131.)

In some countries, where a clause purports to retain title until not only the purchase price, but also any other debts of the buyer to the seller are paid in full, such clauses have been struck down for non-compliance with security registration requirements in those jurisdictions.

22 See Debattista, C. *Bills of Lading in Export Trade*, above, p. 155. See also *Benjamin's Sale of Goods*, above, p. 115, paras. 18.739 *et seq.*

Ltd,[23] where Staughton J stated that: "First, this area of the law is presently a maze if not a minefield, and one had to proceed with caution for every step of the way."[24]

On a general level, it has been noted that the recognition of "*Romalpa*" clauses by the English courts depends largely on a careful judicial assessment of the extent of the reservation of title to be counterbalanced vis-à-vis the rights and interests of third parties.[25]

Indeed, Debattista points out that "*Romalpa*" clauses can be effective only insofar as the goods subject to reservation of title can be ascertained as the seller's goods, and are not mixed together with other third parties' goods of the same specification.[26]

Further, where the clause allows the reservation of title to be overextended onto the proceeds for the resale of the original goods, such a clause will retain its validity only insofar as the proceeds can be identifiable and ascertainable from other goods belonging to the buyer.[27]

Finally, the English courts have been reluctant to recognise "*Romalpa*" clauses that attempt to reserve title to the products of the raw materials and their proceeds, construing such clauses as floating charges which require registration under the Companies Act 2006.[28]

Implied reservations of title

Property of the goods can be retained by the seller even in the absence of specifically expressed contractual clauses through implied reservations of title.

Within the context of contracts concluded on shipment terms, implied reservations of title have been identified in relation to the form and utilisation of bills of lading.

Bills of lading made to the seller's order

Bills of lading are usually drawn to the buyer's order whose name is usually indicated in the consignee box of the bill.

On the contrary, bills of lading made to the seller's order have been considered by courts as *prima facie* evidence of an implied seller's reservation of title of the goods until payment was made by the buyer.

In *Jenkyns v Brown*,[29] Klingender & Co, a trader, purchased corn at New Orleans as an agent of a London merchant. The purchase was made with Klingender's money, and Klingender drew for the amount upon its principal, the bill being, in its body, expressed to be on account of the corn.

Klingender sold the bill to Brown, a third company, at New Orleans, and at the same time handed to Brown a bill of lading of the corn, which had been drawn for

23 *Hendy Lennox Ltd v Grahame Puttik Ltd* [1984] 2 Lloyd's Rep. 422.
24 *Ibid.*, at 428.
25 See C. Debattista, *Bills of Lading in Export Trade*, Tottel, 2008, p.129.
26 *Ibid.*, and see *Aluminium Industrie Vaassen B.V. v Romalpa Aluminium Ltd*, above, 445.
27 *Ibid.*
28 *Ibid.* See Companies Act 2006, sections 860 and 874. See also *Re Peachdart Ltd* [1984] Ch 131; *Borden (UK) Ltd v Scottish Timber Products Ltd* [1981] Ch 25; *Re Bond Worth Ltd* [1979] 3 All ER 919; *Compac Computer v Abercon Group* [1993] BCLC 602; *Modelboard Ltd v Outer Box Ltd* [1993] BCLC 623.
29 *Jenkyns v Brown* (1849) 14 QB 496.

delivery to Klingender's order and endorsed by Klingender. Klingender at the same time empowered Brown to sell the corn if the bill of exchange should not be paid.

The court held that the inference from these facts was that Klingender did not transfer the property in the corn to the plaintiff, subject to a lien, but only transferred the property to the plaintiff on the condition of his paying the bill of exchange and, in the meantime, the corn was the property of the defendant.

In the words of Coleridge J:

> The corn having arrived in England, and the bills of exchange and lading having been forwarded to England by defendant, the bill of exchange was accepted by plaintiff. On its maturity, he offered to take it up: but it was not produced, owing to a mistake of defendant's agent in England as to its place of deposit. On a later day the bill of exchange was presented to plaintiff, who did not pay it: Held defendant under these circumstances, was entitled to retain the corn.
>
> Although Klingender & Co. bought the corn in question abroad as agents for the plaintiff, yet, as they paid for it with their own money, it became their property; and, after the shipment, the cargo continued their property, as there is no evidence of an intention that it should pass, and as the taking of a bill of lading deliverable to their own order is nearly conclusive evidence that it did not pass. By delivering this bill of lading, indorsed to the defendants, as a security for the payment of the bills of exchange drawn on the plaintiff for the value of the cargo, and giving power to sell in case of failure of payment (the bills of exchange having been purchased by the defendant), they passed to the defendant for value a special property in the cargo; and by afterwards sending the invoice with the bills of exchange and letters of advice to the plaintiff they passed to him the general property in the cargo, subject to this special property. Under this arrangement, the plaintiff's right of possession would not arise till the bills should be paid.[30]

Similarly, in *The Parchim*,[31] the Prize Court determined that the owner of goods shipped under a contract of sale and seized as prize, should be identified in accordance with the municipal law of England as codified in the SOGA 1893, that law being based upon mercantile usages common in their general operation to all nations. If the parties contracted with reference to a municipal law which proved to differ from the English law, that fact was considered to be material in considering the intention of the parties as to the passing of the property.

Although property and not risk is the test, the incidence of the risk as between buyer and seller is a very strong indication as to which of them owns the property.

Considering the circumstances which rebut the presumption arising under the SOGA 1893, section 19(2), the court stated that a seller of goods shipped who takes bills of lading in his own name intends to reserve the right of disposal. As stated by Lord Parker of Weddington:

> The English cases, however, on which the Sale of Goods Act was founded seem to show that the appropriation would not be such as to pass the property if it appears or can be inferred that there was no actual intention to pass it. If the seller takes the bill of lading to his own order and parts with it to a third person, not the buyer, and that third person, by possession of the bill of lading, gets the goods, the buyer is held not to

30 *Ibid.*, at 502, 503. See also *Bailey (T.D.), Son & Co. v Ross T. Smyth & Co., Ltd.* (1940) 67 Ll L Rep. 147.

31 *The Parchim* [1918] AC 157.

> have the property so as to enable him to recover from the third party, notwithstanding that the act of the seller was a clear breach of the contract.
>
> [. . .] This seems to be because the seller's conduct is inconsistent with any intention to pass the property to the buyer by means of the contract followed by the appropriation. On the other hand, if the seller deals with the bill of lading only to secure the contract price, and not with the intention of withdrawing the goods from the contract, he does nothing inconsistent with an intention to pass the property, and therefore the property may pass either forthwith subject to the seller's lien or conditionally on performance by the buyer of his part of the contract. [. . .] The prima facie presumption in such a case appears to be that the property is to pass only on the performance by the buyer of his part of the contract and not forthwith subject to the seller's lien. Inasmuch, however, as the object to be attained, namely, securing the contract price, may be attained by the seller merely reserving a lien, the inference that the property is to pass on the performance of a condition only is necessarily somewhat weak, and may be rebutted by the other circumstances of the case.[32]

The presumption under section 19(2) SOGA 1979 and the possibility for the seller to retain title in an implicit manner applies also to f.o.b. contracts, despite doubts having been raised in the past by the doctrine.[33]

Indeed, in *Mitsui & Co Ltd v Flota Mercante Grancolombiana "The Ciudad de Pasto" and "The Ciudad the Neva"*,[34] doubts were raised concerning the effects of the fact that the bills of lading indicating the shipment of a cargo of prawns sold on f.o.b. terms had been made to the seller's order.

It was held by the Court of Appeal that since by the bills of lading the goods were deliverable to the order of the sellers, consequently the *prima facie* presumption was that they reserved the right of disposal and, unless that presumption was displaced, the result was that the property in the prawns did not pass to the buyers until the balance of the price i.e. the 20 per cent had been paid.

As stated by Purchas LJ:

> It is at this point of the learned Judge's judgment, like my Lord, Lord Justice Staughton, that regretfully I find myself unable to follow him in drawing that inference. I therefore direct my attention to see where the difference has arisen.
>
> . . . The relevant dispute before me centered upon whether it was right to conclude that title has passed to Colombia Fisheries at the time of shipment at Cartagena or only at some later, unidentified time. The clear inference is that Colombia Fisheries bought the goods on f.o.b. terms. Therefore unless there was a breach of the agreement, or some failure on the part of their sellers to perform their agreement, the title in the goods should have been passed to Colombia Fisheries at the time of shipment.

32 *Ibid.*, at 170, 171. See also *Wait v Baker* 2 Ex 1; *Gabarron v Kreeft* (1875) LR 10 Ex. 274; *Mirabita v Imperial Ottoman Bank* (1878) 3 Ex D 164; *Van Casteel v Booker* (1848) 2 Ex. 691; *Browne v Hare* (1858) 3 H&N 484; *Joyce v Swann* 17 CB (N.S.) 84.

33 It has been pointed out by Debattista that the doctrine has been in the past reluctant to accept the possibility of application of section 19(2) SOGA 1979 to f.o.b. contracts. Debattista points out that in the past *Carver's Carriage* (13th Edition, Stevens, 1982, para. 1620) raised doubts based on the fact that by virtue of an f.o.b. contract a seller promises to deliver the goods free on board, and consequently to transfer the property of the goods to the buyer at shipment, with no possibility of exceptions unless specified otherwise by the sales contract. Debattista emphasises that Carver's view was antagonised by *Benjamin's Sale of Goods* (above, para. 20.077); and Goode, *Commercial Law* (above, p. 935). See Debattista, *Bills of Lading in Export Trade*, above, p. 117 and footnote n. 56.

34 *Mitsui & Co Ltd v Flota Mercante Grancolombiana "The Ciudad de Pasto" and "The Ciudad the Neva"* [1988] 2 Lloyd's Rep. 208.

The inference which the learned Judge has drawn from the statements before him under the Civil Evidence Act that the goods were bought on f.o.b. terms has not been challenged on appeal. In citing that as one of the leading inferences upon which the learned Judge inferred that the property passed on shipment, it is difficult not to conclude that at this point in his judgment Homer must have nodded in overlooking the fact that in an f.o.b. contract it is still open to the seller to reserve to himself the right of disposal of the goods the subject matter of the contract. If it were otherwise it is unlikely that the learned Judge would have referred to that particular aspect of the case at that point in his judgment.

I now turn to the judgment again where reference is made to s. 19(2) of the Act: I was asked by the defendants to infer that Vikingos had not passed the title to Mitsui U.S.A. on shipment because of the terms in which Vikingos took the bills of lading, which were to their own order. Prima facie taking bills of lading in such a form is an indication that the shipper wishes to reserve the right of disposal of the goods and not at that time to pass the property in the goods to any other person. No reliance before me was placed upon any difference between any foreign legal system and English law and the parties among other things referred me to the Sale of Goods Act and the well known passage in Lord Wright's speech in *Ross T. Smyth v T. Bailey Son & Co.* (1940) 67 Ll.L.Rep. 147; (1940) 45 Com. Cas. 292. However in each case it is a question of evaluating all the evidence of the parties' conduct including the contracts which they have made in order to see whether they have intended that the general property should not pass on shipment. In the present case I do not consider that I should conclude that Vikingos were intending not to perform their obligation to pass the property in the goods on shipment.

There again, with respect to the Judge, he has returned to the error which, in my judgment, he made in the application of the accepted fact that the contract was on f.o.b. terms to the problem of deciding when the property in the goods should pass. He continued then to this finding, which was based upon that erroneous inference:

The correct inference is in my judgment that they were at most merely reserving a special property in order to facilitate the operation of the letter of credit mechanism for payment. Vikingos would have a lien on the bills of lading until they were paid and thereafter the bankers would have a lien. But there is no reason why the general property should not pass down the line to Colombia Fisheries. Further it would be extravagant that the general property should not pass seeing that Vikingos had already been paid 80 per cent of the value of the goods prior to shipment and were only interested in collecting the balance of 20 per cent.

In my judgment, there was simply no evidence from which secondary inferences could be drawn which would entitle the departure from the prima facie presumption arising from the form in which the bills of lading were drawn.[35]

Bills of lading made to the buyer's order

It has been noted that the fact that a bill of lading has been drawn to the buyer's order does not represent, per se, any indication in terms of transfer of property.[36]

Indeed, even when a bill of lading is made to the buyer's order, an implied reservation of title whereby the seller retains the property of the goods until payment may still arise, in case the seller retains the bill of lading and endorses it to the buyer only after money is exchanged.[37]

35 *Ibid.*, at 216.

36 See Debattista, *Bills of Lading in Export Trade*, above, p. 118; *Benjamin's Sale of Goods*, para. 20.83.

37 *Ibid.* See also H. Goitein, The Passing of Property and the Risk under a C.I.F Contract, (1947) 43 *LQR* 81, 84.

In *The Parana* there were other goods purchased by a neutral party from the enemy shipper, either after shipment, or before shipment upon f.o.b. terms, payment against bill of lading, but the bill of lading was not taken up until after the capture of the goods, then the purchased goods were liable to condemnation. The same result follows where (as in the case of *The Parana*) goods have been purchased before shipment and are deliverable by the bill of lading to the purchaser, who has himself effected the insurance, but drafts drawn for the cost and freight price upon a confirmed bank credit established by the purchaser under the terms of the contract are not paid until after the capture. It cannot be inferred from these circumstances that the intention was that the property should pass before shipment.

As held by Lord Summer:

> Cases, in which it has been held that taking the bill of lading in the shipper's own name negatives any unconditional appropriation to the buyer by the delivery of the goods on shipboard and indicates one conditional on the documents being taken up, can throw only an indirect light on the question here involved. Certainly no case was found, in which it was held that taking the bill of lading in the buyer's name, while withholding delivery of it until presentation and taking up of the documents, would not be, as an appropriation, equally conditional. Much reliance was placed on The Parchim 65, a case not only decided on very special facts, but on facts so different from those arising in the present appeal as not in any way to rule it. That case did not in any degree substitute the incidence of the risk for the passing of the general property as the test to be applied. There the sellers of the entire cargo of a named ship took the bills of lading to their own order, but it was held that the presumption of an intention to retain the property till something was done by the buyer after shipment was rebutted by the special circumstances of the case. The contract was unusual. It was on cost and freight terms, but was by no means similar to that now under discussion. With the exception of the form of the bills of lading, which itself was determined by the sellers' agent without either particular instructions or actual knowledge of the terms of the contract, everything pointed to the intention that the property should pass to the buyer on shipment, though he was only to have possession of the cargo and of the bills of lading representing it on subsequently paying the price. Special significance was attached to the fact that, on shipment or at least on notification of it, the cargo was to be at the buyer's risk and he had to pay, lost or not lost. Meantime the documents were held by a bank in medio, neither to be transferred to the buyers without payment, nor to be placed at the sellers' disposal, unless and until the buyers failed to take them up. Incidentally it may be observed that, although the loading was only completed after the outbreak of war, the interval was short, the shipment was made in pursuance of a contract entered into before the war, and no point was taken on behalf of the captors, even if any arose, as to the passing of property afloat during war from an enemy seller to a neutral buyer by delivery of documents. The case does not purport to lay down any general rule, that a particular mode of dealing with a bill of lading must, whenever it occurs and in whatever circumstances, always prove a particular intention. It is not an authority for the contention, that, if the bill of lading is taken in the buyer's name this necessarily proves that the goods shipped are appropriated to the contract, and delivered to the captain as the buyer's bailee, with a consequent inference of the passing of the property to the buyer on shipment.
>
> In the present case it appears to their Lordships that the retention by the seller of the bill of lading was inconsistent with an intention to pass the property. They think that it was "clearly intended by the consignor to preserve his title to the goods until he did a further act by transferring the bill of lading." The special circumstance of the existence of a confirmed banker's credit in this case is only indirectly relevant. It no doubt enhances the likelihood that the bills of lading will eventually be taken up and

> the goods be paid for, and so diminishes the importance to the seller of being still able to say that the goods are his, but it is not direct evidence of intention; it is only a reason why a particular intention is more likely to have been formed in such a case than in others. The intention has still to be inferred, principally from what was done and from the communications made with reference to it, and these point to an intention not to pass the property till the drafts were paid, and it is really rather a reason for intending to get the documents presented and taken up as soon as possible, than for an intention not to retain the ownership even until that could be effected. If the seller was paid or was holder of an enforcible contract from a bank for payment, the sooner he passed the property the better, for he was uninsured, but if he was neither he gained nothing by passing the property away. It was not onerous property.[38]

Similarly, in *The Seven Pioneer*,[39] the contract for the sale of cement provided for payment against the bill of lading. It was held by the High Court of New Zealand that the normal inference under those circumstances should be that the seller had reserved the right of disposal until payment in accordance with the contract had been made; there was nothing in the terms of the contract or the circumstances of this case to displace that inference; however, the bills of lading were never released to the plaintiffs and the plaintiff acquired no rights to the bills of lading until payment was made.

Therefore, the sellers retained a right of disposal over the goods and the property did not pass to the plaintiff under New Zealand law; the plaintiff did not have a sufficient interest in the goods at the time they were damaged to found a claim in negligence.

As stated by Rodney Hansen J:

> (1) Where there is a contract for the sale of specific goods, or where goods are subsequently appropriated to the contract, the seller may, by the terms of the contract or appropriation, reserve the right of disposal of the goods until certain conditions are fulfilled.
> (2) In such case, notwithstanding the delivery of the goods to the buyer, or to a carrier or other bailee for the purpose of transmission to the buyer, the property in the goods does not pass to the buyer until the conditions imposed by the seller are fulfilled.
> (3) Where goods are shipped, and by the bill of lading the goods are deliverable to the order of the seller or his agent, the seller is prima facie deemed to reserve the right of disposal.
> (4) Where the seller of goods draws on the buyer for the price, and transmits the bill of exchange and bill of lading to the buyer together to secure acceptance or payment of the bill of exchange, the buyer is bound to return the bill of lading if he does not honour the bill of exchange, and if he wrongfully retains the bill of lading the property in the goods does not pass to him.
>
> In this case, the bills of lading were all made to the order of Starlink, as buyer and consignee. Pursuant to s. 21(3) the seller is not therefore deemed to have reserved the right of disposal. In *Mitsui & Co. Ltd. v Flota Mercante Grancolombiana S.A. (The Cuidad de Pasto and the Cuidad de Neiva)* [1988] 2 Lloyd's Rep. 208 at p. 215 it was suggested that the statutory presumption may be displaced by naming the buyer as consignee but I agree with the learned authors of *Benjamin's Sale of Goods* at par.

38 *Ibid.* at 515, 516, 517.
39 *The Seven Pioneer* [2001] 2 Lloyd's Rep. 57 NZ.

20–70 that where the buyer is named as consignee, the presumption simply does not arise and a seller should not be taken to have given up his right of disposal merely because the bill is made out to the buyer's order. As Benjamin goes on to point out, retention of the bill of lading gives the seller considerable control over the goods; the buyer is not normally entitled to demand delivery from the carrier without presenting the bill. In cases where the contract provides for payment against the bill of lading, the normal inference should be that the seller has reserved a right of disposal until payment in accordance with the contract has been made.

There is nothing in the terms of the contract or the circumstances of this case to displace that inference. The bills of lading all showed the consignee as being "to order of Starlink Navigation". However, as previously noted, the bills of lading were never released to the plaintiff. The sale and purchase agreement between the plaintiff and Indocement provided for payment:

. . . by T.T. [telegraphic transfer] upon receipt documents (C.A.D.) directly to our Bankers . . .

The plaintiff, accordingly, acquired no right to the bills of lading until payment was tendered. Under the bills of lading themselves the plaintiff had no right to delivery of the goods unless it held the bills. In my view, these matters support the inference that Indocement retained a right of disposal over the goods and property in the goods did not pass to the plaintiff under New Zealand law. It follows that the plaintiff did not have a sufficient interest in the goods at the time they were damaged to found a claim in negligence.[40]

In light of the above, even in the case that a bill of lading is made to the buyer's order (as is often the case), in order to assess the transfer of property, one should always ascertain the seller's behaviour: if the bill of lading is only tendered to the buyer after payment is made, that would entail an implied retention of title by the seller, with the property passing on to the buyer only after money is exchanged.

Transactions "cash against documents"

It is clear on the authorities that in the case where a contract concluded on shipment terms provides for cash against documents as a payment method, property will pass to the buyer at the moment of payment, in derogation of sections 16 and 20A of SOGA 1979.

In *The Miramichi*,[41] a cargo of bushels of wheat sold on c.i.f. terms provided for cash against documents as the payment method. The court held that under those circumstances the sellers had reserved a right of disposal, or a *jus disponendi*, over the goods, which still remained their property, and would so remain until the shipping documents had been tendered to and taken over by the buyers, and the bill of exchange for the price had been paid.[42]

Similarly, in *Re An Arbitration between Shipton, Anderson & Co. and Harrison Brothers & Co.*,[43] a cash against payment clause was held to represent an implied reservation of title for the goods, the property of which was due to pass on to the buyer only after payment was made.

40 *Ibid.*, at 62.
41 *The Miramichi* [1915], 71.
42 *Ibid.*, at 78. On this point see Debattista, *Bills of Lading in Export Trade*, p. 118, footnote 66.
43 In *Re An Arbitration between Shipton, Anderson & Co. and Harrison Brothers & Co.* [1915] 3 KB 676.

Here, the owner of a specific parcel of wheat in a warehouse in Liverpool sold it upon the terms of payment of cash within seven days against the transfer order. In the words of Reading LCJ:

> The first is whether the property in the wheat sold passed to the buyers under the contract. Upon that point the question turns on whether the contract was a sale which comes within s. 18 of the Sale of Goods Act, 1893, or whether it comes within s. 19 of that Act. If the contract was an unconditional contract for the sale of specific goods in a deliverable state, then, by virtue of r. 1 of s. 18, the property in the goods passed to the buyers when the contract was made, and it would be immaterial whether the terms of payment, or the time of delivery, or both, were postponed. By s. 19, where the contract is for the sale of specific goods the seller may, by the terms of the contract, reserve the right of disposal of the goods until certain conditions are fulfilled, in which case the property in the goods does not pass until those conditions are fulfilled. The question in this case depends upon whether or not the right of disposal of the goods had been reserved by the sellers under the terms of the contract until payment had been made. It appears to me that under this contract the sellers did reserve such a right of disposal by making it a term of the contract that cash was to be paid within seven days against transfer order; that the intention of the parties was that they should have this right of disposal until payment had been made; and that, consequently, the property had not passed to the buyers. Therefore the answer to the first question is, in my judgment, that the property in the goods sold had not passed to the buyers under the contract.[44]

The idea that by virtue of a cash against payment transaction sellers retain a *jus disponendi* over the title of the goods until payment is made was further confirmed in *Ginzberg and Others v Barrow Haematite Steel Company, Ltd. and McKellar*.[45]

Here, a cash against documents c.i.f. transaction for the sale of a cargo of 10,000 tons of Indian manganese was held by the court to create by default the seller's title retention of the goods until payment was made.

Indeed, if the contract had been performed according to its terms and the bills of lading had been handed to the first defendants with provisional invoices requiring payment of the price, it was plain that no unconditional appropriation would have taken place and no property would have passed until payment; that the plaintiffs intended merely to expedite delivery without departing from fundamental principles of their c.i.f. contract; that, accordingly, the property in the goods did not pass to the first defendants; and that, therefore, the plaintiffs were entitled to judgment against the first and second defendants for conversion of the goods consumed, and delivery up of the goods in the defendants' possession, or their value.

McNair J held that:

> On the facts set out above the critical question is whether the property in the goods passed to the defendants when the goods were delivered by the ship to the British Railways wagons pursuant to the delivery order in accordance with the instructions of the plaintiffs' London firm in their letter of Jan. 23, 1964. By Sect. 17 of the Sale of Goods Act 1893, it is provided as follows:

44 *Ibid.*, at 680.

45 *Ginzberg and Others v Barrow Haematite Steel Company, Ltd. and McKellar* [1966] 1 Lloyd's Rep. 343.

(1.) Where there is a contract for the sale of specific or ascertained goods the property in them is transferred to the buyer at such time as the parties to the contract intend it to be transferred.

(2.) For the purpose of ascertaining the intention of the parties regard shall be had to the terms of the contract, the conduct of the parties, and the circumstances of the case.

Though this section in terms only applies in the case of a sale of specific or ascertained goods, it is clear law (and accepted by both parties in the present case) that the principles set out in this section also apply to the case of a contract for the sale of unascertained goods: see the speech of Lord Wright in *Ross T. Smyth & Co., Ltd. v T.D. Bailey, Son & Co.* (1940) 45 Com. Cas. 292, at pp. 299 and 300; (1940) 67 Ll.L.Rep. 147, at p. 155.

Sect. 18 then provides as follows: Unless a different intention appears, the following are rules for ascertaining the intention of the parties as to the time at which the property in the goods is to pass to the buyer. There follow four rules dealing with specific goods with which I am not here concerned. Then there follows Rule 5 in the following terms:

(1.) Where there is a contract for the sale of unascertained or future goods by description, and goods of that description and in a deliverable state are unconditionally appropriated to the contract, either by the seller with the assent of the buyer, or by the buyer with the assent of the seller, the property in the goods thereupon passes to the buyer. Such assent may be express or implied, and may be given either before or after the appropriation is made . . .

If this contract had been performed according to its terms and bills of lading indorsed in blank had been handed to the buyers with a provisional invoice requiring payment of the price, I think it is plain that no unconditional appropriation would have taken place, and no property would have passed until payment: see *Shepherd v Harrison* (1871) L.R. 5 H.L. 116, and see the speech of Lord Wright in *Ross T. Smyth & Co., Ltd. v T.D. Bailey, Son & Co.* (1940) 45 Com. Cas. 292, at p. 300; (1940) 67 Ll.L.Rep. 147, at p. 155, . . . The bills of lading were held by the appellants [that is, the sellers]. The contract provided for cash or (at seller's option) an acceptance of seller's draft against documents. That condition for the transfer of the documents had not been fulfilled. The bills of lading were the symbols of the goods, and the appellants, by retaining them, retained as against the respondents [that is, the buyers] title and control over the goods. All the respondents had at that stage was a contractual right to obtain control and thereby become owners upon taking up the documents. . . . that is, by paying for them in cash or accepting the sellers' draft. See, too, *The Glenroy* [1945] A.C. 124 (P.C.), at p. 134, 1 where Lord Porter states that in the case of a normal c.i.f. contract the property would not pass until the documents were taken up and paid for. If the buyer takes the bills of lading and does not within a reasonable time pay in accordance with the invoice accompanying the bills of lading the property does not ordinarily pass. The question whether in a particular case the property does pass depends upon the intention of the parties, and in ascertaining that intention regard shall be paid . . . to the terms of the contract, the conduct of the parties, and the circumstances of the case. . . . (See per Lord Wright, ibid., at pp. 300 and 156 of the respective reports.)

It was argued on behalf of the defendants in the present case that the terms of the contract had been varied by the substitution of a different method of delivery and a different method of payment so that in effect the contract became one for delivery of unascertained goods ex ship and so that the terms as to payment no longer imported a condition upon the passing of the property - payment and delivery, it was said, being merely concurrent obligations. I find it quite impossible to accept this submission. There was no evidence of any intention to vary on the part of the plaintiffs, to make

> such a fundamental variation of the contract, still less any evidence of any agreement to that effect on the part of the defendant company.
>
> It is not uncommon to find in c.i.f. contracts provision for payment against bills of lading or delivery orders. See *Comptoir d'Achat et de Vente du Boerenbond Belge S/A v Luis de Ridder Limitada (The Julia)* [1949] A.C. 293, at p. 309; (1949) 82 Ll.L.Rep. 270, at p. 281, where Lord Porter said this:
>
> > . . . The strict form of c.i.f. contract may, however, be modified: a provision that a delivery order may be substituted for a bill of lading or a certificate of insurance for a policy would not, I think, make the contract concluded upon something other than c.i.f. terms, but in deciding whether it comes within that category or not all the permutations and combinations of provision and circumstance must be taken into consideration. . . .
>
> As it seems to me, the true inference from the facts and the documents in the present case is that the plaintiffs intended merely to expedite the delivery for the benefit of the defendants (albeit they were not themselves in a position to tender bills of lading) without in any way departing from the fundamental principles of their c.i.f. contract the implementation of which would safeguard them against losing the property in the goods until payment was made.[46]

In light of the above, it appears to be clear on the authorities that cash against documents transactions indeed create by default an implied reservation of title, whereby the property of the goods will be retained by the seller until payment is made.[47]

46 *Ibid.*, at 352, 352.

47 See Debattista, *Bills of Lading in Export Trade*, above, p. 118. See also *Carver on Bills of Lading*, above, para. 6.055. See also *Benjamin's Sale of Goods*, above, paras. 21.138 *et seq.*

CHAPTER 9

Performance of a contract concluded on shipment terms: The seller's physical duties

9.1 The performance of international sales contracts

One of the main peculiarities of contracts concluded on shipment terms lies with their performance. Indeed, such contracts are performed by the seller in a dual mode: a) physical mode, which relates to the seller's duties in relation to the goods; and b) documentary duties, which entail the obligation of the seller to tender documents as originally specified in the sales contract.

James Finlay & Co. Ltd. v N.V. Kwik Hoo Tong Handel Maatschappij[1] established the legal proposition of dual performance of contracts concluded on shipment terms: physical and documentary.[2] In the words of Scrutton LJ:

> It is not necessary to discuss whether it is accurate to say that a c.i.f. contract is a sale of documents or a sale of goods. In view of the fact that the goods may be lost before the documents are tendered and before the property has passed, there is a good deal to be said for the view that at any rate a very large proportion of the contract is a sale of documents. But at any rate it is an essential part of the contract that genuine documents relating to goods complying with the contract should be furnished to the buyer.[3]

The separation of the seller's physical duties from documentary obligations gives rise to profound consequences in terms of the legal evaluation of contracts concluded on shipment terms.

Indeed, this scenario entails the need to legally analyse and consider the seller's physical duties separately from the seller's documentary duties, in order to ascertain possible breaches of contract separately.

This chapter shall focus on the seller's duties in relation to the goods: first, a difference between the breach of conditions and warranties will be taken into account in order to establish when one deals with a breach which can be considered fatal to the sale contract.

Thereafter, we shall consider the identification and the classification of physical duties within the context of contracts concluded on shipment terms, in light of

---

1 In *James Finlay & Co. Ltd. v N.V. Kwik Hoo Tong Handel Maatschappij* [1929] 1 KB 400, 411; (1928) 32 Ll L Rep 245.

2 As will be appreciated in the following, the proposition that contracts concluded on shipment terms are performed in a physical and documentary fashion also gives rise to two separate rights of rejection on the buyer's part: the right to reject the documents, and to reject the goods. See chapter 12.

3 *Ibid.*, at 252.

the relevant provisions of SOGA 1979 and customary contractual arrangements in relation to the goods which often characterise international commercial sales.

9.2 Conditions and warranties in a sales contract

The use of the word "condition" appears to have originated in the seventeenth century. A statutory definition of a condition was for the first time enshrined into section 12(2) of the Sale of Goods Act 1930. According to that definition, a condition can be defined as a "stipulation which is so vital to the contract that its complete and exact performance by one party is condition precedent to the obligation of the other party to perform his part".[4]

---

4 See *Chitty on Contracts*, 31st Edition, Sweet & Maxwell, 2012, Volume I, at 12-026. To understand the history of "condition" first we have to understand what is the background of the statute, the Sale of Goods Act 1930. As per the 8th Law Commission Report, the history of this Act is as follows:

> Until the first of July, 1930, the law of sale of goods in India was governed by Chapter VII (sections 76 to 123) Legislation of the Indian Contract Act, 1872. The Indian Contract Act itself being based on the English Common Law, the law relating to the sale of goods in India followed the principles of the English Common Law, including the Law Merchant. The English law of sale of goods was codified in 1893 by the enactment of the Sale of Goods Act which embodied the basic Common Law principles after adapting them to meet the needs of a growing society.
>
> In India, by 1920 it was found that the law relating to the sale of goods contained in Chapter VII of the Indian Contract Act was not adequate to meet the needs of the community and that some of the provisions of this branch of the law required alteration in the light of new developments in mercantile transactions. The accretions to the law made by judicial decisions in England which were embodied in the Sale of Goods Act of 1893 were not to be found in the analogous provisions contained in the Indian Contract Act. It was also considered necessary to embody the law relating to sale of goods in a separate enactment.
>
> Hence, in 1926–27 an exhaustive examination of the case-law bearing on the portions of the Contract Act dealing with the sale of goods was made by the Legislative Department. As a result of this examination, a draft Bill was prepared in 1928. In 1929 a Special Committee consisting of eminent lawyers examined the draft Bill and the draft Bill as revised by this Committee and, subsequently, by a Select Committee of the Legislature, was enacted as the Indian Sale of Goods Act, 1930 (III of 1930), section 65 of which repealed Chapter VII of the Indian Contract Act, 1872.
>
> The Act, as passed, was mainly based on the provisions of the English Act of 1893, modified in the light of subsequent judicial decisions in England and India.
>
> Having carefully Examined the provisions of the scape of Act in the light of judicial decisions in India since 1930, the development of the law relating to the sale of goods in other countries, the suggestions made by various commercial bodies and individuals as well as the requirements of the modern welfare State, we have reached the conclusion that the provisions of the Act do not require any radical change.
>
> Now it's time to know the history of Condition and warranty, which has a very long history in India. We can found the same in famous "Arthasashtra" written by the great Koutilya or Chanakya in almost 4th Century B.C. Arthasastra is considered as one of the best book on "science of political economy" system has ever written.
>
> During Chandragupta's period, in which Kautilya lived, good trade practices were prevalent. For example, "Goods could not be sold at the place of their origin, field or factory. They were to be carried to the appointed markets (panya sala) where the dealer had to declare particulars as to the quantity, quality and the prices of his goods which were examined and registered in the books." Every trader was required to take a license to sell. A trader from outside had to obtain permission. The superintendent of commerce fixed the whole-sale prices of goods as they entered the Customs House. He allowed a margin of profit to fix retail prices. Speculation and cornering to influence prices were prohibited. Thus, the State bore a heavy responsibility for protecting the public against unfair prices and fraudulent transactions. There were severe punishments for smuggling and adulteration of goods. For example, public health was guarded by punishing adulteration of food products of all kinds, including grains, oils, alkalies, salts, scents and medicines.

SOGA 1979 does not postulate a specific definition for a condition of a contract; rather it specifies in section 11 when a condition is to be treated as a warranty.

SOGA 1979, section 11 When condition to be treated as warranty

(2) Where a contract of sale is subject to a condition to be fulfilled by the seller, the buyer may waive the condition, or may elect to treat the breach of the condition as a breach of warranty and not as a ground for treating the contract as repudiated.

(3) Whether a stipulation in a contract of sale is a condition, the breach of which may give rise to a right to treat the contract as repudiated, or a warranty, the breach of which may give rise to a claim for damages but not to a right to reject the goods and treat the contract as repudiated, depends in each case on the construction of the contract; and a stipulation may be a condition, though called a warranty in the contract.

(4) [Subject to section 35A below] Where a contract of sale is not severable and the buyer has accepted the goods or part of them, the breach of a condition to be fulfilled by the seller can only be treated as a breach of warranty, and not as a ground for rejecting the goods and treating the contract as repudiated, unless there is an express or implied term of the contract to that effect [. . .]

(6) Nothing in this section affects a condition or warranty whose fulfilment is excused by law by reason of impossibility or otherwise.

By contrasting the concept of condition with the concept of warranty, SOGA 1979 denotes a condition as a stipulation in a contract the breach of which may give rise to the right of repudiating the sales contract.

Further, SOGA 1979 makes it clear that there is no implied warranty or condition as to quality of fitness of goods for any particular purpose, except those specified in SOGA or any other law.[5]

The ancient law relating to warranties of land was full of subtleties and intricacies; it occupied the attention of the most eminent writers on the English law, and it was declared by Lord Coke, that the learning of warranties was one of the most curious and cunning learnings of the law; but it is now of little use even in England. The warranty was a covenant real, whereby the grantor of an estate of freehold, and his heirs, were bound to warrant the title; and either upon voucher, or judgment in, a writ of warrantia chartae, to yield other lands to the value of those from which there had been an eviction by paramount title the heir of the warrantor was bound only on condition that he had, as assets, other lands of equal value by descent. Warranties were lineal and collateral. Lineal means, when the heir derived title to the land warranted, either from or through the ancestor who made the warranty.

Collateral warranty was when the heir's title was not derived from the warranting ancestor, and yet it barred the heir from claiming the land by any collateral title, upon the presumption that he might thereafter have assets by descent from or through the ancestor; and it imposed upon him the obligation of giving the warrantee other lands, in case of eviction, provided he had assets.

The statute of Anne, annulled these collateral warrantees, which bid become a great grievance. Warranty in its original form, it is presumed, has never been known in the United States. The more plain and pliable form of a covenant has been adopted in its place and this covenant, like all other covenants, has always been held to sound in damages which after judgment may be recovered out of the personal or real estate, as in other cases.

5 See section 14 SOGA 1979, "Implied terms about quality or fitness."

(1) Except as provided by this section and section 15 below and subject to any other enactment, there is no implied condition or warranty about the quality or fitness for any particular purpose of goods supplied under a contract of sale.

(2) Where the seller sells goods in the course of a business, there is an implied term that the goods supplied under the contract are of satisfactory quality.

This is the basic principle of *caveat emptor*, i.e. let the buyer beware. However, there are certain stipulations which are essential for the main purpose of the contract of sale of goods which go to the root of the contract and non-fulfilment of these causes frustration of the contract.

These are termed "conditions". Other stipulations, which are not essential, are termed as "warranties". Both of these are collateral to a contract for the sale of goods, and a contract cannot be avoided for breach of warranty, but the aggrieved party can claim damages.

A stipulation in a contract of sale with reference to goods which are the subject thereof may be a condition or a warranty. As established above, a condition is a stipulation essential to the main purpose of the contract, the breach of which gives rise to a right to treat the contract as repudiated.

A warranty, on the other hand, is a stipulation collateral to the main purpose of the contract, the breach of which gives rise to a claim for damages but not to a right to reject the goods and treat the contract as repudiated. Whether a stipulation in a contract of sale is a condition or a warranty depends in each case on the construction of the contract. A stipulation may be a condition, although called a warranty in the contract.[6]

Whether a particular stipulation in a contract is a condition or a warranty depends on the interpretation of the terms of the contract. Merely stating "conditions of contract" in an agreement does not mean all stipulations mentioned are "conditions", the infringement of which will enable the party not in breach to terminate the contract.[7]

9.3 Express and implied conditions

On a general level, conditions which are agreed to by the parties are commonly referred to as "express conditions".

(2A) For the purposes of this Act, goods are of satisfactory quality if they meet the standard that a reasonable person would regard as satisfactory, taking account of any description of the goods, the price (if relevant) and all the other relevant circumstances.

(2B) For the purposes of this Act, the quality of goods includes their state and condition and the following (among others) are in appropriate cases aspects of the quality of goods –
- (a) fitness for all the purposes for which goods of the kind in question are commonly supplied,
- (b) appearance and finish,
- (c) freedom from minor defects,
- (d) safety, and
- (e) durability.

(2C) The term implied by subsection (2) above does not extend to any matter making the quality of goods unsatisfactory –
- (a) which is specifically drawn to the buyer's attention before the contract is made,
- (b) where the buyer examines the goods before the contract is made, which that examination ought to reveal, or
- (c) in the case of a contract for sale by sample, which would have been apparent on a reasonable examination of the sample.

6 See *Benjamin's Sale of Goods*, above, chapter 3. See also Francis M. Burdick, Conditions and Warranties in the Sale of Goods, *Columbia Law Review* 1(2) (February, 1901), 71–93.

7 *Ibid.*

Nevertheless, usually in a dispute it is the court which decides the nature of a particular clause by the process of interpretation.

If an agreement does not make an event a condition, then the court may supply a term to that effect. Such conditions will be referred to as "implied" conditions, since a court uses the process of implication to determine whether to supply a term that makes an event a condition or not, and if yes, then what term to supply.

The distinction between express and implied conditions is of practical importance because, as will be readily appreciated, the common law doctrine of strict compliance is limited to express conditions.[8]

9.4 Conditions and seller's physical duties

As established above, the breach of a condition entails the elective right of the party not in breach to repudiate the contract.

The crucial question, therefore, is: when does a buyer have the option to reject goods for non-conformity or, in other words, to repudiate a sales contract for a seller's breach of a condition which relates to the physical duties?

Before answering the aforementioned question, there is the need to establish how to identify conditions in relation to the physical duties.

As will be analysed in detail in the following, the seller's physical duties are the duties of the seller which relate to the description, quantity, quality, and sample; further, also, time of shipment and place of shipment are to be considered part of the description of the goods and, hence, the seller's physical duties.[9]

All the terms in the sales contract which relate to the aforementioned aspects of the goods will be, thus, considered to be part of the physical duties of the seller.[10]

Once we identify the terms re physical duties, how do we ascertain whether those terms represent conditions or warranties? This distinction is of the utmost importance as only in the presence of a breach of a physical duty which amounts to a condition will the buyer be entitled to reject the cargo.

The contract itself may make it clear that the buyer's only right in case of non-conformity is to give the buyer an allowance on the price.[11]

---

8 See chapter 10.

9 See *Bowes v Shand* (1877) 2 App Cas 455 (HL), and *Petrotrade v Stinnes Handel* [1995] 1 Lloyd's Rep. 142.

10 As it will be noted in the following (see chapter 10), in order to translate physical duties into documentary duties, the sales contract should saddle the seller with obligations to tender documents which testify as to the description, quantity, quality of the goods, and so on. The failure to do this will entail that the sale contract provides only for physical duties, and that the buyer can only rely on the possibility of rejecting the cargo on arrival in case of a breach of physical duty which amounts to a condition.

11 See, for instance, lines 20–24 of Fosfa 54, which state that: "At time and place of shipment, the oil shall be of good merchantable quality, in good condition and of the agreed description and specifications. If the oil is shipped in more than one tank of the same ship, the analysis details of the oil in each separate tank at loading shall conform to the above. Should the oil on arrival not prove equal to the above, or should the oil contain sea water or other admixture, this contract not to be void, but the oil is to be taken with an allowance to be agreed upon or fixed by arbitration provided always that the oil shipped shall conform to the above. Sweepings shall be accepted with a fair allowance, to be fixed by agreement or by arbitration."

If the contract does not make it explicitly clear whether the parties intended to make non-conformity fatal to the seller, the court or arbitrator will, however, have to try to identify the intention of the parties. This could be done by reading between the lines of the contract in order to ascertain whether the contract itself provides for any guidance, albeit implicit, as to what the parties intended should be the effect of non-conformity.[12]

In the absence of any guidance, implicit or explicit, arising from the sales contract itself, the market could provide an answer, on the basis of whether or not it is common practice within a specific line of trade to treat the type of non-conformity alleged as a breach going to the very identity of the goods sold.[13]

The identification of conditions in relation to the seller's physical duties may prove in practice of difficult execution. Indeed, it is clear on the authorities that not even headings are to be considered as conclusive evidence if we are considering terms which amount to conditions.

Therefore, even terms which are explicitly described by the contract itself as "conditions" of the contract may, in reality, not prove to be such.

In *Schuler v Wickman*,[14] the respondents ("Wickman"), who were a selling organisation, entered into a distributorship agreement with the appellants ("Schuler"), who manufactured panel presses, to promote the sales of panel presses in the UK. The agreement contained (inter alia) the following clauses:

> **Clause 7. Promotion by Sales**
>
> [i.e. Wickman] (a) Subject to Clause 17 Sales will use its best endeavours to promote and extend the sale of Schuler products in the Territory. (b) It shall be a condition of this Agreement that: (i) Sales shall send its representatives to visit the six firms whose names are listed in the Schedule hereto at least once in every week for the purpose of soliciting orders for panel presses; (ii) the same representative shall visit each firm on each occasion unless there are unavoidable reasons preventing the visit being made by that representative in which case the visit shall be made by an alternate representative and Sales will ensure that such a visit is always made by the same alternate representative. Sales agrees to inform Schuler of the names of the representatives and alternate representatives instructed to make the visits required by this Clause.
>
> **[. . .] Clause 11. Duration of Agreement**
>
> (a) This Agreement and the rights granted hereunder to Sales shall commence on the First day of May 1963 and shall continue in force (unless previously determined as hereinafter provided) until the 31st day of December and thereafter unless and until determined by either party upon giving to the other not less than 12 months' notice in writing to that effect expiring on the said 31st day of December 1967 or any subsequent anniversary thereof PROVIDED that Schuler or Sales may by notice in writing to the other determine this Agreement forthwith if: (i) the other shall have committed a material breach of its obligations hereunder and shall have failed to remedy the same within 60 days of being required in writing so to do; or (ii) the other shall cease to carry on business or shall enter into liquidation (other than a members' voluntary liquidation

---

12 See Debattista, *Bills of Lading in Export Trade*, above, p. 122.
13 *Ibid.*
14 *Schuler v Wickman* [1973]2 Lloyd's Rep. 53.

> for the purposes of reconstruction or amalgamation) or shall suffer the appointment of a Receiver of the whole or a material part of the undertaking.

The court was asked to determine whether, on the facts found and the true construction of the documents, Schuler were entitled by reason of breach by Wickman of their obligations under Clause 7(b) of the distributorship agreement (a) to terminate that agreement, or under Clause 11(a)(i)(b) to repudiate that agreement.

It was held by the court that on its true construction, Clause 7 was not a "condition", even though it was stated to be so, for to interpret it otherwise would produce an unreasonable result.

In the words of Reid LJ:

> But on any view the interrelation and consequences of the various provisions of this agreement are so ill-thought out that I am not disposed to discard the natural meaning of the words which I have quoted merely because giving to them their natural meaning implies that the draftsman has forgotten something which a better draftsman would have remembered. If the terms of clause 11 are wide enough to apply to breaches of clause 7 then I am inclined to hold that clause 7 must be read subject to the provisions of clause 11.
>
> It appears to me that clause 11(a)(i) is intended to apply to all material breaches of the agreement which are capable of being remedied. The question then is what is meant in this context by the word "remedy". It could mean obviate or nullify the effect of a breach so that any damage already done is in some way made good. Or it could mean cure so that matters are put right for the future. I think that the latter is the more natural meaning. The word is commonly used in connection with diseases or ailments and they would normally be said to be remedied if they were cured although no cure can remove the past effect or result of the disease before the cure took place. And in general it can only be in a rare case that any remedy of something that has gone wrong in the performance of a continuing positive obligation will, in addition to putting it right for the future, remove or nullify damage already incurred before the remedy was applied. To restrict the meaning of remedy to cases where all damage past and future can be put right would leave hardly any scope at all for this clause. On the other hand, there are cases where it would seem a misuse of language to say that a breach can be remedied. For example, a breach of clause 14 by disclosure of confidential information could not be said to be remedied by a promise not to do it again.
>
> So the question is whether a breach of Wickman's obligation under clause 7(b)(i) is capable of being remedied within the meaning of this agreement. On the one hand, failure to make one particular visit might have irremediable consequences, e.g., a valuable order might have been lost when making that visit would have obtained it. But looking at the position broadly I incline to the view that breaches of this obligation should be held to be capable of remedy within the meaning of clause 7. If that is right and if clause 11 is intended to have general application then clause 7 must be read so that a breach of clause 7(b)(i) does not give to Schuler a right to rescind but only to require the breach to be remedied within 60 days under clause 11(a)(i).
>
> Schuler maintains that the word "condition" has now acquired a precise legal meaning; that, particularly since the enactment of the Sale of Goods Act, 1893, its recognised meaning in English law is a term of a contract any breach of which by one party gives to the other party an immediate right to rescind the whole contract. Undoubtedly the word is frequently used in that sense. There may, indeed, be some presumption that in a formal legal document it has that meaning. But it is frequently used with a less stringent meaning. One is familiar with printed "Conditions of Sale" incorporated into a contract, and with the words "For conditions see back" printed on a ticket. There it simply means that the "conditions" are terms of the contract.

> In the ordinary use of the English language "condition" has many meanings, some of which have nothing to do with agreements. In connection with an agreement it may mean a pre-condition: something which must happen or be done before the agreement can take effect. Or it may mean some state of affairs which must continue to exist if the agreement is to remain in force. The legal meaning on which Schuler relies is, I think, one which would not occur to a layman; a condition in that sense is not something which has an automatic effect. It is a term the breach of which by one party gives to the other an option either to terminate the contract or to let the contract proceed and, if he so desires, sue for damages for the breach.
>
> Sometimes a breach of a term gives that option to the aggrieved party because it is of a fundamental character going to the root of the contract, sometimes it gives that option because the parties have chosen to stipulate that it shall have that effect. Mr. Justice Blackburn said in *Bettini v Gye* (1875) 1 Q.B. 183, at p. 187:
>
>> Parties may think some matter, apparently of very little importance, essential; and if they sufficiently express an intention to make the literal fulfilment of such a thing a condition precedent, it will be one . . .
>
> In the present case it is not contended that Wickman's failures to make visits amounted in themselves to fundamental breaches. What is contended is that the terms of clause 7 "sufficiently express an intention" to make any breach, however small, of the obligation to make visits a condition so that any such breach shall entitle Schuler to rescind the whole contract if they so desire.
>
> Schuler maintains that the use of the word "condition" is in itself enough to establish this intention. No doubt some words used by lawyers do have a rigid inflexible meaning. But we must remember that we are seeking to discover intention as disclosed by the contract as a whole. Use of the word "condition" is an indication.
>
> The fact that a particular construction leads to a very unreasonable result must be a relevant consideration. The more unreasonable the result the more unlikely it is that the parties can have intended it, and if they do intend it the more necessary it is that they shall make that intention abundantly clear.
>
> Clause 7(b) requires that over a long period each of the six firms shall be visited every week by one or other of two named representatives. It makes no provision for Wickman being entitled to substitute others even on the death or retirement of one of the named representatives. Even if one could imply some right to do this, it makes no provision for both representatives being ill during a particular week.[15]

The aforementioned comments of Lord Reid were echoed by Lord Morris, who undertook an interesting legal analysis of the terminology used in a sale contract. He stated that:

> Words are but the instruments by which meanings or intentions are expressed. Often the same word has in differing contexts to do service to convey differing meanings. In contracts of insurance an insurer will often wish to stipulate that his acceptance of a risk is strictly contingent upon the complete accuracy of some statement or representation that has been made to him. The word "warranty" if used by a proposer or an insured person in reference to such a statement or representation may denote much more than a promise for the breach of which (if the statement of representation is inaccurate) damages might be sought. So the word "warranty" may be used to denote one of the meanings that can be given to the word "condition". An insurer may provide that he will only be liable if his insured does this or that: even if "this or

15 *Ibid.*, at 56, 57.

> that" is not of special importance a Court may decide that it was clearly the intention of the parties that there should only be liability if this or that had been done. If in the contract it is stated that such performance is a condition precedent to a right to recover the intention of the parties may be clearly revealed. (See *London Guarantie Company v Fearnley* (1880) 5 App. Cas. 911.)
>
> If it is correct to say, as I think it is, that where there are problems of the construction of an agreement the intention of the parties to it may be collected from the terms of their agreement and from the subject-matter to which it relates, then I doubt whether, save in so far as guidance on principle is found, it is of much value (although it may be of much interest) to consider how Courts have interpreted various differing words in various differing contracts. Nor is it of value to express either agreement or disagreement with the conclusions reached in particular cases.
>
> Just as the word "warranty" may have differing meanings according to the contract so may the word "condition". The words "condition precedent" may have a specific meaning. But the "conditions" of a contract may be no more than its terms or provisions. A condition of a contract may according to the context be a term of it or it may denote something to be satisfied before the contract comes into operation or it may denote something basic to its continuing operation. The case of *Glaholm v Hays* (1841) 2 Man. & G. 257, related to a charter-party one term of which provided that the vessel was to sail from England on or before Feb. 4. The question which there arose was whether that term was a condition precedent upon the non-compliance wherewith the freighters were at liberty to throw up the charter. In giving judgment Chief Justice Tindal said:
>
> Whether a particular clause in a charter-party shall be held to be a condition, upon the non-performance of which by the one party, the other is at liberty to abandon the contract and consider it at an end; or whether it amounts to an agreement only the breach whereof is to be recompensed by an action for damages, must depend upon the intention of the parties to be collected, in each particular case, from the terms of the agreement itself, and from the subject matter to which it relates. It cannot depend, as Lord Ellenborough observes, on any formal arrangement of the words, but (must depend) on the reason and sense of the thing as it is to be collected from the whole contract: See *Ritchie v Anderson* (10 East, 295).
>
> Looking at the language of the charter and the variation of language in the term in question in that case the Court considered that a distinction was intended and that while one set of terms sounded in agreement the one in question sounded in condition. Looking also at the subject-matter the Court considered that construing the term as a condition precedent carried into effect the intention of the parties. [. . .] I conclude therefore, that it was not the intention of the parties to give to the word "condition" in clause 7(b) the meaning contended for by the appellants, viz. - "a stipulation such that any breach of it however slight would give the promisee a right to be quit of his future obligations and sue for damages." The word denoted a stipulation which by reason of its detail had special significance. I agree with the decision of the learned arbitrator whose finding was that "It is an expression which indicates the importance attached by the parties to that stipulation when you come to consider under clause 11(a)(i) whether a party has committed a material breach of its obligations, such obligations including the obligation in clause 7(b)."[16]

It is therefore clear on the authorities that merely placing as many specifications of the goods under a heading entitled "commodity" or "description" does not make those qualities automatically fatal to the sellers.

16 *Ibid.*, at 62, 63.

Indeed, conditions should be interpreted in light of other conditions which can, at times, assume the form of "conditions precedent" capable of overruling other "servant" conditions.

9.5 Implied conditions related to the seller's physical duties

Terms regarding the goods are made "conditions" of the contract if the parties expressly give the option of rejection to the buyer.

Nevertheless, even if the contract is silent in that regard, terms related to description, satisfactory quality, or sample are all made "implied conditions" by SOGA 1979.

Indeed, it is essential under common law to have a sort of "navigation compass" setting up the direction throughout a sales contract and its terms.

As we established above, establishing when a term amounts to a condition is of the utmost importance in order to interpret a sales contract and establish liabilities and possible courses of action in the case of infringement of its terms.

Doing so creates a scenario whereby both the seller and the buyer know where they stand at any given point of an international sales transaction: this ultimately helps ensure the highest degree possible of legal certainty, an element of the foremost importance within the context of highly risky transactions such as contracts concluded on shipment terms.

This is the role of the implied conditions stemming out of SOGA 1979 which relate to description, satisfactory quality, or sample; they integrate the will of the parties to a sales contract, offering guidance in relation to the interpretation of its terms.

The SOGA 1979 implied conditions in relation to the goods shall be subject of scrutiny in the following.

9.6 Section 13 SOGA 1979: Terms describing the goods

Section 13 of the Sale of Goods Act 1979 relates to "sale by description". It reads as follows:

SOGA 1979, section 13 Sale by description

(1) Where there is a contract for the sale of goods by description, there is an implied term that the goods will correspond with the description.
   (1A) As regards England and Wales and Northern Ireland, the term implied by subsection (1) above is a condition.

(2) If the sale is by sample as well as by description it is not sufficient that the bulk of the goods corresponds with the sample if the goods do not also correspond with the description.

(3) A sale of goods is not prevented from being a sale by description by reason only that, being exposed for sale or hire, they are selected by the buyer.

Under section 13, any term which relates to the description of the goods amounts to a condition, the breach of which will entitle the buyer to repudiate the contract and reject the goods.

Sales contracts will describe the goods traded in many ways, some of those details appearing as part of the "commodity", others as "specifications". The question is to endeavour to ascertain what aspects of the description given by traders to the goods sold form part of the "description" of the goods in legal terms.[17]

The contract itself may make it clear that the buyer's only right in case of non-conformity is to give the buyer an allowance on the price, or better practice, derogating de facto section 13 of SOGA 1979.[18]

When the contract fails to make it explicitly clear whether the parties intended to make non-conformity in terms of the description of the goods fatal to the seller, section 13 SOGA 1979 will find application rendering that breach fatal to the seller.

In *Tradax Export S.A. v European Grain & Shipping Co.*,[19] the sellers sold to the buyers 9500 tons of soya bean meal, 5 per cent more or less at seller's option. The contract was drawn up on Gafta 106 which provided, inter alia, that: "Goods in bulk U.S.A. solvent extracted toasted soya bean meal – maximum 7.5% fibre."

The goods were analysed by a Gafta analyst and certificates of analysis were given which showed, inter alia, an excess of fibre content which averaged 9.28 per cent. All the samples were apparently above the level of 7.5 per cent, which was the maximum specified.

The buyers rejected the goods because the fibre content exceeded the contract guarantee and claimed arbitration. The sellers contested that rejection.

It was held by the court that the words "maximum 7.5% fibre" formed part of the description of the goods to which this contract related and were a condition of the contract. The sellers were in breach of a condition of the contract in tendering goods not of the contract description and the buyers were accordingly *prima facie* entitled to reject the goods.

In the words of Bingham J:

> The task of the Court is, to construe the whole of the written contract between the parties in a reasonable and commercial way, against the background of the trade in which the contract was made, in order to ascertain the intentions of the parties. In carrying out its own task the Court will attach weight to the construction put upon the contract by trade arbitrators. The specific object of the construction exercise here is to ascertain whether the words "MAXIMUM 7.5% FIBRE" were words of description used to identify the goods which were to be the subject of the contract, such that any fibre content in excess of this percentage (if not de minimis) would entitle the

17 This section applies where the sale is solely by description. If the buyer sees the actual goods before the sale then section 13 cannot be relied upon, see *Harlington & Leinster v Christopher Hull Fine Art* [1991] 1 QB 564. As made clear on the authorities (see *Arcos v Ranaason* [1933] AC 470, and *Re Moore & Landauer* [1921] 2 KB 519), section 13 simply relates to the description of goods and not quality.

18 For an example of such a term, see Fosfa 54, lines 24 and 25, which states as follows: "At time and place of shipment, the oil shall be of the agreed description and specifications. If the oil is shipped in more than one tank of the same ship, the analysis details of the oil in each separate tank at loading shall conform to the above. Should the oil on arrival not prove equal to the above, or should the oil contain sea water or other admixture, this contract not to be void, but the oil is to be taken with an allowance to be agreed upon or fixed by arbitration provided always that the oil shipped shall conform to the above. Sweepings shall be accepted with a fair allowance, to be fixed by agreement or by arbitration".

19 *Tradax Export S.A. v European Grain & Shipping Co.* [1983] 2 Lloyd's Rep. 100.

buyers to reject goods tendered, or whether they were words relating to quality only, such that any fibre content in excess of this percentage (if not such as to render the goods unmerchantable) would entitle the buyers to damages or an adjustment of the price in their favour but not entitle them to reject the goods. The task of construction should not be conducted in a mechanical, legalistic, old-fashioned or narrow way (see particularly *Ashington Piggeries Ltd. v Christopher Hill Ltd.*, sup., per Lord Diplock at pp. 279 and 501; *Reardon Smith Line Ltd. v Yngvar Hansen-Tangen*, sup., per Lord Wilberforce at pp. 626 and 998C-G).

In my judgment, the words "MAXIMUM 7.5% FIBRE" formed part of the description of the goods to which this contract related and were a condition of the contract. No doubt that conclusion is in part the result of an impression formed by reading the contract as a whole against the background of the facts as found by the Board of Appeal, but there are seven considerations which are not matters of impression only and which I regard as significant:

1. The words appear in the clause of the short form contract which is intended to and does contain the description of the contract goods. This would be the natural place in this form to include a term relating to description.
2. There is no typographical change to indicate that these words are of subsidiary importance compared with the words which precede them, all of which are admittedly words of description.
3. Nothing follows the fibre provision in this clause, and it cannot therefore be said that the clause contains any other provision which is manifestly not descriptive. If the fibre provision is not part of the description, it is the only component of this clause which is not.
4. The contract contained a specific quality clause, to which attention was paid by deletion of the reference to sealed sample. Had the fibre provision been intended to relate to quality only (and not to description as well), this would have been the natural place in the contract to express it, as a supplement to or variation of the provisions "F.A.Q.".
5. The inclusion of a maximum fibre percentage meant that while any percentage below that specified was acceptable any percentage above it by more than a de minimis amount was not. Had the provision been a warranty relating to quality alone, I would not have expected to see a reference to a maximum, but merely the statement of a percentage. It is true that if a warranty of quality had merely said "7.5% fibre", the buyers could theoretically have alleged a breach of warranty if the fibre content fell significantly below that level, but this is commercially wholly unreal since the goods would then have been better than warranted, not worse, so the buyers would have had nothing to gain.
6. The Board of Appeal's findings show that specification of a maximum fibre content (particularly for goods imported into the U.K.) is very uncommon. In the absence of such a provision, a fibre content above normal levels is treated as a matter for price adjustment. This background of practice supports the inference that these parties intended to depart from the usual practice and intended to specify a maximum percentage (a little lower than the norm) failing compliance with which the goods should be liable to rejection.
7. The arbitrators found the maximum fibre provision to be a condition of the contract. The Board of Appeal referred to it as "part of the description of the goods". In the light of the argument they had heard I cannot accept that the Board of Appeal used this language inadvertently. It is said that they did not use it as a legal term of art. I feel sure that Sir MacKenzie Chalmers intended a sale by description in s. 13 of the 1893 Act to mean not some esoteric legal conception but such a sale as a reasonable commercial man would hold to be by description. The Board of Appeal evidently did regard this provision as part

> of the description of the goods even if they did go on to hold (like the umpire in *Arcos v Ronaasen*, sup.) that since the goods were merchantable there should be no right to reject.
>
> So I conclude that "MAXIMUM 7.5% FIBRE" was part of the description of the goods. In arguing that it was not, Mr. Hallgarten accepted that the buyers might have been right had these words, or an expression such as "fibreless", preceded the reference to soya bean meal, or if there had been no dash before the word "MAXIMUM", but these submissions seem to me to reflect the sort of technical, linguistic approach which in other parts of his argument he urged me (as I think rightly) to eschew. He also contended that if this was intended to be a condition, breach of which would entitle the buyers to reject, one would expect to find this clearly spelled out on the face of the document. I would not myself expect it. Contracts of this kind are usually characterized by brevity and the use of a good deal of commercial shorthand. Mr. Rix is in my view right to suggest that it is in the reverse situation, when what would otherwise be grounds for rejection are to be treated as matters for price allowance only, that one most often finds explicit clauses specifying the precise consequences.
>
> It follows that in my view, agreeing with the arbitrators and disagreeing with the Board of Appeal, the sellers were in breach of a condition of the contract in tendering goods not of the contract description and the buyers were accordingly prima facie entitled to reject the goods.[20]

Nevertheless, even if the terms related to the description of the goods clearly amount to conditions by way of explicit reference in the sales contract itself or through the application of section 13 of SOGA, it may be still difficult at times to ascertain whether a specific non-conformity is fatal to the seller.

Under those circumstances, the court or arbitrators will look to evidence from the market as to whether the description of the goods in the contract went to the identity of the commodity sold.[21] In *Marimpex v Dreyfus*,[22] the plaintiffs agreed to sell a quantity of Russian gasoil to the defendants. The sale was a sale by description and the gasoil was described in the contract as "normal Russian gasoil", with no further specifications. It was an express or implied term of the contract that the gasoil would be of merchantable quality.

When the contract was made the gasoil had already been shipped on board the vessel *Zaks Diklo*. It was part of a cargo of 38,278.348 tonnes which had been shipped at Ventspils in Russia under a bill of lading dated 13 July 1992. A volume of 18,000 tonnes was appropriated to the contract.

After the vessel arrived at Hamburg a dispute arose between the parties as to whether the gasoil was of merchantable quality. The defendants submitted that it was neither normal Russian gasoil nor of merchantable quality because it was contaminated by bacteria in such quantities that it was not acceptable in the market. The plaintiffs argued that while like all gasoil it contained bacteria the amount of bacteria was not such as to affect its price or merchantability.

The main issue for decision was whether the gasoil was "normal Russian gasoil", as per contractual description; the problem here lay with the fact that the

20 *Ibid.*, at 104, 105.
21 See Debattista, *Bills of Lading in Export Trade*, above, p. 139.
22 *Marimpex v Dreyfus* [1995] 1 Lloyd's Rep. 167.

sales contract did not contain any specific indications of what are the specific characteristics of "normal Russian gasoil" in terms of amount of bacteria or other foreign bodies.

The court had therefore to turn to the "market" definition of "normal Russian gasoil", i.e. what is the common content of impurity present in gasoil shipped from Russia.

It was eventually held that the contamination of the whole cargo was such that it was not acceptable in the market without treatment or a significant price discount. Indeed, the gasoil was neither normal Russian gasoil nor of merchantable quality; whatever the relevant criteria there could be no doubt that some at least of the gasoil was contaminated to an unacceptable degree.

As stated by Clarke J:

> Mr. Hill's opinion is that the market was much too conservative, both then and now. There is evidence that there is now a common form of clause in contracts for the sale of normal Russian gasoil in which the cost of treating the products with a "bacterial content" of more than 1000 CFUs per litre up to U.S.$3 per tonne is to be borne by the sellers. Mr. Hill takes the view that there is no need to treat oil for domestic use at such low levels of contamination. In the absence of evidence to the contrary I accept that evidence, although for the reasons which I have given I hold that Dreyfus acted reasonably in the light of the advice which they received both as to the level of contamination in this shipment and as to the relevant criteria.
>
> The questions are whether in these circumstances the gasoil was normal Russian gasoil and whether it was of merchantable quality. Mr. Lowe submits that it was normal Russian gasoil because the 1000 CFUs per litre limit was not recognized in the trade at the time and because, even if it was, the description of the cargo as normal Russian gasoil was not describing its quality in terms of the number of bacteria contained within it. He thus submits that the real question is whether the oil was of merchantable quality. In that connection he submits that it was of merchantable quality because in the light of all the knowledge now available it could have been used as domestic fuel or as diesel oil. He relies in particular upon the decisions of the House of Lords in *Henry Kendall & Sons v William Lillico & Sons Ltd.* [1968] 1 Lloyd's Rep. 547; [1969] 2 A.C. 31 (the Hardwick Game Farm case) and in *B.S. Brown & Son Ltd. v Craiks Ltd.* [1970] 1 W.L.R. 752 and upon the decision of the Court of Appeal in *M/S Aswan Engineering Establishment Co. Ltd. v Lupdine Ltd.* [1986] 2 Lloyd's Rep. 347; [1987] 1 W.L.R. 1.
>
> In my judgment the gasoil was neither normal Russian gasoil nor of merchantable quality. Whatever the relevant criteria, there can be no doubt that some at least of the gasoil in shore tank 73 was contaminated to an unacceptable degree. That seems to me to follow from the conclusion of Mr. Hill that 2000 tonnes of it required to be treated. That is some 10 or 11 per cent. of the total consignment. It is true, as Mr. Lowe submits, that Mr. Hill thought that a smaller quantity than that was affected and that the contamination at the bottom was of a different order of magnitude from that further up the tank. But Mr. Hill nevertheless thought that 2000 tonnes should be treated. Such a quantity could not be regarded as de minimis. It is not and cannot be suggested that that part of the cargo was suitable for any use without being treated.[23]

By way of *obiter dictum*, Clarke J thereafter considered the aforementioned scenario in light of section 13 of SOGA 1979:

23 *Ibid.*, at 177.

That conclusion makes it unnecessary to decide whether there was a breach of the condition implied by s. 13(1) of the Act, namely that where (as here) there is a contract of sale of goods by description there is an implied condition that the goods will correspond with the description. However I will express my view shortly. Mr. Lowe submits that the bacterial characteristics of the gasoil are not part of the description and that the description "normal" tells one nothing about the number of bacteria to be expected in the oil. Mr. Howard submits on the other hand that it is well settled that words relating to quality can form part of the description of the goods and that here they do.

Mr. Howard is right to say that words relating to quality can form part of the description: see *Benjamin's* at par. 11–017. The question is whether the word "normal" forms part of the description here. In my judgment it does, at least to some extent. So for example the expression "normal" would give an indication that the pour point of the oil was within certain limits. If it were not, the oil might be Russian but not normal. The word must I think add something to the expression "Russian gasoil." The question is what. It seems to me that it says something about the quality. To come within the description the oil must have attributes which are within those to be expected in normal Russian gasoil.

Thus I would hold that if the gasoil was such that it was so contaminated that it required significant treatment before it could be used for any purpose or alternatively had to be sold at a significant discount it could no longer fairly be described as normal Russian gasoil. In the light of the views of Mr. Hill as to the necessity on any view of treating some 10 per cent. or more of the oil in shore tank 73 I would hold that the oil was not normal Russian gasoil. On the contrary it was abnormal gasoil because a significant part of it could not be used without more than minimal expenditure.

Those conclusions seem to me to make it unnecessary to consider what the position would have been had the whole of the oil been fit for use as domestic oil [. . .] It follows from the conclusions which I have stated above that in 1992 the gasoil was not saleable for any purpose without either treatment or a discount once the potential buyers were aware of the contamination. I accept the evidence of Mr. Caperton that there is no distinction for this purpose between buyers of the gasoil for use as diesel oil or heating oil and buyers for other purposes. Thus none of the potential buyers was willing to buy the gasoil except at a significant discount or perhaps after it had been appropriately treated.

In my judgment the same would be true to-day. Although the position is now, as then, that the oil could in fact be used for heating oil or as diesel oil without ill effects, the market nevertheless regards gasoil with more than 1000 CFUs per litre of bacteria, yeasts or moulds as being unacceptable without treatment. This is shown by the type of contract to which I have already referred in which there is a provision entitling the buyers to have the gasoil treated at the sellers' expense up to a maximum of U.S.$3 per metric tonne. In my judgment in the absence of such treatment the gasoil would be neither merchantable nor "normal" Russian gasoil.[24]

The judgment in *Marimpex v Dreyfus* also touched upon the concept of "merchantable" or "satisfactory quality" under section 14 of SOGA 1979, to which our attention shall now turn.

24 *Ibid.*, at 178, 179.

9.7 Section 14 of SOGA 1979: The implied condition of satisfactory quality

Another implied term in relation to the seller's physical duties which will amount to a condition the breach of which might be fatal to the seller relates the concept of "satisfactory quality" enshrined into section 14 of SOGA 1979.

In 1995, section 14(2) of the SOGA 1979 changed the duty from one of supplying "merchantable" goods to one of supplying "goods of satisfactory quality". Section 14 reads as follows:

SOGA 1979, section 14 Implied terms about quality or fitness

(1) Except as provided by this section and section 15 below and subject to any other enactment, there is no implied condition or warranty about the quality or fitness for any particular purpose of goods supplied under a contract of sale.

(2) Where the seller sells goods in the course of a business, there is an implied term that the goods supplied under the contract are of satisfactory quality.

(2A) For the purposes of this Act, goods are of satisfactory quality if they meet the standard that a reasonable person would regard as satisfactory, taking account of any description of the goods, the price (if relevant) and all the other relevant circumstances.

(2B) For the purposes of this Act, the quality of goods includes their state and condition and the following (among others) are in appropriate cases aspects of the quality of goods –

- (a) fitness for all the purposes for which goods of the kind in question are commonly supplied,
- (b) appearance and finish,
- (c) freedom from minor defects,
- (d) safety, and
- (e) durability.

(2C) The term implied by subsection (2) above does not extend to any matter making the quality of goods unsatisfactory –

- (a) which is specifically drawn to the buyer's attention before the contract is made,
- (b) where the buyer examines the goods before the contract is made, which that examination ought to reveal, or
- (c) in the case of a contract for sale by sample, which would have been apparent on a reasonable examination of the sample.

(2D) If the buyer deals as consumer or, in Scotland, if a contract of sale is a consumer contract, the relevant circumstances mentioned in subsection (2A) above include any public statements on the specific characteristics of the goods made about them by the seller, the producer or his representative, particularly in advertising or on labelling.

(2E) A public statement is not by virtue of subsection (2D) above a relevant circumstance for the purposes of subsection (2A) above in the case of a contract of sale, if the seller shows that –

- (a) at the time the contract was made, he was not, and could not reasonably have been, aware of the statement,
- (b) before the contract was made, the statement had been withdrawn in public or, to the extent that it contained anything which was incorrect or misleading, it had been corrected in public, or
- (c) the decision to buy the goods could not have been influenced by the statement.

(2F) Subsections (2D) and (2E) above do not prevent any public statement from being a relevant circumstance for the purposes of subsection (2A) above (whether or not the buyer deals as consumer or, in Scotland, whether or not the contract of sale is a consumer contract) if the statement would have been such a circumstance apart from those subsections.

(3) Where the seller sells goods in the course of a business and the buyer, expressly or by implication, makes known –
  (a) to the seller, or
  (b) where the purchase price or part of it is payable by instalments and the goods were previously sold by a credit-broker to the seller, to that credit-broker, any particular purpose for which the goods are being bought, there is an implied condition that the goods supplied under the contract are reasonably fit for that purpose, whether or not that is a purpose for which such goods are commonly supplied, except where the circumstances show that the buyer does not rely, or that it is unreasonable for him to rely, on the skill or judgment of the seller or credit-broker.

(4) An implied condition or warranty about quality or fitness for a particular purpose may be annexed to a contract of sale by usage.

(5) The preceding provisions of this section apply to a sale by a person who in the course of a business is acting as agent for another as they apply to a sale by a principal in the course of a business, except where that other is not selling in the course of a business and either the buyer knows that fact or reasonable steps are taken to bring it to the notice of the buyer before the contract is made.

(6) As regards England and Wales and Northern Ireland, the terms implied by subsections (2) and (3) above are conditions.

Liability under SOGA, section 14 is strict and not dependent on proof of fault on the part of the seller. In applying this section, a judge would thus consider whether a reasonable person would regard the goods as of satisfactory quality looking at the stated aspects in addition to all other relevant circumstances. Looking at fitness for purpose, a court of law will consider whether the goods are fit for the purpose for which the goods are commonly supplied.

In addition to the statutory guidance given by section 14 itself, whereby criteria for the determination of satisfactory quality of goods include their state and condition and appearance and finish, freedom from minor defects, safety, and durability, courts would generally apply the acceptability and usability tests to help determine if the goods in question are of satisfactory quality.

The acceptability test looks at whether a reasonable purchaser would have accepted the goods at the same price had they known of the defect. In *Shine v General Guarantee Corp*,[25] the claimant purchased a second hand sports car from a car dealer. The car gave him constant problems and he then discovered that the car had previously been in an accident and had been totally submerged in water. The claimant brought an action under section 14(2). The courts applied the acceptability test asking whether a reasonable purchaser would have accepted the goods at the stated price knowing of the fault. Clearly in this case a reasonable purchaser would not have accepted the goods and therefore the seller was in breach.

25 *Shine v General Guarantee Corp* [1988] 1 All ER 911. See Debattista, *Bills of Lading in Export Trade*, above, p. 169. See also *Benjamin's Sale of Goods*, above, paras. 19.286 *et seq.*

Alongside the acceptability test, in assessing issues related to section 14, courts often use the so called "usability test" "less generous than the acceptability test, this test requires the court to consider if a reasonable purchaser could have used the goods for the purposes for which the goods were commonly supplied".[26]

In *Aswan Engineering v Lupdine*,[27] the claimants purchased some liquid waterproofing from the defendant which was contained in some heavy duty plastic pails. The pails were described as being heavy duty and suitable for storage outside. The claimant stored the pails outside, but they were in Kuwait and the pails were left out in the sun in temperatures of up to 70°C. Consequently, the pails melted and the liquid waterproofing was ruined.

The court applied the usability test asking whether a reasonable user could have used the goods for the purposes for which they are commonly supplied. The court held that there was no breach of section14 as it was the extreme conditions which caused the pails to melt, and a reasonable user could have used the goods without incurring damage.

Likewise, in the aforementioned judgment in *Marimpex v Dreyfus*, the court was asked to determine the "merchantability" and satisfactory quality of a cargo described in the sales contract as "normal Russian gasoil". In applying the "usability test", Clarke J held that:

> In my judgment the gasoil was neither normal Russian gasoil nor of merchantable quality. Whatever the relevant criteria, there can be no doubt that some at least of the gasoil in shore tank 73 was contaminated to an unacceptable degree. That seems to me to follow from the conclusion of Mr. Hill that 2000 tonnes of it required to be treated. That is some 10 or 11 per cent. of the total consignment. It is true, as Mr. Lowe submits, that Mr. Hill thought that a smaller quantity than that was affected and that the contamination at the bottom was of a different order of magnitude from that further up the tank. But Mr. Hill nevertheless thought that 2000 tonnes should be treated. Such a quantity could not be regarded as de minimis. It is not and cannot be suggested that that part of the cargo was suitable for any use without being treated. It follows, in my judgment, that on any view of the meaning of merchantable quality this cargo was not merchantable.

Section 14(6) of the Sale of Goods Act, 1979 provides:

> Goods of any kind are of merchantable quality within the meaning of subsection (2) above if they are as fit for the purpose or purposes for which goods of that kind are commonly bought as it is reasonable to expect having regard to any description applied to them, the price (if relevant) and all the other necessary circumstances.

---

26 See *Dalmare SpA v Union Maritime Ltd* [2012] EWHC 3537 (Comm); [2013] 2 All ER 870; [2013] 2 All ER (Comm) 70; [2013] 1 Lloyd's Rep. 509. Here, a sales contract on the Norwegian Saleform 1993, which provided that the vessel was to be delivered and taken over "as she was" at the time of inspection, fair wear and tear excepted, did not exclude the implied term of satisfactory quality in the SOGA 1979, section 14(2). See also *Bominflot Bunkergesellschaft fur Mineralole mbH & Co KG v Petroplus Marketing AG (The Mercini Lady)* [2012] EWHC 3009 (Comm); [2013] 1 All ER (Comm) 610; [2013] 1 Lloyd's Rep. 360, where a buyer of gasoil was awarded damages for losses arising from the gasoil having been unstable on delivery. Unstable gasoil could not be used for any of the relevant grade of gasoil's usual purposes and therefore the gasoil had not been of satisfactory quality for the purposes of the SOGA 1979, section 14(2).

27 *Engineering v Lupdine* [1987] 1 All ER 135.

> Given that 10 per cent. or more of the gasoil was not fit for any purpose without treatment it follows that the consignment was not fit for the purpose or purposes for which gasoil is commonly bought within the meaning of that sub-section. Moreover there is nothing in any of the cases to which Mr. Lowe has referred which leads to any other conclusion.
>
> Further, as I indicated above, Mr. Hill's initial view that 2000 tonnes should be treated was based upon his assumption that SGS results related only the total of bacteria, yeasts and moulds. When he appreciated that that was not so, he expressed the view that an owner could not be criticized if he decided that the whole cargo should be treated. Moreover he took that view notwithstanding his opinion that at least the cargo above 30cm. could have been used for domestic purposes. In all the circumstances I have reached the conclusion that the consignment was not of merchantable quality and that Marimpex were in breach of the condition of merchantable quality which it is common ground was either express or to be implied into the contract by s. 14(2) of the 1979 Act.
>
> Mr. Lowe submits that that is not so because, even if the oil could have been sold only at a discount, that is of little if any significance unless the discount was very substantial. In this connection he refers to the decision of the House of Lords in *Brown v Craiks* (sup.). However that was a case where the goods could be used for one of the purposes for which such goods were commonly used without any work being done on them. In the instant case the oil could not be used for any purpose unless more than de minimis expenditure was incurred. In these circumstances the oil was not in my judgment merchantable within the meaning of s. 14(6) of the Act.[28]

Within the context of contracts concluded on shipment terms, the concept of "satisfactory quality" assumes a different dimension which invariably needs to be linked with transit of the goods.

Indeed, under contracts concluded on delivery terms, the point of delivery is the point of arrival and the goods must be durable at that point and for as long as they would need to be durable in a physical sale.

The scenario is radically different in a shipment sale where the seller is only bound to ship the goods; to what extent does the physical duty to provide the buyer with goods of satisfactory quality apply? Is that duty extended to the point of discharge, whatever happens on the voyage?

The answer to that question was given in *Mash & Murrell Ltd v Joseph I. Emanuel Ltd*:[29] the seller must deliver goods on board in such a state as to withstand the strains and stresses of a normal voyage.

The case involved a sale by the defendant (vegetable importers) to the plaintiff (vegetable dealers) of 50 tons of Cyprus potatoes c.&f. Liverpool. Upon their arrival at Liverpool, the potatoes were found to be rotten.

A claim was consequently brought by the buyers alleging that: (a) the potatoes were not fit to travel; (b) the sellers were in breach of section 14(1) (implied condition of fitness for purpose) of the Sale of Goods Act, 1893, in that the potatoes were not fit for the purpose of being carried to Liverpool for sale for human consumption; (c) the sellers were in breach of section 14(2) (warranty as to merchantable quality) in that the potatoes, at the time of shipment, were not merchantable as potatoes sold for carriage and delivery to Liverpool by Ionian; and

28 See *Marimpex v Dreyfus* [1995] 1 Lloyd's Rep. 167, at 178.
29 *Mash & Murrell Ltd v Joseph I. Emanuel Ltd* [1961] 2 Lloyd's Rep. 326.

(d) the sellers were in breach of the implied warranty in c.i.f. and c.&f. contracts that goods should be fit to withstand a normal voyage and should arrive sound and fit for sale for human consumption.

It was held by the court that when the potatoes were loaded at the port of origin, they were not fit to travel; the buyers had made known the purpose for which the goods were required (for sale for human consumption after arrival), and the goods were not fit for that purpose on arrival.

In relation to the warranty as to merchantable quality, the court stated that, in the case of goods sold c.&f. terms, the warranty entailed that the goods should remain merchantable for a reasonable period of time (time for normal transit and for disposal), and that the warranty was broken. The sellers were, thus, found in breach of the warranty to ship the goods in such a condition as to be capable of withstanding a normal voyage and to be of merchantable quality on arrival.

In the words of Pearson LJ:

> Does the new term of durability extend that duty to the point of discharge whatever happens on the voyage?
>
> The agreement for sale was made on July 8, 1957, and the potatoes delivered under it had been shipped at Limassol on June 29, 1957. The potatoes were accepted, paid for and disposed of by the plaintiffs. No question arises as to whether the plaintiffs were entitled to reject the goods, or whether the defendants were entitled to recover the price. The only claim in the action is by the plaintiffs for damages for alleged breach of an implied warranty of quality. The learned Judge held that there was an implied warranty, and that the plaintiffs had proved a breach of it by the defendants, and therefore the plaintiffs were entitled to recover damages.
>
> Mr. Ashton Roskill, in presenting this appeal on behalf of the defendants, began by saying that he had two submissions, namely, (1) that, on the assumption that there was a warranty as alleged, the plaintiffs had failed to prove any breach of it, and (2) that there was no warranty as alleged. When he had concluded his argument on the first submission, he was stopped by the Court, and the ensuing arguments by Mr. Roche, on behalf of the plaintiffs, and by Mr. Roskill, in reply, were confined to the first submission. Thus the questions as to the existence and precise nature of the alleged warranty have not been considered in this Court. The warranty which has been assumed for the purposes of the first submission is broadly to the effect that the potatoes were, when supplied, "fit to travel" in the sense that they were on shipment of such quality (including condition) that, after a normal voyage to Liverpool, they would be in a proper state on arrival there. It is not necessary to elaborate what is meant by "a proper state on arrival", because it is common ground that the potatoes on arrival at Liverpool were in an advanced stage of soft-rot and manifestly unfit for human consumption and saleable only as pig food. The assumed warranty is retroactive, in the sense that the defendants, in making on July 8, 1957, the agreement to sell, are assumed to have impliedly warranted that the potatoes were fit to travel on the previous date of shipment, which is June 29, 1957. There was no argument on the question, but, to give some explanation of the retroactive element which was introduced into the assumed warranty, reference was made to two cases, namely, *Monarch Steamship Company, Ltd. v Karlshamns Oljefabriker (A/B)* [1949] A.C. 196; (1948) 82 Ll.L.Rep. 137 – the passage on pp. 229 and 155 of the respective reports per Lord Wright – and the other case mentioned was *Biddell Brothers v E. Clemens Horst Company* [1911] 1 K.B. 934 – in the Court of Appeal per Lord Justice Kennedy at pp. 955 to 956.
>
> The sole question considered in this appeal has been whether the plaintiffs have, on the evidence, proved a breach by the defendants of the assumed warranty. The plaintiffs did not seek to show by direct evidence that the potatoes were not "fit to

> travel" when they were shipped at Limassol on June 29, 1957, but they sought to show it indirectly by inference from the admitted fact that the potatoes were in a bad state when they arrived at Liverpool and from the alleged fact, which they endeavoured to prove, that the voyage from Limassol to Liverpool was a normal voyage. That would be the necessary inference from those facts, because "fit to travel" is taken in this case to mean able to reach Liverpool in good state after a normal voyage.[30]

Within the context of contracts concluded on shipment terms, *Mush & Murrel* thus creates an implied obligation whereby the seller is under the obligation to ship the goods in such a state as to be capable of withstanding transit. Failure to do so will ignite the possibility for the buyer to reject the goods and repudiate the contract.

9.8 Section 15 SOGA 1979: Goods sold as per sample

Where the goods are sold "as per sample", the goods shipped must conform to the sample. Section 15 of the Act states as follows:

> **SOGA 1979, section 15 Sale by sample**
>
> (1) A contract of sale is a contract for sale by sample where there is an express or implied term to that effect in the contract.
> (2) In the case of a contract for sale by sample there is an implied term –
> (a) that the bulk will correspond with the sample in quality;
> (3) As regards England and Wales and Northern Ireland, the term implied by subsection (2) above is a condition.

Section 15 applies to contracts for the sale of goods by sample. This is where a buyer is shown a sample of a unit or a batch of units and then orders a large quantity of those goods. Section 15 simply includes two terms into such a contract: first, that the bulk of the goods will correspond with the quality of the shown sample; second, to a similar effect, that the goods will be free from any defects which would not have been apparent on an inspection of the sample.

9.9 The quantity of the goods: A condition of a contract concluded on shipment terms?

Traditionally, quantity has always been considered part of the description of the goods, breach of which would entitle the buyer to reject the goods and terminate the contract.

Commodity sale standard forms often contain clauses which provide for allowances;[31] without these contractual thresholds, the default position would be that the buyer could reject for breach of description.

---

30 *Ibid.*, at 339.

31 See Fosfa 54 1. Clause 1 Tolerance: "Sellers have the option of shipping 5% more or less of the mean contract quantity. In the event of more than one shipment being made each shipment is to be considered as a separate contract but the tolerance on the mean contract quantity is not to be affected thereby." See also GA 100, clause 2 Quantity, which states as follows: "Sellers shall have the option of shipping a further 3% more or less than the contract quantity. The excess above 2% or the deficiency below 2% shall be settled on the quantity thereof at shipment at market value on the last

Indeed, it is clear on the authorities that even if the seller ships a quantity larger than the agreed quantity, the buyer can reject the cargo.

This is what happened in *Re Keighley Maxtead & Co and Bryant Durant & Co*.[32] Here a contract in writing for the sale of "About 3,000 tons of wheat, 10 per cent more or less, to be shipped by steamer" from India, provided for payment to be made by cash in London within seven days from delivery of the invoice in exchange for the bill or bills of lading.

The contract contained, inter alia, the following clause: "Sellers have option of shipping less than the minimum quantity, in which case the price of the quantity short shipped of the medium quantity will be settled at the value of the day of the appropriation. Sellers can also exceed the maximum quantity, in which case the excess over the medium quantity will remain for their account."

The seller informed the buyer that 3,800 tons had been shipped on Bombay, and that he appropriated 3,000 tons of that shipment to the contract with the buyer, and he subsequently sent the buyer an invoice for 3,000 tons ex Bombay. The bills of lading of the 3,000 tons were two for 1,750 tons each and two for 250 tons each. The seller offered to deliver to the buyer either all the bills of lading or two for 1,750 tons each, but the seller refused to accept the tender or to pay any part of the price.

It was held by the court that the buyers were entitled to delivery of a bill or bills of lading for the amount of wheat which they had bought, and were entitled to refuse the tender made by the sellers.

The seller, instead, indicated in the bill of lading a higher quantity of product than specified in the commercial invoice; that the buyer was at his option to reject the bill on the ground of falsity regarding quantity, and the seller was and should be bound to provide such a bill which should and must contain the description of the specific goods and the specific quantity as per the commercial invoice.

9.10 Section 15A SOGA 1979: The *de minimis* rule

Section 15A of SOGA 1979 lays down the content of the so called *de minimis* rule. It states as follows:

SOGA 1979, section 15 Modification of remedies for breach of condition in non-consumer cases

(1) Where in the case of a contract of sale –

(a) the buyer would, apart from this subsection, have the right to reject goods by reason of a breach on the part of the seller of a term implied by section 13, 14 or 15 above, but

day of discharge of the vessel at the port of destination; the value to be fixed by arbitration, unless mutually agreed. Should sellers exercise the option to ship up to 5% more, the excess over 2% shall be paid for provisionally at contract price. The difference between the contract price and the market price calculated in accordance with the provisions of this clause shall be adjusted in a final invoice. In the event of more than one shipment being made, each shipment shall be considered a separate contract, but the margin of the mean quantity sold shall not be affected thereby."

32 *Re Keighley Maxtead & Co and Bryant Durant & Co* (1894) 7 Asp MLC 418.

(b) the breach is so slight that it would be unreasonable for him to reject them, then, if the buyer does not deal as consumer, the breach is not to be treated as a breach of condition but may be treated as a breach of warranty.

(2) This section applies unless a contrary intention appears in, or is to be implied from, the contract.

(3) It is for the seller to show that a breach fell within subsection (1)(b) above.

Section 15A is based on the Roman law principle *de minimis non curat lex*, which translated into the common law principle whereby judges "will not sit in judgment of extremely minor transgressions of the law".

That is the scope of application of section 15A, which will save a defective physical performance of the seller in the case that the breach committed by the seller is so slight as to render it unreasonable for the buyer to reject the cargo.

What constitutes a "slight breach" capable of triggering the application of section 15A needs to be assessed on a case by case basis and requires judicial intervention.

In *Arcos v Ranaason*,[33] a contract for the sale of a quantity of wooden staves for making barrels described the staves as being half an inch thick. Some of the staves delivered were not half an inch thick but very slightly out. There was nothing wrong with the quality of the wood and they could still be used for the intended purpose of making barrels. The buyer rejected the goods as the price of wood had fallen and he could purchase them cheaper elsewhere.

The House of Lords held that the purchasers were entitled to reject the goods under section 13 as they were not as described.

In the words of Lord Atkin:

> The decisions of the learned judge and of the Court of Appeal appear to me to have been unquestionably right. On the facts as stated by the umpire as of the time of inspection only about 5 per cent. of the goods corresponded with the description: and the umpire finds it impossible to say what proportion conformed at the time of shipment.
>
> It was contended that in all commercial contracts the question was whether there was a "substantial" compliance with the contract: there always must be some margin: and it is for the tribunal of fact to determine whether the margin is exceeded or not. I cannot agree. If the written contract specifies conditions of weight, measurement and the like, those conditions must be complied with. A ton does not mean about a ton, or a yard about a yard. Still less when you descend to minute measurements does ½ inch mean about ½ inch. If the seller wants a margin he must and in my experience does stipulate for it. Of course by recognized trade usage particular figures may be given a different meaning, as in a baker's dozen; or there may be even incorporated a definite margin more or less: but there is no evidence or finding of such a usage in the present case.
>
> No doubt there may be microscopic deviations which business men and therefore lawyers will ignore. And in this respect it is necessary to remember that description and quantity are not necessarily the same: and that the legal rights in respect of them are regulated by different sections of the code, description by s. 13, quantity by s. 30. It will be found that most of the cases that admit any deviation from the contract are cases where there has been an excess or deficiency in quantity which the Court has considered negligible. But apart from this consideration the right view is that the

33 *Arcos v Ranaason* [1933] AC 470. See Debattista, *Bills of Lading in Export Trade*, above, p. 196. See also *Benjamin's Sale of Goods*, above, paras. 20.212 *et seq.*

> conditions of the contract must be strictly performed. If a condition is not performed the buyer has a right to reject. I do not myself think that there is any difference between business men and lawyers on this matter. No doubt, in business, men often find it unnecessary or inexpedient to insist on their strict legal rights. In a normal market if they get something substantially like the specified goods they may take them with or without grumbling and a claim for an allowance. But in a falling market I find that buyers are often as eager to insist on their legal rights as courts of law are ready to maintain them. No doubt at all times sellers are prepared to take a liberal view as to the rigidity of their own obligations, and possibly buyers who in turn are sellers may also dislike too much precision. But buyers are not, as far as my experience goes, inclined to think that the rights defined in the code are in excess of business needs.[34]

Lord Atkin's reference to "microscopic deviations which business men and therefore lawyers will ignore" appears to suggest that, rather than being of wide application, the *de minimis* rule will save the defective performance of a seller only under extreme circumstances.

In *Shipton, Anderson & Co. v Weil Brothers & Co.*,[35] under a contract for the sale of a cargo of wheat weighing 10 per cent more or less than 4500 tons, the sellers tendered a cargo weighing 55 lbs more than the maximum quantity of 4950 tons.

The buyers rejected the whole cargo solely upon the ground that the quantity tendered was 55 lbs in excess of the contract quantity.

The court was asked to decide, inter alia, whether the sellers were only entitled to calculate the 8 per cent on 4500; the excess tendered was so trifling as not to amount to a breach of the contract.

It was held that, as the quantity in excess was so trifling and the sellers had not claimed the price thereof, the sellers had substantially performed the contract, and the buyers were not entitled to reject the cargo under section 30(2) of the Sale of Goods Act, 1893, which provides that "where the seller delivers to the buyer a quantity of goods larger than he contracted to sell, the buyer . . . may reject the whole."

As stated by Lush J:

> Having first decided that, upon the true construction of the contract, the plaintiffs were only entitled to deliver 4950 tons, proceeded: The second question is whether, if the plaintiffs were only entitled to calculate the 8 per cent. on the 4500 tons, which is in my view the true position, the excess in fact tendered was so trifling as not to amount to a breach of the contract. Now the excess quantity is trifling, so trifling that it is quite impossible to suppose that any business man would regard it as in any way affecting the substance of the contract or as making the contract any the more or any the less an advantageous contract to enter into. It is an excess of 55 lbs. in a total cargo of 4950 tons; approximately it is an excess of 1 lb. in every 100 tons tendered. If one considers the excess in money, it seems more trifling still; it is an excess of 4s. on a contract price of over 40,000l.; or putting it again in still plainer figures an excess of 1s. in 10,000l. Counsel for the defendants, however, say that that is an excess which by law entitles the buyer to reject, and they rely upon s. 30, sub-s. 2, of the Sale of Goods Act of 1893. That section says: [His Lordship read the sub-section]. They contend, as they must to be consistent, that any excess that can be measured in weight or in currency would have this effect, that, if it is only sixpence or indeed anything that

34 *Arcos v Ranaason* [1933] AC 470, at 479.
35 *Shipton, Anderson & Co. v Weil Brothers & Co* [1912] 1 KB 574.

can be measured, there is a discrepancy between the contract and the tender which is fatal. I asked if there was any authority for such a contention, and I was referred to the case of *Tamvaco v Lucas*. 5 The difference between the contract quantity and the shipped quantity was, no doubt, not very large in that case, and it was undoubtedly held that the tender was a bad tender because there had been an excess; but I would point out that, as far as I can gather from the arguments and from the judgment, the question was not raised which is raised in this case, whether there can be an excess so trivial that it is not in substance an excess at all. That case was dealt with on the footing that there had been in fact an excessive tender, and the question was whether in the circumstances of that case the buyer could or could not reject. I do not think that that case can be relied upon as an authority for the proposition that any excess, if once it can be measured and put into pounds, shillings, and pence, or put into weight, is of itself necessarily in law an excess which makes the tender bad. I have found a case which I think is more in point. It is true that the actual point was not decided, because it was not necessary to decide it; but there was a dictum of Bingham J. in that case which exactly, in my opinion, applies to this case. The case to which I refer is *Harland v Burstall*. 6 A smaller quantity was there delivered than the contract quantity, thirty loads out of 500, of course a very different proportion to this, and Bigham J. held that there was a deficiency which entitled the buyers to reject. The learned judge says this: "Of course, in carrying out a commercial contract such as this, some slight elasticity is unavoidable; no one supposes that the delivery is to be within a cubic foot of the named quantity, but it must be substantially of the quantity named; and in my judgment 470 loads is not substantially 500." I think that the question is whether there has been a substantial departure from the contract. As I pointed out during the argument, the right to reject is founded upon the hypothesis that the seller was not ready and willing to perform, or had not performed, his part of the contract. The tender of a wrong quantity evidences an unreadiness and unwillingness, but that, in my opinion, must mean an excess or deficiency in quantity which is capable of influencing the mind of the buyer. In my opinion, this excess is not. I agree that directly the excess becomes a matter of possible discussion between reasonable parties, the seller is bound to justify what he has done under the contract; but the doctrine of de minimis cannot, I think, be excluded merely because the statute refers to the tender of a smaller or larger quantity than the contract quantity as entitling a buyer to reject.

I wish to add this. The reason why an excess in tender entitles a buyer to reject is that the seller seeks to impose a burden on the buyer which he is not entitled to impose. That burden is the payment of money not agreed to be paid. It is prima facie no burden on the buyer to have 55 lbs. more than 4,950 tons offered to him, and there is nothing to suggest that these sellers would have ever insisted, or thought of insisting, upon payment of the 4s. over the 40,000l. The sellers' original appropriation appeared to be within the proper quantity. The excess of 55 lbs. appears when the quantity shipped is converted from kilos into tons. If the sellers had expressly or impliedly insisted upon payment of the 4s. upon their view of the contract, the case would have been different; but nothing of that kind can be supposed to have taken place here.[36]

In light of the aforementioned cases, it is of difficult execution to provide guidelines in relation to the application of section 15A of SOGA 1979 to contracts concluded on shipment terms.

Nevertheless, it is important to notice that the *de minimis* rule will apply only to extreme scenarios; sellers, thus, are best advised not to be overly reliant on section 15A as a sort of default mechanism of defence in a case of defective performance of their physical duties.

36 *Ibid.*, at 577, 578.

9.11 Time of shipment

Although not enshrined in SOGA 1979 as an implied term amounting to a condition, it is clear on the authorities that time of shipment is part of the terms describing the goods and is an implied condition of contracts concluded on shipment terms.

Indeed, where a contract stipulates shipment within certain dates, all the goods sold must be shipped by the date or within the period agreed in the sale, and the bill of lading date must conform to the contract.

This was held in *Bowes v Shand*,[37] where two contracts, each for the sale of 300 tons of rice, were made in London. The first contract (which the second exactly followed) was for 300 tons "of Madras rice, to be shipped at Madras, or coast, for this port, during the months of March and/or April, 1874, per Rajah of Cochin". The 600 tons filled 8200 bags.

The vessel arrived at Madras in February, and on the 23 February, 1780 bags were put on board; on 28 February, 3560 bags were put on board, and bills of lading were given for those amounts on the days mentioned. A bill of lading for the remaining 1080 bags was given on the 3 March, but all except 50 bags had been put on board before that day.

In an action for refusing to accept the rice, the defence was that it had not been shipped during the months of March and/or April.

The court held that the contract had not been complied with; indeed, in the case of the shipments in one or more specially chartered vessels, such vessel or vessels must complete the loading of all the cargo within the time stipulated by the contract. In the case of shipments by liner, the cargo shall be loaded on board within the stipulated time.

In the words of Lord Chancellor Cairns LJ:

> The case appears to me, when properly considered, to be an extremely simple one. The action is brought upon two contracts for the sale of rice, which differ only in respect of the price, and therefore it will be sufficient that I should refer to one of the contracts. The first of the two contracts is dated on the 17th of March, 1874; and the sold note, which is written to the Respondents, Shand & Co., runs in these words: "We have this day sold for your account to Bowes, Martin, & Kent, the following Madras rice to be shipped at Madras, or coast, for this port during the months of March and/or April, 1874, about (300) three hundred tons per Rajah of Cochin, eleven and ten pence halfpenny per cwt.; for 'fair pinky.'" That sentence includes all that for the present purpose it is material that I should refer to.
>
> My Lords, so far as the construction of the contract expressed in those words is concerned, unless there be something peculiar to the words by reason of the custom of the trade to which the contract relates, the construction of the contract is for the Court. That has been said so often that I need not refer your Lordships to any authority upon the subject. The Court it is which, when once it is in possession of the circumstances surrounding the contract, and of any peculiarity of meaning which may be attached by reason of the custom of the trade, to any of the words of that contract, has to place the construction upon the contract. I shall assume, in the first place, that there is no word in this contract which is proved by the custom of the trade to have any particular meaning. I shall afterwards consider whether it has been proved that there is any custom attaching a particular meaning to the words used.

37 *Bowes v Shand* (1877) 2 App Cas 455 (HL).

My Lords, looking at the construction of these words, I put aside in the first place some which to any one unaccustomed to a contract of this kind, might appear peculiar, the words and/or, inasmuch as no question has been raised on these words, and it is agreed upon both sides that they are so used simply as a mercantile way of expressing that something is to be done in the months of March and April, or in either of those months. Putting that aside, and looking still at what would be the ordinary and the grammatical meaning of the words, it will I think occur to your Lordships that it is possible that the words which I have read may mean one of two things. It might be held that they mean that the rice which is spoken of, is to be put on board the ship which is mentioned, during some part of the two months specified, the months of March and April, 1874, and that that is the meaning of the words "to be shipped" during those months, or it might be held that they mean that the shipment is to be made continuously and in such a way as that it is to come to a conclusion in one of the months in question, and then a bill of lading, representing the shipment and the contract made on the shipment, is to be given inside of one of those months for the whole of the rice in question.

My Lords, if that is the natural meaning of the words, it does not appear to me to be a question for your Lordships, or for any Court, to consider whether that is a contract which bears upon the face of it some reason, some explanation why it was made in that form, and why the stipulation is made that the shipment should be during these particular months. It is a mercantile contract, and merchants are not in the habit of placing upon their contracts stipulations to which they do not attach some value and importance, and that alone might be a sufficient answer. But, if necessary, a farther answer is obtained from two other considerations. It is quite obvious that merchants making contracts for the purchase of rice, contracts which oblige them to pay in a certain manner for the rice purchased, and to be ready with the funds for making that payment, may well be desirous both that the rice should be forthcoming to them not later than a certain time, and also that the rice shall not be forthcoming to them at a time earlier than it suits them to be ready with funds for its payment. Therefore it may well be that a merchant making a number of rice contracts, ranging over several months of the year, will be desirous of expressing that the rice shall come forward at such times, and at such intervals of time, as that it will be convenient for him to make the payments, and it may well be that a merchant will consider that he has obtained that end if he provides for the shipment of the rice during a particular month, or during particular months, and that he will know that provided he has made that stipulation the rice will not be forthcoming at a time when it will be inconvenient for him to provide the money for the payment. My Lords, there is still another explanation which appears upon part of the evidence in this case; because sufficient appears upon the evidence to shew that these contracts were made for the purpose of satisfying and fulfilling other contracts which Messrs. Bowes, Martin, & Kent, had made with other persons, and it is at least doubtful whether if they had made a contract in any other form than that which is before your Lordships, a contract made in another form, or a contract made without this stipulation as to the shipment during these months, would have been a fulfilment of those other contracts which they desired to be in a position to fulfil.

Therefore, my Lords, still dwelling merely upon the natural meaning of these words, and without any evidence as to their having any particular or customary meaning, I should undoubtedly say, and say without hesitation, that the meaning of this contract must be one of two things. Prima facie, I should say it meant that the shipment must be made, that the rice must be put on board, during the two specified months, and neither before nor after those months. But if the contract does not mean that, the only other meaning which it appears to me it could have is – and as to that I think evidence would be required to shew that by usage it had obtained that meaning – that the shipment should be made in a manner which could be described as continuous, and that it should come to a consummation or completion in one of these months which are here mentioned, and that the bill of lading should be given for the whole and complete shipment at that time. My Lords, if those two meanings be the only possible meanings of this contract, if they be the natural meanings of the contract, then according to neither meaning was the rice in this case put on board in such a way that it could be tendered in fulfilment of the contract; because the whole of the rice was actually on board, not merely at the time when this contract was made, but during the month of February, with the exception of fifty bags, which were put on board on the 2nd of March; and bills of lading had been given during the month of February for all the parcels of the rice with the exception of 1080 of the bags in respect of which a bill of lading was given on the 3rd of March. According, therefore, to neither of those constructions would the rice have been put on board in such a way as to make it a tender in fulfilment of the contract.

My Lords, still dwelling upon the case without reference to what took place at the trial, or to any evidence with regard to any custom, I now turn from this construction, which I submit to your Lordships is the natural and only possible construction, literally, of the words, to the construction which the contract has received in the Court of Appeal. Lord Justice Mellish on this subject speaks in this way. He says: "The real question is, whether in order to fulfil a contract that 600 tons of rice should be shipped in March or April, it is necessary that the whole 600 tons should have been put on board in March or April, or whether it is sufficient that the shipment should have been completed in March or April." He then refers to a case which I shall afterwards have to refer to, and he continues: "The word 'shipped' is, we think, capable of both constructions, and even if it be admitted that its literal meaning would imply that the whole quantity must be put on board during the specified time, that is a construction which seems to put a fresh additional burden on the seller, without any corresponding benefit to the purchaser, and the consequence of adopting it would, we think, be that purchasers would, without any real reason, frequently obtain an excuse for rejecting contracts when prices had dropped." My Lords, I must submit to your Lordships that if it be admitted, as the Lord Justice is willing to admit, that the literal meaning would imply that the whole quantity must be put on board during a specified time, it is no answer to that literal meaning, it is no observation which can dispose of, or get rid of, or displace, that literal meaning, to say that it puts an additional burden on the seller, without a corresponding benefit to the purchaser; that is a matter of which the seller and the purchaser are the best judges. Nor is it any reason for saying that it would be a means by which purchasers without any real cause would frequently obtain an excuse for rejecting contracts when prices had dropped. The non-fulfilment of any term in any contract is a means by which a purchaser is able to get rid of the contract when prices have dropped; but that is no reason why a term which is found in a contract should not be fulfilled.[38]

The words of the Lord Chancellor were echoed by Hearthely LJ, who emphasised the crucial importance of time of shipment within the context of contracts concluded on shipment terms as follows:

I think the meaning of the word "shipped" is sufficiently understood by this time in commerce. But if it were needed I think we have sufficient evidence before us that by the word "shipped" all the witnesses understand put on board. I read the contract therefore as if it said "put on board at Madras, or coast, for this port during the months of March and/or April, 1874."

Now, your Lordships will observe that it is not "in" the months of March and/or April; it is not that the goods are to find themselves on board, and to be there within that period, namely, the months of March and/or April; but it is that they are to be

38 *Ibid.*, at 465.

shipped – that is to say, to be put on board – during those months, implying a continuous act of shipping by which these goods are to be placed in the position in which they are to be placed according to the meaning of the contract. It is not surprising that a state of things has arisen upon which there might be some controversy, for this reason: owing to the distance of the district from which the goods were to come, the parties to the contract of the 17th of March could not, or did not, ascertain the exact state of things at the date of the contract; and in truth the goods which have been tendered to the Defendants were all on board at the very date of the contract itself, namely, on the 17th of March. They had been put there, therefore, of course with no reference whatever to the contract and its terms; and it is not surprising that this shipment or embarcation of the goods made before the contract was entered into, but without knowledge of the contract, should not be found to square with that instrument. The consequence is, that we have here, as it seems to me, an engagement to supply rice to the Defendants, the character of which rice was to be this: it was to be rice to be shipped during these two particular months, March and April, or either of them, and not otherwise.

Now under these circumstances, and with the plain meaning of the contract lying, as it appears to me, on its surface, we are not entitled to speculate on the reasons and motives which have induced those who are engaged in this particular trade, those who have this "usual run," as the witness describes it, of contracts before them from time to time, and who must have pondered upon the matter, to frame their contracts in the manner which pleases them best. We must assume that it is owing to the custom of the trade that they have determined to frame them in this fashion. They do not stipulate either that the goods shall be found on board at such a time, or that the goods shall be on board before the end of the month of April; that would have been a very simple mode of expressing it, if that was what they wished; but they do expressly say that the goods shall be shipped – that is to say, put on board – during these two particular months, or one of them.

Now, the learned Judge who tried the case and addressed the jury in the first instance appears to have reasoned upon the motives which might probably have induced such a contract to be entered into; and also Lord Justice Mellish, in the Court of Appeal, did in some degree consider how far, in his judgment, a reason could be assigned for such a form of contract. Mr. Justice Brett says, in addressing the jury, that if the burden be thrown on him of construing the contract, "I construe it thus: That the meaning of it is, that if the loading has been conducted consecutively with ordinary and reasonable dispatch, and is completed in March or April, so that the vessel, so far as the loading of the cargo is concerned, may sail in March or April, that is sufficient; that is a March or April shipment." He seems there to read the contract, in fact, as I have just expressed it, as if the contract had been that the ship should be loaded before the end of April; that is the construction which, in his view of it, expressed as he expressed it, it would convey. He goes on to say, "That is, if I have to construe it, if there be no generally understood meaning of this phrase in the trade. Now, that seems to me to be the natural meaning of it – I mean in such a produce as rice – where the thing to be shipped is from a country where the produce is grown and where there is no difference in the article itself, which will itself be sent forward, whether it be sent forward in February, March, or April."

My Lords, the view that I take of the contract, I confess, is this, that it is not the article rice only that is sold, but the thing that is sold is the article rice shipped in March or April, and that the article rice shipped in February is not the article which has been purchased by the Defendants.

The Lord Justice says, in very much the same phraseology, that the word "shipped" is capable of the two constructions of meaning – either begun and finished to be put on board, or the putting on board completed in March or April. He says: "The word 'shipped' is capable of both constructions, and even if it be admitted that its literal meaning would imply that the whole quantity must be put on board during the specified time, that is a construction which seems to put a great additional burden on the seller without any corresponding benefit to the purchaser, and the consequence of adopting it would, I think, be that purchasers would, without any real reason, frequently obtain an excuse for rejecting contracts when prices had fallen." Now, with the greatest possible respect, and I am sure no one Judge ever entertained more respect for another than I entertain for the Lord Justice Mellish, I do think that that is a very hazardous way of construing a contract, namely, to say in a class of contracts having a great range, that the Judge can see, upon the face of the contract, a sufficient reason to reject what may be the literal interpretation of it, for that if such literal interpretation is to be applied, there would be an excuse afforded to parties for rejecting contracts. The danger of such a construction is extreme, because it is impossible to know all the causes which may have induced the persons to put words into a contract. If the words have a certain definite meaning, it is dangerous to depart from that meaning until you can arrive at any sound ground upon which you should do so; it is dangerous to depart from it upon a conjecture that it can make no difference to the parties, and especially you cannot reject the literal construction because you think that, unless you reject it, you may be affording an opportunity for an evasive purchaser to escape from his bargain. Of course, as has been already observed, in many cases a purchaser is desirous of escaping from his bargain, and if he finds that the bargain which is attempted to be enforced as against him, is not only burdensome upon him, but is against the letter of his contract, there is nothing in our law which prevents his availing himself of that answer to the case made against him, namely, that he has not entered into the engagement you allege, and if you seek to fasten upon him the engagement, you must first bring him within the four corners of the contract.

What Lord Justice Mellish says is very much like what Mr. Justice Brett said, namely: "The sole object of the purchaser in such a purchase as that now in question in confining the seller to a particular time within which the goods must have been shipped, is, as far as appears, that he may know when the goods are likely to arrive. That object seems as effectually attained by knowing when the shipment will be or has been completed, as by knowing when each part of the goods was put on board." That is, assuming in the first place that the only object you have in view is to know when the ship may arrive, but having assumed that, it farther assumes that your object is to know the latest period at which it may arrive. Now, I apprehend my Lords, that it is important to persons entering into contracts of this description to arrange all their contracts for the whole course of the year, after the calculations they may have made as to what particular times they will be in funds to meet their engagements, and it is just as important to them to know how long it will be before the ship arrives, as to know how soon it will be that the ship will arrive. They do not wish the goods to arrive sooner than the time when they have made their arrangements for them, and they do not wish them to arrive later than the time for which they have made their arrangements. And if they have specifically named the months of March and April, they mean those two months. They do not mean to purchase goods placed on board in the previous month, February, which therefore would, or might arrive, at a different season from that at which they specially engaged by the contract to accept the goods, which goods, by the nature of the contract, are to be paid for immediately on the ship's arrival.

Well, my Lords, that really seems to me to amount to the whole case, because, as regards the evidence which has been produced in this cause, I entirely agree in what has been already said, that that evidence, it it was required at all, or if it is admissible at all, has, if anything, strengthened what appears to my noble and learned friend on the woolsack, and appears also to me, to be the natural construction of the contract. All the witnesses, uniformly, beginning with one of the Plaintiffs themselves (that is a very curious thing), and following through the rest of the witnesses, state distinctly that which the Judge, Justice Brett, at last put to one of those witnesses, "what you mean to say is that March is March and April is April." That is pretty much the case,

> and one could hardly put in a clearer point of view one's own opinion that in reality the contract is simple and easy to be construed, and that "March" in the contract does mean March, and that "April" does mean April, and that the loading "during the months of March and April" does mean a loading during those months.
>
> My Lords, without detaining your Lordships any longer upon the case, which has been so fully and amply gone into, I am content to say that I do not think this case is at all governed by the case of *Alexander v Vanderzee*, nor do I think it necessary to say anything whatever upon that case. I think it is plain upon the construction of the contract that we have before us, and I think that that contract was not performed in such a manner as that the Defendants were compelled to accept, upon the tender to them, goods which were shipped in the month of February, instead of goods which were shipped in the months of March and April, or one of them. The February shipment applied to the whole of the goods with the exception simply of the fifty bags which have been mentioned. We have it in evidence that those fifty bags amounted to four tons weight out of 300 tons, that is to say, one-seventy-fifth part of the whole subject-matter of the contract. It appears to me that the Defendants could not be obliged to accept a tender of those bags separate and distinct from the complete contract they had entered into for the whole 300 tons, the large bulk, indeed almost the entirety, of which was shipped in a different month from that which they had contracted for, and therefore was not of such a character as to be deliverable to them in fulfilment of the contract they had entered into.[39]

Unless it is otherwise specified in the sales contract, the time of shipment thus represents a term intended to be part of the description of the goods and therefore a condition.[40]

This might be interpreted as vexatious to the seller, especially if one considers a scenario whereby the cause of delay is the carrier or the port, and especially where the seller does not, as the shipper under the contract of carriage, have a remedy against the carrier.

Nevertheless, since when it comes to international commercial sales time is of the essence, the classification of time of shipment as a condition of the contract produces a high degree of legal certainty, working at the same time as an incentive on the parties to ship the goods by the stipulated contractual date.[41]

Moreover, the scenario might be mitigated by the introduction of shipping laycan clauses to indicate that the parties did not intend time of shipment to be of the essence.

---

39 *Ibid.*, at 469.

40 See Debattista, C. *Bills of Lading in Export Trade*, above, p. 179. See also *Benjamin's Sale of Goods*, above, paras. 16.286 *et seq.*

41 See *Benjamin's Sale of Goods* (8th Edition, Sweet & Maxwell, 2010) para. 20–050. The first part of para. 20–050 states:

> Time of shipment. It is the duty of the buyer to nominate a ship capable of loading within the shipment period and to give reasonable notice of readiness to load, or such notice as may be required by the express terms of the contract. Failure to give such notice as will enable the seller to load by the end of the shipment period, or to give notice within such time as is specified by the contract, makes the buyer liable in damages and entitles the seller to refuse to deliver, since the time of taking delivery (no less than the time of shipment) is of essence of an fob contract.

9.11.1 Time of shipment: Laycan clauses and their effect

Laycan clauses stipulate the earliest date, when the ship is required by the charterer (e.g. "Laytime for loading shall not commence before"), and the latest date for the commencement of the charter.

In *The Luxmar*,[42] by an oral contract made on or about 12 May 2004 and later evidenced in writing, the claimant (ERG) agreed to sell to the defendant (Chevron) a quantity of gasoline f.o.b. ISAB refinery north side Priolo terminal. The contract contained a laycan clause whereby the buyer was in the position to narrow the shipment period which provided for shipment intended to be 27–30 May 2004, to a two day laycan latest by 21 May 2004.

On 17 May 2004 Chevron nominated the vessel *Luxmar* to load the cargo. On 21 May the laycan was narrowed to 29–30 May 2004.

The vessel arrived at Priolo at 10.00 on 28 May and gave notice of readiness. The cargo was not ready because of technical problems at ERG's plant. The necessary repairs were not completed until 3 June.

On 3 June 2004 Chevron terminated the contract on the basis that ERG's failure to commence loading constituted a repudiatory breach.

ERG asserted that Chevron terminated the contract unlawfully and claimed damages for its breach. Chevron counterclaimed general damages for late delivery in addition to demurrage.

ERG argued that its only obligation under the contract was to load the vessel within the laytime allowed by clause 9, or pay demurrage, if any, in accordance with clause 10. Clause 7 did not impose any other delivery obligation on it, and Chevron had no right to terminate the contract.

Chevron contended that clause 7 imposed a delivery period within which ERG was bound to deliver the cargo. Alternatively, Chevron could justify the termination of the contract because (1) the failure to complete delivery within the laytime provisions was a breach of condition entitling Chevron to terminate, and (2) ERG was in breach of an obligation to deliver within a reasonable time, entitling Chevron to terminate. Chevron claimed general damages for late delivery in addition to demurrage.

At first instance Langley J gave judgment in favour of ERG.[43] He held that clause 7 did not impose a delivery period; it provided for a laycan and no more. Chevron's remedy for the delay was limited to demurrage. There was no obligation on ERG to deliver in a reasonable time, breach of which could justify the termination of the contract. Accordingly, Chevron was liable to ERG for wrongfully terminating the contract. Chevron were not entitled to general damages for delay in addition to demurrage.

Chevron appealed, and it was held by the Court of Appeal that the concept of the laycan in the second paragraph of the delivery clause was an essential part of the clause as a whole and the word "delivery" had to be construed accordingly.

42 *The Luxmar* [2007] 2 Lloyd's Rep. 542.
43 [2006] 2 Lloyd's Rep. 543.

The use of a laydays/cancelling provision in the contract, particularly a provision entitling a vessel to present at any moment up to the end of the delivery period, made the contract a non-traditional f.o.b. contract in that time of delivery had become an obligation which was not of the essence of the contract.

Chevron's submission that they were in any event entitled to terminate the contract because the time for loading had been substantially exceeded would be rejected. A provision that a vessel be loaded within a particular time was not treated as a condition of the contract in shipping cases and there was no reason why the position should be any different in other cases, such as sale cases, where the relevant obligation was to load within the laydays. The innocent party could only terminate after a frustrating time had elapsed.

In the judgment, Longmore LJ digressed on the legal nature of laycan clauses as follows:

> But the delivery clause has to be read as a whole and, when so read, the "laycan" provisions are important. "Laycan" is a word or phrase often to be found in charterparties and, as Rix LJ observed in *Tidebrook Maritime Corporation v Vitol SA (The Front Commander)* [2006] 2 Lloyd's Rep. 251, paras 38 and 39, it is a reference to:
>
> (a) the earliest day upon which an owner can expect his charterer to load and (b) the latest day upon which the vessel can arrive at its appointed loading place without being at risk of being cancelled. The importance of such a laycan period is to enable the charterer to know when he has to have the goods ready for loading, and to enable both parties to know when, if the vessel is late in respect of her . . . expected time of arrival, the charterer can free himself by cancellation from the obligation of chartering the vessel and turn to alternative arrangements. Of course if a vessel arrives early, the owner may permit her to be loaded before the earliest day, and if she arrives late, the charterer can still maintain the charter.
>
> All this is elementary in a shipowner/charterer contract, such as a charterparty. It may also be important to observe that a right of cancellation is just what it says. It is a right to cancel which does not carry with it any right to damages for non-performance: see *Marbienes Compania Naviera SA v Ferrostaal AG (The Democritos)* [1976] 2 Lloyd's Rep. 149 at page 152 per Lord Denning MR.
>
> Sometimes, as in this case, the laycan concept is used in an fob contract. Since, in such a contract, it is the buyer who has the disposition of the vessel, it is the buyer who is in the position of the shipowner and is at risk of the vessel being cancelled if she does not present before the last day of the laycan period. Similarly it is the seller who is in the position of the charterer and is the person entitled to terminate the contract if the vessel has not arrived in time. The seller will not be bound to start loading the vessel before the period starts but will be bound to load as and when, within the laycan period, the vessel is ready to receive the cargo. As Christopher Clarke J put the matter in *SHV Gas Supply & Trading SAS v Naftomar Shipping & Trading Co Ltd Inc (The Azur Gaz)* [2006] 1 Lloyd's Rep. 163:
>
> The term laycan is habitually used in the negotiation of charterparties to refer to the earliest date at which the laydays can commence and the date after which the charter can be cancelled if the vessel has not by then arrived. By extension the term is found in fob sales, so as to provide that the seller can cancel the contract if the vessel, which it is the buyer's duty to procure, does not arrive at the port by the cancellation date.
>
> The laycan provision thus gives the fob seller a right to bring the contract to an end in circumstances in which, without a cancelling provision, he may well have no right to do so. The concomitant of that right is that the buyer is entitled to present the vessel at any time up to 2400 on the last day of the laycan spread, here 30 May. If he is entitled to present the vessel at 2300 (or even 2359) on 30 May, the contract

> cannot be interpreted to mean that the seller must have completed loading by 2400 on that day because that would be a commercial absurdity. In that event, the seller must be entitled (and must also be bound) to load within the laytime provided for by the contract. If he does not do so, he will be in breach of contract. He will not, however, be immediately in repudiatory breach partly because terms as to time of loading a vessel are not traditionally (and for good reason) regarded as conditions of the contract and partly because there would be great practical difficulties if the buyer were able to terminate the contract when the vessel had been partly but not fully loaded.
>
> [. . .] the traditional view (that time of delivery is of the essence of an fob contract) can be retained with the laycan provision by holding that, if notice of readiness is in fact given at such time as would enable the ship to be loaded by the end of the delivery period, time of delivery will be a condition; whereas if notice of readiness is given at a later time but within the cancelling period, only then would the obligation be to complete delivery within the laydays. This is an argument which it is not possible to accept. It is not sensible that an obligation relating to time of delivery should be a condition in one factual circumstance but not in another. It is either a condition or it is not. In the context of the present contract with an entitlement on the part of the buyer to present a vessel at any time up to the last moment for contractual delivery, it cannot, in my judgment, be right to hold that the words "DELIVERY . . . 27–30/05/2004" constitute a condition of the contract.[44]

It was these considerations that led the judge to hold that the concept of the laycan in the second paragraph of the delivery clause was an essential part of the clause as a whole and that the word "delivery" had to be construed accordingly.

Longmore LJ's analysis of the legal consequences of laycan clauses indicates that the use of a laydays/cancelling provision in the contract (particularly a provision entitling a vessel to present at any moment up to the end of the delivery period) makes the contract a non-traditional f.o.b. contract in that time of delivery has become an obligation which is not of the essence of the contract.

That does not come as a surprise, since traders are constantly adapting and even changing traditional f.o.b. contracts in the course of their business. If they want to rely on delivery obligations as they have been traditionally construed, they may well be advised not to employ cancelling provisions but that is, as always, a matter for them.[45]

Aside of the introduction of laycan clauses in the sale contract, in practice, two main mechanisms are used to solve problems of late shipment: a) extensions under the sales contract; and b) a falsely dated bill of lading.

Extensions under the sales contract

Extensions of the time allowed for shipment are the result of bilateral negotiations between the sellers and buyers taking place *ex post facto* after the sales contract is concluded. The seller would be best advised to stipulate for this in the initial contract of sale, as arrangements at a later stage are entirely dependent on the agreement of the buyer who, should it suit him commercially, may fail to give his consent.

44 *Ibid.*, at 546.
45 *Ibid.*, at 547.

Falsely dated bills of lading

Another possible remedy for late shipment is represented by a bill of lading indicating timely shipment, perhaps against the tender of a letter of indemnity holding the carrier harmless against the consequences of misdating a bill of lading.

This practice is not, however, without its difficulties and even risks, as the carrier could refuse to issue such bill, and first and foremost, because the seller is not entitled to demand the issue of such a bill in the first place: the seller qua shipper is only entitled to a bill of lading from the carrier after the carrier has received the goods into his charge, however late that may be under the contract of sale.[46]

Above all, if the fraud on the bill of lading is found out, the seller loses his right to payment, even if he has taken the precaution of demanding payment through a confirmed irrevocable letter of credit.

Even if the seller's fraud is not found out on tender, the buyer may have remedies against the seller for a long time after payment.[47]

No shipment period indicated in the sale contract

A different scenario arises if the sales contract gives no shipment period but incorporates from a charter party an estimated time of arrival at the discharge port. That is what happened in *The Azur Gas*,[48] where the seller agreed to sell to the buyer 2700 mt +/- 5 per cent at sellers' option commercial butane meeting Melilli specifications c.i.f. Tunisia Port-La Goulette or Gabes.

The contract contained the following clauses: "Vessel Azur Gaz Accepted by the Buyer", and "Laycan 17–19 February 2003 consequently ETA Gabes 20 February am La Goulette 19 February pm".

The port of Melilli experienced an unusually long spell of bad weather, which prevented vessels from loading, and the port was substantially inoperative between 15 February and 2 March, save for three periods on 19, 24, and 26 February when larger vessels were able to berth.

The *Azur Gaz* arrived at Melilli on 17 February and tendered notice of readiness. Because of the bad weather she had to lie in the outer roads of Santa Panagia Bay. She was able to anchor on 19 February, but was not able to berth until 3 March.

On 25 February, the buyer cancelled the contract, relying on the failure of the seller to ship within the period 17–19 February.

---

46 See Article III 3(a) of the Hague-Visby Rules, which states as follows:

> After receiving the goods into his charge the carrier or the master or agent of the carrier shall, on demand of the shipper, issue to the shipper a bill of lading showing among other things:
>
> (a) The leading marks necessary for identification of the goods as the same are furnished in writing by the shipper before the loading of such goods starts, provided such marks are stamped or otherwise shown clearly upon the goods if uncovered, or on the cases or coverings in which such goods are contained, in such a manner as should ordinarily remain legible until the end of the voyage.

47 See Debattista, *Bills of Lading in Export Trade*, above, p. 239. Moreover, the bank may have remedies against the carrier: *Standard Chartered Bank v Pakistan National Shipping Corporation (No.2)* [1999] 1 Lloyd's Rep. 747 on assessment of damages; [2003] 1 Lloyd's Rep. 227 on liability; [2000] 2 Lloyd's Rep. 511 on bank's contributory fault.

48 *The Azur Gas* [2006] 1 Lloyd's Rep. 163.

The seller on its part alleged that by cancelling the contract, the buyer was in repudiatory breach, and claimed damages.

The buyer contended that it was entitled to terminate the contract on the basis that (a) the reference to "Laycan Feb 17–19 2003" was to be construed as a reference to a shipment period, and SHV was in breach of its obligation to ship within that period; alternatively (b) there was an implied term that the goods would be shipped within a reasonable time, which had expired by 27 February; alternatively (c) the seller was in breach of its undertaking that the ETAs given were reached honestly and on reasonable grounds.

It was held by the court that the word "laycan" in the contract did not mean "shipment". It applied in its ordinary sense and was consistent with the incorporation of the charter party.

Since there was no expressly agreed shipment period, it was an implied term of the contract that the seller would ship the goods within a reasonable time. The seller was not in breach of that implied term. It could not be blamed for the weather or for the berthing difficulties, and there was no evidence that it was in any way dilatory in shipping the cargo.

Nevertheless, the court established that in the absence of a predetermined time of shipment, an estimated time of arrival had to be given honestly and on reasonable grounds. An estimate was not given on reasonable grounds if an enquiry which ought to have been made was not made, and the answer would have invalidated the estimate.

It was found that the estimate of the time of the vessel's arrival at the discharge port was not based on reasonable grounds in the absence of any information as to the berthing prospects at the loading port. Bad weather, port closure, and berthing difficulties could and did occur at Melilli and other ports in winter. It was not reasonable to assume that in February there would be no problem. An enquiry of someone with knowledge of what was happening at Melilli would have revealed that the port was, on account of bad weather, substantially inoperative on 15, 16, and 17 February and that there was no prospect of *Azur Gaz* berthing immediately upon arrival on 17 February.

Since the ETAs were not based on reasonable grounds, the seller was found in breach of condition and the buyer entitled to terminate as it did.

In the words of Christopher Clark J:

> In my judgment Mrs Pons's estimate of the time of the vessel's arrival at the discharge port was not based on reasonable grounds in the absence of any information whatever as to the berthing prospects at the loading port, which was a port of which she had no experience. Bad weather, port closure and berthing difficulties can and do occur at Melilli and other ports in winter. It was not, in my judgment, reasonably to be assumed that in February there would be no problem. I agree, in this respect, with the comment at para 4.8 of Cooke on Voyage Charters (2nd edn) in respect of estimates of expected arrival given by shipowners:
>
> There will often be circumstances where the owner will be obliged to make enquiries of third parties, such as port agents, in order to ascertain the time likely to be required for obtaining a berth and for cargo handling operations at previous ports. [. . .] an inquiry of someone with knowledge of what was happening at Melilli would have revealed that the port was, on account of bad weather, substantially inoperative on 15, 16 and 17 February and that there was no prospect of Azur Gaz berthing immediately

upon arrival on 17 February. That inquiry could have been made of the owners' agent at Melilli – Vinci Maritima – if necessary through the owners' brokers in Paris, or of ERG, SHV's suppliers, or of SHV's preferred agent at Melilli – Ferrari – even though they were not nominated for the purpose of this charter.

[. . .] If, as I hold, the ETAs were not based on reasonable grounds, SHV (seller) were in breach of condition and Naftomar (buyer) was entitled to terminate as they did: *The Mihalis Angelos* [1971] 1 QB 164, 194, 199–200 and 204–207. Even if the term is to be regarded as an innominate term, the consequences of the invalidity of the estimate were such as to entitle termination by 27 February.[49]

In light of *The Azur Gas*, in the absence of a specified shipment period and in presence of ETAs, it is, thus, essential that the estimated arrival provided by the seller be based on reasonable grounds. Failure to do so will expose the seller to liabilities for breach of contract.

9.12 Place of shipment

Where a place is stipulated for shipment (always under f.o.b. contracts, and sometimes if the contract is stipulated on c.i.f. terms), unless otherwise specified in the sales contract, that place "describes" the goods and is intended to be a condition of the contract.

This entails that the seller qua shipper cannot load the goods at an alternative place rather than the one stipulated in the sales contract, even if that alternative could prove to be more convenient for the carrier, and actually causes no real loss to the other party to the contract of sale.

Petrotrade Inc. v Stinnes Handel[50] involved the plaintiff sellers (Petrotrade) and the defendant buyer (Stinnes) for the sale and purchase of 10,000 tonnes of premium 0.15 leaded gasoline, f.o.b. Antwerp.

Petrotrade were unable to procure a cargo for Antwerp, but succeeded in purchasing 10,000 tonnes of gasoline scavenger-free from the Total refinery at Flushing. Stinnes were unimpressed by this offer. They regarded Petrotrade as in default and would only accept the substitute parcel if it were offered at a price below the contract price.

Petrotrade contended that because Flushing was on the way from the outer anchorage to Antwerp and was closer to the position of Rava than Antwerp, a cargo sold f.o.b. Antwerp could be tendered for delivery at Flushing; in an f.o.b. contract the place of delivery was an innominate term and not a condition and, since Flushing was so close to the BRC refinery at Antwerp and more convenient to the vessel, the buyers would not be deprived of substantially the whole benefit of their contract by the tender of the cargo at that place.

Alternatively, Petrotrade contended that Stinnes was estopped from asserting that delivery at Flushing did not comply with the contract and was precluded from treating the tender at Flushing as non-contractual. The issue was whether Stinnes

49 *Ibid.*, at 172, 173.
50 *Petrotrade Inc. v Stinnes Handel* [1995] 1 Lloyd's Rep. 142.

by words or conduct represented that the Flushing cargo would be acceptable if tendered under the contract.

It was held by the court that in a f.o.b. contract where the buyer had to nominate the ship the precise identification of the delivery point was vital to the buyer; there were strong grounds for classifying the place of shipment as part of the description of the goods and therefore a condition of the contract any breach of which would entitle the buyer to treat the contract as terminated; the delivery to Antwerp was in this contract a condition and any breach of that term, whatever its commercial consequences for the buyers, entitled Stinnes to terminate the contract.

Since it was not established that Total's refinery at Flushing was within the legal limits of the port of Antwerp, or could for any other reason be described as falling within the port of Antwerp, the tender of gasoline for loading at that place could not be a contractual tender to Stinnes within the terms of the sale contract; Stinnes would be entitled to treat such tender as a breach of a condition under the contract.

In the words of Coleman J:

> There is surprisingly little authority on this point. In the current edition of *Benjamin's Sale of Goods* at pars. 18–116 it is stated in relation to overseas sales in general:
>
> It has been settled ever since the decision of the House of Lords in *Bowes v Shand* (1877) 2 App Cas 455 that stipulations as to the time of shipment form part of the description of the goods, and that breach of such stipulations entitles the buyer to reject . . . Stipulations as to the place of shipment and as to the time at which the goods are to be ready for shipment are similarly part of the description of the goods.
>
> The issue in *Bowes v Shand* (1877) 2 App. Cas. 455, was, however, unrelated to the place of shipment and concerned only whether the buyer was entitled to reject a cargo of "Madras rice, to be shipped at Madras, or coast, for (London) during the months of March and/or April, 1874, per Rajah of Cochin" in circumstances where most of the cargo was shipped in February. The House of Lords, in reversing the Court of Appeal's judgment, held that the time of shipment was a condition of the contract. Lord Cairns, L.C. at pp. 467–468 observed:
>
> My Lords, before leaving that part of the case, I must advert to a suggestion which was made at the Bar on behalf of the Respondents, although it does not appear to have been made in the Court below. It was suggested that even if the construction of the contract be as I have stated, still if the rice was not put on board in the particular months, that would not be a reason which would justify the Appellants in having rejected the rice altogether, but that it might afford a ground for a cross action by them if they could shew that any particular damage resulted to them from the rice not having been put on board in the months in question. My Lords, I cannot think that there is any foundation whatever for that argument. If the construction of the contract be as I have said, that it bears that the rice is to be put on board in the months in question, that is part of the description of the subject-matter of what is sold. What is sold is not 300 tons of rice in gross or in general. It is 300 tons of Madras rice to be put on board at Madras during the particular months. The construction may be shewn by evidence to be different from what I have supposed, but if the construction be that which I have supposed, the Plaintiff, who sues upon that contract, has not launched his case until he has shewn that he had tendered that thing which has been contracted for, and if he is unable to shew that, he cannot claim any damages for the non-fulfilment of the contract.
>
> It is to be noted that he treated the time and place of shipment as part of the description and therefore conditions of the contract.
>
> Lord Blackburn at pp. 480–481 also assimilates the contractual status of the place of shipment and the time of shipment:

It was argued, or tried to be argued, on one point, that it was enough that it was rice, and that it was immaterial when it was shipped. As far as the subject-matter of the contract went, its being shipped at another and a different time being (it was said) only a breach of a stipulation which could be compensated for in damages. But I think that that is quite untenable. I think, to adopt an illustration which was used a long time ago by Lord Abinger, and which always struck me as being a right one, that it is an utter fallacy, when an article is described, to say that it is anything but a warranty or a condition precedent that it should be an article of that kind, and that another article might be substituted for it. As he said, if you contract to sell peas, you cannot oblige a party to take beans. If the description of the article tendered is different in any respect it is not the article bargained for, and the other party is not bound to take it. I think in this case what the parties bargained for was rice, shipped at Madras or the coast of Madras. Equally good rice might have been shipped a little to the north or a little to the south of the coast of Madras. I do not know quite what the boundary is, and probably equally good rice might have been shipped in February as was shipped in March, or equally good rice might have been shipped in May as was shipped in April, and I dare say equally good rice might have been put on board another ship as that which was put on board the Rajah of Cochin. But the parties have chosen, for reasons best known to themselves, to say: We bargain to take rice, shipped in this particular region, at that particular time, on board that particular ship, and before the Defendants can be compelled to take anything in fulfilment of that contract it must be shewn not merely that it is equally good, but that it is the same article as they have bargained for – otherwise they are not bound to take it.

That was not a f.o.b. contract. Its characteristics were closer to those of a c.&f. contract. Furthermore, it was not necessary for the decision to reach any conclusion on the contractual status of the place of shipment. However, as I have said, there is now clear authority that time for shipment is a condition of a f.o.b. contract: see *J.J. Cunningham Ltd. v Robert A. Munro & Co. Ltd.* (1922) 13 Ll.L.Rep. 216.

As to f.o.b. contracts, in *Wackerbarth v Masson* (1812) 3 Campb. 270, where the contract was for delivery "free on board a foreign ship" and where the purchaser asked for delivery at the f.o.b. port or by the warehouseman there attorning bailee, it was held by Lord Ellenborough at nisi prius that the seller was entitled to insist on the nomination of a foreign ship to which he could deliver on board and that the buyer was liable for non-performance. He observed that the seller had a right to refuse delivery "as it was not the mode of delivery for which he had stipulated". In other words the seller was under no obligation to deliver otherwise than in exact conformity with the mode of delivery expressed in the contract, notwithstanding the geographical proximity of the warehouse to the vessel's rail.

In *Maine Spinning Co. v Sutcliffe & Co.* (1918) L.J.K.B. 382 the issue was whether under a contract for the sale of wool for "delivery Liverpool" it was open to the buyer to take delivery in the port as distinct from over the ship's rail. Mr. Justice Bailhache held that the contract was in effect for delivery f.o.b. Liverpool and that meant delivery to a ship at Liverpool. It was argued that the plaintiff buyers were entitled to take delivery of the wool anywhere in Liverpool in as much as the provision for delivery on board ship at Liverpool could be waived by the buyer as it was in its own favour. Mr. Justice Bailhache rejected this submission and held that the delivery clause was not wholly in the buyer's favour and could not be waived by them. He applied *Wackerbarth v Masson*, sup.

Both these decisions are entirely consistent with the speech of Lord Blackburn in *Bowes v Shand*, sup. They and it suggest that the place of shipment is a term to be strictly complied with and that in ascertaining what remedies are available to an innocent party one is not concerned with the consequences of the breach, but with the mere fact of breach: any breach of the term would entitle the opposite party to decline to perform further. Indeed, if in a f.o.b. contract time of delivery is a condition, it would be very strange if the place of delivery were only an innominate term to the effect that the right to terminate for breach was dependent on the nature of the breach. Further, given that *Bowes v Shand* was concerned with what was in effect a c. and f. contract, the argument in favour of the place of shipment being a condition in a f.o.b. contract where the buyer has to tender his vessel at the delivery point, would seem to be even stronger. Certainly in c.i.f. contracts the place of shipment has for many years been assumed by text book writers and commercial Judges to be a condition of the contract: see for example, *Aruna Mills Ltd. v Dhanrajmal Gobindram* [1968] 1 Lloyd's Rep. 304; [1968] 1 Q.B. 655 at p. 665 per Mr. Justice Donaldson.

Mr. Smouha relied in support of his submission that place of delivery was an innominate term on the judgment of the Court of Common Pleas in *Neill v Whitworth* (1866) L.R. 1 C.P. 684. There the contract was in substance a c.&f. contract for the sale of cotton: . . . to arrive from Calcutta at Liverpool per ship or ships and to be fair Bengal cotton, the said cotton to be taken from the quay.

The cotton was discharged at Liverpool, but before delivery orders were given to the buyers the cotton was taken into warehouses and there stored. The sellers attempted to tender the cotton in the warehouses, but the buyers rejected this tender as non-contractual and sued for damages for non-delivery. Their claim failed. The Court of Common Pleas, whose judgment was upheld on appeal in the Court of the Exchequer Chamber, held that the clause "the cotton to be taken from the quay" was not a "condition precedent" but a mere stipulation in favour of the seller to the effect that the contract was to deliver the cotton at a reasonable time and under reasonable circumstances although it would be at the buyers' charge from the time it was landed on the quay. The substance of the decision was thus that the sellers were not obliged to do more than discharge on to the quayside but that if, having done so, they warehoused the cotton, the additional charges thereby incurred would be borne by the buyers. The sellers' minimum contractual obligation was to place the cotton on to the quay. Having done that, they had performed their contract. If beyond that they took the goods to a warehouse, that was subsequent to their having placed the goods on to the quay and did not mean that they had disabled themselves from delivery pursuant to the contract. Accordingly, this case does not support the proposition that under a f.o.b. contract the seller can tender the goods at any place other than the named f.o.b. port provided that such other place is more or at least no less, convenient than the f.o.b. port.

It is perfectly true that the tendering of the contract goods at a place not quite inside the named port of delivery may be a breach which would in some cases, such as the present, cause the buyer no great loss and would certainly not deprive him of the whole commercial benefit of the contract of sale. That factor is unquestionably a relevant consideration in testing whether a particular term as to the contractual status of which there is no direct authority is as a matter of construction a condition of the contract. It is, however, not the only consideration. This is made clear by the Court of Appeal in *Bunge Corporation v Tradax Export S.A.* [1980] 1 Lloyd's Rep. 294 and particularly the extremely comprehensive analysis of the current approach to construction in the judgments of Lord Justice Megaw at pp. 307 to 309 and Lord Justice Browne at pp. 309 to 310. In the House of Lords the speeches of Lord Wilberforce and Lord Roskill [1981] 2 Lloyd's Rep. 1 at pp. 5–6 and pp. 11–15; [1981] 1 W.L.R. 711 at pp. 715 to 716 and pp. 724 to 729 are to the same effect. Just as it is relevant, in order to identify the mutual intention of the parties, to investigate whether breaches of the term in question may in some circumstances have the effect of depriving the innocent party of substantially the whole benefit of the contract and in other circumstances not, so it is also necessary to have regard to the commercial and contractual function of the term in question. Is it the kind of provision to which people who make contracts of that kind are likely to attach overriding importance, even if the consequences of non-compliance may in some cases be commercially trivial? Is it a term the contractual function of which is related to other terms of the contract which have been held by the Courts to be conditions?

> In a f.o.b. contract where the buyer has to nominate the ship the precise identification of the delivery point is vital to the buyer. In order to take delivery he in turn has to enter into a contract of affreightment with a carrier which exactly matches the sale contract. If he has chartered a ship to load at a given port where the goods are to be delivered to the ship under the sale contract it is at that port and only at that port that he can require the chartered ship to load. He is not entitled to nominate another port unless the charter-party provides for a loading port range. It will not necessarily do so. The response that he may be able to persuade the carrier to go to a nearby port for a modest extra payment which would be recoverable from the seller in damages is nothing to the point. The fact is that in f.o.b. contracts when the buyer has to nominate the ship the need for the precise matching of the contract of affreightment with the contract of sale, both as to timing and as to place of shipment, is essential and obvious in all cases. Contractual disparity would, in many cases, lead to acute problems for the buyer. It would often give rise to considerable commercial inconvenience. Apart from the need for a matching contract of affreightment, the buyer might have sold the goods forward or arranged to finance their purchase and might for either of those purposes have to tender or deposit bills of lading evidencing shipment at the port of shipment named in his sale contract. It would not be open to him to tender or deposit bills of lading evidencing shipment from a nearby port. The absence of precise correspondence between the actual place of shipment identified in the shipping documents and the contractual place of shipment would thus be likely in many cases to cause severe disruption of the buyer's commercial arrangements with others.
>
> Moreover, if the place of shipment were only an innominate term, disputes would frequently arise as to the buyer's right to reject a tender of goods at a port other than that contracted for. There would be an issue whether it was so far from, or had such different characteristics from, the port of delivery identified in the contract as to deprive the buyer of substantially the whole benefit of the sale contract. The uncertainty to which such disputes would be bound to give rise and the certainty which is achieved if the place of shipment is a condition of the contract is clearly a highly relevant consideration in deciding how to classify the term.
>
> Although judicial authority on the contractual status of the port of shipment in a f.o.b. contract is indeed sparse since the issue has hardly ever been raised for determination, commercial lawyers have for many years assumed that such a term is a condition. There are indeed very strong grounds, which I have identified, for classifying that term, like terms as to the time for performance, in the way in which Lord Blackburn classified it in *Bowes v Shand*, sup. in relation to a c.&f. contract, namely as part of the description of the goods and therefore a condition of the contract any breach of which will entitle the buyer to treat the contract as terminated, regardless of the magnitude of the consequences of the breach. Consequently, paying full regard to the warning given by Lord Justice Roskill in *The Hansa Nord* [1975] 2 Lloyd's Rep. 445 at pp. 457–458; [1976] 1 Q.B. 44 at pp. 70–71 that a Court should not be over ready, unless required by statute or authority so to do, to construe a term in a contract as a condition, I have no doubt that delivery at Antwerp was in this contract a condition and that any breach of that term, whatever its commercial consequences for the buyers, entitled Stinnes to terminate the contract.[51]

Consequently, since it was not established that Total's refinery at Flushing was within the legal limits of the port of Antwerp, or could for any other reason be described as falling within the port of Antwerp, the tender of gasoline for loading at that place could not be a contractual tender to Stinnes within the terms of the

51 *Ibid.*, at 148, 149, 150.

sales contract. Stinnes was therefore entitled to treat such a tender as a breach of condition under that contract.

Although *Petrotrade* refers to an f.o.b. contract, which by its own essence would naturally indicate a place of shipment, the parallel and reference made by Coleman J to *Bowes v Shand* and to sales concluded on c.i.f. terms extends the rationale of place of shipment as a condition of the contract also to c.i.f. contracts indicating a port of origin.

9.13 Declaring shipment in c.i.f. contracts

Whenever goods are sold on c.i.f. or c.& f. terms, although the seller makes the carriage arrangements, the buyer needs to have information regarding the shipment of the goods.

The buyer needs this information either because he needs to organise discharge arrangements, or because such information would facilitate onsales or, in c.& f. contracts, insurance arrangements.[52]

Because of the commercial significance of the information to be passed from seller to buyer, the trading contract will frequently contain clear stipulations about the form which the declaration is to take.[53]

Whether detailed or not, the formal requirements of the notice of appropriation must be strictly complied with, and they are treated by the courts as conditions.

In *Bunge v Tradax*,[54] with reference to f.o.b contracts, the House of Lords held that in a mercantile contract when a term had to be performed by one party as a condition precedent to the ability of the other party to perform another term especially an essential term such as the nomination of a single loading port, the term as to time for the performance of the former obligation would in general fall to be treated as a condition.

Accordingly, the buyers' obligation to give 15 days' loading notice to the sellers was a condition, for until the requisite notice had been given, the sellers could not know for certain which loading port they should nominate so as to ensure that the contract goods would be available for loading on the ship's arrival at that port before the end of the shipment period.[55]

9.13.1 What type of ship must be nominated?

In terms of the type of vessel which needs to be nominated, two issues arise here: first, the ship must comply with any requirements stipulated in the contract of sale; a second issue would revolve around the need, if any, for the ship to be seaworthy.

52 See Debattista, *Bills of Lading in Export Trade*, above, p.216.
53 See Gafta 119.
54 *Bunge v Tradax* [1981] 2 All ER 540.
55 *Ibid.*, at 714–716.

It is clear on the authorities that if the parties have agreed that the vessel nominated must comply with certain requirements, then the nomination of a vessel which does not is a breach by the seller of the sales contract.[56]

In terms of implied duty to nominate a seaworthy ship, rather surprisingly at first sight, it seems that there is no authority for the implication of a duty to nominate a seaworthy vessel, unless of course, the trading contract includes an express term to that effect.

In the absence of such an express obligation in the contract, must the ship nominated be seaworthy? In other words, would the seller be liable to the buyer under the sales contract if it were not?

It has been noted by the doctrine that the answer is probably not.[57] This because the duty of the seller is not so much to provide a seaworthy vessel, but to provide a reasonable contract of carriage, that is to say a contract of carriage which gives the buyer an adequate right of recovery against the carrier if, in breach of the contract of carriage, the vessel was found to be unseaworthy.

This is not to say, of course, that the carrier is not in breach. The carrier is in breach, but of another contract, namely the contract of carriage. The issue here is whether the seller is in breach under the contract of sale.[58]

9.13.2 Inaccurate declarations

If a declaration is validly made, then it binds the seller to perform his contract by tendering documents covering goods on the nominated vessel.

The whole purpose of the declaration is to give the buyer advanced notice of shipment so that he can make arrangements for discharge or onsale. The declaration of shipment within the context of c.i.f. contracts effectively fills in a blank left in the contract of sale.

Once the blank is filled in through nomination of the vessel, then it is as if the contract always contained the name of the nominated ship and the seller's duty is to ship goods on that ship and on no other.[59]

It has been noted that this puts the seller in serious difficulties where he makes a valid declaration under the contract which inaccurately gives the name of a ship other than that on which the goods were in fact shipped.[60]

For here, the bill of lading which the seller gets from the carrier (and therefore the only one which he is going to be able to tender to the buyer for payment) will

56 See *Bergerco v Vegoil* [1984] 1 Lloyd's Rep. 440. In this case, the court held that what was stipulated for was that for the ship to be a contractually permitted ship she had to be a direct ship, one which was not going to call at any port between New Orleans and Bombay for the purpose of loading and unloading cargo; here, the nominated vessel was never at any time a direct vessel which was going direct to Bombay and the term agreed had not been complied with.

57 See Debattista, *Bills of Lading in Export Trade*, above, p.216.

58 *Ibid.*, p. 219.

59 By way of example, see Gafta 100, clause 10(g): "When a valid Notice of Appropriation has been received by Buyers, it shall not be withdrawn except with their consent." See also Gafta 100, clause 10(e): "Every Notice of Appropriation shall be open to correction of any errors occurring in transmission."

60 See C. Debattista, *Bills of Lading in Export Trade*, Tottel, 2008, p. 165.

not tally with the bill of lading which he has, through declaration of the vessel, undertaken to tender.

Now, where the market is rising, it is unlikely that the buyer will raise too much of an issue about this: the buyer has made a good deal and it is not in his interests to reject the goods, albeit shipped on a different vessel.

However, where the market is falling, or where for any other reason the buyer has lost interest in the goods, or at any rate in the goods at the contract price, the buyer may well be inclined to reject the goods, or negotiate a discount with the seller.

9.13.3 Substitution of the vessel

Given the effect of a declaration of shipment, however, the difficult issue is whether, once a vessel has been declared, the seller can then renominate if he discovers that the first nomination was inaccurate.

The position is tolerably clear where the contract itself either specifically gives the seller the right to substitute a vessel for the vessel first nominated, or it specifies the latitude within which the seller can amend his first declaration of shipment.

This is what happened in *The Ballenita*,[61] where the contract entitled the sellers to nominate a vessel three London working days before the expected date of the vessel's arrival.

The court held that the words "or sub" appearing in the contract indicated that the sellers could nominate a substitute after an original nomination had been made, and that to construe the clause as having the effect that the right of substitution lapsed once the three-day period had commenced would be to deprive the sellers of a right given to them by contract. It was not the function of the courts to rewrite the contract for the parties.

In the words of Judge Diamond QC:

> I can find no provision in the contract which indicates either expressly or by necessary implication that the right to substitute was to lapse once a notice of readiness had been given in respect of the original vessel. Equally it can be said that there is nothing in the contract to indicate that the right of substitution was exercisable until some time later, e.g. until discharge of the original vessel had commenced. I have to say however that, if the contract had provided for the right of substitution to be exercisable at any time until the commencement of discharge, I would not have found this surprising. The contract is one on c.i.f. terms modified however to incorporate certain features found in recent years in contracts in the oil trade, such as provisions enabling the sellers to retain flexibility in appropriating goods to the contract until a relatively late stage and provisions dispensing with the use of bills of lading to transfer constructive possession of the goods from the sellers to the buyers before discharge of the oil at the port of destination. In the present case there was no obligation on the sellers to nominate a vessel until three working days prior to arrival and the words "or sub" would seem to indicate a common intention that the sellers might even then retain flexibility in appropriating goods to the contract.

61 *The Ballenita* [1992] 2 Lloyd's Rep. 455. See Debattista, *Bills of Lading in Export Trade*, above, p. 219. See also *Benjamin's Sale of Goods*, above, paras. 14.896 *et seq.*

> Unless, therefore, there is some characteristic in a notice of readiness which can be demonstrated as clearly inconsistent with the preservation of the sellers' right to substitute one vessel for another, I would have considered that, in the context of the present contract, the right of substitution was intended to be exercisable at any stage until the commencement of discharge. This is not to say that there might not be reasons why the right could not in fact be exercised after the vessel had arrived. The second ship would have to be one that was capable of being contractually nominated. It would be necessary that the sellers had not, by representing that they would not substitute another vessel, become estopped from exercising their right of substitution. But, apart from such constraints, it is not apparent to me that the scheme of the contract requires that the right of substitution ought to be held to have lapsed at any time before the commencement of discharge.[62]

If the contract gives no express right to substitute, then there would appear to be no general right to substitute.

It has been noted that the mere addition of the words "or sub" or "or better name" or "or TBN" in the nomination itself does not create such a right.[63] The effect of such words in the declaration of shipment itself has been held only to serve to give the seller "the right to substitute another contractual vessel with a contractual cargo in immediate replacement" of the vessel first nominated.

In *The Marine Star*,[64] it was held on appeal that the seller's nomination amounted to a firm nomination of *Marine Star* pursuant to the nomination clause in the contract. Although the seller's original nomination contained the wording: "Marine Star, substitution", that nomination was held to have the effect of locking *Marine Star* into the contract subject only to the right to substitute another contractual vessel with a contractual cargo in immediate replacement of *Marine Star*.

9.14 Nomination clauses in f.o.b. contracts

Where goods are sold f.o.b., the seller needs to know which ship the buyer is using so as to make the necessary arrangements for putting the goods at the disposal of the buyer at the loading port.

Where goods are sold f.o.b., the seller's duty is to put the goods free on board – but on board what, and where, and when? The seller can only perform his duty to load if the buyer makes appropriate shipping arrangements and tells the seller about them. The buyer therefore has a duty to make effective nomination of a vessel to the seller.

For nomination to be effective under an f.o.b contract, the nomination must be of a vessel which allows the seller to load the goods within the agreed shipment period. If the buyer nominates a vessel which does not allow the seller to load the goods within the shipment period, then that nomination is ineffective.[65]

Again, if the buyer nominates a vessel which is prohibited by law from entering the loadport, then the nomination is ineffective. It is because the seller needs to

62 *The Ballenita* [1992] 2 Lloyd's Rep. 455, 461.
63 See Debattista, *Bills of Lading in Export Trade*, above, p. 236.
64 *The Marine Star* [1993] 1 Lloyd's Rep. 329.
65 See Debattista, *Bills of Lading in Export Trade*, above, p. 236.

know where and when to load the goods that contracts frequently impose a careful timetable on the buyer regarding notification of the vessel to the seller.[66]

In terms of the possibility of substitution, it has been correctly pointed out by the doctrine that the naming of the vessel by an f.o.b. buyer does not "describe" or "identify" the goods in the same way as the declaration of shipment does in a c.i.f. contract.[67]

In other words, different from a c.i.f. nomination which goes back to the original sale contract filling a gap left blank by the parties and therefore having very much a contractual nature, an f.o.b. nomination does not appear to be linked in any way to the original sales contract, which does not contain any transport obligations.[68]

It would seem therefore that, so long as the formal requirements of nomination could still be satisfied, there should be nothing to stop the buyer from substituting a nomination once made – and this is whether or not the contract of sale or the nomination expressly gave the buyer the right to nominate.[69]

Nevertheless, the contract may actually restrict or exclude the buyer's power to renominate, and if that is the case, the buyer shall not be entitled to do so.

Further, even in absence of such a clause, if the seller has acted upon the first nomination and would suffer loss – e.g. warehousing charges – because of the renomination, then it would seem that the seller can, at the very least, recover from the buyer the losses caused by withdrawal of the first nomination.[70]

9.15 Certificate final clauses

"Certificate final" clauses are extremely common in contracts concluded on shipment terms;[71] such clauses turn a physical duty to ship goods of the contract description, sample, or quality into a purely documentary obligation. This entails that insofar as the seller tenders a certificate in relation to the aspect of the physical duties intended to be "final" as per contractual specification (e.g. quantity, quality, sample, etc.), that will satisfy the seller's physical obligations regardless of the effective condition of the goods.

This means that if, for instance, a sales contract stipulates for quality to be final and showing no more than 3 per cent foreign matter in the goods as per a certificate issued by an independent surveyor after the goods are shipped on board, the tender of such a certificate will be considered as "final" in terms of the quality of the goods, relieving the seller from any liability in relation to that specific physical

66 For example, clause 6 of GAFTA 119. See Debattista, *Bills of Lading in Export Trade*, above, p.216.

67 See Debattista, *Bills of Lading in Export Trade*, above, p. 216.

68 By the very nature of an f.o.b. sale, the buyer is to make all the necessary transport arrangements, and he shall do so by stipulating a contract of carriage directly with the carrier.

69 For an example of a contract of sale reserving the right to renominate, see lines 65 and 66 of Gafta 119.

70 See Debattista, *Bills of Lading in Export Trade*, above, p. 216. See also *Benjamin's Sale of Goods*, above, paras. 21.293 *et seq*.

71 For an example of a certificate final clause, see clause 5 of Gafta 119, which provides that the certificate of inspection at the time of loading into the carrying vessel would be final as to quality.

obligation, regardless of the actual quality state of the goods once the cargo reaches the buyer at the port of destination.[72]

Validity under English law

In terms of validity under English law, the legal *standi* of certificate final clauses can be found in section 55 of the SOGA 1979. Section 55 states as follows:

SOGA 1979, section 55 Exclusion of implied terms

(1) Where a right, duty or liability would arise under a contract of sale of goods by implication of law, it may (subject to the Unfair Contract Terms Act 1977) be negatived or varied by express agreement, or by the course of dealing between the parties, or by such usage as binds both parties to the contract.

(2) An express term does not negative a term implied by this Act unless inconsistent with it.

Section 55 thus makes it clear that where a right, duty, or liability would arise under a contract of sale of goods by implication of law, it "may . . . be negatived or varied by express agreement . . ." and a "certificate final" clause provides just such an "express agreement" that no evidence of breach as to an attribute covered by the clause is admissible.[73]

In terms of SOGA 1979, this is the case even if the discrepancy between the goods shipped and the goods promised goes to an obligation implied by the Act itself (e.g. sections 13 or 14).

Furthermore, it deserves to be outlined that the protection normally provided by the Unfair Contract Terms Act 1977 to set aside exclusion clauses does not operate in the context of "international supply contracts".[74]

---

72 This entails that if the goods discharged at the port of destination show more than 3% of foreign matter, the buyer is prevented from claiming the liability of the seller for breach of the physical duty to ship goods containing no more than 3% foreign matter.

73 On this point, see C. Debattista, Certificate Final, or Not?, *Shipping & Transport International*, 2015, 10(3).

74 See Debattista, Certificate Final, or Not?, above. Section 26 of the 1977 Act excludes international commercial sales from its scope of application, by stating that:

(1) The limits imposed by this Act on the extent to which a person may exclude or restrict liability by reference to a contract term do not apply to liability arising under such a contract as is described in subsection (3) below.

(2) The terms of such a contract are not subject to any requirement of reasonableness under section 3 or 4: and nothing in Part 11 of this Act shall require the incorporation of the terms of such a contract to be fair and reasonable for them to have effect.

(3) Subject to subsection (4), that description of contract is one whose characteristics are the following –

 (a) either it is a contract of sale of goods or it is one under or in pursuance of which the possession or ownership of goods passes; and

 (b) it is made by parties whose places of business (or, if they have none, habitual residences) are in the territories of different States (the Channel Islands and the Isle of Man being treated for this purpose as different States from the United Kingdom).

(4) A contract falls within subsection (3) above only if either –

 (a) the goods in question are, at the time of the conclusion of the contract, in the course of carriage, or will be carried, from the territory of one State to the territory of another; or

 (b) the acts constituting the offer and acceptance have been done in the territories of different States; or

The scope of certificate final clauses

On a general level, certificate final clauses are freely agreed by commercial parties in order to bring finality to disputes as to the quality of goods shipped, thus avoiding unnecessary cost in putting forward such disputes. This perspective was emphasised by the Court in *Toepfer v Continental Grain Co.*[75]

Here, the buyers bought from the sellers a quantity of wheat described as "No. 3 Hard Amber Durum Wheat of U.S. origin – quality/condition final at loading as per official certificate c.i.f. certain Italian ports". The contract incorporated the terms and conditions of form 27 of the London Corn Trade Association, which stated (inter alia) that "Official . . . certificates of inspection to be final as to quality." The US Secretary of Agriculture had fixed official grain standards for wheat, and as far as "Durum Wheat" was concerned there were three classes: (i) "Hard Amber Durum Wheat"; (ii) "Amber Durum Wheat"; and (iii) "Durum Wheat".

In each class of wheat there were six grades, consisting of five numerical grades in descending order of merit and one sample grade. The sellers obtained a certificate from an inspector appointed by the Secretary of Agriculture to the effect that the wheat concerned was "No. 3 Hard Amber Durum Wheat", but the inspector had been negligent, and the certificate ought to have described the wheat as "No. 3 Amber Durum Wheat". The mistake was eventually discovered by the buyers, who claimed damages.

It was held by the court that the certificate in certifying that the wheat was "No. 3 Hard Amber Durum Wheat" was certifying the quality of the wheat. Since the certificate was expressly agreed to be final and was binding on both buyer and seller, a mistake made by the certifier (even when afterwards admitted by him to be a mistake) did not invalidate the certificate.

In the words of Cairns LJ:

> When parties enter into a contract on terms that the certificate of some independent person is to be binding as between them, it is important that the Court should not lightly relieve one of them from being bound by a certificate which was honestly obtained and not vitiated by fraud or fundamental mistake on the part of the certifier. When, for instance, as in this case, the certificate called for by the contract is one relating to

---

(c) the contract provides for the goods to be delivered to the territory of a State other than that within whose territory those acts were done.

See also *Air Transworld v Bombardier Inc* [2012] I Lloyd's Rep. 349. In this case, the questions before the court related to the operation of the Unfair Contract Terms Act 1977 to the exclusions of liability in the Aircraft Purchase Agreement (APA) whereby an Angolan company purchased aircraft from a Canadian Company, as incorporated into the Assignment Agreement. UCTA 1977 had no application to an "International Supply Contract" as defined by section 26 of UCTA 1977 and the implied terms could be ousted by agreement. It was held by the court that the APA, properly construed, had the effect of negating the conditions implied by sections 13 and 14 of the SOGA 1979. Although there was no express reference to the exclusion of conditions, it was clear that the first two lines of article 4.1 could only be read as saying that the defendant's obligations were to be found exclusively in the APA and its Appendix. The following lines made it clear that resort was not be had to any other obligation or liability of any kind which arose in law. No one reading the provision could be in any doubt that it was intended that the obligations resting on the seller, and the rights available to the buyer, were only to be found in the APA and in the specification in Appendix A to which it referred. The warranty was given in substitution for all other rights which might be implied by the SOGA 1979.

75 *Toepfer v Continental Grain Co* [1974] 1 Lloyd's Rep.

> the quality of goods sold, the business purpose is to avoid disputes about quality, and that purpose is defeated unless it is made difficult for a party to go behind a valid certificate . . . [f]or the sake of achieving certainty in the great majority of cases, it is worthwhile to take the risk that occasionally a wrong decision will be given and that there will be no means of reconsidering it.[76]

This means that where a certificate is to be conclusive as to the quality of goods, the buyer will be precluded from recovering damages from the seller if, contrary to the statement contained in the certificate, they are not of the contract quality,

Certificate final clauses are drafted with varying degrees of strictness and precision. They range from the extremely specific, making a certificate final, for example, only as to quantity. They can be drawn more widely, as to encompass several specific characteristics, making the certificate final only, say, as to quantity, moisture content, or other specification. Finally, the clause can be drafted in very broad terms, making the certificate final in generic terms as to quality.[77]

It has been correctly noted that "the more widely a "certificate final" clause is drafted and interpreted, the greater the protection it affords the seller – and, if the clause is enforced, the contract consequently comes closer to being a contract for the sale of documents rather than one for the sale of goods covered by documents".[78]

As we established above, the ultimate upshot of a certificate final clause, at any rate one widely drawn and interpreted, is to distil the seller's performance from the physical to the documentary by excluding remedies which the buyer might otherwise have for breach of the seller's physical duties to ship goods of the contract quality.

Indeed, a dexterously drafted certificate final clause can prevent the buyer from: a) proving that the seller failed to ship goods of the contract description, at any rate in the absence of the seller's fraud; b) rejecting the goods on the basis of non-conformity with matters described in the certificate; and c) suing for damages for breach of the duty to ship goods of the contract description.

9.16 English courts' approach to certificate final clauses

English courts have taken an even-handed approach to these clauses, seeking to strike a balance between the position of the seller and the buyer.

The advantages as between buyer and seller of a provision that quality is to be final at loading as per certificate are set out in *Rolimpex Centrala Handlu Zagranicznego v Haji E. Dossa & Sons Ltd.*,[79] where Mr Justice Donaldson said the following:

> A provision that a certificate given at the loading port shall be conclusive may well have great advantages to both parties. Thus, the buyers obtain an inspection at or before shipment by independent experts and can refuse to accept delivery of any goods which do not pass that scrutiny. They could, of course, make an inspection themselves, but, if they sought to reject goods, a dispute would be certain to arise. A conclusive certificate avoids all such disputes. Furthermore, the goods can be sold on similar terms without risk that the sub-buyers will make claims. From the point of view of the

76 *Ibid.*, at 11, 14, 15.
77 See C. Debattista, Certificate Final, or Not?, *Shipping & Transport International*, 2015, 10(3).
78 *Ibid.*
79 *Rolimpex Centrala Handlu Zagranicznego v Haji E. Dossa & Sons Ltd.* [1971] 1 Lloyd's Rep. 380.

> sellers the advantage lies in the avoidance of complaints based on evidence collected in a foreign country long after the goods have left their control, and in the fact that at the time of the inspection they have an opportunity of replacing any goods which do not meet with the approval of the surveyors. Against this background there is no reason to treat as commercially unrealistic the suggestion that the parties intended the surveyor's certificate to be conclusive.[80]

If a seller is always best advised to attempt to insert as many certificate final clauses as the buyer can stomach, such clauses are subject to strict interpretation by English courts, which have carefully interpreted certificate final clauses so as to limit them to what they actually say.

For instance, if a certificate final clause makes a certificate final as to sample, and the goods do not conform to the sample, the buyer has no remedy in respect of the non-conformity of the goods with the sample.

Nevertheless, if the goods are also not of satisfactory quality, then the buyer retains his remedy in respect of that other breach, which remains unaffected by the certificate final clause.

In *W.N. Lindsay & Co. v European Grain and Shipping Agency*,[81] a c.i.f. sales contract for 100 tons of Indian groundnut extractions provided, inter alia, by clause 11, that sampling was mandatory and final, but analysis was permissive, at the option of the buyer only. There was no express provision in the contract as to the effect of the buyer not requiring analysis of the sample within the contract time.

Complaints were put forward by a customer of the buyers that its employees were badly affected by handling the goods, and a microscopic test of a sample at the instance of the buyers (outside the terms of the contract) showed the presence of mowrah meal (which is injurious to livestock). Consequently, the buyers initiated a claim vis-à-vis the sellers for damages.

On appeal, the contention by the sellers was that if the buyers failed to request analysis under clause 11 within the contract time, the buyers were, by implication, debarred thereafter from proving the presence of a contaminating ingredient by analytical evidence, although they might prove it by any other kind of evidence.

It was held by the Court of Appeal that the implication contended for by the sellers was unnecessary and contrary to common sense; that any clause in a contract relied upon as excluding evidence ordinarily admissible was to be strictly construed; that much clearer words than those of clause 11 would be required to modify so drastically the buyers' common law rights in a matter which went to the root of the contract.

As put by Lord Justice Diplock:

> As is the case with many standard commercial contracts which have evolved piecemeal over the years, the drafting is not self-consistent, and the nomenclature employed is not uniform. The usual presumption that the same word is used throughout the contract in the same meaning is less strong than in the case of a contract drafted at one time by a single draftsman.

---

80 *Ibid.*, at 384.

81 *W.N. Lindsay & Co. v European Grain and Shipping Agency* [1963] 1 Lloyd's Rep. 437.

[. . .] We turn now to the vital clause, Clause 11. We approach it in the light of the facts (1) that the contract contains four express stipulations as to the characteristics of the goods apart from their description, namely, one general stipulation as to their being fair average quality, and three separate stipulations as to their content of specific ingredients; (2) that the stipulations as to fair average quality and as to content of oil and albuminoids are each accurately described as a "warranty", for breach thereof does not give rise to a right of rejection; (3) that the more complex stipulation as to sand and/or silica content has some of the characteristics of a "warranty" in that a silica content of between 2.12 per cent. and five per cent. gives rise not to a right of rejection, but to what is in effect liquidated damages; (4) that the Castor Clause contains its own provisions as to analysis; (5) that "allowances" are payable in respect of breaches of all these express stipulations; (6) that the "allowances" in respect of breaches of the three express stipulations as to the content of specific ingredients are fixed by the contract, and their amount is ascertainable only by analysis; and (7) that methods of analysis for oil and albuminoids (proteins) and for sand and silica are prescribed in the Fertilisers and Feeding Stuffs Regulations, 1960.

Clause 11 purports to deal with "Sampling and Analysis." One notes immediately the contrast between the way these two topics are dealt with. Sampling on arrival of the goods is mandatory; but the procedure laid down in the clause for analysis is, on the face of it, permissive only. It comes into operation only "If required by Buyer". Once it has been initiated by the buyer (but not otherwise) both he and the seller acquire rights to require a second test, and there are express provisions as to the finality of the analysis if a second test is required. We need not decide for the purposes of this case whether by necessary implication the first analysis made under this procedure is final and conclusive if neither party requires a second test.

But the clause contains no express provision as to what is to occur if the buyer does not, within the time limit laid down in the clause, require the sample to be tested by analysis for its content of some specific contaminating ingredient, in the present case mowrah meal.

The [seller's] contention is that by necessary implication the buyer is for ever after debarred from proving the presence of that or any ingredient by analytical evidence, although he may prove it by any other kind of evidence.

With great respect, the implication for which the sellers contend appears to us at first sight to be not merely unnecessary, but contrary to common sense. What support (if any) does it derive from the remainder of the clause? It is expressly provided that the buyer, if he requires an analysis, must give instructions to the analyst "specifying what test/s are to be carried out".

[. . .] any clause in a contract relied upon as excluding evidence which would ordinarily be admissible is to be strictly construed – all the more so where the evidence sought to be excluded is directed to the question whether the goods correspond to the description by which they were sold. Much clearer words than those of Clause 11 would be required to modify so drastically the buyer's common-law rights in a matter which goes to the root of the contract into which he has entered.[82]

In his judgment, Lord Justice Diplock clearly emphasises the need to construe certificate final clauses strictly *contra preferentem*.

A similar approach was adopted in the *Bow Cedar*,[83] where the sellers sold to the buyers 500 tonnes of Brazilian crude groundnut oil FFA basis f.o.b., with weight and quality final at loading as per certificate of independent surveyors nominated by sellers.

82 *Ibid.*, at 443, 444, 445.

83 *The Bow Cedar* [1980] 2 Lloyd's Rep. 601.

The goods were found at the time of shipment to actually consist of 250 tonnes of groundnut oil and 250 tonnes of soya bean oil and that, by reason of the admixture with soya bean oil, the goods appropriated to the contract could not properly be described as groundnut oil.

The buyers claimed damages based on the difference between the value of sound groundnut oil and the price realised by the oil as delivered. The sellers denied liability contending that the certificates given on shipment were final and conclusive.

The court found that it was clear from the certificates that there was 0.98 per cent FFA in the sample and 0.18 per cent moisture and impurities, but there was nothing in the certificates to support the suggestion that the surveyors were also certifying that the goods were Brazilian crude groundnut oil. Further, the court stated that it was clear from the form and layout of the certificates that what was being certified was the result of their chemical analysis not the commodity which they were analysing; even if, however, the certificates did certify the commodity as well as the chemical analysis it was plain on the ordinary meaning of the words that the certificates were to be final as to the sort of matters that were covered by the quality clause, including moisture and impurities, and not as to the commodity itself.

The presence of soya bean oil did not affect the quality of the oil, which was excellent, but the goods were not the contract goods and there was nothing in the contract which made certificates final as to the description of the goods.

In the words of Lloyd J:

> It is clear from the terms of that certificate that the independent surveyors were certifying that there was .98 per cent. FFA in the sample and .18 per cent. moisture and impurities. But Mr. Rix, on behalf of the sellers, submits that the certificate goes further than that. He argues that the surveyors were certifying not only that the percentage of FFA moisture and impurities was as stated, but also that the goods were Brazilian crude groundnut oil.
>
> I can see nothing in the certificate which supports that view. On the contrary it is, to my mind, clear that what the surveyors were certifying was the result of their chemical analysis not the commodity which they were analysing.
>
> [. . .] If I am right that the certificates issued by Thionville do not even purport to certify that the oil was groundnut oil, then the sellers' argument does not get off the ground. But if I am wrong about that and if the certificates purport to certify the commodity as well as the chemical analysis, the next question would be whether the contract makes the certificates conclusive in that respect. I do not think it does. I have already set out the main provisions of the "Confirmation of Sale". The "Commodity" is described as Brazilian crude groundnut oil. There is then a term as to quality which provides maximum 3 per cent. FFA and maximum 12 per cent. moisture and impurities. The contract then provides for the "quality" to be final at loading as per certificate.
>
> There was some discussion as to whether that provision should be construed strictly against the sellers as suggested by Lord Justice Diplock, in *W.N. Lindsay & Co. v European Grain and Shipping Agency* [1963] 1 Lloyd's Rep. 437, or whether the words should be given their ordinary businesslike meaning as suggested by Lord Justice Cairns, in *Toepfer v Continental Grain Co.* [1974] 1 Lloyd's Rep. 11. Mr. Grace, on behalf of the buyers, argued that very clear words would be necessary in order to compel the buyers to accept goods which do not comply with their contract description. I assume he is wrong about that. Even so, it seems to me plain on the ordinary meaning of the words, that the certificates were to be final as to the sort of matters that are covered

by the quality clause, for example the percentage of FFA, moisture and impurities, and not as to the commodity itself.

I am confirmed in that view by the fact that it appears also to be the view of the two trade tribunals before whom this case has come. In par. 38 (e) of their award, the Board of Appeal say:

The goods appropriated to this contract did not comply with the contract description of the goods sold and the Thionville certificates, even if final as to quality, do not protect the Sellers from a claim for damages in this instance.

Mr. Rix relied on the decision of the Court of Appeal in *Toepfer v Continental Grain Co*. In that case there was a contract for the sale of No. 3 hard amber durum wheat. The contract provided for quality to be final as per official inspection certificate. The wheat was certified as hard amber wheat, but in fact it was not. The percentage of hard vitreous kernels was too low. The buyers claimed damages. The umpire and the Board of Appeal rejected the buyers' claim; so did the Judge. In the Court of Appeal, the main issue was whether the buyers were bound by a certificate when the person giving the certificate had been negligent. It was held that they were. But there was another point: it was submitted that the certificate was only binding as to quality, not as to description. Since "hard" was part of the description of the goods, and since the wheat did not comply with the contractual description, the buyers argued that the certificate was not binding. The Court of Appeal rejected that argument. It was held that on the facts of that case the quality and description could not be separated. The hardness related to both.

But in the present case the presence of soya bean oil did not affect the quality of the oil in any way. The quality was excellent but the goods were not the contract goods [. . .] There is nothing to suggest that in those circumstances the certificates would have been binding.[84]

It is clear on the authorities that the presence of certificate final clauses is strictly circumscribed to the specific ambit they refer to, and will be strictly applied by the English courts.

Nevertheless, certificate final clauses which render quality or description final are, at times, difficult to interpret.

Distinction between quality and description

It has been correctly pointed out that, especially at a higher level, courts have been careful to limit the impact of a certificate final clause related to quality. Such a clause does not have any impact on the implied condition that goods sold by description must comply with the description as per originally established in the sales contract.[85]

In *Toepfer*,[86] the buyers bought from the sellers a quantity of wheat described as "No. 3 Hard Amber Durum Wheat of U.S. origin – quality/condition final at loading as per official certificate c.i.f. certain Italian ports". A mistake made by the inspector re the grading of the wheat ignited a controversy which involved, inter alia, a learned discussion on the difference between "quality" and "description".

Indeed, the buyers maintained that the certificate tendered by the sellers was only final as to "quality", not final, as to the "description" of the goods.

84 *Ibid.*, at 602, 604, 605.

85 See C. Debattista, Certificate Final, or Not?, *Shipping & Transport International*, 2015, 10(3).

86 *Toepfer* [1974] I Lloyd's Rep. 11.

Lord Denning MR, found the distinction between "quality" and "description" of goods of scarce relevance. In his words:

> We were referred to cases on sale of goods and to the provisions of the statute. I confess that I found the discussion unhelpful. The "description" of goods often includes a statement of their quality. Thus "new-laid eggs" contains both quality and description all in one. "Quality" is often part of the description. In this very case the word "hard" is a word both of quality and of description. If a certificate is final as to the quality "hard", it is final as to that description also. The quality and description cannot be separated. Finality as to one means finality as to the other.[87]

If Lord Denning MR in *Toepfer* found the distinction between quality and description somehow immaterial, that distinction does figure prominently in later cases.

Thus, in the aforementioned *Bow Cedar*,[88] a clause making "weight and quality final at loading as per certificate of independent surveyors nominated by sellers" was caged safely away from description and restricted to quality.

As stated by Lloyd J, the certificates in that case were to be final as to the sort of matters that are covered by the quality clause and not as to the commodity itself.[89]

Subsequently to the *Bow Cedar*, the line of reasoning of the Court of Appeal's decision in *Toepfer* was reconstructed by Lord Diplock in the House of Lords in *Gill & Duffils SA v Berg* & *Co Inc.*[90] Here, the sellers sold to the buyers 500 tonnes of Argentine Bolita beans, with quality final at port of discharge as certificate, indicating that the quality of the lot is equal to one of the sealed sample.

A discrepancy present in the certificate of quality called into question whether the goods were, in fact, consistent with the original contractual description. It was held by the House of Lords that the buyers were not entitled to reject the documents in relation to the 445 tonnes on the grounds that the goods did not comply with the contractual description.

As put by Lord Diplock:

> The words used in a contract of sale that refer to the goods agreed to be sold (not being "specific goods" as defined in s. 62 of the Sale of Goods Act, 1893) often include words that describe a characteristic as to quality or condition that they possess which distinguishes them from other goods of the same general kind. What *Toepfer v Continental Grain* decided was that where the description of the goods agreed to be sold included a statement as to their quality and provided that a certificate as to quality was to be final, the certificate was final as to the correspondence of the goods with that part of the description of them in the contract that referred to their quality (in casu "No. 3 hard amber") notwithstanding that the certificate was proved to have been inaccurate. The conclusion reached by the Court of Appeal in *Toepfer v Continental Grain* is, in my opinion, plainly right. My own preferred analysis of the reason why it is consistent with s. 13 of the Sale of Goods Act, 1893, is that while "description" itself is an ordinary English word, the Act contains no definition of what it means when it speaks in that section of a contract for the sale of goods being a sale "by description". One must look to the contract as a whole to identify the kind of goods that the seller was agreeing to sell and the buyer to buy. In Toepfer's case, it was not "No. 3 hard amber

87 *Ibid.*, at 13.

88 [1980] 2 Lloyd's Rep. 601.

89 See *The Bow Cedar*, above, at 604.

90 *Gill & Duffils SA v Berg & Co Inc* [1984] I Lloyd's Rep. 227.

> durum wheat" simpliciter but durum wheat of U.S. origin for which a certificate had been issued by a U.S. Government official stating that its quality was that which is described in the trade as "No. 3 hard amber".
>
> Similarly, where, as in the instant case, the sale (to use the words of s. 13) is "by sample as well as by description", characteristics of the goods which would be apparent on reasonable examination of the sample are unlikely to have been intended by the parties to form part of the "description" by which the goods were sold, even though such characteristics are mentioned in references in the contract to the goods that are its subject-matter.
>
> My Lords, the c.i.f. contract in the instant case contains provisions opposite the rubrics "quality" and "special conditions and remarks" respectively, which make the certificate of GSC conclusive as to the conformity of the bulk shipment at port of discharge with the sample that had been submitted to the buyers while the contract was in course of negotiation and had been sealed by GSC. It must have been the intention of the parties that the conclusiveness of the certificate would be limited to those characteristics of the contract goods that would be apparent on reasonable examination of the sample.[91]

The purpose and effect of Lord Diplock's interpretation was clearly to circumscribe the finality imposed by the clause as to quality and not to description, thus leaving unaffected by a certificate final clause a buyer's remedies for breach of the seller's duty to ship goods complying with their description, that duty being regarded as too fundamental to brook interference by the clause.[92]

It has been correctly pointed out that, in effect, the judges are here preventing certificate final clauses from doing that which they are expressly allowed to do by section 55 of SOGA 1979, namely, to negative or vary by express agreement a right arising by implication of law, that is to say, a right to recovery for breach of the implied condition of compliance with description.

As we shall discover in the following, that was not the last occasion where certificate final clauses have been curtailed by judicial interpretation.

9.17 Recent developments on certificate final clauses: *The Mercini Lady*

In the last few years, certificate final clauses have been subject to scrutiny again in *The Mercini Lady*.[93]

The initial judgment by Mr Justice Field in the Commercial Court caused much controversy for two reasons. First, it exposed f.o.b. sellers to the risk of goods deteriorating after loading, even in a "certificates final on loading" contract. Second, it decided that standard exclusion wording was ineffective based on a very precise and legalistic interpretation of the wording.

Before the court of first instance decision in *The Mercini Lady*, a "certificate final on loading" clause and a clean certificate would guarantee sellers the utmost

91 *Ibid.*, at 233.

92 See C. Debattista, Certificate Final, or Not? *Shipping & Transport International*, 2015, 10(3).

93 *The Mercini Lady (KG Bominflot Bunkergellschaft fur Mineralole mbh & Co KG v Petroplus Marketing AG)* [2009] EWHC 1088 (Comm) (22 May 2009)).

protection if goods were found deteriorated, outside specification, or in a poor state on discharge.

After the first instance decision, in the absence of an inconsistent contractual term, a condition was to be implied into every f.o.b. contract under section 14 of SOGA 1979, whereby goods were to be of satisfactory quality not only when the cargo was delivered onto the vessel but also for a "reasonable time thereafter". Further, this term should also be implied at common law, with the additional factor that the goods should also remain in accordance with the contractual specification (if any) for such a time.

Essentially this was an extension of the aforementioned longstanding (but seldom applied) rule set out in *Mash & Murrell Ltd v Joseph I Emanuel Ltd*,[94] whereby all c.i.f. contracts would by default include an implied term that goods will be of satisfactory quality when loaded and also in a state capable of enduring the "normal journey" to remain of satisfactory quality upon arrival.

Importantly, in the first instance decision in *The Mercini Lady*, this principle was overextended even in the presence of a certificate final clause as to final quality on loading. Indeed, the court stated that f.o.b. buyers were entitled to expect that the goods will be sufficiently "durable" to be of satisfactory quality upon delivery. With this rationale in mind, the court ruled that this entitlement be protected by the implied "condition".

A second paramount point of the first instance decision related to the exclusion clause present in the contract. The contract had specifically excluded any "guarantees, warranties or representations, express or implied, or merchantability, fitness or suitability of the oil for any particular purpose or otherwise". However, the clause did not contain the word "condition". As a result, this exclusion clause was ineffective in protecting the sellers against the obligations implied pursuant to section 14 SOGA because these are "conditions" as per section 14(6) SOGA.[95]

---

94 *Mash & Murrell Ltd v Joseph I Emanuel Ltd* [1961] 1 All ER 485. See Debattista, *Bills of Lading in Export Trade*, above, p. 159. See also *Benjamin's Sale of Goods*, above, paras. 19.369 *et seq.*

95 See section 14 SOGA, Implied terms about quality or fitness, which states as follows:

(1) Except as provided by this section and section 15 below and subject to any other enactment, there is no implied condition or warranty about the quality or fitness for any particular purpose of goods supplied under a contract of sale.

(2) Where the seller sells goods in the course of a business, there is an implied term that the goods supplied under the contract are of satisfactory quality.

(2A) For the purposes of this Act, goods are of satisfactory quality if they meet the standard that a reasonable person would regard as satisfactory, taking account of any description of the goods, the price (if relevant) and all the other relevant circumstances.

(2B) For the purposes of this Act, the quality of goods includes their state and condition and the following (among others) are in appropriate cases aspects of the quality of goods –

(a) fitness for all the purposes for which goods of the kind in question are commonly supplied,
(b) appearance and finish,
(c) freedom from minor defects,
(d) safety, and
(e) durability.

The term implied by subsection (2) above does not extend to any matter making the quality of goods unsatisfactory –

(a) which is specifically drawn to the buyer's attention before the contract is made,

On appeal, the appellant sellers advanced submissions on the distinction between the obligations of sellers in relation to the satisfactory quality of goods as under SOGA, as distinct from the obligations relating to specifications under the common law. They contended that where the contract contained an express "certificate final on loading" term there was no need to rely on any implied contradictory term.

Additionally, in relation to the exclusion clause, the sellers contended that the commercial approach would be to recognise that the parties intended to exclude the conditions as implied under SOGA. The sellers highlighted the "floodgates" argument that the current approach leads to uncertainty by having to calculate what a "reasonable time" may be in each case. The sellers also offered examples of where the word "guarantee" had been treated as meaning "condition" by the courts.

The respondent buyers replied that in the absence of express wording excluding the guarantee that the goods would remain of such quality and condition after loading there was no rationale for not implying the additional term. Where the parties intended (or rather did not expressly exclude) that the goods would remain of a satisfactory quality for a reasonable time after loading it would be illogical that they did not intend exactly the same for specifications. The buyers also relied on established authority in case law that, to exclude conditions, the word "condition" must be expressly used in the contract.

The Court of Appeal held that there was no such common law implied term as suggested by the buyers. The contract made it clear that the specification had to be met at the time of delivery, that the intention was that the gasoil should be inspected by an independent inspector prior to loading, "basis shoretank", and that the inspector's determination should be conclusive. The sediment was within specification limits at the time of loading and delivery, and therefore, gasoil of the correct specification was delivered.

After delivery the buyer assumed "all risks pertaining thereto" (clause 15). "All risks" included the risk of transport, and the risk of cargo instability. A clause for conclusive inspection and determination on loading replaced or redefined the implied terms as to quality, and prevented any further implication that it was legitimate to take account of changes in the cargo's specification after delivery.

Moreover, the suggested term could not survive section 14(1) of the SOGA 1979, which limited the implication of terms about quality or fitness to the statutory terms contained in the Act.

As for the implied obligations which the sellers said had been excluded, these were not only fundamental obligations of English law, long enshrined in the Sale of Goods Acts, but there was a judicial consensus that such obligations could only be excluded by language which expressly referred to "conditions". It was not open to the court to depart from that long established consensus. Accordingly, the condition implied by section 14(2) of the SOGA 1979 had not been excluded by the contract. As put by Rix LJ:

(b) where the buyer examines the goods before the contract is made, which that examination ought to reveal, or

(c) in the case of a contract for sale by sample, which would have been apparent on a reasonable examination of the sample.

In my judgment, there is nothing to suggest, let alone require the alleged implication. It is accepted by the buyer that the express terms of the contract do not assist, and that the term therefore has to be implied. It is also accepted that the term is novel. Unlike the statutory implication, on which it is modelled, the additional implied term is not a mere interpretation of the meaning and effect of an implied term which exists (subject to exclusion) and exists as a matter of law and statute, but is a total addition to the contract. The analogy with the section 14(2) implication would be to find that the express provisions about the specification mean that the specification has to be met not only at delivery but also for a "reasonable" but uncertain period after delivery. However, there is no legitimate support for such an interpretation, and none for the implication of a term to supply the want of such a meaning.

On the contrary, the contract makes it clear that the specification has to be met at the time of delivery, that the intention is that the gasoil should be inspected by an independent inspector prior to loading, "basis shoretank" (ie not even on the basis of the gasoil in the ship's tanks), and that the inspector's determination should be conclusive (ie final and binding in the absence of fraud or manifest error). It is accepted that, even though the gasoil's sediment was measured by the wrong test, nevertheless the sediment was within specification limits at the time of loading and delivery. Therefore gasoil of the correct specification was delivered. The buyer's acceptance of that fact supplants the want of a valid inspector's certificate. Moreover, the intention of the contract remains, that specification should be determined conclusively at loading. Therefore it matters not that things may change thereafter, or even, if a conclusive determination has once been made, that things may not change but that a new test may show a different result which is outside specification limits. After delivery the buyer "assumes all risks pertaining thereto" (clause 15). All risks are all risks. They include the risk of transport, and they include the risk of cargo instability unless that risk has already been taken by the seller under a term of the contract which relates to the condition of the cargo pre-delivery. But a clause for conclusive inspection and determination on loading replaces or redefines the implied terms as to quality pro tanto. A fortiori it prevents any further implication that it is legitimate to take account of changes in the cargo's specification after delivery.

The question might therefore arise hereafter as to the extent to which clauses 4 and 12 might impinge even with respect to the basic statutory term to be found in section 14(2). Thus a matter of latent inherent vice which could not have been picked up by the quality inspection mandated by clauses 4 and/or 12 may possibly stand outside those clauses so as to give cause to find a breach of an implied term of satisfactory quality. If, however, the alleged vice is in truth something for which the specification and conclusive determination clauses provide, such as here sediment, there may be no room for a separate allegation of breach by reference to the statutory implied term of what is now satisfactory quality or any similar term to be implied at common law. That is I believe, generally speaking, the learning of the jurisprudence on conclusive certification clauses.[96]

Rix LJ then proceeded to analyse the impact of *Mash &Murrel* on a certificate final clause related to quality.

In his words:

Mash & Murrell itself is a warning about inferring from deterioration of even perishable goods during a voyage a conclusion about breach of the statutory implied condition of (then) merchantable quality. Diplock J held that there had been a breach of the implied term. On appeal, however, this court held that the cause of the deterioration was lack of proper ventilation during the voyage: [1962] 1 WLR 16.

96 *Ibid.*, at 448, 449.

> In the circumstances it would be superfluous to discuss whether or not the additional implied term was necessary or not in the light of the acceptance of the section 14(2) term. It could certainly go further than the statutory term, which is not focused on this contract's specification in particular, but more generally on the considerations set out in section 14(2A) and (2B). Therefore, contrary to the submission of Mr Jacobs, the presence of the statutory implied term would not render the additional implied term redundant (at any rate in theory). On the other hand, for the reasons stated above, the additional implied term was simply not part of the intention of the parties to this contract and would not have been understood by reasonable merchants to have been part of its meaning (see *Attorney General of Belize v Belize Telecom Ltd* [2009] 1 WLR 1988, and *Mediterranean Salvage & Towage Ltd v Seamar Trading & Commerce Inc (The Reborn)* [2009] 2 Lloyd's Rep 639). If it had been otherwise, the whole point of a final and binding determination by an independent inspector on loading would be rendered pointless, for the buyer could always say that although the goods were within specification on loading, and had been conclusively determined so to be, they had nevertheless fallen out of specification during the contemplated voyage or within a reasonable time. All certainty in international sale of goods, which such inspection clauses are designed to provide (see *Alfred C Toepfer v Continental Grain Co* [1974] 1 Lloyd's Rep 11) would be utterly broken. Such clauses, plain and express as they are, would simply be a snare and a delusion, because they would always have to make way for the special additional term, even though it was merely implied and not express.
>
> Finally, although it was not a point made at the hearing, it is hard to see how the alleged additional term can survive section 14(1) of the 1979 Act. That provision, which limits the implication of terms about quality or fitness to the statutory terms contained in the 1979 Act, thus retains, in the background, the most fundamental rule of all so far as quality is concerned, namely that, despite the huge inroads made by first the common law and then statute, the underlying principle is still caveat emptor, let the buyer beware.[97]

The Court of Appeal decision has, thus, categorically restored the previous status quo. Indeed, the Commercial Court decision was the source of much controversy, in that it potentially exposed f.o.b. sellers to the risk of goods deteriorating after loading, even in the presence of a certificates final on loading clause.

In addition, it was decided that a standard exclusion clause of a kind that is widely relied upon did not exclude the application of terms implied by the SOGA 1979.

On appeal, Lord Justice Rix put the first instance decision firmly in context. He found that, to the extent that the first instance decision may have created a novel implied term which could avoid the effect of the standard certificate final on loading clause, the decision was wrong; otherwise, all certainty in the international sale of goods, which such inspection clauses are designed to provide, would be utterly broken.

In respect to the exclusion of the terms implied by the SOGA 1979, Lord Justice Rix determined that the first instance decision was correct. However, he suggested that this finding would have little relevance to the express nature of the certificate final on loading clause:

> If . . . the alleged vice [off-spec quality criteria] is in truth something for which the specification and conclusive determination clauses provide . . . there may be no room

97 *Ibid.*, at 450.

> for a separate allegation of breach by reference to the statutory implied term of what is now satisfactory quality or any similar term to be implied at common law.[98]

Therefore, it remains the case that to exclude the effect of any implied statutory terms, the contract must be expressly specific in excluding "statutory implied terms and/or conditions".

Before the first instance decision in *The Mercini Lady*, a "certificate final on loading" provision, coupled with a clean certificate, would have provided incontrovertible protection if the goods deteriorated after loading.

For a while, that confidence was lost and the Commercial Court seemed to provide for certain ongoing obligations for goods to remain "on spec" during the voyage and that the "final" loading certificate did not prevent those ongoing obligations.

After the Court of Appeal decision, certainty in the international sale of goods, which such inspection clauses are designed to provide, has been fully restored. A clause for conclusive inspection and determination on loading replaces or redefines the implied terms as to quality and prevents further terms being implied relating to the cargo after delivery.

Where such a clause is enforced, the seller discharges his responsibilities towards the buyer by presenting documents agreed to be final as between the parties, whether or not the seller actually shipped goods of the contract quality.

The buyer is then left to seek recovery either from the carrier for any discrepancy between the goods as described in the sale contract and the goods discharged, or from the surveying agency, as outlined in the following.

9.18 Certificate final clauses: mistakes and negligence of the surveying agency

Remedies against the surveying agency are often based on the tort of negligent misrepresentation rather than contract.

Nevertheless, it is clear on the authorities that mistakes or negligence of the surveying agent do not impeach the validity of a certificate final clause. In *Toepfer v Continental Grain Co.*,[99] a mistake made by the certifier, even when afterwards admitted by him to be a mistake, did not invalidate the certificate. It remained binding as between seller and buyer.

As put by Lord Denning MR:

> It is said: This certificate was made under a mistake. The Department of Agriculture in the United States have admitted it. They have reprimanded the inspector. They have issued "a formal corrective action" to him. The inspector himself admitted that he made a mistake. On this ground it is said that the certificate is not binding.
>
> Apart altogether from authority, I am clearly of opinion that a mistake by the certifier, even when afterwards admitted by him to be a mistake, does not invalidate the certificate. It remains binding as between seller and buyer and all down the chain. The Board of Appeal in their award set out the commercial reasons which support this view:

98 *Ibid.*, at 448.

99 *Toepfer v Continental Grain Co.* [1974] 1 Lloyd's Rep. 11.

> The commercial purpose of the provisions [for an official certificate to be final as to quality] . . . is to avoid disputes as to quality and to achieve finality in this respect once a proper certificate of inspection had been issued and tendered. A further reason . . . is that differences of opinion are otherwise to be expected among persons experienced in the grain trade in countries outside the United States and Canada as to the correct grading (including both the grade and sub-class) of consignments of U.S. or Canadian grain and such differences would otherwise give rise to numerous disputes.
>
> It must be remembered that numerous persons act on the faith of the certificate, such as the buyers, sub-buyers, bankers lending money and so forth. Good sense requires that the finality of the clause should be upheld by arbitrators and the Courts in full. It is not open to the arbitrator himself to say afterwards: "I have made a mistake".[100]

If the aforementioned reasons are in essence of a commercial nature, they are not deprived of legal foundation.

In the words of Lord Denning MR:

> These commercial considerations are borne out by legal principles. I tried to summarize them in the recent case of *Arenson v Arenson* [1973] 2 Lloyd's Rep. 104 at p. 107; [1973] 2 W.L.R. 553 at p. 559:
>
> > . . . Whenever two persons agree together to refer a matter to a third person for decision, and further agree that his decision is to be final and binding upon them, then, so long as he arrives at his decision honestly and in good faith, the two parties are bound by it. They cannot re-open it for mistake or error on his part of for any reason other than for fraud or collusion . . .
>
> Those words are appropriate here. There is no suggestion of fraud or collusion. It is a case of a mistake or error. Mr. Staughton referred us to *Dean v Prince* [1953] Ch. 590, [1954] Ch. 409, and *Wright v Frodoor* [1967] 1 W.L.R. 506, where it was said that a certificate or valuation can be set aside, not only for fraud, but also for a material mistake or miscarriage, at any rate if it appears on the face of the certificate or is admitted by the certifier. Mr. Staughton relied in particular on what Mr. Justice Harman said in *Dean v Prince* at p. 593. I do not think those cases and those observations apply to a case like the present. They apply at most to contracts which are still executory and a party comes to a Court of equity asking for them to be specifically enforced. They do not apply to contracts which have been executed, as here, contracts for the sale of goods which have been delivered. In such cases the parties, and all those down the chain, are entitled to regard the certificate as final. It cannot be upset, as between them, for mistake of the certifier.[101]

9.19 Rights against the inspecting agency

Where the inspecting agency is fraudulent or negligent in issuing a certificate stating that the goods conform to the contract, the question arises whether the buyer can recover damages from the agency.

100 *Ibid.*, at 13. See Debattista, *Bills of Lading in Export Trade*, above, p. 196. See also *Benjamin's Sale of Goods*, above, paras. 15.096 *et seq.*

101 *Ibid.*, at 14.

Voices to that end were raised in *Sutcliffe v Thackrah*,[102] and in *Arenson v Arenson*,[103] where reference was made to authorities in the courts of the US. These showed that in the US, a certificate cannot, as between the parties, be set aside for mistake of the certifier.[104]

Nevertheless, it might prove very difficult in practice to claim the negligence of the surveying agency. In *The Kriti Palm*,[105] a mistake made by the surveyor in relation to the sampling of the quality of a cargo of gasoil, and a deliberate concealment were not considered as dishonest behaviour capable of giving rise to liabilities.

The importance of drafting

In light of the aforementioned considerations, the importance of carefully crafting certificate final clauses cannot be emphasised enough. Indeed, in order to avoid unwelcome surprises, such clauses need to be extremely well defined about: a) who is to issue the certificate; b) what the certificate is to say; and above all c) as to what the certificate is agreed to be final.

By way of example, let us consider a certificate final clause drafted as follows: "quality as per certificate issued at loadport by shippers to be final and binding

102 *Sutcliffe v Thackrah*, [1973] 2 Lloyd's Rep. 115. Here it was held by Buckley LJ that:

> The principle of law which forbids an action for want of skill or care against an arbitrator or a quasi arbitrator, is just as applicable to a skilled or professional arbitrator as to one who is unskilled and non-professional and that the fact of its being his business makes no difference.
>
> In my judgment, the authorities establish that where a third party is required to decide any matter which is in dispute between other parties or any matter upon which such other parties have opposed interests on which they agree to accept the third party's decision, the third party is performing a quasi-judicial function and falls within the principle of the authorities which I have been discussing. It is true that in the present case there was no formulated dispute between the vendor and the purchaser, but in any case in which the vendor and purchaser leave the price of property which is to be sold to be determined by a third party they must necessarily have opposed interests. In any such case it is unnecessary to find in terms an agreement that they will refer the price to the third party in default of agreement between themselves, for this is precisely the effect of the agreement, even though there is no reference to failure to agree.
>
> In my judgment a clear distinction is to be drawn between the position of a third party who is required to adjudicate in such a way as this and one to whom the parties delegate the function of ascertaining some matter of fact. If a vendor and a purchaser of goods sold by weight delegate to a third party the function of ascertaining the weight of a particular parcel of such goods, they are not seeking an adjudication: they are delegating a ministerial function which with the necessary skill and equipment they could perform themselves and about which, if they did it accurately, no dispute could arise, for the weight of the parcel would be a pure question of fact allowing no room for difference of opinion. *Glanzer v Shepard* (1922) 233 N.Y. 236, was such a case. In my judgment, *Gammel v Ernst and Ernst* (1955) 245 Minn. 249 is to be explained on the same ground. What the defendant firm had to ascertain in that case was the net earnings per share of certain common stock for a particular period. Different accountants using different but acceptable methods of accountancy might well have arrived at different answers to that enquiry. The correctness of any one answer would not be by any means so demonstrably correct as the ascertainment of the weight of particular goods. Nevertheless it is clearly a tenable view that what Messrs. Ernst and Ernst had to ascertain was a fact and that, since the parties selected Messrs. Ernst and Ernst to ascertain it, they agreed to accept the accountancy methods selected by that firm as appropriate to those circumstances. The Court proceeded upon the view that the firm was employed to act not as an "arbiter" but as "an accountant evaluator".

103 *Arenson v Arenson* [1973] 2 Lloyd's Rep. 104.

104 See *Sanitary Farm v Gammel* (1952) 195 F 2d 106: but the negligent certifier is liable in damages to the party injured by his negligence, see *Gammel v Ernst & Ernst* (1955) in the US.

105 *The Kriti Palm* [2007] 1 Lloyd's Rep. 555.

upon both parties, unless it can be proved that testing and/or sampling was incorrectly performed".

Such a clause would confer a certain degree of protection on a buyer in the case of a mistake made by the surveyor which, as established above, would not impeach the finality of the erroneous certificate.

Nevertheless, even the presence of such *caveat emptor* might not transpire, in practice, to be an effective tool of protection for a buyer. In *Apioil v Kuwait*,[106] a contract for the sale of a cargo of Russian straight run fuel oil was subject in terms of quality to a certificate final clause to be considered binding upon the parties, unless mistakes in the sampling could have been proven. The buyers claimed mistakes had been made in the sampling, and were consequently saddled with the burden of proof.[107] As put by Colman J:

> In the event this was not an issue which gives rise to much controversy between the parties. It was accepted that the legal burden of proving the relevant contractual attributes of the SGS certificate fell upon whichever party relied on the certificate as establishing the viscosity of the cargo for the purpose of asserting that party's claim or defence in these two actions. Such party would have to adduce at least prima facie evidence that: (i) the samples which SGS had analysed were taken by SOGEX from the vessel's tanks; (ii) that such samples were fully representative of the quality of the cargo having been taken in accordance with one of the four international sampling standards; and (iii) that such samples were sent for analysis to SGS Holland and were analysed by SGS to give the results shown in the SGS certificate.[108]

Although the burden of proof is a double-edged sword which cuts both ways, and consequently would call into question also the seller in terms of proving the sample was correctly performed, that would result in most circumstances as a more burdensome task for the buyer.

Indeed, proving that a sample was incorrectly performed represents an extremely arduous task for a buyer who is logistically far away from the port of origin where sampling usually takes place.

That is the reason why some traders resorted to the introduction of "manifest error exclusion clauses". In *Galaxy Energy International v Eurobunker*,[109] the sale contract for low sulphur fuel oil contained, inter alia, a certificate final clause whereby the quality as ascertained at loading installation was to be final and binding for both parties "save fraud and manifest error".

The issue for decision was whether, under the terms of the aforementioned clause, the buyers had a real prospect of success in showing that there was a plain and obvious error in relation to the certificate or the procedure leading to the making of the certificate.

The court found that there was no contemporaneous protest by the buyers of the certificate tendered by the seller, and that prejudiced the possibility of the buyer setting aside the validity of the certificate final clause for manifest error.

---

106 *Apioil v Kuwait* [1995] 1 Lloyd's Rep. 124.
107 *Ibid.*, at 131.
108 *Ibid.*
109 *Galaxy Energy International v Eurobunker* [2001] 2 Lloyd's Rep. 725.

Indeed, the court found that if the differing results as shown had given rise to a plain and obvious error, there was no doubt the buyers would have raised the point; they said nothing at the time, and it was difficult to see how it could be said there was a plain and obvious error when nothing was expressed about it at the time the certificate was produced and part of the cargo accepted.

In the words of Thomas J.:

> As was common ground, the question before the Court was whether there was a real prospect of successfully defending the claim by showing that there was a plain and obvious error in relation to the certificate or the procedure leading to the making of the certificate.
>
> If I was to consider the definition of repeatability and reproducibility given by Mr. Chell, the tests of sample A made in November, 2000 and April, 2001 were plainly within the range of repeatability. There was no error evidenced by the re-test, let alone any plain and obvious error. All the other tests at Malta were within the reproducibility range of sample A and thus no error could be inferred from such tests.
>
> However, reading Mr. Chell's report as a whole and taking into account the fact that this is a Part 24 application, I accept that he seems to have taken the view that all the tests in Malta by Saybolt should have been within the repeatability range, even though the tests on sample B and C taken in November, 2000 and the new composite made up in April, 2001 were tests on different samples. He does not explain why this was so, but it may be because he considered that the samples should all have been the same or treated as the same. Accepting this evidence, it points, as he stated in his report, to an inconsistency in the results.
>
> Is this sufficient? I do not consider that it is.
>
> In the first place, I consider that the relevant sample was sample A. The contract provided for a guaranteed specification at the discharge port; the guarantee plainly applied to the cargo sold to the buyers and due for discharge and not to the whole of the cargo on the vessel. Similarly the task of Saybolt at Malta was to re-test the parcel to be discharged by means of a composite sample from the ship's tanks. Their certificate would be a certificate in respect of the composite sample of that cargo and not the other cargo on the vessel. Thus the relevant certification was the certification in respect of the composite sample of that cargo. The relevant sample was sample A; this was re-checked in April, 2001 and the result was within the margin of ±3 deg. C applicable for repeatability. In so far as it might be appropriate to consider the new composite sample prepared in April, 2001, as this was a new sample, then the reproducibility range applied and there was no error when that result is compared with the result in the certificate of Nov. 22, 2000.
>
> Furthermore even assuming that it is appropriate to apply the repeatability range to the new composite sample prepared in April, 2001 (so that the result is outside the range) and/or that it is appropriate to rely upon the test results of samples B and C and apply to them the repeatability range (so that the results are outside the range), then these results would point to an inconsistency, but nothing more. I do not consider that they give rise to any real prospect of showing that there was a plain and obvious error in the certificate or the testing or sampling. On the evidence, there is nothing to show that a plain and obvious error occurred in these tasks; at the highest it shows that if the sampling was done differently, there might have been a different result. This might have been caused by some form of error, but even an error (and not merely the possibility of an error) is not enough. There is no evidence of plain and obvious error.
>
> There is one further point, though it only reinforces the conclusion I have reached. There was no contemporaneous protest by the buyers about the certificate of Nov. 22, 2000. If the differing results as shown on that certificate (which included the notation that sample C had shown a result of 9 deg. C and had been re-tested three times) and/or as compared to the result in Tarragona had given rise to a plain and obvious

> error, then I have no doubt that the buyers would have raised the point. They said nothing at the time; the new evidence in relation to the tests in April, 2001 did not in reality change the position. It is difficult to see how it can be said there was a plain and obvious error when nothing was expressed about it at the time the certificate was produced and part of the cargo accepted.[110]

In light of *Galaxy Energy International v Eurobunker*, even the presence of a manifest error exclusion will not suffice to protect the position of the buyer, unless objections are explicitly and promptly raised by the buyer when the relevant mistaken certification is tendered by the seller.

Elements on the basis of which to determine the extent and classification of what can constitute a manifest error can be found in *Veba Oil v Petrotrade*.[111] Here, a cargo of gasoil was sold on the basis of a contract which provided that the quantity and quality of the cargo was: "to be determined by a mutually agreed independent inspector at the loading installation [Antwerp] in the manner customary at such installations, and such determination shall be final and binding for both parties save fraud or manifest error".

The buyers claimed the invalidity of the certificate tendered by the sellers, on the basis of the fact that it had been performed with a different method compared to that originally established in the sales contract.

The court held that if the error consisted of a departure from instructions then it would not be necessary to ask whether in addition that error amounted to a "manifest error"; it would vitiate the determination in any event.

However, the court also specified that if the inspector's use of the wrong test method ought properly to be regarded as an immaterial departure from their instructions it would not be concluded that it nevertheless constituted a manifest error such as to entitle the buyers to set aside the determination on that basis.

In the words of Lord Justice Simon Brown:

> Although that conclusion is sufficient to dispose of the appeal, I would touch briefly on the alternative basis for decision relied upon by the buyers, the reference in clause 10 to "manifest error". Mr. Justice Morison below went no further than to say that he was "inclined to the view that there was a manifest error here, due to the wrong test being used".
>
> Mr. Justice Morison had previously considered the meaning of "manifest error" in *Conoco (U.K.) Ltd. v Phillips Petroleum Co. U.K. Ltd.* (unreported, Aug. 19, 1996) where, following dicta in earlier cases, he held that manifest error referred to: "oversights and blunders so obvious as to admit of no difference of opinion".
>
> The question then arising is whether it is relevant to consider whether the error is one that affected the result. Considering that question in *Conoco v Phillips*, Mr. Justice Morison said this: . . . it seems to me that there is no room for any debate as to whether the oversight or blunder would or would not have made any material difference to the result. If it could be shown that there was a manifest error then in my judgment that would be an end of the case. If fraud was shown, I cannot accept that it would be open to debate as to whether the fraud did or did not affect the result; so also would manifest error.

110 *Ibid.*, at 730.

111 *Veba Oil v Petrotrade* [2002] 1 Lloyd's Rep. 295.

> I confess to some difficulty with this approach. Fraud, of course, would vitiate the determination irrespective of whether it affected the result: "Fraud or collusion unravels everything" (per Lord Denning in *Campbell v Edwards*). The exception for "manifest error", however, seems to me of a rather different character and to be designed essentially to fill the gap in the law created by the development to which I have already referred: the overthrow of the *Dean v Prince* principle of setting aside determinations for mistake. Nowadays, if parties wish to contract on the basis that they will not be held to mistakes made by the expert in the course of carrying out his instructions, they must needs include a term like this with regard to manifest error. But if they do, is it then really to be said that provided only the mistake is obvious, the determination will be avoided irrespective of whether it could affect the outcome? In this context I am inclined to think not. Take the very error committed in *Frank H. Wright (Constructions) Ltd. v Frodoor Ltd.*, the erroneous inclusion of a "not" in the report. I do not think that that ought properly to be regarded as a "manifest error". Rather I would extend the "definition" of manifest errors as follows: "oversights and blunders so obvious and obviously capable of affecting the determination as to admit of no difference of opinion". . . . If, of course, the error consists of a departure from instructions, then, assuming I am right in my earlier conclusion, it will never be necessary to ask whether in addition that error amounts to a "manifest error": it will vitiate the determination in any event. If, however, I am wrong in my earlier conclusion – if, in short, the inspectors' use of the wrong test method here ought properly to be regarded as an immaterial departure from their instructions – I would not conclude that it nevertheless constituted a manifest error such as to entitle the buyers to set aside the determination on that alternative basis.
>
> That, however, is by the way. For the reasons given earlier, I would hold the determination not to be binding because of the inspectors' material departure from their instructions, and accordingly dismiss this appeal.[112]

Indeed, in this case the manifest error was established, as the inspectors here were required to determine the quality of the cargo using a specific test method. They did not do so and the parties had not agreed to be bound by a determination as to quality by any other method. The determination was accordingly not binding.

Further judicial guidance on the constitutive elements of what can represent a manifest error was given in *The Helen Knutson*.[113] Here, the sale of a cargo of ultra low sulphur auto diesel was subject to a certificate final clause which rendered quality and quantity final and binding save fraud and/or manifest error.

It was held by the court that manifest error might be shown on the face of the determination by an error of arithmetic or by a misplaced decimal point or other typographical error. Under such circumstances, it would be unnecessary to retest a portion of the retained sample to establish the error; thus it could not be said that the suggested implied term was necessary to make the contract work, and, accordingly, the buyers had no real prospect of establishing the alleged implied term based upon business efficacy.

As put by Mr Nigel Tear QC:

> I was referred to *Veba Oil v Petrotrade* [2002] 1 Lloyd's Rep. 295, at p. 302 where the meaning of manifest error was discussed by Lord Justice Simon Brown. He defined it

112 *Veba Oil v Petrotrade* [2002] 1 Lloyd's Rep. 295, 302–304.
113 *The Helen Knutson* [2003] 2 Lloyd's Rep. 686.

as referring to "oversights and blunders so obvious and obviously capable of affecting the determination as to admit of no difference of opinion."

A manifest error may be shown on the face of the determination by an error of arithmetic or by a misplaced decimal point or other typographical error. In such cases it will be unnecessary to retest a portion of the retained sample to establish the error. Thus it cannot be said that the suggested implied term is necessary to make the contract work.

Assuming, in Texaco's favour, that it is permissible, when seeking to establish a manifest error, to have regard to evidence of a retest in addition to that which is stated on the face of the determination (arguably contrary to the decision of Mr. Justice Potter in *Heald Foods Ltd. v Hyde Dairies Ltd. and Others* (unreported Dec. 6, 1996)) the suggested implied term may make it easier in some circumstances to establish a manifest error. It was therefore said that the suggested implied term was very important. However, terms are not implied on the grounds of importance, ease of proof, convenience or reasonableness but on the grounds that they are necessary to make the contract work. I do not consider that the suggested implied term is necessary to make the "manifest error" provision work.[114]

9.20 Certificate final clauses: The current status quo

Due, inter alia, to the aforementioned difficulties in shielding the position of the buyer within the context of certificate final clauses, even in the presence of limitation clauses, the criteria of construction and interpretation of certificate final clauses are being applied increasingly rigorously by courts of law.

As correctly pointed out in the doctrine,[115] in the course of the years, certificate final clauses have been subject to the process of judicial erosion which led English courts to deflect finality away from description. This process has also led the courts to meticulously police contractually agreed methods of inspection, and there is an as yet inchoate fraud exception to finality waiting in the wings.

The recent case of *Aston FFI (Suisse) SA v Lonis Dreyfus Commodities Suisse SA*[116] epitomises the current judicial position of the English courts vis-à-vis certificate final clauses. Here, the sale of Russian milling wheat in bulk was subject to a certificate final clause whereby quality, quantity, and condition were to be considered final at time and place of loading as per certificate to be issued by a third party to be appointed at the buyer's choice.

The contract incorporated Gafta 124, clause 10 of which provided that in the event of non-compliance with the preceding provisions of these rules being raised at arbitration as a defence, any quality and/or condition shall be deemed to be waived and barred, unless the arbitrators or board of appeal, as the case may be, shall in their absolute discretion determine otherwise.

A dispute arose, and the question was whether the buyers were entitled to reject the cargo under the contract absent a contractually compliant certificate.

The court held that there was nothing in the contract nor Gafta 124 which provided either expressly or impliedly that the issuance of an inspection certificate

114 *The Helen Knutson* [2003] 2 Lloyd's Rep. 686, 693.

115 See Debattista, *Bills of Lading in Export Trade*, above, p. 236.

116 *Aston FFI (Suisse) SA v Lonis Dreyfus Commodities Suisse SA* [2015] EWHC 80 (Comm); [2015] 1 Lloyd's Rep. 413.

compliant with a sub-clause of the payment section of the contract was determinative of the quality of the goods, such that the absence of such a contractually compliant certificate would preclude the buyers from rejecting the goods for relevant disconformity.

As put by Eder J:

> It seems to me relatively plain that a compliant certificate was one of the documents which had to be presented by sellers under the contract to obtain "cash"; and, in their turn, by buyers under the letter of credit under the sub-sale. In my view, it necessarily follows that the absence of such a compliant certificate in effect prevented sellers from obtaining "cash" under the contract and also prevented buyers, in their turn, obtaining payment under the letter of credit under the sub-sale (although the latter is not directly relevant to the present case). However, it remains to consider whether buyers were entitled to reject the cargo under the contract absent a contractually compliant certificate.
>
> In considering this aspect of the case, it seems to me important to recognise at the outset that, an fob buyer will (or at least may) ordinarily have two separate rights of rejection, ie a right to reject the documents and a right to reject the goods: see, for example, *Benjamin's Sale of Goods*, 9th Edition, para 20–113. The result is that (subject, of course, to the terms of any particular contract), an fob buyer may be able to reject the goods even if the documents are contractually compliant.
>
> However, the main thrust of his argument was that: (i) as a general proposition, where a contract prescribes a mandatory procedure for (say) inspection of the goods and also provides, in effect, that the results of such inspection as contained in a certificate are "final" as to the quality of the goods, then the buyer can only reject the goods by relying on a contractually compliant certificate demonstrating a relevant (and sufficient) disconformity of the goods; and (ii) the inspection clause of the present contract (read with such parts of GAFTA 124 as were incorporated into the contract) provided in effect for such mandatory procedure, ie it contained an exclusive code for determining the quality and condition of the goods with regard to the matters specified in sub-clauses (5) and (7) of the payment provisions of the GTT.
>
> [. . .] the exclusion of ordinary rights at common law should not be lightly inferred and require clear and unambiguous expression: see *Gilbert-Ash (Northern) Ltd v Modern Engineering (Bristol) Ltd* [1974] AC 689 per Lord Diplock at page 717H; and, specifically in the present context, clear words would be necessary to exclude the independent right to reject the cargo for non-conformity: see, for example, *W N Lindsay & Co Ltd v European Grain & Shipping Agency Ltd* per Diplock LJ at page 445.
>
> [. . .] I accept, of course, that the opening part of the inspection clause in the contract uses the term "final"; that, as I have already stated, this must relate to what has been referred to as the "first survey"; and that the presentation of a contractually compliant inspection certificate (ie an inspection certificate complying with the terms of sub-clause (5) of the payment section of the GTT) is one of the documents which is required by sellers to obtain "cash" under the contract (and also by buyers under the sub-sale). However, there is nothing in the contract nor the GTT nor GAFTA 124 which provides either expressly or impliedly that the issuance of an inspection certificate compliant with sub-clause (5) of the payment section of the GTT is determinative of the quality of the goods such that the absence of such contractually compliant certificate would, in effect, preclude buyers from rejecting the goods for relevant disconformity. On the contrary, it seems to me that the effect of the inspection clause in the contract when read together with note (9) of the GTT is that even if the inspection certificate produced by the first surveyor did not contractually comply with the terms of sub-clause (5) of the payment section of the GTT (so as to prevent sellers from obtaining "cash" under the contract), buyers would be entitled to reject the cargo for relevant disconformity having regard to the totality of the evidence in relation thereto.

> In summary, while I accept in principle that the independent right of an fob buyer to reject the goods may be modified or even excluded by agreement, I do not consider that the words of the contract in the present case have such effect.[117]

Aston FFI (Suisse) SA v Lonis Dreyfus Commodities Suisse SA shows how far the courts have come since the days of Lord Denning MR in *Toepfer v Continental Grain*. In *Aston v Dreyfus*, the High Court appeared to agree with the unremarkable proposition that a seller cannot take advantage of finality where he tenders a certificate which falls short of documentary requirements in the contract; but then the court, having found the certificate in that case to have been compliant, appears boldly to rush to stating that even where a seller tenders a compliant certificate, and absent "clear and unambiguous expression", the buyer can still exercise his right to reject goods for physical non-conformity.

If this is right, then what price now finality, and precisely how clear and unambiguous does a certificate final clause need to be if it is to meet the seller's expectations? This is clearly a field where the turf war between sellers and buyers is bound to go on, either at the early stage when such clauses are, typically, rather hastily conceived and drafted, or at a later stage when lawyers and judges pore over their precise terms.

117 See *Aston FFI (Suisse) SA v Lonis Dreyfus Commodities Suisse SA*, above, 420, 421.

CHAPTER 10

The seller's documentary duties

10.1 Introduction

As established in the previous chapter, one of the peculiarities of contracts concluded on shipment terms lies in the fact that the seller performs his duties in a dual mode: physical duties, and documentary duties.

This chapter aims at exploring the nature of documentary duties within the context of contracts concluded on shipment terms. We shall proceed following the structure of the previous chapter, i.e. by first identifying the seller's documentary duties, and then establishing the nature of breaches of documentary duty which amount to infringements of conditions that entitle buyers to terminate the contract.

10.2 The seller's documentary duties in contracts concluded on shipment terms: Preliminary issues

The importance of documents in international commercial sales cannot be understated. Goods are traded largely on the basis of documents, and it has been sometimes questioned whether we are dealing with a sale of documents rather than goods.[1]

Indeed, one should always bear in mind that, within the context of contracts concluded on shipment terms, a buyer will usually receive documents from the seller before the goods; immediately thereafter, the goods are shipped on board.

At that stage, the buyer will need to make an assessment of the performance of the seller solely on the basis of the conformity of the documents to what was originally established in the sales contract. Indeed, far from the port of loading, and without the possibility of inspecting the cargo, the buyer presented with the documents will need to make a decision as to whether or not to honour the contract in terms of payment.

Although, as it will readily be appreciated, the acceptance of the documents will not usually prevent the buyer from rejecting the cargo for breach of physical duties,[2] the moment of performance of the seller's documentary duties still remains a crucial phase within the context of contracts concluded on shipment

1 See *Vladimir Ilich, The* [1975] 1 Lloyd's Rep. 322. See Debattista, *Bills of Lading in Export Trade*, above, p. 169. See also *Benjamin's Sale of Goods*, above, paras. 18.236 *et seq.*

2 See chapter 12.

terms. Indeed, the buyer will never be in the same position again, as payment is yet to be made and will happen only in the case of documentary compliance.

Apart from payment, documents are of the utmost importance for the buyer also in relation to insurance arrangements, as well as possible claims vis-à-vis the carrier. Documents are, thus, at least of the same importance as the commodity itself.

The first step of our analysis lies with the identification of the seller's documentary duties.

The documents to be tendered by the seller

Contracts concluded on shipment terms are often unclear as to what documents the seller must tender for payment. In *Tamvaco v Lucas*,[3] a cargo of wheat was sold with payment cash in London in exchange for the "usual" shipping documents.

The sellers tendered shipping documents of a cargo answering the description in the contract including, inter alia, a charter party, a bill of lading, and a policy of insurance effected on the cargo.

Evidence was given on behalf of the sellers, which was not contradicted, that the policy tendered was sufficient to protect the interest of the shipper of the cargo at the time of shipment. The buyers refused payment claiming the insurance policy did not cover the value of the cargo and hence the sellers were not ready and willing to tender, nor did they tender, "the usual shipping documents" according to the contract.

The court held that the plaintiffs had so tendered; and that they were not bound to tender as a "shipping document" within the meaning of the contract, a policy covering the full amount of the buyers' risk, as it appeared by the provisional invoice and bill of lading.

As stated by Cockburn CJ:

> I am of opinion that the rule for entering a verdict for the defendants must be discharged. The case is presented to us in this shape. It is admitted that the defendants are liable, having received commission which makes them responsible as del credere agents, if the buyers of this cargo of wheat were bound to accept the shipping documents tendered, and to fulfil the contract by payment, But it is said that there was a defect in one of the shipping documents, viz. the policy of insurance, in consequence of it not being for an amount sufficient to afford the buyers of the cargo such an indemnity against the loss of the cargo as they were entitled to. The question is put as one of pure law, on these very simple and short facts. The terms of the contract being that the payment should take place on the production of the shipping documents, and when the cargo would still be at sea, a provisional invoice was sent in to the defendants, or rather to the buyers of the cargo, which invoice, framed upon the bill of lading, stated the quantity of wheat at a given amount; but the cargo did not realize that amount, for it turned out considerably less. When the policy of insurance is produced, it turns out to be of less amount than the sum at which the total value of the cargo appeared in the provisional invoice and the bill of lading; and it is said that the buyers would be entitled to take advantage of that circumstance, and to refuse to accept the shipping documents, or to pay according to the terms of the contract; inasmuch as the policy of insurance was included in the shipping documents, on the delivery of which payment was to be made, and the policy of insurance was not sufficient to satisfy the provisions

3 *Tamvaco v Lucas* 1861 (30) LJQB 234.

of the contract, being of less amount than the value of the cargo as represented in the provisional invoice. The total value of the cargo, as appearing on the provisional invoice, included the amount of 1001l. 10s. for freight; and it is said, on the part of the plaintiffs, that at all events the insurance was not to cover the freight, but only the value of the cargo, as compounded of the cost of the cargo at the place of shipment, the shipping of it, and the commission and other charges which would be incidental to the shipping of such a cargo, and also the premiums of insurance; and that, if the sum of 1001l. 10s. be therefore deducted, as it ought to be, from the price as per invoice, there would remain uncovered by the policy the comparatively insignificant sum of 24l. 10s. The first question is whether that is a correct view of the matter, and whether the freight ought to be deducted, as not meant to be included in the policy of insurance and covered by it. I think that is the correct view; and, when we are dealing with a policy of insurance as one of the shipping documents to be delivered by the seller to the buyer in order to protect the buyer, I am of opinion that the freight, which the buyer will not have to pay until the cargo has arrived, need not be covered by the policy of insurance.

There still remains, however, when the freight has been deducted, a sum of 24l. 10s. unprotected by the policy. Mr. Smith has argued that a further deduction should be made on the score of discount. In that view I cannot concur, because I think the true period of payment is that fixed by the terms of the contract, and that the discount is only matter of subordinate and independent arrangement between the parties, whereby, in consideration of a more speedy payment by the one party than that which the contract would in strictness require, the other party agrees to make an abatement of a portion of the purchase money. I do not think, therefore, that that touches the difficulty in the case.

Then comes the question, whether the deficiency of 24l. 10s. is a matter which could fairly be objected to on the delivery of such a shipping document as this. On this part of the case, as it is presented to us, I think our decision ought to be in favour of the plaintiffs. The contract provides for payment by the buyers on the delivery of the shipping documents. By that I understand the ordinary and usual shipping documents, as they are understood in contracts of this nature by members of the mercantile community. The policy of insurance is undoubtedly one of these; and, if the policy, instead of being such as is contemplated as an ordinary and usual shipping document, turns out substantially a defective one, and such as would not afford the buyer a reasonable protection and indemnity against risk, which he is entitled to under the terms of such a contract, and the shipping documents be accordingly rejected, and the performance of the contract resisted on that ground, I am far from saying that such ground would not be sufficient to justify a buyer in refusing to fulfil the terms of the contract of purchase and sale. But it becomes a very different question whether the present small and comparatively insignificant deficiency may be made a mere pretext for a departure from the contract, when substantial and bona fide protection is afforded to the buyers by means of the policy.

The defendants submit the question on this part of the case for our consideration, as a mere question of law on this short point. The policy, when produced, turns out to be somewhat less in amount than what appears on the provisional invoice to be the value of the cargo; and it is said that, on that mere simple fact, without more, as a matter of law, the defendants are entitled to say that the buyers were not bound to perform their part of the contract; and that therefore the defendants, who have insured the performance of the contract by their principals, are not bound either. I cannot concur in that proposition taken as a matter of law. As I have before said, there may be facts in any particular case which would justify a buyer in refusing to accept a policy of insurance as one of the shipping documents, if the policy of insurance was substantially inoperative to protect the buyer against the possibility of loss or damage by perils of the sea; but no such question was here submitted as a matter of fact for the consideration of the jury. It was not proposed that it should be submitted to the jury, whether, in the present instance, the policy of insurance was substantially effective as a shipping document, as satisfying that which the buyers had reasonably a right to expect. The question is submitted to us as a mere question of law on the facts as they appear to us on evidence; and, as I have said, I cannot come to a conclusion that the defendants' contention is correct. If the objection could avail them anything, it would only be on the ground that this was not a compliance with the terms of the contract, reference being had to all circumstances of the case, and to how far this policy of insurance was, substantially and practically, a protection to the buyer against sea risk. The defendants not having asked to have the question left to the jury, we must take it, as against them, that this was substantially a good policy of insurance, and one which would have satisfied the exigencies of this contract, as being a shipping document on the production and the delivery of which the buyers would have been bound to pay.

There seems to be another view of this case which is also unfavourable to the defendants. Assuming that, upon a contract of this sort, the shipping documents must be substantially sufficient, yet, as this is a term in the contract introduced for the benefit of the buyer, it certainly is one that may be waived by him. In the present case, it does not appear that the buyer ever repudiated this contract, or denied his liability to be bound by its terms, on the ground that these documents or any of them were insufficient. Long before the shipping documents arrived in this country the buyer repudiated his liability, on the ground that the defendants had exceeded their authority as agents. And, again, when the shipping documents arrived, and it was sought to make the buyers fulfil the terms of the contract, the defendants never for a moment set up the insufficiency of these shipping documents; but they sought to force the contract on the buyers for whom they had acted, as one which the buyers were bound to complete. Now, as has been pointed out by more than one of my learned brothers in the course of the argument, if, at the time these shipping documents were originally tendered, there had been any objection taken on the score of the insufficiency of this policy, there would have been no difficulty (for this was long before the arrival of the cargo) in making good the defect by means of supplementary insurance. I think, therefore, there has been a waiver on the part of the buyers, the principals in the contract, and also a waiver on the part of the defendants, who, as agents, were liable on this del credere contract. There was an absolute and entire waiver of any objection which might by possibility have been taken to the insufficiency of the policy. On every ground, therefore, and in every point of view in which I can look at the case, I cannot but think that the defendants have failed to make out, on this technical objection, any ground why the verdict should be disturbed.

The point comes before us on a rule to enter a verdict for the defendants on an objection taken at the trial; and I understand that objection to be, that the plaintiffs undertook to insure the defendants as to their interest with reference to the contract price, and with reference to the apparent interest of the buyer under the contract. I do not think that, in point of law, that is so. There was some evidence in the case that the policy was one which would be sufficient as a policy on the shipment; and probably the jury would have found in the affirmative, if that point had been left to them. Therefore, I think the defendants must be confined strictly to the objection which is made the ground of their rule, and which really comes to this: "You undertook to insure my interest in the cargo with reference to this contract price; that is, to insure my interest to the extent of 50s. per quarter." Now, the validity of that objection depends on the nature of the contract. This is not a contract, as I understand it, for the seller to ship free on board a particular ship to be found by the vendee; but it is one of the usual contracts to sell a cargo which is to come by a ship sailing at a particular time, and is covered by the usual policy that would be taken in such a case. I do not think the construction of the contract is that these parties engaged to ship the cargo: if it had been to be shipped by these particular parties other questions might arise; and, as Mr. Honyman put it, it might be an ingredient, if the contract had been so worded, that they should ship and insure in accordance with their knowledge that the value to the buyer was this precise amount. I doubt very much whether that would be so; but, in the present case, I am of opinion that the plaintiffs were at liberty to buy a cargo in the market of any wheat corresponding with that mentioned in the contract, which should be shipped from the 1st of October to the 15th of November, not in any particular ship, but in any ship answering the description "A 1 English or a first class foreign vessel, not Greek or Turk." Therefore I think it is clear that the present case is one of those in which a person is bargaining for a cargo or which shall answer the description on its shipment, or which shall answer the description on the seller ordering it to be shipped in a particular manner, or by buying a shipment which is already at sea. That being the contract, we must see how this supposed obligation to insure to the extent of the interest of the parties on that contract, that is, to the amount of the contract price, including the freight, can arise. Now, I think it very true that this contract is for a shipment which shall be insured, because the price is to be 50s. "including freight and insurance;" it must, therefore, be a cargo by a ship which is bringing goods on freight, and there must be a bill of lading, there must be the charter party, and there must be a policy of insurance; and the question is, what is the meaning of that word "insurance," coupled with the phrase "cash in London in exchange for shipping documents"? I do not think that, on this contract, the seller himself was bound to insure. I think it is one of those contracts in which the insurance "runs," as it has been expressed, as the bill of lading, and the charter party runs, with the interest in the cargo, as one of the three shipping documents; and I think that, if the original shipper had insured, which he ought to have done, or, if the person who knew of the shipments had insured in London, in either of those cases the policy so effected would be the one to which such a contract as this would refer. I think that appears unanswerably to be the true view, when we consider that these documents go along with the property, into whosoever hands it may come. The object is to have these kinds of cargoes saleable in the market; and that, although the cargo has not arrived, the owner may realize his money, and the cargo be sold over and over again before it comes to this country. It seems to me a monstrous thing to say, with reference to every contract of sale of this description, that there must be a policy to cover the full price. The phrase "shipping documents," I think, shews that the policy connected with the shipping and effected at that time would be the document meant. I do not mean to say that if, by any accident, there were no insurance when the cargo was shipped, the contract might not be answered by making a policy in London; but I think the contract contemplates a policy made with reference to the shipment. I quite agree with what my Lord has said, that the policy must be a bona fide policy. I take it that, if there was an illusory insurance, that would not do; because the contract is for a price covering freight and insurance. It appears to me, as I said before, to contemplate, not only that the cargo shall come on freight, but that it shall come in one of the particular class of ships named, and be insured; and therefore if there was an illusory insurance I think the buyer might say, "You have not sent it insured." I think, therefore, the terms of the contract relate to the policy on the shipment; that the insurance must cover the value of the goods, and the cost of the insurance, as at the port of loading; but that it need not include the freight or profit at the port of discharge. The buyer buys what the seller sells, and puts himself, in effect, in his shoes. I think the first man, if he buys from the original shipper, puts himself in his shoes, as it were, and takes the policy from him – supposing the policy is a right policy with regard to the first shipper, – and whether it be or not is not determined by the value which the buyer thinks the goods will bear when they come to England. That being so, the only question is one of fact. Is this a document fairly to be taken as a shipping document, accompanying the rest of the papers, and a fair bona fide policy? No point was made as to that at the trial. There was some evidence on which the jury might have so found; but, no point having been made of it, I think we should be doing wrong if we were to send the case down for a new trial on account of any doubt of that kind, the objection at the trial being merely that the

> plaintiffs ought to have calculated the amount of insurance so as to cover the cost of 50s. I think that justice was done in this case, and that the point of law on which the defendants insist is against them. The rule must therefore be discharged.[4]

Confusion might also arise in the case of incorporation of standard forms, which might contain surprising clauses regarding documents.[5]

10.3 Identification of the seller's documentary duties

The main issue lies with what documents the seller must tender for payment, and what documents the buyer can insist on before he pays.

First, if the payment method is via a letter of credit,[6] the letter of credit will indicate all the documents the seller needs to tender to the confirming bank in order to be paid. The letter of credit thus represents an exhaustive statement of the seller's documentary duties; nevertheless, a letter of credit can be ambiguous in practice.

In *Credit Agricole Indosuez v Muslim Commercial Bank Ltd*,[7] a letter of credit for a cargo of Iranian raw cotton provided for, inter alia, the presentation by the seller of original documents along with eight copies each of invoice, packing list, weight and measurement list, bill of lading, and certificate of origin.

No weight and measurement list and no certificate of origin were sent by Credit Agricole to the Muslim Commercial Bank within the mechanism of the letter of credit.

The issue at stake for the court's decision was whether the weight and measurement list and certificate of origin were to be considered as essential documents against which negotiation and payment were agreed to be made under the terms of the letter of credit.

Albeit indicated in the letter of credit, the credit did not specify whether the aforementioned documents were to be considered as a condition *sine qua non* of the credit itself, as required by a clause of the credit, which specified that the instructions for the issuance of the credit itself must state precisely the document(s) against which payment, acceptance, or negotiation were to be made.

It was held by the court that the letter of credit left one in genuine doubt as to whether the documents which it referred to were stipulated documents essential to the operation of the credit, and that it did not state precisely that a weight and

---

4 *Ibid.*, at 238, 239.

5 By way of example, see Fosfa 54, ll 103–4, whereby it is stated that the bill of lading must identify the ship's tank into which the oil is loaded, and, if commingled, the bill must indicate the total commingled quantity. What if the bill of lading then fails to do this?

6 See chapter 11. A letter of credit is a document from a bank guaranteeing that a seller will receive payment in full as long as certain delivery conditions have been met. In the event that the buyer is unable to make payment on the purchase, the bank will cover the outstanding amount.

Letters of credit are often used in international transactions to ensure that payment will be received where the buyer and seller may not know each other and are operating in different countries. In this case the seller is exposed to a number of risks such as credit risk, and legal risk caused by the distance, differing laws, and difficulty in knowing each party personally. A letter of credit provides the seller with a guarantee that they will get paid as long as certain delivery conditions have been met. For this reason, the use of letters of credit has become a very important aspect of international trade.

7 *Credit Agricole Indosuez v Muslim Commercial Bank Ltd* [2000] 1 Lloyd's Rep. 275.

measurement list and a certificate of origin were documents against which payment or negotiation was to be made.

As put by Sir Christopher Staughton:

> One can see at a glance that this is a hotchpotch or amalgam of terms that require documents to be provided, terms as to what documents should contain, terms as to performance of the sale contract, terms as to performance of the letter of credit contract and terms which may or may not be one of those things.
>
> [. . .] It seems to me that the letter of credit leaves one in genuine doubt as to whether cl. 9 is stating that the documents which it refers to are stipulated documents, essential to the operation of the credit. It certainly does not, as required by art. 5(b), state precisely that a weight and measurement list, and a certificate of origin, are documents against which payment or negotiation is to be made.[8]

Inconsistencies and or ambiguities in terms of establishing the seller's documentary duties will lead to the interpretation and construction of such duties by courts of law, the results of which might vary and will need to be determined on a case by case basis.

Identification of seller's documentary duties in cash against documents transactions

If the sales contract provides for cash against documents as the payment method, whereby the buyer pays cash vis-à-vis the production of documents by the seller, the contract itself will be a crucial means for the identification of the seller's documentary duties.

As we established in the previous chapter, the seller is subject to physical duties in the first place, and those duties are enshrined in the terms of the contract which deal with description, quantity, quality, sample, time of shipment, place of shipment, etc. Those terms will not automatically saddle the seller with any documentary duty, unless it is otherwise specified by the contract itself.

In other words, just by virtue of the fact that a sales contract indicates a commodity of "Russian Gasoil of Class A quality", that does not translate into a seller's documentary duty to tender certificates which attest to the origin or the quality of the gasoil. On the contrary, unless the contract itself makes it explicit that the seller is under the duty to tender such documents, the seller shall not bear such obligations.

That is the reason why a buyer is best advised to translate all the physical duties of a contract concluded on shipment terms into documentary duties.

Documents and deadlines for presentation

In terms of the time limit for presentation of documents, that will depend entirely on whether the transaction is to be perfected cash against documents or via a letter of credit.

Cash against documents transactions will seldom stipulate deadlines for the presentation of documents by the seller. Indeed, such deadlines are not germane

8 *Ibid.*, at 278.

to the nature of contracts concluded on shipment terms, which see the seller being paid only after he tenders the documents in conformity with what was originally established in the sale contract.

In that regard, no deadline is therefore necessary in order to accelerate the tender of documents by a seller, whose desire to get paid by the buyer as soon as possible acts as the most effective incentive.

Nevertheless, if the contract provides for such a deadline, the seller will have to abide by it, and the buyer will be in the position to reject documents (in case of non-conformity) only after the deadline expires.

In *Toepfer v Lenersan-Poortman*,[9] the sale of Canadian rapeseed was subject by contractual specification to the tender of documents by telegraphic transfer not later than 20 days after the date of the bill of lading.

The buyers refused to accept the documents tendered by the seller outside the deadline established in the sales contract, and the court was asked to ascertain whether the deadline for presentation amounted to a condition of the contract.

At first instance, Donaldson J held that the obligations imposed by the "payment against document" clause were mutual, and the clause defined neither the latest nor the earliest date for payment but the date.

According to Donaldson J, the parties had substituted a timetable of their own making for that which would have been provided by the mercantile law, and that timetable was intended to bind both parties. Indeed, in commodity contracts it was clear law that provisions as to the time of shipment and the time of appropriation were prima facie in the "condition" category and there was no reason to distinguish provisions as to the time for the presentation of documents.

The Court of Appeal endorsed the conclusions drawn by Donaldson J, finding that on the construction of the payments clause, the buyers and sellers each agreed to do all that was necessary on their part for the carrying out of the exchange on the prescribed date for payment, and that the sellers' obligation was to tender documents in time for the buyers to take up and pay for them on that date, and the buyers' obligation was to take up and pay for the documents on that date.

The sellers' obligation to tender documents in time was a condition of the contract and the buyers were entitled on breach of that term to treat the contract as at an end and to reject the documents accordingly.

In the words of Brandon LJ:

> We examine the question of the sellers' obligation under the payment clause first apart from any authority upon it. In doing so we shall look at two aspects of the matter, the aspect of co-operation and the aspect of certainty.
>
> First, the aspect of co-operation. It is a general principle of the law of contract that, where the parties have agreed that something shall be done, which cannot effectively be done unless both co-operate in doing it, the construction of the contract is that each agrees to do all that is necessary to be done on his part for the carrying out of that thing, though there be no express words to that effect. See Chitty on Contracts, 24th. ed., vol. 1, pars. 788 and 1491, and cases there cited.

9 *Toepfer v Lenersan-Poortman* [1980] 1 Lloyd's Rep. 143.

If that general principle is applied to this particular case, the result appears to us to be this. The payment to be made by the buyers under the payment clause is, by the express terms of that clause, a payment against documents, that is to say an exchange of cash for documents. The clause further provides that such exchange is to take place by the earlier of two specified dates, which we shall call the prescribed date for payment. The exchange cannot be effectively carried out on the prescribed date for payment unless both the sellers and the buyers co-operate in achieving that result. The construction of the contract, therefore, should be that the sellers and the buyers each agree to do all that is necessary on their part for the carrying out of the exchange on the prescribed date for payment. It follows that the sellers should be under an implied obligation to tender documents in time for the buyers to take up and pay for them on that date.

Second, the aspect of certainty. If the contention put forward for the sellers is correct, the effect of a payment clause in the terms here concerned would as we understand it, be this. The only obligation of the sellers would be to send forward the documents with due dispatch. This might result in their tendering the documents at three different times in relation to the prescribed date for payment. First, the sellers might tender the documents before the prescribed date for payment: in that case the buyers would be entitled to take up and pay for them forthwith, but would not be obliged to do so until the prescribed date. Secondly, the sellers might tender the documents on or just before the prescribed date for payment: in that case the buyers would be obliged to take up and pay for them on that date. Thirdly, the sellers might tender the documents after the prescribed date for payment (including in certain circumstances after the arrival of the vessel): in that case the buyers' obligation to pay against them on the prescribed date would be postponed until such later tender.

If that indeed is the effect of the clause, it produces a somewhat uncertain situation for the buyers so far as both their rights and obligations are concerned.

If the contention for the buyers is correct, the rights and obligations of the parties are much more clear-cut. The sellers' obligation is to tender the documents in time for the buyers to take up and pay for them on the prescribed date for payment. The buyers' obligation is to take up and pay for the documents on that date.

In our view the Court should, when dealing with a commercial contract of this kind, prefer a construction of it which produces reasonable certainty in the rights and obligations of both parties to one which does not.

Looking at the matter, therefore, from both the co-operation aspect and the certainty aspect we would, apart from authority, prefer the construction of the clause contended for by the buyers.

Turning now to authority, we were referred to a number of cases in which the effect of terms as to payment similar to those contained in the payment clause in the present case was considered. While there appears to be no express decision on the point, there are observations in the cases supporting both views with regard to it.

The view that the clause does not impose any obligation on the sellers different from their common law obligation is supported by the observations of Mr. Justice Sellers in *Colin & Shields v W. Weddel & Co. Ltd.* [1952] 1 Lloyd's Rep. 390, at p. 395. The correctness of those observations was, however, doubted by both Lord Justice Singleton and Lord Justice Denning in the same case on appeal: see [1952] 2 Lloyd's Rep. 9, at pp. 17–18 and p. 19 respectively.

The contrary view, that the clause imposes an obligation on the sellers with regard to the tender of documents corresponding to that imposed on the buyers with regard to payment, is supported, firstly, by the observations of Lord Justice Swinfen Eady in *Karberg (Arnhold) & Co. v Blythe, Greene, Jourdain & Co.* [1916] 1 K.B. 495 at p. 504; secondly, by the doubts of Lord Justice Singleton and Lord Justice Denning in *Colin & Shields v W. Weddel & Co. Ltd.* referred to above; and, thirdly, by the observations of Mr. Justice Diplock in *Tricerri Ltd. v Crosfields & Calthrop Ltd.* [1958] 1 Lloyd's Rep. 236, at p. 242.

> The balance of authority is, therefore, in favour of the view which we have indicated that we should reach without it, and confirms us in that view.
>
> On the footing that the payment clause imposed on the sellers an obligation to tender documents in time to enable the buyers to pay against them by the prescribed date for payment, which was on the facts 20 days after the date of the bills of lading, it is clear that they failed to do so. The second question for consideration, therefore, is whether such failure entitled the buyers to reject the documents.
>
> It appears that this question was argued and decided in the Court below solely by reference to the point whether the obligation concerned was a condition of the contracts in the strict sense on the one hand, or an intermediate or innominate term of the kind discussed in *Hong Kong Fir Shipping Co. Ltd. v Kawasaki Kisen Kaisha Ltd.* [1971] 2 Lloyd's Rep. 478; [1962] 2 Q.B. 26 on the other, and without regard to the terms of cl. 10 (the default clause) in FOSFA 12, which was, as indicated earlier, expressly incorporated into the contracts.
>
> Dealing with the case in that way, the question for decision remains the same as it was before Mr. Justice Donaldson, namely, whether the sellers' obligation with regard to the time for tendering documents was a condition of the contract rather than an innominate term, so as to entitle the buyers to reject documents tendered late.
>
> With regard to that question we accept that Courts today tend to be reluctant to accord to a term in a contract the status of a condition unless it is clearly expressed to be one. It must further be recognised that, despite s. 11 (1) (b) of the Sale of Goods Act, 1893, contracts of sale do not differ from other contracts in this respect: *Cehave N.V. v Bremer m.b.H. (The Hansa Nord)* [1975] 2 Lloyd's Rep. 445; [1976] 1 Q.B. 44. In accordance with that approach, the House of Lords in *Bremer v Vanden* [1978] 2 Lloyd's Rep. 109, held that a term in a standard form of GAFTA agreement incorporated into a c.i.f. contract for the sale of soya bean meal, which provided that notice of prohibition of performance was to be given without delay, was not a condition but an innominate term.
>
> On the other hand, terms relating to the time of performance by sellers of their obligations under c.i.f. contracts have, in general, been held to be conditions. That was decided, so far as a term relating to the time of shipment is concerned, in *Bowes v Shand* (1887) 2 App. Cas. 455; and again, so far as a term relating to notice of appropriation is concerned, in *Reuter v Sala* (1879) 4 C.P.D. 239. The reason is, no doubt, the need for certainty in commercial transactions already referred to earlier: compare *The Mihalis Angelos* [1970] 2 Lloyd's Rep. 43; [1971] 1 Q.B. 164, by Lord Justice Megaw at pp. 55 and 205. It is difficult to see any good reason why a term in a c.i.f. contract relating to the time for the sellers to tender documents should not equally, and for the same reason, be regarded as a condition.[10]

Interestingly, the Court of Appeal drew a parallel with the decision in *Bowes v Shand*,[11] which, as noted above,[12] established time of shipment as a condition of contracts concluded on shipment terms.

Indeed, within the context of such contracts, time is of the utmost importance. It does not come as a surprise, therefore, that if the trading contract expressly stipulates the tender of documents by a certain time, that deadline will amount to a condition, the breach of which entitles buyers to reject documents which are otherwise perfectly compliant.[13]

---

10 *Toepfer v Lenersan-Poortman* [1980] 1 Lloyd's Rep. 143, 146, 147.
11 *Bowes v Shand* (1887) 2 App Cas. 455
12 See paragraph 10.2, above.
13 *Ibid.*

10.4 When is a documentary breach a breach of a condition?

Similar to the approach in the previous chapter with respect to the physical duties of the seller, we shall now turn our attention to the identification of breaches of conditions when it comes to the seller's documentary duties.

The aforementioned distinction between warranties and conditions also stands with regard to documentary duties;[14] the breach of a warranty will only give rise to damages, whereas the breach of a condition has a much more severe impact on the contract, potentially leading to its termination.

When it comes to documentary duties, English law has traditionally adopted the principle of strict compliance: any breach, no matter how slight, will entail a breach of a condition which entitles the buyer to reject documents and terminate the contract.

Nevertheless, as it will be readily appreciated, within the context of contracts concluded on shipment terms the principle of strict compliance appears to have been established very much *sub silentio*, as the authorities confronting the issue are scarce and conflicting.

In *The Hansa Nord*,[15] according to two contracts the sellers sold to the buyers a quantity of US citrus pulp pellets, c.i.f. Rotterdam. In the case of each contract delivery was to be by instalments and, by clause 7, shipment was to be made "in good condition". Shipments were made in part performance of the two contracts by the vessel *Hansa Nord*, and when the vessel arrived in Rotterdam, the buyers rejected the entire cargo on the grounds that the shipment had not been in good condition.

Although the case primarily related to the seller's physical duties, documentary duties were considered by way of *obiter dictum* by Roskill LJ, who stated that:

> The seller's obligation regarding documentation had long been made sacrosanct by the highest authority and that the express or implied provisions in a c.i.f. contract in those respects were of the class . . . any breach of which justified rejection.[16]

The aforementioned *dictum* perfectly encapsulates the principle of strict compliance in documentary duties. Unfortunately, the case fails to assert such an important principle with authority, as the primary issue considered by the court was a possible breach of physical duties by the seller. Moreover, no mention or specific reference is made to the "highest authority" allegedly establishing such an important principle.

Although it has been correctly noted that there seems to be a certain judicial reluctance to challenge the proposition that documentary duties are conditions, on the other hand it is also true that finding an authority which clearly asserts the principle of strict compliance appears to be an arduous endeavour.

14 See chapter 10.
15 *The Hansa Nord* [1976] QB 44.
16 *Ibid.*, at 54.

The reason for this lies in the fact that, in the vast majority of the circumstances, issues arise in relation to the seller's physical duties rather than documentary duties, as documents are tendered, more often than not, without apparent defects.

In this regard, one needs to bear in mind that once a breach of a condition is identified in relation to physical duties, that would suffice in solving a dispute, conferring the right on a buyer to terminate the contract. Reference to the seller's documentary duties would be, at that stage, utterly superfluous and redundant.

10.4.1 Strict compliance preferable

One significant argument in support of the principle of strict compliance is the certainty of application.[17] Indeed, this concept is often preferred by judges in light of the rigour of conditions vis-à-vis the "haze of innominate terms".[18]

In *SIAT di dal Ferro v Tradax Overseas*,[19] the issue at stake was whether the contract of carriage stipulated by the seller within the context of a c.i.f. transaction was in conformity with what was originally established by the sale contract.

In deciding the dispute, Megaw LJ embarked upon a disquisition on the importance of certainty within the context of identification of the nature of documentary breaches. In his words:

> I have already referred by way of example to the defects affecting the insurance certificate tendered in purported compliance with the sellers' contractual duty as regards the group 4 documents. There are, as I have already indicated, recorded in the findings of the Board of Appeal, numerous other defects in other documents in the several groups. Some of them may be regarded as falling within the category of de minimis departures from the contractual obligation. Others of them, though they could not sensibly be described as minimal, were, it was argued for the sellers, of such a nature, both individually and cumulatively, that the buyers were not entitled in law to reject the documents by reason of them: the buyers' remedy, it was said, was, having taken up and paid for the documents, to claim damages from the sellers for such loss as they might be able to prove that they had suffered.
>
> That involves a question of principle about which there may be a dispute. There are authoritative pronouncements which at least suggest that, in this area of obligations as to documents in c.i.f. contracts, any defect – any breach – other than one within the de minimis category, entitles the buyers to reject the documents: the buyer is not obliged, at peril of being himself held to be in grave breach of contract if he makes the wrong decision (often a decision which has to be made quickly and, through no fault of his, on incomplete and imperfect information), to weigh and assess the risks and possibilities as to the seriousness of the consequences to him of the documentary defects, should he accept the documents. That, I believe, was the sort of consideration which Lord Justice Roskill had in mind when, in his judgment in *Cehave N.V. v Bremer Handelsgesellschaft m.b.H.* [1975] 2 Lloyd's Rep. 445; [1976] 1 Q.B. 44, at pp. 457 and 70F, he said:
>
> . . . Mr. Lloyd ultimately persuaded me that the seller's obligation regarding documentation had long been made sacrosanct by the highest authority and that the express or implied provisions in a c.i.f. contract in those respects were of the class, accepted

17 See Debattista, *Bills of Lading in Export Trade*, above, p.363.
18 *Ibid.*
19 *SIAT di dal Ferro v Tradax Overseas* [1980] 1 Lloyd's Rep. 53.

by Lord Justice Diplock in the *Hong Kong Fir* case, [1961] 2 Lloyd's Rep. 478; [1962] 2 Q.B. 25, at pp. 493–495 and 69–72 any breach of which justified rejection.

But, if so, the question would arise whether it is a desirable or defensible distinction; or whether it would lead to anomalies and uncertainties in an area of the law where such degree of certainty as can fairly be achieved is obviously commercially desirable. Again, ought the essential nature of the buyers' rights, when he is faced with defective documents, to vary according to whether he is or is not in a string of buyers of the same goods; whether at the date of the tender of the defective documents he has or has not resold, whether on the same or different contractual terms; or whether thereafter he might desire to resell by passing on the documents, rather than taking delivery of the goods on his own account?

It should not be forgotten also, in this context, that the law, in the absence of a contractual term to the contrary, allows a seller who has presented defective documents to represent, tendering correct documents, so long as he does so before the last permissible date provided by the terms of the contract, or, in the absence of contractual terms, the date for presentation provided by the term which in those circumstances is implied by law. So that, if the correctness of the documents is a condition of the contract, in the Sale of Goods Act sense of the word "condition", the seller may have an opportunity to remedy even serious breaches before the buyer becomes entitled to treat the contract as repudiated.

I do not find it necessary to decide this question of principle. That is because there is in this case one type of documentary defect, common to all the three groups, which, in my judgment, is of such a nature that the buyers were entitled to reject the documents in each of the groups, on both the first and the second presentations: that is, apart from any special protection given to the sellers by the documents clause. There was a grave, and, for what that may matter, unexplained, failure by the sellers to provide documents containing or evidencing a contract or contracts of carriage of the contractual goods from the contractual port of loading to the contractual destination.[20]

The importance of certainty when it comes to the identification of conditions within the context of documentary duty was further emphasised by Lord Ruskill in *Bunge Corporation v Tradax Export SA*.[21] Here, the court was asked whether specific documentary imperfections amounted to breaches of condition. Lord Ruskill pointed out that:

My Lords, it is beyond question that there are many cases in the books where terms, the breach of which do not deprive the innocent party of substantially the whole of the benefit which he was intended to receive from the contract, were nonetheless held to be conditions any breach of which entitled the innocent party to rescind. Perhaps the most famous is *Bowes v Shand* (1877) 2 App. Cas. 455. *Reuter v Sala* (1879) 4 C.P.D. 239, is another such case. Both these cases were decided before the Sale of Goods Act, 1893, was enacted. But that Act only codified the relevant common law. I think Mr. Buckley was entitled to say that these two, and other similar cases, largely turned upon the fact that the breach complained of was part of the description of the goods in question and that would therefore today be a statutory condition under s. 13 of the Sale of Goods Act. But there are many other cases, modern and less modern, where terms in contracts for the sale of goods have been held to be conditions any breach of which will give rise to a right to rescind. Though s. 10 (1) of the Sale of Goods Act provides that, unless a different intention appears, terms as to the time of payment are not deemed to be of the essence of a contract of sale, there are many cases, notably

20 *Ibid.*, at 63.

21 *Bunge Corporation v Tradax* [1981] 1 WLR 711.

those in connection with the opening of bankers' credits and the payment against documents, where the relevant obligations have been held to be a condition a breach of which will entitle the innocent party to rescind. No useful purpose will be served by listing all those cases cited in argument on either side. Many are usefully collected in the judgment of Mr. Justice Diplock, as he then was in *Ian Stach Limited v Baker Bosley Ltd.* [1958] 2 Q.B. 130 at pp. 139–144, and I would emphasize in this connection the need for certainty in this type of transaction to which that learned Judge referred at pp. 143 and 144 of his judgment. Parties to commercial transactions should be entitled to know their rights at once and should not, when possible, be required to wait upon events before those rights can be determined. Of course, in many cases of alleged frustration or of alleged repudiatory delay it may be necessary to await events upon the happening or non-happening of which rights may well crystallize. But your Lordships' House has recently reiterated in a series of cases arising from the withdrawal of ships on time charter for non-payment of hire the need for certainty where punctual payment of hire is required and has held that the right to rescind automatically follows a breach of any such condition.

My Lords, I find nothing in the judgment of Lord Justice Diplock in the Hong Kong Fir case which suggests any departure from the basic and long standing rules for determining whether a particular term in a contract is or is not a condition and there is much in the judgment of Lord Justice Sellers with which Lord Justice Upjohn, as he then was, expressly agreed, to show that those rules are still good law and should be maintained. They are enshrined in the oft quoted judgment of Lord Justice Bowen, as he then was, in *Bentsen v Taylor* [1893] 2 Q.B. 274 at p. 28.

There is no way of deciding that question except by looking at the contract in the light of the surrounding circumstances, and then making up one's mind whether the intention of the parties, as gathered from the instrument itself, will best be carried out by treating the promise as a warranty sounding only in damages, or as a condition precedent by the failure to perform which the other party is relieved of his liability.

That well-known passage will be found quoted by Lord Justice Sellers at pp. 488 and 60 of the reports in the Hong Kong Fir case. I would add a reference in this connection to the judgment of Lord Justice Scrutton in *Comptoir Commercial Anversois v Power* [1920] 1 K.B. 868 at p. 899.

My Lords, the judgment of Lord Justice Diplock in the Hong Kong Fir case is, if I may respectfully say so, a landmark in the development of one part of our law of contract in the latter part of this century. The learned Lord Justice showed by reference to detailed historical analysis, contrary to what had often been thought previously, that there was no complete dichotomy between conditions and warranties and that there was a third class of term, the innominate term. But I do not believe the learned Lord Justice ever intended his judgment to afford an easy escape route from the normal consequences of rescission to a contract breaker who had broken what was, upon its true construction, clearly a condition of the contract by claiming that he had only broken an innominate term. Of course when considering whether a particular term is or is not a condition it is relevant to consider to what other class or category that term, if not a condition, might belong. But to say that is not to accept that the question whether or not a term is a condition has to be determined solely by reference to what has to be proved before rescission can be claimed for breach of a term which has already been shown not to be a condition but an innominate term. Once it is appreciated that the whole of the passages on pp. 493 and 494 and 69 and 70 of the learned Lord Justice's judgment are directed to the consequences of a term which is not a condition but an innominate term and not to the question of whether or not a particular term is a condition, the difficulties mentioned by Lord Justice Megaw in his judgment if the passages in question are read too literally, and as the appellants invite your Lordships to read them, disappear. The only criticism I would respectfully venture of these passages is the use of the adverb "expressly" in the passage I have already quoted from the middle of the full paragraph on pp. 494 and 70. Surely the same result must follow whether the legal consequences of the breach are also "impliedly" provided for in the contract upon that contract's true construction? In venturing this amendment to what the learned Lord Justice said, I derive comfort from the fact that my noble and learned friend, Lord Diplock himself in *Photo Production Ltd. v Securicor Transport Ltd.* [1980] 1 Lloyd's Rep. 545; [1980] A.C. 827 at pp. 553 and 849 speaks of the case where the contracting parties have agreed.

[. . .] whether by express words or by implication of law . . . that any . . . failure by one party to perform a particular primary obligation ("condition" in the nomenclature of the Sale of Goods Act 1893), irrespective of the gravity of the event that has in fact resulted from the breach, shall entitle the other party to elect to put an end to all primary obligations of both parties remaining unperformed.

Thus, I think it legitimate to suggest an amendment to the passage in [1961] 2 Lloyd's Rep. 478; [1962] 2 Q.B. 26 at pp. 494 and 70 either by deleting the word "expressly" or by adding the words "or by necessary implication".

My Lords, your Lordships' House had to consider a similar problem in relation to a different clause (cl. 21) in a different GAFTA contract in *Bremer Handelsgesellschaft m.b.H. v Vanden Avenne-Izegem P.V.B.A.* [1978] 2 Lloyd's Rep. 109. My noble and learned friend Lord Wilberforce said at p. 113:

Automatic and invariable treatment of a clause such as this runs counter to the approach, which modern authorities recognise, of treating such a provision as having the force of a condition (giving rise to rescission or invalidity), or of a contractual term (giving rise to damages only) according to the nature and gravity of the breach. The clause is then categorised as an innominate term. This doctrine emerged very clearly in the *Hong Kong Fir* case in relation to the obligation of seaworthiness, and was as applied to a contract for sale of goods made on GAFTA form 100 in *The Hansa Nord*, a decision itself approved by this House in the Reardon Smith case. In my opinion, the clause may vary appropriately and should be regarded as such an intermediate term: to do so would recognise that while in many, possibly most, instances, breach of it can adequately be sanctioned by damages, cases may exist in which, in fairness to the buyer, it would be proper to treat the cancellation as not having effect. On the other hand, always so to treat it may be often be unfair to the seller, and unnecessarily rigid.

The passage I have just quoted was directed to cl. 21 of the contract there in question. All members of your Lordships' House were of the opinion that that clause was not a condition because it was insufficiently definitive or precise – see the speeches of my noble and learned friends, Lord Salmon at p. 128, and Lord Russell of Killowen at p. 130. But it is important to observe that your Lordships' House had also to consider cl. 22 of that contract. All members of your Lordships' House held that cl. 22 was a condition – see the speeches of my noble and learned friends, Lord Wilberforce at p. 116, and Lord Salmon at p. 128. I venture to emphasize the statement in the former passage that accurate compliance with the stipulation in question was essential to avoid commercial confusion in view of the possibility of long string contracts being involved, a point of especial importance in the present case.

In short, while recognizing the modern approach and not being over ready to construe terms of conditions unless the contract clearly requires the Court so to do, none the less the basic principles of construction for determining whether or not a particular term is a condition remain as before, always bearing in mind on the one hand the need for certainty and on the other the desirability of not, when legitimate, allowing rescission where the breach complained of is highly technical and where damages would clearly be an adequate remedy. It is therefore in my opinion wrong to use the language employed by Lord Justice Diplock in the Hong Kong Fir case as directed to the determination of the question which terms of a particular contract are conditions and which are only innominate terms. I respectfully agree with what Lord Justice Megaw said in the passage in his judgment in the instant case at [1980]

> 1 Lloyd's Rep. 294 at pp. 307, 308. The explanation of the passage which he quotes is that which I have just given.[22]

Similarly, the importance of identifying breaches of documentary duties as breaches of conditions under strict terms was emphasised in *Soon Seng Co Ltd v Glencore Grain Ltd*,[23] where the buyer rejected documents claiming, inter alia, that the bill of lading was to be drawn on liner terms.

The sellers appealed contending that the sales contract contained no requirements at all that the bills of lading should be on liner terms and, if that was wrong, any such requirement was an innominate or intermediate term, breach of which did not justify rejection of the documents.

Here it was held by the court that the contracts contemplated performance involving the presentation of shipping documents including invoices and bills of lading. That, indeed, was the scheme of a c.&f. sale; the documents would identify the agreed cost, freight, and destination and would give the buyers contractual rights as against the carriers as to delivery for such freight and at such destination; "liner terms" referred to responsibility for, inter alia, discharge, a matter directly involving the carrier; when the sale contract price clause referred to "liner terms" the natural conclusion was that it referred to a right which the buyers were to be given against the carriers.

So viewed, the contract remained from shipment an essentially documentary transaction under which the buyers parted with payment in return for continuous protection, inter alia, against the carrier.

These were transactions which were to be performed *prima facie* by shipping the goods, by arranging their carriage, and by delivering the shipping documents; the sellers were bound under each contract to make a "proper" contract of affreightment and to procure a "proper" bill of lading; and in the context, a proper contract and bill of lading meant a contract and a bill not merely covering carriage to the destination but also providing for discharge at the destination on liner terms.

Therefore, the presence in the bill of lading of provision for discharge on liner terms was a condition precedent to the buyers' obligation to take up the documents. As it is of the nature of documentary requirements that they should be strictly complied with, and the sellers did not in fact tender complying bills, the contracts were not performed and the sellers were in breach through non-delivery.

In delivering his judgment, Mance J reconsidered the judicial position relating to the importance of sellers' documentary duties in international commercial sales. In his words:

> The sellers' reliance on *Cehave N.V. v Bremer Handelsgesellschaft m.b.H. (The Hansa Nord)* [1975] 2 Lloyd's Rep. 445; [1976] 1 Q.B. 44 is answered by the same consideration. Lord Justice Roskill there said at p. 457, col. 2; p. 70E-G:
>
> > I was at one time troubled by the fact that to accept Mr Lloyd's argument on this branch of the law might involve the acceptance of different standards in the case of c.i.f. contracts between the performance of a seller's obligations regarding

22 *Bunge Corporation v Tradax* [1981] 1 WLR 711, at 736.
23 *Soon Seng Co Ltd v Glencore Grain Ltd* [1996] 1 Lloyd's Rep. 398.

> the shipping documents which the seller has to procure and tender to the buyer and the seller's obligations regarding the goods which he has to procure, ship and cause to be delivered. Thus a bill of lading claused as to the apparent good order and condition of the goods shipped would be a bad tender and could at once be rejected by or on behalf of the buyer; yet if Mr Lloyd be right, the defects in the condition of the goods which led to that clausing of the bill of lading would not automatically justify the rejection of the goods. At first sight this seems inconsistent, but Mr Lloyd ultimately persuaded me that the seller's obligation regarding documentation had long been made sacrosanct by the highest authority and that the express or implied provisions in a c.i.f. contract in those respects were of the class, accepted by Lord Justice Diplock in *Hongkong Fir Shipping Co. Ltd. v Kawasaki Kisen Kaisha Ltd.* [1961] 2 Lloyd's Rep. 478; [1962] 2 Q.B. 26, any breach of which justified rejection.

This passage was cited by Lord Justice Megaw in the S.I.A.T. case, where Lord Justice Megaw said in this context:

> There are authoritative pronouncements which at least suggest that, in this area of obligations as to documents in c.i.f. contracts, any defect – any breach – other than one within the de minimis category, entitles the buyers to reject the documents: the buyer is not obliged, at peril of being himself held to be in grave breach of contract if he makes the wrong decision (often a decision which has to be made quickly and, through no fault of his, on incomplete information), to weigh and assess the risks and possibilities as to the seriousness of the consequences to him of the documentary defects, should he accept the documents. That, I believe, was the sort of consideration which Lord Justice Roskill had in mind . . .

Lord Justice Megaw went on to suggest that he viewed the principle as applicable whether or not the contract involved presentation of documents under a banker's credit or direct to the buyer, but he did not find it necessary to decide this because on any view the failure of the Ancona/Ravenna bills to specify the contractual destination justified their rejection. If necessary, I would follow and apply the indications as to the general principle regarding non-conforming documentation contained in both Lord Justice Roskill's and Lord Justice Megaw's judgments. But, whatever the general principle, the failure of the bills to cover the discharging operation in accordance with the sale contract in my view justified rejection. The consequences of such a failure must necessarily be uncertain, and the buyers were under no obligation either to bear or to attempt to assess the costs and risks involved in the bills of lading being on "free in and out" terms, as distinct from liner terms.[24]

The following passage of Mance J's judgment elegantly conceptualises the importance of documentary strict compliance within the context of contracts concluded on shipment terms:

> In principle, I consider that presence in the bills of lading of provision for discharge on liner terms was a condition precedent to buyers' obligation to take up the documents. It is of the nature of documentary requirements that they should be strictly complied with. This is so whether or not a third party such as a bank is involved in the transaction. A buyer presented with shipping documents must make a judgment on the documents whether or not they are acceptable. He does not, at least normally, have the goods available for inspection at that stage. He cannot evaluate how significant any documentary discrepancy will or may prove. He is entitled to know where he stands.

24 *Ibid.*, at 401.

> All these factors point to a strict view of compliance with documentary requirements such as the present. The strictness may sometimes be mitigated by the sellers' ability to correct and re-present the documents, a point made by Lord Justice Megaw in the S.I.A.T. case, at pp. 62–63. But whether or not that course would have been open, compliance with the present documentary requirement was in my judgment a condition precedent to any obligation on the part of buyers to take up the documents. Since the sellers did not in fact re-present complying bills, the contracts were not performed and the sellers were in breach through non-delivery.[25]

The analysis of Mance J in the aforementioned passage lays down the conceptual foundations of the principle of strict compliance in documentary duties. Indeed, as the learned judge specified in his judgment, the importance of strict compliance of documents does not derive from the fact that documents are prepared in a clinical environment and can be double-checked and scrutinised so as to avoid mistakes.

The real rationale for the adoption of the principle of strict compliance in documentary duties lies with the fact that, within the context of contracts concluded on shipment terms, by default the buyer receives the documents first; at that point, the buyer will check compliance of the documents and pay the seller.

In that specific moment of time, the buyer cannot inspect the goods, and needs to make an informed assessment of the compliance of the seller's performance on the face of the documents alone. In the case that documents are not compliant, the buyer, as elegantly put by Mance J in *Soon Seng Co Ltd v Glencore Grain Ltd*, is not in the position to evaluate the nature of the documentary imperfection vis-à-vis the cargo. In other words, the buyer cannot possibly ascertain the impact of a documentary breach (as slight as it may be) on the cargo.

Consequently, in legal teleological terms, strict compliance has the advantage of conferring the highest possible degree of certainty on a scenario otherwise thwarted by severe ambiguity.[26]

10.4.2 Authorities against strict compliance

Part of the doctrine did question, in the past, the adoption of documentary strict compliance, on the basis of the necessity to avoid sharp practice and the possibility of saving an effective performance of the seller in the presence of a slight breach.

A case often quoted as an authority allegedly contrary to the principle of documentary strict compliance is *Jydsk Andels-Foderstofforretning v Grands Moulins de Paris*.[27] Here, a sale of bran saw the buyers refusing to take up the documents on the grounds that the contract called for a maximum of 440,000 kilos, whereas the certificates of weight presented to them showed 441,470 kilos.

The buyers were found not entitled to terminate the contract by Mackinnon J, who held as follows:

25 *Ibid.*, at 402.

26 For a discussion on arguments in support of strict compliance, see Debattista, *Bills of Lading in Export Trade*, above, p.363.

27 *Jydsk Andels-Foderstofforretning v Grands Moulins de Paris* [1931] 39 Lloyd's Rep. 223.

> I have stated a good many of the facts which are stated in the case. They also find this as a natural incident of bran as an article of commerce: that bran is not liable to a natural increase in weight, but is subject to increase or decrease in the course of transit according to circumstances.
>
> I understand that to mean that it is not subject to a natural increase in weight only, in the sense that ice is subject to a natural decrease in weight, but that the weight of bran may go up or down according as it goes into moist or dry conditions, according as moisture is attracted to or repelled from it. That leads us to a matter which is fairly obvious, that it is quite consistent with the sellers having shipped not an ounce or a gramme more than the contract weight of bran, namely, 8800 50 kilo bags – quite consistent with their having shipped them of that weight – and their weighing a little more at Rouen by reason of having attracted some moisture during their transport down the River Seine. But I do not think that the certificate of weight required by this contract is a certificate of weight at Paris; I think what the contract requires is a certificate of weight at the port of shipment, namely, Rouen, and, in fact, the certificate of weight did show this slight increase – an excess of weight at Rouen. It is to be noted that after the sale in Denmark, or at the sale, the bags were weighed again, and it is apparent that they had gone down a little in weight, though they were still somewhat in excess of the contract quantity, although only half of the excess that was found by the certificates at Rouen. It seems to be, incidentally, an example of that rise and fall of the weight of bran which is stated by the Appeal Committee to be its natural incident.
>
> In the circumstances which I have stated, I think that the award of Mr. Ward was right upon a very simple ground, namely, that this excess of weight was a matter so negligible that it did not entitle the buyers to reject the whole parcel of goods. I think it would be a different matter if, upon a contract for 440 tons, they were being called upon to accept and to pay for 441 tons or 44112 tons; but when they are only being called upon to accept and to pay according to the contract for 440 tons, and it is found that they are asked to take delivery of an extra 1 or 112 tons for nothing, and when that is in regard to a subject-matter which, as is found by the arbitrators, and as must be commercially well known to the parties, is liable to have its weight increased or decreased by reason of the natural changes in the atmosphere, I think that in those circumstances the buyers were not entitled to reject these goods, and that in the circumstances it was a good tender.[28]

Part of the doctrine has emphasised that it is not clear whether the learned judge treated the issue as a breach of physical duties rather than documentary duties.[29]

It is the opinion of this author that it is possible to evince from the aforementioned passage of the judgment that emphasis was indeed put on the physical aspect of the performance, rather than on the documentary obligations. Indeed, the description of how a cargo of bran is subject to physical fluctuations during transit, alongside the accent put on the inability to reject the cargo, appear to point towards the conclusion that the case was considered and adjudicated in terms of physical duties and acceptance of the cargo, rather than on documentary aspects.

The case might just represent, therefore, an example of the application of the *de minimis* rule which, as established in the previous chapter, applies to the physical duties of the seller and it is enshrined in the aforementioned section 15A SOGA 1979.[30]

28 *Ibid.*, at 227, 228.

29 See Debattista, *Bills of Lading in Export Trade*, above, p.363.

30 See chapter 9.

Another case cited vis-à-vis the principle of strict compliance is *Moralice (London) Ltd v ED & F Man.*[31] The case saw documents for a cargo of sugar being rejected by banks within the mechanism of a letter of credit, as the certificate of quantity showed the cargo being in shortage by three bags.

The court held that the banks were entitled to reject documents which did not exactly comply, and that though the *de minimis* rule would have applied to such short shipment as between buyer and seller under a normal contract of sale, that rule could not be applied where payment was to be made against documents in accordance with a letter of credit.

In the words of MacNair J:

> The next question is as to the effect of that contract. I think that, as a matter of construction, it is reasonably clear that when the defendants say that they are prepared to hold the plaintiffs harmless from any consequence which arose from their being three bags short shipped, what they mean is – or more accurately, what the language they use means is – that they will indemnify the plaintiffs against the plaintiffs' own indemnity to the bank, because that is the matter which the parties had under consideration at the time.
>
> If that is so, the next question I have to consider is whether the plaintiffs did in fact incur any liability to the bank. The determination of that issue, as it seems to me, depends upon whether or not I take the view that these documents, showing the deficiency of the 300 kilos, were documents which the bank would have been obliged to take up. Clearly the bank would not be obliged to take up those documents, seeing that they were documents which differed from the documents required by the credit, unless it is true to say that the maxim de minimis non curat lex, or, as it is sometimes called, the rule of insignificance, applies (a) on the facts of this case, and (b) as between confirming banker and the beneficiary of the credit – namely, the seller.
>
> On the first question (a), I think that as between a buyer and a seller, if the contract was not complicated by the intervention of a letter of credit, and seeing that the seller was not calling upon the buyer to pay for 500 tons, but only for 500 tons less 300 kilos, it would be a case in which the maxim or rule I have already referred to would apply, and would fall within cases like *Shipton, Anderson & Co. v Weil Bros. & Co., Ltd.* (1912) 17 Com. Cas. 153, that being a decision of Mr. Justice Lush, and the case of *Jydsk Andels-Foderstofforretning v Grands Moulins de Paris* (1931) 39 Ll.L.Rep. 223, a decision of Mr. Justice MacKinnon; because, as between buyer and seller, a deficiency of 300 kilos out of 500,000 kilos is, in the words of those judgments, quite insignificant or negligible.[32]

It is the opinion of the author that *Moralice (London) Ltd v ED & F Man* cannot possibly be considered as an authority against the principle of strict compliance and in favour of the application of the *de minimis* rule to the sellers' documentary duties.

Indeed, the reference to the possibility of application of the *de minimis* rule to documentary duties was done in the judgment by way of *obiter*, and it also appears clear from the judgment that the emphasis of the legal analysis of MacNair J is on the sellers' physical duties, rather than on the documentary counterpart.

Further, in legal teleological terms, overextending the application of the *de minimis* rule from the seller's physical duties onto the documentary obligations appears to be a conceptually erroneous task.

31 *Moralice (London) Ltd v ED & F Man* [1954] 21 Lloyd's Rep. 527.

32 *Ibid.*, at 532.

First, as established in the previous chapter, section 15A SOGA 1979, which contains the *de minimis* rule, is a section falling within the physical duties of the seller, whose scope of application would be to save the physical performance of the seller in a world of commodities which is far from being perfect and absolute.

Second, it has been rightly emphasised that the *ex post* introduction of section 15A into SOGA 1979 was accompanied by a memorandum specifying that section 15A was not to be intended as a major change in the law.[33]

The last authority against the principle of strict compliance is *Tradax Internacional SA v Goldschmidt SA*.[34] Here, a cargo of barley sold on f.o.b. terms was not supposed to contain more than 4 per cent foreign matter as per contractual specification in terms of quality.

The seller tendered a certificate of quality showing that the cargo contained 4.10 per cent foreign matter. The tender was in breach of the documentary strict compliance but it was, nonetheless, regarded as a "good tender" by the court, as it reflected the reality of the situation of the cargo, and the breach was commercially insignificant.

In the words of Slynn J:

> If the documents did not include a quality final certificate or if the quality final certificate which was included dealt with goods other than barley it seems to me that the buyer could refuse the documents. Equally if the certificate dealt only with weight and failed to deal with quality it may well be that the documents could be refused without more. But here the certificate is a good certificate in that it does state what is the quality, what is the percentage of impurities. It shows that there was not a full compliance with the contractual term as to quality and it does what it was intended to do. It is a valid document capable, as Mr. Hallgarten says, of being transferred as part of a subsequent sale.
>
> The question here, it seems to me, is not whether the document can be rejected because it did in itself not comply with the contractual terms relating to the provisions as to a certificate, but because it shows that the goods did not comply with the contractual terms.
>
> It is accepted that the provision as to impurities was not part of the description of the goods so there was no implied condition under s. 13 of the Sale of Goods Act, 1893, entitling rejection on non-compliance. Nor is any condition implied by s. 14 of the Sale of Goods Act, 1893, relied on. Accordingly it seems to me that on the basis of what was said in the case of *The Hansa Nord* [1975] 2 Lloyd's Rep. 445; [1976] Q.B. 44 at pp. 451 and 61 by Lord Denning, M.R., and at pp. 457 and 70H-71B by Lord Justice Roskill and what was said in *Hong Kong Fir Shipping Co. Ltd. v Kawasaki Kisen Kaisha Ltd.* [1961] 2 Lloyd's Rep. 478; [1962] 2 Q.B. 26, in the absence of any clear agreement or prior decision that this was to be a condition, the Court should lean in favour of construing this provision as to impurities as an intermediate term, only a serious and substantial breach of which entitled rejection.
>
> At pp. 445 and 61 of The Hansa Nord, Lord Denning, M.R., stresses that in the ordinary case where there is a deviation between the goods and the contractual provisions the buyer does not have the right to reject the whole cargo unless the breach was serious and substantial. Where the discrepancy is a minor discrepancy the buyer is bound to accept the goods. He should not reject them unless there is a serious and

33 See Debattista, *Bills of Lading in Export Trade*, above, p.363.

34 *Tradax Internacional SA v Goldschmidt SA* [1977] 2 Lloyd's Rep. 604.

substantial breach clearly attributable to the seller. At pp. 457 and 70, Lord Justice Roskill said:

In my view, a Court should not be over ready, unless required by statute or authority so to do, to construe a term in a contract as a "condition" any breach of which gives rise to a right to reject rather than as a term any breach of which sounds in damages – I deliberately avoid the use of the word "warranty" at this juncture. In principle contracts are made to be performed and not to be avoided according to the whims of market fluctuation and where there is a free choice between two possible constructions, I think the Court should tend to prefer that construction which ensures performance and not encourage avoidance of contractual obligations.

If there had been no provision as to a quality final certificate I would have had no doubt whatever that the present breach of the provision as to impurities would not have entitled rejection of the goods but would have entitled the buyers only to an allowance. Does it make any difference that the quality final certificate whose purpose is to finalise quality between the buyer and the seller (and which is otherwise valid) shows this minor breach, which but for the final certificate must be met by a prior allowance.

In my judgment, on the terms of the present contract, it does not make any difference. The buyers here had to consider whether the breach established by the quality final certificate was substantial and serious or went to the root of the contract or, on the other hand, whether it was of such a kind that they should have been satisfied with a price adjustment. There was, on the findings of the Board of Appeal, only one answer to that. Those findings are in strong terms and show that commercial men (to whose conclusions on these matters I must and do attach great weight) considered that this kind of deviation in quality would not be treated as entitling a rejection either of a quality final certificate (the quality final certificate being otherwise valid) or the goods. Accordingly I hold that the buyers were not entitled automatically to reject the document because of this statement in the quality final certificate that the goods contained 4.1 per cent. impurities.

The second issue which has been argued and which arises if I am wrong on the first issue, is whether on the facts of the present case the buyers lost the right to reject either documents or goods by reason of their acceptance or waiver.

The buyers contend that their only right to reject in the events which happened was a right to reject the documents. That could only arise on presentation of the documents, and when the quality final certificate was presented it was rejected. It is irrelevant what the buyers did in relation to the goods and even though the buyers, through their agents, knew of the defect in the documents which would eventually be tendered, their failure to take any step then to reject cannot be treated as a waiver or acceptance of the documents. This was at most an anticipatory breach. Any knowledge of an impending breach is irrelevant and cannot affect the position. Moreover, what the buyers did by putting the goods into a silo to prevent demurrage accruing did not affect the sellers' right any more than if they had left the goods on the ship. Accordingly it is said that there is no question of any acceptance for the purposes of s. 11(1)(c) and s. 35 of the Sale of Goods Act, 1893.

It is said moreover that there can only be a waiver if there is a clear and unequivocal representation that the contractual right to documents was being abandoned and a reliance on that representation by the sellers (see *Finagrain v Kruse* [1976] 2 Lloyd's Rep. 508, especially per Lord Justice Megaw at pp. 534/5), and that it is impossible to read into par. 11 of the award a finding that the buyers represented that they were not going to reject the documents, particularly as at that stage the sellers were themselves relying on the quality final certificate to resist complaints about defects in the goods. Nor is there a finding that the sellers knew the buyers were aware of the defect in the quality final certificate.[35]

35 *Ibid.*, at 610, 611.

In *Tradax Internacional SA v Goldschmidt SA*, the buyers were therefore prevented from rejecting the certificate of quality showing a percentage of impurities slightly higher compared to that originally established in the sales contract, due to the fact that the certificate of quality so tendered was a good certificate, doing what it was intended to do, i.e. to show that "there was not a full compliance with the contractual term as to quality."[36]

With the greatest respect, this line of reasoning does not seem to sit well with the nature of a documentary presentation within the context of international commercial sales.

Indeed, within that context, a "good" documentary tender is a tender of a document which reflects the reality as per the sales contract or, in other words, what was originally established in the sales contract, not the actual reality.

If this line of reasoning were to be applied to other documents, e.g. a bill of lading dated outside the shipment period, that tender could also be saved as a bill of lading so dated would be a "good" document reflecting the reality.

The application of such rationale on a large scale would have severe consequences for the legal assessment of a seller's documentary performance within the context of contracts concluded on shipment terms.

That is the reason why, as has been noted by the doctrine, the authority of the first part of Slynn J's judgment must be called into question (although the result is, with respect, amply justified by the second part of the ratio, based on estoppel).[37]

Overall, it is suggested that the adoption of the principle of strict compliance as the governing criterion of the seller's documentary duties is not only preferable, but essential, in order to guarantee a satisfactory functioning of contracts concluded on shipment terms.

Indeed, if one can understand the rationale for the introduction of a *de minimis* rule aimed at protecting the seller in terms of physical performances at times of difficult execution, one must also consider, on the other hand, the different nature of documentary duties.

Within the context of international commercial sales, goods are traded on the face of documents and, as put by Kerr LJ in *Procter & Gamble*,[38] "this is not a trade in goods, but in contracts for the shipment of goods".

Buyers and sellers have elected to trade not only goods but also documents and, as established above, goods are traded by merchants via the endorsement of the documents. This entails that, as previously mentioned, in the vast majority of circumstances the buyer will need to make an informed assessment of the performance of sellers on the basis of the documents alone, without the possibility of inspecting the cargo.

The risks and uncertainty inherently embedded in such a scenario can easily be understood, as well as the consequent need for the law to ensure the highest possible degree of certainty.

---

36 *Ibid.*, at 612.

37 See Debattista, *Bills of Lading in Export Trade*, above, p.217. See also Benjamin's *Sale of Goods*, above, paras. 18.396 *et seq.*

38 *Proctor & Gamble Philippine Manufacturing Corp v Becker* [1988] 2 Lloyds Rep. 21, 29.

It is submitted that only by endorsing the principle of strict compliance when it comes to documentary duties can the law create a scenario of efficiency and stability.

Indeed, far from shielding only the buyer's position, the principle of strict compliance also crafts an alcove of certainty in relation to the legal status quo of the seller; each party knows where it stands and what the remedies are at any given moment of time within the context of a transaction concluded on shipment terms.

Thus, the principle of strict compliance avoids unnecessary uncertainties, curtails litigation, and creates efficiencies within the context of transactions otherwise destined to a perpetual limbo of ambiguity.

CHAPTER 11

Letters of credit and contracts concluded on shipment terms

11.1 Letters of credit as vehicles of payment in international commercial sales

A letter of credit is a document from a bank guaranteeing that a seller will receive payment in full as long as certain delivery conditions have been met.

The bank that writes the letter of credit "will act on behalf of the buyer and make sure that all delivery conditions have been met before making the payment to the seller. Most letters of credit are governed by rules promulgated by the International Chamber of Commerce (ICC) known as Uniform Customs and Practice for Documentary Credits (UCP). Letters of credit are typically used by importing and exporting companies, particularly for large purchases, and will often negate the need for the buyer to pay a deposit before delivery is made."[1]

11.2 Mechanisms governing documentary credits

Letters of credit accomplish their purpose by substituting the credit of the bank for that of the customer, for the purpose of facilitating trade.

Commercial letter of credit:

Commercial letters of credit have been used for centuries to facilitate payment in international trade.

Letters of credit used in international transactions are governed by the UCP. The general provisions and definitions of the ICC are binding on all parties. Domestic collections in the US are governed by the Uniform Commercial Code (UCC).

In legal terms, a commercial letter of credit is a "contractual agreement between a bank, known as the issuing bank, on behalf of one of its customers, authorising another bank, known as the advising or confirming bank, to make payment to the beneficiary."[2]

The quintessential elements of a letter of credit comprise a payment undertaking given by a bank (issuing bank), on behalf of a buyer (applicant) to pay a seller (beneficiary) for a given amount of money on presentation of specified documents

1 D. Muraleedharan, *Modern Banking: Theory and Practice*, PHI Learning Private LTd, second edition, 2014, at pp.66–67.

2 See "Understanding Letters of Credit" at crfonline.com

representing the supply of goods within specified time limits. Documents must conform to terms and conditions set out in the letter of credit.

The issuing bank, on the request of its customer, opens the letter of credit. The issuing bank makes a commitment to honour drawings made under the credit. The beneficiary is normally the provider of goods and/or services. Essentially, the issuing bank replaces the bank's customer as the payor.

The beneficiary is entitled to payment as long as he can provide the documentary evidence required by the letter of credit. The letter of credit is a distinct and separate transaction from the contract on which it is based. All parties deal in documents and not in goods.

The issuing bank is not liable for performance of the underlying contract between the customer and beneficiary. Indeed, the issuing bank's obligation to the buyer is to examine all documents to ensure that they meet all the terms and conditions of the credit.

Upon requesting demand for payment, the beneficiary warrants that all conditions of the agreement have been complied with. If the beneficiary (seller) conforms to the letter of credit, the seller must be paid by the bank.

The issuing bank's liability to pay and to be reimbursed from its customer becomes absolute upon the completion of the terms and conditions of the letter of credit. Under the provisions of the UCP 600, the bank is given a reasonable amount of time after receipt of the documents to honour the draft.

The issuing bank's role is to provide a guarantee to the seller that if compliant documents are presented, the bank will pay the seller the amount due and examine the documents, and will only pay if these documents comply with the terms and conditions set out in the letter of credit.[3]

The credit opened by the buyer with the issuing bank can be either advised or confirmed by a correspondent bank.

An advising bank, usually a foreign correspondent bank of the issuing bank, will advise the beneficiary. Generally, "the beneficiary would want to use a local bank to ensure that the letter of credit is valid. In addition, the advising bank would be responsible for sending the documents to the issuing bank. The advising bank has no other obligation under the letter of credit. If the issuing bank does not pay the beneficiary, the advising bank is not obligated to pay.

The correspondent bank may confirm the letter of credit for the beneficiary. At the request of the issuing bank, the correspondent obligates itself to ensure payment under the letter of credit. The confirming bank would not confirm the credit until it evaluated the country and bank where the letter of credit originates. The confirming bank is usually the advising bank."[4]

3 Typically, the documents requested will include a commercial invoice, a transport document such as a bill of lading or airway bill, and an insurance document; but there are many others. Letters of credit deal in documents, not goods.

4 See D. Muraleedharan, *Modern Banking: Theory and Practice*, above at p. 68.

11.3 The legal traits of letters of credit

Step-by-step process

The buyer and seller agree on a sale, and the seller wants a letter of credit to guarantee payment. The buyer applies to his bank for a letter of credit in favour of the seller. Thereafter, the buyer's bank approves the credit risk of the buyer, issues and forwards the credit to its correspondent bank (advising or confirming). The correspondent bank is usually located in the same geographical location as the seller (beneficiary).

The advising bank will authenticate the credit and forward the original credit to the seller (beneficiary).

The seller (beneficiary) ships the goods, then verifies and develops the documentary requirements to support the letter of credit. Documentary requirements may vary greatly depending on the perceived risk involved in dealing with a particular company.

The seller presents the required documents to the advising or confirming bank to be processed for payment.

The advising or confirming bank examines the documents for compliance with the terms and conditions of the letter of credit. If the documents are correct, the advising or confirming bank will claim the funds by debiting the account of the issuing bank, waiting until the issuing bank remits, after receiving the documents. The issuing bank will examine the documents for compliance. If they are in order, the issuing bank will debit the buyer's account. Thereafter, the issuing bank will forward the documents to the buyer.

Legal connotations

In legal teleological terms, each of the different stages of a letter of credit postulates a specific legal relationship. The relationship between the buyer/applicant and the issuing bank can be described as a bilateral contractual relationship which will give rise to bilateral liabilities.

Once the letter of credit has been opened, this entails an undertaking by the issuing bank towards the seller entailing the promise of payment of the sum indicated in the credit vis-à-vis the production of the documents indicated in the credit itself. This means that there is a "unilateral" contract between the issuing bank and the seller, whereby the issuing bank promises to pay the seller upon satisfactory tender of the documents listed in the letter of credit.

As established above, it is unlikely that the issuing bank will deal directly with the seller; rather, it will appoint an advising/confirming bank with whom the issuing bank has a bilateral contract.

Finally, if the credit is to be confirmed, the confirming bank will add its own unilateral undertaking/promise of payment to the seller; this entails that, whenever a credit is confirmed, the seller has two unilateral promises of payment, one from the issuing bank, and the other stemming from the confirming bank. The seller does not have any obligations towards the confirming bank or the issuing bank; his obligations will always lie with the buyer according to the original sales contract.

This means that a seller/beneficiary of a credit will be in the position to sue a confirming bank and/or an issuing bank in case of violation of the credit obligations under the UCP 600.

Conversely, a confirming bank/issuing bank is not in the position to sue a seller/beneficiary of a letter of credit. This shall be object of scrutiny in the following. For the moment our analysis will be devoted to unfolding the legal issues related to the different phases of a letter of credit, starting from the opening stage.

11.4 When must a letter of credit be opened?

Two main scenarios need to be distinguished here: a) where the sales contract stipulates a time, the letter of credit will have to be opened by the agreed time; b) if the sales contract does not stipulate a time, it is clear on authority that the letter of credit must be opened by the commencement of the shipment period.

Uncertainty in relation to the deadline emerged in *Pavia v Thurmann-Nielsen.*[5] Here the dispute arose in relation to sales contracts for a cargo of Brazilian groundnuts. The sales contracts provided for payment via letter of credit, and the buyer failed to open the credit by the shipment period.

The question of law submitted for the decision of the court was whether, on the facts as found and the true construction of the contracts, the credit should have been opened by the buyers or made available to the sellers by the commencement of the shipment period.

The Court of Appeal held that in a contract for the sale of goods c.i.f., shipment at the option of the seller over a prolonged period, which provides for payment by confirmed credit, the buyer, in the absence of express stipulation, must open the credit and make it available to the seller at the beginning of the shipment period.

The seller is entitled, before shipment, to be assured that he will on shipment be paid. If the buyer is anxious not to have to put the credit machinery in motion until shortly before the seller is ready to ship, a provision for that purpose must be inserted in the contract.

In the words of Somervell J:

> My view is that the contract would be unworkable if, as suggested by Mr. Widgery, the buyer under it was under no obligation until a date, which he could not possibly know, and which there is no machinery for his finding out, namely, when the seller actually has the goods down at the port ready to be put on to the ship. There are no words in the contract which would justify us in arriving at that result and there is no reason why we should imply any such term into this contract. I do not think it is a question of implication. I think when a seller is given a right to ship over a period and there is machinery for payment, that machinery must be available over the whole of that period. If the buyer is anxious, as he might be if the period of shipment is a long one, not to have to put the credit machinery in motion until shortly before the seller is likely to want to ship, then he must put in some provision by which the credit shall be provided 14 days after a cable received from the seller, or the like. In the absence

5 *Pavia v Thurmann-Nielsen* [1952] 2 QB 84.

> of any provision of that kind, I think the answer which the judge gave to the question posed is plainly right, and the appeal should be dismissed.[6]

Somervell J's arguments were echoed by Lord Denning, who stated as follows:

> The sale of goods across the world is now usually arranged by means of confirmed credits. The buyer requests his banker to open a credit in favour of the seller, and in pursuance of that request the banker, or his foreign agent, issues a confirmed credit in favour of the seller. This credit is a promise by the banker to pay money to the seller in return for the shipping documents. Then the seller, when he presents the documents, gets paid the contract price. The conditions of the credit must be strictly fulfilled, otherwise the seller would not be entitled to draw on it.
>
> The question in this case is this: In a contract which provides for payment by confirmed credit, when must the buyer open the credit? In the absence of express stipulation, I think the credit must be made available to the seller at the beginning of the shipment period. The reason is because the seller is entitled, before he ships the goods, to be assured that, on shipment, he will get paid. The seller is not bound to tell the buyer the precise date when he is going to ship; and whenever he does ship the goods, he must be able to draw on the credit. He may ship on the very first day of the shipment period. If, therefore, the buyer is to fulfil his obligations he must make the credit available to the seller at the very first date when the goods may be lawfully shipped in compliance with the contract. The appeal should be dismissed.[7]

The linkage between the opening of the credit and shipment period created by *Pavia v Thurmann-Nielsen* is of solid foundation. Indeed, the rationale of letters of credit is to guarantee payment to a seller who would otherwise be about to ship the goods without knowing whether he will ever be paid by the buyer.

A similar issue to that in *Pavia v Thurmann-Nielsen* subsequently arose in *Sinason-Teicher Inter-American Grain corpn. v Oilcakes and Oilseed Trading Co Ltd*,[8] albeit here the obligation of the buyer was not to provide payment via letter of credit, but rather with a banker's guarantee.

The sellers argued that the guarantee had to be provided as soon as reasonably possible, with the counter argument of the buyers being that the guarantee was to be ready by the first shipment date.

On appeal, it was held by the court that guarantees and letters of credit were analogous and that what was a reasonable time for tendering was a question of fact based on commercial considerations and the purpose of the contract.

In this case, the event guaranteed was the presentation of the contract documents and the court held that the question of whether the guarantee was furnished within a reasonable time had to be considered in the light of the event guaranteed, i.e. that the documents would be taken up on first presentation.

The buyers' obligation was to provide a guarantee within a reasonable time before the first shipment date.

As put by Lord Denning:

---

6 *Ibid.*, at 88.

7 *Ibid*, at 89.

8 *Sinason-Teicher Inter-American Grain corpn. v Oilcakes and Oilseed Trading Co Ltd* [1954] 2 Lloyd's Rep. 327.

The contract contained no express provision as to the time when the English buyers should give the bank guarantee, and the question is when it should have been given. The American sellers said that it should have been given at latest by Sept. 9, 1952, and that because it was not given by that time they were entitled to and did cancel the contract on Sept. 10, 1952. The English buyers said that they were not bound to give the guarantee by that date and that the cancellation by the American sellers amounted to a repudiation of the contract.

I must say that the American sellers, at the time they cancelled, had got a wrong view of the contract. They thought they had a right to be given the guarantee immediately after the making of the contract, which was certainly not the case.

[. . .] We were referred to *Pavia & Co., S.P.A. v Thurmann-Nielsen* [1952] 2 Q.B. 84; [1952] 1 Lloyd's Rep. 153. I agree with what Mr. Justice Devlin said about that case. It does not decide that the buyer can delay right up to the first date for shipment. It only decides that he must provide the letter of credit at latest by that date. The correct view is that, if nothing is said about time in the contract, the buyer must provide the letter of credit within a reasonable time before the first date for shipment. The same applies to a bank guarantee: for it stands on a similar footing.

The Appeal Committee of the London Corn Trade Association found all the facts in a most comprehensive statement and they said this:

The sellers were at all times aware of the practice and procedure with regard to this switch transaction and the need to obtain the German guarantees before the English buyers could establish their guarantee or letter of credit.

In so far as it is a question of fact we find, and in so far as it is a matter of law we hold, that the buyers' obligation was to provide a bank guarantee within a reasonable time before 1st October, 1952, and that such reasonable time had not arrived by the 10th September, 1952.

That finding of the Appeal Committee is decisive against the sellers here to-day. But, furthermore, the Appeal Committee found that on any view, even if the obligation was simply to provide the guarantee within a reasonable time in all the circumstances the guarantee was provided within that time: they said that the proper form was lodged with the Bank of England on the 8th September and approval obtained on the 9th September, 1952. Until such approval by the Bank of England had been obtained the buyers could not furnish a guarantee or letter of credit to the sellers and the buyers were entitled to a reasonable period of time after such approval to obtain such guarantee and so far as it is a question of fact we find, and in so far as it is a matter of law we hold, that such reasonable time had not elapsed by the 10th September.[9]

Unfortunately, *Sinason-Teicher Inter-American Grain corpn. v Oilcakes and Oilseed Trading Co Ltd* does create a certain level of uncertainty as the concept of "reasonable period before shipment" was not defined by the court.

If one could see *Sinason-Teicher* as a further mechanism of protection for sellers compared to *Pavia*, one can also not help wondering whether the concept of "reasonable period before shipment" refers to the time necessary for the seller to make the necessary arrangements for goods to be shipped, or if that concept can even be extended to preparatory phases such as the manufacturing process.[10]

9 *Ibid.*, at 330, 331. In relation to f.o.b. contracts, see *Ian Stach Ltd v Baker Bosley Ltd* [1958] 2 QB 130. Here the court held that in a contract for the sale of goods f.o.b. which provides for shipment over a period within which the buyer is entitled to call for the shipment of the goods at any time, and which is financed by a banker's confirmed irrevocable credit, the *prima facie* rule is that the credit must be opened by the buyers at the latest by the first day of the shipment period.

10 On this point see Jack, *Documentary Credits*, Tottel Publishing, 2009, p. 48.

11.5 Making a letter of credit which conforms to the contract of sale

Although, as will be readily appreciated, a letter of credit is destined to become, in legal teleological terms, completely disjointed with the actual sale contract it originates from, care needs to be used in order to delineate its traits when the contract is drafted.

More specifically, when parties agree on payment through letter of credit, the contract should indicate clearly what type of letter of credit must be opened, the documents the seller must tender to the confirming bank, and when the letter of credit is to be opened.

Indeed, there is no duty on the banks to ensure that the documents tendered by the seller for payment are either reasonable or usual: their only duty is to pay against the documents described in the letter of credit.

One should also consider the letter of credit as the essential vehicle for payment, with the documents to be tendered as the trigger. In this regard, the position of the seller is easily ascertained, in the sense that the seller is best advised to always wait for the communication that a letter of credit has been opened before commencing the loading operation of the cargo.

No letter of credit opened by the buyer will entail no shipment by the seller, as would a different letter of credit compared to what was originally established in the sales contract.

Indeed, the buyer must instruct the issuing bank to issue a letter of credit which conforms with any terms the parties have agreed regarding the tender of documents for payment.

In *Cereal v ED&F*,[11] a contract for the sale of a cargo of sugar on f.o.b. terms provided for payment by letter of credit to be available at sight against the shipping documents. The buyers opened a letter of credit, which required presentation of a bill of lading dated no later than 31 October. The sellers insisted that under the contract a bill of lading might have a date in November, and that the letter of credit should accordingly provide for a bill of lading dated in October or November. The buyers, on their part, maintained that the letter of credit complied with the terms of the contract. When the sellers failed to withdraw their demand for amendment of the letter of credit, the buyers treated the sellers' conduct as a repudiatory breach, and terminated the contract.

It was held by the court that the sales contract did not require the letter of credit to contain a last date for shipment and, hence, that the letter of credit was not in accordance with the terms of the contract.

As put by Walker J:

> My task on the preliminary question is to construe the contract having regard to its particular terms and factual matrix.
>
> What that construction involves is that the period within which the sellers must stow the cargo is the period of time needed in order to stow the cargo on board a vessel presenting in October. True, it does not specify an end period with a fixed date.

---

11 *Cereal v ED&F* [2008] 1 Lloyd's Rep. 355.

> That, however, may be in the interests of the buyer, avoiding the need to nominate a vessel on which the cargo could be stowed by 31 October. I accept that as a matter of commercial reality a letter of credit will usually need to specify fixed dates which are to be specified in the bill of lading or other evidence of completion of shipment. Accordingly, in a case where the contract itself does not identify a fixed deadline, the buyer will have to make a reasonable estimate of when shipment will be complete. To an extent the buyer may need to make inquiries of others. That however does not seem to me to be in the same league as the uncertainty which caused concern to Diplock J in the Ian Stach case, where the construction rejected by Diplock J would have meant that at the time the shipping period started the seller would not have from the banker any assurance that if he performed his part of the contract he would receive payment. I agree with the panel that contracts for the sale of goods not uncommonly require a party to make a reasonable estimate of the time needed for a particular purpose. A similar example to that of the panel is the need for a buyer, when an fob contract fixes a date for completion of loading, to nominate a vessel which is capable of loading the goods by the fixed date.[12]

If the letter of credit opened by the buyer is different to the one agreed in the sales contract, the buyer will be in fatal breach of the contract of sale, entitling the seller to terminate, or threaten to terminate, the contract of sale if it so suits him.

Alternatively, the seller is entitled to insist that the letter of credit is to be amended to tally with the sales contract.

However, if the seller agrees to the changes, then the contract of sale has effectively been varied by agreement of the parties. To this end, it is much safer for such alterations of the contract of sale to be documented, if possible through a simple exchange of faxes confirming agreement, rather than through simple inaction by the seller/beneficiary.

A lack of reaction by the seller could be interpreted by the court as an implicit acceptance of the terms of the letter of credit unilaterally modified by the buyer.

In *Glencore v Lorico*,[13] a letter of credit opened for the sale of a cargo of Turkish wheat sold on f.o.b. terms required the sellers to present bills of lading with the wording "freight pre-paid" printed on their face. That requirement was unilaterally introduced by the buyers into the letter of credit and immediately explicitly rejected by the sellers who, nevertheless, remained silent vis-à-vis the subsequent insistence of the buyers.

On appeal, it was held that absent any special agreement, the sellers were entitled to see a conforming letter of credit in place before they began shipment of the goods, and that their obligation was to ship the contract goods on board the vessel provided by the buyers for carriage on whatever terms as to freight, and otherwise the buyers had agreed with the shipowners.

The sellers were expressly free of any obligation to pay freight and in the normal course they could not be sure before shipment that the shipowner would issue freight prepaid bills of lading, unless they were prepared if necessary to pay the amount of freight themselves or unless some other guaranteed payment mechanism was already in place.

12 *Cereal v ED&F* [2008] 1 Lloyd's Rep. 355, 358, 359.
13 *Glencore v Lorico* [1997] 2 Lloyd's Rep. 386.

It was abundantly clear that the buyers' own assurances could not be enough to serve as a guarantee to the sellers that "freight pre-paid" bills of lading would be issued when the shipment was complete; that would have meant that the security of a bank guarantee for the payment of the price under the letter of credit would dissolve.

Thus, the buyers' contention that the letter of credit terms were in conformity with the contract was contrary both to the underlying concept of the f.o.b. contract and to the essential commercial purpose of the letter of credit.

Indeed, the freight prepaid requirement, unless it was a term of the sale contract itself, was introduced by the buyers and immediately rejected by the sellers; the buyers maintained their requirement, and it was of the essence of their case that the sellers made no further reference to it before the contract came to an end.

The court found that sellers thereafter did not act inconsistently with their previous refusal, and their silence could not be regarded as an acceptance of the buyers' demand; the buyers could not allege that there was a fresh agreement as regards this term of the letter of credit which had the effect either of supplementing or varying the requirements of the sale contract.

Ultimately, the buyers were not entitled to require the sellers to procure and produce freight prepaid bills of lading in order to receive payment under the letter of credit opened by them; the buyers failed to open a letter of credit conforming with the sales contract and they were thereby in breach of contract. As put by Evans LJ:

> The first issue, therefore, is whether the buyers under a sale contract on what are described as normal f.o.b. terms are entitled to open a letter of credit which requires the sellers to present "freight pre-paid" bills of lading if they are to receive payment from the buyers' bank. Absent any special agreement, the sellers are entitled to see a conforming letter of credit in place before they begin shipment of the goods, and then their obligation is to ship the contract goods on board the vessel provided by the buyers, for carriage on whatever terms as to freight and otherwise the buyers have agreed with the shipowner. The sellers are expressly free of any obligation to pay freight (special terms apart, f.o.b. is the antithesis of c.&f. – cost and freight) and in the normal course they cannot be sure before shipment that the shipowner will issue freight pre-paid bills of lading, unless they are prepared if necessary to pay the amount of freight themselves, or unless some other guaranteed payment mechanism is already in place. I would put the matter broadly in that way, because it may be that an undertaking from the shipowner himself, or a third party guarantee of the payment of freight following due shipment of the goods, would suffice. It is unnecessary to consider that aspect further in the present case, because all that was offered by the buyers was their own assurance that the freight would be paid, by them or on their behalf. It is abundantly clear, in my judgment, that the buyers' own assurance cannot be enough to serve as a guarantee to the sellers that "freight pre-paid" bills of lading will be issued when shipment is complete. That would mean, as the Judge pointed out, that the security of a bank guarantee for the payment of the price, which is what the letter of credit mechanism provides, would be destroyed. I therefore agree with the Judge's observations that the buyers' contention, that the letter of credit terms were in conformity with the contract, is contrary both to the underlying concept of the f.o.b. contract (subject always to what special terms may be agreed in a particular case) and to the essential commercial purpose of the letter of credit machinery.
>
> [. . .] It is a long established rule of law that a contracting party, who, after he has become entitled to refuse performance of his contractual obligations, gives a wrong reason for his refusal, does not thereby deprive himself of a justification which in fact

> existed, whether he was aware of it or not . . . [per Mr. Justice Greer in *Taylor v Oakes, Roncoroni & Co.* (1922) 127 L.T. 267 at p. 269].
>
> The buyers' duty was to open a conforming letter of credit by the beginning of the shipment period (this is the prima facie rule: *Ian Stach Ltd. v Baker Bosley Ltd.* [1958] 2 Q.B. 130). Under the sale contract as varied, therefore, they were required to do this by Apr. 1. The sellers demanded a price increase and insisted on more onerous payment terms on that day. Undoubtedly, the buyers were entitled to regard this demand as a refusal by the sellers to ship goods on the contract terms. They contend, however, that the sellers . . . did not convey any acceptance of a termination. It made an extra contractual demand based on a false premise (that the vessel was late) (Skeleton argument par. 4.2) . . . and that if the sellers had specified the letter of credit defect as a reason for their attitude, then they would or might have been able to dispense with the freight pre-paid requirement, after making some further arrangements with the receivers. The correct legal analysis, Mr. Havelock-Allan submits, is that the contract remained in existence after Apr. 1, because it was not terminated; the sellers waived the buyers' breach, or alternatively they extended the time within which the buyers might open a conforming letter of credit; therefore, they could or might still have remedied the defect, if it had been relied upon by the sellers in their message of Apr. 1.
>
> Mr. Justice Longmore rejected this submission, on the ground that a contractual letter of credit had to be in place . . . strictly before the first day for shipment . . . In fact, therefore, the buyers could not have put the position right at the time when the point could have been but was not taken. He also said, however, that . . . the refusal to perform was as early as 1st. April, or (perhaps more likely) when the sellers took no steps to conform to the requirement of the buyers' solicitors letter on or about 6th. April.[14]

It appears clear from *Glencore v Lorico* that the initial explicit refusal of the sellers of the new conditions of the letter of credit unilaterally modified by the seller was crucial in determining the rejection by the seller of the new conditions.

The sellers' subsequent silence vis-à-vis the buyer's insistence of presentation of bills of lading carrying the wording "freight pre-paid" was considered consistent with their initial rejection of the unilaterally amended terms of the letter of credit.

This appears to suggest that a tacit response of a seller to a unilaterally modified letter of credit by the buyer could be interpreted by the court as an implicit acceptance of the new terms.

11.6 Non-explicit reaction of a seller to a modified letter of credit

Sellers have been taken to agree to a change in their documentary duties where they have failed to object to the letter of credit, and, shipped the goods.

In *Panoutsos v Hadley*,[15] a contract made in September for the sale and shipment of 4000 tons of flour, to be shipped to Greece not later than 7 November, provided that "each shipment shall be deemed a separate contract", and that payment should be "by confirmed bankers' credit". The buyer opened a bankers' credit which was not in fact "confirmed"; and the seller, with notice of that fact, made some shipments and received payment therefore by means of the credit, and

14 *Ibid.*, at 394, 395.

15 *Panoutsos v Hadley* [1917] 2 KB 475.

also obtained from the buyer an extension of time to 30 November for shipment of the balance of the flour. On 25 November the seller cancelled the contract as to the shipment of the balance of the flour, without any previous notice, upon the ground that the credit was not in accordance with the contract.

It was held by the court that the seller, by waiving for a time the breach of the condition as to a confirmed credit, was not thereby bound to act upon that credit up to the end of the contract, but that he was not entitled to cancel the contract without giving the buyer reasonable notice of his intention to cancel so as to give the buyer an opportunity of complying with the condition.

As put, on appeal, by Viscount Reading CJ:

> The question put to the Court is "whether or not upon the above findings of fact" – to which must now be added "coupled with our findings of fact" – there was any evidence upon which the arbitrators could properly find that the sellers had waived the term in the contract that payment should be by "confirmed bankers' credit." It was therefore admitted that there was no confirmed bankers' credit, but the buyer contended that there had been a waiver of that condition of the contract. In answer to that the sellers said that there had been no such waiver, and if there had been a waiver that they were entitled at any time to insist upon the condition being performed. The buyer replied that no doubt the sellers were entitled to insist upon the performance of the condition, but that, having waived its performance hitherto, they must give reasonable notice to the buyer of their intention to insist upon its performance in the future so as to give him an opportunity of putting the credit right. Bailhache J. held that the sellers must be taken to have waived the performance of the condition, that the buyer was entitled to reasonable notice, and that such notice had not in fact been given. He therefore answered the question in favour of the buyer.
>
> In my opinion the learned judge was right. It is open to a party to a contract to waive a condition which is inserted for his benefit. If the sellers chose to ship without the safeguard of a confirmed bankers' credit, they were entitled to do so, and the buyer performed the contract by paying for the goods shipped, though there was no confirmed bankers' credit, inasmuch as that condition had been waived. If at a later stage the sellers wished to avail there was no confirmed bankers' credit, in as much as that conditions themselves of the condition precedent, in my opinion there was objective justification in the facts to prevent them from demanding the performance condition if they had given reasonable notice to the buyer that they would not ship unless there was a confirmed bankers' credit. If they had done that and the buyer had failed to comply with the condition, the buyer would have been in default, and the sellers would have been entitled to cancel the contract without being subject to any claim by the buyer for damages.
>
> In *Bentsen v Taylor, Sons & Co.* (I) Bowen L.J. stated the law as to waiver thus: "Did the defendants by their acts or conduct lead the plaintiff reasonably to suppose that they did not intend to treat the contract for the future as at an end, on account of the failure to perform the condition precedent?" Reading sellers for defendants and buyer for plaintiff in that passage, it applies exactly to the present case. The sellers did lead the buyer to think so, and when they intended to change that position it was incumbent on them to give reasonable notice of that intention to the buyer so as to enable him to comply with the condition which up to that time had been waived.
>
> The case of *In re Tyrer & Co. and Hessler & Co.* (2) was cited as an authority for the proposition that the moment the sellers chose to avail themselves of the failure to perform the condition precedent they could put an end to the contract without giving the buyer an opportunity of remedying the default which had hitherto been waived. That case is not an authority for that proposition. It shows that, where there are stipulated times in a charterparty for payment of the hire of a ship and a power to withdraw the ship if the payment is not made at the stipulated time, the mere fact

> that there has been default in payment at one or more stipulated times, of which advantage has not been taken, does not entitle the party in default at a subsequent time to a notice so as to enable him to comply with the condition before the right to withdraw arises. That is a totally different case from the present. I cannot find any authority to support the proposition that, when one party has led another to believe that he may continue in a certain course of conduct without any risk of the contract being cancelled, the first-mentioned party can cancel the contract without giving any notice to the other so as to enable the latter to comply with the requirement of the contract. It seems to me to follow from the observations of Bowen L.J. in *Bentsen v Taylor, Sons & Co.* (1) that there must be reasonable notice given to the buyer before the sellers can take advantage of the failure to provide a confirmed bankers' credit. That is the decision of Bailhache J.
>
> The only question which remains is whether reasonable notice has been given. We have more material before us than Bailhache J. had when he came to the conclusion that no reasonable notice had been given. 1 am not prepared to draw the inference of fact that reasonable notice had been given before the sellers cancelled the contract. If notice had been given on October 27, and on November 25 the sellers had cancelled the contract, I should have thought that that would have been ample notice to enable the buyer to provide the confirmed credit in New York. But I cannot find any such notice on the part of the sellers of their intention to insist upon the performance of the condition. [His Lordship referred to the letters, and said that the conclusion he came to was that the sellers were content to make shipments upon the credit opened on October 16, which they knew from the letter of that date was not a confirmed bankers' credit, until they determined to cancel, which they did on November 25 without giving reasonable notice of their intention to cancel.]
>
> The result is that the decision of Bailhache J. is right, and the appeal must be dismissed.[16]

A similar fate would be incurred by a seller if, instead of reacting explicitly vis-à-vis the unilateral modifications of the letter of credit done by a buyer, he were to put forward an unrelated request to the buyer, such as an extension of shipment period.

This is what happened in the *Enrico Furst v Fischer*,[17] where a contract for the sale of cast iron piping, f.o.b. London, provided for credit to be opened immediately in London for 70 per cent by a confirming bank.

Contrary to what was established in the sales contract, the credit was just "advised" by an advising bank in London and not confirmed. This entailed that the sellers never received any undertaking promising payment vis-à-vis the tender of documents by the bank based in London, as per the original arrangements made in the sales contract.

The sellers were late in shipping the goods and, rather than rejecting the unilateral modification of the credit made by the seller, they asked for an extension of the shipping time.

The court found that the buyers were in breach in that the credit did not comply with the contract terms because it was not opened in London or irrevocable in London; nevertheless, the sellers treated it as valid in its nature and requested an extension.

16 *Panoutsos v Hadley* [1917] 2 KB 475, 477, 478, 479.
17 *Enrico Furst v Fischer* [1960] 2 Lloyd's Rep. 340.

In the words of Diplock J:

> I hold that a letter of credit in this form did not comply with the contract. It was not an irrevocable letter of credit opened in London and payable in London, because, although irrevocable so far as Swiss-Israel Trade Bank was concerned, Westminster Bank, Ltd., did not add their confirmation, and could have resiled from the credit at any time. It seems to me that such a credit is not an irrevocable credit opened in London, and, in forming that view (which I should have done even without the assistance of expert evidence), I am confirmed by the expert evidence of the banking witnesses who were called before me for the plaintiffs themselves. It will be noted that in one other respect the credit did not comply with the terms of the contract, namely, so far as the weight certificate is concerned. It will also be noted that Westminster Bank, Ltd., had themselves added the words "S.S. Co's" before the words "Bills of Lading", although those words did not appear in the instructions which they had obtained from the Swiss-Israel Trade Bank.
>
> On receipt of the credit, the defendants wrote to the plaintiffs, on Mar. 20, complaining about it. They raised no point about its not having been confirmed by Westminster Bank, Ltd. and thus not complying (as I have held) with the terms of the contract in that respect. They did, however, ask for amendments to the terms of the credit, the relevant requests being, first, to amend the provision as to the weight certificate by substituting weight certificates by Cawood Wharton & Co., Ltd.; secondly, to amend the shipment date to April and the availability to May 10, the credit being for shipment "during March", and the availability being to Apr. 15; and, thirdly, they requested the plaintiffs to amend the provision as to bills of lading.
>
> [. . .] I have already held that the credit did not comply in its nature with the terms of the contract, because it was not opened in London or irrevocable in London. The plaintiffs say: "Nevertheless, even if that be so, the defendants waived their right to insist upon the credit complying strictly with the contract", and they rely upon the letters of Mar. 20 and 24, to which I have already referred. I have no doubt that the defendants, when they received the letter of credit, took no point on its not being "an irrevocable credit opened in London". They took plenty of points, but they did not take that one. They treated it as valid in its nature and requested the plaintiffs to extend it, which they did. No doubt the reason that they did not take any point about it is that, with a reputable bank like Swiss-Israel Trade Bank, it made no real commercial difference whether the Westminster Bank, Ltd., added their own undertaking or not.
>
> In those circumstances, subject to what I hope he will not mind me calling an ingenious argument put forward by Mr. MacCrindle, it seems to me to be a classic case of waiver, indistinguishable, indeed (without going into any more esoteric argument), from the decision in *Panoutsos v Raymond Hadley Corporation of New York* [1917] 2 K.B. 473. That was a case where the contract called for a "confirmed bankers' credit". An unconfirmed credit was opened, and the sellers, taking no point about it, shipped on the unconfirmed credit. Giving the judgment of the Court of Appeal – a very strong Court of Appeal, consisting of Viscount Reading, C.J., Lord Cozens-Hardy, M.R., and Lord Justice Scrutton – Viscount Reading said this (ibid., at p. 478):
>
> If the sellers chose to ship without the safeguard of a confirmed bankers' credit, they were entitled to do so, and the buyer performed his part of the contract by paying for the goods shipped, though there was no confirmed bankers' credit, inasmuch as that condition had been waived. If at a later stage the sellers wished to avail themselves of the condition precedent, in my opinion there was nothing in the facts to prevent them from demanding the performance of the condition if they had given reasonable notice to the buyer that they would not ship unless there was a confirmed bankers' credit. If they had done that and the buyer had failed to comply with the condition, the buyer would have been in default, and the sellers would have been entitled to cancel the contract without being subject to any claim by the buyer for damages.

In *Bentsen v Taylor, Sons & Co.* [1893] 2 Q.B. 274, at p. 283, Bowen L.J. stated the law as to waiver thus: "Did the defendants by their acts or conduct lead the plaintiff reasonably to suppose that they did not intend to treat the contract for the future as at an end, on account of the failure to perform the condition precedent?"

Then there is another passage which I should read (sup., at p. 479):

> I cannot find any authority to support the proposition that, when one party has led another to believe that he may continue in a certain course of conduct without any risk of the contract being cancelled, the first-mentioned party can cancel the contract without giving any notice to the other so as to enable the latter to comply with the requirement of the contract. It seems to me to follow from the observations of Bowen L.J. in *Bentsen v Taylor, Sons & Co.*, sup., that there must be reasonable notice given to the buyer before the sellers can take advantage of the failure to provide a confirmed bankers' credit.

If one substituted for the words "if the sellers chose to ship without the safeguard of a confirmed bankers' credit" the words "if the sellers chose to invite the buyers to amend at their own trouble and expense the credit without insisting upon it being confirmed", then, until they have given notice, they cannot rely upon the buyers' breach as a breach of condition of the contract.

Mr. MacCrindle, however, argues that any waiver created by the letter of Mar. 20 or Mar. 24, as to the character of the credit, was a conditional waiver. The defendants, he says, were offering to treat the contract as subsisting provided that three conditions were fulfilled: first, that the credit was extended (as it was); secondly, the provision as to weight notes was amended (as it was); and, thirdly, that the words "S.S. Co.'s" were eliminated, or, if the letter of May 24 had been included, further amendments were made in order to enable the defendants to charter. It matters not, he argues, that the defendants were not entitled under the contract itself to insist on the third condition; it was a condition of any waiver contained in those letters, and unless it is complied with, says Mr. MacCrindle, to the letter, the plaintiffs cannot rely upon waiver of the term as to the nature of the credit.

This argument, with great respect, seems to me to confuse waiver with variation of the terms of a contract. The letters on which the defendants rely do not purport to be an offer to vary the terms of the contract as respects the nature of the credit; they purport to treat the contract as still subsisting and to insist upon its fulfilment. In so far as their specific requirements were justified by the terms of the contract, they were complied with by the plaintiffs before the expiry of the delivery date.

Waiver does not vary the terms of the contract, as the many cases decided while Sect. 4 of the Sale of Goods Act, 1893, and the Statute of Frauds, 1677, were still in force show; see, for example, *Hickman v Haynes and Another* (1875) L.R. 10, C.P. 598, and *Besseler Waechter Glover & Co. v South Derwent Coal Company, Ltd.* [1938] 1 K.B. 408; (1937) 59 Ll.L.Rep. 104. Waiver is conduct on the part of a party to a contract which affects his remedies for a breach of contract by the other party. The general principle was laid down as long ago as 1888 by Lord Justice Bowen in *Birmingham and District Land Company v London and North Western Railway Company* (1888) 40 Ch.D. 268.

The classic passage, at p. 286, is this:

> The truth is that the proposition is wider than cases of forfeiture. It seems to me to amount to this that if persons who have contractual rights against others induce by their conduct those against whom they have such rights to believe that such rights will either not be enforced or will be kept in suspense or abeyance for some particular time, those persons will not be allowed by a Court of Equity to enforce the rights until such time has elapsed, without at all events placing the parties in the same position as they were before.

The proposition was, in its general form, stated again more recently in *Charles Rickards, Ltd. v Oppenhaim* [1950] 1 K.B. 616, at p. 623, where Lord Justice Denning said, after discussing the problems which arose as regards Sect. 4 of the Sale of Goods Act, 1893:

> If the defendant, as he did, led the plaintiffs to believe that he would not insist on the stipulation as to time, and that, if they carried out the work, he would accept it, and they did it, he could not afterwards set up the stipulation as to the time against them. Whether it be called waiver or forbearance on his part, or an agreed variation or substituted performance, does not matter. It is a kind of estoppel. By his conduct he evinced an intention to affect their legal relations. He made, in effect, a promise not to insist on his strict legal rights. That promise was intended to be acted on, and was in fact acted on. He cannot afterwards go back on it. I think not only that that follows from *Panoutsos v Raymond Hadley Corporation of New York* [1917] 2 K.B. 473, a decision of this Court, but that it was also anticipated in *Bruner v Moore* [1904] 1 Ch. 305. It is a particular application of the principle which I endeavoured to state in *Central London Property Trust, Ltd. v High Trees House, Ltd.* [1947] K.B. 130. For myself, I should prefer to say that, in relation to sale of goods, it was a particular application of Sect. 11 (1) (a) of the Act, which says:

(a) Where a contract of sale is subject to any condition to be fulfilled by the seller, the buyer may waive the condition, or may elect to treat the breach of such condition as a breach of warranty, and not as a ground for treating the contract as repudiated.

Where a buyer undertakes to open a credit of a particular kind by a specified time as in this case, the undertaking involves two separable parts: first, that he will open the credit of the particular kind, and, secondly, that he will do so by the specified time. If by his conduct the seller leads the buyer to suppose, and to act upon the supposition, that he, the seller, will not insist upon the opening of the credit within the specified time, he waives his right to treat the failure to open the credit within the specified time as a breach of condition entitling him to repudiate the contract, but he does not thereby waive his right to have the credit of the particular kind opened within a reasonable time, and to treat failure to open it as a breach of condition if it is not opened in a reasonable time.

What is a reasonable time, however, depends upon all the circumstances, including the conduct of the seller, and, if his conduct is such as to induce the buyer to suppose, and to act upon the supposition, that there is no urgency about performance of the obligation, then a reasonable time does not expire until the seller has given to the buyer reasonable notice of his intention to insist upon the performance of this part of his undertaking. Until that notice has been given and a reasonable time thereafter has elapsed, the seller cannot rely upon the breach of the undertaking to open the credit in the contractual form as a ground for treating the contract as repudiated, although he may treat it as a breach of warranty.

Consequently, if he himself, during that period, wrongfully repudiates the contract, it is not open to him to say: "All I have done is to elect to treat the buyers' repudiation of the contract as rescinding it", for he had no right to do that.

But, whether this is the correct analysis or not, it seems to me that the defendants, by calling for the amendment of the credit in respects other than the absence of any irrevocable undertaking by Westminster Bank, Ltd., itself to pay the drafts drawn under it, waived their right to treat the failure of the plaintiffs to fulfil their undertaking in this respect as a breach of condition until they had given the plaintiffs reasonable notice of their intention to do so.[18]

18 *Ibid.*, at 348, 349, 350.

In light of *Enrico Furst v Fischer*, in the case of unilateral modification of a letter of credit by a buyer, the reaction of a seller needs to be unequivocal and clearly voiced towards the rejection of the altered credit; any different request might be interpreted as an implicit acceptance of the alterations unilaterally made by the buyer.

A seller who tenders documents under previous instalments will find himself in a similar situation. In *Alan v El Nasr*,[19] two sales contracts for coffee beans provided for payment via letter of credit. The buyers resold the coffee to sub-buyers who opened an irrevocable letter of credit.

The letter of credit was expressed in terms of payment in sterling and did not conform with the contracts in a number of respects; but the sellers accepted the confirmation in those terms and began to operate the credit, asked for an extension of the date, and presented documents including invoices expressed in sterling against payment in sterling.

When the final 221 tons under the second contract had been loaded, the sellers prepared an invoice, again expressed in sterling, against payment of the price for the 221 tons; nevertheless, before they presented the documents, sterling was devalued.

The sellers thereafter claimed that Kenya shillings were the currency of account in the original contracts, and that the buyers were liable to pay an additional sum as dictated by the conversion rate of the new currency to be used instead of sterling.

On appeal, the Court of Appeal held that the money of account of the original contracts construed by their proper law was Kenya shillings, the decisive factor being the expression of the price in "shs.", an abbreviation appropriate to Kenya shillings but not to shillings in sterling currency.

Moreover, the court held that the sellers, by accepting payment under a sterling letter of credit, had irrevocably waived their right to be paid in Kenyan currency (or, according to Megaw LJ and Stephenson LJ, had accepted a variation of the sales contract) so that when the whole price had been paid under that letter of credit the buyers had discharged their whole contractual obligation and could not be required to pay more.

In the words of Lord Denning:

> In many cases – and our present case is one – the letter of credit does not conform. Then negotiations may take place as a result of which the letter of credit is modified so as to be satisfactory to the seller. Alternatively, the seller may be content to accept the letter of credit as satisfactory as it is, without modification. Once this happens, then the letter of credit is to be regarded as if it were a conforming letter of credit. It will rank accordingly as conditional payment.
>
> There are two cases on this subject. One is *Panoutsos v Raymond Hadley Corporation of New York* [1917] 2 K.B, 473; but the facts are only to be found fully set out in 22 Com.Cas. 207. The other is *Enrico Furst & Co. v W.E. Fischer Ltd.* [1960] 2 Lloyd's Rep. 340. In each of those cases the letter of credit did not conform to the contract of sale. In each case the non-conformity was in that it was not a confirmed credit. But the sellers took no objection to the letter of credit on that score. On the contrary, they asked for the letter of credit to be extended: and it was extended.

19 *Alan v El Nasr* [1972] 2 QB 189.

In each case the sellers sought afterwards to cancel the contract on the ground that the letter of credit was not in conformity with the contract. In each case the court held that they could not do so.

What is the true basis of those decisions? is it a variation of the original contract? or a waiver of the strict rights thereunder? or a pro- G promissory estoppel precluding the seller from insisting on his strict rights? or what else?

In Enrico Furst, Diplock J. said it was a "classic case of waiver."

I agree with him. It is an instance of the general principle which was first enunciated by Lord Cairns L.C. in *Hughes v Metropolitan Railway Co.* (1877) 2 App.Cas. 439, and rescued from oblivion by *Central London JJ Property Trust Ltd. v High Trees House Ltd.* [1947] K.B. 130. The principle is much wider than waiver itself: but waiver is a good instance of its application. The principle of waiver is simply this: If one party, by his conduct, leads another to believe that the strict rights arising under the contract will not be insisted upon, intending that the other should act on that belief, and he does act on it, then the first party will not afterwards be allowed to insist on the strict legal rights when it would be inequitable for him to do so: see *Plasticmoda Societa per Azioni v Davidsons (Manchester) Ltd.* [1952] 1 Lloyd's Rep. 527, 539. There may be no consideration moving from him who benefits by the waiver. There may be no detriment to him by acting on it. There may be nothing in writing. Nevertheless, the one who waives his strict rights cannot afterwards insist on them. His strict rights are at any rate suspended so long as the waiver lasts. He may on occasion be able to revert to his strict legal rights for the future by giving reasonable notice in that behalf, or otherwise making it plain by his conduct that he will thereafter insist upon them: *Tool Metal Manufacturing Co. Ltd. v Tungsten Electric Co. Ltd.* [1955] 1 W.L.R. 761. But there are cases where no withdrawal is possible. It may be too late to withdraw: or it cannot be done without injustice to the other party. In that event he is bound by his waiver. He will not be allowed to revert to his strict legal rights. He can only enforce them subject to the waiver he has made.

Instances of these principles are ready to hand in contracts for the sale of goods. A seller may, by his conduct, lead the buyer to believe that he is not insisting on the stipulated time for exercising an option: *Bruner v Moore* [1904] 1 Ch. 305. A buyer may, by requesting delivery, lead the seller to believe that he is not insisting on the contractual time for delivery: *Charles Rickards Ltd. v Oppenhaim* [1950] 1 K.B. 616, 621. A seller may, by his conduct, lead the buyer to believe that he will not insist on a confirmed letter of credit: *Plasticmoda* [1952] 1 Lloyd's Rep. 527, but will accept an unconfirmed one instead: *Panoustsos v Raymond Hadley Corporation of New York* [1917] 2 K.B. 473; *Enrico Furst & Co. v W.E. Fischer* [1960] 2 Lloyd's Rep. 340. A seller may accept a less sum for his goods than the contracted price, thus inducing him to believe that he will not enforce payment of the balance: *Central London Property Trust Ltd. v High Trees House Ltd.* [1947] K.B. 130 and *D. & C. Builders Ltd. v Rees* [1966] 2 Q.B. 617, 624. In none of these cases does the party who acts on the belief suffer any detriment. It is not a detriment, but a benefit to him, to have an extension of time or to pay less, or as the case may be. Nevertheless, he has conducted his affairs on the basis that he has that benefit and it would not be equitable now to deprive him of it.

The judge rejected this doctrine because, he said, "there is no evidence of the buyers having acted to their detriment." I know that it has been suggested in some quarters that there must be detriment. But I can find no support for it in the authorities cited by the judge. The nearest approach to it is the statement of Viscount Simonds in the *Tool Metal* case [1955] 1 W.L.R. 761, 764, that the other must have been led "to alter his position," which was adopted by Lord Hodson in *Ajayi v R.T. Briscoe (Nigeria) Ltd.* [1964] 1 W.L.R. 1326, 1330. But that only means that he must have been led to act differently from what he otherwise would have done. And if you study the cases in which the doctrine has been applied, you will see that all that is required is that the one should have "acted on the belief induced by the other party." That is how Lord Cohen put it in the *Tool Metal* case [1955] 1 W.L.R. 761, 799, and that is how I would put it myself.

> The judge also rejected the doctrine because of something which was said in the recent case of *Woodhouse A.C. Israel Cocoa Ltd. S.A. v Nigerian Produce Marketing Co. Ltd.* [1971] 2 Q.B. 23 about estoppel: but no question of waiver arose there: no question of letters of credit; or anything of that kind. It has no application here and neither counsel relied in any way upon it before us.
>
> [. . .] Applying the principle here, it seems to me that the sellers, by their conduct, waived the right to have payment by means of a letter of credit in Kenyan currency and accepted instead a letter of credit in sterling. It was, when given, conditional payment, with the result that, on being duly honoured (as it was), the payment was no longer conditional. It became absolute, and dated back to the time when the letter of credit was given and acted upon. The sellers have, therefore, received payment of the price and cannot recover more.[20]

Per curiam, the effect on the buyer's liability of establishing a confirmed irrevocable letter of credit depends on the terms of the particular sales contract. On the present facts (according to Megaw LJ, even if there had been no variation or waiver), once the letter of credit was opened by the buyers and accepted by the sellers through the bank, it operated as a conditional discharge of the buyers' obligation to pay the price; and when the payment was actually made under it the buyers were wholly discharged from their contractual obligation.

According to Lord Denning MR, where a contract of sale stipulates for payment by confirmed irrevocable letter of credit, the letter when given and accepted (a) does not operate as absolute payment unless the seller so stipulates; (b) does operate as a conditional payment of the price analogous to the giving of a bill of exchange or a cheque; and (c) is not merely a mode of payment.

Where one party to a contract has by his conduct induced the other party to believe that he will not insist on his strict legal rights under the contract, the party who has waived his rights cannot afterwards insist on them if the other party has acted on that belief differently from the way in which he would otherwise have acted. It is not necessary for the other party to show that he has acted to his detriment.

A similar fate is to await a seller who objects to some defects but not to others. This is what happened in *Ficom v Sociedad Cadex*,[21] where a sales contract for Bolivian coffee provided for payment via letter of credit, whose original terms had been modified by the buyers in relation to the destination of the goods, the extension of the shipment period, and the quality certificate.

The sellers advised the buyers that they would accept the first two aforementioned amendments, but would not agree to the third as "it was not agreed initially".

When the sellers presented the documents for drawing under the letter of credit, including the quality certificate, they were refused payment under the letter of credit, since the documents did not conform to the documents required under the letter of credit in a number of respects and particularly in relation to the quality certificate.

The court held that, on the authorities, parties to a contract of sale under which payment was to be made by means of a letter of credit could, by subsequently

20 *Ibid.*, at 213, 214.

21 *Ficom v Sociedad Cadex* [1980] 2 Lloyd's Rep. 118.

agreeing to terms of the letter of credit which differed from those specified in the sales contract, thereby vary their contractual obligations under the sales contract.[22]

The terms of the letter of credit as opened by the buyers through the confirming bank were agreed by the parties, and that agreement was a binding agreement on the parties, although it was difficult to reconcile the letter of credit, as it appeared to contemplate that defects in quality should not give rise to a right of rejection while the letter of credit contemplated that there might be rejection of the documents if the quality certificate was not in accordance with the documents required for presentation under the letter of credit; such inconsistency did not of itself detract from the binding effect of the letter of credit.

The agreement so made was supported by consideration in that since the sales contract was silent as to the terms of the letter of credit contemplated by the sales contract, the definition of these terms was a matter of mutual benefit, and acceptance of the terms by each party was therefore supported by consideration moving from the other.

Consequently, the letter of credit as established was binding, once accepted, on both parties, and the sellers could only draw on the letter of credit if they tendered a quality certificate in accordance with the requirements of the letter of credit; they were unable to do so, and the buyers were therefore entitled to bring the contract to an end.

As put by Robert Goff J:

> In the present case, I am concerned with a contract of sale in which the terms of the letter of credit – and in particular of the documents to be presented under the letter of credit – were undefined in the sale contract. Now, in such a case, it is a commonplace that a letter of credit will be opened thereafter – sometimes preceded by a pre-advice by the buyer of the terms of the proposed credit followed by detailed negotiations of the terms so proposed – resulting in a letter of credit being issued in precise terms acceptable to both parties. Often the letter of credit so agreed will take the form which is usually employed in the particular trade. Now, although it is impossible to formulate any general rule, in such a case the terms of the letter of credit so agreed may well become binding contractually upon the parties. If so, and if they depart in any respect from the terms (express or implied) of the original sale contract, they will constitute a binding variation of that contract: if they simply fill a gap in the original sale contract, then they will operate to supplement that contract. It is of importance to the parties that the terms of the letter of credit, if so agreed by them, should become binding, because on that basis the buyer will enter into a binding arrangement with his own bank, which in turn will enter into a binding arrangement with the issuing bank instructed to issue the letter of credit to the seller, the terms of which will in their turn become binding as between the issuing bank and the seller. An example of a case in which such a binding variation of a sale contract was entered into is the case of *Alan v El Nasr*, to which I have previously referred; I refer in particular to the judgment of Lord Justice Megaw in that case at pp. 327 and 217–218 of the respective reports.
>
> Such a case may be contrasted with a case where the letter of credit established departs in some particular respect from the terms required by the sale contract, and the sellers forbear from insisting upon precise compliance with the terms of the sale

22 A somewhat similar case might arise where the sale contract did not define the terms of the proposed letter of credit so that the letter of credit, as subsequently agreed, might fill the contractual gap and so supplement the terms of the sale contract, as was the case here.

> contract in that particular respect. In such a case, particularly where the quality should not give rise to a right of rejection but rather should be dealt with by way of an allowance against the price; whereas the letter of credit, as opened, contemplates that there may be a rejection of the documents, and so no right to payment, if the quality certificate was not in accordance with the documents required for presentation under the letter of credit. But such an inconsistency does from time to time occur where there is a contract of sale under which payment is to be made by letter of credit (for an example, which was referred to me in the course of this argument, see *The Hansa Nord*, [1975] 2 Lloyd's Rep. 445); and the mere fact that inconsistency of this kind does occur does not of itself detract from the binding effect of the letter of credit. The fact is, in my judgment, that in the present case the parties supplemented the silent agreement by defining the terms of the letter of credit, even though they did so in terms which were in certain respects inconsistent with the original sale contract; having done so, in my judgment the letter of credit became binding upon the parties. The matter goes beyond a mere equitable estoppel; there was an offer by the buyers of a letter of credit in specified terms, and that offer was accepted by the sellers, in circumstances where the parties intended that those terms, once accepted, should be mutually binding upon them.
>
> Lastly, I am satisfied that the agreement so made was supported by a consideration. Mr. Donaldson submitted that that was not so. The foundation of his submission was that the addition of the requirement of the quality certificate went beyond what was required by normal trade custom, and was solely for the benefit of the buyers; accordingly, he submitted, consideration was not furnished for that requirement. I do not think that is right. Where, as here, the sale contract is silent as to the terms of the letter of credit contemplated by the sale contract, the definition of those terms is a matter of mutual benefit and acceptance of the terms by each party is therefore supported by consideration moving from the other. In my judgment it is not possible in such a case to isolate one particular facet of the terms so agreed and to argue that that particular term was for the benefit of one party only and so unsupported by consideration moving from the other. I therefore reject Mr. Donaldson's submission that the buyer's argument founders for want of consideration.
>
> My conclusion is that the letter of credit as established was binding, once accepted, on both parties. It follows that the sellers could only draw on the letter of credit if they tendered a quality certificate in accordance with the requirements of the letter of credit so established. That, it is plain, they were unable to do.[23]

A seller facing a modified letter of credit is, in light of the aforementioned authorities, best advised to unequivocally and explicitly react vis-à-vis the amended credit. Failure to do so will entail the seller complying with the newly established obligations.

11.7 Unclear letters of credit

Letters of credit may often be, in practice, unclear in regard to the documentary requirements therein enshrined. By way of example, let us consider a scenario whereby the sales contract does not enlist a specific document to be presented under the credit, but the document is thereafter required by the letter of credit.

For instance, what if the sales contract fails to mention tender of a quality certificate which is then required under the letter of credit? This is what happened in *Newman Industries v Indo-British Industries*,[24] where the letter of credit opened by

23 *Ibid*., at 132, 133.

24 *Newman Industries v Indo-British Industries* [1956] 2 Lloyd's Rep. 219.

the buyer for the sale of a second hand generator required a certificate of guarantee of satisfactory performance initially not accounted for in the sales contract.

According to the court, the contract did not contain, nor was intended to contain, a guarantee for future performance, and the attempted introduction of such a guarantee came too late to be incorporated as a new term.

As held by Sellers J:

> That guarantee, I am satisfied, was the guarantee which was referred to in the tender, namely, that the unit would be "completely stripped, overhauled and tested." There was some oral evidence that prior to this tender in February there had been some conversation between Mr. Chaudhury, a representative of the third parties who was over in London, Mr. J. Reynolds, of the defendants, and a representative of the plaintiffs, and that some mention was then made of a guarantee. I accept that there was some mention of a guarantee, but it was in the terms of or to the effect of, that which appeared in the plaintiffs' tender when that was sent to the defendants. I am perfectly satisfied from all the documents in this case and the evidence I have heard that there was no suggestion in those early days of the plaintiffs giving any guarantee for future performance in respect of this second-hand plant. I accept that they would not have given one. It was not their practice or intention, and any reliance which has been sought to be placed in this case upon such a conversation, by the defendants or the third parties, is not acceptable.
>
> [. . .] There is no indication there of any guarantee given by the plaintiffs for the future performance of the goods sold, and I can say now that the effort which was made to attach to this bargain which was being negotiated between the parties any standard conditions of sale which were customary in the trade must on the facts wholly fail. The evidence which was given in support did not establish the attitude which was taken up, that there were such things in the trade as standard conditions with regard to guarantees for the future; but even if there were, that printed statement of the conditions, referred to expressly by the last part of the letter acknowledging the order sent by the plaintiffs, would entirely negative any such implication in this particular contract.
>
> [. . .] Nowhere had a term been indicated before as to a guarantee for any period in the future. Now there was a request for "at least 12 months from date of installation," and I am satisfied it was that requirement, so stated by the third parties, coming at that stage after the defendants had concluded their transactions with the plaintiffs, which placed Mr. Reynolds, who was acting for the most part on behalf of the defendants, in the difficulty from which he never found a way of extricating himself in a business sense, although I think abundant opportunity presented itself so to do.
>
> [. . .] That, in very prolonged outline (a course which I thought to be necessary) is the material on which this case has to be decided, and I have come to the conclusion, on that material, that the documents relied on by the plaintiffs in the statement of claim, as amended, do constitute a contract for the sale of this generator set between the plaintiffs and the defendants and that it contains no guarantee for future performance. I also hold that there was a similar contract between the defendants and the third parties with no guarantee for future performance on the documents relied on by the defendants in their statement of claim against the third parties.
>
> Assuming that I am wrong about that, and that the letter of credit of May 4 ought also to be taken into account as a contractual document, it makes no difference, in my view, as to the contract for the sale of the goods. It is true I had no application before me to rectify that document, but it is clear, accepting the terms used in the letter of credit with regard to the guarantee, that there was no intention in the minds of anybody, plaintiffs, defendants or third parties, to give any guarantee for future performance. That clause in the letter of credit related only to that which had been promised throughout from the first tender, namely, a guarantee as to the performance on test and trial after overhaul, and it would be nothing but unjust to use that unfortunate clause to invoke

> any other interpretation. The indent which the third parties sent after they had effected the contract with the defendants, who then had themselves contracted with Newman's, came too late, unless the parties were agreeable, to incorporate a new term into the bargain. The effect of what was done by the defendants, in my view, was to endeavour, on behalf of the third parties, to get this extra and additional guarantee, this guarantee for future performance. They never succeeded in doing it before the date arrived for the delivery of the documents to them, although they got something going a very long way towards it afterwards. It was still not accepted by the plaintiffs as a contractual obligation and it was not a contractual obligation of the bargain as originally made. That is the view I have formed about the method which Mr. Reynolds adopted in advancing his request to the plaintiffs as revealed in the subsequent correspondence which took place. I therefore find, as I have said, that there was a contract of sale on f.o.b. terms between the plaintiffs and the defendants and likewise between the defendants and the third parties, which again, I think, was on f.o.b. terms with additional terms thereto which do not alter the nature of the transaction, in my view.[25]

In case a new documentary requirement is added in the credit by the buyer, it is clear from *Newman Industries v Indo-British Industries* that the answer as to whether or not the buyer is in breach of his contract of sale depends on whether or not there was a course of dealing between the parties; and on whether or not there is a recognised trade practice regarding the document now required by the buyer through the letter of credit.

A different scenario could see a seller tendering documents mentioned neither in the sale nor in the credit. This scenario poses problems if the "extra" document shows up an inconsistency in other documents.

The UCP 600 lays down the conditions for banks to assess the presentation of documents by the seller within the context of letters of credit. Banks' responsibilities consist of the determination of compliance of the documents tendered by the seller (with the relevant time limits), and of specific obligations in case of refusal to honour the credit when there are discrepancies between the tender of documents and the credit. We shall consider such obligations in turn in the following.

11.8 Banks' responsibilities when documents are tendered for payment

Within the context of documentary credits, a bank's basic duty is to examine documents on their face for a complying presentation, as per Article 14(a) UCP 600, which imposes on banks a duty to examine documents in order to:

> **Article 14(a) UCP 600**
>
> determine, on the basis of the documents alone, whether or not the documents appear on their face to constitute a complying presentation.

Compliance is of the utmost importance as payment is only made by banks vis-à-vis a complying presentation.

25 *Ibid.*, at 229, 230, 234.

The banks' obligations do not, as will be readily appreciated, amount to much. A whole cluster of articles in the UCP 600 ensure that banks will look only at the documents and not beyond them.

To this end, Article 34 UCP 600 contains a specific disclaimer on the effectiveness of documents as follows:

> **Article 34 UCP 600**
>
> A bank assumes no liability or responsibility for the form, sufficiency, accuracy, genuineness, falsification or legal effect of any document, or for the general or particular conditions stipulated in a document or superimposed thereon; nor does it assume any liability or responsibility for the description, quantity, weight, quality, condition, packing, delivery, value or existence of the goods, services or other performance represented by any document, or for the good faith or acts or omissions, solvency, performance or standing of the consignor, the carrier, the forwarder, the consignee or the insurer of the goods or any other person.[26]

According to Article 34, banks are relieved of any concerns about accuracy, genuineness, and falsification of documents; this entails that banks are not saddled with any concerns of falsification or forgery of documents by the seller. Their duty is to examine the documents on their face in order to determine compliance with the credit.

It has been correctly noted that Articles 14 and 34 of the UCP 600 represent significant changes in terms of banks' duties compared to the previous versions of the UCP 600.[27]

Indeed, under the UCP 500, banks were subject to the duty to examine the documents stipulated in the credit with reasonable care in order to ascertain whether or not the documents appeared on their face to constitute a complying presentation.[28]

The qualification of "reasonable care" had been the object of much debate, and some guidance re the definition of that proposition can be found in *Kredietbank Antwerp v Midland Bank plc.*[29]

> The professional expertise of a trading bank includes knowledge of the UCP rules and of their practical application. This necessarily involves a degree of judgment, and for this reason the administrative task of checking whether documents conform with the requirements of the credit is supervised by experienced senior managers to whom problems are taken and by whom decisions are made.[30]

Under the current status quo as established by the UCP 600, the standard benchmarks for banks' examination of documents is just the determination of compliance solely on the basis of what appears on the face of the documents tendered by the seller.

26 See Jack's *Documentary Credits*, 2009, Tottel, p. 170.
27 *Ibid.*
28 See Article 13 UCP 500.
29 *Kredietbank Antwerp v Midland Bank plc.* [1999] CLC 1108.
30 *Ibid.*, at 1110.

11.9 The principle of autonomy of documentary credits

The principle of autonomy of documentary credit is enshrined in Article 4 of the UCP 600.

Article 4 UCP 600 Credits v. contracts

> a. A credit by its nature is a separate transaction from the sale or other contract on which it may be based. Banks are in no way concerned with or bound by such contract, even if any reference whatsoever to it is included in the credit. Consequently, the undertaking of a bank to honour, to negotiate or to fulfil any other obligation under the credit is not subject to claims or defences by the applicant resulting from its relationships with the issuing bank or the beneficiary.
>
> A beneficiary can in no case avail itself of the contractual relationships existing between banks or between the applicant and the issuing bank.
>
> b. An issuing bank should discourage any attempt by the applicant to include, as an integral part of the credit, copies of the underlying contract, proforma invoice and the like.

Banks are, thus, not required to familiarise themselves with any of the infinitely various terms, conventions, or esoteric understandings of the sales transactions themselves: their role is limited to the demanding, but essentially clerical, task of scrutinising the documents tendered under the credit to establish that they conform to the terms of the credit.[31]

As Lord Diplock said in *Commercial Banking Company of Sydney Ltd v Jalsard Pty Ltd*:[32]

> The banker is not concerned as to whether the documents for which the buyer has stipulated serve any useful commercial purpose or as to why the customer called for tender of a document of a particular description. Both the issuing banker and his correspondent bank have to make decisions as to whether a document which has been tendered by the seller complies with the requirements of a credit.[33]

An early illustration of the principle of autonomy of documentary credit arose in *Urquhart, Lindsay & Co Ltd v Eastern Bank Ltd.*[34] Here, the sellers entered into a contract with the buyers in Calcutta to manufacture and ship machinery by instalments over several months at agreed prices, but subject to a stipulation that, should the cost of labour or wages increase, there should be a corresponding increase in the purchase price.

The buyers were also to open a "confirmed irrevocable credit" in favour of the plaintiffs with a bank in England, and to pay for each shipment as it took place. In pursuance of this arrangement, the defendants, who were the buyers' bankers in London, wrote to the sellers stating that they would pay bills drawn on the buyers to the extent of £70,000, the bills to be accompanied by documents and to be received before 14 April 1921, "this to be considered a confirmed irrevocable credit".

---

31 *Glencore International AG v Bank of China* [1996] CLC 95 112 A-C.
32 *Commercial Banking Company of Sydney Ltd v Jalsard Pty Ltd* [1973] AC 279, 286.
33 *Ibid.*
34 *Urquhart, Lindsay & Co Ltd v Eastern Bank Ltd* [1922] 1 KB 318.

The sellers shipped two instalments under the contract and received payment under the letter of credit. The buyers then found that the invoices included an increase in the purchase price on account of wages and materials, and instructed the defendants only to pay so much of the next invoices as represented the original prices.

The bank accordingly refused to pay the bill presented on the next shipment and the sellers then cancelled the contract, claiming damages from the bank as on a repudiation by the buyers

The court held that, the credit being irrevocable, the refusal of the defendants to take and pay for the particular bills on presentation of the proper documents constituted a repudiation of the contract as a whole, and that the sellers were entitled to damages so reckoned.

In the words of Rowlatt J:

> In my view the defendants committed a breach of their contract with the plaintiffs when they refused to pay the amount of the invoices as presented. Mr. Stuart Bevan contended that the letter of credit must be taken to incorporate the contract between the plaintiffs and their buyers; and that according to the true meaning of that contract the amount of any increase claimed in respect of an alleged advance in manufacturing costs was not to be included in any invoice to be presented under the letter of credit, but was to be the subject of subsequent independent adjustment. The answer to this is that the defendants undertook to pay the amount of invoices for machinery without qualification, the basis of this form of banking facility being that the buyer is taken for the purposes of all questions between himself and his banker or between his banker and the seller to be content to accept the invoices of the seller as correct. It seems to me that so far from the letter of credit being qualified by the contract of sale, the latter must accommodate itself to the letter of credit. The buyer having authorized his banker to undertake to pay the amount of the invoice as presented, it follows that any adjustment must be made by way of refund by the seller, and not by way of retention by the buyer.[35]

Similarly, another legal paradigm for the autonomy of credits can be found in *Westpac Banking Corpn v South Carolina National Bank*,[36] where the Privy Council held that it was erroneous for the court below to consider the circumstances under which a bill of lading was issued, rather than confine its legal analysis to the documents alone.

As put by Lord Goff of Chievely:

> Their Lordships approach the matter as follows. First, they are unable to accept the proposition that the words "Shipped on Board" make the bill internally inconsistent. True it is that the bill is on a "received for shipment" form and for that reason refers to Columbus America as the intended vessel; but there is nothing inconsistent in a document which states that the specified goods have been received for shipment on board a named vessel and have in fact been shipped on board that vessel. Their Lordships feel bound to say, with all respect, that the majority of the Court of Appeal fell into error in their approach to the construction of the bill of lading. For, as appears from the judgment of Mr. Justice Priestley, he went beyond the terms of the document itself and sought to draw inferences of fact as to what had occurred at the time when the document was issued. In particular, he inferred that the bill of lading was

35 *Ibid.*, at 322.
36 *Westpac Banking Corpn v South Carolina National Bank* [1986] 1 Lloyd's Rep. 311.

> in fact the receipt which was issued for the goods received at Sydney, and that it was in fact so issued at the time when those goods were so received. In their Lordships' view there was no sufficient basis for either inference. Some other more informal receipt may have been provided by the agents at Sydney at the time when the goods were received there, to be replaced later by the bill of lading issued at Newcastle; and in any event the bill of lading may have been signed and issued at Newcastle at some date after the date of the receipt of the goods at Sydney. Be that as it may, it is well settled that a bank which issues a letter of credit is concerned with the form of the documents presented to it, and not with the underlying facts. It forms no part of the bank's function, when considering whether to pay against the documents presented to it, to speculate about the underlying facts. For that reason, the Court of Appeal erred in approaching the problem by seeking to draw the inferences of fact to which their Lordships have referred.[37]

The principle of autonomy of documentary credits was further emphasised by Lord Diplock in his seminal decision in *United City Merchants (investments) Ltd v Royal Bank of Canada*. In his words:

> So the point falls to be decided by reference to first principles as to the legal nature of the contractual obligations assumed by the various parties to a transaction consisting of an international sale of goods to be financed by means of a confirmed irrevocable documentary credit. It is trite law that there are four autonomous though interconnected contractual relationships involved. (1) The underlying contract for the sale of goods, to which the only parties are the buyer and the seller; (2) the contract between the buyer and the issuing bank under which the latter agrees to issue the credit and either itself or through a confirming bank to notify the credit to the seller and to make payments to or to the order of the seller (or to pay, accept or negotiate bills of exchange drawn by the seller) against presentation of stipulated documents; and the buyer agrees to reimburse the issuing bank for payments made under the credit. For such reimbursement the stipulated documents, if they include a document of title such as a bill of lading, constitute a security available to the issuing bank; (3) if payment is to be made through a confirming bank the contract between the issuing bank and the confirming bank authorizing and requiring the latter to make such payments and to remit the stipulated documents to the issuing bank when they are received, the issuing bank in turn agreeing to reimburse the confirming bank for payments made under the credit; (4) the contract between the confirming bank and the seller under which the confirming bank undertakes to pay to the seller (or to accept or negotiate without recourse to drawer bills of exchange drawn by him) up to the amount of the credit against presentation of the stipulated documents.
>
> Again, it is trite law that in contract (4), with which alone the instant appeal is directly concerned, the parties to it, the seller and the confirming bank, "deal in documents and not in goods", as art. 8 of the Uniform Customs puts it. If, on their face, the documents presented to the confirming bank by the seller conform with the requirements of the credit as notified to him by the confirming bank, that bank is under a contractual obligation to the seller to honour the credit, notwithstanding that the bank has knowledge that the seller at the time of presentation of the conforming documents is alleged by the buyer to have, and in fact has already, committed a breach of his contract with the buyer for the sale of the goods to which the documents appear on their face to relate, that would have entitled the buyer to treat the contract of sale as rescinded and to reject the goods and refuse to pay the seller the purchase price. The whole commercial purpose for which the system of confirmed irrevocable documentary credits has been developed in international trade is to give to the seller an assured

37 *Ibid.*, at 315.

right to be paid before he parts with control of the goods that does not permit of any dispute with the buyer as to the performance of the contract of sale being used as a ground for non-payment or reduction or deferment of payment.[38]

Similarly, banks are also not concerned with goods or trade practices. This can be evinced by Article 5 of the UCP 600.

Article 5 UCP 600 Documents v. goods, services or performance

Banks deal with documents and not with goods, services or performance to which the documents may relate.

Trade practices of the commodity concerned are, in particular, of no concern to the banks in deciding whether or not to accept the documents.

In *Rayner v Hambro's Bank*,[39] a bank received instructions from a customer to open a confirmed credit in favour of the plaintiffs covering a cargo of "Coromandel groundnuts." The bank opened the credit and notified the plaintiffs that it was available against the invoice and bills of lading for "Coromandel groundnuts." The plaintiffs presented bills of lading for "machine-shelled groundnut kernels" accompanied by an invoice for "Coromandel groundnuts." The bank refused payment, and the plaintiffs sued them for breach of the undertaking in the letter of credit. Evidence was accepted by Atkinson J that "machine-shelled groundnut kernels" were, and were universally understood in the trade to be, identical with "Coromandel groundnuts". He gave judgment for the plaintiffs, and the bank appealed.

It was held, reversing the judgment of Atkinson J, that where the customer of a bank instructs the bank to open a credit, the bank acts at its peril if it departs from the precise terms of the mandate, and that, therefore, the action failed.

As held by Mackinnon J:

The legal result of a banker issuing a letter of credit has been considered in various cases to which I do not think it is necessary to refer, but two passages which have been mentioned by Goddard L.J., seem to me to sum up the position in general terms with the greatest accuracy. In *English, Scottish and Australian Bank, Ld. v Bank of South Africa*, Bailhache J. said: "It is elementary to say that a person who ships in reliance on a letter of credit must do so in exact compliance with its terms. It is also elementary to say that a bank is not bound or indeed entitled to honour drafts presented to it under a letter of credit unless those drafts with the accompanying documents are in strict accord with the credit as opened." And Lord Sumner in *Equitable Trust Co. of New York v Dawson Partners, Ld.* said: "It is both common ground and common sense that in such a transaction the accepting bank can only claim indemnity if the conditions on which it is authorized to accept are in the matter of the accompanying documents strictly observed. There is no room for documents which are almost the same, or which will do just as well. Business could not proceed securely on any other lines. The bank's branch abroad, which knows nothing officially of the details of the transaction thus financed, cannot take upon itself to decide what will do well enough and what will not. If it does as it is told, it is safe; if it declines to do anything else, it is safe; if it departs from the conditions laid down, it acts at its own risk." The defendant bank were told by their Danish principals to issue a letter of credit under which they were

38 [1983] 1 AC 168

39 *Rayner v Hambro's Bank* [1943] KB 37.

> to accept documents – an invoice and bills of lading – covering "Coromandel groundnuts in bags." They were offered bills of lading covering "machine-shelled groundnut kernels." The country of origin was stated to be British India. The words in that bill of lading clearly are not the same as those required by the letter of credit. The whole case of the plaintiffs is, in the words of Lord Sumner, that "they are almost the same, or they will do just as well." The bank, if they had accepted that proposition, would have done so at their own risk. I think on pure principle that the bank were entitled to refuse to accept this sight draft on the ground that the documents tendered, the bill of lading in particular, did not comply precisely with the terms of the letter of credit which they had issued.
>
> Atkinson J., however, in his judgment says: "A sale of Coromandel groundnuts is universally understood to be a sale of machine-shelled kernels that is, dry decorticated, and there is a standard form of contract, No. 37, used in the trade. The marking C.R.S. is short for 'Coros,' which is itself an abbreviation for 'Coromandels.' If a bag of kernels is marked 'C.R.S.,' it means that it is a bag of Coromandel groundnuts." That is stating the effect of evidence given by persons who deal in groundnuts in Mincing Lane, and when Atkinson J. says that it is "universally understood," he means that these gentlemen from Mincing Lane have told him: "We dealers in Mincing Lane all understand these things. We understand that 'Coromandel groundnuts' are machine shelled groundnut kernels, and we understand when we see 'C.R.S.' that that means 'Coromandels.'" It is suggested that as a consequence the bank, when this bill of lading for machine-shelled groundnut kernels with C.R.S. in the margin was brought to them, ought to be affected with this special knowledge of those witnesses who deal in these things on contracts in Mincing Lane. I think that is a perfectly impossible suggestion. To begin with, this case does not concern any transaction in Mincing Lane. It is a transaction with Denmark, and for aught I know and for aught the evidence proved, the people in Denmark know nothing about this business usage of Mincing Lane. Moreover, quite apart from that special application of the relevant considerations, it is quite impossible to suggest that a banker is to be affected with knowledge of the customs and customary terms of every one of the thousands of trades for whose dealings he may issue letters of credit. A homely illustration is suggested by the books in front of me. If a banker were ordered to issue a letter of credit with respect to the shipment of so many copies of the "1942 Annual Practice" and were handed a bill of lading for so many copies of the "1942 White Book," it would be entirely beside the mark to call a lawyer to say that all lawyers know that the "1942 White Book" means the "1942 Annual Practice." It would be quite impossible for business to be carried on, and for bankers to be in any way protected in such matters, if it were said that they must be affected by a knowledge of all the details of the way in which particular traders carry on their business. [His Lordship dealt with certain other contentions of the plaintiffs which do not call for a report.] For these reasons, I think that this appeal succeeds, that the judgment in favour of the plaintiffs must be set aside, and judgment entered for the defendants with costs, here and below.[40]

Mackinnon's position was fully endorsed by Goddard LJ, who stated as follows:

> I agree. It seems to me that Atkinson J. has based his judgment on the consideration that the bank was affected in some way by this custom of the trade, and, secondly, that he has considered whether what the bank required was reasonable or unreasonable. I protest against the view that a bank is to be deemed affected by knowledge of the trade of its various customers, but, quite apart from that, even if the bank did know of this trade practice by which "Coromandel groundnuts" can be described as "machine-shelled groundnut kernels," I do not think that would be conclusive of the case.

40 *Ibid.*, at 40–42.

> There are three parties concerned in a banker's credit – the person who requests the bank to establish the credit, the bank which establishes it, and the beneficiary who can draw on it. The person who requests the bank to establish the credit can impose what terms he likes. If he says to the bank: "I want a bill of lading in a particular form," he is entitled to it. If the bank accepts the mandate which its customer gives it, it must do so on the terms which he imposes. The bank, as between itself and the beneficiary can impose extra terms if it likes. For instance, in this case, the bank imposes a term: "All drafts drawn hereagainst must contain the clause: 'Drawn under confirmed credit No. 14597.'" The bank can say to the beneficiary: "These are the terms on which the bank will pay," and if it has only been authorized by its customer to pay on certain terms it must see that those terms are included in the notification which it gives to the beneficiary, and it must not pay on any other terms. If it does pay on any other terms, it runs the risk of its customer refusing to reimburse it. It does not matter whether the terms imposed by the person who requires the bank to open the credit seem reasonable or unreasonable. The bank is not concerned with that. If it accepts the mandate to open the credit, it must do exactly what its customer requires it to do. If the customer says: "I require a bill of lading for Coromandel groundnuts," the bank is not justified, in my judgment, in paying against a bill of lading for anything except Coromandel groundnuts, and it is no answer to say: "You know perfectly well that 'machine-shelled groundnut kernels are the same as Coromandel groundnuts.'" For all the bank knows, its customer may have a particular reason for wanting "Coromandel groundnuts" in the bill of lading. At any rate, that is the instruction which the customer has given to the bank, and if the bank wants to be reimbursed and remunerated by its customer, it must show that it has performed his mandate. If I employ someone at a remuneration to pay money for me on getting a receipt in a particular form and he pays the money without getting the receipt in that form, he has not carried out the duty which I imposed on him. It would be no answer for him to say: "Well, I got a receipt which in fact gives you all reasonable protection." My answer to that would be: "You are not concerned with the protection which you have given me. You are concerned to carry out the orders which I gave you, and you have not done it."
>
> In my opinion, in this case, whether the bank knew or did not know that there was this trade practice to treat "Coromandel groundnuts" and "machine-shelled groundnut kernels" as interchangeable terms, is nothing to the point. They were told to establish a credit, and to pay against a bill of lading describing particular goods, and the beneficiary under that credit presented a bill of lading which was not what they had promised to pay against. Therefore, it seems to me, whether it is reasonable or unreasonable for their principals to say that they want a bill of lading for "Coromandel groundnuts," or whether the bank had or had no knowledge of some of the trade practices which are referred to, is not the question. The question is "What was the promise which the bank made to the beneficiary under the credit, and did the beneficiary avail himself of that promise?" In my opinion, in the present case, he did not, and, therefore, I think that the bank was justified in refusing to pay. The other matters are, in my opinion, quite irrelevant, though the judge seems to have paid particular attention to them. I agree that this appeal should be allowed.[41]

Similarly, in *Credit Agricole v Credit Suisse*,[42] the issue was whether a confirming bank, the claimants, were entitled to an indemnity under a letter of credit issued by the defendants, a bank. Essentially, this issue depended upon the proper interpretation of the terms of the letter of credit, which provided for documents "to

41 *Ibid.*, at 43.
42 *Credit Agricole v Credit Suisse* [2001] 1 All ER (Comm) 1088.

be accepted as presented", in the light of the UCP 600 and factual and expert banking evidence.

As held by Morrison J:

> It seems to me the whole tenor of the case as originally constructed was that there was a date on the railway bills which the document checkers were reasonably entitled to rely upon as satisfying the time condition in the L/C, even though, by the time the documents were finally presented the 20 day period had expired . . . As an additional argument it was being suggested that because of the words in Field 78, CFSB were obliged to pay as soon as the Claimants had confirmed that they had "taken up documents in conformity with the terms of the credit" whether or not the documents were actually in conformity. I regard the contemporary Swift message from the Claimants rejecting CFSB's rejection of the documents as ambiguous. But even if the Claimants had been saying all along that Field 48 was overridden, that was certainly not the way the case was understood by CFSB or by either expert.
>
> It was common ground between the experts that the time provision in the UCP [21 days of shipment unless otherwise agreed] was fundamental. The railway bills were in standard form for this type of rail journey and such documents will frequently have been in front of the Claimant's document checkers. As already noted, the box at the bottom left hand-side of the bill contains a place for a date stamp of the sending station. Mr Palmer said that in his experience this box was frequently not properly completed. Mr Helbling disagreed. He had never seen a bill in the form which did not have the proper stamp indicating the date when the goods were shipped. It is to be noted that the genuine bills in relation to this cargo all have the proper stamp upon them. I have been shown no bill which is improperly stamped. Having regard to the significance of the time of shipment it is probable that such statements are invariably correctly stamped otherwise they would be rejected. I find as a fact that Mr Elliott knew or ought to have known that the bottom left hand box was the proper place for the indication of the date of the document. His explanation for why he completed the check sheet as he did was unconvincing and implausible. The only sensible inference to be drawn from the contemporary documents is that the Claimants believed that the 20 day requirement was met because of the two dates of 18/19 June. Further, when he was asked about the usual place for a date stamp indicating the date of the transport document he was evasive. In my view Mr Helbling was obviously right when he said that "it would not be reasonable for a bank to consider the date of 18 June or 19 June affixed below the delivery term . . . as being the date of despatch of the goods." That is so, whether or not Mr Elliott and his team could be expected to understand a limited amount of German. But I would have thought that the words "bahnhof" or "bahnhofs" would be part of the language known to document checkers. When Mr Palmer said that he himself did not know those words, and indeed mispronounced them as he came to the witness box, I did not believe him. He was, for a number of years, Assistant General Manager of an Austrian bank in London in charge of all trade and lending. He had frequently seen transport bills in the standard form. I find it incredible that he did not know the word for railway station in the German language.
>
> Mr Palmer suggested that the words "to be accepted as presented" were used because rail transport bills in relation to rail journeys in middle and eastern Europe were notoriously difficult to follow, especially where the prime language of the document was Russian, Cyrillic script which document checkers could not sensibly be required to read or understand. Mr Helbling, for his part, accepted that parts of the bills might be incomprehensible, and hence the need for them to be accepted as presented, but that the time requirements of the UCP were so fundamental that the words could not properly be taken to mean that an undated transport bill must be accepted.

> Mr Helbling was well qualified to give his opinion to the Court. His CV is impressive. He has chaired the Expert's panel of the ICC Docdex procedures which include the resolution of documentary credit disputes and gives advice to the ICC's Commission on Banking. He has been a representative to the ICC of the Swiss National ICC Committee. He struck me as a careful and very well qualified expert witness. I have no hesitation in preferring his opinions to those of Mr Palmer, despite the latter's own qualifications and expertise. At the end of the day, however, there was not much between their evidence, as Mr Palmer properly conceded that had he been the document checker he would not have been prepared to certify conformity with the conditions in the L/C. He would have needed further information. It seems to me that on the material before him, Mr Elliott was not reasonably entitled to regard the documents as conforming to the conditions. He fell below the international standard banking practice referred to in the Articles of the UCP. He erroneously believed that the dates he identified were those stated under rubric DDU. But he knew the meaning of the INCOTERM and cannot reasonably have thought that the dates there referred to the date of the transport bills nor the date of shipment. In any event, the earlier dates on some of the bills should have alerted him to the problem. He should have noticed an absence of a date stamp in the usual place and thus he failed to give effect to the provisions of Article 28. He should have concluded that he was not satisfied that the documents were in conformity and the Claimants should have refused to pay.
>
> I reject the argument that the conditions of the L/C were ambiguous or obscure and that Mr Elliott can say that even if he were wrong he cannot be said to have acted unreasonably. In my judgment, the words "to be accepted as presented" cannot sensibly be regarded as making the fulfilment of the time condition otiose. It would make no commercial sense for that to be so. It would render Article 28 of no effect. To dis-apply that Article, much stronger words would be required. There is no conflict between the words "to be accepted as presented" and the period for presentation expressly agreed between the parties to the L/C. If a transport bill is undated or bears no discernible date indicating when the goods were received for shipment, then the Bank could not be satisfied that the documents were in conformity. If a Bank cannot be satisfied that the documents as tendered were in conformity without further inquiry then the tender is a bad one and the documents should be rejected. This principle is entirely in accordance with the opinions of the ICC Commission of Banking Experts, to which this Court should give weight. The 21 day rule is regarded as fundamental and requires the bank to satisfy itself that it has been complied with. In this case the Claimants could not have been satisfied with the tender because of the absence of any convincing date stamp indicating when the goods were received.[43]

It is, thus, clear that banks' duties are to be assessed only in relation to the credit, with no consideration for the underlying contractual obligations between sellers and buyers, the nature of the goods, or trade practices.

This brings us to the next step in our analysis of documentary credits, i.e. what is a complying presentation by the seller, and how is compliance to be ascertained by banks?

11.10 What is a complying presentation?

Two issues need to be unfolded here: a) what must the documents comply with and b) how strictly must the documents comply to those benchmark criteria?

43 *Ibid.*, at paras. 19–23.

As to the first question, see Articles 15 and 2 of the contract for the bank's central obligation and for the definition of a complying presentation.

The UCP 600 itself provides some indications through Articles 2 and 15.

Article 2 UCP 600

Complying presentation means a presentation that is in accordance with the terms and conditions of the credit, the applicable provisions of these rules and international standard banking practice.

The constitutive elements to determine compliance are, thus, the terms and conditions of the credit, the applicable provisions of the UCP 600, and international standard banking practice. What is "international standard banking practice"? ISBP is the short and well-known name of the ICC publication No: 645: International Standard Banking Practice for the Examination of Documents under Documentary Letters of Credit. The ISBP was approved by the ICC banking commission in October 2002. After this approval, the ISBP became an official ICC document. The UCP rules are written in a general manner. They are not detailed enough to cover the day to day practice. The ISBP was prepared in order to fill the gap between general principals of UCP and the daily practice. UCP 500 was the latest version of the rules which were governing documentary letters of credit at the time ISBP was being prepared. So, the ISBP was first constituted with the aim of explaining the UCP 500 rules more explicitly. Another aim of the drafting commission of the ISBP was to achieve internationally accepted standards for examination of documents under documentary letters of credit. In order to succeed in this aim, the commission asked various ICC national committees and members to send checklists on how documents were examined in their organisations. After 14 meetings and four different drafts, the ISBP was finally put into its final shape. It is important to note that the ISBP cannot in any way change the UCP 600 rules which apply to letters of credit, but the ISBP is a valuable supplementary guide to the UCP.[44]

---

44 In the Preliminary Considerations section there is an expanded paragraph on the risks that arise when a beneficiary accepts a letter of credit which requires the presentation of a document that is to be issued, signed, or countersigned by the applicant. The expanded text in the revised ISBP emphasises that the beneficiary of the letter of credit should consider the appropriateness of this requirement carefully or seek an amendment. Having encountered a number of letters of credit with similar clauses in recent months, all issued by banks in the Middle East, this is without doubt a real issue. In one recent instance the presentation of a document, which had to be signed by a specifically named individual within the applicant's organisation, represented 30% of the value of the letter of credit, but competitive forces meant that the beneficiary had reluctantly made a commercial decision to allow this onerous clause to remain in the letter of credit. I sincerely hope that they obtain this document signed in accordance with those terms and get paid!

2. Virgule (a diagonal mark (/) used especially to separate alternatives): in all honesty this is not a word I have encountered prior to reading the revised ISBP. However, it is very relevant if used (ISBP suggests that virgules are not used) on a SWIFT MT700 in the goods description, for example in field 45A it reads Red/Blue/Yellow sweatshirts according to PO number 76598654 dated 30th August 2013, with no further clarification on the letter of credit. ISBP provides guidance that the documents presented could evidence only Red or only Blue or only Yellow, or any combination of them. This is valuable clarification for every documentary credit practitioner.
3. Certificates, certifications, declarations, and statements. The ISBP now states that when a certificate, declaration, or statement is required by the letter of credit, the document is to be signed.

As to the second question, i.e. how strictly must the documents comply to those

---

Most of my clients have told me that they would of course routinely sign such documents, but again this elucidation is helpful. It is unusual to come across a letter of credit which does not call for some form of certificate evidencing that . . . has taken place, so it is an important point to note.

4. Copy transport documents. If the letter of credit calls for copy transport documents rather than originals, the ISBP states that UCP 600 articles 19–25 which relate to transport documents does not apply. Copy transport documents are to be examined only to the extent expressly stated in the credit, otherwise according to UCP 600 sub-article 14(f), which effectively means that the documents appear to fulfil the function of the required document and that there is no conflict regarding the data on the document, with any other document stipulated in the letter of credit.
5. The ISBP contains an expanded segment which refers to expressions which should not be used in UCP 600, but if these expressions are used, how to interpret them. New additions are "shipping company" and "documents acceptable as presented" and an expanded explanation of "third party documents not acceptable". Perhaps the most onerous expression is "documents acceptable as presented" which almost seems to undermine the very use of a letter of credit. The ISBP provides clarity that if this expression is used a presentation may consist of one or more of the stipulated documents provided they are presented within the expiry date of the credit and the drawing amount is within that which is available under the credit. The documents will not otherwise be examined for compliance under the credit or UCP 600, including whether they are presented in the required number of originals or copies. This fresh interpretation does at least provide some criteria, albeit very scant, should this set phrase be encountered.
6. Shipping marks – As a former documentary examiner for a bank, I am conditioned to want to see exact mirror images when comparing documents to letter of credit. This is not necessarily the case or indeed correct, but it is, for me, a natural reaction. With this in mind, the ISBP indicates that if a letter of credit states that the details of a shipping mark are to be evidenced on specific documents, these details must be shown but not necessarily in the exact same sequence as expressed in the letter of credit. Some of my clients have commented that this is a surprise to them as they would never consider presenting documents which contain shipping marks in any other sequence to that required in the letter of credit, but it is worth noting these revised guidelines in the ISBP.
7. Invoices. Perhaps one of the areas that causes the most debate amongst documentary credit practitioners is the description of goods on the invoice compared to the description as stated within the letter of credit. The previous version of ISBP mentions there is no need for a mirror image when comparing the description of goods on the invoice to the description on the letter of credit. The ISBP reinforces UCP 600 Article 18 which uses the word "correspond" when stating how the goods' descriptions should be represented on the invoice compared to the letter of credit. The ISBP expands upon this by mentioning that invoices may also indicate data in respect of the goods, services, or performance, provided that they do not appear to refer to a different nature, classification, or category of the goods, services, or performance. An example is provided using an invoice which describes the goods as "imitation suede shoes" whereas the letter of credit's description is "suede shoes". This would be considered unacceptable as ISBP deems that this would represent a change in nature, classification, or category of the goods. The tried and tested policy of quoting goods description on the invoice verbatim, as per the description on the letter of credit is still the best course of action.
8. Bills of Lading. "A Bill of Lading may be issued by any entity other than a carrier or master (captain), provided it meets the requirements of UCP 600 Article 20" is an important statement made in the ISBP. In consideration of this if the letter of credit has a stipulation such as "freight forwarder's bills of lading are not acceptable" or words of similar effect, this has no meaning in the context of the title, format, content, or signing of a bill of lading unless the credit provides specific requirements detailing how the bill of lading is to be issued and signed. In the absence of these requirements, such a stipulation is to be disregarded, and the bill of lading presented is to be examined according to the requirements of UCP 600 Article 20. So in effect such clauses are totally superfluous and will be disregarded. This interpretation has been warmly welcomed, rather unsurprisingly by many freight forwarders as this is a very clear section and leaves the documentary practitioner in no doubt about what is acceptable.
9. Country named on bills of lading. I ran a public workshop recently in London, where a delegate mentioned that a well-known bank had recently raised a discrepancy relating to the fact that a

benchmark criteria, there are a number of senses in which the level of compliance is not absolutely strict: some leeway is recognised in the context of description of the goods, their quantity and typographical errors ("typos"). As we shall discover in the following, it may be, however, that the UCP 600 has introduced a more rigorous – or at any rate more confusing – test of "linkage" between the documents.

11.11 Strict compliance and the UCP 600

As established above, the common law principle of strict compliance with documentary duties is an influential and efficient tool for governing the seller's documentary duties within the context of contracts concluded on shipment terms.

Has the principle of strict compliance been embraced by the UCP 600? As will be readily appreciated, three areas of the UCP 600 appear to have deviated from strict compliance, i.e. a) the Articles of the UCP 600 governing the description of the goods as it appears on documents; b) the quantity of the goods; and c) by way of case law interpretation, typos in the documents tendered by the seller.

11.11.1 Description of the goods on the commercial invoice

As we shall soon discover in the following, the UCP 600 allows a certain amount of leeway in the description of the goods in most of the documents, apart from the commercial invoice, which needs to strictly comply with the credit in terms of the description under Article18 of the UCP 600.

Article 18 UCP 600 Commercial invoice

a. A commercial invoice:
   i. must appear to have been issued by the beneficiary (except as provided in article 38);

---

letter of credit had stated: port of loading – Felixstowe UK, and their bill of lading had shown the port of loading as "Felixstowe" but had not, unsurprisingly, mentioned "UK". The ISBP is quite clear on this issue – a bill of lading is to indicate the port of loading stated in the credit. When a credit indicates the port of loading by also stating the country in which the port is located, the name of the country need not be stated. So the bank in question has erroneously raised this as a discrepancy. This interpretation also applies to air waybills, with no need for a country to be stated on the document.

10. Air Waybills. There are some very important elements in the ISBP which relate to air waybills. The carrier is to be identified by its name and not merely by its IATA code, so for example British Airways needs to be stated rather than just "BA" or Singapore Airlines must be stated rather than just "SQ". However, the airport can be identified using its IATA code without stating the full name of the airport, so LHR is perfectly acceptable for London Heathrow and LAX is similarly fine when the airport is Los Angeles.

These ten elements of the ISBP are not placed in any order of importance but as previously mentioned they have all come up in conversations with clients since the introduction of the revised ISBP. My personal opinion is that these revised guidelines had a very soft launch after their approval in April this year, and it appears that many companies who use letters of credit are unaware of the revision and some are totally unaware of ISBP in any event. There is an official launch arranged by the ICC in London in October but this seems a little late since the latest version will have been in existence for a number of months when that launch takes place. In any event the latest version represents a much more comprehensive edition than previously, with improved clarity and shorter, more easily understood paragraphs and is a must for everyone who has any involvement with the collation/production of documents against letters of credit.

ii. must be made out in the name of the applicant (except as provided in sub-article 38 (g));
iii. must be made out in the same currency as the credit; and
iv. need not be signed.

b. A nominated bank acting on its nomination, a confirming bank, if any, or the issuing bank may accept a commercial invoice issued for an amount in excess of the amount permitted by the credit, and its decision will be binding upon all parties, provided the bank in question has not honoured or negotiated for an amount in excess of that permitted by the credit.
c. The description of the goods, services or performance in a commercial invoice must correspond with that appearing in the credit.

Clearly, Article 18(c) of the UCP 600 fully embraces the principle of strict compliance when it comes to the description of the goods as it appears on the commercial invoice.

For guidance on the meaning of the word "correspond" used by Article 18(c), it is possible to refer to the case *Glencore v Bank of China*.[45]

Although the case offered indications on the counterpart Article 37(c) enshrined in the UCP 500, it can still be referred to in order to interpret Article 18(c) by way of analogy.

The case dealt with a contract of sale whereby the plaintiffs (Glencore) sold to the buyers, Shan He Trade Co. Ltd., 1500 tonnes of aluminium ingots c.i.f. Zhangjiagang. The payment clause provided for an irrevocable letter of credit payable against presentation of various documents including a commercial invoice, producer's weight/packing list, and a certificate of origin.

The issuing bank (the Bank of China) rejected the documents, inter alia, on the grounds that copies of the commercial invoices described the origin of the goods shipped as "Any Western Brand – Indonesia (Inalum Brand)", whereas the letter of credit described the goods as "Any Western Brand".

The court held that where the compliance of the goods as invoiced was concerned, there was no real difference between a point being made about the documents and a point being made about the goods. In any event the discrepancy complained of was a point being made about the documents in the context of the rejection of documents under a documentary credit, and the sale contract itself unlike the letter of credit did not refer to "Western brand" under the rubric of "Origin" but to "Western, excluding India/Egypt".

The submission that this alleged discrepancy was a complaint about the compliance of goods, as invoiced, with the contractual origin was rejected, as well as the submission that the origin of the goods was not part of their description being rejected.[46]

It did not seem to be obvious to the court that a reasonable banker ought to regard "Western" as being used in a geopolitical or commercial rather than a geographical sense, so as to embrace Indonesia. It was found equally not obvious that

45 *Glencore v Bank of China* [1996] 1 Lloyd's Rep. 135, 153, 154.

46 See also *Bulgrains & Co Ltd v Shinhan Bank* [2013] EWHC 2498 (QB). In this case, the omission of an ampersand or the word "and" from the name of a company in documents presented under a letter of credit was a material discrepancy entitling a bank to reject the presentation.

the goods could not have an origin different from their port of shipment; and, in any event, the plaintiffs could not succeed where the alleged discrepancy was an invitation to litigation as the reference "Indonesia (Inalum Brand)" was.

Consequently, the Bank of China's objection to the 800 tonne letter of credit was valid and the plaintiffs' claim for declaratory relief in respect of the letter of credit failed.

In the words of Rix J:

> I reject the submission that the origin of the goods is not part of their description. A reference to their origin is to be found within the paragraph of the credit defining the "Commodity", which is part of, if not all of, the description of the goods. [. . .] That said, there is no authority which precisely covers the present situation, which is one where under a credit governed by the UCP the invoice correctly reproduces the goods' description but then adds an additional or qualifying phrase which goes outside and beyond the language of the credit, and for good measure does so in terms relevant to origin in circumstances where the certificate of origin itself, which also contains that additional language, is not objected to. In my judgment, however, the closest authority, albeit one not relating to an UCP credit, is *Rayner v Hambros*, for there the correct description in the invoice was qualified by a different description in the bill of lading. In this case, as in that, it is irrelevant, in the absence of evidence helpful to the beneficiary as to banking practice or as to the knowledge of a reasonable banker, that in the merchants' trade the two descriptions are compatible. It does not seem to me to be obvious that a reasonable banker would or ought to regard "western" as being used in a geo-political or commercial, rather than a geographical, sense so as to embrace Indonesia, despite the reference to "shipment from far eastern port". It is not obvious to me that goods cannot have an origin different from their port of shipment. In any event, the plaintiffs cannot succeed where the alleged discrepancy is an invitation to litigation, as it seems to me the reference to "Indonesia (Inalum Brand)" is. Even though the terms of art. 37(c) may fall short of the requirement of complete identity between the language of the credit relating to description and the language of the invoice, it does not seem to me that additional language which is prima facie inconsistent with the language of the credit, and at the very least introduces an element of ambiguity and doubt, falls within any latitude which is intended to reflect the distinction between correspondence and identity referred to in the cited passage from "UCP 500 & 400 Compared". Nor does the present case seem to me to come within that element of flexibility, such as it is, which is encompassed within Mr. Justice Donaldson's language in *M. Golodetz & Co. Inc. v Czarnikow-Rionda Co. Inc.* [1979] 2 Lloyd's Rep. 450 at p. 451, where he said: A tender of documents which, properly read and understood, calls for further inquiry or are such as to invite litigation is clearly a bad tender. But the operative words are "properly read and understood". I fully accept that the clause on this bill of lading makes it unusual, but properly read and understood it calls for no inquiry . . .
>
> That language would justify Mr. Justice Leggatt's acceptance of "ex" as the equivalence of "previous name" (see *The Messiniaki Tolmi*); it might also justify some additional language, albeit not sanctioned in the credit, which throws no doubt on the fulfilment of the credit's requirements. That, however, is not, it seems to me, this case.
>
> The only aspect of the matter which has given me pause is the failure to object to the reference to Indonesian origin in the certificate of origin, coupled with the structure of the UCP's requirements as to the standard for examination of the documents and for the giving of notice of discrepancies to be found in arts. 13 and 20. Article 13 emphasizes that "all documents" have to be examined "with reasonable care" and continues.
>
> Documents which appear on their face to be inconsistent with one another will be considered as not appearing on their face to be in compliance with the terms and conditions of the Credit.

Article 20 limits the discrepancies of which complaint can be made to the discrepancies of which notice is given within seven banking days. If therefore no objection is taken to Indonesian origin in the certificate of origin, the document which is most concerned with origin, and if the bank is required to examine all documents with reasonable care (which might be said to exclude the riposte that the fact that a documentary banker has nodded or blinked over one document is no reason why he cannot object to another whose deficiencies he has observed), should he be entitled to say, as a reasonable banker, that the representation of the invoice that an Indonesian brand falls within the description of "western brand" means that the invoice does not correspond with the credit, or at any rate invites a dispute as to whether it does? Nevertheless, Mr. Hofmeyr conceded that the fact that no objection was taken to one document does not preclude objection, even the self-same objection, to another document. Moreover, albeit in the context of a somewhat different argument, Lord Justice Lloyd in *Seaconsar v Bank Markazi* appears to have been of the view that a deficiency in one document cannot be cured by reference to another (at p. 240). I would therefore be prepared to regard Mr. Hofmeyr's concession as well founded.

For these reasons, the Bank of China's first objection to the 800 tonne letter of credit is valid, and on this ground alone the plaintiffs' claim for declaratory relief in respect to this letter of credit must fail.[47]

11.11.2 Description of the goods in documents other than the commercial invoice

Article 14 UCP 600 provides the standards for examining documents as follows:

Article 14 UCP 600 Standard for examination of documents

a. A nominated bank acting on its nomination, a confirming bank, if any, and the issuing bank must examine a presentation to determine, on the basis of the documents alone, whether or not the documents appear on their face to constitute a complying presentation.
b. A nominated bank acting on its nomination, a confirming bank, if any, and the issuing bank shall each have a maximum of five banking days following the day of presentation to determine if a presentation is complying. This period is not curtailed or otherwise affected by the occurrence on or after the date of presentation of any expiry date or last day for presentation.
c. A presentation including one or more original transport documents subject to articles 19, 20, 21, 22, 23, 24 or 25 must be made by or on behalf of the beneficiary not later than 21 calendar days after the date of shipment as described in these rules, but in any event not later than the expiry date of the credit.
d. Data in a document, when read in context with the credit, the document itself and international standard banking practice, need not be identical to, but must not conflict with, data in that document, any other stipulated document or the credit.
e. In documents other than the commercial invoice, the description of the goods, services or performance, if stated, may be in general terms not conflicting with their description in the credit.
f. If a credit requires presentation of a document other than a transport document, insurance document or commercial invoice, without stipulating by whom the document is to be issued or its data content, banks will accept the document as presented if its content appears to fulfil the function of the required document and otherwise complies with sub-article 14 (d).

47 *Glencore v Bank of China* [1996] 1 Lloyd's Rep. 135, 153, 154.

g. A document presented but not required by the credit will be disregarded and may be returned to the presenter.
h. If a credit contains a condition without stipulating the document to indicate compliance with the condition, banks will deem such condition as not stated and will disregard it.
i. A document may be dated prior to the issuance date of the credit, but must not be dated later than its date of presentation.
j. When the addresses of the beneficiary and the applicant appear in any stipulated document, they need not be the same as those stated in the credit or in any other stipulated document, but must be within the same country as the respective addresses mentioned in the credit. Contact details (telefax, telephone, email and the like) stated as part of the beneficiary's and the applicant's address will be disregarded. However, when the address and contact details of the applicant appear as part of the consignee or notify party details on a transport document subject to articles 19, 20, 21, 22, 23, 24 or 25, they must be as stated in the credit.
k. The shipper or consignor of the goods indicated on any document need not be the beneficiary of the credit.
l. A transport document may be issued by any party other than a carrier, owner, master or charterer provided that the transport document meets the requirements of articles 19, 20, 21, 22, 23 or 24 of these rules.

According to Article 14(e) UCP 600, in documents other than the commercial invoice, the description of the goods, services or performance, if stated, may be in general terms not conflicting with their description in the credit.

Contrary to what Article 18(c) does in relation to the description of the goods appearing on the commercial invoice, Article 14(e) does not embrace the principle of strict compliance when it comes to other documents, allowing banks a certain degree of leverage in assessing compliance.

Nevertheless, what do the words "not conflicting with" enshrined in Article 14(e) mean? Yet again, guidance on the relevant phrase in Article 37(c) of the UCP 500 found in *Banque de l'Indochine v Rayner*[48] can be equally applicable to Article 14(e) UCP 600.

In *Banque de l'Indochine v Rayner*, the issues object of controversy involved, inter alia, discrepancies between the description of the goods as appearing in the credit, and the description enshrined in a certificate of origin.

As put by Sir John Donaldson MR:

> The sections of the Uniform Customs and Practice which are material for this purpose are:
>
> **"B. Liabilities and responsibilities**
>
> "Article 7 Banks must examine all documents with reasonable care to ascertain that they appear on their face to be in accordance with the terms and conditions of the credit. Documents which appear on their face to be inconsistent with one another will be considered as not appearing on their face to be in accordance with the terms and conditions of the credit . . .

48 *Banque de l'Indochine v Rayner* [1983] 1 Lloyd's Rep. 228.

"C.3 Commercial invoices

"Article 32 . . . (c) The description of the goods in the commercial invoice must correspond with the description in the credit. In all other documents the goods may be described in general terms not inconsistent with the description of the goods in the credit.

"C.4 Other documents

"Article 33 When other documents are required, such as warehouse receipts, delivery orders, consular invoices, certificates of origin, of weight, of quality or of analysis etc. and when no further definition is given, banks will accept such documents as tendered."

No complaint is or was made by the bank about the commercial invoice. The argument has turned upon the other documents. It seems that the sugar came from two different sources. As a result some of the documents related to quantities smaller than the total contract quantity. Thus, whilst there was only one commercial invoice and one bill of lading, there were two certificates of weight, quality and packing, two certificates of origin and three E.U.R. 1 certificates. The crux of the argument was the extent to which these documents had on their face to be linked to each other and to the commercial invoice.

Mr. Buckley, for the merchants, submits that in the light of article 33 it is sufficient if the various certificates purport to be certificates of the type called for, describe the goods at least in general terms and cover the full quantity of goods mentioned in the invoice. In particular, in the light of article 7, it is not necessary that the documents should on their face be linked one to the other, provided that they are not inconsistent with each other.

Mr. Saville, for the bank, submits that there must be sufficient linkage to prove that the documents, if accurate, all relate to the parcel of goods which are the subject of the commercial invoice. In support of this submission he referred us to *In re an Arbitration between Reinhold & Co. and Hansloh* (1896) 12 T.L.R. 422, where the certificate of quality did not mention that the bags concerned were marked with an "F" and the bill of lading referred to bags so marked. The Divisional Court held that this was a bad tender, since there was no evidence that the bags shipped were those which were the subject matter of the certificate. He also relied upon the decision of McNair J. in *Bank Melli Iran v Barclays Bank (Dominion, Colonial & Overseas)* [1951] 2 Lloyd's Rep. 367, that a certificate that a number of vehicles were in new condition was defective in that it failed to identify the vehicles. From these authorities, the correctness of which has never been doubted, he sought to extract the principle that it is not sufficient to produce a certificate of quality or other supporting document called for by the credit, if that document is merely "not inconsistent" with the other documents and, in particular, the commercial invoice. It must, he submitted, be consistent and only consistent if it is to render the letter of credit operative. For my part, I would accept this submission in a case to which the U.C.P. does not apply. However, that is not this case.

Article 7 undoubtedly supports Mr. Buckley's submission and I do not consider that any of the documents produced were necessarily inconsistent with each other. This is not surprising if, as I suspect is the case, the documents in fact relate to the sugar concerned. His submission also gains support from the second sentence of article 32 (c) in that again I do not think that the description of the goods in any of the documents is inconsistent with the description in the credit. Article 33 adds little. It entitles and requires the bank to accept a document purporting to be a certificate of quality or whatever as being such a certificate. All the documents tendered purport to be documents of the kind called for by the credit.

> So far so good from the point of view of the merchants. But there is another obstacle in their way. There is, in my judgment, a real distinction between an identification of "the goods," the subject matter of the transaction, and a description of those goods. The second sentence of article 32 (c) gives latitude in description, but not in identification. For example, the E.U.R. certificate or certificate of origin could identify "the goods" by reference to marks on the bags or by reference to a hold in the vessel which they occupied provided that no other goods were in the hold. Having so identified "the goods" they could then describe them as "sugar" simpliciter since this description is not inconsistent with "E.E.C. White Crystal Sugar Category No. 2, Minimum Polarisation 99.8 degrees Moisture Maximum 0.08 per cent." But however general the description, the identification must, in my judgment, be unequivocal. Linkage between the documents is not, as such, necessary, provided that each directly or indirectly refers unequivocally to "the goods." This seems to me to be the proper and inevitable construction to place upon article 32 (c) if the specified documents are to have any value at all. It is here that the merchants are in difficulties.
>
> No problem arises with the commercial invoice or the bill of lading, the latter showing 40,000 polythene lined unmarked jute bags of white crystal sugar weighing 2,018.6 metric tons gross loaded on the Markhor at Antwerp bound for Djibouti in transit for The Yemen. There are two quality certificates, which in total have the same gross weight as that shown in the bill of lading and, by calculation from the net weights, the same number of bags. However, one refers to the sugar to which it relates as having been loaded on the "M.V. Markhor or substitute." Clearly this could be a different vessel and accordingly refer to a different parcel of sugar. There are two certificates of origin. One refers to consignment by "M.V. Markhor or substitute," the other to "Transports mixtes à destination Djibouti Port in Transit Yemen." The quantities are correct, but the certificates might refer to two other parcels of sugar. There are three E.U.R. 1 certificates. The total quantities are correct, but one names Tate & Lyle for account their principals as consignees, another Rayners for account their principals and the third Rayners simpliciter. Two give no indication of the method of transport, one says simply "Fer." One refers to preferential terms between France and Djibouti and the other to France and Yemen Nord. Clearly these certificates could relate to the goods, but they do not necessarily do so. This will not do.[49]

Similarly, in *Bank Melli Iran v Barclays*,[50] a dispute arose between the issuing bank (Bank Melli Iran) and the confirming bank, Barclays, which paid the seller despite the presence of a discrepancy between the description of the goods as appearing in the credit, which indicated 100 Chevrolet trucks in new condition, vis-à-vis a certificate issued by the US government official that purchase had been made of 100 "new, good" Chevrolet trucks.

It was held that the accepting bank was required to act strictly in accordance with the mandate of the issuing bank, and that in this case the British bank were shown to have authorised payment against documents which did not fully comply with the mandate of the Persian bank; but that the subsequent course of action of the Persian bank (principals in the transaction) did not indicate any intention to reject the documents and was consistent only with their acceptance of the action of the British bank (agents in the transaction) in paying against the documents tendered. Judgment was entered for the British bank.

49 See P. Todd, *Bills of Lading and Bankers' Documentary Credits*, 4th Edition, Informa, 2007, p. 139.
50 *Bank Melli Iran v Barclays* [1951] 2 Lloyd's Rep. 357.

As stated by McNair J:

> I now proceed to examine the documents tendered. (1) The invoice tendered was in the following terms:
>
> > To 100 "one ton" Chevrolet truck in new condition ex site at [Belcèle] near Antwerp, Belgium . . . £40,000.
>
> I feel no doubt at all that the phrase "in new condition" is not or may not be synonymous with the term "new." It is, of course, true that the term "new" is capable of different meanings in relation to different subject-matters. For example, the term "new" when applied to wine, as in the phrase "putting new wine into old bottles," has clearly a different meaning from what it bears when applied to a motor car; but "in new condition" in relation to a motor vehicle seems to me to be essentially different from "new."
>
> [. . .] The document accepted as complying with the requirement of a "U.S.A. Government undertaking confirming that the trucks" (or "the said trucks") "are new" was in the following terms. I consider that the document is clearly defective in two respects: (1) The description of the trucks as "new (comma) good" may clearly connote something different from the description "new." It may have a special trade meaning in relation to motor vehicles. It is sufficient to say that it is not the same. (2) But the more important defect, in my judgment, is that the certificate does not purport to relate to any specific trucks; the trucks as to which the certificate is given are not identified as the trucks covered by the invoice or a fortiori by the delivery order, which did not come into existence until some five or six weeks after the date of the certificate.
>
> To the objection that a certificate identifying the goods was impracticable and, therefore, Barclays Bank were entitled to accept the next best, there are, in my judgment, at least two answers: (1) that there was no practical difficulty in identifying the trucks by number or otherwise in the delivery order and relating the certificate to the trucks so identified; and (2) that if Barclays Bank considered the requirements impracticable it was their duty to refer back to Bank Melli for further instructions. In my judgment, this certificate plainly did not comply with the terms of their mandate.
>
> The delivery order (apart from not identifying the trucks) described the trucks as "new (hyphen) good." It was suggested that the phrase "new-good" comes into existence by the accident of the typist striking the wrong key. This may be so; but the result was that in this delivery order this composite word "new-good" appeared. In my judgment, this description, like the description "new, good" or "in new condition" is not the same as "new."
>
> I accordingly hold without hesitation that the documents against which the first payment of £40,000 was made were not in accordance with the bank's mandate, and that the allegations set out in par. 4 of the points of claim are established.[51]

11.12 The UCP 600 and quantity

The UCP 600 also appears to deviate from the common law principle of documentary strict compliance in relation to the quantity of the goods.

Indeed, Article 30 UCP 600 confers on a bank a certain amount of leeway when it comes to the determination of compliance in relation to the quantity of the goods.

51 *Ibid.*, at 374, 375.

Article 30 UCP 600 Tolerance in credit amount, quantity and unit prices

a. The words "about" or "approximately" used in connection with the amount of the credit or the quantity or the unit price stated in the credit are to be construed as allowing a tolerance not to exceed 10% more or 10% less than the amount, the quantity or the unit price to which they refer.
b. A tolerance not to exceed 5% more or 5% less than the quantity of the goods is allowed, provided the credit does not state the quantity in terms of a stipulated number of packing units or individual items and the total amount of the drawings does not exceed the amount of the credit.
c. Even when partial shipments are not allowed, a tolerance not to exceed 5% less than the amount of the credit is allowed, provided that the quantity of the goods, if stated in the credit, is shipped in full and a unit price, if stated in the credit, is not reduced or that sub-article 30 (b) is not applicable. This tolerance does not apply when the credit stipulates a specific tolerance or uses the expressions referred to in sub-article 30 (a).

The tolerance of 5 per cent, more or less, granted to banks by Article 30 UCP 600 does not find application whenever the credit states the quantity in terms of a stipulated number of packing units or individual items, and the total amount of the drawings does not exceed the amount of the credit.

Likewise, the tolerance is not to be applied whenever the credit stipulates a specific tolerance.

11.13 Letters of credit and typographical errors

The common law principle of strict compliance would not tolerate any documentary defect, not even the slightest, as a typographical error ("typo").

In light of the relevant case law, it is probably true to say that, within the context of documentary credits, banks are not to reject presentations because of "discrepancies" which are purely the result of typographical errors.

In *Seaconsar v Bank Markazi*,[52] a discrepancy found in the documents tendered by the seller in relation to the requirement that the *procès-verbal* had to bear the letter of credit number and the buyer's name, was not found, on appeal by Lloyd and Beldam LJJ (Stuart-Smith LJ, dissenting) to be trivial.

Indeed, the Court of Appeal found that there was an express requirement that the documents presented should be listed in the sense that each of them was to contain the letter of credit number and the name of the defendants' principal; whatever the reason for this, the requirement was clear and Bank Melli could not ignore this requirement; the absence of the letter of credit number and the name of the defendants' principal from the *procès-verbal* called for some explanation and Bank Melli were entitled to reject the documents.

As held by Beldam LJ:

> The first issue was whether the documents presented on Dec. 1 conformed with the stipulations in the letter of credit. A paying bank can only safely accept documents which are strictly in accordance with the stipulations in its mandate. In Lord Sumner's oft-quoted words:

52 *Seaconsar v Bank Markazi* [1993] 1 Lloyd's Rep. 236, 240.

There is no room for documents which are almost the same, or which will do just as well. Business could not proceed securely on any other lines. The bank's branch abroad, which knows nothing officially of the details of the transaction thus financed, cannot take upon itself to decide what will do well enough and what will not. If it does as it is told, it is safe; if it declines to do anything else, it is safe; if it departs from the conditions laid down, it acts at its own risk. See *Equitable Trust Company of New York v Dawson Partners, Ltd.* (1926) 27 Ll.L. Rep. 49 at p. 52.

The document on which Bank Melli based its rejection was the procès verbal of goods confirmed by the authorized representative of Deputy Ministry of Defence for Logistic, Iran. The letter of credit stipulated that all documents and packages should bear the letter of credit number and the name of the Ministry of Defence for Logistic, Iran. The procès verbal of loading certifying that the second shipment had been made in accordance with the terms of the contract was signed by the authorized representative, Mohammad Taghi Eskandari, but the name of the Deputy Ministry of Defence for Logistic, Iran, did not appear on the document. Nor did the letter of credit number. The appellant argues that the procès verbal was one of a set of documents which clearly referred to the consignment of goods in question and that read together there could be no doubt that it related to the same consignment and was signed on behalf of the authorized representative of the Ministry of Defence, Iran. Additionally the respondent argued that the same discrepancy had appeared on the procès verbal of loading of the first consignment but Bank Melli had permitted an alteration to be made so that it conformed with the stipulations. The appellants rely on a principle which they contended was supported by the judgment of Mr. Justice Parker, as he then was, in *Banque de l'Indochine et de Suez S.A. v J.H. Rayner (Mincing Lane) Ltd.* [1982] 2 Lloyd's Rep. 476; [1983] 1 Q.B. 711 that documents tendered as part of a set and at the same time could be read or linked together to establish compliance. I do not, however, read Mr. Justice Parker's judgment in this sense. At p. 482, col. 1; p. 721E he said:

I have no doubt that so long as the documents can be plainly seen to be linked with each other, are not inconsistent with each other or with the terms of the credit, do not call for inquiry and between them state all that is required in the credit, the beneficiary is entitled to be paid. I also accept, as did Mr. Saville, that Lord Sumner's statement cannot be taken as requiring rigid meticulous fulfillment of precise wording in all cases. Some margin must and can be allowed, but it is slight, and banks will be at risk in most cases where there is less than strict compliance. They may pay on a reasonable interpretation (see *Commercial Banking Co. of Sydney Ltd. v Jalsard Pty. Ltd.* [1973] A.C. 279, 285–286) where instructions are ambiguous, but where the instructions from the issuing bank are clear they are obliged to see to it that the instructions are complied with and entitled to refuse payment to the beneficiary unless they are.

From the closing words of this passage it is clear that the Court was there dealing with a case in which the mandate to the paying bank did not expressly require each document to bear on its face specified particulars. In the present case the mandate from the respondents was clear and required expressly that the conditions be fulfilled, otherwise the bank would be taking a risk in paying against them. Accordingly they were rightly rejected and I do not regard the appellants as having a good arguable case to the contrary.[53]

An interesting passage of the judgment is where Lloyd LJ makes reference, by way of example, to a "trivial" discrepancy which would not reasonably require a bank to reject the documents presented by the seller.

In Lloyd LJ's words:

53 *Ibid.*, at 254, 255.

> I cannot regard as trivial something which, whatever may be the reason, the credit specifically requires. It would not, I think, help to attempt to define the sort of discrepancy which can properly be regarded as trivial. But one might take, by way of example, *Bankers Trust Co. v State Bank of India* [1991] 2 Lloyd's Rep. 443 where one of the documents gave the buyer's telex number as 931310 instead of 981310. The discrepancy in the present case [i.e. the failure to put the letter of credit number and the buyer's name on one of the documents tendered when the letter of credit stipulated for such details on every document tendered] is not of that order.[54]

Indeed, the case *Bankers Trust Co. v State Bank of India*[55] referred to by Lloyd LJ in *Seaconsar v Bank Markazi* represents a paradigm of a trivial documentary discrepancy which could be saved within the context of letters of credit.

Here, the nature of the discrepancies related, inter alia, with the fact that on one of the documents tendered by the seller the telex number of the buyers' New Jersey office was given as 931310 instead of 981310. Such discrepancy was found by the court to be of a trivial nature.

It is, therefore, eminently clear that in the aforementioned areas of description of the goods, quantity, and typos, the UCP 600 deviates from the principle of strict compliance, allowing banks a certain amount of leverage.

11.14 Compliance achieved through fraud

As established above, on the basis of the principle of autonomy of documentary credits, a credit by its nature is a separate transaction from the sale or other contract on which it may be based. Banks are in no way concerned with or bound by such a contract, even if any reference whatsoever to it is included in the credit.

Such clear detachment is crucial when it comes to the question of compliance achieved through fraud.

Indeed, in cases of fraud on the part of the seller, where the letter of credit is irrevocable, the buyer can only obtain an injunction to prevent the bank from making payment on tender of conforming documents against evidence that the fraud has come to the notice of the bank.

In *Czarnikow-Rionda Sugar Trading Inc v Standard Bank London Ltd*,[56] the buyers sought an injunction on the basis of the "exception in the case of what is called established or obvious fraud to the knowledge of the bank".

The Court of Appeal held that the interests in the integrity of banking contracts under which banks made themselves liable on their letters of credit or their guarantees was so great that not even fraud could be allowed to intervene, unless the fraud came to the notice of the bank (a) in time, i.e. in any event before the beneficiary was paid, and (b) in such a way that it could be said that the bank had knowledge of fraud.[57]

---

54 *Ibid.*, at 240.

55 *Bankers Trust Co. v State Bank of India* [1991] 2 Lloyd's Rep. 443.

56 *Czarnikow-Rionda Sugar Trading Inc v Standard Bank London Ltd* [1999] 2 Lloyd's Rep. 187 (CA).

57 See also *Alternative Power Solution Ltd v Central Electricity Board* [2014] UKPC 31; [2014] 4 All ER 882 (Privy Council). In this case, the Mauritian Court of Appeal had wrongly upheld an interim injunction restraining a bank from debiting a purchaser's account under a letter of credit where there

In the absence of the fraud exception a buyer could no more seek to prevent his seller from drawing on the letter of credit for which the seller had stipulated than the buyer could prevent his bank from making payment under it.

As held by Rix J:

> The context of a final trial on the effect of the fraud exception is comparatively rare. In that context it is interesting to see what Mr. Justice Waller had to say about the test of fraud (at p. 617):
>
> It is simply not for a bank to make enquiries about the allegations that are being made one side against the other. If one side wishes to establish that a demand is fraudulent it must put the irrefutable evidence in front of the bank. It must not simply make allegations and expect the bank to check whether those allegations are founded or not . . . [I]t is not the role of a bank to examine the merits of allegations of breach of contract. To hold otherwise would place banks in a position where they would in effect have to act as Courts in deciding whether to make payment or not. Of course, if a beneficiary were to admit to the bank that it had no right to make the demand, then a totally different situation would arise.
>
> In the light of these authorities, it seems to me that, even if I assume for the sake of argument that Rionda has otherwise brought itself within the fraud exception, its claim against Standard for a pre-trial injunction must fail on the balance of convenience alone. I would seek to put the matter in the following way.
>
> The interest in the integrity of banking contracts under which banks made themselves liable on their letters of credit or their guarantees is so great that not even fraud can be allowed to intervene unless the fraud comes to the notice of the bank (a) in time, i.e. in any event before the beneficiary is paid, and (b) in such a way that it can be said that the bank had knowledge of the fraud. Whether that interest is viewed in terms of the importance that must be attached to the honouring of banking commitments, or in terms of the lifeblood of commerce and in particular international commerce, it has been amply recognized in case after case. Unless the banking commitment can be insulated from disputes between merchants, international trade would become impossible.
>
> If it were simply a matter of claim between two merchants who are in contractual relations with one another, let us say a buyer and a seller, no special rules would be necessary. A good arguable claim for relief by a buyer, alleging fraud, against a seller, could be dealt with on normal principles. Once, however, a letter of credit arrangement has been set up, the special rule that only the fraud exception permits interference comes into play.
>
> Thus, in the absence of the fraud exception, a buyer can no more seek to prevent his seller from drawing on the letter of credit for which the seller has stipulated than the buyer can seek to prevent his bank from making payment under it. The reason is that otherwise the special rule could be subverted, and the integrity and insulation of banking contracts could be overthrown, simply by the device of injuncting the beneficiary rather than the bank. The formulation of the fraud exception, to the extent that it requires the timely knowledge of the bank and not merely that of the beneficiary (who, ex hypothesi knows of his own fraud), emphasizes the distinctiveness of this rule. In this connection, *Themehelp v West* represents either a genuine distinction, based on the fact that the claim against the beneficiary alone was brought at an early stage, well before the question of enforcement of the guarantee arose; or the decision must be regarded as undermined by the concession there that a claim against a beneficiary, as distinct from a claim against a bank, was not covered by prior authority. In any

---

had been insufficient evidence that the bank was aware of a fraud by the seller. The test for an injunction at the interlocutory stage was whether it was seriously arguable that, on the material available, the only realistic inference was that the beneficiary of the letter of credit could not honestly have believed in the validity of its demands on the performance bonds and that the bank was aware of that fact.

> event, the present case, although it involves a claim against the beneficiary, USR, also involves a claim against a bank, Standard, and does not come at an early stage, but long after negotiation of documents and transfer of the goods, and is therefore not within any Themehelp exception.
>
> An additional dimension of complexity is superimposed by the fact that a final decision on the beneficiary's alleged fraud cannot be reached at a merely pre-trial hearing. Of course, the fraud exception is framed in such terms, requiring the fraud to be clear and to come to the timely knowledge of the bank, that in one sense there ought not to be a difference between a pre-trial application and the final trial. But life and the law are not perhaps as simple as that, and the difference between the tests formulated for the pre-trial stage and for final trial emphasize the difficulty. However, the fact that the claimant gets the benefit of a lower standard of proof for the purposes of a pre-trial hearing, places on the Court, as I believe the cases demonstrate, an additional requirement to be careful in its discretion not to upset what is in effect a strong presumption in favour of the fulfilment of the independent banking commitments.
>
> It is in this context that one comes to Mr. Justice Kerr's "insuperable difficulty". The same considerations that compel the narrowness of the exception which the Courts have allowed to the fulfilment of the banking commitments continue to operate at the level of balance of convenience.[58]

Payment in the face of fraud could not be a mere matter of discretion by a bank; it must be either within its mandate or not and either a matter of obligation or not.

11.15 How long does the bank have to examine and to pay?

Articles 14(b), 15, and 16 set out a detailed procedure which the banks must follow on presentation if they are to protect themselves against actions by the seller or the buyer.

Article 14 UCP 600 Standard for examination of documents

a. A nominated bank acting on its nomination, a confirming bank, if any, and the issuing bank must examine a presentation to determine, on the basis of the documents alone, whether or not the documents appear on their face to constitute a complying presentation.
b. A nominated bank acting on its nomination, a confirming bank, if any, and the issuing bank shall each have a maximum of five banking days following the day of presentation to determine if a presentation is complying. This period is not curtailed or otherwise affected by the occurrence on or after the date of presentation of any expiry date or last day for presentation.
c. A presentation including one or more original transport documents subject to articles 19, 20, 21, 22, 23, 24 or 25 must be made by or on behalf of the beneficiary not later than 21 calendar days after the date of shipment as described in these rules, but in any event not later than the expiry date of the credit.
d. Data in a document, when read in context with the credit, the document itself and international standard banking practice, need not be identical to, but must not conflict with, data in that document, any other stipulated document or the credit.
e. In documents other than the commercial invoice, the description of the goods, services or performance, if stated, may be in general terms not conflicting with their description in the credit.

58 *Czarnikow-Rionda Sugar Trading Inc v Standard Bank London Ltd* [1999] 2 Lloyd's Rep. 187 (CA), 202.

f. If a credit requires presentation of a document other than a transport document, insurance document or commercial invoice, without stipulating by whom the document is to be issued or its data content, banks will accept the document as presented if its content appears to fulfil the function of the required document and otherwise complies with sub-article 14 (d).
g. A document presented but not required by the credit will be disregarded and may be returned to the presenter.
h. If a credit contains a condition without stipulating the document to indicate compliance with the condition, banks will deem such condition as not stated and will disregard it.
i. A document may be dated prior to the issuance date of the credit, but must not be dated later than its date of presentation.
j. When the addresses of the beneficiary and the applicant appear in any stipulated document, they need not be the same as those stated in the credit or in any other stipulated document, but must be within the same country as the respective addresses mentioned in the credit. Contact details (telefax, telephone, email and the like) stated as part of the beneficiary's and the applicant's address will be disregarded. However, when the address and contact details of the applicant appear as part of the consignee or notify party details on a transport document subject to articles 19, 20, 21, 22, 23, 24 or 25, they must be as stated in the credit.
k. The shipper or consignor of the goods indicated on any document need not be the beneficiary of the credit.
l. A transport document may be issued by any party other than a carrier, owner, master or charterer provided that the transport document meets the requirements of articles 19, 20, 21, 22, 23 or 24 of these rules.

According to Article 14(b), a bank has a maximum of five banking days . . . to determine if a presentation is complying.

If compliance is attested, a bank is compelled to honour the credit under Article 15 UCP 600.

Article 15 UCP 600 Complying presentation

a. When an issuing bank determines that a presentation is complying, it must honour.
b. When a confirming bank determines that a presentation is complying, it must honour or negotiate and forward the documents to the issuing bank.
c. When a nominated bank determines that a presentation is complying and honours or negotiates, it must forward the documents to the confirming bank or issuing bank.

When a bank determines that a presentation is complying, it must honour the credit and forward the documents up the chain. But, what in the case of a non-complying presentation?

Article 16 UCP 600 deals with the issues of non-complying presentation as follows:

Article 16 UCP 600 Discrepant documents, waiver and notice

a. When a nominated bank acting on its nomination, a confirming bank, if any, or the issuing bank determines that a presentation does not comply, it may refuse to honour or negotiate.

b. When an issuing bank determines that a presentation does not comply, it may in its sole judgement approach the applicant for a waiver of the discrepancies. This does not, however, extend the period mentioned in sub-article 14 (b).

c. When a nominated bank acting on its nomination, a confirming bank, if any, or the issuing bank decides to refuse to honour or negotiate, it must give a single notice to that effect to the presenter.
   The notice must state:
   i. that the bank is refusing to honour or negotiate; and
   ii. each discrepancy in respect of which the bank refuses to honour or negotiate; and
   iii. a) that the bank is holding the documents pending further instructions from the presenter; or
        b) that the issuing bank is holding the documents until it receives a waiver from the applicant and agrees to accept it, or receives further instructions from the presenter prior to agreeing to accept a waiver; or
        c) that the bank is returning the documents; or
        d) that the bank is acting in accordance with instructions previously received from the presenter.

d. The notice required in sub-article 16 (c) must be given by telecommunication or, if that is not possible, by other expeditious means no later than the close of the fifth banking day following the day of presentation.

e. A nominated bank acting on its nomination, a confirming bank, if any, or the issuing bank may, after providing notice required by sub-article 16 (c) (iii) (a) or (b), return the documents to the presenter at any time.

f. If an issuing bank or a confirming bank fails to act in accordance with the provisions of this article, it shall be precluded from claiming that the documents do not constitute a complying presentation.

g. When an issuing bank refuses to honour or a confirming bank refuses to honour or negotiate and has given notice to that effect in accordance with this article, it shall then be entitled to claim a refund, with interest, of any reimbursement made.

11.16 Rejection for non-compliance

According to Article 16(a) UCP 600, when a bank determines that a presentation does not comply, it may refuse to honour it. As will be readily appreciated, in the case that a credit is not honoured by a bank, the bank is subject to specific obligations.

In light of Article 16(b), when a bank determines that a presentation does not comply, it may in its sole judgement approach the applicant for a waiver of the discrepancies, although if it does so, this will not extend the maximum period of five banking days that banks have at their disposal in order to examine documents.

It appears clear from the wording of Article 16(b) that the possibility for a bank to approach the buyer for a waiver in case of discrepancies between the documents tendered by the seller and the credit is not an obligation pending on the banks' shoulders.

The Article simply allows for that possibility, conferring full discretion on the banks. Past authority suggests that the Article does not allow fishing expeditions by the bank, asking the buyer whether he is generally happy with the documents.

In *Banker's Trust Co. v State Bank of India*,[59] the Court of Appeal was asked to assess, inter alia, whether it is permissible for banks to consult and or release documents to the buyers.

The court held (Lloyd LJ, dissenting) that it was accepted that consultation by the issuing bank with the buyers as to whether the buyers would or would not wish to take up the documents, having regard to the discrepancies found by the issuing bank, was not prohibited expressly or impliedly by any provisions of the code including in particular the words "on the basis of the documents alone".

Further, the court found that it was also accepted that the practice of undertaking such consultation was in the interest of both parties to the relevant contract; there was no valid ground for supporting the contention that time reasonably spent in carrying out that consultation was to be excluded from the assessment of the reasonable time prescribed by Article 16.

The reasonable time on its express terms included the examination of the documents and the determination; and an issuing bank was acting within a reasonable time in making its determination if it consulted where necessary its applicant for the purposes described.

Article 16 UCP did not contemplate a period of time for the applicant (buyers) to go through the documents to see if it could find further discrepancies; while the bank might consult the customer it was still the bank which had to make the decision whether to reject.

As put by Sir John Megaw:

> I agree with the view expressed by Lord Justice Farquharson. The answer on the question of principle does not affect the result of this appeal; but, in my view, if the question of principle were to be decided in accordance with the submissions of the defendants, the consequences would be of considerable, and perhaps unwelcome, practical importance. If the view which I take as to the construction of art. 16(b) of the Code is correct, those consequences do not arise. It is for that reason that I venture to add what I fear is more than the conventional formula of "a few words of my own" on that issue.
>
> The issue, as defined by Lord Justice Lloyd, is whether the "reasonable time" in art. 16(c) includes time for the issuing bank to consult with its customer, the applicant, when the issuing bank has found discrepancies in the documents, and thus is required by art. 16(b) to determine whether to take up the documents or to refuse them. It has not been argued, and it could not be argued, that the issuing bank is not obliged to make a determination when discrepancies are found. Article 16(b) says: ". . . it must determine . . ."
>
> Since the issuing bank "must determine", it could not be suggested that the "reasonable time" for such determination excludes time reasonably taken in ascertaining and considering any matter relevant to the determination, unless, on the true construction of the Code, and in particular art. 16, it is provided that the consideration of that matter is to be excluded.
>
> It is, therefore, necessary to consider whether the consultation by the issuing bank as to whether, on the discrepancies found by the bank, the applicant would wish the bank to take up or to refuse the documents, is, or may be, relevant to the determination. If it is otherwise relevant is it excluded by the words "on the basis of the documents alone"?

---

59 *Banker's Trust Co. v State Bank of India* [1991] 2 Lloyd's Rep. 443.

The approach to those questions should be in accordance with Lord Diplock's words in *The Antaios* [1984] 2 Lloyd's Rep. 235 at p. 238, col. 2; [1985] A.C. 191 at p. 201:

> . . . I take this opportunity of re-stating that if detailed semantic and syntactical analysis of words in a commercial contract is going to lead to a conclusion that flouts business commonsense, it must be made to yield to business commonsense.

I should refer also to Lord Diplock's statement in *United City Merchants (Investments) Ltd. v Royal Bank of Canada* [1982] 2 Lloyd's Rep. 1 at p. 6, col. 1; [1983] 1 A.C. 168 at p. 182:

> It is trite law that there are four autonomous though interconnected contractual relationships involved.

The metaphor "autonomous" means only that one does not read into any one of the four contracts the terms of any one the other three contracts. But the "genesis and the aim of the transaction" (Lord Wilberforce's words in another authority) are not to be ignored where they may be relevant to assist in the interpretation of the terms of the contract.

The relevant facts appearing on the evidence have been summarized in the judgments of Lord Justice Lloyd and Lord Justice Farquharson. It is beyond doubt on the evidence that the practice of issuing banks in London in respect of import credits (this was an import credit), when they have found discrepancies in the documents, is commonly, if not universally, to consult the applicant as to whether, on those discrepancies, it would or would not wish the issuing bank nevertheless to accept the documents. Under the practice, the issuing bank may, if it sees fit, allow the applicant also to see the documents. Mr. Procter's evidence, accepted by the Judge, was that: "In the vast majority of cases" the applicant, when consulted, expressed the wish that the issuing bank should accept the documents. Another witness said that this occurred in about 90 per cent. of the cases when the applicant was consulted. If, for any reason, the issuing bank had not received from the applicant the so-called "waiver" – the request that the issuing bank should accept the documents – by the end of the time which the issuing bank regarded as a reasonable time for making its determination, it would notify the remitting bank (or, where applicable, the beneficiary of the credit, the seller) that the documents were refused. I need not stress the obvious advantages to the parties, the banks, as well as to their respective customers, which derive from the exercise of this practice. I agree with Lord Justice Lloyd's view that it must be in the interest of all parties. As Mr. Procter said: "It saves everyone a lot of time and trouble". On that evidence it has to be accepted that the practice of consultation is reasonable as between the issuing and the remitting bank. For example, as a result, in nine cases out of 10 the documents will be accepted; whereas, without this practice, in all those cases the probability is that the documents would be rejected, with, at best, an indication from the issuing bank that it might, at some time in the future, seek the consent of the remitting bank, or the seller, to change its decision and to accept the documents.

Why, then, should the time reasonably taken for such consultations (which, on the evidence to which I shall refer later, is treated by at least one London clearing bank as being reasonably taken as the by no means insignificant time of 24 hours) not be included in the "reasonable time" which art. 16 permits for the examination and determination by the issuing bank? The contrary conclusion, as it appears to me, in Lord Diplock's words, "flouts business common sense".

The defendants' answer, as I understand it, involves acceptance that, as it is put by Lord Justice Lloyd: "Of course there is nothing in the Code to prohibit consultation". If the Code were to be construed as containing such a prohibition, it would inevitably upset the whole of the existing practice of London banks. That is because, as a result, any "determination" under art. 16(b) by an issuing bank, however timeously made, would make the refusal of the documents vulnerable to the invocation by the remitting bank of art. 16(e), invalidating the rejection, on the simple and unanswerable ground: "In your determination you took into account that which you are prohibited by the Code from taking into account – consultation as to your customer's wishes".

As I understand it, then, it is accepted that consultation by the issuing bank with the applicant as to whether the applicant would or would not wish to take up the documents, having regard to the discrepancies found by the issuing bank, is not prohibited, expressly or impliedly, by any provision of the Code, including in particular, the words "on the basis of the documents alone". As I understand it, also, it is accepted that the practice of undertaking such consultation is in the interest of both parties to the relevant contract. Once those two propositions are accepted, I am, with all respect, unable to see any valid ground supporting the contention that time reasonably spent in carrying out that consultation, in order to assist the issuing bank in the determination which it is required by art. 16(b) to make, is to be excluded from the assessment of the reasonable time prescribed by art. 16(c). The reasonable time on its express terms includes the examination of the documents and the determination. The time reasonably taken in the determination whether to take up or to refuse the documents is no less a proper element in the assessment of the art. 16(c) reasonable time than is the time reasonably spent in the examination of the documents. Both factors equally come into the account, because both equally are required to be undertaken by the issuing bank in the fulfilment of its contractual obligations under art. 16.

It has been argued by the defendants that, while the issuing bank is not prohibited by the contract from consulting the applicant, nevertheless its right to do so does not arise from the Code: hence any time occupied in this exercise does not come within the scope of the reasonable time visualized or prescribed by art. 16(b) and (c). Its right to consult the applicant, it is said, if I have understood the argument correctly, arises from the general right of waiver: a general, non-contractual, right whereby anyone is entitled to ignore – to place no legal reliance on – an infringement of a legal right. I must confess that I do not understand how any question of the common law right of waiver is of any relevance. The applicant cannot waive a breach of the autonomous contract between the banks, though its wish as to whether the issuing bank should take up or refuse the documents may be highly relevant to the banks' determination. So far as waiver by the issuing bank is concerned, the provisions of the contract – art. 16 of the Code – are intended to provide for the circumstances in which what may be described as a "deemed waiver" by the issuing bank will arise. It will arise if the issuing bank does not complete its task of examining the documents, making its determination and notifying the remitting bank in the prescribed form within a reasonable time. There is nothing that I can see in the general law of non-contractual waiver which has the slightest bearing on the question whether consultation with the applicant is or is not properly to be taken into account in deciding whether, under the terms of art. 16, the reasonable time for the carrying out by the issuing bank of its duties under that article has or has not been complied with.

I have said that in my opinion the consequences as affecting the existing practice of at least the majority of London banks would be substantial, and possibly serious, if the defendants' submissions were right on this question of principle.[60]

The possibility for a bank to approach a buyer for a waiver in the case of discrepancies, as per Article 16(b) UCP 600, encapsulates a possibility, which does not translate into any obligation, nor overextend the powers of the banks in terms of assessment of documents.[61]

60 *Ibid.*, at 455, 456, 457.

61 This is an issue of the utmost importance, since liabilities could otherwise arise within the context of contracts concluded on shipment terms. Let us consider the following scenario: what would happen if Article 16(b) UCP 600 provided for an obligation for banks to consult buyers in cases of

11.17 Banks' obligations in case of refusal to honour

According to Article 16(c), (d), and (e) UCP 600, when a bank determines that the presentation is not complying, it must give a "single notice" by telecommunication or if that is not possible by other expeditious means, stating each discrepancy on the basis of which it is refusing to honour. It must also return the documents to the presenter "at any time".

The content of the obligation of having to state all the discrepancies has been, in the course of the years, elaborated on by courts in relation to previous versions of the UCP.

In *The Royan*,[62] the behaviour of an issuing bank was called into question in terms of content of the notice of rejection of the documents presented by the seller.

The Court of Appeal held that Article 8(e) of the UCP (as it then was) did not require a precise form of words to be used. According to the court, the banks communication made it clear that they were not accepting the documents; their reasons for rejecting the documents were well known to both parties, and there was a valid rejection of the documents in relation to the first and second shipments before the credit had expired.

In the words of Lloyd LJ:

> Mr. Hapgood's second argument was that if Sumitomo were in position to reject the documents, they never in fact did so, because they never indicated that they were holding the documents at the disposal of Rabobank, as required by art. 8(e) of the Uniform Customs. Nor did they state their reasons for rejecting the documents.
>
> But art. 8(e) of the Uniform Customs, assuming it applied between Sumitomo and Rabobank at all, does not require a precise form of words to be used. Sumitomo's telexes of Nov. 16 and 18 made it abundantly clear that they were not accepting the documents. It was unnecessary for them to say, in so many words, that they were holding the documents at Rabobank's disposal. Their reasons for rejecting the documents were well known to both parties. So I would not accept Mr. Hapgood's second argument. In my view there was a valid rejection of the documents in relation to the first and second shipments before the credit had expired.[63]

In *The Lena*,[64] a detailed bank's notice of discrepancies was called into question under the UCP code. The court found the note of rejection to be specific and detailed enough and complying in terms of the obligations enshrined in Article 8 UCP (as it was then).

As held by Parker J:

> Article 8 (1) is not of significance. I set out art. 8 (2) to (4).
>
> (2) Payment, acceptance or negotiation against documents which appear on their face to be in accordance with the terms and conditions of a credit by a bank authorised to do so, binds the party giving the authorisation to take up the documents and reimburse the bank which has effected the payment, acceptance or negotiation.

---

discrepancies, and a bank were not to consult a buyer? A buyer keen to accept defective documents due to market value fluctuations for the goods sold, could have been in the position to initiate a legal course of action vis-à-vis the bank for damages.

62 *The Royan* [1988] 2 Lloyd's Rep. 250.

63 *Ibid.*, at 254.

64 *The Lena* [1981] 1 Lloyd's Rep. 68.

(3) If, upon receipt of the documents, the issuing bank considers that they appear on their face not to be in accordance with the terms and conditions of the credit, that bank must determine, on the basis of the documents alone, whether to claim that payment, acceptance or negotiation was not effected in accordance with the terms and conditions of the credit.

(4) If such claim is to be made, notice to that effect, stating the reasons therefor, must be given by cable or other expeditious means to the bank from which the documents have been received and such notice must state that the documents are being held at the disposal of such bank or are being returned thereto. The issuing bank shall have a reasonable time to examine the documents.

It is contended by the plaintiffs that Cripps Warburg, who are a bank, negotiated the draft against documents which appeared on their face to be in accordance with the terms of the credit and was authorized to do so by the Janata Bank. The Janata Bank was therefore bound to take up the documents and reimburse Cripps Warburg under art. 8 (2) or, if it considered that the documents appeared on their face not to be in order it must decide, under art. 8 (3), whether to claim that negotiation was not in accordance with the terms of the credit and, if it so decided, it was then obliged to inform Cripps Warburg promptly and give its reasons. There being therefore a duty to state reasons, the Janata Bank is precluded from relying on anything not raised.

On the face of it this argument appears somewhat startling, for Cripps Warburg's position does not, at any rate at first sight, seem to be that of an authorized negotiating bank having effected a negotiation pursuant to authority from the Janata Bank. It is the more startling when on the face of the credit it is stated that the Janata Bank are authorized to negotiate drafts under the credit. It is contended, however, that the Janata Bank did authorize Cripps Warburg to negotiate the drafts by virtue of their undertaking to all drawers, endorsers and bona fide holders of the drafts drawn under and strictly in compliance with the terms of the credit. The argument runs thus. Under s. 2 of the Bills of Exchange Act a holder is defined as including "a payee . . . who is in possession". Cripps Warburg were therefore holders and the Janata Bank's undertaking included them. Hence they were authorized to negotiate the draft and they did so, for s. 31 (1) of the Act requires for negotiation no more than a transfer from one person to another in such a manner as to constitute the transferee the holder of the bill.

This argument is in my judgment unsound. In the first place the Janata Bank did not expressly authorize Cripps Warburg to negotiate the drafts against the stipulated documents. It is clear from the wording of art. 8 (2) itself and from par. (b) of the General Provisions and Definitions of U.C.P. that a "bank authorised" is intended to refer to a confirming or advising bank or perhaps some other specified bank. The meaning cannot be extended by reason of the Janata Bank's undertaking to cover any one who happens to be an endorser or payee of the draft and who happens also to be a bank. Secondly, this was a bill payable to order and under s. 31 (3) it is negotiated by endorsement and delivery. There was here no negotiation at all. Cripps Warburg were the original "order" payees of the bill and it was delivered to them. True such delivery constituted them "holders" but the delivery constituted "issue" of the bill, not "negotiation". Thirdly, whatever they did was not done against documents. There was merely an assignment coupled with an obligation to provide some of the documents, which were in the event not provided. The argument presented is ingenious but artificial and I reject it.[65]

65 *Ibid.*, at 96.

11.17.1 Returning the documents to the seller

According to Article 16(e) UCP 600, a nominated bank acting on its nomination, a confirming bank, if any, or the issuing bank may, after providing notice required by sub-Article 16(c)(iii)(a) or (b), return the documents to the presenter at any time.

Article 16(e) does not indicate a specific deadline for the documents to be returned to the seller; that gave rise to controversies in past and recent times.

In *Bankers Trust Co v State Bank of India*,[66] the telex sent by a bank to the seller saying "Documents held at your risk and will be at your disposal after payment to us", was held to be in breach of the relevant – and identical – Article of the UCP 400: "after payment to us" was held not to be putting the documents at the disposal of the seller.

As held by Farquarson LJ:

> I do not consider that the terms of the relevant articles are in complete accord with either of these approaches.
>
> Article 16, pars. (b) and (c) provide for the issuing bank to have a reasonable time to complete two tasks: 1) to examine the documents submitted by the presenting bank. 2) where the documents are not in accordance with the terms and conditions of the credit, to determine on the basis of the documents alone whether to take them up or to refuse them and claim that on their face they appear to be discrepant.
>
> The question is: what steps may be taken by the bank within the time limit in arriving at its determination? If the task of the issuing bank is restricted to the examination of the documents, there is no room for it to make any "determination". If it discovers any discrepancies its function is simply to reject the documents. The making of a determination in my judgment implies something more. As Sir John Megaw pointed out in argument, it may be that one or more of the documents presented is in a foreign language in which none of the bank's staff is versed; or the technical nature of other documents may require an explanation from an expert. When a task has to be completed in a reasonable time that must mean reasonable in all the circumstances, and the circumstances would include the need for consultations of that nature. Similarly, if it is the custom among bankers, as the evidence disclosed, to enquire of the applicant for a letter of credit whether it wished the bank to reject the documents in reliance on the discrepancies it has found, it should be permitted to do so within the ambit of the reasonable time required to make its determination: I would hold that an issuing bank is acting within a reasonable time in making its determination if it consults where necessary a translator, an expert in the commodity being sold, or its applicant for the purposes described. Other circumstances which will no doubt be taken into account in determining what is a reasonable time, are the complication of the transaction, the number and complexity of the documents involved and, for example, the fact that the documents are being considered by the staff of a large bank at a busy financial centre. In the vast majority of cases where an applicant is consulted about discrepancies found in the documents, it can be done shortly by a telephone call or fax transmission. On the evidence it would be unusual to submit the documentation to the applicant for its inspection. If such a submission were made it could only be for the purpose of seeking the applicant's opinion on the correct course to take in the light of discrepancies already found. Article 16 does not, in my judgment, contemplate a period of time for the applicant to go through the documents, as in the present case, to see if it could find further discrepancies. While the bank may consult the customer for the limited purpose set out, it is still the bank which has to make the decision whether to reject.

66 *Bankers Trust Co v State Bank of India* [1991] 2 Lloyd's Rep. 443.

> The provision that the bank should arrive at its decision on the basis of the documents alone does not, in my judgment, prohibit consultations of this kind. It is merely to emphasize that the decision must be based on the discrepancies in the documents and not on any defect in the goods.
>
> Accordingly I am of the opinion that the time taken by the appellant in Stage 2, beyond the limited consultation referred to, as well as Stage 3, which would have been unnecessary if the applicant had not searched for further discrepancies in the documents, was in excess of a reasonable time.
>
> A further point was taken by the respondent that the rejection telex sent by the appellant on Sept. 30 was in breach of art. 16(d) of UCP.[67]

Farquarson LJ's judgment was echoed by Sir John Megaw LJ, who stated as follows:

> As regards the question of construction of the provision of art. 16(d) of the Code, as to "holding documents at the disposal of . . . the presentor", I agree with the reasons given by Lord Justice Lloyd for rejecting the submissions of the plaintiffs.
>
> I also agree that, on the facts, the plaintiffs' notice of rejection of the documents was not given within a reasonable time, and hence the appeal fails on that issue also. But, with diffidence, I have found myself unable to agree with Lord Justice Lloyd's opinion as to the question of principle which has been argued before us. I agree with the view expressed by Lord Justice Farquharson. The answer on the question of principle does not affect the result of this appeal; but, in my view, if the question of principle were to be decided in accordance with the submissions of the defendants, the consequences would be of considerable, and perhaps unwelcome, practical importance. If the view which I take as to the construction of art. 16(b) of the Code is correct, those consequences do not arise. It is for that reason that I venture to add what I fear is more than the conventional formula of "a few words of my own" on that issue.
>
> The issue, as defined by Lord Justice Lloyd, is whether the "reasonable time" in art. 16(c) includes time for the issuing bank to consult with its customer, the applicant, when the issuing bank has found discrepancies in the documents, and thus is required by art. 16(b) to determine whether to take up the documents or to refuse them. It has not been argued, and it could not be argued, that the issuing bank is not obliged to make a determination when discrepancies are found. Article 16(b) says: "it must determine . . ."
>
> Since the issuing bank "must determine", it could not be suggested that the "reasonable time" for such determination excludes time reasonably taken in ascertaining and considering any matter relevant to the determination, unless, on the true construction of the Code, and in particular art. 16, it is provided that the consideration of that matter is to be excluded.[68]

Neither Article 16 of UCP 400 nor the special terms of the letter of credit entitled the issuing bank to retain the documents as security for repayment by the defendants; the last sentence of Article 16(d) showed that the issuing bank had to give notice that it was holding the documents at the disposal of the confirming bank before being entitled to claim any refund from the confirming bank.

A similar issue arose in the relatively recent *Fortis Bank*[69] litigation. Here, the issuing bank Indian Overseas Bank ("IOB"), the defendant in the proceedings, opened five letters of credit in respect of five contracts of sale concluded between the seller Stemcor and buyer SESA International for the trade of containerised

67 *Ibid.*, at 453, 454.
68 *Ibid.*, at 455.
69 *Fortis Bank SA/NV v Indian Overseas Bank* [2011] EWCA Civ 58.

scrap. Three of the five letters of credit were confirmed by the appellant, Fortis Bank London, whilst for the remaining two, Fortis Bank acted as an advising bank.

Following the presentation of the documents by Stemcor, which Fortis Bank considered consistent with the letters of credit, the seller was paid and the documents were forwarded to IOB by Fortis Bank in November 2008. Having discovered some discrepancies, IOB gave notice to Fortis Bank under UCP 600 Article 16(c) stating that it was returning the documents in respect of all the presentations except for five presentations where it purported to exercise the option in sub-Article 16(c)(iii)(a) to hold the documents, pending further instructions from the presenter. Those further instructions were given, on terms, by Fortis Bank on 13 January 2009. IOB did not return any of the documents until 16 February 2009.

The claimants obtained summary judgment[70] in respect of all five letters of credit issued by IOB, and in respect of three remaining issues on 28 January 2010[71] when Hamblen J gave judgment for the claimants. Hamblen J implied a term to the effect that IOB, once it had elected to return the documents under Article 16, was under an obligation under that Article to do so with reasonable promptness. As IOB had failed to return the documents, it was precluded under sub-Article 16(f) from relying on the discrepancies it had detected. IOB appealed.

The appeal of IOB revolved around two main issues: (i) whether IOB was precluded under sub-Article 16(f) from relying on the discrepancies; and (ii) whether the bill of lading date was the date of shipment on board. Fortis and Stemcor – the seller under the sale contract and beneficiary of the letters of credit – cross-appealed on a third issue: (iii) whether there was a discrepancy in the beneficiary's consolidated certificate.

Both the appeal and cross-appeal were dismissed. Starting with the third issue, as the judge had found, there was indeed a discrepancy, in that each letter of credit stated that the negotiating bank had been advised to despatch original shipping documents only by air courier service to the letter of credit opening bank "at our cost", whereas the documents presented under each letter of credit certified that this had taken place "at issuing bank's cost". "Our" referred back to the first word of the clause, "we", which referred to Stemcor, not Fortis Bank. The discrepancy could not be regarded as so trivial as to be ignored, such as a mistake of name or obvious error discernable from the document. As for the second bill of lading issue, the terms of the letter of credit required presentation within 21 days of the date of the bill of lading. The bill of lading contained a "shipped on board" date and an "issued" date. It was held that the latter was to be taken as the date of the bill of lading and that therefore presentation thereof was within time according to the terms of the letter of credit.

In relation to the first and main issue, i.e. the failure to return the documents promptly, it was held that UCP 600 Article 16(f) would preclude IOB from claiming that the documents did not constitute a complying presentation. While IOB did indeed have to return the documents, the question was whether the obligation to do so promptly arose under the UCP 600. On a proper construction of UCP

70 [2009] EWHC 2303 (Comm).
71 [2010] EWHC 84 (Comm).

sub-Article 16(c), there was an obligation to act in accordance with the notice given and return the documents promptly. IOB had been in breach of that obligation.

In the words of Thomas LJ:

> The generally accepted approach a court should take to the construction of the UCP is set out in the judgment of Sir Thomas Bingham MR in *Glencore International AG v Bank of China* [1996] 1 Lloyd's Rep 135 at page 148 col 2:
>
> "Practice is generally governed by the UCP, a code of rules settled by experienced market professionals and kept under review to ensure that the law reflects the best practice and reasonable expectations of experienced market practitioners. When courts, here and abroad, are asked to rule on questions such as the present they seek to give effect to the international consequences underlying the UCP."
>
> [. . .] In my view, a court must recognise the international nature of the UCP and approach its construction in that spirit. It was drafted in English in a manner that it could easily be translated into about 20 different languages and applied by bankers and traders throughout the world. It is intended to be a self-contained code for those areas of practice which it covers and to reflect good practice and achieve consistency across the world. Courts must therefore interpret it in accordance with its underlying aims and purposes reflecting international practice and the expectations of international bankers and international traders so that it underpins the operation of letters of credit in international trade. A literalistic and national approach must be avoided.
>
> I turn therefore to consider first the commercial practice of international bankers and traders which arises when an issuing bank rejects documents, as that is essential to identify any underlying aim and purpose relevant to the issue.
>
> The evidence of practice was clear. As I have mentioned, the judge heard expert evidence from two bankers; Stemcor and Fortis called Mr Gary Collyer, a technical adviser to the ICC since 1996, a member of the ICC Banking Commission and Chairman of the ICC Drafting Group responsible for the revision of UCP 500 to create UCP 600. IOB called Mr Roger Jones, a retired banker who is chairman of the ICC UK Banking Committee and also a member of the ICC Banking Commission. Their reports contained evidence of practice. They also set out their views on the drafting of the UCP, its scope and other matters to which I refer at para 50. Their oral evidence encompassed the issues raised in the reports.
>
> The judge succinctly summarised their evidence on practice at various paragraphs of his judgment:
>
> "Mr Collyer stated that where 'return' is indicated, the return of documents should occur immediately or at the very latest during the course of the following 'working day' and that where 'hold' is indicated and the presenter instructs the issuing bank to return documents it is international banking practice to comply promptly with instructions received from the presenter, especially instructions relating to the disposal of documents.
>
> Mr Jones said that "best practice" entails the "speedy" return of documents and, based on his own experience of UK practice, that would normally be within a day or two unless there is a good reason why not. However, Mr Jones also said that there is certainly room for limited divergence in market practice dependent on "local conditions" and referred in this context to matters such as weather conditions, religious holidays, the means by which the documents are in fact returned and courier pick-up times. I was referred to a number of ICC Opinions under UCP 500 in which it was recognised that the issuing bank would be liable if it failed to act in accordance with the required statement it had made, although none of them specifically addressed the issue of preclusion. The experts said that the requirement to act in accordance with the disposal statement made related back to the 1963 revision of UCP, although it was thought that the consequent preclusion was introduced in the 1970s. It has therefore long been the position under UCP that the issuing bank is required to act in accordance with its disposal statement.

It was the evidence of both experts that the reasonable expectation of a presenting bank which received an Article 16 disposal notice would be that the issuing bank would act as stated. That would be not only good practice, but normal and expected practice.

The expert evidence in this case is that it is normal and expected international banking practice for documents to be returned and document disposal instructions to be complied with promptly."

[. . .] Neither the UCP nor any ICC paper provided a specific time or a time such as "without delay" or a means by which the documents should be returned:

"Notwithstanding the absence of a specific requirement or specific guidance in this regard, there is a market expectation that, consistent with the reading of Articles 13 and 14, international standard banking practice and the importance associated with possession of the documents, especially title documents, the timely return of dishonoured commercial documents requires priority processing, as delay in returning the documents may prejudice the beneficiary's rights and security.

While the Experts do not have the authority to establish such a standard concerning an exact time period to return the documents once notice is sent, the Experts agree that once the notice is sent stating that the documents are being returned, documents should be returned without delay and by expeditious means."

It was common ground that there had been no change in practice since UCP 500.

It therefore seems to me indisputable that the practice of bankers and international traders is that, on rejection, the issuing bank must hold the documents in accordance with the instructions of the presenter or return them promptly and without delay.

Is an obligation to act in accordance with the notice to be found in sub-article 16(c) of UCP 600 as a matter of construction?

In my view construing the UCP in accordance with the approach to construction I have set out at paras 26 to 29, sub-article 16(c) contains an obligation to act in accordance with the notice. These are the principal reasons for my view.

First, the issuing bank has no option but to comply with the option it has chosen. It is fundamental to the operation of letters of credit that, when the issuing bank determines that the documents do not conform, it may reject them. If it does, then it cannot be entitled to retain the documents, as it is implicit in rejection that it has refused to accept them. It must either hold them at the disposal of or in accordance with the instructions of the presenter or return them. Therefore once the issuing bank has rejected the documents, it cannot do anything else but act in accordance with its chosen option. Thus, it was not necessary to spell out in the sub-article the issuing bank's obligation to act in accordance with the notice. It was implicit in the wording of the article.

Second, the obligation to act in accordance with the notice is what is required by the standard international banking and trading practice set out at paras 31 to 35 above. It is necessary to make letters of credit work in practice so that the presenter can deal with the goods which are represented by the documents which the issuing bank has rejected. The consequences of the inability of the presenter to deal with the documents are too well known to need enumeration; illustrations are obvious such as in the case of a perishable cargo, or where the market falls or where the ship arrives and seeks to discharge the cargo.

Submissions were made on behalf of IOB that there was no need for such an obligation, as letters of indemnity might be used to procure delivery. The fact that one consequence might in certain circumstances be overcome by the presenter providing a letter of indemnity to the carrier cannot be relevant to the existence of the obligation. Another submission made on behalf of IOB was that the presenter would have a remedy by bringing an action for conversion of the documents, if they were not returned. However, that submission implicitly accepts and confirms the position that the issuing bank has no right to retain the documents; if it has no right to retain, it is impossible to understand what the issuing bank is entitled to do other than to return the documents or hold them at the disposal of the presenter in accordance with its instructions or pending instructions.

> It would make no commercial sense, contrary to the submissions of IOB, if, having made an election to return the documents, the issuing bank was not obliged to do anything. It would have the absurd consequence that the documents of title would remain with the bank which had rejected them and the presenter would be unable to deal with them. It was hardly surprising that Mr Jones, the expert called by IOB, could not think of any reason why the issuing bank should not be obliged to act in accordance with the notice given under sub-article 16(c). Furthermore, as the UCP is intended to be a self-contained code for the areas which it covers, it would make no sense to interpret the UCP in such a way that the obligation to act in accordance with the notice was omitted from its scope.
>
> It is also clear from the evidence of practice to which I have referred that an issuing bank that elects to return documents is expected to do so promptly and without delay. Taking into consideration the necessity for the presenter to be able to deal with the documents, it is clear in my view that if the issuing bank elects to return the documents, it must do so with reasonable promptness. I accept that the notice under sub-article 16(c) has to be given within the specified time of five banking days and what is reasonable promptness does not produce an equivalent exact time. However, I cannot accept that interpreting the provision in this way is likely to give rise to any real uncertainty. It is likely to be very clear whether the issuing bank has acted with reasonable promptness.[72]

On appeal, the most important issue was in relation to the scenario which arises when an issuing bank, having rejected documents presented under a letter of credit, serves notice that it is returning the documents to the presenter.

Upholding the judgment of Hamblen J, the Court of Appeal held that when an issuing bank gives notice under Article 16 of UCP 600, it is, on the proper construction of that Article, under the obligation to return the documents promptly. If it does not, the bank is consequently precluded from claiming that the documents do not comply with the credit and will then be bound to honour the credit notwithstanding the discrepancies.

The line of reasoning for this is of easy understanding: as emphasised numerous times above, the importance of documents within the context of contracts concluded on shipment terms cannot be understated. Goods are traded on the basis of documents, and if these are retained by a bank, a seller is essentially prevented from re-tendering documents, or from trading them with another accommodating buyer, bearing the liabilities vis-à-vis the first buyer.

Exactly as at first instance, the Court of Appeal was willing to uphold a purposive interpretation of the UCP 600 to accord with its underlying aims and purposes, reflecting in this way the international banking practice and the reasonable expectations of international banks and traders.

The Court of Appeal, having decided the case on the interpretation of the UCP 600, appeared significantly more reluctant than the judge at first instance to alternatively imply a term into the UCP 600. Thomas LJ notably commented that "there would be real difficulties in using a rule of national law as to the implication of terms to write an obligation into the UCP" (at para. 55).

English courts have in the past implied terms in an attempt to amend discrepancies between the UCP and the expectations of the market.

72 *Fortis Bank SA/NV v Indian Overseas Bank* [2011] 2 Lloyd's Rep. 30, 38, 39, 40.

In *Bankers Trust Co v State Bank of India*,[73] Hirst J held that in spite of the absence of any express wording to that effect in Article 14(d) UCP 400, it was implied that the rejection telex referred to "all" the discrepancies in the documents tendered by the seller in the case of non-compliance. Imposing this implied obligation on the issuing bank was deemed necessary in order to enhance business efficacy.

In the present judgment, the Court of Appeal judgment reaches the same result via the less intrusive tool of a purposive interpretation of the UCP 600.

The judgment should be welcomed by the trading community. In international trade, time is of the essence, and a prompt return of the documents to the beneficiaries is of the utmost importance not only in order to enable them to re-tender the documents, but also in order to allow a possible resale to a different, more accommodating buyer.

Indeed, the crucial point here is the following: on rejecting the documents, the bank must put the seller in a position to sell the goods directly outside the letter of credit, thus mitigating his loss – and, incidentally, any remedy he may have against the bank.

That is the reason why in the case that the bank retains the documents, the seller can sue the bank for damages representing the difference between the sum due under the credit and the amount realised by the onsale of the documents.

Nevertheless, the judicial creation of obligations within the framework of the UCP could give rise to uncertainty. The aim of the UCP is to create a practical and efficient framework of rules designed to assist the parties involved in documentary credits; this means that banks need to operate and base their decisions on the wording of the UCP and, to a certain extent, that was exactly what the IOB did.

Judicial interpretation should not be designed to encourage banks to start second-guessing judicial perceptions of the purpose of the UCP 600, let alone the existence of implied terms whenever the wording of the UCP 600 is ambiguous. Interpretation must be the exception rather than the rule. *Fortis Bank*, thus, represents a lesson to be taken into account in future revisions of the UCP 600.[74]

11.18 Payment under reserve

In order to avoid complications, advising/confirming banks frequently pay under reserve. On a general level, a payment under reserve can be defined as a provisional payment made to the beneficiary of a letter of credit where the documents submitted under the requirements of the credit present discrepancies.

The advising/confirming bank (which advances the payment) holds the balance pending confirmation from the issuing bank regarding the acceptance of documents, and has recourse against the beneficiary for the advanced payment if the issuing bank refuses to accept the documents.

The precise meaning of "payment under reserve" will ultimately depend on the specific arrangement come to between the beneficiary and the bank.

---

73 *Bankers Trust Co v State Bank of India* [1991] 1 Lloyd's Rep. 587.

74 See Lista, A., The Need for Speed: Court of Appeal Interprets UCP 600, *STL* 30, March 2011, 2.

The advising/confirming bank will want to claw back the payment immediately on the rejection of the documents by the issuing bank or the buyer for any reason. On the other hand, the beneficiary will want any clawback to occur only if there is a binding decision by a court or arbitrator that the documents in fact failed to conform.

In *Banque de l'Indochine et de Suez v J.H. Rayner (Mincing Lane) Ltd*,[75] the plaintiff bank notified the defendant sugar merchants of, and themselves confirmed, an irrevocable letter of credit opened by a Djibouti bank in favour of the defendants by order of the buyers under a contract of sale. The defendants tendered documents under the credit and requested payment of the amount due thereunder, some $1,010,000.

After examining the documents, the plaintiffs considered that the tender was defective. Following a telephone conversation between representatives of the parties, the plaintiffs remitted the amount requested to the defendants' bank stating by letter of the same day that "as arranged" payment was effected "under reserve" owing to specified discrepancies which included (i) the absence of a certificate that the vessel belonged to a member of an International Shipping Conference; (ii) the bill of lading was "not portmarked, vessel not responsible for incorrect delivery . . . extra expense . . . to be borne by consignees"; (iii) difficulty in relating certificates of weight, quality, packing and certificates of origin, and EUR1 certificates to the remaining documents and to the letter of credit. No indication was given as to the consequences of the payment being made under reserve.

The issuing bank in Djibouti stated that the buyers refused to lift the reserve in view of the discrepancy in the documents. The plaintiffs claimed that since the documents had been rejected for the specified discrepancies they were entitled to repayment of the sum paid under reserve.

The court found that the tender of the documents was bad both as to individual documents and as a set, and that the plaintiffs were entitled to the return of their money with interest.

On appeal by the defendants, it was held by the court, dismissing the appeal, that, although the expression "payment under reserve" had no defined and generally accepted meaning, the parties had meant by their use of the expression that the defendants would be bound to repay the money on demand if the Djibouti bank should reject the documents either on its own initiative or on the buyers' instructions.

In the words of Parker J:

> There is no authority as to the consequences of a payment under a letter of credit being made under reserve in respect of irregularities although such payments are frequently made and this is recognised both in the textbooks and in the Uniform Customs and Practice for Documentary Credit (1974 rev.) ("U.C.P."), article 8 (g) of which provides:
>
> "If the remitting bank draws the attention of the issuing bank to any irregularities in the documents or advises such bank that it has paid, accepted or negotiated under reserve or against a guarantee in respect of such irregularities, the issuing bank shall not thereby be relieved from any of its obligations under this article. Such guarantee or reserve concerns only the relations between the remitting bank and the beneficiary."
>
> This article does not mention a third method of dealing with irregularities, real or supposed, which is also commonly used, namely, a letter of indemnity by which the beneficiary, in consideration of the payment being made notwithstanding the

75 *Banque de l'Indochine et de Suez v J.H. Rayner (Mincing Lane) Ltd.* [1983] 1 All ER 1137.

irregularities, promises to indemnify the confirming bank against any loss it may suffer by reason of so paying.

It is clear from the evidence that no uniform banking practice exists either as to the form of the indemnity or guarantee which is used in the case of payment notwithstanding irregularities, nor as to the consequences of a payment being made under reserve. There was evidence that payment was normally made under reserve only when the beneficiary was a reputable and valued customer of the remitting bank but no one appears really to have considered what the consequences would be.

If there is no dispute but that there are irregularities justifying nonpayment, there appears to be no difficulty. The natural import of paying under reserve is that if the remitting bank does not, by reason of the irregularities, recover payment, the beneficiary will pay back. It is where, however, as here, there is dispute as to the validity of the alleged irregularities, that the problem arises.

In the absence of any established custom the question I have to determine is what is the meaning of the expression "in the light of surrounding circumstances" or, as it is now called, "the factual matrix." The circumstances in which such payments, and in particular the present payment, are made are (i) that the remitting bank genuinely believes that there are one or more discrepancies justifying non-payment; (ii) that the beneficiary believes that the bank is wrong and that he is entitled to payment; and (iii) that both parties hope that, notwithstanding the alleged irregularities, the issuing bank will take up the documents and reimburse the remitting bank.

The question which arises appears to me to be "did the parties, in such circumstances, by paying and accepting under reserve intend that the bank should be entitled to repayment notwithstanding that it was in law obliged to pay when it did? Or was it merely intended that the position of the bank should be protected to the extent that the customer should not thereafter be entitled to resist a demand for repayment on the ground that the payment was unqualified and that he was therefore entitled to retain the payment even if one or more of the irregularities was in law valid?"

The first of these two possibilities appears to me to import into the expression "under reserve" more than the words can fairly bear.

It would do more than reserve something. It would create a right, albeit perhaps temporary, to have money repaid notwithstanding that at the time of original payment that money was contractually payable. A more natural and, as I think, commercially sensible meaning to give to the words is that the bank reserves the right to have the money back if it was not at the date of payment contractually payable.

Such a meaning is, moreover, one which accords with the realities of the situation. At the time of the payment under reserve the beneficiary either is or is not entitled to payment. If he is entitled to payment the bank should have paid him without reserve and he should in justice be entitled to retain that which was from the start due to him. I find it impossible to suppose that either he or the bank intended by the use of the words to put him under an obligation to repay and then claim against the bank. On the other hand there is every reason to protect the bank from being unable to reclaim even if at least one of the discrepancies was valid. It is this protection only which in my judgment the bank obtains when a payment is made and accepted under reserve.

The matter may be tested by reference to the circumstances of this case. One of the alleged discrepancies advanced by the bank is now accepted by them as being invalid. Had that been the only discrepancy and payment had been made under reserve in respect of that alone the issuing bank might have been prepared to accept the documents, in which case the reserve would have been lifted and the beneficiary retained payment. Suppose, however, the issuing bank had refused on the particular ground and the confirming bank had then demanded repayment. Suppose, further, that the beneficiary had refused repayment on the ground that the objection was invalid. Could such a defence be struck out and judgment given for the bank with no stay of execution, leaving the beneficiary to a counterclaim, the trial of which might keep him out of money which was rightly his for years? I do not consider that it could. His case vis-a-vis the bank is that the bank have reserved the right to have the money back if they were right, not to have it back even if they were wrong. This is what in my judgment the reserve gives the bank. To achieve the results for which the bank contend, clearer words would be required.

It should be noted, furthermore, that Mr. Saville's contention produces within itself difficulties. He says that repayment is to be made if either (a) the issuing bank rejects for one of the specified reasons, or (b) if any of the specified reasons was in law valid albeit not relied on by the issuing bank. Alternative (b) will not arise if alternative (a) applies. Alternative (b) therefore presupposes that the issuing bank has rejected for a reason other than one of the specified reasons. But it is accepted that in such a case the reserve will not avail the confirming bank. The two are therefore inconsistent. If, however, the issuing bank reject for a reason other than one of the specified reasons, so that the confirming bank does not get paid, there appears to be no reason why it should not recover from the beneficiary if, but only if, it can show that one of the specified reasons was in law valid. Mr. Megrah accepts that it can. Alternative (b) therefore marries with the defendants' contention but not with that of the plaintiffs. Even if it could be reconciled with such contention it produces the result that in certain cases the confirming bank would have to establish that a specified reason was in law valid and that in others it need not do so, and neither from the evidence nor on principle can I see any basis upon which such a distinction could be made.[76]

The position of Parker J was fully endorsed by Sir John Donaldson MR, who, on his part, held as follows:

It seems that it is not unusual for a confirming bank to be asked to pay on documents which in its view do not fully comply with the terms of the letter of credit. The bank then has to decide whether (a) to refuse payment, (b) to pay, taking an indemnity from the beneficiary in respect of any loss or damage resulting from the deficiency in the documentation or (c) to pay the beneficiary "under reserve." Which course is adopted depends upon the extent and importance of the deficiencies as perceived by the confirming bank, the likelihood of the bank at whose request the credit was opened ("the issuing bank") and that bank's customer refusing to accept the correctness of any payment to the beneficiary and the credit worthiness, and value attached by the paying bank to the goodwill, of the person seeking to draw on the letter of credit. It is a tribute to the standing of J.H. Rayner (Mincing Lane) Ltd., the defendants, in the City of London that, notwithstanding the bank's conviction that the documents were seriously defective, they paid them "under reserve."

The use of the expression "payment under reserve," as denoting the character of a payment, is, we were told, widespread and would undoubtedly serve a very useful purpose if it had a defined and generally accepted meaning. Unfortunately it seems that it has not. If this is correct, banks will be most unwise to use it without at the same time stating precisely what they mean by it. In the longer term the International Chamber of Commerce, who are the authors and guardians of the Uniform Customs and Practice for Documentary Credits might like to turn their minds to this problem when undertaking the next revision. Meanwhile we have to determine what the parties meant by the expression when they used it on this occasion.

It is common ground that it relates to the circumstances in which the beneficiary can be called upon to repay the money which he has been paid under the letter of credit. The competing submissions are that (1) the money is repayable on demand if the issuing bank, in reliance upon some or all of the deficiencies alleged by the confirming bank, declines to reimburse the confirming bank or to ratify the payment, the beneficiary then being left to sue the confirming bank; (2) money is repayable if, but only

76 *Ibid.*, at 845, 846, 847.

if, the circumstances in (1) exist and the beneficiary accepts that the documentation was defective or this is established in a suit brought by the confirming bank against the beneficiary. If (2) is correct, the only effect of the qualification upon the payment, albeit an important effect, is that the beneficiary cannot resist an order for repayment on the basis that the payment itself had been made under a mistake of law. This was the submission accepted by the judge and his reasons appear in his judgment ante, p. 846B–D; [1982] 2 Lloyd's Rep. 476, 479.

The point is clearly one of difficulty. Mr. Saville characterised the view of the judge as "a lawyer's view" as contrasted with "a commercial view" and I think that this is right. It depends for its validity upon the parties having had it well in mind that money payable under a mistake of law is irrecoverable and wishing to do no more than eliminate this defence. This seems to me to be an improbable premise, when the parties are a commercial bank and a commodity merchant. As I see it, the dialogue to be imputed to the parties goes something like this:

Merchant: "These documents are sufficient to satisfy the terms of the letter of credit and certainly will be accepted by my buyer. I am entitled to the money and need it."

Bank: "If we thought that the documents satisfied the terms of the letter of credit, we would pay you at once. However we do not think that they do and we cannot risk paying you and not being paid ourselves. We are not sure that your buyer will authorise payment, but we can of course ask."

Merchant: "But that will take time and meanwhile we shall have a cash flow problem."

Bank: "Well the alternative is for you to sue us and that will also take time."

Merchant: "What about your paying us without prejudice to whether we are entitled to payment and then your seeing what is the reaction of your correspondent bank and our buyer?"

Bank: "That is all right, but if we are told that we should not have paid, how do we get our money back?"

Merchant: "You sue us."

Bank: "Oh no, that would leave us out of our money for a substantial time. Furthermore it would involve us in facing in two directions. We should not only have to sue you, but also to sue the issuing bank in order to cover the possibility that you might be right. We cannot afford to pay on those terms."

Merchant: "All right. I am quite confident that the issuing bank and my buyer will be content that you should pay, particularly since the documents are in fact in order. You pay me and if the issuing bank refuses to reimburse you for the same reason that you are unwilling to pay, we will repay you on demand and then sue you. But we do not think that this will happen."

Bank: "We agree. Here is the money 'under reserve'."[77]

In *Bankers Trust*, what the parties meant with their payment under reserve agreement was that "payment was to be made under reserve in the sense that the beneficiary would be bound to repay the money on demand if the issuing bank should reject the documents, whether on its own initiative or on the buyer's instructions.

Such arrangement would be regarded as a binding agreement made between the confirming bank and the beneficiary by way of a compromise to resolve the impasse created by the uncertainty of their respective legal obligations and rights." [78]

77 *Ibid.*, at 854, 855.

78 *Ibid.*, at p.773.

CHAPTER 12

Rejection and termination of contracts concluded on shipment terms

12.1 Introduction

This chapter aims at analysing the last phase of the life cycle of a sales contract concluded on shipment terms, i.e. rejection and termination of the contract.

As established above, one of the peculiarities of contracts concluded on shipment terms lies with the dual mode of performance by a seller, i.e. physical and documentary.

We have seen that these two sellers' duties are independent from one another, giving rise to the buyer's two separate and independent rights of rejection; as will be readily appreciated in the following, this scenario gives rise to some intricate consequences in terms of rejection and termination of contract.

We shall cover the matter by considering in the first place whether the seller can cure documentary defects.

Thereafter, the separation between the seller's physical duties and documentary duties will be subject to scrutiny, with the view to ascertaining the legal consequences arising from that scenario.

12.2 Is there any right of the seller to cure a documentary defect?

The principle of strict compliance would appear, *prima facie*, incompatible with the possibility of the seller curing a documentary defect.

Nevertheless, part of the doctrine has, in the past, advocated such a possibility. This is based on the common law rule which gives the defaulting party the right to cure defective performance within the time allowed by the contract for such performance.[1]

The authority often quoted for this proposition is *Borrowman v Free*.[2] In this case, the sales contract provided for a specific time frame for the tender of the declaration of shipment by the seller.

A first nomination was made by the seller and rejected by the buyers as outside the contractual specification. A second nomination was thereafter issued by the

1 See *Benjamin's Sale of Goods*, above, para. 12–044.

2 *Borrowman v Free* (1878) 4 QBD 500. See A. Apps, The Right to Cure Defective Performance, *LMCQ*, 525.

sellers and again rejected by the buyers, who claimed the sellers had no right to retender.

On appeal, the court held that the sellers were entitled to renominate the vessel, curing, therefore, a previous defective documentary performance, since the renomination happened within the time limit established by the sale contract.

As put by Bramwell LJ:

> I think that this judgment cannot be supported. I will deal first with the second point, which has been made before us on behalf of the defendants, namely, that the plaintiffs were not in a condition to tender the cargo of the Maria D., because it did not then belong to them. I think that this point was not taken at the trial, and if it had been the plaintiffs would have been able to meet it. I think that that is clear upon the construction of the documents and upon the facts before the Court. All that the sellers were bound to do under the contract of sale was to name the ship and to send on the invoice within the proper time. This they did, and the buyers were then to declare their option as to the mode of payment. It was contended at the trial that the tender was insufficient, because it was not accompanied with the shipping documents of the Maria D. I think it clear that it was unnecessary that at the time of the tender the sellers should have them in their possession. The performance of the contract does not depend upon that circumstance. As I have already said, before us the contention has been urged that the cargo of the Maria D. was not the plaintiffs'. Now, I quite allow that although a contention is not formally made at the trial, yet if it is obvious upon the face of the evidence it may be urged before us when the case is considered in all its aspects. This objection, however, is of a doubtful nature. Moreover, the plaintiffs might have met it by evidence that they had previously bought it; but, even if they had not bought it, the objection seems to me unsustainable; it is quite competent for a man to sell what does not belong to him: before the time for performance he may have bought it or procured the assignment of it, and be ready to fulfil his contract. The contention for the defendants is not maintainable either in the shape taken at the trial or in the form urged before us.
>
> As to the main point in the case I cannot agree with the view of Denman, J. In due course after the contract had been entered into the Charles Platt arrived, but the shipping documents had not reached the plaintiffs when they offered her cargo to the defendants. The latter objected that under the contract they were not bound to take it without the shipping documents. This objection was not allowed by the plaintiffs, and the question was referred to arbitration. The arbitrator was of opinion that the plaintiffs could not insist upon the tender. It is unnecessary to express any opinion as to the decision of the arbitrator. The plaintiffs then offered a second ship, the Maria D., within the time limited by the contract. It has been argued that by the tender of the Charles Platt the option of the plaintiffs was determined, and that the position of the parties is the same as if the Charles Platt had been named in the contract, and that no other ship could be declared. I do not think this argument maintainable. Suppose that a clause had been inserted, that no ship was to be declared whose shipping documents had not then arrived in England. A clause of that kind would be repugnant to the theory that the contract is to be treated as if the Charles Platt had been the ship named in it. The case may be shortly stated as follows: if the Charles Platt was a proper ship, the plaintiffs were entitled to tender her cargo; if she was not, they were entitled to withdraw the tender, and instead of the cargo of the Charles Platt to offer that of the Maria D. The defendants have relied upon *Gath v Lees* 2, but the decision is distinguishable. In that case cotton was "to be delivered at seller's option in August or September, 1864." The seller elected to exercise that option in August, and notice that it would be so exercised was accepted by the buyers. The seller had a right to exercise that option; but in this case, upon the defendants' hypothesis, the plaintiffs by naming the Charles Platt, exercised their option in an improper manner; therefore

> they had a right to withdraw their tender, and to exercise it in a proper manner. That case shews that this action is maintainable.[3]

Bramwell LJ's judgment was echoed by Brett LJ who, for his part, stated as follows:

> I also think that the judgment of Denman, J., must be reversed. The plaintiffs offered, and were ready and willing, to deliver the cargo of the Maria D., but the defendants refused to accept it. The defendants say that the plaintiffs might in fact be ready and willing to offer the cargo, but that they could not do so in law, because they could not at the time tender the bills of lading. This objection seems to me unsustainable, for the shipping documents might have been delivered within a reasonable time. The objection that the defendants were not possessed of the cargo of the Maria D. was not raised at the trial, and cannot be taken now. It was further argued that if the cargo of the Maria D. could be properly tendered, it was not tendered in point of fact, and that the tender of it was not waived by the defendants. I am of opinion that they did waive it, for they insisted that they were not bound to accept the tender of any vessel after the plaintiffs had offered the Charles Platt.[4]

It is suggested that it would be quite erroneous to consider the rationale of *Borrowman v Free* as the legal foundation for asserting the right of a seller to cure documentary defects within the context of contracts concluded on shipment terms.

The reason for this is that, in *Borrowman v Free*, the seller was allowed to rectify a declaration of shipment/nomination of the vessel/notice of appropriation within the time limit established in the sales contract itself.

Indeed, contracts concluded on shipment terms often include deadlines for the declaration of shipment; the importance of a declaration of shipment cannot be understated as it is necessary for the buyer in order to identify the vessel on board which goods have been shipped and, consequently, to make the necessary arrangements in order to collect the cargo at the port of destination.

Within the context of a c.i.f. sale (as in *Borrowman v Free*), the notice of appropriation is very much related and inherent to the contract itself, rather than to its performance. One might suggest that a notice of appropriation in a c.i.f sale goes back to the original sales contract, filling a gap invariably left blank in the sales contract itself, i.e. the name of the vessel on board of which the cargo is shipped.

At the time when a c.i.f. sale is concluded, the sales contract contains indications regarding the seller's transport obligations, but it will not specify the name of the vessel to be used by the seller (doing so would expose the seller to serious liabilities should the vessel specifically indicated in the sales contract become unavailable for any reason).

Indeed, as elegantly put by Donaldson J in the *Vladimir Ilich*:[5]

> It is important to remember that an appropriation is a matter of contract, not of performance. That comes later. Accordingly, validity depends upon form and timing and not upon substance or factual accuracy.[6]

3 *Borrowman v Free* (1878) 4 QBD 500, 502, 503.
4 *Ibid.*, at 504.
5 *Vladimir Ilich* [1975] 1 Lloyd's Rep. 322.
6 *Ibid.*, at 329.

If the notice of appropriation, rather than belonging to the performance sphere of a contract concluded on shipment terms, is of a contractual nature, one would find it very difficult to consider the *Vladimir Ilich* as authority for the assertion of the possibility for a seller to cure documentary defects, since we are in the performance phase of the contract, i.e. a moment completely separated in legal teleological terms from the contract itself.[7]

Authorities in favour of the seller's right to cure documentary defects

Apart from the aforementioned *Borrowman v Free*, attempts have been made to contemplate some case law *dicta* as authoritative propositions for the seller's right to cure documentary defects.

The first of such *obiter dicta* relates to the judgment in *SIAT di dal Ferro v Tradax*,[8] where Megaw LJ said:

> The question would arise whether it is a desirable or defensible distinction; or whether it would lead to anomalies and uncertainties in an area of the law where such degree of certainty as can fairly be achieved is obviously commercially desirable. Again, ought the essential nature of the buyers' rights, when he is faced with defective documents, to vary according to whether he is or is not in a string of buyers of the same goods; whether at the date of the tender of the defective documents he has or has not resold, whether on the same or different contractual terms; or whether thereafter he might desire to resell by passing on the documents, rather than taking delivery of the goods on his own account?
>
> It should not be forgotten also, in this context, that the law, in the absence of a contractual term to the contrary, allows a seller who has presented defective documents to represent, tendering correct documents, so long as he does so before the last permissible date provided by the terms of the contract, or, in the absence of contractual terms, the date for presentation provided by the term which in those circumstances is implied by law. So that, if the correctness of the documents is a condition of the contract, in the Sale of Goods Act sense of the word "condition", the seller may have an opportunity to remedy even serious breaches before the buyer becomes entitled to treat the contract as repudiated.
>
> I do not find it necessary to decide this question of principle. That is because there is in this case one type of documentary defect, common to all the three groups, which, in my judgment, is of such a nature that the buyers were entitled to reject the documents in each of the groups, on both the first and the second presentations: that is, apart from any special protection given to the sellers by the documents clause.[9]

Contrary to what part of the doctrine states,[10] with the utmost respect, it is not possible to consider *SIAT di dal Ferro v Tradax* as an authoritative proposition for the seller's right to cure a documentary performance. Indeed, it is very clear from the aforementioned passage that Megaw J was speaking *obiter*, and did not decide the specific legal question with authority.

---

7 See Debattista, *Bills of Lading in Export Trade*, above, p.217.

8 *SIAT di dal Ferro v Tradax* [1980] 1 Lloyd's Rep. 53.

9 *Ibid.*, at 62, 63.

10 See A. Apps, The Right to Cure Defective Performance, *LMCQ*, 535. See Debattista, *Bills of Lading in Export Trade*, above, p. 198. See also *Benjamin's Sale of Goods*, above, paras. 21.063 *et seq.*

Similarly, in *Soon Hua Seng Co Ltd v Glencore Grain Ltd*,[11] by way of *obiter dictum* Mance J stated that:

> The strictness [of documentary duties] may sometimes be mitigated by the sellers' ability to correct and re-present the documents, a point made by Lord Justice Megaw in the S.I.A.T. case, at pp. 62–63. But whether or not that course would have been open, compliance with the present documentary requirement was in my judgment a condition precedent to any obligation on the part of buyers to take up the documents. Since the sellers did not in fact re-present complying bills, the contracts were not performed and the sellers were in breach through non-delivery.[12]

In this case, Mance J recalls *obiter* the aforementioned Megaw LJ's *dictum* in *SIAT di dal Ferro v Tradax* without in essence deciding the question with authority.

Further *obiter dictum* allegedly supporting the possibility for the seller to cure documentary defects arises in *The Kanchenjunga*.[13] Here, Lord Goff said as follows:

> We can see these principles at work in the law of sale of goods. If goods are tendered which are not in conformity with the contract, the buyer is entitled to reject them. However, as is recognized by s. 11(2) of the 1979 Act, where a contract of sale is subject to a condition to be fulfilled by the seller, the buyer may . . . elect to treat the breach of the condition as a breach of warranty . . .
>
> Of course, if the buyer rejects the goods as not conforming with the contract, and the time for delivery has expired, the buyer can without more sue the seller for damages for non-delivery. If the time for delivery has not yet expired, the seller is still entitled to make a fresh tender which conforms with the contract, in which event the buyer is bound to accept the goods so tendered: see *Borrowman Phillips & Co. v Free & Hollis* (1878) 4 Q.B.D. 500. If the buyer elects to accept non-contractual goods, he is bound by his election and is limited to his right of action for damages for breach of warranty, the exercise of that right being consistent with his having waived his right to reject the good.[14]

Although the *dictum* in this case comes from the House of Lords, it has been correctly noted that the case related to the nomination of a safe port under a charter party, rather than the performance of the seller in a sales contract concluded on shipment terms.[15]

Above all, a common thread appears to link the various aforementioned *obiter dicta* and the related proposition allegedly suggesting the possibility for a seller to cure documentary defects, i.e. the existence of a time limit for the presentation of documents.

Indeed, as correctly pointed out by the doctrine, whenever time is of the essence, strict compliance with the time for performance is a condition of the contract, any breach of which will entitle the innocent party to elect to terminate the contract, no matter how trivial and whether it causes any loss.[16]

Here lies one of the keys for the legal determination of the possibility for the seller to cure documentary defects when it comes to contracts concluded on shipment terms: if the condition *sine qua non* of the right of a seller to cure documentary

---

11 *Soon Hua Seng Co Ltd v Glencore Grain Ltd* [1996] 1 Lloyd's Rep. 398.

12 *Ibid.*, at 403.

13 *The Kanchenjunga* [1990] 1 Lloyd's Rep. 391.

14 *Ibid.*, at 399.

15 See Debattista, *Bills of Lading in Export Trade*, above, p.217.

16 See A. Apps, The Right to Cure Defective Performance, *LMCQ*, 535.

defects lies with the existence of a time limit for the presentation of documents, that excludes such a possibility within the context of international commercial sales.

Indeed, the presence of a time limit for the presentation of the documents by the seller is non-germane and utterly alien to such contracts, which seldom provide for a deadline for the presentation of documents. The reason for this is that the seller already has the best possible incentive for tendering the documents required by the sales contract, i.e. payment. If the seller does not tender the documents, no payment will be made by the buyer who, for his part, maintains a strong contractual position until payment is made.

Further, one should never forget the peculiar nature of contracts concluded on shipment terms, and the repercussions for the legal dimension of such contracts. Indeed, documents are tendered by the seller after the goods are shipped on board and, if one considers a sale down a string of buyers, often when the goods are already afloat.

If the documents tendered by the seller show a defective performance, those defects will invariably be reflected by the status quo of the goods, which is destined in the vast majority of circumstances to remain immutable, regardless of the presentation of new "cured" documents.

By way of example, if within the context of a sales contract for a cargo of potatoes of "class A quality", the certificate of quality tendered by the seller to the buyer after the cargo is shipped on board shows that the potatoes are actually of inferior specification and/or defective in terms of quality, such tender cannot possibly be saved or cured.

The reason is that, even if the seller amends his documentary performance by re-tendering a certificate of quality consistent with what was originally established in the sales contract, that new "cured" tender cannot possibly replace the cargo shipped, which is destined to remain a defective cargo.

In other words, once the cargo is shipped, it would prove very difficult, if not impossible, for a seller to replace the cargo by simply replacing the documents initially tendered, as the cargo will remain the exact same one originally shipped by the seller.

Thus, to claim a general right for the seller to cure documentary duties when it comes to international commercial sales appears to be, at best, an overstatement.[17]

12.3 Rejection in cash against documentary transactions

Where a buyer of goods in a domestic sale is presented with goods which do not conform in a serious way with the terms of the contract of sale, his most persuasive

17 If that is arguably true when it comes to cash against documents transactions, the scenario is radically different in the case that the sales contract provides for payment via letter of credit. In that case, the seller can re-tender where the bank rejects the documents, so long as he can still comply with the time requirements of the letter of credit.

Nevertheless, it needs to be emphasised that this is not because of some general right of cure: rather, it is because under the separate and independent contract, i.e. the letter of credit between the seller and the confirming bank, the seller does not actually promise the confirming bank to tender the documents by a given date; it is simply that if he does not, then he will not be paid.

That being the case, since there is no bilateral contractual relationship between the seller and the confirming bank, the seller is not in breach, and there is no breach to cure: re-tender would simply be performance of the seller's condition for payment under the letter of credit.

remedy against the seller is to reject the goods and cancel the contract. This remedy – or the threat of it – is equally, if less justly, available to a buyer who wishes to lower the price against a falling market.

Where the sale is concluded on shipment terms, the notion of terminating the contract by rejection is rather more difficult, both because of the additional costs involved in rejecting the goods, and also because the seller actually performs two types of duties, the tender of documents and the delivery of goods.[18]

12.3.1 The two rights of rejection

The seller's duties to ship the goods and to tender documents are mirrored by the buyer's remedies of rejecting documents and goods.

These remedies are separate and independent, that is to say, the buyer's reaction to one mode of performance does not affect his rights regarding the other mode of performance.

In *Finlay (James) & Co. Ltd. v M.V. Kwik Hoo Tong Handel Maatschappij*,[19] the seller under a c.i.f. contract tendered to the buyer a bill of lading which stated, not fraudulently but contrary to the fact, that the shipment had taken place in the contract month. Being unaware of this fact at the time of the tender, the buyer accepted the shipment, and entered into sub-contracts for the sale of a portion of the goods, those sub-contracts containing a clause that "the bill or bills of lading shall be conclusive evidence of the date of shipment".

The sub-purchasers refused to take delivery, alleging that the shipment had not been made during the contract month. The buyer under the original contract then ascertained that the goods had not been shipped during the contract month.

It was held by the court that the buyer was entitled to damages for the breach by the seller of his obligation to deliver a bill of lading stating the date of shipment correctly, the measure of damages being the difference between the market price and the contract price of the goods.

In analysing the nature of c.i.f. contracts, Scrutton LJ reached the following conclusions:

> The point involved is a comparatively short one, but it is interesting and somewhat difficult on the question of the measure of damages. It arises in this way : a Dutch firm sold sugar to Finlay & Co., a well known English firm which also carries on business in India. The contract was for the shipment of sugar in three monthly instalments, the third of these being for September, 1920, and it is only in relation to the September shipment that the question arises. Since the decision in *Bowes v Shand* (2) it has been well settled that on a sale of goods a condition as to the time of shipment is vital and is of the essence of the contract. Accordingly, if a person has contracted to sell a September shipment, it is useless for him to tender an October shipment and say that the difference is very little. In this case the Dutch firm had on September 30 sugar at a port in Java, ready for shipment, which would have satisfied the contract, and the ship on which the sugar was intended to be shipped had arrived at or off the port on that date. None of the sugar, however, was in fact loaded on the ship in September.

18 See Debattista, *Bills of Lading in Export Trade*, above, p. 297.

19 *Finlay (James) & Co. Ltd. v M.V. Kwik Hoo Tong Handel Maatschappij* [1929] 1 KB 400.

Consequently the Dutch firm broke their contract with Finlay & Co. But more happened than that. Under a c.i.f. contract the sellers have not only to ship goods under the contract for carriage to the port of destination, they have to furnish the buyers with certain documents, among others (1.) a contract for the carriage of the goods, so that if they are lost during the voyage, in circumstances for which the ship is responsible, the buyers can recover their loss from the shipowner; and (2.) a policy of insurance covering the contract goods, so that if they are lost during the voyage by a risk covered by the policy the buyers can recover from the underwriters. It is unnecessary to discuss whether it is accurate to describe a c.i.f. contract as a sale of documents or as a sale of goods. In view of the fact that the goods may be lost before the documents are tendered and before the property has passed, there is a good deal to be said for the view that the contract is for a sale of documents; but at any rate it is an essential part of the contract that genuine documents relating to the goods complying with the contract should be tendered to the buyer.[20]

The idea of separation between a seller's documentary and physical duties, which give rise to two separate and independent rights of rejection on the buyer's part, was further emphasised in *Kwei Tek Chao & Others v British Traders and Shippers Ltd.*[21]

Here the court stated that under a c.i.f. contract a buyer had a right to reject the documents and a right to reject the goods, those rights being separate and distinct in law, and his right to damages on a breach of the seller's obligation to present a correct bill of lading vested when the bill was tendered; and that the right could not be affected by any action the buyer might take on a subsequent breach by the seller to deliver goods in accordance with the contract, whether the buyer elected to treat the subsequent breach as a breach of condition or as a breach of warranty.[22] As elegantly put by Devlin J:

I do not think that that is the right view of the matter. There is not, in my judgment, one right to reject; there are two rights to reject. A right to reject is, after all, only a particular form of a right to rescind the contract. Wherever there is a breach of condition there is a right to rescind the contract, and if there are successive breaches of different conditions committed one after the other, each time there is a breach there is a right to rescind in respect of that breach. A right to reject is merely a particular form of the right to rescind, which involves the rejection of a tender of goods or of documents; and a rightful rejection of either is a rescission which brings the contract to an end.

Here, therefore, there is a right to reject documents, and a right to reject goods, and the two things are quite distinct. A c.i.f. contract puts a number of obligations upon the seller, some of which are in relation to the goods and some of which are in relation to the documents. So far as the goods are concerned, he must put on board at the port of shipment goods in conformity with the contract description, but he must also send forward documents, and those documents must comply with the contract. If he commits a breach the breaches may in one sense overlap, in that they flow from the same act. If there is a late shipment, as there was in this case, the date of the shipment being part of the description of the goods, the seller has not put on board goods which

20 *Ibid.*, at 406, 407.

21 *Kwei Tek Chao & Others v British Traders and Shippers Ltd.* [1954] 2 QB 459.

22 Before jumping the gun, and rejecting documents or cargo, the buyer needs to be certain of being in the presence of a breach of a condition. Failure to do so will expose the buyer to serious liabilities. See *Glencore Energy UK Ltd v Cirrus Oil Services Ltd* [2014] EWHC 87 (Comm); [2014] 1 All ER (Comm) 513; [2014] 2 Lloyd's Rep. Here a seller of crude oil was awarded damages under SOGA 1979, section 50(2) and (3) after the buyer refused to accept the cargo. The award was designed to compensate the seller for the loss of the bargain and did not relate to lost profits.

> conform to the contract description, and therefore he has broken that obligation. He has also made it impossible to send forward a bill of lading which at once conforms with the contract and states accurately the date of shipment.
>
> Thus the same act can cause two breaches of two independent obligations. However that may be, they are distinct obligations, and the right to reject the documents arises when the documents are tendered, and the right to reject the goods arises when they are landed and when after examination they are found not to be in conformity with the contract. There are many cases, of course, where the documents are accepted but the goods are subsequently rejected. It may be that if the actual date of shipment is not in conformity with the contract, and the error appears from the documents, the buyer, by accepting the documents, not only loses his right to reject the documents, but also his right to reject the goods, but that would be because he had waived in advance reliance on the date of shipment.[23]

Devlin J's analysis of separation and independence between the two rights of rejection within the context of contract concluded on shipment terms is particularly interesting in legal teleological terms.

Breaches of physical duties may, in practice, overlap with breaches of documentary duties; by way of example, a bill of lading dated outside the contractual shipment period represents a simultaneous breach of documentary duties (i.e. the duty to tender a bill of lading of contractual specification) and a breach of physical duties (i.e. the physical duty to ship the goods in time).[24]

As specified by Devlin J, such areas of overlap do not erode the legal and conceptual distinction, separation, and independence between the two sets of duties of the seller, which give rise to two separate rights of rejection on the buyer's part.

Such distinction is of particular relevance within the context of contracts concluded on shipment terms. One should never forget the mechanisms governing international commercial sales, and their practical and legal consequences. Indeed, one of the peculiarities of such transactions lies with the fact that the buyer is destined to receive, in the vast majority of circumstances, the documents before the goods.

Due to the existence of two separate and independent rights of rejection, a buyer accepting complying documents is not thereafter prevented from rejecting the goods in the case that the cargo turns out to be in the end of non-contractual specification. This functions extremely efficiently within the context of contracts concluded on shipment terms, offering protection to a buyer who is presented with forged documents by the seller.

A counterfactual scenario seeing the buyer in possession of a single right of rejection would entail that the buyer is no longer in the position of rejecting the goods after having accepted documents which, although *prima facie* tallying with what was originally established in the sales contract, did not in the end reflect the real status quo of the goods.

The importance of distinguishing between the seller's physical and documentary duties and the related buyer's rights of rejection cannot be overstated; nevertheless,

23 *Kwei Tek Chao & Others v British Traders and Shippers Ltd.* [1954] 2 QB 459, at 480, 481.

24 As established above, time of shipment is to be considered as part of the physical duties of the seller and amount to a condition of contracts concluded on shipment terms (*Bowes v Shand* (1877) 2 App Cas 455 (HL)).

as will readily be appreciated, far from being straightforward, such distinction may give rise in practice to intricate scenarios in terms of hidden documentary defects, action for damages, and acceptance of clearly defective documents by the buyer.

12.4 Hidden documentary defects

The first idiosyncratic consequence of the two rights of rejection lies with a scenario where the seller presents the buyer with falsified documents which are perfectly consistent with what was originally established in the sales contract, and bear no consequences/reflection on the condition of the cargo.

Let us consider a scenario where the seller presents the buyer with a falsified bill of lading with the buyer having no knowledge of the falsification. In that case, the buyer is compelled to accept the documents and, by the same token also the goods if, upon arrival, they are perfectly consistent with the sales contract.

What if the buyer was to discover at a later stage that the bill of lading has been falsified? Can he initiate an action for damages vis-à-vis the seller? If so, how are damages going to be computed? The answers to these questions lie with the two aforementioned cases, *Finlay James*, and *Kwei Teck Chao*.

In *Finlay James*, buyers discovered a falsification in the documents tendered by the seller after having sold the goods at auction making a loss. They were able to sue the original sellers for damages, which were calculated in terms of the difference between the contractual price and the price that the goods were sold for at auction. The rationale for this can be found in the words of Scrutton LJ:

> After the war, and possibly earlier, a lax practice *N. v KWIK* began by which shippers of goods which should have been, H.M. but were not, shipped at the end of a particular month had a bill of lading provided for them dated as in the month of shipment, when it should have been dated after the month of shipment. Sometimes that was done on the shipper giving a letter of indemnity to the shipowner, where upon the latter did what he ought not to have done – namely, misdate the bill of lading. Sometimes it was done by alleging a custom whereby a bill of lading might be dated in September when in fact the goods were not shipped, but which were ready for shipment or were in lighters ready for shipment, in that month. Whatever the reason, the practice was most undesirable, and certainly is not one which I should expect a great shipping line to countenance for a moment. But for some reason those who shipped the sugar on behalf of the Dutch firm obtained mate's receipts dated September 30, although the goods were not in the custody of the ship on that date, and took from the ship a bill of lading dated September 30. As under the contract the sellers had to provide Finlay & Co. with a bill of lading so that under it delivery might be obtained from the ship, and a policy of insurance, the Dutch firm sent forward the bill of lading which was wrongly dated. On receiving it, apparently in order, as it stated that shipment was in September, Finlay & Co. paid the contract price. The market had fallen heavily, and consequently they paid more than the market value of the sugar at that time. If the bill of lading had been correctly dated Finlay & Co. would have rejected the tender and kept the price in their pocket. Finlay & Co. had in fact subsold a portion of the 300 tons, and when they tendered the bill of lading to their sub-purchasers, the latter refused to take it on the ground that the sugar was not shipped in September. Whether the sub-purchasers had information which justified that view or whether they merely rejected.
>
> Accordingly, under the sub-contracts Finlay & Co. might sue the sub-purchasers, but there were circumstances giving rise to suspicion, and Finlay & Co. sued the Dutch firm

> for breach of contract, and Wright J., having come to the conclusion on the evidence that the sugar was not shipped in September, awarded them as damages the difference between the price paid by Finlay & Co. and the value of the sugar at the time of the delivery in Bombay. It is said for the appellants that that is quite the wrong measure of damage. They contend that Finlay & Co. have lost nothing – because they have obtained goods of exactly the same value as they would have got under a September shipment. The judge rejected that contention, and took the view that it was a condition of the contract not only that the goods should be shipped in September but that a genuine bill of lading should be delivered showing the right date of shipment, i.e., September. As he said, if the bill of lading had shown that the shipment was in October, the tender would have been rejected by Finlay & Co., who would have kept in their pocket the price they paid under the contract, and the loss by the fall in the market would properly have fallen on the Dutch firm, because of their breach of contract in presenting an incorrect bill of lading. I agree with that view. Finlay & Co. do not claim the difference between the market value of the goods delivered and the price they would have got under the sub-contracts. If they had been claiming that difference in price as their damages, the question of the exact effect of *Hall v Pirn (Junior) & Co.* (1) and its relation to *Williams Bros. v Agius* (2) would have arisen directly, and we might have been compelled to give the enlightenment for which Mr. Jowitt asked.[25]

The damages awarded in *Finlay James* relate to a scenario whereby a buyer discovers that documents have been falsified after selling the goods over and making a loss.

What is the outcome of a different scenario whereby the buyer, after having accepted the documents and goods, discovers that the documents have been forged, and has retained possession of goods the market value of which has in the meantime decreased?

That was the scenario subject to scrutiny in the *Kwei Teck Chao* case. Here, the court allowed the buyer's course of action vis-à-vis the seller to recover damages. Indeed, it was held that under a c.i.f. contract a buyer had a right to reject the documents and a right to reject the goods, those rights being separate and distinct in law, and his right to damages on a breach of the seller's obligation to present a correct bill of lading vested when the bill was tendered.

That right could not be affected by any action the buyer might take on a subsequent breach by the seller to deliver goods in accordance with the contract, whether the buyer elected to treat the subsequent breach as a breach of condition or as a breach of warranty.

The damages were not therefore limited to the difference in value, if any, between an October shipment and a November shipment. The true measure of the damages was held to be the difference between the contract price and the market price of the goods.

In the words of Devlin J:

> I now have to assess the damages which flow from the breach of contract which I have found in this case to have been committed, that is, the delivery by the sellers to the buyers of forged bills of lading, with the result that the buyers, who accepted them, lost the right to reject which they could have exercised had they known, as they ought to have known from the bills of lading, the true date of shipment.

25 *Finlay (James) & Co. Ltd. v M. V. Kwik Hoo Tong Handel Maatschappij* [1929] 1 KB 400, at 409, 410.

The principle upon which the damages fall to be assessed. I have also already considered, and I have held that the damages are to be determined in accordance with the decision of the Court of Appeal in *James Finlay & Co. Ld. v N.V. Kwik Hoo Tong H.M.1.* The facts in that case were very similar to those in the present case, but the dates are important. In *James Finlay & Go. Ld. v N.V. Kwik Hoo Tong H.M.1* the ship arrived with the goods on board before the documents were tendered; the date of its arrival being November 9, 1920. The documents were tendered on November 12, and the ship completed her discharge on November 15. The goods were rejected by the purchasers, were sold by auction in December 1920, and it was not until some considerable time later, in 1922, that the buyer discovered that the bill of lading was false, and brought his action for damages. The measure of damage was held to be the difference between the contract price of the goods and the market price, as evidenced by the price obtained at the auction.

The dates referred to are to be found in the report of the case in Lloyd's List Reports, 2 and that report makes it clear that the market price did not fluctuate between the date of tender, November 12, and the date when the goods were sold, December 10. It had, however, fallen considerably below the contract price, and the buyer was thus enabled to obtain by way of damages compensation for the fall in the market. That followed because, had he exercised his right to reject, he would have been able to do so, and by so doing would in effect have relieved himself of the result of the fall in the market.

The basis upon which that conclusion was reached is stated by Wright J. in the court of first instance. Having explained the measure of damage, he said: "The measure of damages in such a case, in my judgment, is that which I have explained, and it seems to me exactly to fall within the language of section 53, subsection (2), of the Sale of Goods Act, 1893 namely, the estimated loss directly and naturally resulting, in the ordinary course of events, from the breach of warranty."

Applying that measure, I should not have thought that there would be any difficulty in principle on the facts in this case. The dates and figures in the present case are that the contract price was £590 per ton, the documents were tendered while the voyage was still continuing, on November 10, 1951, and by that date the price had fallen. It is common ground that the reason why the price fell was because of an embargo placed by the Chinese authorities upon the importation of goods of this type from Hongkong. That embargo, in the words of one of the witnesses, "knocked the market to pieces." One of the matters which I shall have to consider is whether there was really a market at all, but there were, at any rate, quotations, although they are said to be, and many of them are in fact given as, "nominal" quotations. The nominal quotation on November 10 was 3–65 cents per lb., which worked out at the equivalent of £504 sterling per ton, so that by that date the market price had, upon any view, fallen to some extent. By December 17, the date when the goods arrived, the quotations had fallen still further, and the comparable figure in sterling per ton was £330.

I have already in my earlier judgment dealt with the date upon which the plaintiffs knew or ought to have known that they had a right to reject, and it is unnecessary for me now to say more than that for the purpose of this judgment I can take it as being not later than December 17, 1952. This is not, therefore, a case like the Kwik Hoo Tong case, in which that knowledge was not acquired until some time afterwards. The date when delivery was taken from the ship was a date on which the plaintiffs knew a great deal, and it is sufficient for the purpose of the judgment in this case to say that they knew enough to enable them to reject, because the case for the plaintiffs is that on or before December 17 and until the present day the goods were substantially worthless, so that the exact date does not matter.

So far as the principle is concerned, the buyer is, upon the measure as set out by Wright J., entitled to be put in the same position as he would have been in if he had exercised his right to reject. He has the goods, he has parted with his money, and therefore he wants to relieve himself of the goods and recover his money. If that is done he will be in the same position as he would have been in if he had never parted with his money and had never received the goods. Accordingly, the reasonable course for him is, as soon as he ascertains that he has a right to compensation, in that the bills of lading were false, to sell the goods then, or within a reasonable time thereafter, for what they will fetch, and to obtain from the seller the difference between the price obtained for the goods and the contract price which he pays. In that way he will be put in almost precisely the same position as if he had rejected the goods. In other words, the measure is the difference between the contract price and the price at which the buyer has sold the goods. Whether that is put as the price which the buyer actually gets for the goods, or whether it is put as the market price obtainable for the goods on the day when the buyer should sell them, I do not think matters very much. It is put in both ways in the course of the judgment in the Court of Appeal in *James Finlay & Co. Ld. v N.V. Kwilt Hoo Tong H.M.*, but if one bears in mind the principle that the buyer is bound to mitigate his damage, then as soon as he knows of his rights he must sell the goods. He cannot do so before he does know his rights, and "as soon as" means within a reasonable time thereafter. If he chooses not to sell the goods he is not to be put in any better or worse position by delaying for his own purposes, so that, in substance, it is the price which he actually gets on selling them, or the price which he actually could get if he did sell them.

Upon that principle, the only difficulty which arises is due to the fact that upon the plaintiffs' case the buyer could not have sold the goods at any time on or after December 17, 1951, in the Hongkong market, that is to say, at any time after he knew of December 17 and until the present day the goods were substantially worthless, so that the exact date does not matter. In those circumstances a difficulty may arise in attempting to find his rights to compensation. Before I deal with that, which is a difficulty arising purely upon the facts of this case, I must deal with the objection which Mr. Eoskill has advanced to the principle as I have just stated it. Mr. Eoskill submits that the true measure of damage is the difference between the contract price and the price at which the buyer could have bought corresponding goods in the market on November 10, 1951, that being the date when the documents were tendered, and when, therefore, his right to reject the goods arose.

Mr. Eoskill concedes, of course, that that was not the date taken in *James Finlay & Co. v Kwik Hoo TongS* the principle of which case I am applying, but he has pointed out that in that case the market price at the date of tender was the same as the market price at the time of the auction, and therefore there was, as he puts it, tersely, "no money in the point." It is quite clear that it never occurred to anybody to take the date of tender as being the relevant date. It is clear also from the terms of Wright J.'s judgment that he was not taking the date of tender. There is nothing to show that he considered the date of tender as being in any way relevant, but, as Mr. Eoskill says, there being nothing in the point, it was not argued, and it is open to him now.

In my judgment, his argument is fallacious in two respects, first, because I do not think that November 10, 1951, was the relevant date, and secondly, because it takes the buying price instead of the selling price. With regard to the first point, the breach for which damage is being awarded is, in effect, the breach of the duty imposed by the contract to give, by means of the bills of lading, correct information about the date of shipment. The bills of lading were false, although the defendants themselves were not privy to the fraud, but they were, by those who perpetrated the fraud, intended to be acted upon and to deceive, among others, the plaintiffs, and the plaintiffs were so deceived. It seems to me to be quite illogical to say that the plaintiffs must be expected as reasonable men to act in the same way as if they had not been deceived.

As to the consequences of a wrong which deceives the aggrieved party, whether it be a tort or a breach of contract, the aggrieved party cannot be expected to act in such a manner as to compensate himself until he has ascertained the fact. It seems to me quite fictitious to talk of the buyers having to be treated as if they had gone out into the market and bought goods on November 10, when, in fact, they had supposed that they had already taken up goods which were in accordance with the contract, and they had no notion, and could have had no notion, that rights with regard to the contract.

That I still believe to be a correct statement of the law, but it does not state, and it does not require, that the amount is to be determined by reference to the conditions which existed on the day when the breach was committed. The right to damages then vests, the measure is then decided upon, as it were, in law; but it may well be that the amount cannot be ascertained until subsequent events have determined it. That must be so, of course, in every case of fraud, where the damages cannot be quantified until it is seen what means of mitigation are open to the aggrieved party when he knows the facts.

Mr. Eoskill objects to the consideration of the question of fraud, because he says that the position is different in tort from what it would be in damages for breach of contract. I do not know that it is, but the matter is not peculiar to fraud. If one takes, for example, a case of wrongful dismissal, the right to damages vests on the date of the breach, which is the date of the wrongful dismissal. The measure of damages is then determined once and for all, and it is the difference between the salary or wages which the plaintiff would have earned under the contract for the remaining period of the contract, and such salary or wages as he has been able to get by obtaining comparable work during the period of the contract which he did not serve with his former employer. The amount is still unsettled; it cannot be ascertained until it is seen what alternative remuneration the plaintiff is able to secure, and it would add nothing to the point to say that upon the date of the breach there happened to be a job vacant which was precisely the same as the one from which the plaintiff had been dismissed, at precisely the same salary, if the plaintiff did not know about it and could not, by the exercise of reasonable diligence, have obtained it. I think, therefore, that the relevant date is not the date of breach, but the date when the plaintiffs could, acting with reasonable diligence, and after they knew of their rights, have resold the goods on the market and obtained the best price they could for them.

The second fallacy in Mr. Eoskill's argument is that he takes the buying price and not the selling price. That is not generally a matter of importance. The margin between the two is not ordinarily great, but in this case it happens to be of considerable importance. It is common ground that the quotations represent the price at which anybody could buy Kongalite in Hongkong. It may be that the plaintiffs could have bought it for less, but it is disputed that the quotations represented the price a seller could necessarily obtain when the market was so constricted that there was no longer the ordinary small margin between the buying and selling price.

In my judgment, the buying price has nothing to do with the calculation which I have to make. It is no doubt true that if the goods had been rejected, the buyer, if he had wanted to provide himself with similar goods for the purpose of fulfilling his contract of resale, could have gone out in the market as on the day of the rejection and bought them, and the difference between the contract price and the lower buying price would have been the profit which he made by virtue of the rejection, and which in one sense he has lost because he did not reject. It is also true that if a buyer rejected and wanted to claim damages against the seller, the measure of damages, which could only arise at all if the market had risen and not fallen, would be the price at which he bought goods in order to put himself in the same position.

But those calculations, and the relevance of the buying price, depend upon the fact that the buyer has not got the goods. He has returned them, and is putting himself in the same position, so far as he can, as if the contract goods had been delivered. Therefore he has to buy. In this case the buyer has received the goods, and a calculation which supposes, incorrectly and notionally, that he should go out and buy another quantity of the same goods, has nothing to do with the reality of the matter. What he wishes to do in those circumstances, in order to put himself in the same position, is to sell the goods, not to buy them, and one would think, therefore, that the measure

> I have stated, and which seems to me to follow the principle to which I have referred, would be the right one.
>
> Therefore, the only difficulty which arises is due to the fact that there cannot be fixed with any degree of certainty the price at which the buyer could have sold on the market on December 17 or thereafter. There is a substantial body of evidence to show that the quotations were merely nominal quotations, and many of them are indeed so described. There were some sales; there is no specific evidence of the quantity sold, but the general evidence is that they were all very small sales, and that in fact no substantial sales at all were taking place during the relevant period. That evidence comes from a number of sources, but I heard yesterday the evidence of Mr. Sulke, a partner in the plaintiff firm, who was dealing with the matter, and I have no hesitation in acting upon it. He seemed to me to be a good and reliable witness, and his evidence is corroborated and fortified by much other evidence given in the course of the case.
>
> The conclusion which I draw from that evidence is that there was no market in which these goods could be sold, in the ordinary sense; that the market had gone to pieces, and that the only demand for this material being from the mainland, an enormous surplus was built up in the godowns in Hongkong, which nobody was willing to take, and the only outlet was small sales. The test of the matter, after all, is that Mr. Sulke has a quantity of this material on his hands, and I am satisfied that his evidence is true when he says that he has endeavoured to sell it, has failed so to do, and still cannot sell it. When I say that he has endeavoured to sell "it" that requires modification. He has not, or at any rate he did not for a considerable period after the event, endeavour to sell the 20 tons which were the subject-matter of the contract, because he supposed that they were not his property; but he had another 10 tons of a similar material, which he endeavoured but has been unable to sell. I am satisfied, therefore, that the plaintiffs' case is made out when they say that this commodity was virtually unsaleable in the Hongkong market. But "virtually unsaleable" does not mean that the goods have no value for the purpose of the calculation of damages. They have not yet been sold, and it is possible that they may never be sold, but it is also possible that trade may revive and that some sort of a market may be found for them if they are held on to long enough. They therefore have some value, although it may be a speculative one, but that possibility in itself is something which must be valued.
>
> The only sale of any quantity which the evidence reveals is a sale at 50 cents per lb., that is, £70 per ton. The plaintiffs are content to take that as being evidence of the salvage value of the goods, and that is therefore the figure which, for the purpose of this calculation of value, I place upon them. The only other observation which I would make is that with regard to Mr. Eoskill's contention that, there being no sellers' market in Hongkong, it was the duty of the plaintiffs in such circumstances to seek a market elsewhere. I need not say more about that than that I am not satisfied on the evidence that there was any market elsewhere in which the plaintiffs, acting reasonably, could have resold this quantity of these goods.
>
> Accordingly, the damages will be calculated on the basis of the difference between the contract price of £590 per ton less the figure of £70 per ton, upon the contract quantity of 20 tons.[26]

The idea of linking the calculation of damages with fluctuations in the market value of the goods has been subject to judicial criticism. The ordinary measure of damages in the case of delayed shipment of goods is made plain by the authority of *Taylor & Sons Ltd. v Bank of Athens*.[27] Here, in analysing the legal nature of damages under such circumstances, McCardie J stated that:

---

26 *Kwei Tek Chao & Others v British Traders and Shippers Ltd.* [1954] 2 QB 459, at 492–497.
27 *Taylor & Sons Ltd. v Bank of Athens* [1922] 10 Lloyd's Rep. 88.

I therefore cannot deal with this case on the footing that it is a claim for damages by the buyers for delay. How then does the matter stand as to Sect. 53 of the Sale of Goods Act? Now it seems reasonably clear that this case does not fall within Sub-sect. 3 of Sect. 53. That Sub-sect., as I have said, refers to "breach of warranty of quality." I do not forget Sect. 62 (the definition clause of the Act) which provides that "'quality of goods' includes their state or condition." But even though a broad meaning be given to the word "quality" it can scarcely include the state of things now before me when considered in the light of *Bowes v Shand* (sup.). In *Bostock v Nicholson* [1904] 1 K.B. 734, Mr. Justice Bruce said: "Sub-sect. 3 of Sect. 53 relates only to a breach of warranty of quality." So too, in *Benjamin on Sale*, 6th Edition, 1143, the learned author points out that Sub-sect. 3 of Sect. 53 covers only cases of breach of warranty of quality. "In the case," he adds, "of breach of warranty of description or of fitness the buyer's damages are regulated by Sub-sect. 2 only." I therefore turn to Sub-sect. 2 and consider how it bears on the case before me. It is a very important Sub-section, for it is the one which applies to a vast number of the cases which come before the Courts.

I point out that there is here no question at all of special damages within Sect. 54 of the Act. Contrast, for example, the facts in *Bostock v Nicholson* (sup.). Now the Subsection says that the measure of damages for breach of warranty is the estimated loss directly and naturally resulting, in the ordinary course of events, from the breach of warranty. It is vital to observe that the damage must result from the breach of warranty, as distinguished from a loss through having entered into the contract. It does not extend, I think, to a case where the loss results not from the breach of warranty but from an unfortunate or improvident bargain which the buyer may have made. Market falls are not generally due to a vendor's default. A buyer cannot, I think, save perhaps in very exceptional circumstances, attribute to his seller a loss which, in substance and in fact, arises not from the seller's breach but from a fall in market values. To impose the burden of such a loss would be to saddle him with something for which he is wholly free from blame. Although the present is not a case of delay, yet I think that the guiding principle of *Wertheim v Chicoutimi Pulp Co.* (sup.) is one which should here be applied. At page 307 the Board said:- It is the general intention of the law that in giving damage for breach of contract the party complaining should, so far as it can be done by money, be placed in the same position as he would have been in if the contract had been performed. (*Irvine v Midland Railway Co., Ireland* (1880) 6 L.R. Irish, page 63, approved by Palles, C.B., in *Hamilton v Magill* (1883), 12 L.R. Irish, at page 202.) That is a ruling principle. It is a just principle.

In the case now before me the buyers would, even if the sellers had fulfilled their bargain, have suffered the loss of £4 per ton by reason of the fall in market values. The breach of contract committed by the seller was not assessable save at a nominal sum, inasmuch as there was no difference in value at the material time between locust beans shipped in August and locust beans shipped in September.[28]

McCardie J's reluctance to link damages to fluctuations in the market value of the goods was expressed as follows:

It is vital to observe that the loss "must result from the breach of warranty, as distinguished from a loss through having entered into the contract. It does not extend, I think, to a case where the loss results not from the breach of warranty but from an unfortunate or improvident bargain which the buyer may have made. Market falls are not generally due to a vendor's default. A buyer cannot, I think, save perhaps in very exceptional circumstances, attribute to his seller a loss which, in substance and in fact, arises not from the seller's breach, but from a fall in market values. To impose the

28 *Ibid.*, at 90.

> burden of such a loss on the seller would be to saddle him with something for which he is wholly free from blame".[29]

Taylor & Sons Ltd. v Bank of Athens was distinguished in *Finlay James*, where the facts were substantially the same except that the buyer, instead of suing for damages for failure to ship within the contract time, sued, as he was able to do in that case, for damages for failure to deliver a correct bill of lading.

McCardie J's approach to damages in *Taylor & Sons Ltd. v Bank of Athens* has sound foundations. Indeed, linking the measure of damages to market variations it may appear, *prima facie*, quite peculiar especially if one considers that market oscillations in terms of value of the goods have nothing to do with the seller's behaviour.[30]

Nevertheless, the scenario whereby a buyer is somehow "forced" to accept falsified documents and at a later stage to also accept the goods as consistent with what was originally established in the sale contract, is equally atypical.

Under those circumstances, the buyer must be in the position to act vis-à-vis the seller and recover damages; nevertheless, the calculation of the measure of damages is altogether a complex matter.

In order to solve this conundrum, one may look at the general principles of the law when it comes to the possibility of initiating an action for damages. Damages are always linked to the nature of the breach, in the sense that if there is no breach (and loss for that matter), damages cannot be claimed or awarded.

What is the nature of damages claimed by a buyer "forced" to accept documents which are, *prima facie*, of contractual specification but which, in reality, conceal defects?

Those damages are linked to the failure of the seller to honestly perform his documentary duties; as a result, the buyer was deprived of his sacrosanct right to reject the defective documents presented by the seller, terminate the contract, not pay for the goods, or reach a settlement with the seller obtaining a discount or other form of compensation (the most likely scenario in practice).

Having established the nature of the breach, it is now possible to endeavour to calculate the measure of the damages by taking into account what McCardie J stated, inter alia, in *Taylor & Sons Ltd. v Bank of Athens,* i.e. that:

> It is the general intention of the law that in giving damage for breach of contract the party complaining should, so far as it can be done by money, be placed in the same position as he would have been in if the contract had been performed.[31]

This passage is of the utmost importance as it encapsulates in legal teleological terms the essence of the computation of damages in the case of breach of contract, i.e. the concept of putting the party not in breach in the position that he should have been, had the contract been regularly performed.

---

29 *Ibid.*

30 On this point, see Debattista, *Bills of Lading in Export Trade*, above, p. 297. See also *Benjamin's Sale of Goods*, above, paras. 21.236 *et seq*. See also I. Carr, *International Trade Law*, Routledge, 2013, p.569.

31 *Taylor & Sons Ltd. v Bank of Athens* [1922] 10 Lloyd's Rep. 88, 90.

And that is exactly what the courts did in *Finlay James* and *Kweck Tech Chao*, where the calculation of damages was computed on the basis of the difference between the contractual price and the price for which the goods were sold at auction (*Finlay James*, where the buyer made a loss), or the market value of the goods on the day the falsification was discovered (*Kweck Tech Chao*, where the buyer retained possession of the goods).

Although *prima facie* linked to fluctuations in the market value of the goods, it is submitted that the calculation of damages as per *Finlay James* and *Kweck Tech Chao* is the only possible means to attempt somehow to move "back in time", placing the buyer in the position he should have been, had the seller performed in an honest fashion.

Indeed, had the seller performed honestly, presenting the buyer with a bill of lading dated outside the shipment period, the buyer would have been in the position to reject the documents, terminate the contract, or obtain the cargo at a discounted price.

12.5 Defects confined to the documents alone

In both the aforementioned cases, *Finlay James* and *Kweck Tech Chao*, the hidden documentary defects discovered at a later stage by the buyer, i.e. bills of lading falsely dated within the shipment period reflected a breach of the physical duty to ship the goods in time.

What if the hidden documentary defects discovered by the buyer after having accepted a cargo of contractual specifications remain confined to the documents alone? This is what happened in *Procter & Gamble Philippine Manufacturing Corporation v Kurt A. Becher GmbH & Co. K.G.*,[32] where the date on the bill of lading did not correspond to the shipment date, which fell, nevertheless, within the shipment period originally established in the sales contract.

Here we are clearly dealing with a scenario whereby the documentary defects remained confined to the documents alone, as the cargo was shipped within the shipment time, but the bill of lading did not carry the exact date of shipment.

The buyers' attempt to claim damages vis-à-vis the seller was thwarted on appeal by the fact that the Court of Appeal found that their remedy was confined to recovering the actual financial loss, if any, suffered by them by reason of the breach.

Since the buyers had suffered no financial loss, they were not capable of recovering any damages from the sellers.

As held by Kerr LJ:

> The whole basis of the decision in James Finlay was that one of the sellers' obligations under a c.i.f. contract is to present a correctly dated bill of lading. This obligation has the character of a condition, in the sense that the buyer is entitled to reject a tender of documents which include an incorrectly dated bill of lading, and thus entitled to refuse to pay for the goods. On a falling market it is self-evident that buyers would have availed themselves of this right if they had known that the tendered bill of lading

32 *Procter & Gamble Philippine Manufacturing Corporation v Kurt A. Becher GmbH & Co. K.G.* [1988] 2 Lloyd's Rep. 21.

was misdated. As Lord Justice Scrutton said in James Finlay at pp. 249 and 409, the buyers would in that event have kept the price in their pocket. And in James Finlay and Kwei Tek Chao the buyers accordingly recovered full damages on this basis. No more need be said by way of introduction.

One then comes to the buyers' seductive submission on these lines. Mr. Russell said that it followed that if the buyers had known in this case that the bill of lading had been misdated they would have rejected the documents, refused to pay the price and left the sellers to face the loss resulting from the fall in the market. As a statement of what would have happened if the buyers had known the true facts this is obviously true. But it does not provide the correct test in law. The issue is not what the buyers would have done if they had known the true facts. The first question is: what would have been the buyers' rights if the sellers had not committed the breach on which the buyers rely?

That this is the correct analysis of the issue is not only apparent from the passages cited from the judgments in James Finlay, but also as a matter of general principle. The object of an award of damages for breach of contract is to put the innocent party in the same position so far as money can do it as if the contract had not been broken. So put, the answer to the present problem becomes obvious. If there had been no breach, then the bill of lading under contract 83/703 would have been dated Feb. 6 or 10 instead of Jan. 31. In that event the buyers would have had no right to reject it or to refuse to pay for the goods. They would only have been entitled to the contractual allowance for shipment in February. In relation to contract 83/701 the position would have been different. A correctly dated bill of lading would have revealed the sellers' breach of condition in relation to the date of shipment, whereas an incorrect date concealed this breach. On that basis, following James Finlay, the buyers were rightly awarded full damages under contract 83/701. But the Board of Appeal was wrong in drawing no distinction in relation to contract 83/703 and awarding full damages in both cases. The incorrectly dated bill of lading tendered under the latter contract concealed no similar breach.

The correctness of this analysis is supported by two other general considerations.

First, as was pointed out by Mr. Justice McCardie in *Taylor v Bank of Athens*, the position would of course be entirely different if the sellers had themselves been involved in the false dating of the bill of lading and could therefore have been sued in fraud. In that event the buyers would have recovered full damages because the measure of damages in claims for fraud is different. In cases of fraudulent misrepresentation the innocent party is entitled to be put in the same position as if the representation had not been made, not as if it had been true: see *Doyle v Olby (Ironmongers) Ltd.* [1969] 2 Q.B. 158 and *Saunders v Edwards* [1987] 1 W.L.R. 1116 at p. 1121. In that event, therefore, the measure of damages would have assumed that no bill of lading had been presented at all and placed the buyers in the same position as if they had kept the price of the goods in their pocket. But there was no basis for any such claim in the present case, and we also heard no argument about the possible relevance of the Misrepresentation Act 1967. I therefore say no more about this.

The second aspect which one must bear in mind is that the buyers' apparent misfortune is no different in principle from other situations where an "innocent" party may be unaware in time that the other party has committed a breach of condition. When he subsequently discovers this he may be compelled to treat it as no more than a breach of warranty. The damages recoverable for a breach of warranty may well turn out to be greatly different from what would have been the "innocent" party's position if he had known of the breach of condition in time to be able to rescind the contract. In financial terms the difference is between compensation for a breach of contract and putting the innocent party in the same position as if he had never entered into the contract at all. *Taylor v Bank of Athens* provides a good illustration in a similar context. Unfortunately for the buyers, no reliance was placed on the breach involved in the tender of a wrongly dated bill of lading, as subsequently in James Finlay. The shipment had been made out of time on a falling market, and if the buyers had been aware of this they would, of course, have refused to pay against the documents. But the sellers were equally innocent, and by the time the truth came out the buyers were left only with the measure of damages under s. 53(2). But no loss connected with the fall in the market flowed from the fact that the shipment was a few days late; nor any other loss. So the buyers were left with nominal damages only. Strictly, as both Counsel agreed, if Mr. Justice Leggatt had not ordered the repayment of 312 per cent. of the price as damages, his order should have included an award of nominal damages.[33]

Kerr LJ's judgment was echoed by Nichols LJ who, for his part, stated that:

Although the sole question on this appeal concerns damages, it is necessary to note at once, because this is at the heart of the arguments advanced on behalf of the buyers, that a right to damages is not the only remedy which a buyer has in respect of a misdated bill of lading. Before us it was common ground that the buyers in the present case were entitled to reject the bill of lading when it was tendered. They were entitled to reject the bill of lading because it misstated the date of shipment. They were entitled to reject the bill for this reason, even though the goods had been shipped within the shipment period. If the buyers had exercised that right then, unless the sellers had been able to re-tender another, correct bill of lading, that would have been the end of the matter: the buyers would have kept the price, and they would not have suffered the loss they did by reason of the fall in the market.

That remedy, of rejection of the shipping documents when tendered, was one of the remedies available in respect of the sellers' breach of cl. 6. In the event the buyers were unable to have recourse to that remedy, because they did not know of the inaccuracy in the bill of lading when it was tendered. So, perforce, the buyers' remedy in respect of the sellers' breach of cl. 6 was confined to a right to recover damages.

It is at this point, as it seems to me, that some confusion has crept into the buyers' case. It is trite law that the basic, general principle applicable in awarding damages for breach of contract is that the innocent party is to be placed, so far as money can do this, in the same position as he would have been in if the contract had been performed. If in the circumstances the breach caused no financial loss, only nominal damages are recoverable by the innocent party. This, on principle, will be so even if the breach in respect of which damages are being claimed is a breach of a condition which would have enabled the innocent party to reject the documents or goods altogether, had he known of the existence of the breach before, by accepting the documents or goods, it became too late for him to exercise the remedy of rejection. In such a case the remedy of rejection may afford an innocent party a much more valuable form of relief. But when that remedy ceases to be available, and the innocent party is confined to his remedy in damages, he is not entitled to assess his damages by reference to what his financial position would have been if the primary remedy of rejection had been exercised by him. For better or worse, his claim, as a claim for damages, is then confined to making good the loss sustained by him by reason of the breach of the contract. Quantifying that loss requires, in general, a comparison to be made between the innocent party's actual financial position and what his financial position would have been had the contract been duly performed.

This accords with the approach adopted in s. 53(1) and (2) of the Sale of Goods Act, 1979:

(1) Where there is a breach of warranty by the seller, or where the buyer elects (or is compelled) to treat any breach of a condition on the part of the seller

33 *Ibid.*, at 27, 28, 29.

as a breach of warranty, the buyer is not by reason only of such a breach of warranty entitled to reject the goods; but he may –

(a) set up against the seller the breach of warranty in diminution or extinction of the price or,

(b) maintain an action against the seller for damages for the breach of warranty.

(2) The measure of damages for breach of warranty is the estimated loss directly and naturally resulting, in the ordinary course of events, from the breach of warranty.

There is no suggestion in that section that the measure of the damages recoverable for breach of warranty in a case where there has been a breach of condition which the buyer has been compelled to treat as a warranty is any different from the measure of the damages recoverable in any other case of breach of warranty.

[. . .] I do not think that the existence of the disparity in the efficacy of the two remedies, rejection and damages, in a case where the breach causes little or no financial loss to a buyer, casts doubt on the correctness of this analysis of the measure of the damages recoverable for such a breach. The disparity arises from the availability of the right of rejection in such a case, namely, even where the breach of condition has caused little or no financial damage to the innocent party. If there is an anomaly here, it lies in the availability of the remedy of rejection in such a case, not in the measure of damages applicable in such a case. As I see it, this is the short and complete answer to the buyers' contention that damages in respect of the tender of the misdated bill of lading are to be assessed on the footing that the buyers were thereby wrongfully deprived of a right to reject the documents and the goods. They did not lose that right by reason of the breach. Had there been no breach of cl. 6 the buyers would have had no right to reject the bill of lading or the goods. What the buyers lost, in the event, was the opportunity to exercise one of the remedies (rejection) afforded by the law in respect of the breach. They lost the opportunity to exercise that remedy, not because of the breach of cl. 6, but because they did not know of the existence of the breach at the time. But, as I have sought to indicate, having lost the opportunity to exercise the remedy of rejection in respect of the breach, thenceforth the buyers' remedy in respect of the breach was confined to recovering the actual financial loss, if any, suffered by them by reason of the breach.

[. . .] In particular, it was submitted, first, that since the tender of the bill of lading was a bad tender, the comparison to be made is between the financial position of the buyers (a) having accepted the bad tender and (b) having rejected the bad tender. I cannot accept this formulation. The comparison is between the financial position of the buyers in the events which happened (viz. having accepted the bad tender) and what their financial position would have been if the bill of lading had stated accurately the date of shipment (viz. having accepted a good tender).

If that comparison is made, the extent of the loss of the buyers was that, unknown to themselves, they had been given an unmerchantable bill of lading. As to that, I do not doubt that there may be cases where a buyer suffers loss by payment of the price against a bill of lading which was unmerchantable because it mis-stated the date of shipment even though the actual date of shipment was within the contract period. Such a buyer might, by reason of the unmerchantability of the bill, be unable to sell the goods, or complete a prior sale of the goods, whilst the goods were still afloat. In such a case the buyers' prima facie measure of damages would be the difference between the market value of the goods when he ought to have been able to deal with them (viz. when the bill of lading was tendered and accepted) and the market value of the goods when he became able to deal with them (viz. when the goods were delivered). In the present case the impact of cl. 27 would also have to be considered with regard to any claim for loss of profit on sub-sales. I do not pursue these points, however, because no claim under any of these heads was advanced in this case before such a claim emerged, as an alternative claim, in the course of the argument of this

> appeal. Neither before the arbitrators nor before the Judge did the buyers claim that pending the arrival of the cargo in Rotterdam and its delivery to the buyers they had suffered loss by reason only of the bill of lading being unmerchantable because of the inaccuracy in it. What was claimed was the difference between the price paid by the buyers on tender of shipping documents.[34]

The judgment in *Procter & Gamble* appears to be, with respect, idiosyncratic regarding the issue of damages. It would appear that where the buyer accepts documents with hidden defects which do not conceal any physical defect with the goods, the buyer can neither pull out of the trading contract nor sue for damages.

Although the lack of a perceivable loss under normal circumstances would unquestionably prevent any buyer from recovering damages, the scenario arising in *Procter & Gamble* must be considered within the context of contracts concluded on shipment terms.

Here the seller's documentary and physical duties are quite distinct; consequently, there is no need for any reflection of a breach of a documentary duty onto a breach of physical duty in order for a buyer's claim to arise.

Furthermore, although no identifiable loss was ascertained, a bill of lading falsely dated is of no use to an aware buyer; a buyer in possession of such a bill is not in the position to endorse the goods over whilst they are in transit, nor to trade them.

This violates the core and essence of international commercial sales, i.e. the trading of the goods through the endorsement of the documents.

As a result, it is rather difficult to postulate the possibility of a seller remaining unharmed after having tendered a document which frustrates the possibility of the buyer endorsing the goods over.

In the absence of tangible loss, damages could have been awarded nominally in order to compensate the position of a buyer "stuck" with a bill of lading on a cargo that is untradable.

12.6 Acceptance of clearly defective documents: The *Panchaud Freres* doctrine

Where the buyer accepts documents which contain noticeable defects, what effect does that acceptance have on his right to reject the goods?

If the right to reject documents is separate and independent of the right to reject goods, then surely the answer to this question should be none. Indeed, the fact that the buyer decided to accept clearly defective documents should bear no consequence on his right to reject the goods.

On the other hand, to give the buyer the right to reject goods in these circumstances would be to allow him to "blow hot and cold" on the contract depending on what was happening to the market price of the commodity concerned. How have the courts resolved this dilemma?

34 *Ibid.*, at 31–32.

The seminal decision on this matter is *Panchaud Freres*.[35] Here a sales contract for Brazilian yellow maize c.i.f. Antwerp provided, inter alia, for shipment to take place from (a) Brazilian port/s not north of Santos during the period of June/July, 1965.

The sales contract incorporated all the terms and conditions of the London Corn Trade Association contract form No. 77, which provided, inter alia, that the bill of lading was to be considered proof of date of shipment in the absence of evidence to the contrary.

Pursuant to the contract, the sellers tendered to the buyers, inter alia, a bill of lading in respect of 200 metric tons of Brazilian yellow maize shipped on the *African Night*. The bill of lading was dated 31 July 1965.

Other shipping documents tendered included a certificate of quality, which stated, in respect of the 200 tons: "Loaded on August 10 to 12, 1965." On arrival of the vessel at Antwerp, the buyers refused to take delivery of the 200 tons on the grounds that the number of bags did not correspond with the number stated in the bill of lading.

The sellers conceded that they had breached the contract by reason of the false date on the bill of lading, but contended that the buyers had waived the breach through the acceptance of clearly defective documents.

In appeal, the court held that buyers, by taking up documents and paying for them, were precluded from complaining of late shipment or of a defect in the bill of lading. The Court of Appeal found that if a man, who is entitled to reject goods on a certain ground, so conducts himself as to lead the other to believe that he is not relying on that ground, then he cannot afterwards set it up as a ground of rejection, when it would be unfair or unjust to allow him so to do. In the words of Lord Denning:

> This doctrine of estoppel by conduct underlies the dictum of Mr. Justice Devlin (as he then was) in *Kwei Tek Chao and Others (trading as Zung Fu Co.) v British Traders and Shippers Ltd. N.V. Handelsmaatschappij J. Smits Import-Export, Third Party* [1954] 2 Q.B. 459, at pp. 480 and 481; [1954] 1 Lloyd's Rep. 16, at pp. 48 and 49. It is so very apposite that I will read it in full:
>
> [. . .] If there is a late shipment, as there was in this case, the date of the shipment being part of the description of the goods, the seller has not put on board goods which conform to the contract description, and therefore he has broken that obligation. He has also made it impossible to send forward a bill of lading which at once conforms with the contract and states accurately the date of shipment. Thus the same act can cause two breaches of two independent obligations.
>
> However that may be, they are distinct obligations, and the right to reject the documents arises when the documents are tendered, and the right to reject the goods arises when they are landed and when after examination they are found not to be in conformity with the contract. There are many cases, of course, where the documents are accepted but the goods are subsequently rejected. It may be that if the actual date of shipment is not in conformity with the contract, and the error appears from the documents, the buyer, by accepting the documents, not only loses his right to reject the documents, but also his right to reject the goods, but that would be because he had waived in advance reliance on the date of shipment. [. . .]

35 *Panchaud Freres* [1970] 1 Lloyd's Rep. 53.

> Mr. Justice Devlin used the word "waived". But he used it in its popular sense. Not in its legal sense. When "waiver" is used in its legal sense, it only takes place when a man, with knowledge of a breach, does an unequivocal act which shows that he has elected to affirm the contract as still existing instead of disaffirming it as, for instance, in waiver of forfeiture: see *Matthews v Smallwood* [1910] 1 Ch. 777. In the present case Mr. Justice Roskill thought that Mr. Justice Devlin had used "waived" in that sense: and he held that these buyers had not waived the right to reject for late shipment because they had not got actual knowledge of that breach. At most they had constructive notice of it: and our commercial law sets its face resolutely against any doctrine of constructive notice: see *Manchester Trust v Furness* [1895] 2 Q.B. 539, at p. 545, by Lord Justice Lindley, and *Greer v Downs Supply Company* [1927] 2 K.B. 28, at p. 36, by Lord Justice Scrutton.
>
> The present case is not a case of "waiver" strictly so called. It is a case of estoppel by conduct. The basis of it is that a man has so conducted himself that it would be unfair or unjust to allow him to depart from a particular state of affairs which another has taken to be settled or correct see the cases I referred to in *Central Newbury Car Auctions Ltd. v Unity Finance Ltd. and Another. Mercury Motors, Third Parties* [1957] 1 Q.B. 371, at p. 380. Applied to the rejection of goods, the principle may be stated thus: If a man, who is entitled to reject goods on a certain ground, so conducts himself as to lead the other to believe that he is not relying on that ground, then he cannot afterwards set it up as a ground of rejection, when it would be unfair or unjust to allow him so to do. Mr. Lloyd gave a good illustration. Suppose, he said, in this case the bill of lading had contained the true date of shipment – Aug. 12 – (whereas the last date under the contract was July 31): so that, when the buyer took up the documents, he could have seen, if he had read it, that the date of shipment was Aug. 12. If he did not trouble to read it, but instead took up the documents and paid for them, he could not afterwards reject the goods on the ground of late shipment. Even though he had not read the bill of lading – and so was ignorant of the late shipment – he could not afterwards reject the goods on that ground: for the simple reason that he had the full opportunity of finding out from the contract documents what the real date of shipment was: and yet he did not trouble to do so. It would not be fair or just to allow him afterwards to reject the goods. Mr. Evans was inclined to accept this illustration as correct. Another instance can be given from the ordinary sale of goods. If a buyer does not choose to examine the goods when they arrive, and puts it off beyond a reasonable time, he loses his right to reject; see sect. 35 of the Sale of Goods Act, 1893. Although he did not know they were not in conformity with the contract, nevertheless, by letting a reasonable time go by, he loses his right to reject.
>
> It seems to me that this case falls within that principle. If the buyers had read the shipping documents when they took them up and paid for them – as they could and should have done – they would have read this certificate of quality and seen that the date of shipment was really Aug. 12: and that someone had put July 31 on to the bill of lading so as to make it appear that the goods had been shipped in accordance with the contract, whereas, in fact they had not. If the buyers choose not to read the documents, they must put up with the consequences.[36]

The effects of the *Panchaud Freres* doctrine entail that a buyer who decides to accept clearly defective documents is thereafter estopped from rejecting goods on similar grounds.

This means that if a buyer accepts a bill of lading clearly dated outside the shipment period, he will no longer be in the position to reject the goods for breach of

36 *Ibid.*, at 56, 57, 58.

the corresponding physical duty to ship the goods on time once the goods reach the port of destination, and vice versa.

The effects of the *Panchaud Freres* doctrine should not be overextended, in the sense that the buyer accepting documents evidently defective is still in the position to reject the goods on different grounds.[37]

The implications of the *Panchaud Freres* doctrine place it in conceptual terms within the category of exceptions of the principle of separation and independence of the two buyer's rights of rejection.

The rationale of *Panchaud Freres* is sound: the judgment does not attempt to erode the separation between the seller's physical and documentary duties; rather, it creates a legal mechanism capable of estopping a buyer from using legal principles in order to speculate on the market value of the goods.[38]

Nevertheless, the consequences of *Panchaud Freres* for the possibility of a buyer accepting clearly defective documents to initiate an action vis-à-vis the seller have been the object of much debate, as we shall discover in the following.

12.7 Acceptance of clearly defective documents and actions for damages

The judgment in *Panchaud Freres* does not deal with the implications of the acceptance of defective documents for the possibility of recovering damages from the seller.

That matter has been dealt with by two conflicting judgments, *Kleinjan & Holst v Bremer Handels*[39] and *Vargas v Cremer*.[40]

In *Kleinjan & Holst v Bremer Handels*, the sellers tendered patently defective documents which were accepted by the buyers, who subsequently initiated an action for damages vis-à-vis the sellers for breach of contract.

The court held that it was the duty of the seller to tender shipping documents complying with the original sales contract and, by failing to do so, they were in

37 For instance, a buyer accepting a bill of lading showing late shipment could still reject the cargo by reason of breaches of other physical duties, e.g. cargo of inferior quality or of non-contractual description. In terms of reflections on SOGA 1979, see section 35A(1) of the Act. Prior to the amendments, termination for breach of condition was a black-and-white remedy: the buyer could not accept some goods and reject the rest. If he accepted some goods, he was then thrown onto his remedy in damages for the damaged goods.

This is why parties are careful in commodity contracts to allow for price adjustments. Section 35A now allows the buyer to reject the non-conforming goods while accepting the rest: "If the buyer has the right to reject the goods . . . but accepts some of the goods, including, where there are any goods unaffected by the breach, all such goods, he does not by accepting them lose his right to reject the rest."

It is important to note that this new section does not force the buyer to accept the conforming goods: it simply gives him the option of so doing and rejecting the rest. He may still reject the lot, possibly an attractive option in a falling market, and in this sense, price adjustment clauses are still necessary if the seller wants to close off the buyer's right of rejection.

38 See Debattista, *Bills of Lading in Export Trade*, above at p. 216.

39 *Kleinjan & Holst v Bremer Handels* [1972] 2 Lloyd's Rep. 11. See Debattista, *Bills of Lading in Export Trade*, above, p. 321. See also *Benjamin's Sale of Goods*, above, paras. 21.096 *et seq*. See J. Chua, *Law of International Trade*, Sweet & Maxwell, 2009, p. 363.

40 *Vargas v Cremer* [1987] 1 Lloyd's Rep. 394.

breach of a condition of the contract which gave rise to the buyer's right to claim damages.

As held by Cooke J:

> I now come to the question of damages. The argument of the sellers, as I understand it, is this. The buyers in this case have accepted the documents and have accepted the goods. Therefore, by virtue of sect. 11 (1) (c) of the Sale of Goods Act, 1893, the breach of any condition to be fulfilled by the sellers can only be treated as a breach of warranty. The only breach of warranty on which it is now open to the buyers to rely is a warranty that the goods would be shipped on the Mahout. Applying the principles of sect. 53 of the Sale of Goods Act, the measure of damages for such a breach is the difference in value between goods shipped on the Mahout and goods shipped on the Mahsud, and since there is no such difference in value or, at any rate, none has been established, the buyers are entitled to recover nominal damages only. That, as I understand it, is the gist of Mr. Boyd's argument on this part of the case and in support of it he relies on the decision of Mr. Justice McCardie in *Taylor and Sons Ltd. v Bank of Athens* (1922) 27 Com. Cas. 142. I think it is convenient to begin from what I hope are generally accepted principles. Where the sellers are in breach of a term of the contract which in Sale of Goods Act terminology is a condition, the buyers may, if they act at the right time, rescind the contract. If for any reason the buyers are unable to act at the right time or if they elect not to rescind, then the right of rescission is lost, but since the fact remains that the sellers are in breach of the term in question the buyers are entitled to recover damages for that particular breach in accordance with whatever measure is appropriate to it. No doubt in the case where the buyers elect not to rescind they may, at the same or some other time, waive also their right to recover damages for the particular breach in question. Such a waiver is perhaps in normal circumstances unlikely. In any event, an election not to rescind for the breach does not of itself import a waiver of the right to recover damages for it. One turns then to consider what happened in this case. The findings in par. 10 of the special case appear to me to show that on Feb. 15, 1971, the buyers were minded to reject the documents tendered. That is to say, the buyers were minded to rescind the contract on the ground of the sellers' breach of condition in failing to tender documents complying with the notice of appropriation of Feb. 5. On Feb. 16 the buyers accepted the documents and paid the contract price. They did so pursuant to the agreement contained in the exchange of telex messages on that date. By that agreement the rights of the buyers are reserved. Where a person's rights are reserved then prima facie it is all of his rights which are reserved and not merely some of them. I think that all of the buyers' rights were reserved in this case including their right to recover damages for the sellers' breach of contract in failing to tender shipping documents in accordance with the notice of Feb. 5.
>
> What then is the measure of damages appropriate to that breach? In my view, it is the difference between the contract price of the goods and their market price at the date of the breach. In *James Finlay & Co. Ltd. v N. V. Kwik Hoo Tong Handel Maatschappij* [1929] 1 K.B. 400, the sellers under a c.i.f. contract tendered to the buyers a bill of lading which stated, not fraudulently but contrary to the fact, that shipment had taken place in the contract month. In the belief that the bill of lading was correctly dated, the buyers paid the contract price. Subsequently the buyers learned that the goods had not been shipped during the contract month. It was held by the Court of Appeal, affirming the judgment of Mr. Justice Wright ([1928] 2 K.B. 604), that the buyers were entitled to recover damages for the breach by the sellers of their obligation to deliver a bill of lading correctly stating the date of shipment and that the measure of such damages was the difference between the market price and the contract price of the goods. Now it is true that in Finlay's case the buyers were misled by a wrongly-dated bill of lading and accepted the shipment on the basis that the bill of lading was

correctly dated. In the present case it cannot be said that the buyers were misled into believing that the documents tendered were in accordance with the contract, for indeed at the very time when the documents were tendered the buyers were maintaining that they were not in accordance with the contract. But by accepting the documents while reserving their rights the buyers must be taken to have reserved their right to take the point that the documents were not in accordance with the contract and to recover damages on that basis. In my view, the decision in Finlay's case lays down a general rule as to the measure of damages in cases where the sellers have broken a condition of the contract by failing to tender proper documents and the buyers, not having rescinded, are entitled to recover damages for the breach. The reasons why the buyers have not rescinded are immaterial. Whether they have been misled or have elected not to rescind with full knowledge of the facts the position is the same, namely, that if they had rescinded, they would not have had to pay a price (viz. the contract price) in excess of the market price of the goods at the time of the breach.

It remains to consider the case of *Taylor and Sons Ltd. v Bank of Athens*, sup. In that case Taylor's bought from the bank locust beans under a contract which provided that the beans should be shipped and the bills of lading dated in July and/or August, 1919. Relying on an assertion of the sellers that the bills of lading were dated Aug. 31, 1919, the buyers accepted the documents tendered, paid the price and received the goods. Subsequently the buyers discovered that although the bills of lading were dated Aug. 31, they had been signed in September, and that shipment had not taken place during the contract months. The buyers went to arbitration but, perhaps unfortunately, their claim for damages as formulated in the arbitration was not based on a breach of contract in tendering a bill of lading bearing the wrong date. The breach of contract complained of was a failure to ship the goods within the proper period. For that breach of contract the measure of damages was held by Mr. Justice McCardie to be the difference at the material time between the market price of beans shipped in August and the market price of beans shipped in September. That was a nominal sum only. I think it is fair to say that the decision in Taylor's case has been generally accepted as correctly stating the measure of damages for the particular breach complained of in that case. It is clear, however, from the decisions of Mr. Justice Wright and of the Court of Appeal in the James Finlay case that Taylor's case is not to be taken as laying down the measure of damages where the breach complained of is a failure to tender correct shipping documents. That is the breach complained of in this case and, in my view, the measure of damages in this case is that which I have stated. It was argued on behalf of the sellers that the effect of the agreement of Feb. 16, 1971, was that the buyers were reserving only the right to recover damages for the difference in value, if any, between pellets shipped by the Mahsud. It follows from what I have said that that is, in my view, much too restricted an interpretation of the rights which the buyers were reserving. Such a difference in value was likely to be nominal only, and it is absurd to think that both buyers and sellers did not have in mind on Feb. 16, the real point of commercial substance, which was the difference between the contract price of the goods and their market value at the time when the documents were tendered. But the view which I have formed as to the meaning of the agreement of Feb. 16 is not based on speculation as to what was in the minds of the parties but on the language used in the telex messages themselves.

For these reasons, I am of the opinion that the measure of damages in this case is the difference between the contract price of the goods and the market price of similar goods at the time when the documents were tendered.[41]

With respect, the judgment in *Kleinjan* appears to be quite idiosyncratic; it is, undoubtedly true that by tendering defective documents the seller was in breach

41 *Kleinjan & Holst v Bremer Handels* [1972] 2 Lloyd's Rep. 11, at 20, 21, 22.

of contract. Nevertheless, it is likewise undeniable that the buyer was in a position to reject the seller's tender as evidently non-compliant with what was originally established in the sale contract.

In other words, in *Kleinjan* we are dealing with a scenario where the buyer (quite different from the buyers in *Finlay James* and in *Kwek Teck Chao*) has not been deprived of his right to reject the documents. On the contrary, the buyer here could clearly notice that the documents were defective but elected, nonetheless, to accept them as it was convenient for him to do so at that particular moment in time.

Consequently, allowing a buyer to recover damages from the seller at a later stage does not appear to be consistent with the legal position of a buyer who, by accepting evidently defective documents, de facto elected to condone a breach of contract by the seller.

Under such circumstances, a buyer should, therefore, be estopped from recovering damages from the seller at a later stage, regardless of the fact that he accepted the documents reserving the right to sue the seller for breach of contract.

The judgment in *Kleinjan* appears to suggest otherwise, and it is interesting to note that the damages were computed in terms of the difference between the contract price of the goods and the market price of similar goods at the time when the documents were tendered.

The aforementioned measure of damages allocated in *Kleinjan* had to be established on the basis of a different "formula" compared to the ones established in *Finlay James* and in *Kwek Teck Chao*; indeed, in *Kleinjan* the nature of the breach is radically different compared to the two aforementioned judgments, as the buyer had not been deprived of his right to reject the documents by the seller.

A completely different scenario arose in the judgment of *Vargas v Cremer*, where buyers accepting clearly defective documents had been prevented at a later stage from recovering damages from the sellers.

Here, Saville J held as follows:

> In *Kleinjan & Holst N.V. Rotterdam v Bremer Handelgesellschaft mbH* [1972] 2 Lloyd's Rep. 11 at pp. 21–22 Mr. Justice Cooke, said, in the context of a case where the buyers had taken up the documents in circumstances where they would have been entitled to reject them:- What then is the measures of damages appropriate to that breach? In my view it is the difference between the contract price of the goods and the market price at the date of the breach. In *James Finlay & Co v N.V. Kwik Hoo Ton Handel Maatschappij* (1928) 32 Ll.L.Rep. 245; [1929] 1 K.B. 400, the sellers under a cif contract tendered to the buyers a bill of lading which stated, not fraudulently but contrary to the facts, that shipment had taken place in the "contract month". In the belief that the Bill of Lading was correctly dated, the buyers paid the contract price. Subsequently the Buyers learned that the goods had not been shipped during the contract month. It was held by the Court of Appeal, affirming the judgment of Mr. Justice Wright [1928] 2 K.B. 604, that the buyers were entitled to recover damages for the breach by sellers of their obligation to deliver a bill of lading correctly stating the date of shipment and that the measure of such damages was the difference between the market price and contract price of the goods. Now it is true that in Finlay's case the buyers were misled by a wrongly dated bill of lading and accepted the shipment on the basis that the bill of lading was correctly dated. In the present case it cannot be said that the buyers were misled into believing that the documents tendered were in accordance with the contract, for indeed at the very time when the documents were tendered the buyers were maintaining that

they were not in accordance with the contract. But by accepting the documents while reserving their rights the buyers must be taken to have reserved their rights to take the point that the documents were not in accordance with the contract and to recover damages on that basis. In my view, the decision in Finlay's case lays down a general rule as to the measure of damage in cases where the Sellers have broken a condition of the contract by failing to tender the proper documents and the Buyers, not having rescinded, are entitled to recover damages for the breach. The reasons why the Buyers have not rescinded are immaterial. Whether they have been misled or have elected not to rescind with full knowledge of the facts the position is the same, namely, that if they had rescinded, they would not have had to pay a price (viz. the contract price) in excess of the market price of the goods at the time of the breach.

The actual decision in this case can be supported on the grounds that there the parties had made a special agreement, to the effect that the buyers would take the goods on the basis that if they were entitled to reject them, then damages would be assessed on the basis that they had exercised that right. However, I am unable to agree that in the absence of such an agreement the law is as stated by Mr. Justice Cooke in the latter parts of the passage which I have cited. In Finlay's case, it is clear that the Court of Appeal proceeded on the basis that the contract contained not only a term that the goods would be shipped in the stipulated month but also a term that the documents would show the true date of shipment; that there was a breach of this latter term; and that but for that breach the buyers (who were ignorant of the true position) would have rejected the documents for late shipment (i.e. for breach of the former term) – see in particular the judgments of Lord Justice Scrutton, at pp. 249 and 409 and Lord Justice Greer, at pp. 252 and 413–414. In such a case the loss of the right to reject is a result of the breach of the latter term – just as it was in *Kwei Tek Chao v British Traders & Shippers Ltd.* [1954] 1 Lloyd's Rep. 16; [1954] 2 Q.B. 459 – so that damages are properly based on the difference between the contract price and the market price at the time of the breach, rather than on the difference in value between the goods as they in fact were and their value had they been in accordance with the terms of the contract.

If the buyers know of the breach, however, then the position is different, for without more there is then no causal connection between the breach and the loss of the right to reject. The buyers know that they may reject if they wish to do so – the breach does not cause them to accept the documents. In such a case to award damages where the documents have been accepted on the basis of the difference between the contract and market prices at the date of the breach is to award damages that simply do not flow from the breach. The damages that flow from the breach in such circumstances are represented (in the ordinary case at least) by the difference between the value of the goods as warranted and their value in fact. I should add that to my mind acceptance of the documents together with a reservation of all rights would (in the absence of a special agreement made with the sellers) make no difference where the buyers know the true position: they can only reserve what rights they have – if they choose to accept the documents with knowledge of the breach, then the rights they have are the rights attached to that case, and not those that would exist if they had taken a different course of action.

In the present case too it cannot be said that the breach resulted in the loss of the right to reject the documents, because in no sense did the breach lead the buyers to accept the documents – thus (unlike Finlay's case and Kwei Tek Chao) there is simply no causal connection between the breach and the loss of the right to reject. The loss sustained by the buyers from the breach in question is not therefore to be based on the loss of the right to reject, but on the difference (if any) between the value of the goods as warranted and their value in fact.

In the present case Mr. Justice Hobhouse also remitted the award to the Board of Appeal to state whether there was any difference in market value between goods with a maximum fat content of 15 per cent. and goods with a fat content of 15.73 per

> cent. – and in the supplemental award the Board of Appeal found that there was no difference whatsoever.
>
> As to the "prudent course" adopted by the buyers, or the "commercial impracticability" of the buyers doing otherwise than they did, it seems to me that on my reasoning these are simply irrelevancies, for the conduct adopted by the buyers was not the result of the breach – that conduct was not caused or dictated by the fact that the documents showed an excess of fat, but doubtless by the fall in the market which was quite unrelated to the breach in this case and the buyer's desire to secure themselves with regard to what they asserted were their rights. Of course, other things being equal, the buyers are entitled, as Mr. Havelock-Allan submitted, to fair compensation for the breach – but what the Board of Appeal awarded is in my judgment neither fair nor compensation, since in effect the Board of Appeal awarded the buyers the difference between the contract price and the market (or more accurately the resale) price of the goods, in circumstances where the breach relied upon in fact caused the buyers no loss at all.[42]

Saville J's judgment in *Vargas* leaves open a conflict of views on the rights of a buyer who accepted clearly defective documents.

Here, the buyers were not allowed to claim damages against the seller, as they elected to accept documents openly differing from what was originally established in the sale contract.

The possibility of accepting clearly defective documents by reserving the right to sue the seller for breach of contract was coldly dismissed by Saville J, since buyers can only reserve what rights they have; if they choose to accept the documents with knowledge of the breach, then the rights they have are the rights attached to that case, and not those that would exist if they had taken a different course of action.[43]

It is worth emphasising that the judgment in *Vargas* goes beyond the impossibility for a buyer to sue the seller for damages after accepting clearly defective documents. Indeed, the buyer is equally estopped from recovering damages in the case of discovery of hidden defects in any other documents tendered by the seller.

This might be considered overly harsh for a buyer who will no longer be, therefore, in a position to initiate an action against a seller who, in this case, deprived him of the right to reject the forged documents in the first place.

Nevertheless, since the buyers had accepted the clearly defective documents, the breach of condition was, by virtue of SOGA, 1893, section 11(1)(c), reduced to a breach of warranty. Damages were awarded accordingly, with the measure of damages for breach of warranty being the difference between the contract price and the market price.

42 *Vargas v Cremer* [1987] 1 Lloyd's Rep. 394, at 398, 399.
43 *Ibid.*, at 399.

CHAPTER 13

The Vienna Convention (CISG) on Contracts for the International Sale of goods

13.1 The scope of the Vienna Convention for the international sale of goods

As we established in the first chapter, the Convention for Contracts for the International Sale of Goods, known as the 1980 Vienna Convention or CISG, is the latest in a line of attempts at creating a uniform set of rules regulating international sales.

The Vienna Convention came into force in 1988; nevertheless, it must be said that most commodity sales expressly exclude its application.

Where a sales contract is subject to English law, the Vienna Convention will not find application because the UK has not as yet become a party to the Convention.

For these reasons, it is not necessary for this book to cover the Convention in its entirety. The intention here is simply to select those parts of the Convention to which a trader should be alert if asked to negotiate with another party on Vienna Convention terms, with the view of drawing parallels and making distinctions with English law.

To this end, the relevant Articles will be dealt with in three major categories: a) scope of application; b) formation of the contract; and c) sale of goods.

Scope of application of the CISG

The ambit of function of the Vienna Convention (CISG) on the international sale of goods is expressed in Article 1.

Article 1 CISG

(1) This Convention applies to contracts of sale of goods between parties whose places of business are in different States:
  (a) when the States are Contracting States; or
  (b) when the rules of private international law lead to the application of the law of a Contracting State.

(2) The fact that the parties have their places of business in different States is to be disregarded whenever this fact does not appear either from the contract or from any dealings between, or from information disclosed by, the parties at any time before or at the conclusion of the contract.

(3) Neither the nationality of the parties nor the civil or commercial character of the parties or of the contract is to be taken into consideration in determining the application of this Convention.

According to Article 1(1)(a), the CISG applies to contracts for the sale of goods between parties whose places of business are in different states, when the states are contracting states. Given the significant number of contracting states, this is the usual path to the CISG's applicability.

The CISG also applies if the parties are situated in different countries (which need not be contracting states) and the conflict of law rules lead to the application of the law of a contracting state.

For instance, a contract between a Japanese trader and a Brazilian trader may contain a clause that arbitration will be in Sydney under Australian law with the consequence that the CISG would apply. A number of states have declared that they will not be bound by this condition.[1]

The CISG is intended to apply to commercial goods and products only, and parties to a contract may exclude or vary the application of the CISG.[2]

Article 7 of the CISG governs the issues related to the interpretation of the Convention itself.

Article 7 CISG

(1) In the interpretation of this Convention, regard is to be had to its international character and to the need to promote uniformity in its application and the observance of good faith in international trade.

(2) Questions concerning matters governed by this Convention which are not expressly settled in it are to be settled in conformity with the general principles on which it is based or, in the absence of such principles, in conformity with the law applicable by virtue of the rules of private international law.

Interpretation of the CISG is, thus, to take account of the "international character" of the Convention, the need for uniform application, and the need for good faith in international trade.

Disputes over the interpretation of the CISG are to be resolved by applying the "general principles" of the CISG or, where there are no such principles but the matters are governed by the CISG (a *praeter legem* gap), by applying the rules of private international law.[3]

A key point of controversy was whether or not a contract requires a written memorial to be binding, and this issue is dealt with by Article 11 of the CISG.[4]

Article 11 CISG

A contract of sale need not be concluded in or evidenced by writing and is not subject to any other requirement as to form. It may be proved by any means, including witnesses.

---

1 The CISG allows contracting states to lodge reservations (called "declarations" in the CISG's own language) in reference to opting out of Article 1(1)(b), which allows for the application of the CISG in cases when the rules of private international law point at the law of a contracting state as the law applicable to the contract for the sale of goods. More specifically, China, Germany, Czech Republic, Saint Vincent and the Grenadines, Singapore, Slovakia, and the US have opted out. See http://www.uncitral.org/uncitral/en/uncitral_texts/sale_goods/1980CISG_status.html at 22 December 2007.

2 See Articles 6 and 7 of the CISG.

3 See Article 7 CISG.

4 See Fritz Enderlein and Dietrich Maskow, *A Commentary on the United Nations Convention on Contracts for the International Sale of Goods*, 1992, Oceana Publications, at p. 9.

The CISG allows for a sale to be oral or unsigned.[5] In many nations oral contracts are accepted, and those states had no objection to signing the CISG.

Nevertheless, in some countries, contracts are not valid unless written, and states with a strict written requirement exercised their ability to exclude those Articles relating to oral contracts, enabling them to sign as well.[6]

It is worth emphasising that the CISG is not a complete qualification by its own definition. Indeed, the Convention allows parties to derogate from or vary the effects of its provisions, according to Article 6.

Article 6 CISG

The parties may exclude the application of this Convention or, subject to Article 12, derogate from or vary the effect of any of its provisions.

Apart from the possibility of derogating from its provisions, the Convention also leaves behind gaps to be filled in by the applicable national law under due consideration of the conflict of law rules applicable at the place of jurisdiction.

By way of example, this is self-evident in Article 5.

Article 5 CISG

This Convention does not apply to the liability of the seller for death or personal injury caused by the goods to any person.

13.2 The interaction between the Convention and the Incoterms®

In terms of correlations between the Convention and the Incoterms®, Article 9 states as follows:

Article 9 CISG

(1) The parties are bound by any usage to which they have agreed and by any practices which they have established between themselves.

(2) The parties are considered, unless otherwise agreed, to have impliedly made applicable to their contract or its formation a usage of which the parties knew or ought to have known and which in international trade is widely known to, and regularly observed by, parties to contracts of the type involved in the particular trade concerned.

The interconnections between trade usages and the Convention in general is not entirely clear. Nevertheless, it is of the utmost importance to attempt to define this relationship as the vast majority of contracts concluded on shipment terms incorporate in one way or another trade usage terms.

The first thing to do is to distinguish between two scenarios: (a) where the parties agreed that the contract is to be interpreted in accordance with a set of standard terms (e.g. Incoterms® or Fosfa contracts), and (b) where no reference to trade usage terms is made in the sales contract in terms of interpretation.

5 See Article 11 CISG.

6 More specifically, Argentina, Belarus, Chile, China, Hungary, Latvia, Lithuania, Paraguay, the Russian Federation, and Ukraine are not bound by Article 11 CISG.

The solution to scenario (a) is to be found in the aforementioned Article 9 of the CISG, which allows the contractual intention of the parties, where contrary to the Convention, to supersede the rules enshrined into the Convention itself.[7]

If, on the other hand, the parties have not made reference to the Incoterms® or any other set of standard terms (scenario (b)), then the question is whether the rules of interpretation as set out in the trade usage terms are relevant.

Part of the doctrine appears to suggest that even if specific reference to the Incoterms® has not been made by the contracting parties, their contract should be interpreted in accordance with trade usage terms.[8]

A possible methodological approach in case the contract incorporates some of the most well known and established of the terms referred to in the Incoterms® (e.g. c.i.f. and f.o.b. terms), would be to consider that, in conformity with Article 9(2) of the Convention, the parties have impliedly incorporated the trade rules in their contract as a "usage of which the parties knew or ought to have known and which in international trade is widely known to, and regularly observed by, in the particular trade concerned".[9]

Nevertheless, arguments can be raised against such an approach; indeed, a court may find it difficult to accept that a certain clause of the Incoterms® has become a usage in respect of a certain kind of trade.

Indeed, it appears that, with the exception of bulk oil sales, where multinational corporations of equal bargaining power regularly incorporate and thus observe the Incoterms®, the Incoterms® have not become a normative custom practice in other types of trade.[10]

Furthermore, in some legal systems, if the parties have not specifically referred to the Incoterms® in the sales contracts, the courts will interpret trade usage terms in light of the case law (UK) or according to statutory requirements (USA), thus increasing the risk of non-uniform interpretation.[11]

Another possible approach in case of non-specific reference to trade usage terms by the sales contract could be the interpretation of the terms of the contract in accordance with Article 8 of the Convention.

---

7 See ICC 6653/1993 (1993) Journal du Droit International (JDI) 1040–1047, 1053–1056. See also Case Law on UNCITRAL texts (CLOUT) abstract no. 103. High Arbitration Court of Russian Federation: Information Letter 10 of 25 December 1996 Comments by A Muranov in ‹http://cisgw3.law.pace.edu/cases›. Finally, see also Corte di Appello di Genova (Case 211/24–03–1995), where an FOB contract for the sale of raw oil was construed in accordance with the NIOC standard terms, as the parties had made express reference to them (see ‹http://soi.cnr.it/~crdcs/crdcs/it240395a.htm›).

8 See Derains, *Transfer des risques de livraison*, in Derains and Ghestin, *"La Convention de Vienne sur la vente international et les Incoterms"* (1990) 127, 137. Derans points out that Greek courts have quite often used the Incoterms® as interpretative criteria of the parties' intention even if the parties had not referred to them.

9 See D. Flambouras, *Transfer of Risk in the Contract of Sale Involving Carriage of Goods: A Comparative Study in English, Greek Law and the United Nations Convention on Contracts for the International Sale of Goods*, Worcester College, Oxford, available at www.jus.uio.no.

10 E.g. dry commodities. See F. Enderlein and D. Maskow, *United Nations Convention on Contracts for the International Sale of Goods*, Oceana Publications, 2002, p. 257.

11 On this point see Sono, UNCITRAL and the Vienna Sales Convention (1984) 18 *Int'l Law* 7, 12, and D. Flambouras, *Transfer of Risk in the Contract of Sale Involving Carriage of Goods: A Comparative Study in English, Greek Law and the United Nations Convention on Contracts for the International Sale of Goods*, above, p. 39.

Article 8 CISG

(1) For the purposes of this Convention statements made by and other conduct of a party are to be interpreted according to his intent where the other party knew or could not have been unaware what that intent was.
(2) If the preceding paragraph is not applicable, statements made by and other conduct of a party are to be interpreted according to the understanding that a reasonable person of the same kind as the other party would have had in the same circumstances.
(3) In determining the intent of a party or the understanding a reasonable person would have had, due consideration is to be given to all relevant circumstances of the case including the negotiations, any practices which the parties have established between themselves, usages and any subsequent conduct of the parties.

Under Article 8 CISG, a court of law could construe the terms of the contract in accordance with the Incoterms®, if the parties had referred to them in their previous transactions, or if they were considered as prevailing and of binding usage. These factors are amongst the circumstances prescribed by Article 8(3) in order to determine the contracting parties' intention.

Nevertheless, such an approach will not always be successful, as the parties' intention is, more often than not, unclear.

If the court cannot decide that the parties had intended to incorporate the Incoterms® in accordance with Article 8 (interpretation of contractual statements) or in accordance with Article 9 (trade usages), then recourse to the methodology of Article 7 (interpretation of the Convention) will be necessary.

The recourse to the "international character" of the Convention, the need for uniform application, and the need for good faith in international trade as per the aforementioned Article 7 of the CISG, could enable a court to reconcile the interpretation of trade usage terms with the Convention itself.

If no reconciliation is possible in accordance with Article 7, recourse to the applicable law by virtue of the rules of private international law of the forum would then be deemed to be necessary.[12]

It is submitted that reference to the applicable law should be considered as a weapon of last resort, as its application may indeed generate much complexity in terms of uncertainty, non-uniform application of the Convention, and recourse to older and conflicting domestic authorities.[13]

By way of example, one might consider f.o.b. contracts, where issues of lack of uniform interpretation might arise due to the variants of f.o.b terms in different legal systems.[14]

---

12 See D. Flambouras, "Transfer of Risk in the Contract of Sale involving Carriage of Goods: A Comparative Study in English, Greek Law and the United Nations Convention on Contracts for the International Sale of Goods", Worcester College, Oxford, available at www.jus.uio.no.

13 On this point see H.J. Berman and M. Ladd, Risk of Loss in Documentary Transactions etc. (1988) 21 *Cornell Int'l L J* 423, 432. See also D. Flambouras, *Transfer of Risk in the Contract of Sale Involving Carriage of Goods: A Comparative Study in English, Greek Law and the United Nations Convention on Contracts for the International Sale of Goods*, above, p. 40.

14 An example of f.o.b. variants is an f.o.b. "buyer's place of business" contract under the UCC. Under such terms, the contract assumes the nature of a contract on delivery terms, and this entails a complete change of the legal nature of an f.o.b. contract (which is normally concluded on shipment terms).

In light of the aforementioned considerations, it is submitted that the courts should not be reluctant to interpret the parties' intentions so as to conclude that the Incoterms® have been implicitly incorporated.

Finally, a scenario whereby the parties may intend a trade usage to be interpreted in accordance with the rules of a national law and not the Convention or the Incoterms® (e.g. English law in the case of c.i.f contracts) can be also theorised.

Under such circumstances, the parties are well advised to make their intentions clear, as many courts would be willing to refer to the Incoterms® through Article 9 of the CISG, rather than involve themselves in interpreting the parties' intentions in accordance with Article 8, or in finding the applicable law in accordance with Article 7.[15]

It can be therefore concluded that, overall, the interaction between the Vienna Convention and trade usage terms is not regulated very efficiently by the Convention.

This renders it imperative for contracting parties to devise mechanisms of interactions themselves, whether by incorporating the ICC's Incoterms® or any other set of standard terms and by expressly excluding the Convention itself, or by explicitly stating that the rules laid down in the standard terms shall supersede the Convention or otherwise.[16]

13.3 Formation of a contract under the Vienna Convention

Articles 14–24 of the CISG deal with the formation of a contract. According to Article 14, an offer to contract must be addressed to a person, be sufficiently definite – that is, describe the goods, quantity, and price – and indicate an intention for the offeror to be bound on acceptance.

Article 14 CISG

(1) A proposal for concluding a contract addressed to one or more specific persons constitutes an offer if it is sufficiently definite and indicates the intention of the offeror to be bound in case of acceptance. A proposal is sufficiently definite if it indicates the goods and expressly or implicitly fixes or makes provision for determining the quantity and the price.

(2) A proposal other than one addressed to one or more specific persons is to be considered merely as an invitation to make offers, unless the contrary is clearly indicated by the person making the proposal.

It has been noted that the formation of a contract under Article 14 is a compromise between different legal traditions. The main controversy referred to the

15 See D. Flambouras, *Transfer of Risk in the Contract of Sale Involving Carriage of Goods: A Comparative Study in English, Greek Law and the United Nations Convention on Contracts for the International Sale of Goods*, above, p. 40. On this point, see also F. Enderlein and D. Maskow, *United Nations Convention on Contracts for the International Sale of Goods*, Oceana Publications, 2002, p. 263.

16 As for example the Gafta No. 79, 79A and 100 contracts provide in their final terms. See also D. Flambouras, *Transfer of Risk in the Contract of Sale Involving Carriage of Goods: A Comparative Study in English, Greek Law and the United Nations Convention on Contracts for the International Sale of Goods*, above, p. 42.

question of whether a contract should be formed with the dispatch or receipt of the statement of acceptance.

Here the continental European thinking based on Roman law heritage clearly dictates the way in which the receipt of the statement of acceptance is the prerequisite for the formation of a contract.

The Anglo-American doctrine found its way into the Convention through the general possibility to revoke the offer.[17]

According to Article 14, a proposal is aimed at concluding a contract only when it expresses the intention of the offeror to be bound. The offer is one of the two statements of will which lead to the conclusion of a contract. Hence, the relationship under a contract is a relationship of intention. The intention to be bound is not excluded because of the fact that the contract is to be concluded under a condition.

A proposal for the conclusion of a contract does not automatically contain the intention to be bound; it may also be aimed at taking up negotiations on a sale.[18]

In the absence of intention to be bound, lacking provisions could be integrated by *jus dispositivum,* i.e. "the law adopted by consent, or the body of permissive general international law outside of *jus cogens* which accommodates opting-out, adjustment, or derogation, within private agreements".[19]

Some formulations in the offer might cause doubt as to the intention to be bound. In some instances, the intention to be bound can be seen "from the clarity with which the goods are specified. As far as the intention to be bound is the result of an error, questions of validity are touched upon which do not come under the CISG. Non-binding offers do not contain an intention to be bound."[20]

The CISG does not appear to recognise common law unilateral contracts;[21] nevertheless, subject to clear indication by the offeror, Article 14(2) treats any proposal not addressed to a specific person as only an invitation to make an offer.

Further, where there is no explicit price or procedure to implicitly determine price, parties are assumed to have agreed upon a price based upon that "generally charged at the time of the conclusion of the contract for such goods sold under comparable circumstances".[22]

17 See F. Enderlein and D. Maskow, *A Commentary on the United Nations Convention on Contracts for the International Sale of Goods*, Oceana Publications, 1992, p. 54.

18 This could be the case in particular if the proposal at first only contains the category and quantity of the goods. See F. Enderlein and D. Maskow, *A Commentary on the United Nations Convention on Contracts for the International Sale of Goods*, above, p. 54.

19 See Fritz Enderlein and Dietrich Maskow, *A Commentary on the United Nations Convention on Contracts for the International Sale of Goods*, 1992, Oceana Publications, at p. 54.

20 *Ibid.*

21 See, for instance, *Carlill v Carbolic Smoke Ball Company* (1892) 2 QB 484. This seminal case concerned a flu remedy called the "carbolic smoke ball". The manufacturer advertised that buyers who found it did not work would be awarded £100, a considerable amount of money at the time. The company was found to have been bound by its advertisement, which was construed as an offer which the buyer, by using the smoke ball, accepted, creating a contract. The Court of Appeal held that the essential elements of a contract were all present, including offer and acceptance, consideration, and an intention to create legal relations.

22 See Article 55 CISG.

On a general level, an offer may be revoked provided the withdrawal reaches the offeree before or at the same time as the offer, or before the offeree has sent an acceptance. This is dealt with by Articles 15 and 16(1), as follows:

Article 15 CISG

(1) An offer becomes effective when it reaches the offeree.
(2) An offer, even if it is irrevocable, may be withdrawn if the withdrawal reaches the offeree before or at the same time as the offer.

Article 16 CISG

(1) Until a contract is concluded an offer may be revoked if the revocation reaches the offeree before he has dispatched an acceptance.
(2) However, an offer cannot be revoked:
   (a) if it indicates, whether by stating a fixed time for acceptance or otherwise, that it is irrevocable; or
   (b) if it was reasonable for the offeree to rely on the offer as being irrevocable and the offeree has acted in reliance on the offer.

Some offers may not be revoked; this happens, for example, according to Article 16(2)(b), when the offeree reasonably relied upon the offer as being irrevocable.

13.3.1 Acceptance under the CISG

The CISG requires a positive act to indicate acceptance; silence or inactivity are not considered an acceptance under Article 18, as outlined in the following:

Article 18 CISG

(1) A statement made by or other conduct of the offeree indicating assent to an offer is an acceptance. Silence or inactivity does not in itself amount to acceptance.
(2) An acceptance of an offer becomes effective at the moment the indication of assent reaches the offeror. An acceptance is not effective if the indication of assent does not reach the offeror within the time he has fixed or, if no time is fixed, within a reasonable time, due account being taken of the circumstances of the transaction, including the rapidity of the means of communication employed by the offeror. An oral offer must be accepted immediately unless the circumstances indicate otherwise.
(3) However, if, by virtue of the offer or as a result of practices which the parties have established between themselves or of usage, the offeree may indicate assent by performing an act, such as one relating to the dispatch of the goods or payment of the price, without notice to the offeror, the acceptance is effective at the moment the act is performed, provided that the act is performed within the period of time laid down in the preceding paragraph.

On a general level, a contract is created by way of exchange of two corresponding statements of intention: the offer and the acceptance. Nevertheless, according to Article 18, whenever there is agreement between the parties (e.g. by way of signing a document) there will also be a contract, even if offer and acceptance are not identifiable.[23]

The statement of acceptance does not expressly have to declare acceptance of the offer; it is necessary that assent to the offer is expressed by the offeree. The statement or conduct is interpreted pursuant to Article 8, and it must express assent to the offer. The mere "acknowledgment of receipt of the offer will, thus, not suffice; neither will an expression of interest in it."[24]

The offeree may also express his assent through conduct implying an intent, e.g. by opening a letter of credit in the amount of the price. Under those circumstances, the act which is to express assent to an offer has to refer clearly to the offer.

It has been noted that it is not clear why the offeree should not inform the offeror of his decision to accept the offer. After all, for both parties, "clarification is needed as regards the conclusion of the contract, and only such conduct should be deemed to be considered an acceptance which becomes directly effective towards the other party."[25]

In relation to the acceptance phase, the CISG attempts to resolve the common situation where an offeree's reply to an offer accepts the original offer, but attempts to change the conditions. This is dealt with by Article 19.

Article 19 CISG

(1) A reply to an offer which purports to be an acceptance but contains additions, limitations or other modifications is a rejection of the offer and constitutes a counter-offer.
(2) However, a reply to an offer which purports to be an acceptance but contains additional or different terms which do not materially alter the terms of the offer constitutes an acceptance, unless the offeror, without undue delay, objects orally to the discrepancy or dispatches a notice to that effect. If he does not so object, the terms of the contract are the terms of the offer with the modifications contained in the acceptance.
(3) Additional or different terms relating, among other things, to the price, payment, quality and quantity of the goods, place and time of delivery, extent of one party's liability to the other or the settlement of disputes are considered to alter the terms of the offer materially.

Article 19 of the CISG treats any change to the original conditions as a rejection of the offer. Indeed, an offer modified in its conditions is considered as a counter offer, unless the modified terms do not materially alter the terms of the offer.

To this end, "changes to price, payment, quality, quantity, delivery, liability of the parties, and arbitration conditions may all materially alter the terms of the offer."[26]

Nevertheless, that will have to be assessed on a case by case basis, and the main question revolves around whether the modifications are material or immaterial.

It has been noted that a vast gap exists here between theory and practice. In practice, most of the acceptances would actually be counter offers, since it would suffice for the parties to "have differing jurisdictional clauses in their business

23 See F. Enderlein and D. Maskow, *A Commentary on the United Nations Convention on Contracts for the International Sale of Goods*, above, p. 65.

24 *Ibid.*

25 *Ibid.*, at p. 65.

26 *Ibid.*, at p. 71.

conditions; and the buyer and the seller regularly exchange their offers and acceptances on printed forms or together with their different business conditions".[27]

Above all, even actual additions or modifications will not be considered a counter offer, in case they do not materially alter the terms of the offer. What is considered as material will entirely depend on the circumstances of each case.

Indeed, since what is unimportant to one party may be important to the other, and vice versa, the question which will have to be asked is whether the modifications to the original offer will cause the offeror additional efforts or difficulties or increase his risks.

"Neutral" modifications will be generally regarded as immaterial. Immaterial/ neutral modifications could be, for instance, that a "certain packaging of the goods was prescribed, but a more suitable packaging could be used to avoid additional costs or that global delivery dates are specified."[28]

13.4 Sale of goods

Articles 25–88 of CISG are devised to regulate the sale of goods, the obligations of the seller, the obligations of the buyer, and the transfer of risk.

13.4.1 Seller's duties

Article 30 of the CISG defines the duties of the seller, "stating the obvious",[29] in terms of delivering the goods, handing over any documents relating to them, and transfering the property in the goods, as required by the contract.

> **Article 30 CISG**
>
> The seller must deliver the goods, hand over any documents relating to them and transfer the property in the goods, as required by the contract and this Convention.

Seller's physical duties

The Vienna Convention therefore embraces the dual mode of performance of the seller's duties which characterises the common law approach, and which has been subject to scrutiny in the above.

Exactly as with English law, the physical duties of the seller compel him to ship the goods of the quality, quantity, and description established by the original sale contract. The physical obligations are enshrined in Article 35 CISG, as follows:

> **Article 35 CISG**
>
> (1) The seller must deliver goods which are of the quantity, quality and description required by the contract and which are contained or packaged in the manner required by the contract.

27 *Ibid.*, at p. 71.

28 *Ibid.*

29 J. Ziegel and C. Samson, *Report to the Uniform Law Conference of Canada on Convention on Contracts for the International Sale of Goods,* (1981) Toronto 168–305.

(2) Except where the parties have agreed otherwise, the goods do not conform with the contract unless they:
   (a) are fit for the purposes for which goods of the same description would ordinarily be used;
   (b) are fit for any particular purpose expressly or impliedly made known to the seller at the time of the conclusion of the contract, except where the circumstances show that the buyer did not rely, or that it was unreasonable for him to rely, on the seller's skill and judgement;
   (c) possess the qualities of goods which the seller has held out to the buyer as a sample or model;
   (d) are contained or packaged in the manner usual for such goods or, where there is no such manner, in a manner adequate to preserve and protect the goods.

(3) The seller is not liable under subparagraphs (a) to (d) of the preceding paragraph for any lack of conformity of the goods if, at the time of the conclusion of the contract, the buyer knew or could not have been unaware of such lack of conformity.

Article 35 CISG encompasses concepts all too familiar to English law, including the implied obligation of the seller to provide the buyer with goods "fit for purpose" or otherwise of satisfactory quality.

Further, the seller is also obliged to deliver goods that are not subject to claims from a third party for infringement of industrial or intellectual property rights in the state where the goods are to be sold, as per Articles 41 and 42 below.

Article 41 CISG

The seller must deliver goods which are free from any right or claim of a third party, unless the buyer agreed to take the goods subject to that right or claim. However, if such right or claim is based on industrial property or other intellectual property, the seller's obligation is governed by Article 42.

Article 42 CISG

(1) The seller must deliver goods which are free from any right or claim of a third party based on industrial property or other intellectual property, of which at the time of the conclusion of the contract the seller knew or could not have been unaware, provided that the right or claim is based on industrial property or other intellectual property:
   (a) under the law of the State where the goods will be resold or otherwise used, if it was contemplated by the parties at the time of the conclusion of the contract that the goods would be resold or otherwise used in that State; or
   (b) in any other case, under the law of the State where the buyer has his place of business.

(2) The obligation of the seller under the preceding paragraph does not extend to cases where:
   (a) at the time of the conclusion of the contract the buyer knew or could not have been unaware of the right or claim; or
   (b) the right or claim results from the seller's compliance with technical drawings, designs, formulae or other such specifications furnished by the buyer.

Seller's documentary duties

The seller's documentary duties are enshrined in Article 34 of the Vienna Convention which states as follows:

> **Article 34 CISG**
>
> If the seller is bound to hand over documents relating to the goods, he must hand them over at the time and place and in the form required by the contract. If the seller has handed over documents before that time, he may, up to that time, cure any lack of conformity in the documents, if the exercise of this right does not cause the buyer unreasonable inconvenience or unreasonable expense. However, the buyer retains any right to claim damages as provided for in this Convention.

The documents to be tendered by the seller are in the first place documents of title (bills of lading, warehouse receipts, etc.) which are handed over in place of the goods and allow the buyer to have disposal over the goods.

Specific indications re the seller's documentary duties have to be found in the original sales contract, or may arise by trade custom practice (e.g. the incorporation of the Incoterms®).

According to Article 34, documents must be handed over at the time and place required by the contract. As far as documents relating to the goods are concerned, a transfer may be envisaged through the banks involved, depending on the terms of payment.

It has been noted that, in the case that the contract mentions nothing about date and place, "the principle of good faith will probably require the seller to hand over the documents to the buyer in such a way that the latter can take over the goods from the carrier when they arrive and bring them through customs."[30]

Seller's transport obligations

Similar to section 32(2) of SOGA 1979, the Vienna Convention provides for the seller's implied transport obligations codified by Article 32 as follows:

> **Article 32 CISG**
>
> (1) If the seller, in accordance with the contract or this Convention, hands the goods over to a carrier and if the goods are not clearly identified to the contract by markings on the goods, by shipping documents or otherwise, the seller must give the buyer notice of the consignment specifying the goods.
>
> (2) If the seller is bound to arrange for carriage of the goods, he must make such contracts as are necessary for carriage to the place fixed by means of transportation appropriate in the circumstances and according to the usual terms for such transportation.
>
> (3) If the seller is not bound to effect insurance in respect of the carriage of the goods, he must, at the buyer's request, provide him with all available information necessary to enable him to effect such insurance.

Article 32 of the Vienna Convention encompasses the concept of "reasonable contract" of carriage enshrined in section 32(2) of SOGA 1979, by imposing on a

30 See F. Enderlein and D. Maskow, *A Commentary on the United Nations Convention on Contracts for the International Sale of Goods*, above, p. 99.

c.i.f. seller the obligation of making contracts of carriage as necessary for carriage to the place fixed by means of transportation appropriate in the circumstances and according to the "usual" terms for such transportation.

As to the circumstances which have to be taken into account by the seller in making the "usual" transport arrangements, these include the category and quantity of the goods, their packaging, the distance which will have to be covered by transport, the available means of transportation, and existing transport routes.

In the case of perishable goods, "cold storage wagons could be appropriate means of transportation or, depending on the nature of the goods, fast means of transportation like an aircraft or express train.

Further, the seller must choose the usual transport routes and avoid unnecessary transhipment or unnecessary unloading. Some of the trade terms, e.g. c.i.f., contain duties pertaining to the seller and, if applicable, will supersede the CISG."[31]

13.4.2 Buyer's obligations

Under Articles 60 and 53 of the Convention, the duty of the buyer is to take all steps "which could reasonably be expected" to take delivery of the goods, and to pay for them.

> **Article 60 CISG**
>
> The buyer's obligation to take delivery consists:
>
> (a) in doing all the acts which could reasonably be expected of him in order to enable the seller to make delivery; and
> (b) in taking over the goods.

> **Article 53 CISG**
>
> The buyer must pay the price for the goods and take delivery of them as required by the contract and this Convention.

The buyer is also obliged to promptly examine the goods under Article 38 of the Convention, as outlined below.

> **Article 38 CISG**
>
> (1) The buyer must examine the goods, or cause them to be examined, within as short a period as is practicable in the circumstances.
> (2) If the contract involves carriage of the goods, examination may be deferred until after the goods have arrived at their destination.
> (3) If the goods are redirected in transit or redispatched by the buyer without a reasonable opportunity for examination by him and at the time of the conclusion of the contract the seller knew or ought to have known of the possibility of such redirection or redispatch, examination may be deferred until after the goods have arrived at the new destination.

31 *Ibid.*, at p. 96.

From the context of Article 38, it can be evinced that the inspection of the goods does not represent a real "obligation" of the buyer, but it could rather be defined as a "burden to examine the goods within a short time".[32]

Consequently, the buyer's failure to inspect the goods does not amount to a breach of contract. Rather, if the buyer does not comply with his "obligation" to examine the goods the buyer may lose, as will be readily appreciated in the following, his rights vis-à-vis the seller that would devolve from a lack of conformity.

It is, however, decisive for retaining his rights that he gives notice of a lack of conformity; the examination only serves a preparatory task to give such a notice. The duty to examine the goods also applies to an *aliud*.

13.5 Transfer of risk

Articles 66–69 CISG regulate the transfer of risk. According to Article 66, once the risk is transferred to the buyer, the buyer is under the obligation to pay for the price of the goods, despite the goods having been damaged or completely lost in transit.

Article 66 CSIG

> Loss of or damage to the goods after the risk has passed to the buyer does not discharge him from his obligation to pay the price, unless the loss or damage is due to an act or omission of the seller.

From the formulation of Article 66, it follows that the risk postulated therein refers in the first place to the risk of having to pay for the goods.

It has been noted that "the distinction between the risk to pay for the goods, and the risk to perform is not made in many countries, and that where it is made, that distinction is relevant only in the event that the buyer has to take the goods at the seller's place."[33]

In general, under the CISG the risk to pay and the risk to perform pass at the same time. This is also the attitude of the Incoterms® in regard to this problem.

The risk of having to pay "informs of those conditions which have to be fulfilled by the seller for the obligation to pay the price not to end (and/or be reduced) in case the goods are destroyed or damaged in transit."[34]

This aspect of bearing the risk needs to be read in conjunction with the seller's liability under Article 36, paragraph 1, of the CISG for a lack of conformity which exists at the time when the risk is passed. Apart from that, the bearing of the risk has no influence on the emergence or settlement date of the obligation to pay the price.

One of the consequences of the transfer of risk under the Vienna Convention is that, when the seller is obligated to deliver again (or to deliver missing parts, to repair, etc),[35] the seller might not only lose his right to obtain the price because

32 *Ibid.*, at p. 112.
33 *Ibid.*, at 190.
34 *Ibid.*, p. 112.
35 See the remedy for specific performance in section 13.7.

the risk materialises again, but he might also have to deliver once again, which of course would revive his right to obtain the price.[36]

Nevertheless, on a general level, the risk of having to perform passes "with the risk of having to pay the price; at least it passes with it at the latest and is not revived when the price risk comes back to the seller. Once the risk has passed, the seller does not have to deliver again.

In case goods are damaged by action or omission of the seller, the seller retains the risk for the goods under Article 66 of the Convention."[37]

36 See F. Enderlein and D. Maskow, *A Commentary on the United Nations Convention on Contracts for the International Sale of Goods*, above, p. 190.

37 This has been subject to fierce criticism by the doctrine. Enderlein and Maskow point out that: "Obviously, the risk shall not pass and/or fall back to the seller when there is such an exception. This is an unfortunate rule.

The reservation, when interpreted narrowly, covers problems which are already solved in different places and, when interpreted broadly, leads to undesirable or even foolish results. The commentators have to make a choice between the two. There are those who want to have the reservation valid only when the conduct of the seller amounted to a breach of an obligation and/or a breach of contract.

Since the restriction cannot simply be ignored we are, in view of the existing dilemma, in favour of a restrictive interpretation. We assume here that the act or omission of the seller has to be in breach of contract or at least in breach of obligation. A difference which in our belief exists in comparison with Article 36, paragraph 2 (which could also justify a different wording) is that the seller cannot exempt himself pursuant to Article 79. The half-sentence commented on thus has the effect that the buyer, in certain cases of performance in breach of contract, is granted further rights in regard to retaining the price apart from the rights provided for in such cases which actually are sufficient because of the risk not passing, or even the falling back. The conduct of the seller, which insofar as it is relevant, must have a close connection, in our view, with the motives due to which the regulation on the passing of the risk was established. Furthermore, there must be a direct relation to the contract and its performance in time and substance.

Instances which are possible in this context include, above all, a lack of conformity of the goods which starts to have an effect only after the risk has passed and possibly leads to the total destruction of the goods, or damage to a part of the goods which is actually not affected by the lack of conformity, or unfit packaging, such as omission of packaging for transport at sea. The acts of the seller must not necessarily be breaches of contract, although this will typically be the case. Anyway, the relevant, but rather abstractly formulated, rule should not in general be extended to torts because they require examination of different conditions. It is, therefore, not advisable for such reasons to grant the buyer the option not to pay the price.

In an f.o.b. contract the seller damages the goods when he removes his containers. Since this probably is no breach of contract but rather a tort and the buyer cannot, therefore, invoke the rights he would have because of a breach of contract, the latter should at least be permitted to reduce the price to the extent to which this is allowed under the applicable law of tort. This example is proof that the rule does not meet its objective, for the fact alone that the seller damages the goods is no justification for presuming his responsibility for it, e.g. the buyer may have placed the goods in violation of regulations. Proceeding on the legal and political principle underlying the rule the buyer would have to bear the risk for he will be the one to have the goods normally insured. There was no reason for the seller to do so. When the insurance company indemnifies the buyer, the taking back of the price, wholly or in part, would presuppose that he hands over the proceeds from it to the seller. But this situation is not provided for in the Convention. Besides, we do not understand why the buyer should be in a particularly favourable position when the seller causes the damage, for the latter in this regard finds himself in a situation which is hardly different from that of any third party. Where the damaging of the goods by the seller was a tort and the buyer, therefore, has claims against the seller, the general possibilities of setting off against the price requirement are applicable under the decisive law, and the buyer is thus satisfied.

A very narrow interpretation could be used to counteract the fact that, because of the lack of a time limit for the relevant conduct of the seller, acts which happen a very long time after the risk has passed or whose effect is felt only at a late point will be taken into account, and so the system of claims

Article 67 of the Convention regulates the transfer of risk in relation to scenarios where goods are handed over by a seller to a carrier. It states as follows:

Article 67 CISG

(1) If the contract of sale involves carriage of the goods and the seller is not bound to hand them over at a particular place, the risk passes to the buyer when the goods are handed over to the first carrier for transmission to the buyer in accordance with the contract of sale. If the seller is bound to hand the goods over to a carrier at a particular place, the risk does not pass to the buyer until the goods are handed over to the carrier at that place. The fact that the seller is authorized to retain documents controlling the disposition of the goods does not affect the passage of the risk.

(2) Nevertheless, the risk does not pass to the buyer until the goods are clearly identified to the contract, whether by markings on the goods, by shipping documents, by notice given to the buyer or otherwise.

Article 67 creates a very similar scenario as the common law rule which sees the transfer of risk retroactively shifted from the seller onto the buyer "on shipment".

Nevertheless, Article 67 denotes a certain ambiguity in reference to the precise event which triggers the transfer of risk, which is described as the moment when goods are "handed over" to the first carrier.

It has been noted that since losses occur or damage is often caused during the process of loading/unloading, it may be necessary to define the concept of "handing over" the goods to the carrier more clearly.

One suggestion is to proceed on the assumption that "the risk bearing becomes effective at the end of the handing over because it is more exactly stipulated than the beginning of that process".[38]

This is consistent with the Incoterms® rules. According to these rules, "the handing over is generally fully perfumed when the goods are on the vehicle of the carrier taking them over and/or when the latter does the loading himself, the goods were provided ready for loading, or only handed over into the keeping of the carrier.

Where the goods are composed of several units which are transported separately, nothing can be said against a risk passing per unit."[39]

---

from breach of contract is thereby fundamentally modified. This exceptional rule cannot, in general, be played off against the system of claims in the event of lack of conformity of the goods.

Furthermore, lawful conduct of the seller, which in interaction with accidents leads to loss or damage of the goods, should not be regarded as a reason for the falling back of the risk. This refers, for instance, to the case that the risk is passed in such a way that the buyer commits a breach of contract by not taking delivery of the goods under Article 69, paragraph 1, and the seller then takes appropriate measures under Article 85 to preserve the goods, which however accidentally lead to their destruction. The same applies where the seller exercises his lawful right to stop the goods in transit. Even more obvious is the non-applicability of this rule in its abstract form when the seller has chosen a carrier for that part of the transportation for which the buyer bears the risk, and when the goods perish in the keeping of the carrier. If this were not so, the scheme of risk-bearing of the Convention would be completely distorted. The problems that may result between the seller and the buyer from the possible engagement of inappropriate carriers should also not be solved invoking the provisions on risk bearing." See F. Enderlein and D. Maskow, *A Commentary on the United Nations Convention on Contracts for the International Sale of Goods*, above, p.189.

38 See F. Enderlein and D. Maskow, *A Commentary on the United Nations Convention on Contracts for the International Sale of Goods*, above, p. 193.

39 *Ibid.*

Nevertheless, contrary to the common law rules on the transfer of risk, Article 67(2) of the Convention subjects the transfer of risk to the additional element of the clear identification of the goods sold.

This requirement was added in order to prevent the seller from "abusing a lack of identification in the contract in order to shift the blame for losses or damage onto the buyer. It has been noted that the requirements for an identification in the contract are determined by this function and hence must not be too strict in an abstract way".[40]

The identification requirements include, in particular, markings which are directly made on the goods due to specific contractual agreements or as a result of specific transport regulations.

Packing lists which are added to the goods may also contain identifying information, including markings made by the seller, which point to the buyer, such as his name, his trademarks or other means of advertising, which also have an identifying effect.

In the case of sale of goods in bulk, the seller is best advised to indicate not only the ship by which the goods are sent, but as far as possible, the part/section of the ship where the batch of goods is stored.

The transfer of risk within the context of string sales is dealt with by Article 68.

Article 68 CISG

> The risk in respect of goods sold in transit passes to the buyer from the time of the conclusion of the contract. However, if the circumstances so indicate, the risk is assumed by the buyer from the time the goods were handed over to the carrier who issued the documents embodying the contract of carriage. Nevertheless, if at the time of the conclusion of the contract of sale the seller knew or ought to have known that the goods had been lost or damaged and did not disclose this to the buyer, the loss or damage is at the risk of the seller.

Quite different from the common law, in the case that goods are sold down a string, according to Article 68, the risk is transferred from the seller to the buyer at the time of the conclusion of the contract.

This solution was not part of the early stage draft of the CISG and was adopted later at the diplomatic conference at the insistence of Pakistan, who was supported by other developing countries.

Article 68 prevents a retroactive passing of the risk and, by any means this has to be considered as inappropriate from the point of view of trade requirements as it is, in the vast majority of circumstances, extremely difficult to establish when a loss occurred or damage was caused to goods in transit.

Conversely, this exertion becomes irrelevant when the passing of the risk takes place with the handing over to the carrier, as under English law. As we have established above, in that event it is the buyer, hence the party who receives the goods and can initiate the necessary measures against the carrier or insurer, who bears the risk for the goods whilst in transit. This creates welcome efficiencies and avoids a string of international litigation.

40 *Ibid.*, at p. 194.

It is, indeed, often the basic rule adopted in Article 68 which creates particular difficulties for the exporter of goods.

The practical effect of the rule critically reviewed here is reduced by the fact that the burden of proof in regard to the goods having been affected by a risk already at the time of the conclusion of the contract, according to the customary proof rules, as they apply also to performance in breach of contract, lies with the buyer. It is, therefore, the latter who is affected by the uncertainties involved.

Further complexities arise from the fact that, in case goods are lost in transit, Article 68 subjects the transfer of risk to the knowledge of the seller that the cargo was lost.

That is a legal position on the opposite site to the spectrum arising from the *Olympia Oil*[41] litigation, which established the irrelevance of the seller's knowledge that the cargo was lost in transit in terms of exemption to the rule whereby the transfer of risk is retroactively shifted from the seller onto the buyer "on or as from shipment".

The appeal of the English legal status quo in relation to the transfer of risk lies, as we have appreciated in the above,[42] with the efficiencies arising from the assertion of the retroactive shift of the risk, which is ultimately beneficial for both sellers and buyers. Indeed, if the sellers would not be prepared to bear the risk for the goods whilst in transit and in the possession of a third party, namely the carrier, the buyer is also well protected by the carriage and insurance documents.

Conversely, the scenario endorsed by Article 68 of the Vienna Convention generates serious difficulties for buyers who, in the case that the loss or damage to the cargo was within the knowledge of their sellers, will have to initiate legal action with two extremely cumbersome burdens of proof, i.e. that the cargo was damaged or lost before the contract of sale was concluded (a circumstance very difficult to prove), and that the seller had knowledge of that scenario, an element even more difficult to assert, considering that the seller is usually located in a different part of the globe from the buyer.

Already from the foregoing analysis it may be concluded that the Vienna Convention is not an appropriate legal framework for contracts subject to the major trade usages.

This is, at the very least, particularly true for c.i.f. and f.o.b. contracts. In these cases, it will need to be accepted that risk transfers on shipment or when the goods are put on board a named vessel, and not in accordance with Article 67 which refers to handing over of the goods to the first inland carrier or the sea carrier's control.

Furthermore, in the case of bulk shipments, the Convention does not seem to provide satisfactory solutions. Indeed, we have established that Article 67(2) does not allow for risk to pass unless goods are clearly identified, endorsing the non-retrospective transfer of risk as the default rule.

Article 68 states that only if (a) the circumstances so indicate, (b) the contract or a usage entitles the seller to deliver a collective consignment, and (c) the seller did not know of the loss or deterioration, may risk pass retrospectively from shipment.

41 See chapter 7.
42 *Ibid.*

This solution does not seem to be appropriate, and cannot be considered as an example of clarity and certainty, by reason of the problems related to the vagueness of the concept of "indicative circumstances", and the problems related to the proof of knowledge in the case of deterioration or damage during transit. The problem becomes even more serious if one considers that the vast majority of commodities commerce is performed on c.i.f. and f.o.b. terms.

13.6 Remedies

The approach adopted by the Convention in relation to remedies is rather different to that of the common law.

The remedies of the buyer and seller depend upon the character of a breach of the contract. As will be readily appreciated, termination of the contract will arise only in the case that a breach is fundamental according to what is established in Article 25 of the Convention.

13.6.1 Fundamental breach

The concept of fundamental breach is of crucial importance in order to fully appreciate the nature of the remedies allowed by the Convention. This concept is enshrined in Article 25.

Article 25 CISG

A breach of contract committed by one of the parties is fundamental if it results in such detriment to the other party as substantially to deprive him of what he is entitled to expect under the contract, unless the party in breach did not foresee and a reasonable person of the same kind in the same circumstances would not have foreseen such a result.

Fundamental breach is a concept of the utmost importance, as it enables an innocent party to avoid the contract without losing any rights to damages.

The distinction between fundamental breach and simple breach of contract is the basic criterion for the classification of breaches of contract. This criterion offers a wide scope of interpretation, and this scenario invariably leads to uncertainties which have been subject to much debate at international level.[43]

There is a certain awkwardness in the definition of fundamentality, and that is probably the result of a compromise. The concept of fundamental breach refers to two essential criteria: a) the party against whom the breach was committed, the aggrieved party; and b) the foreseeability of that breach.

The elements which define a substantial detriment are extremely complex. Indeed, the detriment itself is characterised in its conceptuality by three aspects: a) there

43 See F. Enderlein and D. Maskow, *A Commentary on the United Nations Convention on Contracts for the International Sale of Goods*, above, p. 79; See Michida, Cancellation of Contract, 27 *Am J Comp L* 279, 285 (1979); Eorsi, A Propos the 1980 Vienna Convention on Contracts for the International Sale of Goods, 31 *Am J Comp L* 333, 338 (1983); See Honnold, The Draft Convention on Contracts for the International Sale of Goods: An Overview, 27 *Am J Comp L* 223 (1979); Berman and Kaufman, The Law of International Commercial Transactions, 19 *Harv Int'l L J* 221, 270 (1978).

has to be a relevant detriment to the aggrieved party; b) it has to be fundamental; and c) it needs to be proportionate to the expectations justified under the contract.

It has been correctly noted that, far from being static, the concept of "relevant detriment" in many instances occurs only when the breach of contract continues. Hence, "one of the greatest difficulties in ascertaining the fundamentality of a breach is to determine the time when the detriment has become so great that the prerequisites are met".[44]

To this end, the parties themselves may, from the outset, characterise as fundamental certain categories of non-fulfilment of obligations, e.g. by determining that time is of the essence. This would correspond to the principle of contract autonomy and can also be done by invoking established practices.

According to the doctrine, the term "detriment" should be interpreted in a broad sense, so as to entail that the "purpose the aggrieved party pursued with the contract was foiled and, therefore, led to his losing interest in the performance of the contract; from this follows his interest in avoiding the contract".[45]

Although most aspects within the context of commercial relations can be reduced to issues relating to damages, this does not appear to be the central issue here. Quite on the contrary, when compensation for damages can serve as an adequate remedial action, this should be an indication of the fact that there is no detriment within the meaning of the Convention.

Detriment can be proved, however, when "the aggrieved party in remaining bound to the contract is hindered in his commercial or manufacturing activities in such a way that he can no longer be expected to continue holding on to it".[46]

Hence, detriment can be a very complex phenomenon, and "it must be in existence at the time of the avoidance of the contract, as what matters most in commercial relations are economic results rather than formal fulfilment of obligations".[47]

It needs to be emphasised that a fundamental breach of contract must constitute also a non-fulfilment of a contractual obligation.[48]

---

44 See F. Enderlein and D. Maskow, *A Commentary on the United Nations Convention on Contracts for the International Sale of Goods*, above, p. 80.

45 *Ibid.*, above, p. 79; Eorsi, A Propos the 1980 Vienna Convention on Contracts for the International Sale of Goods, 31 *Am J Comp L* 333, 338 (1983).

46 See F. Enderlein and D. Maskow, *A Commentary on the United Nations Convention on Contracts for the International Sale of Goods*, above, p. 80.

47 *Ibid.*, at p. 80. As to the concept of substantiality, the doctrine pointed out that there is a tautology between substantial and fundamental as characterising a breach of contract; that repetition seems to have been unavoidable in order to ensure congruence of the *definiens* and the *definiendum*.

48 By way of example, the doctrine has emphasised that a "violation of the time for performance constitutes a fundamental breach of contract under Article 25 of the Convention only when the other party cannot use the late delivery for the purpose envisaged in the contract. When the contract stipulates that time is of the essence, or uses such customary terms as "fixed", "absolutely", "precisely", "at the latest", it could be considered as an agreement, where non-fulfilment of this condition will have to be regarded as a fundamental breach of contract. Proof that the legal prerequisites of such breach are not fulfilled is then inadmissible.

By the same token, a violation of the qualitative requirements (non-conforming delivery) is to be considered fundamental under the Convention, when the non-conformity considerably impedes the fitness for use of the goods and when it is irreparable. Whether or not a reparable lack of conformity is fundamental depends on the time element. Had the violation of the time for delivery been fundamental, much would speak in favour of considering a reparable fundamental lack of conformity to be a fundamental breach of contract. If this is not the case, a non-conforming delivery can then expand into

To what extent a non-fulfilment of an obligation is fundamental depends on its relevance for the achievement of the purpose of the contract. In regard to the most important obligations (delivery, payment, acceptance) the possibility of avoidance can be achieved by using the mechanism of the Nachfrist.[49]

In the event of a non-fulfilment of another obligation, avoidance is possible only when it is to be regarded as fundamental. That there is indeed a "non-fulfilment will practically become obvious only after a period of waiting for fulfilment.

Even in the presence of a fundamental breach, avoidance of the contract could be set aside if the breach was not or could not be foreseen as fundamental by the party in breach".[50]

It has been pointed out by the doctrine that it is assumed that if a party knows the far-reaching consequences of a breach of contract for the other party and is not sure of his possibility of fulfilling, then he either does not conclude the contract at all or makes increased efforts to prevent its violation.[51] Therefore, the fundamentality of a breach is made dependent not only on its consequences but also on its foreseeability by the other party.

The rights of the aggrieved party are thus limited in the event that the other party did not foresee special consequences which make up the fundamentality of the breach of contract.

If the breach is fundamental, the innocent party is substantially deprived of what it expected to receive under the contract.

Provided that under the circumstances established above, i.e. an objective test shows that the breach could not have been foreseen, then the contract may be avoided and the aggrieved party may claim damages.

Where part performance of a contract has occurred, then the performing party "may recover any payment made or goods supplied; this is in conflict with the common law approach, where there is generally only a right to claim the value of the goods, and no right to recover goods supplied is allowed, unless title has been retained or damages are inadequate".

13.7 Breach not fundamental

If the breach is not fundamental, then the contract is not avoided and, as will be established, remedies may be sought including specific performance, a claim for replacing the goods, and damages.

---

a fundamental breach of contract when the lack is not removed". See F. Enderlein and D. Maskow, *A Commentary on the United Nations Convention on Contracts for the International Sale of Goods*, above, p. 80.

49 The CISG incorporated, inter alia, the notion of *Nachfrist* from German law. However, the CISG, "unlike German law, does not require a party to offer an additional period of time under which a prospectively defaulting party may perform under the contract. It merely permits a party to offer such an additional period of time. The substantive difference between the two approaches is both obvious and important". See Fritz Enderlein and Dietrich Maskow, *A Commentary on the United Nations Convention on Contracts for the International Sale of Goods*, above, at p. 80.

50 See Fritz Enderlein and Dietrich Maskow, *A Commentary on the United Nations Convention on Contracts for the International Sale of Goods*, above, at p. 80.

51 See F. Enderlein and D. Maskow, *A Commentary on the United Nations Convention on Contracts for the International Sale of Goods*, above, p. 80.

The first remedy mentioned by the Convention in the case of a non-fundamental breach is that of compelling performance enshrined in Article 46, which embraces the general civil law principle that an injured party is entitled to require performance.[52]

Article 46 CISG

(1) The buyer may require performance by the seller of his obligations unless the buyer has resorted to a remedy which is inconsistent with this requirement.
(2) If the goods do not conform with the contract, the buyer may require delivery of substitute goods only if the lack of conformity constitutes a fundamental breach of contract and a request for substitute goods is made either in conjunction with notice given under article 39 or within a reasonable time thereafter.
(3) If the goods do not conform with the contract, the buyer may require the seller to remedy the lack of conformity by repair, unless this is unreasonable having regard to all the circumstances. A request for repair must be made either in conjunction with notice given under article 39 or within a reasonable time thereafter.

This Article stipulates the right of the buyer to performance of a contract, i.e. is an expression of the civil law principle *maxim pacta sunt servanda* (agreements must be kept). This concept entails the idea of a contractual relationship of almost sacred and religious connotations, and it derives from the impact that Christian religion had on the laws of continental Europe. If *pacta sunt servanda*, or agreements must be kept, it derives that remedies are shaped so as to allow the rectification of the performance of the party not in breach, "saving" the "pact".

The right to require specific performance is laid down in many legal systems, but not under common law where, as established above, the primary remedy in the case of a breach of contract is not the request of specific performance; rather, it is a claim for damages.

Pursuant to Article 46 of the CISG, the buyer can insist on performance as long as the seller has not delivered. The right to performance also covers the event in which the seller has delivered only part of the goods or delivered goods to the wrong place,[53] or in which documents are lacking.[54]

13.7.1 Goods not conforming to the contract

If the goods do not conform with the contract, the buyer may require the seller to remedy the lack of conformity by repair, unless this is unreasonable having regard to all the circumstances. A request for repair must be made either in conjunction with notice given under Article 39 or within a reasonable time thereafter.

Article 39 CISG

(1) The buyer loses the right to rely on a lack of conformity of the goods if he does not give notice to the seller specifying the nature of the lack of conformity within a reasonable time after he has discovered it or ought to have discovered it.

---

52 See Treitel, *Remedies for Breach of Contract*, Oxford University Press, (1988), p. 73.
53 According to Article 31 CISG.
54 According to Article 34 CISG.

(2) In any event, the buyer loses the right to rely on a lack of conformity of the goods if he does not give the seller notice thereof at the latest within a period of two years from the date on which the goods were actually handed over to the buyer, unless this time limit is inconsistent with a contractual period of guarantee.

Notice of non-conformity under Article 39 of the Convention serves several purposes: it allows the seller to examine the goods himself, to substitute or repair them, and to collect or obtain evidence which he might need in a probable dispute with the buyer. The buyer's notice should enable the seller to take the necessary steps to remedy the non-conformity. For this reason, an exact description of the non-conformity is required. The notice should relate the essential result of the examination of the goods.

The parties may agree whether and which means of evidence have to be attached to the notice.

The concept of reasonable time has been interpreted as a relatively short time period, as it is in the interests of the buyer himself to inform the seller because the latter can do nothing to cure the lack before he becomes aware of it.[55]

The reasonable time commences at the time of discovery of the non-conformity. In the case of apparent defects, this will usually be the time of the taking over and examination of the goods.[56]

13.7.2 Right to require substitute goods

According to Article 46(2), if the goods do not conform with the contract, the buyer may require delivery of substitute goods only if the lack of conformity constitutes a fundamental breach of contract, and a request for substitute goods is made either in conjunction with notice given under Article 39 or within a reasonable time thereafter.

13.8 Damages

In terms of damages, Article 74 of the Convention specifies as follows:

Article 74 CISG

Damages for breach of contract by one party consist of a sum equal to the loss, including loss of profit, suffered by the other party as a consequence of the breach. Such damages may not exceed the loss which the party in breach foresaw or ought to have foreseen at the time of the conclusion of the contract, in the light of the facts and

55 See F. Enderlein and D. Maskow, *A Commentary on the United Nations Convention on Contracts for the International Sale of Goods*, above, p. 116.

56 *Ibid.* In regard to latent defects, Enderlein and Maskow point out that the time of discovery of the non-conformity will be the time of commencement of the use of the goods, the time of putting them into operation, or even later. If the buyer already discovers defects before taking over the goods, the reasonable time also commences at the time of discovery, i.e. before taking delivery.

matters of which he then knew or ought to have known, as a possible consequence of the breach of contract.

According to Article 74, damages that may be awarded conform to the common law rules established in the seminal judgment *Hadley v Baxendale.*[57] This case set the basic rule to determine consequential damages from a breach of contract, i.e. a breaching party is liable for all losses that the contracting parties should have foreseen, but it is not liable for any losses that the breaching party could not have foreseen on the information available to him.[58]

---

57 *Hadley v Baxendale* [1854] EWHC J70.

58 The claimants, Mr Hadley and another, were millers and mealmen and worked together in a partnership as proprietors of the City Steam-Mills in Gloucester. They cleaned grain, ground it into meal and processed it into flour, sharps, and bran. A crankshaft of a steam engine at the mill had broken and Hadley arranged to have a new one made by W. Joyce & Co. in Greenwich. Before the new crankshaft could be made, W. Joyce & Co. required that the broken crankshaft be sent to them in order to ensure that the new crankshaft would fit together properly with the other parts of the steam engine. Hadley contracted with the defendants Baxendale and Ors, who were operating together as common carriers under the name Pickford & Co., to deliver the crankshaft to the engineers for repair by a certain date. Baxendale failed to deliver on the date in question, causing Hadley to lose business. Hadley sued for the profits he lost due to Baxendale's late delivery, and the jury awarded Hadley damages of £25. Baxendale appealed, contending that he did not know that Hadley would suffer any particular damage by reason of the late delivery.

The question raised by the appeal in this case was whether a defendant in a breach of contract case could be held liable for damages that the defendant was not aware would be incurred from a breach of the contract. The Court of Exchequer, led by Baron Sir Edward Hall Alderson, declined to allow Hadley to recover lost profits in this case, holding that Baxendale could only be held liable for losses that were generally foreseeable, or if Hadley had mentioned his special circumstances in advance. The mere fact that a party is sending something to be repaired does not indicate that the party would lose profits if it is not delivered on time. The court suggested various other circumstances under which Hadley could have entered into this contract that would not have presented such dire circumstances, and noted that where special circumstances exist, provisions can be made in the contract voluntarily entered into by the parties to impose extra damages for a breach.

In the words of Alderson B: "Now we think the proper rule in such a case as the present is this: Where two parties have made a contract which one of them has broken, the damages which the other party ought to receive in respect of such breach of contract should be such as may fairly and reasonably be considered either arising naturally, *i.e.*, according to the usual course of things, from such breach of contract itself, or such as may reasonably be supposed to have been in the contemplation of both parties, at the time they made the contract, as the probable result of the breach of it. Now, if the special circumstances under which the contract was actually made were communicated by the plaintiffs to the defendants, and thus known to both parties, the damages resulting from the breach of such a contract, which they would reasonably contemplate, would be the amount of injury which would ordinarily follow from a breach of contract under these special circumstances so known and communicated. But, on the other hand, if these special circumstances were wholly unknown to the party breaking the contract, he, at the most, could only be supposed to have had in his contemplation the amount of injury which would arise generally, and in the great multitude of cases not affected by any special circumstances, from such a breach of contract. For, had the special circumstances been known, the parties might have specially provided for the breach of contract by special terms as to the damages in that case, and of this advantage it would be very unjust to deprive them. Now the above principles are those by which we think the jury ought to be guided in estimating the damages arising out of any breach of contract . . .

But it is obvious that, in the great multitude of cases of millers sending off broken shafts to third persons by a carrier under ordinary circumstances, such consequences would not, in all probability, have occurred, and these special circumstances were here never communicated by the plaintiffs to the defendants. It follows, therefore, that the loss of profits here cannot reasonably be considered such a consequence of the breach of contract as could have been fairly and reasonably contemplated by both the parties when they made this contract." See *Hadley v Baxendale*, above, 152.

The foreseeability element of Article 74 deals with the possibility that in some circumstances the losses may be extreme and unpredictable.[59]

It has been argued that the "test of foreseeability is substantially broader and consequently more generous to the aggrieved party".[60] Consequently, the party who breaches cannot be held liable for all damages resulting from his breach, but only for the damages he foresaw or should have foreseen.

The subjective component of Article 74 becomes very important when a party to a contract is aware of unusual losses that might occur in the case of a later breach. Therefore, at the end of forming a contract, if a party feels "that breach of the contract by the other party would cause him exceptionally heavy losses or losses of an unusual nature, he may make this known to the other party with the result that if such damages are actually suffered they may be recovered".[61]

With the objective portion of the foreseeability test of the CISG, the damages a reasonable person in the same situation would have anticipated might also become important. Indeed, due to the objective component of the damages provision, a party who breaches a contract cannot avoid paying restitution by claiming that he did not foresee the damage.[62]

Because of the subjective component of Article 74's foreseeability test, parties to a contract governed by the CISG who could potentially have unusually large losses if the contract is breached are "best advised to make these dangers known to the other party, so that the subjective prong will be implicated. However, part of the doctrine points out that notifying the other party also creates objective foreseeability".[63]

Articles 75 and 76 of the Convention deal with the calculation of damages in the case that the contract has been avoided.

Article 75 concerns damages in the case of avoidance and substitute transactions.

Article 75 CISG

If the contract is avoided and if, in a reasonable manner and within a reasonable time after avoidance, the buyer has bought goods in replacement or the seller has resold the goods, the party claiming damages may recover the difference between the contract price and the price in the substitute transaction as well as any further damages recoverable under article 74.

Here we are dealing with a concrete calculation of damages (in contrast to the abstract manner of Article 76 as considered in the following).

59 See J. Honnold, *Uniform Law for International Sales under the 1980 United Nations Convention 50,* (2nd Edition, Kluwer, 1991), p. 514.

60 J. Ziegel and C. Samson, *Report to the Uniform Law Conference of Canada on Convention on Contracts for the International Sale of Goods* (1981) Toronto 168–305.

61 See A.H. Kritzer, *Guide to Practical Applications of the United Nations Convention on Contracts for the International Sale of Goods* (Kluwer, 1989), p.476.

62 *Ibid.*, at p. 302.

63 See K.S. Cohen, Achieving a Uniform Law Governing International Sales: Conforming the Damage Provisions of the United Nations Convention on Contracts for the International Sale of Goods and the Uniform Commercial Code, *Journal of International Law*, 2005, 26(3), 13; See also Eric C. Schneider, Consequential Damages in the International Sale of Goods: Analysis of Two Decisions, 16 *U Pa. J Int'l Bus L*, 1995, 615, 634, at 635.

If the party who is true to the contract can carry out the substitute transaction according to the original terms, he does not suffer losses. If the terms he can agree are even better, he may keep the difference and need not hand it over, for instance, to the party in breach.

The difference in price between the avoided contract and the contract which was newly concluded can, however, be the result of different terms, e.g. a guarantee or of different auxiliary costs (e.g. packaging, transportation).[64]

Further damages are recoverable under the general rule of Article 74. This means, however, that any further damage is limited as to its foreseeability. In this case, too, it is a prerequisite that the injured party claims damages and proves the loss.

Article 76 deals with damages in the case of avoidance and no substitute transactions.

Article 76 CISG

(1) If the contract is avoided and there is a current price for the goods, the party claiming damages may, if he has not made a purchase or resale under article 75, recover the difference between the price fixed by the contract and the current price at the time of avoidance as well as any further damages recoverable under article 74. If, however, the party claiming damages has avoided the contract after taking over the goods, the current price at the time of such taking over shall be applied instead of the current price at the time of avoidance.

(2) For the purposes of the preceding paragraph, the current price is the price prevailing at the place where delivery of the goods should have been made or, if there is no current price at that place, the price at such other place as serves as a reasonable substitute, making due allowance for differences in the cost of transporting the goods.

The abstract calculation of the damages provided for in Article 76 is possible only when the obligee has not effected a substitute transaction, with the reasons for his inaction being irrelevant here.

It has been noted that, in the case that the "obligee effects a cover transaction and then measures his damages according to the abstract method because this is more favourable to him, he acts dishonestly and violates the principle of good faith".[65]

The abstract method of calculating damages does not require the obligee "to have tried concluding a substitute transaction. It cannot be excluded that the obligee first measures the loss abstractly and then proceeds to a cover transaction. There can be no objection against it if this is more favourable to him and if, in so doing, he uses the market developments in his favour".[66]

Interestingly, this position is very much alien to the doubts expressed under common law in *Taylor & Sons Ltd. v Bank of Athens*,[67] where objections were raised by the court in relation to the possibility of calculating damages via a linkage to market value fluctuations of the goods.[68]

---

64 See F. Enderlein and D. Maskow, *A Commentary on the United Nations Convention on Contracts for the International Sale of Goods*, above, p. 220.

65 *Ibid.*, above, p. 223.

66 *Ibid.*

67 *Taylor & Sons Ltd. v Bank of Athens* (1922) 10 Ll L Rep 88; (1922) 27 Com Cas 142.

68 See chapter 12.

Should it become clear, however, that a cover transaction is possible only "under more unfavourable terms and this transaction is carried out within a reasonable time, additional differences in price can be claimed as further damages".

When the obligee purchases and sells continuously and, therefore, no contract can qualify as a substitute purchase or sale, losses can also be calculated abstractly under Article 76.

Some authors assume that it is always at the "buyer's discretion to decide whether he measures his losses according to the abstract or the concrete method, hence an abstract calculation would be admissible in the case of a substitute transaction".[69]

13.8.1 Obligation to mitigate the loss

The concept of the obligation to mitigate losses is alien to the common law and enshrined in Article 77 of the Vienna Convention.

> **Article 77 CISG**
>
> A party who relies on a breach of contract must take such measures as are reasonable in the circumstances to mitigate the loss, including loss of profit, resulting from the breach. If he fails to take such measures, the party in breach may claim a reduction in the damages in the amount by which the loss should have been mitigated.

Article 77 postulates an obligation to mitigate losses. It has been correctly noted that fulfilment of this obligation by one party does not entail a claim for damages but rather leads to a situation where the party who is true to the contract cannot claim full compensation for damages.[70]

The extent of the obligation to mitigate losses enshrined in Article 77 should not be overstated; indeed, Article 77 simply entails that the party claiming damages only has to take such measures as are reasonable under the circumstances. Such measures may "frequently include a cover purchase or sale, and can also include the possibility that the buyer himself remedies defective goods delivered to the buyer."[71]

13.9 Case analysis

This section shall consider a few selected cases decided under the Vienna Convention, in an attempt to illustrate the differences with the common law.

---

69 See F. Enderlein and D. Maskow, *A Commentary on the United Nations Convention on Contracts for the International Sale of Goods*, above, p. 224.

70 *Ibid.*

71 *Ibid.* Enderlein and Maskow point out that "the question of whether the obligation to mitigate losses indeed referred only to the reduction of damages. An American proposal to extend that principle to other remedies was rejected. The example given related to a seller who continues manufacture of a machine even though the buyer has informed him that he has no more use for the machine ordered and would refuse to take delivery of it. If the seller nonetheless continues manufacture of the machine and sues [page 308] for performance, i.e. taking delivery and payment, he will have no obligation to mitigate losses because he claims the price and no damages".

Regarding this problem, the suggestion was to treat the obligation to mitigate losses under Article 77, paragraph 1, as a genuine obligation the breach of which will entail an obligation to compensate for damage. In the case of the example given, the buyer would have to pay the full price, but he would also have the right to claim damages.

For this purpose, attention shall focus primarily on the case law revolving around the concept of fundamental breach enshrined in Article 25, and the possibility for a buyer to terminate the contract.

As established above, in order to qualify as fundamental, a breach must be of a certain nature and weight. The aggrieved party must have suffered such detriment as to substantially deprive it of what it was entitled to expect under the contract.

For example, buyers cannot normally expect that delivered goods will comply with regulations and official standards in the buyer's country.[72]

In CLOUT case No. 123,[73] the delivery of mussels with a cadmium content exceeding recommended levels in the buyer's country had not been regarded as a fundamental breach (or, indeed, as a breach at all) since the buyer could not have expected that the seller would meet those standards and since the consumption of the mussels in small portions as such did not endanger a consumer's health.

Nevertheless, in CLOUT case No. 123, the court established three exceptions from the rule that the seller need not know and observe the standards in the buyer's country, as follows: (a) if the standards in both countries are identical; (b) if, before or at the conclusion of the contract, the buyer informed the seller about these standards; or (c) if due to special circumstances the seller knew or should have known about those standards because, e.g., it particularly specialised in exports to the buyer's country or had a branch office there.[74]

On a general level, specific patterns which constitute fundamental breaches can be identified from the international jurisprudence on the Vienna Convention.

Indeed, it has been established on various occasions that complete failure to perform a basic contractual duty constitutes a fundamental breach of contract unless the party has a justifying reason to withhold its performance. This happened in the past especially in relation to a final non-delivery scenario,[75] as well as in the case of final non-payment.[76]

---

72 See CLOUT case No. 123 [Bundesgerichtshof, Germany, 8 March 1995]. See CLOUT case No. 418 [U.S. District Court, Eastern District of Louisiana, United States 17 May 1999] (in the same sense and relying on CLOUT case No. 123 [Bundesgerichtshof, Germany, 8 March 1995]); CLOUT case No. 426 [Oberster Gerichtshof, Austria, 13 April 2000], also in *Internationales Handelsrecht* 2001, 117. See also Audiencia Provincial de Granada [Spain, 2 March 2000], *Internationales Handelsrecht* 2002, 82 (delivery of chicken meat that did not comply with slaughtering regulations in the buyer's country held no breach at all); Oberster Gerichtshof, Austria, 25 January 2006, *Internationales Handelsrecht* 2006, 110 (delivery of pig liver the import of which was rejected because it did not comply with import regulations).

73 CLOUT case No. 123 [Bundesgerichtshof, Germany, 8 March 1995].

74 See *UNCItRAL Digest of Case Law on the United Nations Convention on Contracts for the International Sale of Goods*, 2012 Edition, p. 120.

75 See CLOUT case No. 90 [Pretura circondariale di Parma, Italy, 24 November 1989] (only partial and very late delivery); CLOUT case No. 136 [Oberlandesgericht Celle, Germany, 24 May 1995] (see full text of the decision).

76 CLOUT case No. 130 [Oberlandesgericht Düsseldorf, Germany, 14 January 1994]; CLOUT case No. 468 [Tribunal of International Commercial Arbitration at the Russian Federation Chamber of Commerce and Industry, Russian Federation, 5 October 1998]; CLOUT case No. 578 [U.S. District Court, Western District of Michigan, United States, 17 December 2001]; CLOUT case No. 810 [China International Economic and Trade Arbitration Commission, People's Republic of China, 8 April 1999] (refusal to open a letter of credit); CLOUT case No. 983 [China International Economic and Trade Arbitration Commission, People's Republic of China, 10 May 2005] (even final partial non-payment can amount to fundamental breach).

Nevertheless, in the case that only a minor part of the contract is not performed (e.g. one delivery out of several deliveries is not made), the failure to perform has been considered by the courts as a simple, non-fundamental breach of contract.[77]

On the other hand, a "final and unjustified announcement of the intention not to fulfil one's own contractual obligations has been found to constitute a fundamental breach".[78]

Similarly, a "buyer's refusal to open a letter of credit as required by the contract has been held to constitute a fundamental breach".[79]

13.9.1 Case law on late performance

On a general level, it appears clear from the case law that late performance (e.g. late delivery of the goods or late payment of the price) does not in itself constitute a fundamental breach of contract.[80] Two interesting elements deserve consideration here: first, the Vienna Convention's idea of delivery as a legal teleological foundation of the seller's obligations is completely alien to English law. Indeed, we have previously dwelled on the importance of the classification of international commercial sales as contracts concluded on shipment terms, rather than on delivery terms. This shifts the focus of the legal analysis of the physical obligations of the seller to the moment of shipment, not of delivery, as to what the seller is promising to the buyer, rather than delivery, to ship the goods in conformity to that originally established in the sale contract.

Another interesting element of differentiation lies with the fact that, in the case of late delivery or late payment, the Convention allows the aggrieved party to fix an additional period of time for performance.[81] As noted above, such remedies of specific performance are completely alien to the common law, where the principle of strict compliance hardly allows a seller to rectify his performance.

---

77 See CLOUT case No. 275 [Oberlandesgericht Düsseldorf, Germany, 24 April 1997]; also Brandenburgisches Oberlandesgericht, Germany, 18 November 2008 *Internationales Handelsrecht* 2009, 105.

78 See CLOUT case No. 136 [Oberlandesgericht Celle, Germany, 24 May 1995]. In that case the seller gave notice that he had sold the specified good to another buyer. See also CLOUT case No. 595 [Oberlandesgericht München, Germany, 15 September 2004] (seller's refusal to deliver on the assumption that the contract had been cancelled was a fundamental breach) (see full text of the decision); Tribunal of International Commercial Arbitration at the Russian Federation Chamber of Commerce, Russian Federation, 4 April 1997 (Arbitral award No.387/1995), Unilex (final refusal to pay the price).

79 See CLOUT case No. 631 [Supreme Court of Queensland, Australia, 17 November 2000], citing CLOUT case No. 187 [U.S. District Court, Southern District of New York, United States, 23 July 1997] (see full text of the decision). See also CLOUT case No. 986 [China International Economic and Trade Arbitration Commission, People's Republic of China, 4 February 2002].

80 Corte di Appello di Milano, Italy, 20 March 1998, Unilex (late delivery); CLOUT case No. 275 [Oberlandesgericht Düsseldorf, Germany, 24 April 1997] (late delivery); CLOUT case No. 301 [Court of Arbitration of the International Chamber of Commerce, 1992 (Arbitral award No. 7585)] (late payment); CLOUT case No. 859 [Superior Court of Ontario, Canada, 6 October 2003] (late delivery, assuming on the facts a fundamental breach).

81 See Articles 49(1)(b) and 64(1)(b) of the Vienna Convention. See also CLOUT case No. 301 [Court of Arbitration of the International Chamber of Commerce, 1992 (Arbitral award No. 7585)].

Defects in the goods:
In the case of defective goods, under the Vienna Convention, the buyer can terminate the contract only in the case that the non-conformity of the goods can be properly regarded as a fundamental breach of contract.[82]

It is, thus, essential to know under what conditions delivery of non-conforming goods constitutes a fundamental breach. Court decisions on this point have found that a non-conformity concerning quality remains a mere non-fundamental breach of contract, as long as the buyer (without unreasonable inconvenience) can use the goods or resell them even at a discount.[83] Here, it is interesting to note how the Vienna Convention translates into a legal prerogative what under English law would be a matter of out of court negotiations.[84]

By way of example, the delivery of frozen meat that was too fat and too moist, and that consequently was worth 25.5 per cent less than meat of the contracted quality (according to an expert opinion), was not regarded as a fundamental breach of contract, since the buyer had the opportunity to resell the meat at a lower price or to otherwise process it.[85]

On the other hand, if the non-conforming goods cannot be used or resold with reasonable efforts, this would constitute a fundamental breach and entitles the buyer to declare the contract avoided.[86] This has been held to be the case whenever goods "suffered from a serious and irreparable defect although they were still usable to some extent."[87]

Courts have considered a breach to be fundamental without reference to possible alternative uses or resale by the buyer, when the goods turned out

82 Article 49(1)(a) Vienna Convention.

83 See CLOUT case No. 171 [Bundesgerichtshof, Germany, 3 April 1996]; CLOUT case No. 248 [Bundesgericht, Switzerland, 28 October 1998]. See the *UNCItRAL Digest of Case Law on the United Nations Convention on Contracts for the International Sale of Goods*, 2012 Edition, p. 120.

84 As established above, the common law principle of strict compliance generates an efficient and certain legal scenario, whereby the buyer can terminate the contract in the case of a breach of condition by the seller (or vice versa). The legal possibility of termination is, of course, only one of the possible courses of action available to the party not in breach, who is likely to negotiate a settlement/discount before proceeding with termination.

85 See CLOUT case No. 248 [Bundesgericht, Switzerland, 28 October 1998]; CLOUT case No. 988 [China International Economic and Trade Arbitration Commission, People's Republic of China, 2000] (holding that delivery of non-conforming souvenir coins of which the buyer resold 75 per cent did not constitute a fundamental breach).

86 See CLOUT case No. 150 [Cour de Cassation, France, 23 January 1996] (artificially sugared wine); CLOUT case No. 79 [Oberlandesgericht Frankfurt a.M., Germany, 18 January 1994] (shoes with cracked leather) (see full text of the decision); Landgericht Landshut, Germany, 5 April 1995, Unilex (T-shirts that shrink by two sizes after the first washing); Bundesgericht, Switzerland, 18 May 2009 *Internationales Handelsrecht* 2010, 27 (packaging machine reached only one-third of the agreed level of production). See *UNCItRAL Digest of Case Law on the United Nations Convention on Contracts for the International Sale of Goods*, above, at p. 120.

87 E.g. flowers which were supposed to flourish the whole summer but did so only for part of it. See CLOUT case No. 107 [Oberlandesgericht Innsbruck, Austria, 1 July 1994]. For a similar case see CLOUT case No. 992 [Copenhagen District Court, Denmark, 19 October 2007] (pony bought for riding competitions that proved to be incurably lame held to constitute a fundamental breach); [Bundesgericht, Switzerland, 18 May 2009] *Internationales Handelsrecht* 2010, 27 [Hamm, Germany, 2 April 2009] (packaging machine reached only one-third of the agreed level of production).

to have major defects, and conforming goods were needed for manufacturing other products.[88]

The same conclusion has been reached where the non-conformity of the goods resulted from added substances, the addition of which was illegal both in the country of the seller and the buyer.[89]

Problems do arise when goods are defective but repairable. Indeed, this scenario under the Vienna Convention gives rise to a certain level of legal uncertainty, an "easy repairability has been found in the past to preclude the possibility for the buyer to claim the presence of a fundamental breach".[90]

Courts have also been reluctant to consider a breach fundamental whenever the seller offers and performs a speedy repair without any inconvenience to the buyer.[91]

From the aforementioned analysis, the differences in terms of remedies for breach of physical duties between the Vienna Convention and at common law appear to be eminently clear.

If, at common law, the identification of a breach of condition (such as description, quantity, quality, sample, time of shipment, and place of shipment) would suffice to terminate the contract, quite the opposite can be said about a breach of physical duty regulated by the Vienna Convention.

Indeed, as established above, the concept of fundamental breach enshrined in Article 25 of the Vienna Convention renders the buyer's remedies difficult to identify and execute, giving rise overall to serious legal uncertainty.

As will be readily appreciated, the same considerations are equally valid in the case of a seller's breach of documentary duties, as considered in the following.

---

88 See CLOUT case No. 138 [U.S. Court of Appeals for the Second Circuit, United States, 6 December 1995] (compressors with lower cooling capacity and higher power consumption than the goods contracted for, which were required for the manufacture of air conditioners by the buyer); CLOUT case No. 150 [Cour de Cassation, France, 23 January 1996] (artificially sugared wine) (see full text of the decision); CLOUT case No. 315 [Cour de Cassation, France, 26 May 1999] (metal sheets absolutely unfit for the foreseen kind of manufacture by the buyer's customer) (see full text of the decision); see also Tribunale di Busto Arsizio, Italy, 13 December 2001, published in Rivista di Diritto Internazionale Privato e Processuale, 2003, 150–155, also available on Unilex (delivery of a machine totally unfit for the particular use made known to the seller and that was incapable of reaching the promised production level represented a "serious and fundamental" breach of the contract, since the promised production level was an essential condition for the conclusion of the contract; the lack of conformity therefore was a basis for avoidance); Bundesgericht, Switzerland, 18 May 2009, Internationales Handelsrecht 2010, 27 (even after numerous attempts to correct problems, packaging machine reached only one-third of the agreed level of production).

89 See the *UNCItRAL Digest of Case Law on the United Nations Convention on Contracts for the International Sale of Goods*, above, p. 119. See Hof's-Gravenhage, The Netherlands, 23 April 2004, *Nederlands Jurisprudentie* 2004 no. 713 (delivery of flour with carcinogenic addition that was forbidden in the Netherlands but not in Mozambique – the place of delivery and use – held to constitute a fundamental breach).

90 See Handelsgericht des Kantons Zürich, Switzerland, 26 April 1995, Schweizerische Zeitschrift für Internationales und Europäisches Recht 1996, 51; Oberlandesgericht Köln, Germany, 14 October 2002, Internationales Handelsrecht 2003, 15; CLOUT case No. 937 [Cantonal Court of the Jura, Switzerland, 26 July 2007).

91 See CLOUT case No. 152 [Cour d'appel, Grenoble, France, 26 April 1995]; CLOUT case No. 282 [Oberlandesgericht Koblenz, Germany, 31 January 1997].

13.9.2 Case law on breach of documentary duties

Just as with breach of physical duties, in order for the contract to be terminated under the Vienna Convention, the violation of documentary obligations needs to amount to a fundamental breach.[92]

In order for a contract to be void, it is indeed necessary that the breach of the seller's documentary duties deprives the aggrieved party of the main benefit of the contract, and that this result could have been foreseen by the other party.

Thus, the courts have stated that there is no fundamental breach in the case of delivery of incorrect certificates pertaining to the goods if either the goods were nevertheless merchantable or if the buyer himself could – at the seller's expense – easily acquire the correct certificates.[93]

This is what happened in the cobalt sulphate case,[94] where a Dutch seller and a German buyer concluded several contracts for the sale of cobalt sulphate with specific technical qualities, and of British origin.

The buyer declared the contracts avoided on the following grounds: the cobalt delivered was of a lower quality than that agreed to under the contracts; the cobalt was produced in South Africa and not in the UK as indicated in the contracts; the seller had delivered non-conforming certificates of origin and quality. The seller denied the buyer's right to avoid and brought suit to recover the purchase price.

The German Supreme Court held that the buyer had not validly avoided the contracts and awarded the seller the full price.

As to the buyer's argument that it was entitled to avoid the contracts under Article 49(1)(b) CISG, because the goods were of a kind different from that agreed upon in the contracts and therefore their delivery constituted a non-delivery, the court stated that the CISG, contrary to German domestic law, does not make any difference between delivery of goods of different kind (*aliud*) and delivery of non-conforming goods.

The court stressed that, pursuant to Article 7 CISG, in the interpretation of the Convention recourse to domestic law is as a rule not admissible. Yet avoidance was impossible also under Article 49(1)(a) CISG.

According to the court, in the system of the Convention the remedy of avoidance for non-conformity of the goods represents the last resort in respect to the other remedies available to the buyer, such as price reduction or damages.

Here lies the full embracing of the principle *pacta sunt servanda*, i.e. the idea of a contract intended almost as a "pact" having religious connotations to it, and the consequent need for the legal remedies to try to "save" the contract and keep it "alive" rather than terminating it.

This approach lies as far as it can possibly be from the strict compliance approach at common law, where a breach of a physical or documentary condition would suffice to bring the contract to an end.

92 As established above, the Vienna Convention embraces the dual type of performance of obligations typical of contracts concluded on shipment terms at common law.

93 See CLOUT case No. 171 [Bundesgerichtshof, Germany, 3 April 1996].

94 See case VIII ZR 51/95, Germany 3 April 1996 Supreme Court (cobalt sulphate case).

In the cobalt sulphate case, the seller's tender of non-conforming documents did not amount to a fundamental breach of contract. In determining whether the non-conformity is fundamental, i.e. deprives the buyer substantially of what it is entitled to expect under the contract,[95] whether the buyer can still make use of the goods or resell them in the usual commercial relationships without incurring any unreasonable difficulties is decisive. The fact that the buyer might be forced to resell the goods at a lower price is not to be considered in itself an unreasonable difficulty.

In the case at hand, the tender of a certificate of origin showing that the cobalt sulphate was of South African origin rather than of British origin as per what was originally established in the sales contract, did not amount to a breach of fundamental nature which would have enabled the buyer to terminate the contract, as the buyer was not held to be substantially deprived of what he was entitled to receive, i.e. cobalt sulphate.

This was despite the alleged difficulties for the buyer in exporting the goods to India (the buyer's primary resale market) due to the then existing embargo against goods produced in South Africa.[96]

Interestingly, the court, although admitting that the delivery of non-conforming documents could amount to a fundamental breach, denied "that this was so in the case at hand, since the buyer could have easily obtained the right certificates of origin by itself and the right certificate of quality through expert examination. Moreover, the non-conformity of the documents did not prevent the buyer from taking delivery of the goods and disposing of them".[97]

Yet again, if considered under common law, the outcome of the case would have been diametrically opposite, with the buyer in the position to terminate the contract for breach of documentary strict compliance by the seller.

Similarly, the facts of a case decided by the Swiss Bundesgericht in 1998 were more straightforward. The contract was for the sale of frozen meat. The meat which was delivered did not live up to the agreed standards. As a consequence, the value of the delivered goods was about 25 per cent less than agreed. The Swiss Bundesgericht explicitly referred to the cobalt sulphate judgment of the German Bundesgerichtshof and held that there was no fundamental breach as the delivered meat could have been reasonably sold on by the buyer for a lower price (which might then have been compensated for by a claim for damages).

---

95 See Article 25 CISG.

96 See case report at: unilex.info "The court did not follow that line of argument because the buyer had neither been able to name potential buyers in those countries or to adduce evidence of earlier sales in these countries, nor had he even alleged that it would have been impossible or unreasonable to make another use of the goods in Germany or to export them into another country. The actual decision of the case thus is based on procedural reasons, namely on the lack of proof by the buyer. It is, however, an interesting question just what the court would have decided if the buyer actually had proven that he could not resell the goods in a considerable proportion of the world. In light of the reasoning adopted, it seems likely that the court would have told the buyer to look for a country where there was no embargo, to sell the goods there (albeit for a lower price) and claim damages for the losses incurred by doing so (for instance for the price difference)".

97 See case report at: unilex.info.

Both the highest German and Swiss courts therefore attached considerable weight to the question of whether the buyer could make some other reasonable use of the non-conforming goods. They have, for example, refused the right to terminate a contract if it is possible and reasonable for the buyer to resell the goods in the ordinary course of business, albeit for a lower price.

Likewise, a typographical error in a bill of lading ("1999" instead of "1998") does not constitute a fundamental breach and does not entitle the buyer to refuse payment. The unjustified denial of contract rights of the other party – e.g. a refusal to recognise the validity of a retention of title clause and the seller's right to possession of the goods, or the unjustified denial of a valid contract after having taken possession of samples of the goods – can amount to a fundamental breach of contract.

The same equally applies to situations whereby "resale restrictions have been substantially violated, or when the buyer, under an f.o.b. contract, refuses to perform its obligation to hire a ship so that it is impossible for the seller to deliver the goods f.o.b".[98]

98 See P. Huber, "Typically German? – Two Contentious German Contributions to the CISG" Belgrade Law Review, Year LIX (2011) no. 3 pp. 150–161.

APPENDIX I

Sale of Goods Act 1979

Sale of Goods Act 1979

1979 CHAPTER 54

An Act to consolidate the law relating to the sale of goods. [6th December 1979]

BE IT ENACTED by the Queen's most Excellent Majesty, by and with the advice and consent of the Lords Spiritual and Temporal, and Commons, in this present Parliament assembled, and by the authority of the same, as follows:—

PART I

CONTRACTS TO WHICH ACT APPLIES

Contracts to which Act applies.

1.—(1) This Act applies to contracts of sale of goods made on or after (but not to those made before) 1 January 1894.

(2) In relation to contracts made on certain dates, this Act applies subject to the modification of certain of its sections as mentioned in Schedule 1 below.

(3) Any such modification is indicated in the section concerned by a reference to Schedule 1 below.

(4) Accordingly, where a section does not contain such a reference, this Act applies in relation to the contract concerned without such modification of the section.

PART II

FORMATION OF THE CONTRACT

Contract of sale

Contract of sale.

2.—(1) A contract of sale of goods is a contract by which the seller transfers or agrees to transfer the property in goods to the buyer for a money consideration, called the price.

(2) There may be a contract of sale between one part owner and another.

(3) A contract of sale may be absolute or conditional.

(4) Where under a contract of sale the property in the goods is transferred from the seller to the buyer the contract is called a sale.

(5) Where under a contract of sale the transfer of the property in the goods is to take place at a future time or subject to some condition later to be fulfilled the contract is called an agreement to sell.

(6) An agreement to sell becomes a sale when the time elapses or the conditions are fulfilled subject to which the property in the goods is to be transferred.

Capacity to buy and sell.

3.—(1) Capacity to buy and sell is regulated by the general law concerning capacity to contract and to transfer and acquire property.

(2) Where necessaries are sold and delivered to a minor or to a person who by reason of mental incapacity or drunkenness is incompetent to contract, he must pay a reasonable price for them.

(3) In subsection (2) above " necessaries " means goods suitable to the condition in life of the minor or other person concerned and to his actual requirements at the time of the sale and delivery.

Formalities of contract

How contract of sale is made.

4.—(1) Subject to this and any other Act, a contract of sale may be made in writing (either with or without seal), or by word of mouth, or partly in writing and partly by word of mouth, or may be implied from the conduct of the parties.

(2) Nothing in this section affects the law relating to corporations.

Subject matter of contract

Existing or future goods.

5.—(1) The goods which form the subject of a contract of sale may be either existing goods, owned or possessed by the seller, or goods to be manufactured or acquired by him after the making of the contract of sale, in this Act called future goods.

(2) There may be a contract for the sale of goods the acquisition of which by the seller depends on a contingency which may or may not happen.

(3) Where by a contract of sale the seller purports to effect a present sale of future goods, the contract operates as an agreement to sell the goods. PART II

6. Where there is a contract for the sale of specific goods, and the goods without the knowledge of the seller have perished at the time when the contract is made, the contract is void. Goods which have perished.

7. Where there is an agreement to sell specific goods and subsequently the goods, without any fault on the part of the seller or buyer, perish before the risk passes to the buyer, the agreement is avoided. Goods perishing before sale but after agreement to sell.

The price

8.—(1) The price in a contract of sale may be fixed by the contract, or may be left to be fixed in a manner agreed by the contract, or may be determined by the course of dealing between the parties. Ascertainment of price.

(2) Where the price is not determined as mentioned in subsection (1) above the buyer must pay a reasonable price.

(3) What is a reasonable price is a question of fact dependent on the circumstances of each particular case.

9.—(1) Where there is an agreement to sell goods on the terms that the price is to be fixed by the valuation of a third party, and he cannot or does not make the valuation, the agreement is avoided; but if the goods or any part of them have been delivered to and appropriated by the buyer he must pay a reasonable price for them. Agreement to sell at valuation.

(2) Where the third party is prevented from making the valuation by the fault of the seller or buyer, the party not at fault may maintain an action for damages against the party at fault.

Conditions and warranties

10.—(1) Unless a different intention appears from the terms of the contract, stipulations as to time of payment are not of the essence of a contract of sale. Stipulations about time.

(2) Whether any other stipulation as to time is or is not of the essence of the contract depends on the terms of the contract.

(3) In a contract of sale "month" prima facie means calendar month.

PART II

When condition to be treated as warranty.

11.—(1) Subsections (2) to (4) and (7) below do not apply to Scotland and subsection (5) below applies only to Scotland.

(2) Where a contract of sale is subject to a condition to be fulfilled by the seller, the buyer may waive the condition, or may elect to treat the breach of the condition as a breach of warranty and not as a ground for treating the contract as repudiated.

(3) Whether a stipulation in a contract of sale is a condition, the breach of which may give rise to a right to treat the contract as repudiated, or a warranty, the breach of which may give rise to a claim for damages but not to a right to reject the goods and treat the contract as repudiated, depends in each case on the construction of the contract; and a stipulation may be a condition, though called a warranty in the contract.

(4) Where a contract of sale is not severable and the buyer has accepted the goods or part of them, the breach of a condition to be fulfilled by the seller can only be treated as a breach of warranty, and not as a ground for rejecting the goods and treating the contract as repudiated, unless there is an express or implied term of the contract to that effect.

(5) In Scotland, failure by the seller to perform any material part of a contract of sale is a breach of contract, which entitles the buyer either within a reasonable time after delivery to reject the goods and treat the contract as repudiated, or to retain the goods and treat the failure to perform such material part as a breach which may give rise to a claim for compensation or damages.

(6) Nothing in this section affects a condition or warranty whose fulfilment is excused by law by reason of impossibility or otherwise.

(7) Paragraph 2 of Schedule 1 below applies in relation to a contract made before 22 April 1967 or (in the application of this Act to Northern Ireland) 28 July 1967.

Implied terms about title, etc.

12.—(1) In a contract of sale, other than one to which subsection (3) below applies, there is an implied condition on the part of the seller that in the case of a sale he has a right to sell the goods, and in the case of an agreement to sell he will have such a right at the time when the property is to pass.

(2) In a contract of sale, other than one to which subsection (3) below applies, there is also an implied warranty that—

(*a*) the goods are free, and will remain free until the time when the property is to pass, from any charge or encumbrance not disclosed or known to the buyer before the contract is made, and (*b*) the buyer will enjoy quiet possession of the goods except so far as it may be disturbed by the owner or other person entitled to the benefit of any charge or encumbrance so disclosed or known. PART II

(3) This subsection applies to a contract of sale in the case of which there appears from the contract or is to be inferred from its circumstances an intention that the seller should transfer only such title as he or a third person may have.

(4) In a contract to which subsection (3) above applies there is an implied warranty that all charges or encumbrances known to the seller and not known to the buyer have been disclosed to the buyer before the contract is made.

(5) In a contract to which subsection (3) above applies there is also an implied warranty that none of the following will disturb the buyer's quiet possession of the goods, namely—

(*a*) the seller;

(*b*) in a case where the parties to the contract intend that the seller should transfer only such title as a third person may have, that person;

(*c*) anyone claiming through or under the seller or that third person otherwise than under a charge or encumbrance disclosed or known to the buyer before the contract is made.

(6) Paragraph 3 of Schedule 1 below applies in relation to a contract made before 18 May 1973.

Sale by description.

13.—(1) Where there is a contract for the sale of goods by description, there is an implied condition that the goods will correspond with the description.

(2) If the sale is by sample as well as by description it is not sufficient that the bulk of the goods corresponds with the sample if the goods do not also correspond with the description.

(3) A sale of goods is not prevented from being a sale by description by reason only that, being exposed for sale or hire, they are selected by the buyer.

(4) Paragraph 4 of Schedule 1 below applies in relation to a contract made before 18 May 1973.

Implied terms about quality or fitness.

14.—(1) Except as provided by this section and section 15 below and subject to any other enactment, there is no implied condition or warranty about the quality or fitness for any particular purpose of goods supplied under a contract of sale.

(2) Where the seller sells goods in the course of a business, there is an implied condition that the goods supplied under the

PART II contract are of merchantable quality, except that there is no such condition—

(*a*) as regards defects specifically drawn to the buyer's attention before the contract is made; or

(*b*) if the buyer examines the goods before the contract is made, as regards defects which that examination ought to reveal.

(3) Where the seller sells goods in the course of a business and the buyer, expressly or by implication, makes known—

(*a*) to the seller, or

(*b*) where the purchase price or part of it is payable by instalments and the goods were previously sold by a credit-broker to the seller, to that credit-broker,

any particular purpose for which the goods are being bought, there is an implied condition that the goods supplied under the contract are reasonably fit for that purpose, whether or not that is a purpose for which such goods are commonly supplied, except where the circumstances show that the buyer does not rely, or that it is unreasonable for him to rely, on the skill or judgment of the seller or credit-broker.

(4) An implied condition or warranty about quality or fitness for a particular purpose may be annexed to a contract of sale by usage.

(5) The preceding provisions of this section apply to a sale by a person who in the course of a business is acting as agent for another as they apply to a sale by a principal in the course of a business, except where that other is not selling in the course of a business and either the buyer knows that fact or reasonable steps are taken to bring it to the notice of the buyer before the contract is made.

(6) Goods of any kind are of merchantable quality within the meaning of subsection (2) above if they are as fit for the purpose or purposes for which goods of that kind are commonly bought as it is reasonable to expect having regard to any description applied to them, the price (if relevant) and all the other relevant circumstances.

(7) Paragraph 5 of Schedule 1 below applies in relation to a contract made on or after 18 May 1973 and before the appointed day, and paragraph 6 in relation to one made before 18 May 1973.

(8) In subsection (7) above and paragraph 5 of Schedule 1 below references to the appointed day are to the day appointed for the purposes of those provisions by an order of the Secretary of State made by statutory instrument.

Sale by sample

15.—(1) A contract of sale is a contract for sale by sample where there is an express or implied term to that effect in the contract. Sale by sample.

(2) In the case of a contract for sale by sample there is an implied condition—

(*a*) that the bulk will correspond with the sample in quality;

(*b*) that the buyer will have a reasonable opportunity of comparing the bulk with the sample;

(*c*) that the goods will be free from any defect, rendering them unmerchantable, which would not be apparent on reasonable examination of the sample.

(3) In subsection (2)(*c*) above "unmerchantable" is to be construed in accordance with section 14(6) above.

(4) Paragraph 7 of Schedule 1 below applies in relation to a contract made before 18 May 1973.

PART III

EFFECTS OF THE CONTRACT

Transfer of property as between seller and buyer

16. Where there is a contract for the sale of unascertained goods no property in the goods is transferred to the buyer unless and until the goods are ascertained. Goods must be ascertained.

17.—(1) Where there is a contract for the sale of specific or ascertained goods the property in them is transferred to the buyer at such time as the parties to the contract intend it to be transferred. Property passes when intended to pass.

(2) For the purpose of ascertaining the intention of the parties regard shall be had to the terms of the contract, the conduct of the parties and the circumstances of the case.

18. Unless a different intention appears, the following are rules for ascertaining the intention of the parties as to the time at which the property in the goods is to pass to the buyer. Rules for ascertaining intention.

Rule 1.—Where there is an unconditional contract for the sale of specific goods in a deliverable state the property in the goods passes to the buyer when the contract is made, and it is immaterial whether the time of payment or the time of delivery, or both, be postponed.

Rule 2.—Where there is a contract for the sale of specific goods and the seller is bound to do something to the goods for the purpose of putting them into a deliverable state, the property does not pass until the thing is done and the buyer has notice that it has been done.

A 5

PART III

Rule 3.—Where there is a contract for the sale of specific goods in a deliverable state but the seller is bound to weigh, measure, test, or do some other act or thing with reference to the goods for the purpose of ascertaining the price, the property does not pass until the act or thing is done and the buyer has notice that it has been done.

Rule 4.—When goods are delivered to the buyer on approval or on sale or return or other similar terms the property in the goods passes to the buyer:—

(*a*) when he signifies his approval or acceptance to the seller or does any other act adopting the transaction ;

(*b*) if he does not signify his approval or acceptance to the seller but retains the goods without giving notice of rejection, then, if a time has been fixed for the return of the goods, on the expiration of that time, and, if no time has been fixed, on the expiration of a reasonable time.

Rule 5.—(1) Where there is a contract for the sale of unascertained or future goods by description, and goods of that description and in a deliverable state are unconditionally appropriated to the contract, either by the seller with the assent of the buyer or by the buyer with the assent of the seller, the property in the goods then passes to the buyer; and the assent may be express or implied, and may be given either before or after the appropriation is made.

(2) Where, in pursuance of the contract, the seller delivers the goods to the buyer or to a carrier or other bailee or custodier (whether named by the buyer or not) for the purpose of transmission to the buyer, and does not reserve the right of disposal, he is to be taken to have unconditionally appropriated the goods to the contract.

Reservation of right of disposal.

19.—(1) Where there is a contract for the sale of specific goods or where goods are subsequently appropriated to the contract, the seller may, by the terms of the contract or appropriation, reserve the right of disposal of the goods until certain conditions are fulfilled ; and in such a case, notwithstanding the delivery of the goods to the buyer, or to a carrier or other bailee or custodier for the purpose of transmission to the buyer, the property in the goods does not pass to the buyer until the conditions imposed by the seller are fulfilled.

(2) Where goods are shipped, and by the bill of lading the goods are deliverable to the order of the seller or his agent, the seller is prima facie to be taken to reserve the right of disposal.

(3) Where the seller of goods draws on the buyer for the price, and transmits the bill of exchange and bill of lading to the buyer together to secure acceptance or payment of the bill of exchange, the buyer is bound to return the bill of lading if he does not honour the bill of exchange, and if he wrongfully retains the bill of lading the property in the goods does not pass to him.

Risk prima facie passes with property.

20.—(1) Unless otherwise agreed, the goods remain at the seller's risk until the property in them is transferred to the buyer, but when the property in them is transferred to the buyer the goods are at the buyer's risk whether delivery has been made or not.

(2) But where delivery has been delayed through the fault of either buyer or seller the goods are at the risk of the party at fault as regards any loss which might not have occurred but for such fault.

(3) Nothing in this section affects the duties or liabilities of either seller or buyer as a bailee or custodier of the goods of the other party.

Transfer of title

Sale by person not the owner.

21.—(1) Subject to this Act, where goods are sold by a person who is not their owner, and who does not sell them under the authority or with the consent of the owner, the buyer acquires no better title to the goods than the seller had, unless the owner of the goods is by his conduct precluded from denying the seller's authority to sell.

(2) Nothing in this Act affects—

(*a*) the provisions of the Factors Acts or any enactment enabling the apparent owner of goods to dispose of them as if he were their true owner;

(*b*) the validity of any contract of sale under any special common law or statutory power of sale or under the order of a court of competent jurisdiction.

Market overt.

22.—(1) Where goods are sold in market overt, according to the usage of the market, the buyer acquires a good title to the goods, provided he buys them in good faith and without notice of any defect or want of title on the part of the seller.

(2) This section does not apply to Scotland.

(3) Paragraph 8 of Schedule 1 below applies in relation to a contract under which goods were sold before 1 January 1968 or (in the application of this Act to Northern Ireland) 29 August 1967.

PART III

Sale under voidable title.

23. When the seller of goods has a voidable title to them, but his title has not been avoided at the time of the sale, the buyer acquires a good title to the goods, provided he buys them in good faith and without notice of the seller's defect of title.

Seller in possession after sale.

24. Where a person having sold goods continues or is in possession of the goods, or of the documents of title to the goods, the delivery or transfer by that person, or by a mercantile agent acting for him, of the goods or documents of title under any sale, pledge, or other disposition thereof, to any person receiving the same in good faith and without notice of the previous sale, has the same effect as if the person making the delivery or transfer were expressly authorised by the owner of the goods to make the same.

Buyer in possession after sale.

25.—(1) Where a person having bought or agreed to buy goods obtains, with the consent of the seller, possession of the goods or the documents of title to the goods, the delivery or transfer by that person, or by a mercantile agent acting for him, of the goods or documents of title, under any sale, pledge, or other disposition thereof, to any person receiving the same in good faith and without notice of any lien or other right of the original seller in respect of the goods, has the same effect as if the person making the delivery or transfer were a mercantile agent in possession of the goods or documents of title with the consent of the owner.

(2) For the purposes of subsection (1) above—

(*a*) the buyer under a conditional sale agreement is to be taken not to be a person who has bought or agreed to buy goods, and

(*b*) " conditional sale agreement " means an agreement for the sale of goods which is a consumer credit agreement within the meaning of the Consumer Credit Act 1974 under which the purchase price or part of it is payable by instalments, and the property in the goods is to remain in the seller (notwithstanding that the buyer is to be in possession of the goods) until such conditions as to the payment of instalments or otherwise as may be specified in the agreement are fulfilled.

1974 c. 39.

(3) Paragraph 9 of Schedule 1 below applies in relation to a contract under which a person buys or agrees to buy goods and which is made before the appointed day.

(4) In subsection (3) above and paragraph 9 of Schedule 1 below references to the appointed day are to the day appointed for the purposes of those provisions by an order of the Secretary of State made by statutory instrument.

26. In sections 24 and 25 above " mercantile agent " means a mercantile agent having in the customary course of his business as such agent authority either—

PART III

Supplementary to sections 24 and 25.

(*a*) to sell goods, or

(*b*) to consign goods for the purpose of sale, or

(*c*) to buy goods, or

(*d*) to raise money on the security of goods.

PART IV

PERFORMANCE OF THE CONTRACT

Duties of seller and buyer.

27. It is the duty of the seller to deliver the goods, and of the buyer to accept and pay for them, in accordance with the terms of the contract of sale.

Payment and delivery are concurrent conditions.

28. Unless otherwise agreed, delivery of the goods and payment of the price are concurrent conditions, that is to say, the seller must be ready and willing to give possession of the goods to the buyer in exchange for the price and the buyer must be ready and willing to pay the price in exchange for possession of the goods.

Rules about delivery.

29.—(1) Whether it is for the buyer to take possession of the goods or for the seller to send them to the buyer is a question depending in each case on the contract, express or implied, between the parties.

(2) Apart from any such contract, express or implied, the place of delivery is the seller's place of business if he has one, and if not, his residence; except that, if the contract is for the sale of specific goods, which to the knowledge of the parties when the contract is made are in some other place, then that place is the place of delivery.

(3) Where under the contract of sale the seller is bound to send the goods to the buyer, but no time for sending them is fixed, the seller is bound to send them within a reasonable time.

(4) Where the goods at the time of sale are in the possession of a third person, there is no delivery by seller to buyer unless and until the third person acknowledges to the buyer that he holds the goods on his behalf; but nothing in this section affects the operation of the issue or transfer of any document of title to goods.

(5) Demand or tender of delivery may be treated as ineffectual unless made at a reasonable hour; and what is a reasonable hour is a question of fact.

PART IV

(6) Unless otherwise agreed, the expenses of and incidental to putting the goods into a deliverable state must be borne by the seller.

Delivery of wrong quantity.

30.—(1) Where the seller delivers to the buyer a quantity of goods less than he contracted to sell, the buyer may reject them, but if the buyer accepts the goods so delivered he must pay for them at the contract rate.

(2) Where the seller delivers to the buyer a quantity of goods larger than he contracted to sell, the buyer may accept the goods included in the contract and reject the rest, or he may reject the whole.

(3) Where the seller delivers to the buyer a quantity of goods larger than he contracted to sell and the buyer accepts the whole of the goods so delivered he must pay for them at the contract rate.

(4) Where the seller delivers to the buyer the goods he contracted to sell mixed with goods of a different description not included in the contract, the buyer may accept the goods which are in accordance with the contract and reject the rest, or he may reject the whole.

(5) This section is subject to any usage of trade, special agreement, or course of dealing between the parties.

Instalment deliveries.

31.—(1) Unless otherwise agreed, the buyer of goods is not bound to accept delivery of them by instalments.

(2) Where there is a contract for the sale of goods to be delivered by stated instalments, which are to be separately paid for, and the seller makes defective deliveries in respect of one or more instalments, or the buyer neglects or refuses to take delivery of or pay for one or more instalments, it is a question in each case depending on the terms of the contract and the circumstances of the case whether the breach of contract is a repudiation of the whole contract or whether it is a severable breach giving rise to a claim for compensation but not to a right to treat the whole contract as repudiated.

Delivery to carrier.

32.—(1) Where, in pursuance of a contract of sale, the seller is authorised or required to send the goods to the buyer, delivery of the goods to a carrier (whether named by the buyer or not) for the purpose of transmission to the buyer is prima facie deemed to be a delivery of the goods to the buyer.

(2) Unless otherwise authorised by the buyer, the seller must make such contract with the carrier on behalf of the buyer as may be reasonable having regard to the nature of the goods and the other circumstances of the case ; and if the seller omits to do

so, and the goods are lost or damaged in course of transit, the buyer may decline to treat the delivery to the carrier as a delivery to himself or may hold the seller responsible in damages.

(3) Unless otherwise agreed, where goods are sent by the seller to the buyer by a route involving sea transit, under circumstances in which it is usual to insure, the seller must give such notice to the buyer as may enable him to insure them during their sea transit; and if the seller fails to do so, the goods are at his risk during such sea transit.

Risk where goods are delivered at distant place.

33. Where the seller of goods agrees to deliver them at his own risk at a place other than that where they are when sold, the buyer must nevertheless (unless otherwise agreed) take any risk of deterioration in the goods necessarily incident to the course of transit.

Buyer's right of examining the goods.

34.—(1) Where goods are delivered to the buyer, and he has not previously examined them, he is not deemed to have accepted them until he has had a reasonable opportunity of examining them for the purpose of ascertaining whether they are in conformity with the contract.

(2) Unless otherwise agreed, when the seller tenders delivery of goods to the buyer, he is bound on request to afford the buyer a reasonable opportunity of examining the goods for the purpose of ascertaining whether they are in conformity with the contract.

Acceptance.

35.—(1) The buyer is deemed to have accepted the goods when he intimates to the seller that he has accepted them, or (except where section 34 above otherwise provides) when the goods have been delivered to him and he does any act in relation to them which is inconsistent with the ownership of the seller, or when after the lapse of a reasonable time he retains the goods without intimating to the seller that he has rejected them.

(2) Paragraph 10 of Schedule 1 below applies in relation to a contract made before 22 April 1967 or (in the application of this Act to Northern Ireland) 28 July 1967.

Buyer not bound to return rejected goods.

36. Unless otherwise agreed, where goods are delivered to the buyer, and he refuses to accept them, having the right to do so, he is not bound to return them to the seller, but it is sufficient if he intimates to the seller that he refuses to accept them.

Buyer's liability for not taking delivery of goods.

37.—(1) When the seller is ready and willing to deliver the goods, and requests the buyer to take delivery, and the buyer does not within a reasonable time after such request take delivery of the goods, he is liable to the seller for any loss occasioned by his neglect or refusal to take delivery, and also for a reasonable charge for the care and custody of the goods.

PART IV

(2) Nothing in this section affects the rights of the seller where the neglect or refusal of the buyer to take delivery amounts to a repudiation of the contract.

PART V

RIGHTS OF UNPAID SELLER AGAINST THE GOODS

Preliminary

Unpaid seller defined.

38.—(1) The seller of goods is an unpaid seller within the meaning of this Act—

(*a*) when the whole of the price has not been paid or tendered;

(*b*) when a bill of exchange or other negotiable instrument has been received as conditional payment, and the condition on which it was received has not been fulfilled by reason of the dishonour of the instrument or otherwise.

(2) In this Part of this Act " seller " includes any person who is in the position of a seller, as, for instance, an agent of the seller to whom the bill of lading has been indorsed, or a consignor or agent who has himself paid (or is directly responsible for) the price.

Unpaid seller's rights.

39.—(1) Subject to this and any other Act, notwithstanding that the property in the goods may have passed to the buyer, the unpaid seller of goods, as such, has by implication of law—

(*a*) a lien on the goods or right to retain them for the price while he is in possession of them;

(*b*) in case of the insolvency of the buyer, a right of stopping the goods in transit after he has parted with the possession of them;

(*c*) a right of re-sale as limited by this Act.

(2) Where the property in goods has not passed to the buyer, the unpaid seller has (in addition to his other remedies) a right of withholding delivery similar to and co-extensive with his rights of lien or retention and stoppage in transit where the property has passed to the buyer.

Attachment by seller in Scotland.

40. In Scotland a seller of goods may attach them while in his own hands or possession by arrestment or poinding; and such arrestment or poinding shall have the same operation and effect in a competition or otherwise as an arrestment or poinding by a third party.

Unpaid seller's lien

PART V

41.—(1) Subject to this Act, the unpaid seller of goods who is in possession of them is entitled to retain possession of them until payment or tender of the price in the following cases:— Seller's lien.

(*a*) where the goods have been sold without any stipulation as to credit;

(*b*) where the goods have been sold on credit but the term of credit has expired;

(*c*) where the buyer becomes insolvent.

(2) The seller may exercise his lien or right of retention notwithstanding that he is in possession of the goods as agent or bailee or custodier for the buyer.

42. Where an unpaid seller has made part delivery of the goods, he may exercise his lien or right of retention on the remainder, unless such part delivery has been made under such circumstances as to show an agreement to waive the lien or right of retention. Part delivery.

43.—(1) The unpaid seller of goods loses his lien or right of retention in respect of them— Termination of lien.

(*a*) when he delivers the goods to a carrier or other bailee or custodier for the purpose of transmission to the buyer without reserving the right of disposal of the goods;

(*b*) when the buyer or his agent lawfully obtains possession of the goods;

(*c*) by waiver of the lien or right of retention.

(2) An unpaid seller of goods who has a lien or right of retention in respect of them does not lose his lien or right of retention by reason only that he has obtained judgment or decree for the price of the goods.

Stoppage in transit

44. Subject to this Act, when the buyer of goods becomes insolvent the unpaid seller who has parted with the possession of the goods has the right of stopping them in transit, that is to say, he may resume possession of the goods as long as they are in course of transit, and may retain them until payment or tender of the price. Right of stoppage in transit.

45.—(1) Goods are deemed to be in course of transit from the time when they are delivered to a carrier or other bailee or custodier for the purpose of transmission to the buyer, until the buyer or his agent in that behalf takes delivery of them from the carrier or other bailee or custodier. Duration of transit.

PART V

(2) If the buyer or his agent in that behalf obtains delivery of the goods before their arrival at the appointed destination, the transit is at an end.

(3) If, after the arrival of the goods at the appointed destination, the carrier or other bailee or custodier acknowledges to the buyer or his agent that he holds the goods on his behalf and continues in possession of them as bailee or custodier for the buyer or his agent, the transit is at an end, and it is immaterial that a further destination for the goods may have been indicated by the buyer.

(4) If the goods are rejected by the buyer, and the carrier or other bailee or custodier continues in possession of them, the transit is not deemed to be at an end, even if the seller has refused to receive them back.

(5) When goods are delivered to a ship chartered by the buyer it is a question depending on the circumstances of the particular case whether they are in the possession of the master as a carrier or as agent to the buyer.

(6) Where the carrier or other bailee or custodier wrongfully refuses to deliver the goods to the buyer or his agent in that behalf, the transit is deemed to be at an end.

(7) Where part delivery of the goods has been made to the buyer or his agent in that behalf, the remainder of the goods may be stopped in transit, unless such part delivery has been made under such circumstances as to show an agreement to give up possession of the whole of the goods.

How stoppage in transit is effected.

46.—(1) The unpaid seller may exercise his right of stoppage in transit either by taking actual possession of the goods or by giving notice of his claim to the carrier or other bailee or custodier in whose possession the goods are.

(2) The notice may be given either to the person in actual possession of the goods or to his principal.

(3) If given to the principal, the notice is ineffective unless given at such time and under such circumstances that the principal, by the exercise of reasonable diligence, may communicate it to his servant or agent in time to prevent a delivery to the buyer.

(4) When notice of stoppage in transit is given by the seller to the carrier or other bailee or custodier in possession of the goods, he must re-deliver the goods to, or according to the directions of, the seller; and the expenses of the re-delivery must be borne by the seller.

Re-sale etc. by buyer

Effect of sub-sale etc. by buyer.

47.—(1) Subject to this Act, the unpaid seller's right of lien or retention or stoppage in transit is not affected by any sale or other disposition of the goods which the buyer may have made, unless the seller has assented to it.

(2) Where a document of title to goods has been lawfully transferred to any person as buyer or owner of the goods, and that person transfers the document to a person who takes it in good faith and for valuable consideration, then—

(*a*) if the last-mentioned transfer was by way of sale the unpaid seller's right of lien or retention or stoppage in transit is defeated ; and

(*b*) if the last-mentioned transfer was made by way of pledge or other disposition for value, the unpaid seller's right of lien or retention or stoppage in transit can only be exercised subject to the rights of the transferee.

Rescission: and re-sale by seller

Rescission: and re-sale by seller.

48.—(1) Subject to this section, a contract of sale is not rescinded by the mere exercise by an unpaid seller of his right of lien or retention or stoppage in transit.

(2) Where an unpaid seller who has exercised his right of lien or retention or stoppage in transit re-sells the goods, the buyer acquires a good title to them as against the original buyer.

(3) Where the goods are of a perishable nature, or where the unpaid seller gives notice to the buyer of his intention to re-sell, and the buyer does not within a reasonable time pay or tender the price, the unpaid seller may re-sell the goods and recover from the original buyer damages for any loss occasioned by his breach of contract.

(4) Where the seller expressly reserves the right of re-sale in case the buyer should make default, and on the buyer making default re-sells the goods, the original contract of sale is rescinded but without prejudice to any claim the seller may have for damages.

PART VI

ACTIONS FOR BREACH OF THE CONTRACT

Seller's remedies

Action for price.

49.—(1) Where, under a contract of sale, the property in the goods has passed to the buyer and he wrongfully neglects or refuses to pay for the goods according to the terms of the contract, the seller may maintain an action against him for the price of the goods.

PART VI

(2) Where, under a contract of sale, the price is payable on a day certain irrespective of delivery and the buyer wrongfully neglects or refuses to pay such price, the seller may maintain an action for the price, although the property in the goods has not passed and the goods have not been appropriated to the contract.

(3) Nothing in this section prejudices the right of the seller in Scotland to recover interest on the price from the date of tender of the goods, or from the date on which the price was payable, as the case may be.

Damages for non-acceptance.

50.—(1) Where the buyer wrongfully neglects or refuses to accept and pay for the goods, the seller may maintain an action against him for damages for non-acceptance.

(2) The measure of damages is the estimated loss directly and naturally resulting, in the ordinary course of events, from the buyer's breach of contract.

(3) Where there is an available market for the goods in question the measure of damages is prima facie to be ascertained by the difference between the contract price and the market or current price at the time or times when the goods ought to have been accepted or (if no time was fixed for acceptance) at the time of the refusal to accept.

Buyer's remedies

Damages for non-delivery.

51.—(1) Where the seller wrongfully neglects or refuses to deliver the goods to the buyer, the buyer may maintain an action against the seller for damages for non-delivery.

(2) The measure of damages is the estimated loss directly and naturally resulting, in the ordinary course of events, from the seller's breach of contract.

(3) Where there is an available market for the goods in question the measure of damages is prima facie to be ascertained by the difference between the contract price and the market or current price of the goods at the time or times when they ought to have been delivered or (if no time was fixed) at the time of the refusal to deliver.

Specific performance.

52.—(1) In any action for breach of contract to deliver specific or ascertained goods the court may, if it thinks fit, on the plaintiff's application, by its judgment or decree direct that the contract shall be performed specifically, without giving the defendant the option of retaining the goods on payment of damages.

(2) The plaintiff's application may be made at any time before judgment or decree.

PART VI

(3) The judgment or decree may be unconditional, or on such terms and conditions as to damages, payment of the price and otherwise as seem just to the court.

(4) The provisions of this section shall be deemed to be supplementary to, and not in derogation of, the right of specific implement in Scotland.

Remedy for breach of warranty.

53.—(1) Where there is a breach of warranty by the seller, or where the buyer elects (or is compelled) to treat any breach of a condition on the part of the seller as a breach of warranty, the buyer is not by reason only of such breach of warranty entitled to reject the goods; but he may—

(*a*) set up against the seller the breach of warranty in diminution or extinction of the price, or

(*b*) maintain an action against the seller for damages for the breach of warranty.

(2) The measure of damages for breach of warranty is the estimated loss directly and naturally resulting, in the ordinary course of events, from the breach of warranty.

(3) In the case of breach of warranty of quality such loss is prima facie the difference between the value of the goods at the time of delivery to the buyer and the value they would have had if they had fulfilled the warranty.

(4) The fact that the buyer has set up the breach of warranty in diminution or extinction of the price does not prevent him from maintaining an action for the same breach of warranty if he has suffered further damage.

(5) Nothing in this section prejudices or affects the buyer's right of rejection in Scotland as declared by this Act.

Interest, etc.

Interest, etc.

54. Nothing in this Act affects the right of the buyer or the seller to recover interest or special damages in any case where by law interest or special damages may be recoverable, or to recover money paid where the consideration for the payment of it has failed.

PART VII

SUPPLEMENTARY

Exclusion of implied terms.

1977 c. 50.

55.—(1) Where a right, duty or liability would arise under a contract of sale of goods by implication of law, it may (subject to the Unfair Contract Terms Act 1977) be negatived or varied by express agreement, or by the course of dealing between the parties, or by such usage as binds both parties to the contract.

PART VII

(2) An express condition or warranty does not negative a condition or warranty implied by this Act unless inconsistent with it.

(3) Paragraph 11 of Schedule 1 below applies in relation to a contract made on or after 18 May 1973 and before 1 February 1978, and paragraph 12 in relation to one made before 18 May 1973.

Conflict of laws.

56. Paragraph 13 of Schedule 1 below applies in relation to a contract made on or after 18 May 1973 and before 1 February 1978, so as to make provision about conflict of laws in relation to such a contract.

Auction sales.

57.—(1) Where goods are put up for sale by auction in lots, each lot is prima facie deemed to be the subject of a separate contract of sale.

(2) A sale by auction is complete when the auctioneer announces its completion by the fall of the hammer, or in other customary manner; and until the announcement is made any bidder may retract his bid.

(3) A sale by auction may be notified to be subject to a reserve or upset price, and a right to bid may also be reserved expressly by or on behalf of the seller.

(4) Where a sale by auction is not notified to be subject to a right to bid by or on behalf of the seller, it is not lawful for the seller to bid himself or to employ any person to bid at the sale, or for the auctioneer knowingly to take any bid from the seller or any such person.

(5) A sale contravening subsection (4) above may be treated as fraudulent by the buyer.

(6) Where, in respect of a sale by auction, a right to bid is expressly reserved (but not otherwise) the seller or any one person on his behalf may bid at the auction.

Payment into court in Scotland.

58. In Scotland where a buyer has elected to accept goods which he might have rejected, and to treat a breach of contract as only giving rise to a claim for damages, he may, in an action by the seller for the price, be required, in the discretion of the court before which the action depends, to consign or pay into court the price of the goods, or part of the price, or to give other reasonable security for its due payment.

Reasonable time a question of fact.

59. Where a reference is made in this Act to a reasonable time the question what is a reasonable time is a question of fact.

PART VII

Rights etc. enforceable by action.

60. Where a right, duty or liability is declared by this Act, it may (unless otherwise provided by this Act) be enforced by action.

Interpretation.

61.—(1) In this Act, unless the context or subject matter otherwise requires,—

"action" includes counterclaim and set-off, and in Scotland condescendence and claim and compensation;

"business" includes a profession and the activities of any government department (including a Northern Ireland department) or local or public authority;

"buyer" means a person who buys or agrees to buy goods;

"contract of sale" includes an agreement to sell as well as a sale;

"credit-broker" means a person acting in the course of a business of credit brokerage carried on by him, that is a business of effecting introductions of individuals desiring to obtain credit—

(*a*) to persons carrying on any business so far as it relates to the provision of credit, or

(*b*) to other persons engaged in credit brokerage;

"defendant" includes in Scotland defender, respondent, and claimant in a multiplepoinding;

"delivery" means voluntary transfer of possession from one person to another;

"document of title to goods" has the same meaning as it has in the Factors Acts;

"Factors Acts" means the Factors Act 1889, the Factors (Scotland) Act 1890, and any enactment amending or substituted for the same; 1889 c. 45. 1890 c. 40.

"fault" means wrongful act or default;

"future goods" means goods to be manufactured or acquired by the seller after the making of the contract of sale;

"goods" includes all personal chattels other than things in action and money, and in Scotland all corporeal moveables except money; and in particular "goods" includes emblements, industrial growing crops, and things attached to or forming part of the land which are agreed to be severed before sale or under the contract of sale;

"plaintiff" includes pursuer, complainer, claimant in a multiplepoinding and defendant or defender counter-claiming;

PART VII

"property" means the general property in goods, and not merely a special property;

"quality", in relation to goods, includes their state or condition;

"sale" includes a bargain and sale as well as a sale and delivery;

"seller" means a person who sells or agrees to sell goods;

"specific goods" means goods identified and agreed on at the time a contract of sale is made;

"warranty" (as regards England and Wales and Northern Ireland) means an agreeement with reference to goods which are the subject of a contract of sale, but collateral to the main purpose of such contract, the breach of which gives rise to a claim for damages, but not to a right to reject the goods and treat the contract as repudiated.

(2) As regards Scotland a breach of warranty shall be deemed to be a failure to perform a material part of the contract.

(3) A thing is deemed to be done in good faith within the meaning of this Act when it is in fact done honestly, whether it is done negligently or not.

(4) A person is deemed to be insolvent within the meaning of this Act if he has either ceased to pay his debts in the ordinary course of business or he cannot pay his debts as they become due, whether he has committed an act of bankruptcy or not, and whether he has become a notour bankrupt or not.

(5) Goods are in a deliverable state within the meaning of this Act when they are in such a state that the buyer would under the contract be bound to take delivery of them.

(6) As regards the definition of "business" in subsection (1) above, paragraph 14 of Schedule 1 below applies in relation to a contract made on or after 18 May 1973 and before 1 February 1978, and paragraph 15 in relation to one made before 18 May 1973.

Savings: rules of law etc.

62.—(1) The rules in bankruptcy relating to contracts of sale apply to those contracts, notwithstanding anything in this Act.

(2) The rules of the common law, including the law merchant, except in so far as they are inconsistent with the provisions of this Act, and in particular the rules relating to the law of principal and agent and the effect of fraud, misrepresentation, duress or coercion, mistake, or other invalidating cause, apply to contracts for the sale of goods.

(3) Nothing in this Act or the Sale of Goods Act 1893 affects the enactments relating to bills of sale, or any enactment relating to the sale of goods which is not expressly repealed or amended by this Act or that. PART VII 1893 c. 71.

(4) The provisions of this Act about contracts of sale do not apply to a transaction in the form of a contract of sale which is intended to operate by way of mortgage, pledge, charge, or other security.

(5) Nothing in this Act prejudices or affects the landlord's right of hypothec or sequestration for rent in Scotland.

Consequential amendments, repeals and savings. 1978 c. 30.

63.—(1) Without prejudice to section 17 of the Interpretation Act 1978 (repeal and re-enactment), the enactments mentioned in Schedule 2 below have effect subject to the amendments there specified (being amendments consequential on this Act).

(2) The enactments mentioned in Schedule 3 below are repealed to the extent specified in column 3, but subject to the savings in Schedule 4 below.

(3) The savings in Schedule 4 below have effect.

Short title and commencement.

64.—(1) This Act may be cited as the Sale of Goods Act 1979.

(2) This Act comes into force on 1 January 1980.

SCHEDULES

Section 1.

SCHEDULE 1

MODIFICATION OF ACT FOR CERTAIN CONTRACTS

Preliminary

1.—(1) This Schedule modifies this Act as it applies to contracts of sale of goods made on certain dates.

(2) In this Schedule references to sections are to those of this Act and references to contracts are to contracts of sale of goods.

(3) Nothing in this Schedule affects a contract made before 1 January 1894.

Section 11: *condition treated as warranty*

2. In relation to a contract made before 22 April 1967 or (in the application of this Act to Northern Ireland) 28 July 1967, in section 11(4) after " or part of them," insert " or where the contract is for specific goods, the property in which has passed to the buyer,".

Section 12: *implied terms about title etc.*

3. In relation to a contract made before 18 May 1973 substitute the following for section 12:—

Implied terms about title, etc.

12. In a contract of sale, unless the circumstances of the contract are such as to show a different intention, there is—

(*a*) an implied condition on the part of the seller that in the case of a sale he has a right to sell the goods, and in the case of an agreement to sell he will have such a right at the time when the property is to pass ;

(*b*) an implied warranty that the buyer will have and enjoy quiet possession of the goods ;

(*c*) an implied warranty that the goods will be free from any charge or encumbrance in favour of any third party, not declared or known to the buyer before or at the time when the contract is made.

Section 13: *sale by description*

4. In relation to a contract made before 18 May 1973, omit section 13(3).

Section 14: *quality or fitness* (*i*)

5. In relation to a contract made on or after 18 May 1973 and before the appointed day, substitute the following for section 14:—

Implied terms about quality or fitness.

14.—(1) Except as provided by this section and section 15 below and subject to any other enactment, there is no implied condition or warranty about the quality or fitness for any particular purpose of goods supplied under a contract of sale. SCH. 1

(2) Where the seller sells goods in the course of a business, there is an implied condition that the goods supplied under the contract are of merchantable quality, except that there is no such condition—

(*a*) as regards defects specifically drawn to the buyer's attention before the contract is made ; or

(*b*) if the buyer examines the goods before the contract is made, as regards defects which that examination ought to reveal.

(3) Where the seller sells goods in the course of a business and the buyer, expressly or by implication, makes known to the seller any particular purpose for which the goods are being bought, there is an implied condition that the goods supplied under the contract are reasonably fit for that purpose, whether or not that is a purpose for which such goods are commonly supplied, except where the circumstances show that the buyer does not rely, or that it is unreasonable for him to rely, on the seller's skill or judgment.

(4) An implied condition or warranty about quality or fitness for a particular purpose may be annexed to a contract of sale by usage.

(5) The preceding provisions of this section apply to a sale by a person who in the course of a business is acting as agent for another as they apply to a sale by a principal in the course of a business, except where that other is not selling in the course of a business and either the buyer knows that fact or reasonable steps are taken to bring it to the notice of the buyer before the contract is made.

(6) Goods of any kind are of merchantable quality within the meaning of subsection (2) above if they are as fit for the purpose or purposes for which goods of that kind are commonly bought as it is reasonable to expect having regard to any description applied to them, the price (if relevant) and all the other relevant circumstances.

(7) In the application of subsection (3) above to an agreement for the sale of goods under which the purchase price or part of it is payable by instalments any reference to the seller includes a reference to the person by whom any antecedent negotiations are conducted ; and section 58(3) and (5) of the Hire-Purchase Act 1965, section 54(3) and (5) of the Hire-Purchase (Scotland) Act 1965 and section 65(3) and (5) of the Hire-Purchase Act (Northern Ireland) 1966 (meaning of antecedent negotiations and

1965 c. 66.
1965 c. 67.
1966 c. 42. (N.I.).

SCH. 1

related expressions) apply in relation to this subsection as in relation to each of those Acts, but as if a reference to any such agreement were included in the references in subsection (3) of each of those sections to the agreements there mentioned.

Section 14: *quality or fitness* (*ii*)

6. In relation to a contract made before 18 May 1973 substitute the following for section 14:—

Implied terms about quality or fitness.

14.—(1) Subject to this and any other Act, there is no implied condition or warranty about the quality or fitness for any particular purpose of goods supplied under a contract of sale.

(2) Where the buyer, expressly or by implication, makes known to the seller the particular purpose for which the goods are required, so as to show that the buyer relies on the seller's skill or judgment, and the goods are of a description which it is in the course of the seller's business to supply (whether he is the manufacturer or not), there is an implied condition that the goods will be reasonably fit for such purpose, except that in the case of a contract for the sale of a specified article under its patent or other trade name there is no implied condition as to its fitness for any particular purpose.

(3) Where goods are bought by description from a seller who deals in goods of that description (whether he is the manufacturer or not), there is an implied condition that the goods will be of merchantable quality; but if the buyer has examined the goods, there is no implied condition as regards defects which such examination ought to have revealed.

(4) An implied condition or warranty about quality or fitness for a particular purpose may be annexed by the usage of trade.

(5) An express condition or warranty does not negative a condition or warranty implied by this Act unless inconsistent with it.

Section 15: *sale by sample*

7. In relation to a contract made before 18 May 1973, omit section 15(3).

Section 22: *market overt*

8. In relation to a contract under which goods were sold before 1 January 1968 or (in the application of this Act to Northern Ireland) 29 August 1967, add the following paragraph at the end of section 22(1):—

"Nothing in this subsection affects the law relating to the sale of horses."

Section 25: *buyer in possession*

9. In relation to a contract under which a person buys or agrees to buy goods and which is made before the appointed day, omit section 25(2).

Section 35: *acceptance*

10. In relation to a contract made before 22 April 1967 or (in the application of this Act to Northern Ireland) 28 July 1967, in section 35(1) omit "(except where section 34 above otherwise provides)".

Section 55: *exclusion of implied terms* (*i*)

11. In relation to a contract made on or after 18 May 1973 and before 1 February 1978 substitute the following for section 55:—

Exclusion of implied terms.

55.—(1) Where a right, duty or liability would arise under a contract of sale of goods by implication of law, it may be negatived or varied by express agreement, or by the course of dealing between the parties, or by such usage as binds both parties to the contract, but the preceding provision has effect subject to the following provisions of this section.

(2) An express condition or warranty does not negative a condition or warranty implied by this Act unless inconsistent with it.

(3) In the case of a contract of sale of goods, any term of that or any other contract exempting from all or any of the provisions of section 12 above is void.

(4) In the case of a contract of sale of goods, any term of that or any other contract exempting from all or any of the provisions of section 13, 14 or 15 above is void in the case of a consumer sale and is, in any other case, not enforceable to the extent that it is shown that it would not be fair or reasonable to allow reliance on the term.

(5) In determining for the purposes of subsection (4) above whether or not reliance on any such term would be fair or reasonable regard shall be had to all the circumstances of the case and in particular to the following matters—

(*a*) the strength of the bargaining positions of the seller and buyer relative to each other, taking into account, among other things, the availability of suitable alternative products and sources of supply;

(*b*) whether the buyer received an inducement to agree to the term or in accepting it had an opportunity of buying the goods or suitable alternatives without it from any source of supply;

SCH. 1

(c) whether the buyer knew or ought reasonably to have known of the existence and extent of the term (having regard, among other things, to any custom of the trade and any previous course of dealing between the parties);

(d) where the term exempts from all or any of the provisions of section 13, 14 or 15 above if some condition is not complied with, whether it was reasonable at the time of the contract to expect that compliance with that condition would be practicable;

(e) whether the goods were manufactured, processed, or adapted to the special order of the buyer.

(6) Subsection (5) above does not prevent the court from holding, in accordance with any rule of law, that a term which purports to exclude or restrict any of the provisions of section 13, 14 or 15 above is not a term of the contract.

(7) In this section "consumer sale" means a sale of goods (other than a sale by auction or by competitive tender) by a seller in the course of a business where the goods—

(a) are of a type ordinarily bought for private use or consumption; and

(b) are sold to a person who does not buy or hold himself out as buying them in the course of a business.

(8) The onus of proving that a sale falls to be treated for the purposes of this section as not being a consumer sale lies on the party so contending.

(9) Any reference in this section to a term exempting from all or any of the provisions of any section of this Act is a reference to a term which purports to exclude or restrict, or has the effect of excluding or restricting, the operation of all or any of the provisions of that section, or the exercise of a right conferred by any provision of that section, or any liability of the seller for breach of a condition or warranty implied by any provision of that section.

(10) It is hereby declared that any reference in this section to a term of a contract includes a reference to a term which although not contained in a contract is incorporated in the contract by another term of the contract.

(11) Nothing in this section prevents the parties to a contract for the international sale of goods from negativing or varying any right, duty or liability which would otherwise arise by implication of law under sections 12 to 15 above.

(12) In subsection (11) above "contract for the international sale of goods" means a contract of sale of goods made by parties whose places of business (or, if they have none, habitual residences) are in the territories of different States (the Channel Islands and the Isle of Man being treated for this purpose as different States from the United Kingdom) and in the case of which one of the following conditions is satisfied:— SCH. 1

(*a*) the contract involves the sale of goods which are at the time of the conclusion of the contract in the course of carriage or will be carried from the territory of one State to the territory of another; or

(*b*) the acts constituting the offer and acceptance have been effected in the territories of different States; or

(*c*) delivery of the goods is to be made in the territory of a State other than that within whose territory the acts constituting the offer and the acceptance have been effected.

Section 55: exclusion of implied terms (ii)

12. In relation to a contract made before 18 May 1973 substitute the following for section 55:—

Exclusion of implied terms.

55. Where a right, duty or liability would arise under a contract of sale by implication of law, it may be negatived or varied by express agreement, or by the course of dealing between the parties, or by such usage as binds both parties to the contract.

Section 56: conflict of laws

13.—(1) In relation to a contract made on or after 18 May 1973 and before 1 February 1978 substitute for section 56 the section set out in sub-paragraph (3) below.

(2) In relation to a contract made otherwise than as mentioned in sub-paragraph (1) above, ignore section 56 and this paragraph.

(3) The section mentioned in sub-paragraph (1) above is as follows:—

Conflict of laws.

56.—(1) Where the proper law of a contract for the sale of goods would, apart from a term that it should be the law of some other country or a term to the like effect, be the law of any part of the United Kingdom, or where any such contract contains a term which purports to substitute, or has the effect of substituting, provisions of the law of some other country for all or any of the provisions of sections 12 to 15 and 55 above, those sections shall, notwithstanding that term but subject to subsection (2) below, apply to the contract.

SCH. 1

(2) Nothing in subsection (1) above prevents the parties to a contract for the international sale of goods from negativing or varying any right, duty or liability which would otherwise arise by implication of law under sections 12 to 15 above.

(3) In subsection (2) above "contract for the international sale of goods" means a contract of sale of goods made by parties whose places of business (or, if they have none, habitual residences) are in the territories of different States (the Channel Islands and the Isle of Man being treated for this purpose as different States from the United Kingdom) and in the case of which one of the following conditions is satisfied:—

(*a*) the contract involves the sale of goods which are at the time of the conclusion of the contract in the course of carriage or will be carried from the territory of one State to the territory of another; or

(*b*) the acts constituting the offer and acceptance have been effected in the territories of different States; or

(*c*) delivery of the goods is to be made in the territory of a State other than that within whose territory the acts constituting the offer and the acceptance have been effected.

Section 61(1): *definition of "business"* (*i*)

14. In relation to a contract made on or after 18 May 1973 and before 1 February 1978, in the definition of "business" in section 61(1) for "or local or public authority" substitute ", local authority or statutory undertaker".

Section 61(1): *definition of "business"* (*ii*)

15. In relation to a contract made before 18 May 1973 omit the definition of "business" in section 61(1).

Section 63.

SCHEDULE 2

CONSEQUENTIAL AMENDMENTS

War Risks Insurance Act 1939 (2 & 3 Geo. 6 c.57)

1. In section 15(1)(*e*) of the War Risks Insurance Act 1939 for "section sixty-two of the Sale of Goods Act 1893" substitute "section 61 of the Sale of Goods Act 1979".

Law Reform (*Frustrated Contracts*) *Act* 1943 (6 & 7 Geo. 6 c. 40)

2. In section 2(5)(*c*) of the Law Reform (Frustrated Contracts) Act 1943 for "section seven of the Sale of Goods Act 1893" substitute "section 7 of the Sale of Goods Act 1979".

Frustrated Contracts Act (Northern Ireland) 1947 (c.2) SCH. 2

3. In section 2(5)(*c*) of the Frustrated Contracts Act (Northern Ireland) 1947 for "section seven of the Sale of Goods Act 1893" substitute "section 7 of the Sale of Goods Act 1979".

Hire-Purchase Act 1964 (c. 53)

4. In section 27(5) of the Hire-Purchase Act 1964 (as originally enacted and as substituted by Schedule 4 to the Consumer Credit Act 1974)— 1974 c. 39.

(*a*) in paragraph (*a*) for "section 21 of the Sale of Goods Act 1893" substitute "section 21 of the Sale of Goods Act 1979";

(*b*) in paragraph (*b*) for "section 62(1) of the said Act of 1893" substitute "section 61(1) of the said Act of 1979".

Hire-Purchase Act 1965 (c. 66)

5. In section 20 of the Hire-Purchase Act 1965—

(*a*) in subsection (1) for "Section 11(1)(*c*) of the Sale of Goods Act 1893" substitute "Section 11(4) of the Sale of Goods Act 1979";

(*b*) in subsection (3) for "sections 12 to 15 of the Sale of Goods Act 1893" substitute "sections 12 to 15 of the Sale of Goods Act 1979".

6. In section 54 of the Hire-Purchase Act 1965 for "section 25(2) of the Sale of Goods Act 1893" substitute "section 25(1) of the Sale of Goods Act 1979".

7. In section 58(1) of the Hire-Purchase Act 1965 for "the Sale of Goods Act 1893" substitute "the Sale of Goods Act 1979".

Hire-Purchase (Scotland) Act 1965 (c. 67)

8. In section 20 of the Hire-Purchase (Scotland) Act 1965 for "1893" substitute "1979".

9. In section 50 of the Hire-Purchase (Scotland) Act 1965 for "section 25(2) of the Sale of Goods Act 1893" substitute "section 25(1) of the Sale of Goods Act 1979".

10. In section 54(1) of the Hire-Purchase (Scotland) Act 1965 for "the Sale of Goods Act 1893" substitute "the Sale of Goods Act 1979".

Hire-Purchase Act (Northern Ireland) 1966 (c. 42)

11. In section 20 of the Hire-Purchase Act (Northern Ireland) 1966—

(*a*) in subsection (1) for "Section 11(1)(*c*) of the Sale of Goods Act 1893" substitute "Section 11(4) of the Sale of Goods Act 1979";

(*b*) in subsection (3) for "1893" substitute "1979".

12. In section 54 of the Hire-Purchase Act (Northern Ireland) 1966 for "section 25(2) of the Sale of Goods Act 1893" substitute "section 25(1) of the Sale of Goods Act 1979".

SCH. 2 13. In section 62(5) of the Hire-Purchase Act (Northern Ireland) 1966 (as originally enacted and as substituted by Schedule 4 to the Consumer Credit Act 1974)—

(*a*) in paragraph (*a*) for " 1893 " substitute " 1979 " ;

(*b*) in paragraph (*b*) for " section 62(1) of the said Act of 1893 " substitute " section 61(1) of the said Act of 1979 ".

14. In section 65(1) of the Hire-Purchase Act (Northern Ireland) 1966 for " the Sale of Goods Act 1893 " substitute " the Sale of Goods Act 1979 ".

Uniform Laws on International Sales Act 1967 (c. 45)

15. For section 1(4) of the Uniform Laws on International Sales Act 1967 substitute the following:—

" (4) In determining the extent of the application of the Uniform Law on Sales by virtue of Article 4 thereof (choice of parties)—

(*a*) in relation to a contract made before 18 May 1973, no provision of the law of any part of the United Kingdom shall be regarded as a mandatory provision within the meaning of that Article ;

(*b*) in relation to a contract made on or after 18 May 1973 and before 1 February 1978, no provision of that law shall be so regarded except sections 12 to 15, 55 and 56 of the Sale of Goods Act 1979 ;

(*c*) in relation to a contract made on or after 1 February 1978, no provision of that law shall be so regarded except sections 12 to 15 of the Sale of Goods Act 1979 ".

Supply of Goods (Implied Terms) Act 1973 (c. 13)

16. In section 14(1) of the Supply of Goods (Implied Terms) Act 1973 (as originally enacted and as substituted by Schedule 4 to the
1974 c. 39. Consumer Credit Act 1974) for " Section 11(1)(*c*) of the principal Act " substitute " Section 11(4) of the Sale of Goods Act 1979 ".

17. For the definition of " consumer sale " in section 15(1) of the Supply of Goods (Implied Terms) Act 1973 substitute—

" consumer sale " has the same meaning as in section 55 of the Sale of Goods Act 1979 (as set out in paragraph 11 of Schedule 1 to that Act).

Consumer Credit Act 1974 (c.39)

18. In section 189(1) of the Consumer Credit Act 1974, in the definition of " goods ", for " section 62(1) of the Sale of Goods Act 1893 " substitute " section 61(1) of the Sale of Goods Act 1979 ".

Unfair Contract Terms Act 1977 (c. 50)

19. In section 6 of the Unfair Contract Terms Act 1977—

(*a*) in subsection (1)(*a*) for " section 12 of the Sale of Goods Act 1893 " substitute " section 12 of the Sale of Goods Act 1979 " ;

(*b*) in subsection (2)(*a*) for " section 13, 14 or 15 of the 1893 Act " substitute " section 13, 14 or 15 of the 1979 Act ". Sch. 2

20. In section 14 of the Unfair Contract Terms Act 1977, in the definition of " goods ", for " the Sale of Goods Act 1893 " substitute " the Sale of Goods Act 1979 ".

21. In section 20(1)(*a*) and (2)(*a*) of the Unfair Contract Terms Act 1977 for " 1893 " substitute (in each case) " 1979 ".

22. In section 25(1) of the Unfair Contract Terms Act 1977, in the definition of " goods ", for " the Sale of Goods Act 1893 " substitute " the Sale of Goods Act 1979 ".

SCHEDULE 3

Section 63

Repeals

Chapter	Short title	Extent of repeal
56 & 57 Vict. c. 71.	Sale of Goods Act 1893.	The whole Act except section 26.
1967 c. 7.	Misrepresentation Act 1967.	Section 4. In section 6(3) the words ", except section 4(2),".
1967 c. 14 (N.I.)	Misrepresentation Act (Northern Ireland) 1967.	Section 4.
1973 c. 13.	Supply of Goods (Implied Terms) Act 1973.	Sections 1 to 7. Section 18(2).
1974 c. 39.	Consumer Credit Act 1974.	In Schedule 4, paragraphs 3 and 4.
1977 c. 50.	Unfair Contract Terms Act 1977.	In Schedule 3, the entries relating to the Sale of Goods Act 1893.

SCHEDULE 4

Section 63.

Savings

Preliminary

1. In this Schedule references to the 1893 Act are to the Sale of Goods Act 1893. 1893 c. 71.

Orders

2. An order under section 14(8) or 25(4) above may make provision that it is to have effect only as provided by the order (being provision corresponding to that which could, apart from this Act, have been made by an order under section 192(4) of the Consumer Credit Act 1974 bringing into operation an amendment or repeal making a change corresponding to that made by the order under section 14(8) or 25(4) above). 1974 c. 39.

SCH. 4

Offences

3. Where an offence was committed in relation to goods before 1 January 1969 or (in the application of this Act to Northern Ireland) 1 August 1969, the effect of a conviction in respect of the offence is not affected by the repeal by this Act of section 24 of the 1893 Act.

1893 Act, section 26

4. The repeal by this Act of provisions of the 1893 Act does not extend to the following provisions of that Act in so far as they are needed to give effect to or interpret section 26 of that Act, namely, the definitions of "goods" and "property" in section 62(1), section 62(2) and section 63 (which was repealed subject to savings by the
1908 c. 49. Statute Law Revision Act 1908).

Things done before 1 January 1894

5. The repeal by this Act of section 60 of and the Schedule to the 1893 Act (which effected repeals and which were themselves repealed subject to savings by the Statute Law Revision Act 1908) does not affect those savings, and accordingly does not affect things done or acquired before 1 January 1894.

6. In so far as the 1893 Act applied (immediately before the operation of the repeals made by this Act) to contracts made before 1 January 1894 (when the 1893 Act came into operation), the 1893 Act shall continue so to apply notwithstanding this Act.

Printed in the UK by The Stationery Office Limited
under the authority and superintendence of Carol Tullo, Controller of
Her Majesty's Stationery Office and Queen's Printer of Acts of Parliament

Dd 758472 5/00 519168 19585

1st Impression December 1979
9th Impression May 2000

APPENDIX II

Carriage of Goods by Sea Act 1992

ELIZABETH II

Carriage of Goods by Sea Act 1992

1992 CHAPTER 50

An Act to replace the Bills of Lading Act 1855 with new provision with respect to bills of lading and certain other shipping documents. [16th July 1992]

BE IT ENACTED by the Queen's most Excellent Majesty, by and with the advice and consent of the Lords Spiritual and Temporal, and Commons, in this present Parliament assembled, and by the authority of the same, as follows:—

Shipping documents etc. to which Act applies.

1.—(1) This Act applies to the following documents, that is to say—

(a) any bill of lading;

(b) any sea waybill; and

(c) any ship's delivery order.

(2) References in this Act to a bill of lading—

(a) do not include references to a document which is incapable of transfer either by indorsement or, as a bearer bill, by delivery without indorsement; but

(b) subject to that, do include references to a received for shipment bill of lading.

(3) References in this Act to a sea waybill are references to any document which is not a bill of lading but-

(a) is such a receipt for goods as contains or evidences a contract for the carriage of goods by sea; and

(b) identifies the person to whom delivery of the goods is to be made by the carrier in accordance with that contract.

(4) References in this Act to a ship's delivery order are references to any document which is neither a bill of lading nor a sea waybill but contains an undertaking which—

(a) is given under or for the purposes of a contract for the carriage by sea of the goods to which the document relates, or of goods which include those goods; and

(b) is an undertaking by the carrier to a person identified in the document to deliver the goods to which the document relates to that person.

(5) The Secretary of State may by regulations make provision for the application of this Act to cases where a telecommunication system or any other information technology is used for effecting transactions corresponding to—

(a) the issue of a document to which this Act applies;

(b) the indorsement, delivery or other transfer of such a document; or

(c) the doing of anything else in relation to such a document.

(6) Regulations under subsection (5) above may—

(a) make such modifications of the following provisions of this Act as the Secretary of State considers appropriate in connection with the application of this Act to any case mentioned in that subsection; and

(b) contain supplemental, incidental, consequential and transitional provision;

and the power to make regulations under that subsection shall be exercisable by statutory instrument subject to annulment in pursuance of a resolution of either House of Parliament.

Rights under shipping documents.

2.—(1) Subject to the following provisions of this section, a person who becomes—

(a) the lawful holder of a bill of lading;

(b) the person who (without being an original party to the contract of carriage) is the person to whom delivery of the goods to which a sea waybill relates is to be made by the carrier in accordance with that contract; or

(c) the person to whom delivery of the goods to which a ship's delivery order relates is to be made in accordance with the undertaking contained in the order,

shall (by virtue of becoming the holder of the bill or, as the case may be, the person to whom delivery is to be made) have transferred to and vested in him all rights of suit under the contract of carriage as if he had been a party to that contract.

(2) Where, when a person becomes the lawful holder of a bill of lading, possession of the bill no longer gives a right (as against the carrier) to possession of the goods to which the bill relates, that person shall not have any rights transferred to him by virtue of subsection (1) above unless he becomes the holder of the bill—

(a) by virtue of a transaction effected in pursuance of any contractual or other arrangements made before the time when such a right to possession ceased to attach to possession of the bill; or

(b) as a result of the rejection to that person by another person of goods or documents delivered to the other person in pursuance of any such arrangements.

(3) The rights vested in any person by virtue of the operation of subsection (1) above in relation to a ship's delivery order—

(a) shall be so vested subject to the terms of the order; and

(b) where the goods to which the order relates form a part only of the goods to which the contract of carriage relates, shall be confined to rights in respect of the goods to which the order relates.

(4) Where, in the case of any document to which this Act applies—

(a) a person with any interest or right in or in relation to goods to which the document relates sustains loss or damage in consequence of a breach of the contract of carriage; but

(b) subsection (1) above operates in relation to that document so that rights of suit in respect of that breach are vested in another person,

the other person shall be entitled to exercise those rights for the benefit of the person who sustained the loss or damage to the same extent as they could have been exercised if they had been vested in the person for whose benefit they are exercised.

(5) Where rights are transferred by virtue of the operation of subsection (1) above in relation to any document, the transfer for which that subsection provides shall extinguish any entitlement to those rights which derives—

(a) where that document is a bill of lading, from a person's having been an original party to the contract of carriage; or

(b) in the case of any document to which this Act applies, from the previous operation of that subsection in relation to that document;

but the operation of that subsection shall be without prejudice to any rights which derive from a person's having been an original party to the contract contained in, or evidenced by, a sea waybill and, in relation to a ship's delivery order, shall be without prejudice to any rights deriving otherwise than from the previous operation of that subsection in relation to that order.

Liabilities under shipping documents.

3.—(1) Where subsection (1) of section 2 of this Act operates in relation to any document to which this Act applies and the person in whom rights are vested by virtue of that subsection—

(a) takes or demands delivery from the carrier of any of the goods to which thc document relates;

(b) makes a claim under the contract of carriage against the carrier in respect of any of those goods; or

(c) is a person who, at a time before those rights were vested in him, took or demanded delivery from the carrier of any of those goods,

that person shall (by virtue of taking or demanding delivery or making the claim or, in a case falling within paragraph (c) above, of having the rights vested in him) become subject to the same liabilities under that contract as if he had been a party to that contract.

(2) Where the goods to which a ship's delivery order relates form a part only of the goods to which the contract of carriage relates, the liabilities to which any person is subject by virtue of the operation of this section in relation to that order shall exclude liabilities in respect of any goods to which the order does not relate.

(3) This section, so far as it imposes liabilities under any contract on any person, shall be without prejudice to the liabilities under the contract of any person as an original party to the contract.

Representations in bills of lading.

4. A bill of lading which—

(a) represents goods to have been shipped on board a vessel or to have been received for shipment on board a vessel; and

(b) has been signed by the master of the vessel or by a person who was not the master but had the express, implied or apparent authority of the carrier to sign bills of lading,

shall, in favour of a person who has become the lawful holder of the bill, be conclusive evidence against the carrier of the shipment of the goods or, as the case may be, of their receipt for shipment.

Interpretation etc.

5.—(1) In this Act—

"bill of lading", "sea waybill" and "ship's delivery order" shall be construed in accordance with section 1 above;

"the contract of carriage"—

(a) in relation to a bill of lading or sea waybill, means the contract contained in or evidenced by that bill or waybill; and

(b) in relation to a ship's delivery order, means the contract under or for the purposes of which the undertaking contained in the order is given;

"holder", in relation to a bill of lading, shall be construed in accordance with subsection (2) below;

"information technology" includes any computer or other technology by means of which information or other matter may be recorded or communicated without being reduced to documentary form; and

"telecommunication system" has the same meaning as in the Telecommunications Act 1984. (1984 c. 12.)

(2) References in this Act to the holder of a bill of lading are references to any of the following persons, that is to say—

(a) a person with possession of the bill who, by virtue of being the person identified in the bill, is the consignee of the goods to which the bill relates;

(b) a person with possession of the bill as a result of the completion, by delivery of the bill, of any indorsement of the bill or , in the case of a bearer bill, of any other transfer of the bill;

(c) a person with possession of the bill as a result of any transaction by virtue of which he would have become a holder falling within paragraph (a) or (b) above had not the transaction been effected at a time when possession of the bill no longer gave a right (as against the carrier) to possession of the goods to which the bill relates;

and a person shall be regarded for the purposes of this Act as having become the lawful holder of a bill of lading wherever he has become the holder of the bill in good faith.

(3) References in this Act to a person's being identified in a document include references to his being identified by a description which allows for the identity of the person in question to be varied, in accordance with the terms of the document, after its issue; and the reference in section 1(3)(b) of this Act to a document's identifying a person shall be construed accordingly.

(4) Without prejudice to sections 2(2) and 4 above, nothing in this Act shall preclude its operation in relation to a case where the goods to which a document relates—

(a) cease to exist after the issue of the document; or

(b) cannot be identified (whether because they are mixed with other goods or for any other reason);

and references in this Act to the goods to which a document relates shall be construed accordingly.

(5) The preceding provisions of this Act shall have effect without prejudice to the application, in relation to any case, of the rules (the Hague-Visby Rules) which for the time being have the force of law by virtue of section 1 of the Carriage of Goods by Sea Act 1971. 1971 c. 19.

6.—(1) This Act may be cited as the Carriage of Goods by Sea Act 1992. Short title, repeal, commencement and extent.

(2) The Bills of Lading Act 1855 is hereby repealed. 1855 c. 111.

(3) This Act shall come into force at the end of the period of two months beginning with the day on which it is passed; but nothing in this Act shall have effect in relation to any document issued before the coming into force of this Act.

(4) This Act extends to Northern Ireland.

PRINTED IN THE UNITED KINGDOM BY PAUL FREEMAN
Controller and Chief Executive of Her Majesty's Stationery Office
and Queen's Printer of Acts of Parliament

APPENDIX III

Conlinebill 2016

First published 1949, revised 1950, 1952, 1973, 1974, 1976, 1978, 2000, 2016

BIMCO

CONLINEBILL 2016

LINER BILL OF LADING

Page 1

Shipper	Bill of Lading No.	Reference No.
Consignee or Order	Notify address	Vessel
Pre-carriage by**	Port of loading	
Place of receipt by pre-carrier**	Port of discharge	
Place of delivery by on-carrier**		

Container No./Seal No./Marks and Nos.	Number and kind of packages, description of cargo	Gross weight, kg	Measurement, m^3

PARTICULARS DECLARED BY THE SHIPPER BUT NOT ACKNOWLEDGED BY THE CARRIER

Total number of Containers/Packages or Units received by the Carrier

Shipper's declared value

Declared value charge

SHIPPED on board in apparent good order and condition (unless otherwise stated herein) the total number of Containers/Packages or Units indicated in the Box opposite entitled "Total number of Containers/Packages or Units received by the Carrier" and the cargo as specified above, weight, measure, marks, numbers, quality, contents and value unknown, for carriage to the Port of discharge or so near thereunto as the vessel may safely get and lie always afloat, to be delivered in the like good order and condition at the Port of discharge unto the lawful holder of the Bill of Lading, on payment of freight as indicated to the left plus other charges incurred in accordance with the provisions contained in this Bill of Lading. In accepting this Bill of Lading the Merchant† expressly accepts and agrees to all its stipulations on both Page 1 and Page 2, whether written, printed, stamped or otherwise incorporated, as fully as if they were all signed by the Merchant.

One original Bill of Lading must be surrendered duly endorsed in exchange for the cargo or delivery order, whereupon all other Bills of Lading to be void.

IN WITNESS whereof the Carrier, Master or their Agent has signed the number of original Bills of Lading stated below right, all of this tenor and date.

Freight details and charges	Date shipped on board	Place and date of issue	Number of original Bills of Lading

Carrier:……………………………………………………………………(insert name, principal place of business)

Signature:……………………………………………………………………(Carrier*/Master*/Agent*)

**Delete as appropriate*

If signed by an Agent indicate with a tick ☑ whether for and on behalf of:

☐ Master; or

☐ Carrier

Agent……………………………………………………………………(insert name)

** Applicable only when pre-/on-carriage is arranged in accordance with Clause 8.

† As defined hereinafter (Cl. 1).

v. 1.1. Dated 26 May 2016. Clause 12 (General Average) updated to refer to York-Antwerp Rules 2016.

CONLINEBILL 2016
NEGOTIABLE LINER BILL OF LADING
Page 2

1. Definition.
"Merchant" includes the shipper, the receiver, the consignor, the consignee, the holder of the Bill of Lading, the owner of the cargo and any person entitled to possession of the cargo.

2. Notification.
Any mention in this Bill of Lading of parties to be notified of the arrival of the cargo is solely for the information of the Carrier and failure to give such notification shall not involve the Carrier in any liability nor relieve the Merchant of any obligation hereunder.

3. Liability for Carriage Between Port of Loading and Port of Discharge.
(a) The International Convention for the Unification of Certain Rules of Law relating to Bills of Lading signed at Brussels on 25 August 1924 ("the Hague Rules") as amended by the Protocol signed at Brussels on 23 February 1968 ("the Hague-Visby Rules") and as enacted in the country of shipment shall apply to this Contract. When the Hague-Visby Rules are not enacted in the country of shipment, the corresponding legislation of the country of destination shall apply, irrespective of whether such legislation may only regulate outbound shipments.
When there is no enactment of the Hague-Visby Rules in either the country of shipment or in the country of destination, the Hague-Visby Rules shall apply to this Contract save where the Hague Rules as enacted in the country of shipment or, if no such enactment is in place, the Hague Rules as enacted in the country of destination apply compulsorily to this Contract.
The Protocol signed at Brussels on 21 December 1979 ("the SDR Protocol 1979") shall apply where the Hague-Visby Rules apply, whether mandatorily or by this Contract.
The Carrier shall in no case be responsible for loss of or damage to cargo arising prior to loading, after discharging, or with respect to deck cargo and live animals.
(b) If the Carrier is held liable in respect of delay, consequential loss or damage other than loss of or damage to the cargo, the liability of the Carrier shall be limited to the freight for the carriage covered by this Bill of Lading, or to the limitation amount as determined in sub-clause 3(a), whichever is the lesser.
(c) The aggregate liability of the Carrier and/or any of its servants, agents or independent contractors under this Contract shall, in no circumstances, exceed the limits of liability for the total loss of the cargo under sub-clause 3(a) or, if applicable, the Additional Clause.

4. Law and Jurisdiction.
Disputes arising out of or in connection with this Bill of Lading shall be exclusively determined by the courts and in accordance with the law of the place where the Carrier has its principal place of business, as stated on Page 1, except as provided elsewhere herein.

5. The Scope of Carriage.
The intended carriage shall not be limited to the direct route but shall be deemed to include any proceeding or returning to or stopping or slowing down at or off any ports or places for any reasonable purpose connected with the carriage including bunkering, loading, discharging, or other cargo operations and maintenance of Vessel and crew.

6. Substitution of Vessel.
The Carrier shall be at liberty to carry the cargo or part thereof to the Port of discharge by the said or other vessel or vessels either belonging to the Carrier or others, or by other means of transport, proceeding either directly or indirectly to such port.

7. Transhipment.
The Carrier shall be at liberty to tranship, lighter, land and store the cargo either on shore or afloat and reship and forward the same to the Port of discharge.

8. Liability for Pre- and On-Carriage.
When the Carrier arranges pre-carriage of the cargo from a place other than the Vessel's Port of loading or on-carriage of the cargo to a place other than the Vessel's Port of discharge, the Carrier shall contract as the Merchant's Agent only and the Carrier shall not be liable for any loss or damage arising during any part of the carriage other than between the Port of loading and the Port of discharge even though the freight for the whole carriage has been collected by him.

9. Loading and Discharging.
(a) Loading and discharging of the cargo shall be arranged by the Carrier or its Agent.
(b) The Merchant shall, at its risk and expense, handle and/or store the cargo before loading and after discharging.
(c) Loading and discharging may commence without prior notice.
(d) The Merchant or its Agent shall tender the cargo when the Vessel is ready to load and as fast as the Vessel can receive including, if required by the Carrier, outside ordinary working hours notwithstanding any custom of the port. If the Merchant or its Agent fails to tender the cargo when the Vessel is ready to load or fails to load as fast as the Vessel can receive the cargo, the Carrier shall be relieved of any obligation to load such cargo, the Vessel shall be entitled to leave the port without further notice and the Merchant shall be liable to the Carrier for deadfreight and/or any overtime charges, losses, costs and expenses incurred by the Carrier.
(e) The Merchant or his Agent shall take delivery of the cargo as fast as the Vessel can discharge including, if required by the Carrier, outside ordinary working hours notwithstanding any custom of the port. If the Merchant or its Agent fails to take delivery of the cargo the Carrier's discharging of the cargo shall be deemed fulfilment of the contract of carriage. Should the cargo not be applied for within a reasonable time, the Carrier may sell the same privately or by auction. If the Merchant or its Agent fails to take delivery of the cargo as fast as the Vessel can discharge, the Merchant shall be liable to the Carrier for any overtime charges, losses, costs and expenses incurred by the Carrier.
(f) The Merchant shall accept its reasonable proportion of unidentified loose cargo.

10. Freight, Charges, Costs, Expenses, Duties, Taxes and Fines.
(a) Freight, whether paid or not, shall be considered as fully earned upon loading and non-returnable in any event. Unless otherwise specified, freight and/or charges under this Contract are payable by the Merchant to the Carrier on demand. Interest at Libor (or its successor) plus 2 per cent. shall run from fourteen days after the date when freight and charges are payable.
(b) The Merchant shall be liable for all costs and expenses of fumigation, gathering and sorting loose cargo and weighing onboard, repairing damage to and replacing packing due to excepted causes, and any extra handling of the cargo for any of the aforementioned reasons.
(c) The Merchant shall be liable for any dues, duties, taxes and charges which under any denomination may be levied, *inter alia*, on the basis of freight, weight of cargo or tonnage of the Vessel.
(d) The Merchant shall be liable for all fines, penalties, costs, expenses and losses which the Carrier, Vessel or cargo may incur through non-observance of Customs House and/or import or export regulations.
(e) The Carrier is entitled in case of incorrect declaration of contents, weights, measurements or value of the cargo to claim double the amount of freight which would have been due if such declaration had been correctly given. For the purpose of ascertaining the actual facts, the Carrier shall have the right to obtain from the Merchant the original invoice and to have the cargo inspected and its contents, weight, measurement or value verified.

11. Lien.
The Carrier shall have a lien on all cargo for any amount due under this contract and the costs of recovering the same and shall be entitled to sell the cargo privately or by auction to satisfy any such claims.

12. General Average and Salvage.
General Average shall be adjusted, stated and settled in London according to the York-Antwerp Rules 2016, in respect of all cargo, whether carried on or under deck. In the event of accident, danger, damage or disaster before or after commencement of the voyage resulting from any cause whatsoever, whether due to negligence or not, for which or for the consequence of which the Carrier is not responsible by statute, contract or otherwise, the Merchant shall contribute with the Carrier in General Average to the payment of any sacrifice, losses or expenses of a General Average nature that may be made or incurred, and shall pay salvage and special charges incurred in respect of the cargo. If a salving vessel is owned or operated by the Carrier, salvage shall be paid for as fully as if the salving vessel or vessels belonged to strangers.

13. Both-to-Blame Collision Clause.
If the Vessel comes into collision with another vessel as a result of the negligence of the other vessel and any act, negligence or default of the Master, Mariner, Pilot or the servants of the Carrier in the navigation or in the management of the Vessel, the Merchant will indemnify the Carrier against all loss or liability to the other or non-carrying vessel or her Owner in so far as such loss or liability represents loss of or damage to or any claim whatsoever of the owner of the cargo paid or payable by the other or non-carrying vessel or her Owner to the owner of the cargo and set-off, recouped or recovered by the other or non-carrying vessel or her Owner as part of its claim against the carrying vessel or Carrier. The foregoing provisions shall also apply where the Owner, operator or those in charge of any vessel or vessels or objects other than, or in addition to, the colliding vessels or objects are at fault in respect of a collision or contact.

14. Government directions, War, Epidemics, Ice, Strikes, etc.
(a) The Master and the Carrier shall have liberty to comply with any order or directions or recommendations in connection with the carriage under this contract given by any Government or Authority, or anybody acting or purporting to act on behalf of such Government or Authority, or having under the terms of the insurance on the Vessel the right to give such orders or directions or recommendations.
(b) Should it appear that the performance of the carriage would expose the Vessel or any cargo onboard to risk of seizure, damage or delay, in consequence of war, warlike operations, blockade, riots, civil commotions or piracy, or any person onboard to risk of loss of life or freedom, or that any such risk has increased, the Master may discharge the cargo at the Port of loading or any other safe and convenient port.
(c) Should it appear that epidemics; quarantine; ice; labour troubles, labour obstructions, strikes, lockouts (whether onboard or on shore); difficulties in loading or discharging would prevent the Vessel from leaving the Port of loading or reaching or entering the Port of discharge or there discharging in the usual manner and departing therefrom, all of which safely and without unreasonable delay, the Master may discharge the cargo at the Port of loading or any other safe and convenient port.
(d) The discharge, under the provisions of this Clause, of any cargo shall be deemed due fulfilment of the contract of carriage.
(e) If in connection with the exercise of any liberty under this Clause any extra expenses are incurred they shall be paid by the Merchant in addition to the freight, together with return freight, if any, and a reasonable compensation for any extra services rendered to the cargo.

15. International Group of P&I Clubs/BIMCO Himalaya Clause for bills of lading and other contracts 2014
(a) For the purposes of this contract, the term "Servant" shall include the owners, managers, and operators of vessels (other than the Carrier); underlying carriers; stevedores and terminal operators; and any direct or indirect servant, agent, or subcontractor (including their own subcontractors), or any other party employed by or on behalf of the Carrier, or whose services or equipment have been used to perform this contract whether in direct contractual privity with the Carrier or not.
(b) It is hereby expressly agreed that no Servant shall in any circumstances whatsoever be under any liability whatsoever to the Merchant or other party to this contract (hereinafter termed "Merchant") for any loss, damage or delay of whatsoever kind arising or resulting directly or indirectly from any act, neglect or default on the Servant's part while acting in the course of or in connection with the performance of this contract.
(c) Without prejudice to the generality of the foregoing provisions in this clause, every exemption, limitation, condition and liberty contained herein (other than Art III Rule 8 of the Hague/Hague-Visby Rules if incorporated herein) and every right, exemption from liability, defence and immunity of whatsoever nature applicable to the carrier or to which the carrier is entitled hereunder including the right to enforce any jurisdiction or arbitration provision contained herein shall also be available and shall extend to every such Servant of the carrier, who shall be entitled to enforce the same against the Merchant.
(d) (i) The Merchant undertakes that no claim or allegation whether arising in contract, bailment, tort or otherwise shall be made against any Servant of the carrier which imposes or attempts to impose upon any of them or any vessel owned or chartered by any of them any liability whatsoever in connection with this contract whether or not arising out of negligence on the part of such Servant. The Servant shall also be entitled to enforce the foregoing covenant against the Merchant; and
(ii) The Merchant undertakes that if any such claim or allegation should nevertheless be made, it will indemnify the carrier against all consequences thereof.
(e) For the purpose of sub-paragraphs (a)-(d) of this clause the Carrier is or shall be deemed to be acting as agent or trustee on behalf of and for the benefit of all persons mentioned in sub-clause (a) above who are its Servant and all such persons shall to this extent be or be deemed to be parties to this contract.

16. Stowage.
(a) The Carrier shall have the right to stow cargo by means of containers, trailers, transportable tanks, flats, pallets, or similar articles of transport used to consolidate goods.
(b) The Carrier shall have the right to carry containers, trailers, transportable tanks and covered flats, whether stowed by the Carrier or received by him in a stowed condition from the Merchant, on or under deck without notice to the Merchant.

17. Shipper-Packed Containers, trailers, transportable tanks, flats and pallets.
(a) If a container has not been filled, packed or stowed by the Carrier, the Carrier shall not be liable for any loss of or damage to its contents and the Merchant shall cover any loss or expense incurred by the Carrier, if such loss, damage or expense has been caused by:
(i) negligent filling, packing or stowing of the container;
(ii) the contents being unsuitable for carriage in container; or
(iii) the unsuitability or defective condition of the container unless the container has been supplied by the Carrier and the unsuitability or defective condition would not have been apparent upon reasonable inspection at or prior to the time when the container was filled, packed or stowed.
(b) The provisions of sub-clause (i) of this Clause also apply with respect to trailers, transportable tanks, flats and pallets which have not been filled, packed or stowed by the Carrier.
(c) The Carrier does not accept liability for damage due to the unsuitability or defective condition of reefer equipment or trailers supplied by the Merchant.

18. Return of Containers.
(a) Containers, pallets or similar articles of transport supplied by or on behalf of the Carrier shall be returned to the Carrier in the same order and condition as handed over to the Merchant, normal wear and tear excepted, with interiors clean and within the time prescribed in the Carrier's tariff or elsewhere.
(b) The Merchant shall be liable to the Carrier for any loss, damage to, or delay, including demurrage and detention incurred by or sustained to containers, pallets or similar articles of transport during the period between handing over to the Merchant and return to the Carrier.

ADDITIONAL CLAUSE
U.S. Trade. Period of Responsibility.
(i) In case the Contract evidenced by this Bill of Lading is subject to the Carriage of Goods by Sea Act of the United States of America, 1936 (U.S. COGSA), then the provisions stated in said Act shall govern before loading and after discharge and throughout the entire time the cargo is in the Carrier's custody and in which event freight shall be payable on the cargo coming into the Carrier's custody.
(ii) If the U.S. COGSA applies, and unless the nature and value of the cargo has been declared by the shipper before the cargo has been handed over to the Carrier and inserted in this Bill of Lading, the Carrier shall in no event be or become liable for any loss or damage to the cargo in an amount exceeding USD 500 per package or customary freight unit.

APPENDIX IV

Fosfa 54 Cif form

By permission of FOSFA International Ltd, (www.fosfa.org)

FEDERATION OF OILS, SEEDS AND FATS ASSOCIATIONS LIMITED
FOSFA INTERNATIONAL

CONTRACT FOR VEGETABLE AND MARINE OIL IN BULK
CIF DELIVERED WEIGHTS

Revised and Effective from 1st September 2008

54

Reference Nos
....
....
....

SELLERS: ....

....

BUYERS: ....

....

BROKERS: ....

....

Date: ....

*An asterisk denotes alternative wording, and should be matter of agreement between the parties.

Sellers have agreed to sell and Buyers have agreed to buy .... say .... metric tons

.... OIL

at .... say .... per metric ton

net delivered weight, cost insurance and freight to ....

as per Bill/s of Lading dated or to be dated during ....

from ....

Payment in .... as per Payment Clause

SPECIAL CONDITIONS: ....

....

....

1. TOLERANCE: Sellers have the option of shipping 5% more or less of the mean contract quantity. In the event of more than one shipment being made each shipment is to be considered as a separate contract but the tolerance on the mean contract quantity is not to be affected thereby.

2. QUALITY, CONDITION AND SPECIFICATIONS: Minimum flash point of 250°F (121°C).
The FFA content shall be expressed as follows:
If as Lauric acid, calculated on a molecular weight of 200; if as Palmitic acid, calculated on a molecular weight of 256; if as Oleic acid, calculated on a molecular weight of 282.

....

....

....

At time and place of shipment, the oil shall be of good merchantable quality, in good condition and of the agreed description and specifications.
If the oil is shipped in more than one tank of the same ship, the analysis details of the oil in each separate tank at loading shall conform to the above.
Should the oil on arrival not prove equal to the above, or should the oil contain sea water or other admixture, this contract not to be void, but the oil is to be taken with an allowance to be agreed upon or fixed by arbitration provided always that the oil shipped shall conform to the above.
Sweepings shall be accepted with a fair allowance, to be fixed by agreement or by arbitration.

3. DECLARATION OF DESTINATION: The goods are sold for shipment to ....

but Buyers have the option to declare ....

as the port/s of destination with a minimum of .... metric tons to any one port. To exercise this option Buyers shall declare

the port/s of destination to Sellers by any means of rapid written communication, not later than 16.00 hours on ....
The Notices Clause and the Non-Business Days Clause shall not apply to such declaration.

4. SHIPMENT AND CLASSIFICATION: Shipment in good condition in ship/s which comply with the FOSFA Qualifications and Operational Procedures for Ships Engaged in the Carriage of Oils and Fats in Bulk for Edible and Oleo-chemical Use in force at the date of the Bill of Lading.
The oil is to be shipped on a ship which, after loading in one or more origin ports, will proceed directly or indirectly on a geographically normal route from the port/s of shipment to the port/s of destination.
For the purposes of this contract the words 'ship' or 'ships' shall mean any full-powered engine-driven ship.
Transhipment shall only be allowed under a through Bill of Lading and shall be restricted to the area of origin and/or customary transhipment ports in the area of destination for the goods specified in the contract, provided that transhipment at origin is completed within the original contract shipment period and/or agreed extension period.
In case of transhipment at origin, Shipping documents shall include FOSFA Certificate of Compliance, Cleanliness and Suitability of Ship's Tank and a FOSFA Combined Masters Certificate in respect of the ocean carrier. In the event of such transhipment at origin the Declaration of Shipment shall include the name of the ocean carrier and transhipment location. Nothing in this clause shall affect the Master's rights or ships obligations under Maritime Law.

5. INSURANCE: Insurance in accordance with the Institute/FOSFA Trades Clauses (A) and the Institute War and Strikes Clauses (FOSFA Trades)— including risk of contamination irrespective of percentage on each tank or on the whole—to be effected at Sellers' option with first class underwriters and/or companies who are domiciled in the UK or for the purpose of any legal proceedings accept a British domicile and provide an address for service of process in London but for whose solvency the Sellers shall not be responsible. Claims to be payable in the currency of the contract. Policies and/or Certificates and/or Letters of Insurance required under this contract shall be for not less than 5% over the invoice amount including freight.
Buyers shall accept insurance including Exclusion Clauses on the FOSFA Insurance Exclusion Clause List.
In the event that Buyers receive an allowance under the Quality, Condition and Specifications Clause, Buyers to return the insurance policy to Sellers in order that they make any recovery thereunder. Any benefit under the insurance in respect of loss in weight shall be for Sellers' account.

6. WAR RISKS INSURANCE: War risks insurance shall be effected on the terms and conditions in force and approved at the time of shipment by the Institute of London Underwriters (Institute War Clauses [FOSFA Trades]). Any expense for covering war risks insurance in excess of ½ % shall be for account of Buyers.
The rate of insurance shall not exceed the rate ruling in London at the time of shipment or date of ship's sailing whichever may be adopted by underwriters.
Notice of extra expense to be borne by Buyers shall be given by Sellers at the time of declaration under this contract or not later than 3 business days after the rate has been agreed with underwriters whichever is the later. Failure to give such notice shall invalidate the Sellers' claim unless in the opinion of arbitrators the delay is justifiable.

7. DECLARATION OF SHIPMENT: Notice stating ship's name, date of Bill/s of Lading and approximate quantity shipped shall be despatched by first Sellers to their Buyers not later than 10 days after the date of the Bill/s of Lading. Notices by intermediate Sellers shall be accepted by their Buyers although received by them after such time, if from the 10th day after the date of the Bill/s of Lading such notices have been passed on with due despatch.
The date of the "on board" Bill/s of Lading shall be considered proof of the date of the shipment in the absence of conclusive evidence to the contrary.
Notices shall be deemed to be under reserve for errors and/or delays in transmission. Any slight variation in the ship's name shall not invalidate the declaration. A valid declaration cannot be withdrawn except with the Buyers' consent. Should the ship arrive before receipt of declaration of shipment and extra expenses be incurred, such expenses are to be paid by Sellers.
Should extra lighterage expenses be incurred owing to Sellers tendering less than 50 tons for a contract of a greater quantity, the extra costs to be borne by Buyers and Sellers equally.
The provisions of this clause to be inoperative if the goods have been sold afloat.
Presentation of documents does not constitute a notice under the terms of this clause.

8. SUPERINTENDENTS: Reference in the contract to superintendents, surveyors or representatives shall mean member superintendents of FOSFA International.
The use of member superintendents shall be mandatory except where:
(i) the contract or national laws or regulations require the use of Governmental or other agencies not recognised by FOSFA International;
(ii) no member superintendent/s is/are available or proximate to the port/s concerned.

9. ANALYSTS: Reference in the contract to analysts shall mean analysts who are members of FOSFA International and represented in the Oils and Fats Section.
The use of member analysts shall be mandatory except where the contract or regulations require the use of Governmental or other analysts.

10. PAYMENT AND SHIPPING DOCUMENTS: Payment shall be made by Buyers in the above-named place for 98% of invoice amount by cash against complete set of shipping documents—
*(a) on presentation;
*(b) on or (at Buyers' option) before arrival of the ship at the port of destination but not later than 45 days from the date of the Bill of Lading, whichever is the earlier, unless documents are presented thereafter. If Buyers elect to call for documents before arrival of ship, then payment shall be made against documents as soon as presented;

*(c) . . . .

. . . .

. . . .

. . . .

If Sellers choose to present documents to Buyers through the intermediary of a bank/s all bank charges incurred including those raised by Buyers bank shall be for Sellers' account unless Buyers demand presentation through a bank of their choice in which case those bank charges shall be for Buyers account.
Any charges for telegraphic remittance of funds to Sellers shall be for Buyers account.
Shipping documents shall consist of—
(1) Commercial invoice;
(2) Full set of clean "on board" Bill/s of Lading and/or Ship's Delivery Order/s and/or other Delivery Order/s in negotiable and transferable form, such other Delivery Order/s guaranteed by a first class bank if required by Buyers;
  (i) If the Bill/s of Lading does/do not indicate that Freight has been paid, the amount of freight shall be deducted from the invoice amount and paid by Buyers on Sellers' behalf. Buyers to send copy of the freight note to Sellers for final invoicing purposes. If freight is to be paid in a currency other than the currency of this contract, the conversion in the final invoice shall be made at the rate of exchange on the day of actual freight payment:
  (ii) If the Bill/s of Lading refer/s to a Charter Party and/or any other documents relating to the freight booking, Sellers shall be responsible for any detrimental consequences from clauses of such documents being contrary to the terms of this contract. If such Bill/s of Lading is/are signed by parties other than the Master then the Bill/s of Lading shall be accompanied by photostat copy of written authority from shipowner or Master authorising the signatory to the Bill/s of Lading:
  (iii) The Bill/s of Lading must identify the ship's tank/s into which the oil is loaded but should the oil be commingled with other parcels the Bill/s of Lading must indicate the total commingled quantity:
  (iv) Delivery Order/s shall be accompanied by non-negotiable or photostat copy of the relative Bill/s of Lading if required by Buyers.
(3) Policy/ies and/or Insurance Certificate/s and/or Letter/s of Insurance in the currency of the contract. Letter/s of Insurance shall specify the insurance company/ies and/or underwriter/s and policy number/s and shall be guaranteed by a first class bank if required by Buyers. After payment Letter/s of Insurance shall be substituted by policy/ies and/or certificate/s on request;
(4) FOSFA Certificate of Compliance, Cleanliness and Suitability of Ship's Tank from superintendents in the form in force at the date of the Bill/s of Lading.
(5) Certificate of Analysis, based on independently sealed samples taken from the relevant ship's tank/s at time of loading, and issued by an independent certified analyst;
(6) A Certificate of Origin and/or other documents as per the Duties, Taxes, Etc Clause of the contract where applicable;
(7) A FOSFA Combined Master's Certificate in the form in force at the date of the Bill/s of Lading;
(8) A copy of the notice to the Master instructing him to follow the FOSFA Heating Instructions;
(9) Certificate/s from superintendents certifying:
  (a) the shipped weight (litre weight in air) ascertained at port of loading and specifying at what point the weight was ascertained;
  (b) particulars of the time and place of loading, sampling and establishment of shipped weight;
  (c) that pre-shipment and contractual loading samples were drawn in accordance with the Sampling and Analysis Clause and quoting details of the seals applied.

In relation to items (4) and (7), the immediate previous cargo in the tank/s receiving the oils or fats shall not have been a product appearing on the FOSFA List of Banned Immediate Previous Cargoes in force at the date of the Bill/s of Lading. The Restrictions beyond the Immediate Previous Cargo on the FOSFA List of Banned Immediate Previous Cargoes shall apply.
Buyers are to accept photostat or certified copy/ies of items (4), (5), (7) and (9) relating to the whole parcel/s.
Buyers agree to accept Bill/s of Lading containing the Chamber of Shipping War Risk Clause and/or any other recognised War Risk Clause.
Should documents be presented with incomplete set/s of Bill/s of Lading, payment shall be made provided that delivery of such Bill/s of Lading be guaranteed, such guarantee to be signed, if required by Buyers, by a first class bank. Acceptance of this guarantee shall not prejudice Buyers' rights under this contract.
Should Sellers have failed to present shipping documents on arrival of the ship at destination, Buyers shall take delivery under a guarantee acceptable to the shipowners to be provided by the Buyers, such guarantee to be signed by a first class bank if required by the shipowners. Buyers shall pay for the documents when presented. Any reasonable extra expenses, including costs of such guarantee or extra handling charges incurred by reason of the failure of Sellers to provide such documents, shall be borne by Sellers and allowed for in the final invoice. In the event that Buyers take delivery as above and Sellers fail to provide shipping documents and if the guarantee provided by Buyers as above is encashed by the shipowners, Sellers shall be responsible for all damages, costs and consequences arising from their failure to present documents. Buyers shall inform Sellers immediately there is a claim against the guarantee and Sellers shall have the right to be joined in any legal action arising therefrom.
Payment shall not be deemed to have been effected before receipt of cleared funds by the payee or his bank. If payment is agreed to be by bank transfer, the party shall effect payment to the payee's bank on or before the due date for payment and payment instructions shall specify a value date not later than the second bank working day after the day of payment.
Any monies due by either party to the contract to the other for final invoices and/or accounts for items on shipments fulfilling this contract shall be settled by either party not later than 21 days from the date of the invoice, (except as otherwise provided under awards of arbitration or appeal as governed by the other provisions in the contract), and if not settled a dispute shall be deemed to have arisen which may be referred to arbitration.

11. INTEREST: If any payment is not made on or before the due date for payment, interest shall be payable.
If there is no due date for payment, interest shall be payable if there has been an unreasonable delay in payment. Interest payable shall be appropriate to the currency involved. If the amount of interest is not mutually agreed, a dispute shall be deemed to exist which shall be settled by arbitration in accordance with the Arbitration Clause.
Nothing in this clause shall affect a party's rights to invoke the provisions of the Default Clause in a case where a failure to effect timely payment could give rise to a claim under that clause.

12. CHARTER PARTY: If the Bill/s of Lading refer/s to a Charter Party, then, if required by Buyers, Sellers shall provide a copy of the Charter Party.

13. UNASCERTAINED GOODS: In every instance where a parcel of goods sold by this contract forms an unidentified part of a larger identified quantity of goods of the same description, whether in packages or in bulk, no separation or distinction shall be necessary and, until separation and identification of the parcel sold hereby from the larger quantity has taken place, the Buyer of the parcel is a pro rata owner of the whole of the larger quantity in common with Seller/s and Buyer/s of other parts of the larger quantity.

14. DISCHARGE: The oil shall be discharged at the port of destination at a berth suitable for the discharge of oils or, if practicable and mutually agreed, and provided the ship is willing to and can safely berth, at Buyers' own or appointed premises within harbour limits. Buyers shall take delivery with customary quick despatch after notice of readiness has been given by the shipowner or representative/s in accordance with the Bill/s of Lading, Charter party or Contract of Affreightment. Otherwise Buyers to be liable to pay demurrage at the rate stipulated in the Charter Party or Contract of Affreightment.

Sellers are responsible for all expenses for pumping out, for connecting to ship's outlet/s and for sweepings and/or puddling, but discharging expenses arising after the oil has passed the ship's rail shall be for Buyers' account. Any loose collected remaining in the ship's tank/s to be discharged by the Sellers and delivered to the Buyers at the discharging berth in packages to be provided by the Buyers. If the packages are supplied by the Buyers but the residue is not delivered such residue or unpumpable oil shall not be included in the delivered weight.

15. WEIGHTS: At loading: The shipping weight shall be ascertained by a Superintendent appointed by Sellers at their expense by gauging either in officially calibrated land tank/s or tank barge/s from which the oil is delivered or by delivery via certified weigh scales, or from tank cars which, if not calibrated, shall be weighed before and after loading by single weighing only (front and back axle weighing not allowed). If none of these methods is possible then the shipping weight to be ascertained by the most practicable alternative means.

At discharge: Buyers' superintendents shall ascertain the weight at Buyers' expense conjointly with Sellers' superintendents, if in attendance, by gauging either in officially calibrated tank/s or tank barge/s in which the oil is received or by overside delivery to certified weigh scales, or in rail/road tank cars which, if not calibrated, shall be weighed before and after loading by single weighing only (front and back axle weighing not allowed). If none of these methods is possible then the discharged weight to be ascertained by the most practicable alternative means. In the event of disagreement between Buyers' and Sellers' superintendents on the question of mass per volume (litre weight in air), sealed samples shall be submitted to an analyst whose decision shall be final.

If establishment of weights is not completed within 5 working days after discharge Sellers may submit an interim invoice which shall become due and payable based on Bill of Lading weights. Weights shall then be established as soon as it is deemed practicable by the superintendents representing the parties and a final invoice shall be issued accordingly.

16. ADJUSTMENT OF OUTTURN: Any excess over or deficit under the mean contract quantity arrived at without taking into consideration the margin of 5% more or less, and the quantity delivered, is to be settled at the price fixed by the appropriate Price Settlement Committee appointed by and published by the Federation, or, if no price is fixed by the Federation then at the market price to be mutually agreed or fixed by arbitration for the day of arrival of the last ship to arrive at the berth/place where the contracted goods are to be discharged at the port of destination.

17. SAMPLING AND ANALYSIS: General: Sampling shall be done in accordance with the method in ISO 5555. Should either party fail to appoint a superintendent then the samples drawn by the superintendent present shall be the valid samples for the purposes of analysis and/or arbitration. The analyses shall be carried out in accordance with the methods laid down in the FOSFA International Standard Contractual Methods List.

The certificate/s shall bear the FOSFA International official seal.

Details of seals and labels shall be given on both loading and discharge survey reports and analysis certificate/s.

All samples drawn under the terms of this contract when delivered to FOSFA International or to the analyst/s to become and be their absolute property.

Pre-shipment Samples: To ensure samples are available in the event of a contamination claim not less than five pre-shipment samples of the oil loaded shall be taken at the ship's rail or the nearest practicable point prior to loading. These samples are to remain sealed with Sellers' superintendents at origin but be available on demand to any receiver in the event of a contamination claim. Samples to be kept for three months from date of Bill of Lading.

At loading: Not less than five samples representative of the oil to be drawn from each ship's tank/s and sealed by superintendent for analysis. Two sets of these samples shall be handed to the Master with instructions to hand over to the Receivers at port of discharge or their superintendents. Tests to be made from a set of sample/s by an analyst in the country of shipment, who shall issue the appropriate certificate. The remaining sets of samples to be retained by the superintendent at the port of loading.

At discharge: Buyers' and Sellers' superintendents shall conjointly draw five representative samples during discharge at the ship's rail or the nearest practicable point thereafter and seal for analysis and/or arbitration purposes. Any unpumpable and/or off-quality oil discharged and stored separately shall be sampled and analysed separately.

Buyers or their superintendents shall retain three sealed samples and, if required, shall send one sealed sample with due despatch for analysis to an analyst. The remaining two sealed samples shall be retained by Sellers or their superintendents. If Buyers fail to send a sample for analysis Sellers have the right to submit a sample and the results of this analysis shall stand as the first analysis. The analysis fee shall be equally divided between Sellers and Buyers.

Buyers and Sellers have the right to claim at their own expense a second and/or third analysis for any one or more individual specification. The party requesting such analysis shall, within five business days after receipt of the preceding analysis, notify the other party, arrange for a sealed sample to be sent to another analyst, and give the necessary instructions to the analyst. If two analyses are made the mean of the two results, and if three analyses are made, the mean of the two results closest to each other, as the case may be, shall be binding and form the basis of final settlement. Where the results of the three analyses are such that the above formula does not apply, the mean of the three shall be taken as final.

Parties shall pass on certificates of analysis with due despatch.

18. DUTIES, TAXES, ETC: All export duties, taxes, levies, etc., present or future in country of origin/port of shipment shall be for Sellers' account.

All import duties, taxes, levies, etc., present or future in port of discharge/country of destination shall be for Buyers' account.

Where the goods are entitled to free entry into or preferential duty in the port of destination named in this contract, Sellers shall furnish together with the shipping documents a Certificate of Origin and/or necessary document/s in the form valid at the time of shipment, otherwise Sellers shall be responsible for any extra duty incurred by Buyers through the non-production of such Certificate and/or document/s.

If the eventual country of destination is different from that named in the contract, then Sellers, at Buyers' request, shall, if possible, supply the appropriate Certificate of Origin for the country of final destination.

19. NOTICES: Notices to be despatched by any means of rapid written communication. All notices shall be under reserve for errors in transmission. Notices shall be passed on with due despatch by intermediate Buyers and Sellers. Any notices received after 16.00 hours on a business day shall be deemed to have been received on the following business day. Notice from a broker shall be a valid notice under this contract.

20. NON-BUSINESS DAYS: Should the time limit for doing any act or giving any notice expire on a Saturday, Sunday or any public holiday in the country where the party required to do the act or give the notice resides or carries on business or in the country where the act has to be done or the notice has to be received or on any day which the Federation shall declare to be a non-business day the time so limited shall be extended until the first business day thereafter. All business days shall be deemed to end at 16.00 hours Mondays to Fridays inclusive. The contract shipment period not to be affected by this clause.

21. ODD DAYS: In any month containing an odd number of days the middle day shall be reckoned as belonging to both halves of the month.

22. FORCE MAJEURE: Should shipment of the goods or any part thereof be prevented at any time during the last 30 days of the contract shipment period by reason of Act of God, strikes, lockouts, riots, civil commotions, fires or any other cause comprehended by the term Force Majeure at port/s of loading or elsewhere preventing transport of the goods to such port/s, the time allowed for shipment shall be extended to 30 days beyond the termination of such cause, but should the contract shipment period be less than 30 days such extension shall be limited to the number of days allowed for shipment under the contract shipment period.

Should such cause exist for a period of 60 days beyond the contract shipment period the contract or any unfulfilled part thereof so affected shall be cancelled.

Sellers invoking this clause shall notify Buyers with due despatch.

When goods of a specific origin are sold with the option of shipment from alternative ports and shipment from all alternative ports is not prevented Sellers may only invoke this clause with regard to the specific port/s provided that the port/s has/have been notified to Buyers as the intended port/s of loading prior to or within seven days of the occurrence but if the occurrence commences within the last seven days of the contract shipment period the port/s of loading to be notified not later than the first business day following the contract shipment period. Shipment after the contract shipment period shall be limited to the port/s so nominated. Buyers have no claim against Sellers for delay in shipment or cancellation under this clause provided that Sellers shall have supplied to their Buyers, if required, satisfactory evidence justifying delay or non-fulfilment to establish any claim for extension or cancellation under this clause.

In case of default after extension the default date shall be similarly deferred.

23. PROHIBITION: In the event, during the contract shipment period, of prohibition of export or any other executive or legislative act by or on behalf of the Government of the country of origin or of the territory where the port/s of shipment named herein is/are situate, or of blockade or hostilities, restricting export, whether partially or otherwise, any such restriction shall be deemed by both parties to apply to this contract and to the extent of such total or partial restriction to prevent fulfilment whether by shipment or by any other means whatsoever and to that extent this contract or any unfulfilled portion thereof shall be extended by 30 days.

In the event of shipment during the extended period still proving impossible by reason of any of the causes in this clause the contract or any unfulfilled part thereof shall be cancelled. Sellers invoking this clause shall advise Buyers with due despatch. If required, Sellers must produce proof to justify their claim for extension or cancellation under this clause.

24. BANKRUPTCY/INSOLVENCY: If before the fulfilment of this contract, either party shall suspend payment, notify any of his creditors that he is unable to meet his debts or that he has suspended payment or that he is about to suspend payment of his debts, convene, call or hold a meeting of his creditors, propose a voluntary arrangement, apply for an official moratorium, have an administration order made, have a winding up order made, have a receiver or manager appointed, convene, call or hold a meeting to go into liquidation (other than for reconstruction or amalgamation), become subject to an Interim Order under Section 252 of the Insolvency Act 1986 or have a Bankruptcy Petition presented against him the contract shall forthwith be closed, either at the actual or estimated market price then current for similar goods or, at the option of the other party, at a price to be ascertained by re-purchase or re-sale and the difference between the contract price and such closing-out price shall be the amount which the other party shall be entitled to claim or shall be liable to account for under this contract. Should either party be dissatisfied with the price ascertained by re-purchase or re-sale, then the matter shall be referred to arbitration. If no re-purchase or re-sale takes place and if the parties cannot agree to a closing-out price, then on application of either party, the closing-out price shall be fixed by a sole arbitrator appointed by the Federation subject to the right of appeal under the Federation's Rules of Arbitration and Appeal.

25. CIRCLE: Where a Seller repurchases from his Buyer, or from any subsequent Buyer, the same goods or part thereof, a circle shall be considered to exist as regards the particular goods so repurchased, and the provisions of the Default Clause shall not apply. (For the purpose of this clause the same goods shall mean goods of the same description, of the same country of origin, of the same quality and, where applicable, of the same analysis warranty, for shipment to the same port/s of destination during the same period of shipment.) Different currencies shall not invalidate the circle.

If the goods are not declared or, having been declared, documents are not presented as a result of a circle having been established, invoices based on the mean contract quantity shall be settled between each Buyer and his Seller in the circle by payment by each Buyer to his Seller of the excess of the Seller's invoice amount over the lowest invoice amount in the circle.

Where the circle includes contract/s expressed in different currencies, the lowest invoice amount shall be replaced by the market price on the first business day for contractual shipment and invoices shall be settled between each Buyer and his Seller in the circle by payment of the difference between the market price and the relevant contract price in the currency of the contract. Failing amicable agreement the market price shall be that declared by a Price Settlement Committee of the Federation appointed for that purpose on application of either party.

Such settlement shall be due for payment not later than 15 consecutive days after the last day for declaration or, should the circle not be established before the expiry of this time, then settlement shall be due for payment not later than seven days after the circle is established. No circle shall be considered to exist if its existence is not established within 45 days after the last day of shipment.

All Sellers and Buyers shall give every assistance to the establishment of the circle and where a circle shall have been established same shall be binding on all parties to the circle. Should any party in the circle commit prior to the due date for payment any act comprehended in the Bankruptcy/Insolvency Clause, the invoice amount for the goods calculated at the closing-out price as provided for in the Bankruptcy/Insolvency Clause, shall be taken as the basis for settlement instead of the lowest invoice amount in the circle, and in this event each Buyer shall make payment to his Seller or each Seller shall make payment to his Buyer of the difference between the closing-out price and the contract price, as the case may be.

In the event of a claim under the Prohibition Clause or the Force Majeure Clause, the date for settlement shall be deferred until the expiry of the extended shipment period. Thereafter, if the contract is cancelled under the terms of the Prohibition Clause or the Force Majeure Clause, this clause is not applicable.

26. DEFAULT: In default of fulfilment of this contract by either party, the other party at his discretion shall, after giving notice, have the right either to cancel the contract, or the right to sell or purchase, as the case may be, against the defaulter who shall on demand make good the loss, if any, on such sale or purchase. If the party liable to pay shall be dissatisfied with the price of such sale or purchase, or if neither of the above rights is exercised, the damages, if any, shall, failing amicable settlement, be determined by arbitration. The damages awarded against the defaulter shall be limited to the difference between the contract price and the actual or estimated market price on the day of default. Damages to be computed on the mean contract quantity. If the arbitrators consider the circumstances of the default justify it they may, at their absolute discretion, award damages on a different quantity and/or award additional damages.

Prior to the last day for making a declaration of shipment a Seller may notify his Buyer of his inability to ship but the date of such notice shall not become the default date without the agreement of the Buyer. If, for any other reason, either party fails to fulfil the contract and is declared to be in default by the other party and default is either agreed between the parties or subsequently found by arbitrators to have occurred, then the day of the default shall, failing amicable settlement, be decided by arbitration.

27. DOMICILE: This contract shall be deemed to have been made in England and the construction, validity and performance thereof shall be governed in all respects by English law. Any dispute arising out of or in connection therewith shall be submitted to arbitration in accordance with the Rules of the Federation. The serving of proceedings upon any party by sending same to their last known address together with leaving a copy of such proceedings at the offices of the Federation shall be deemed good service, rule of law or equity to the contrary notwithstanding.

28. INTERNATIONAL CONVENTIONS: The following shall not apply to this contract:—

(a) the Uniform Law on Sales and the Uniform Law on Formation to which effect is given by the Uniform Laws on International Sales Act 1967;
(b) the United Nations Convention on Contracts for the International Sale of Goods of 1980;
(c) the United Nations Convention on the Limitation Period in the International Sale of Goods of 1974 and the amending Protocol of 1980.

29. ARBITRATION: Any dispute arising out of this contract, including any question of law arising in connection therewith, shall be referred to arbitration in London (or elsewhere if so agreed) in accordance with the Rules of Arbitration and Appeal of the Federation of Oils, Seeds and Fats Associations Limited, in force at the date of this contract and of which both parties hereto shall be deemed to be cognizant.

Neither party hereto, nor any persons claiming under either of them, shall bring any action or other legal proceedings against the other of them in respect of any such dispute until such dispute shall first have been heard and determined by the arbitrators, umpire or Board of Appeal (as the case may be), in accordance with the Rules of Arbitration and Appeal of the Federation, and it is hereby expressly agreed and declared that the obtaining of an Award from the arbitrators, umpire or Board of Appeal (as the case may be), shall be a condition precedent to the right of either party hereto or of any person claiming under either of them to bring any action or other legal proceedings against the other of them in respect of any such dispute.

APPENDIX V

Gafta 119 Fob form

Reproduced with kind permission from GAFTA

Effective 1st April 2012

Contract No.119

GENERAL CONTRACT FOR FEEDINGSTUFFS IN BAGS OR BULK FOB TERMS

** delete/specify as applicable* *Date*..

SELLERS..

INTERVENING AS BROKERS..

BUYERS..
have this day entered into a contract on the following terms and conditions.

1. GOODS..
In bulk or in bags. If in bags, in new and/or second-hand bags of suitable strength to withstand ordinary wear and tear to port of destination. Bags of each mark shall be of uniform weight and shall be properly marked.

2. QUANTITY ....5% more or less at Buyers' option.
In the event of the quantity contracted being a full and complete cargo and/or cargoes the margin of contract quantity shall be 10% more or less, any excess or deficiency over 5% shall be settled at the FOB price on date of last bill of lading; value shall be fixed by arbitration unless mutually agreed. In the event of more than one delivery being made each delivery shall be considered a separate contract, but the margin on the mean quantity sold shall not be affected thereby. Each mark/parcel shall stand as a separate delivery.

3. PRICE..
* per tonne of 1000 kilograms }
} gross weight, delivered Free on Board Buyers' vessel at ....
* per ton of 1016 kilograms or 2240 lbs. }

4. BROKERAGE..................................per tonne, to be paid by Sellers on the mean contract quantity, goods lost or not lost, contract fulfilled or not fulfilled unless such non-fulfilment is due to the cancellation of the contract under the terms of the Prohibition or Force Majeure Clause. Brokerage shall be due on the day shipping documents are exchanged, or if the goods are not delivered then the brokerage shall be due on the 30th consecutive day after the last day for delivery.

5. QUALITY ....

***Official** .... certificate of inspection, at time of loading into the ocean carrying vessel, shall be final as to quality.

Warranted to contain not less than ....
% of oil and protein combined and not more than 1.50% of sand and/or silica. Should the whole, or any portion, not turn out equal to warranty, the goods must be taken at an allowance to be agreed or settled by arbitration as provided for below, except that for any deficiency of oil and protein there shall be allowances to Buyers at the following rates, viz.: 1% of the contract price for each of the first 3 units of deficiency under the warranted percentage; 2% of the contract price for the 4th and 5th units and 3% of the contract price for each unit in excess of 5 and proportionately for any fraction thereof. When the combined content of oil and protein is warranted within a margin (as for example 40%/42%) no allowance shall be made if the analysis ascertained as herein provided be not below the minimum, but if the analysis results below the minimum warranted the allowance for deficiency shall be computed from the mean of the warranted content. For any excess of sand and/or silica there shall be an allowance of 1% of the contract price for each unit of excess and proportionately for any fraction thereof. Should the goods contain over 3% of sand and/or silica the Buyers shall be entitled to reject the goods, in which case the contract shall be null and void, for such quantity rejected. For the purpose of sampling and analysis each mark/parcel shall stand as a separate shipment. The right of rejection provided by this Clause shall be limited to the mark/parcel or marks/parcels found to be defective.
Condition. Delivery shall be made in good condition.

6. PERIOD OF DELIVERY
Delivery during .... at Buyers' call.

Nomination of Vessel. Buyers shall serve not less than..consecutive day's notice of the name and probable readiness date of the vessel and the estimated tonnage required. Buyers have the right to substitute the nominated vessel, but in any event the original delivery period and any extension shall not be affected thereby. Provided the vessel is presented at the loading port in readiness to load within the delivery period, Sellers shall if necessary complete loading after the delivery period and carrying charges shall not apply. In case of re-sales a provisional notice shall be passed on without delay, where possible, by telephone and confirmed on the same day in accordance with the Notices Clause.

In any month containing an odd number of days the middle day shall be accepted as being in both halves of the month, except for pricing purposes the middle day shall be considered to be in the first half of the month.

7. SHIPMENT AND CLASSIFICATION

Shipment by first class mechanically self-propelled vessel(s) suitable for the carriage of the contract goods, classed in accordance with the Institute Classification Clause of the International Underwriting Association in force at the time of shipment, excluding tankers and vessels which are either classified in Lloyd's Register or described in Lloyd's Shipping Index as "Ore/Oil" vessels.

8. LOADING

Vessel(s) to be clean and fit and to load in accordance with the custom of the port of loading unless otherwise stipulated. Bill of lading shall be considered proof of delivery in the absence of evidence to the contrary.

9. EXTENSION OF DELIVERY

The contract period of delivery shall be extended by an additional period of not more than 30 consecutive days, provided that Buyers serve notice claiming extension not later than the next business day following the last day of the delivery period. In this event Sellers shall carry the goods for Buyers' account and all charges for storage, interest, insurance and other such normal carrying expenses shall be for Buyers' account, unless the vessel presents in readiness to load within the contractual delivery period.

Any differences in export duties, taxes, levies etc, between those applying during the original delivery period and those applying during the period of extension, shall be for the account of Buyers. If required by Buyers, Sellers shall produce evidence of the amounts paid. In such cases the Duties, Taxes, Levies Clause shall not apply.

Should Buyers fail to present a vessel in readiness to load under the extension period, Sellers shall have the option of declaring Buyers to be in default, or shall be entitled to demand payment at the contract price plus such charges as stated above, less current FOB charges, against warehouse warrants and the tender of such warehouse warrants shall be considered complete delivery of the contract on the part of Sellers.

10. ICE ....

11. PAYMENT

(a) By cash in .... against the

following shipping documents ....

(b) No clerical error in the documents shall entitle the Buyers to reject them or delay payment, but Sellers shall be responsible for all loss or expense caused to Buyers by reason of such error, and Sellers shall on request of Buyers furnish an approved guarantee in respect thereto.

(c) Amounts payable under this contract shall be settled without delay. If not so settled, either party may notify the other that a dispute has arisen and serve a notice stating his intention to refer the dispute to arbitration in accordance with the Arbitration Rules.

(d) **Interest**. If there has been unreasonable delay in any payment, interest appropriate to the currency involved shall be charged. If such charge is not mutually agreed, a dispute shall be deemed to exist which shall be settled by arbitration. Otherwise interest shall be payable only where specifically provided in the terms of the contract or by an award of arbitration. The terms of this clause do not override the parties' contractual obligation under sub-clause (a).

12. EXPORT LICENCE - If required, to be obtained by Sellers.

13. DUTIES, TAXES, LEVIES, ETC.

All export duties, taxes, levies, etc., present or future, in country of origin, or of the territory where the port or ports of shipment named herein is/are situate, shall be for Sellers' account.

14. INSURANCE

Marine and war risk insurance including strikes, riots, civil commotions and mine risks to be effected by Buyers with first class underwriters and/or approved companies. Buyers shall supply Sellers with confirmation thereof at least 5 consecutive days prior to expected readiness of vessel(s). If Buyers fail to provide such confirmation, Sellers shall have the right to place such insurance at Buyers' risk and expense.

15. WEIGHING

The terms and conditions of GAFTA Weighing Rules No.123 are deemed to be incorporated into this contract. Final at time and place of loading, as per GAFTA registered superintendent certificate at Sellers' choice and expense. Buyers have the right to attend at loading.

16. SAMPLING, ANALYSIS AND CERTIFICATE OF ANALYSIS

The terms and conditions of GAFTA Sampling Rules No. 124 are deemed to be incorporated into this contract. Samples shall be taken at time and place of loading. The parties shall appoint superintendents, for the purposes of supervision and sampling of the goods, from the GAFTA Register of Superintendents. Unless otherwise agreed, analysts shall be appointed from the GAFTA Register of Analysts

17. PROHIBITION

In case of prohibition of export, blockade or hostilities or in case of any executive or legislative act done by or on behalf of the government of the country of origin or of the territory where the port or ports of shipment named herein is/are situate, restricting export, whether partially or otherwise, any such restriction shall be deemed by both parties to apply to this contract and to the extent of such total or partial restriction to prevent fulfilment whether by shipment or by any other means whatsoever and to that extent this contract or any unfulfilled portion thereof shall be cancelled. Sellers shall advise Buyers without delay with the reasons therefor and, if required, Sellers must produce proof to justify the cancellation.

18. LOADING STRIKES

(a) Should delivery of the goods or any part thereof be prevented at any time during the last 28 days of guaranteed time of delivery or at any time during guaranteed contract period if such be less than 28 days, by reason of riots, strikes or lock-outs at port(s) of loading or elsewhere preventing the forwarding of the goods to such port(s), then Sellers shall be entitled at the resumption of work after termination of such riots, strikes or lock-outs to as much time, not exceeding 28 days, for delivery from such port(s) as was left for delivery under the contract prior to the outbreak of the riots, strikes or lock-outs, and in the event of the time left for delivery under the contract being 14 days or less, a minimum extension of 14 days shall be allowed.

(b) In the event of further riots, strikes or lock-outs occurring during the time by which the guaranteed time of delivery has been extended by reason of the operation of the provisions of paragraph (a), the additional extension shall be limited to the actual duration of such further riots, strikes or lock-outs. In case of non-delivery under the above circumstances the date of default shall be similarly deferred.

(c) If delay in delivery is likely to occur for any of the above reasons, Sellers shall serve notice on their Buyers within 7 consecutive days of the occurrence, or not less than 21 consecutive days before the commencement of the contract period, whichever is later, if they intend to claim an extension for delivery, such notice shall limit the port(s) for delivery after expiry of contract period to those for which an extension is claimed.

(d) If required by Buyers, Sellers must provide documentary evidence to establish any claim for extension under this clause.

19. FORCE MAJEURE ....

20. CIRCLE

Where Sellers re-purchase from their Buyers or from any subsequent Buyer the same goods or part thereof, a circle shall be considered to exist as regards the particular goods so re-purchased, and the provisions of the Default Clause shall not apply. (For the purpose of this clause the same goods shall mean goods of the same description, from the same country of origin, of the same quality, and, where applicable, of the same analysis warranty, for delivery from the same port(s) of loading during the same period of delivery). Different currencies shall not invalidate the circle.

Subject to the terms of the Prohibition Clause in the contract, if the circle is established before the goods are delivered, or if the goods are not delivered invoices based on the mean contract quantity, or if the goods have been delivered invoices based on the delivered quantity, shall be settled by all Buyers and their Sellers in the circle by payment by all Buyers to their Sellers of the excess of the Sellers' invoice amount over the lowest invoice amount in the circle. Payment shall be due not later than 15 consecutive days after the last day for delivery, or, should the circle not be ascertained before the expiry of this time, then payment shall be due not later than 15 consecutive days after the circle is ascertained.

Where the circle includes contract expressed in different currencies the lowest invoice amount shall be replaced by the market price on the first day for contractual delivery and invoices shall be settled between each Buyer and his Seller in the circle by payment of the differences between the market price and the relative contract price in the currency of the contract.

All Sellers and Buyers shall give every assistance to ascertain the circle and when a circle shall have been ascertained in accordance with this clause same shall be binding on all parties to the circle. As between Buyers and Sellers in the circle, the non-presentation of documents by Sellers to their Buyers shall not be considered a breach of contract. Should any party in the circle prior to the due date of payment commit any act comprehended in the Insolvency Clause of this contract, settlement by all parties in the circle shall be calculated at the closing out price as provided for in the Insolvency Clause, which shall be taken as a basis for settlement, instead of the lowest invoice amount in the circle. In this event respective Buyers shall make payment to their Sellers or respective Sellers shall make payment to their Buyers of the difference between the closing out price and the contract price.

21. NOTICES

All notices required to be served on the parties pursuant to this contract shall be communicated rapidly in legible form. Methods of rapid communication for the purposes of this clause are defined and mutually recognised as: - either telex, or letter if delivered by hand on the date of writing, or telefax, or E-mail, or other electronic means, always subject to the proviso that if receipt of any notice is contested, the burden of proof of transmission shall be on the sender who shall, in the case of a dispute, establish, to the satisfaction of the arbitrator(s) or board of appeal appointed pursuant to the Arbitration Clause, that the notice was actually transmitted to the addressee. For the purpose of serving notices in a string, any notice received after 1600 hours on a business day shall be deemed to have been received on the business day following. In case of resales/repurchases all notices shall be served without delay by sellers on their respective buyers or vice versa. A notice to the Brokers or Agent shall be deemed a notice under this contract.

22. NON-BUSINESS DAYS

Saturdays, Sundays and the officially recognised and/or legal holidays of the respective countries and any days, which GAFTA may declare as non-business days for specific purposes, shall be non-business days. Should the time limit for doing any act or serving any notice expire on a non-business day, the time so limited shall be extended until the first business day thereafter. The period of delivery shall not be affected by this clause.

23. DEFAULT

In default of fulfilment of contract by either party, the following provisions shall apply: -

(a) The party other than the defaulter shall, at their discretion have the right, after serving notice on the defaulter, to sell or purchase, as the case may be, against the defaulter, and such sale or purchase shall establish the default price.

(b) If either party be dissatisfied with such default price or if the right at (a) above is not exercised and damages cannot be mutually agreed, then the assessment of damages shall be settled by arbitration.

(c) The damages payable shall be based on, but not limited to, the difference between the contract price and either the default price established under (a) above or upon the actual or estimated value of the goods, on the date of default, established under (b) above.

(d) In all cases the damages shall, in addition, include any proven additional expenses which would directly and naturally result in the ordinary course of events from the defaulter's breach of contract, but shall in no case include loss of profit on any sub-contracts made by the party defaulted against or others unless the arbitrator(s) or board of appeal, having regard to special circumstances, shall in his/their sole and absolute discretion think fit.

(e) Damages, if any, shall be computed on the quantity called for if any but, if no such quantity has been declared then on the mean contract quantity, and any option available to either party shall be deemed to have been exercised accordingly in favour of the mean contract quantity.

24. INSOLVENCY

If before the fulfilment of this contract, either party shall suspend payments, notify any of the creditors that he is unable to meet debts or that he has suspended or that he is about to suspend payments of his debts, convene, call or hold a meeting of creditors, propose a voluntary arrangement, have an administration order made, have a winding up order made, have a receiver or manager appointed, convene, call or hold a meeting to go into liquidation (other than for re-construction or amalgamation) become subject to an Interim Order under Section 252 of the Insolvency Act 1986, or have a Bankruptcy Petition presented against him (any of which acts being hereinafter called an "Act of Insolvency") then the party committing such Act of Insolvency shall forthwith serve a notice of the occurrence of such Act of Insolvency on the other party to the contract and upon proof (by either the other party to the contract or the Receiver, Administrator, Liquidator or other person representing the party committing the Act of Insolvency) that such notice was thus served within 2 business days of the occurrence of the Act of Insolvency, the contract shall be closed out at the market price ruling on the business day following the serving of the notice. If such notice has not been served, then the other party, on learning of the occurrence of the Act of Insolvency, shall have the option of declaring the contract closed out at either the market price on the first business day after the date when such party first learnt of the occurrence of the Act of Insolvency or at the market price ruling on the first business day after the date when the Act of Insolvency occurred. In all cases the other party to the contract shall have the option of ascertaining the settlement price on the closing out of the contract by re-purchase or re-sale, and the difference between the contract price and the re-purchase or re-sale price shall be the amount payable or receivable under this contract.

25. DOMICILE

This contract shall be deemed to have been made in England and to be performed in England, notwithstanding any contrary provision, and this contract shall be construed and take effect in accordance with the laws of England. Except for the purpose of enforcing any award made in pursuance of the Arbitration Clause of this contract, the Courts of England shall have exclusive jurisdiction to determine any application for ancillary relief, (save for obtaining security only for the claim or counter-claim), the exercise of the powers of the Court in relation to the arbitration proceedings and any dispute other than a dispute which shall fall within the jurisdiction of arbitrators or board of appeal of the Association pursuant to the Arbitration Clause of this contract. For the purpose of any legal proceedings each party shall be deemed to be ordinarily resident or carrying on business at the offices of The Grain and Feed Trade Association, (GAFTA), England, and any party residing or carrying on business in Scotland shall be held to have prorogated jurisdiction against himself to the English Courts or if in Northern Ireland to have submitted to the jurisdiction and to be bound by the decision of the English Courts. The service of proceedings upon any such party by leaving the same at the offices of The Grain and Feed Trade Association, together with the posting of a copy of such proceedings to his address outside England, shall be deemed good service, any rule of law or equity to the contrary notwithstanding.

26. ARBITRATION

(a) Any and all disputes arising out of or under this contract or any claim regarding the interpretation or execution of this contract shall be determined by arbitration in accordance with the GAFTA Arbitration Rules, No 125, in the edition current at the date of this contract, such Rules are incorporated into and form part of this Contract and both parties hereto shall be deemed to be fully cognisant of and to have expressly agreed to the application of such Rules.

(b) Neither party hereto, nor any persons claiming under either of them shall bring any action or other legal proceedings against the other in respect of any such dispute, or claim until such dispute or claim shall first have been heard and determined by the arbitrator(s) or a board of appeal, as the case may be, in accordance with the Arbitration Rules and it is expressly agreed and declared that the obtaining of an award from the arbitrator(s) or board of appeal, as the case may be, shall be a condition precedent to the right of either party hereto or of any persons claiming under either of them to bring any action or other legal proceedings against the other of them in respect of any such dispute or claim.

(c) Nothing contained under this Arbitration Clause shall prevent the parties from seeking to obtain security in respect of their claim or counterclaim via legal proceedings in any jurisdiction, provided such legal proceedings shall be limited to applying for and/or obtaining security for a claim or counterclaim, it being understood and agreed that the substantive merits of any dispute or claim shall be determined solely by arbitration in accordance with the GAFTA Arbitration Rules, No 125.

27. INTERNATIONAL CONVENTIONS

The following shall not apply to this contract: -

(a) The Uniform Law on Sales and the Uniform Law on Formation to which effect is given by the Uniform Laws on International Sales Act 1967.

(b) The United Nations Convention on Contracts for the International Sale of Goods of 1980.

(c) The United Nations Convention on Prescription (Limitation) in the International Sale of Goods of 1974 and the amending Protocol of 1980.

(d) Incoterms.

(e) Unless the contract contains any statement expressly to the contrary, a person who is not a party to this contract has no right under the Contract (Rights of Third Parties) Act 1999 to enforce any term of it.

Sellers .... Buyers ....

Printed in England and issued by

GAFTA

(THE GRAIN AND FEED TRADE ASSOCIATION)

9 LINCOLN'S INN FIELDS, LONDON WC2A 3BP

119/5

APPENDIX VI

UCP 600

Uniform Customs and Practice for Documentary Credits (2007 revision)

Article 1

Application of UCP 600

The *Uniform Customs and Practice for Documentary Credits, 2007 Revision*, ICC Publication No. 600 ("UCP 600") are rules that apply to any documentary credit ("credit") (including, to the extent to which they may be applicable, any standby letter of credit) when the text of the credit expressly indicates that it is subject to these rules. They are binding on all parties thereto unless expressly modified or excluded by the credit.

Article 2

Definitions

For the purpose of these rules:

Advising bank means the bank that advises the credit at the request of the issuing bank.

Applicant means the party on whose request the credit is issued.

Banking day means a day on which a bank is regularly open at the place at which an act subject to these rules is to be performed.

Beneficiary means the party in whose favour a credit is issued.

Complying presentation means a presentation that is in accordance with the terms and conditions of the credit, the applicable provisions of these rules and international standard banking practice.

Confirmation means a definite undertaking of the confirming bank, in addition to that of the issuing bank, to honour or negotiate a complying presentation.

Confirming bank means the bank that adds its confirmation to a credit upon the issuing bank's authorization or request.

Credit means any arrangement, however named or described, that is irrevocable and thereby constitutes a definite undertaking of the issuing bank to honour a complying presentation.

Honour means:

a. to pay at sight if the credit is available by sight payment.
b. to incur a deferred payment undertaking and pay at maturity if the credit is available by deferred payment.
c. to accept a bill of exchange ("draft") drawn by the beneficiary and pay at maturity if the credit is available by acceptance.

Issuing bank means the bank that issues a credit at the request of an applicant or on its own behalf.

Negotiation means the purchase by the nominated bank of drafts (drawn on a bank other than the nominated bank) and/or documents under a complying presentation, by advancing or agreeing to advance funds to the beneficiary on or before the banking day on which reimbursement is due to the nominated bank.

Nominated bank means the bank with which the credit is available or any bank in the case of a credit available with any bank.

Presentation means either the delivery of documents under a credit to the issuing bank or nominated bank or the documents so delivered.

Presenter means a beneficiary, bank or other party that makes a presentation.

Article 3

Interpretations

For the purpose of these rules:

Where applicable, words in the singular include the plural and in the plural include the singular.

A credit is irrevocable even if there is no indication to that effect.

A document may be signed by handwriting, facsimile signature, perforated signature, stamp, symbol or any other mechanical or electronic method of authentication.

A requirement for a document to be legalized, visaed, certified or similar will be satisfied by any signature, mark, stamp or label on the document which appears to satisfy that requirement.

Branches of a bank in different countries are considered to be separate banks.

Terms such as "first class", "well known", "qualified", "independent", "official", "competent" or "local" used to describe the issuer of a document allow any issuer except the beneficiary to issue that document.

Unless required to be used in a document, words such as "prompt", "immediately" or "as soon as possible" will be disregarded.

The expression "on or about" or similar will be interpreted as a stipulation that an event is to occur during a period of five calendar days before until five calendar days after the specified date, both start and end dates included.

The words "to", "until", "till", "from" and "between" when used to determine a period of shipment include the date or dates mentioned, and the words "before" and "after" exclude the date mentioned.

The words "from" and "after" when used to determine a maturity date exclude the date mentioned.

The terms "first half" and "second half" of a month shall be construed respectively as the 1st to the 15th and the 16th to the last day of the month, all dates inclusive.

The terms "beginning", "middle" and "end" of a month shall be construed respectively as the 1st to the 10th, the 11th to the 20th and the 21st to the last day of the month, all dates inclusive.

Article 4

Credits v. contracts

a. A credit by its nature is a separate transaction from the sale or other contract on which it may be based. Banks are in no way concerned with or bound by such contract, even if any reference whatsoever to it is included in the credit.

Consequently, the undertaking of a bank to honour, to negotiate or to fulfil any other obligation under the credit is not subject to claims or defences by the applicant resulting from its relationships with the issuing bank or the beneficiary.

A beneficiary can in no case avail itself of the contractual relationships existing between banks or between the applicant and the issuing bank.

b. An issuing bank should discourage any attempt by the applicant to include, as an integral part of the credit, copies of the underlying contract, proforma invoice and the like.

Article 5

Documents v. goods, services or performance

Banks deal with documents and not with goods, services or performance to which the documents may relate.

Article 6

Availability, expiry date and place for presentation

a. A credit must state the bank with which it is available or whether it is available with any bank. A credit available with a nominated bank is also available with the issuing bank.

b. A credit must state whether it is available by sight payment, deferred payment, acceptance or negotiation.

c. A credit must not be issued available by a draft drawn on the applicant.

d. i. A credit must state an expiry date for presentation. An expiry date stated for honour or negotiation will be deemed to be an expiry date for presentation.

   ii. The place of the bank with which the credit is available is the place for presentation. The place for presentation under a credit available with any bank is that of any bank. A place for presentation other than that of the issuing bank is in addition to the place of the issuing bank.

e. Except as provided in sub-article 29 (a), a presentation by or on behalf of the beneficiary must be made on or before the expiry date.

Article 7

Issuing bank undertaking

a. Provided that the stipulated documents are presented to the nominated bank or to the issuing bank and that they constitute a complying presentation, the issuing bank must honour if the credit is available by:

   i. sight payment, deferred payment or acceptance with the issuing bank;

   ii. sight payment with a nominated bank and that nominated bank does not pay;

   iii. deferred payment with a nominated bank and that nominated bank does not incur its deferred payment undertaking or, having incurred its deferred payment undertaking, does not pay at maturity;

   iv. acceptance with a nominated bank and that nominated bank does not accept a draft drawn on it or, having accepted a draft drawn on it, does not pay at maturity;

   v. negotiation with a nominated bank and that nominated bank does not negotiate.

b. An issuing bank is irrevocably bound to honour as of the time it issues the credit.

c. An issuing bank undertakes to reimburse a nominated bank that has honoured or negotiated a complying presentation and forwarded the documents to the issuing bank. Reimbursement for the amount of a complying presentation under a credit available by acceptance or deferred payment is due at maturity, whether or not the nominated bank prepaid or purchased before maturity. An issuing bank's undertaking to reimburse a nominated bank is independent of the issuing bank's undertaking to the beneficiary.

Article 8

Confirming bank undertaking

a. Provided that the stipulated documents are presented to the confirming bank or to any other nominated bank and that they constitute a complying presentation, the confirming bank must:
   i. honour, if the credit is available by
      a) sight payment, deferred payment or acceptance with the confirming bank;
      b) sight payment with another nominated bank and that nominated bank does not pay;
      c) deferred payment with another nominated bank and that nominated bank does not incur its deferred payment undertaking or, having incurred its deferred payment undertaking, does not pay at maturity;
      d) acceptance with another nominated bank and that nominated bank does not accept a draft drawn on it or, having accepted a draft drawn on it, does not pay at maturity;
      e) negotiation with another nominated bank and that nominated bank does not negotiate.
   ii. negotiate, without recourse, if the credit is available by negotiation with the confirming bank.

b. A confirming bank is irrevocably bound to honour or negotiate as of the time it adds its confirmation to the credit.

c. A confirming bank undertakes to reimburse another nominated bank that has honoured or negotiated a complying presentation and forwarded the documents to the confirming bank. Reimbursement for the amount of a complying presentation under a credit available by acceptance or deferred payment is due at maturity, whether or not another nominated bank prepaid or purchased before maturity. A confirming bank's undertaking to reimburse another nominated bank is independent of the confirming bank's undertaking to the beneficiary.

d. If a bank is authorized or requested by the issuing bank to confirm a credit but is not prepared to do so, it must inform the issuing bank without delay and may advise the credit without confirmation.

Article 9

Advising of credits and amendments

a. A credit and any amendment may be advised to a beneficiary through an advising bank. An advising bank that is not a confirming bank advises the credit and any amendment without any undertaking to honour or negotiate.

b. By advising the credit or amendment, the advising bank signifies that it has satisfied itself as to the apparent authenticity of the credit or amendment and that the advice accurately reflects the terms and conditions of the credit or amendment received.

c. An advising bank may utilize the services of another bank ("second advising bank") to advise the credit and any amendment to the beneficiary. By advising the credit or amendment, the second advising bank signifies that it has satisfied itself as to the apparent authenticity of the advice it has received and that the advice accurately reflects the terms and conditions of the credit or amendment received.

d. A bank utilizing the services of an advising bank or second advising bank to advise a credit must use the same bank to advise any amendment thereto.

e. If a bank is requested to advise a credit or amendment but elects not to do so, it must so inform, without delay, the bank from which the credit, amendment or advice has been received.

f. If a bank is requested to advise a credit or amendment but cannot satisfy itself as to the apparent authenticity of the credit, the amendment or the advice, it must so inform, without delay, the bank from which the instructions appear to have been received. If the advising bank or second advising bank elects nonetheless to advise the credit or amendment, it must inform the beneficiary or second advising bank that it has not been able to satisfy itself as to the apparent authenticity of the credit, the amendment or the advice.

Article 10

Amendments

a. Except as otherwise provided by article 38, a credit can neither be amended nor cancelled without the agreement of the issuing bank, the confirming bank, if any, and the beneficiary.

b. An issuing bank is irrevocably bound by an amendment as of the time it issues the amendment. A confirming bank may extend its confirmation to an amendment and will be irrevocably bound as of the time it advises the amendment. A confirming bank may, however, choose to advise an amendment without extending its confirmation and, if so, it must inform the issuing bank without delay and inform the beneficiary in its advice.

c. The terms and conditions of the original credit (or a credit incorporating previously accepted amendments) will remain in force for the beneficiary until the beneficiary communicates its acceptance of the amendment to the bank that advised such amendment. The beneficiary should give notification of acceptance or rejection of an amendment. If the beneficiary fails to give such notification, a presentation that complies with the credit and to any not yet accepted amendment will be deemed to be notification of acceptance by the beneficiary of such amendment. As of that moment the credit will be amended.

d. A bank that advises an amendment should inform the bank from which it received the amendment of any notification of acceptance or rejection.

e. Partial acceptance of an amendment is not allowed and will be deemed to be notification of rejection of the amendment.

f. A provision in an amendment to the effect that the amendment shall enter into force unless rejected by the beneficiary within a certain time shall be disregarded.

Article 11

Teletransmitted and pre-advised credits and amendments

a. An authenticated teletransmission of a credit or amendment will be deemed to be the operative credit or amendment, and any subsequent mail confirmation shall be disregarded.

If a teletransmission states "full details to follow" (or words of similar effect), or states that the mail confirmation is to be the operative credit or amendment, then the teletransmission will not be deemed to be the operative credit or amendment. The issuing bank must then issue the operative credit or amendment without delay in terms not inconsistent with the teletransmission.

b. A preliminary advice of the issuance of a credit or amendment ("pre-advice") shall only be sent if the issuing bank is prepared to issue the operative credit or amendment. An issuing bank that sends a pre-advice is irrevocably committed to issue the operative credit or amendment, without delay, in terms not inconsistent with the pre-advice.

Article 12

Nomination

a. Unless a nominated bank is the confirming bank, an authorization to honour or negotiate does not impose any obligation on that nominated bank to honour or negotiate, except when expressly agreed to by that nominated bank and so communicated to the beneficiary.

b. By nominating a bank to accept a draft or incur a deferred payment undertaking, an issuing bank authorizes that nominated bank to prepay or purchase a draft accepted or a deferred payment undertaking incurred by that nominated bank.

c. Receipt or examination and forwarding of documents by a nominated bank that is not a confirming bank does not make that nominated bank liable to honour or negotiate, nor does it constitute honour or negotiation.

Article 13

Bank-to-bank reimbursement arrangements

a. If a credit states that reimbursement is to be obtained by a nominated bank ("claiming bank") claiming on another party ("reimbursing bank"), the credit must state if the reimbursement is subject to the ICC rules for bank-to-bank reimbursements in effect on the date of issuance of the credit.

b. If a credit does not state that reimbursement is subject to the ICC rules for bank-to-bank reimbursements, the following apply:

   i. An issuing bank must provide a reimbursing bank with a reimbursement authorization that conforms with the availability stated in the credit. The reimbursement authorization should not be subject to an expiry date.

   ii. A claiming bank shall not be required to supply a reimbursing bank with a certificate of compliance with the terms and conditions of the credit.

   iii. An issuing bank will be responsible for any loss of interest, together with any expenses incurred, if reimbursement is not provided on first demand by a reimbursing bank in accordance with the terms and conditions of the credit.

iv. A reimbursing bank's charges are for the account of the issuing bank. However, if the charges are for the account of the beneficiary, it is the responsibility of an issuing bank to so indicate in the credit and in the reimbursement authorization. If a reimbursing bank's charges are for the account of the beneficiary, they shall be deducted from the amount due to a claiming bank when reimbursement is made. If no reimbursement is made, the reimbursing bank's charges remain the obligation of the issuing bank.

c. An issuing bank is not relieved of any of its obligations to provide reimbursement if reimbursement is not made by a reimbursing bank on first demand.

Article 14

Standard for examination of documents

a. A nominated bank acting on its nomination, a confirming bank, if any, and the issuing bank must examine a presentation to determine, on the basis of the documents alone, whether or not the documents appear on their face to constitute a complying presentation.

b. A nominated bank acting on its nomination, a confirming bank, if any, and the issuing bank shall each have a maximum of five banking days following the day of presentation to determine if a presentation is complying. This period is not curtailed or otherwise affected by the occurrence on or after the date of presentation of any expiry date or last day for presentation.

c. A presentation including one or more original transport documents subject to articles 19, 20, 21, 22, 23, 24 or 25 must be made by or on behalf of the beneficiary not later than 21 calendar days after the date of shipment as described in these rules, but in any event not later than the expiry date of the credit.

d. Data in a document, when read in context with the credit, the document itself and international standard banking practice, need not be identical to, but must not conflict with, data in that document, any other stipulated document or the credit.

e. In documents other than the commercial invoice, the description of the goods, services or performance, if stated, may be in general terms not conflicting with their description in the credit.

f. If a credit requires presentation of a document other than a transport document, insurance document or commercial invoice, without stipulating by whom the document is to be issued or its data content, banks will accept the document as presented if its content appears to fulfil the function of the required document and otherwise complies with sub-article 14 (d).

g. A document presented but not required by the credit will be disregarded and may be returned to the presenter.

h. If a credit contains a condition without stipulating the document to indicate compliance with the condition, banks will deem such condition as not stated and will disregard it.

i. A document may be dated prior to the issuance date of the credit, but must not be dated later than its date of presentation.

j. When the addresses of the beneficiary and the applicant appear in any stipulated document, they need not be the same as those stated in the credit or in any other stipulated document, but must be within the same country as the respective addresses mentioned in the credit. Contact details (telefax, telephone, email and the like) stated as part of the beneficiary's and the applicant's address will be disregarded. However, when the address and contact details of the applicant appear as part of the consignee or notify party details on a transport document subject to articles 19, 20, 21, 22, 23, 24 or 25, they must be as stated in the credit.

k. The shipper or consignor of the goods indicated on any document need not be the beneficiary of the credit.

l. A transport document may be issued by any party other than a carrier, owner, master or charterer provided that the transport document meets the requirements of articles 19, 20, 21, 22, 23 or 24 of these rules.

Article 15

Complying presentation

a. When an issuing bank determines that a presentation is complying, it must honour.

b. When a confirming bank determines that a presentation is complying, it must honour or negotiate and forward the documents to the issuing bank.

c. When a nominated bank determines that a presentation is complying and honours or negotiates, it must forward the documents to the confirming bank or issuing bank.

Article 16

Discrepant documents, waiver and notice

a. When a nominated bank acting on its nomination, a confirming bank, if any, or the issuing bank determines that a presentation does not comply, it may refuse to honour or negotiate.

b. When an issuing bank determines that a presentation does not comply, it may in its sole judgement approach the applicant for a waiver of the discrepancies. This does not, however, extend the period mentioned in sub-article 14 (b).

c. When a nominated bank acting on its nomination, a confirming bank, if any, or the issuing bank decides to refuse to honour or negotiate, it must give a single notice to that effect to the presenter.

The notice must state:

i. that the bank is refusing to honour or negotiate; and

ii. each discrepancy in respect of which the bank refuses to honour or negotiate; and

iii. a) that the bank is holding the documents pending further instructions from the presenter; or

b) that the issuing bank is holding the documents until it receives a waiver from the applicant and agrees to accept it, or receives further instructions from the presenter prior to agreeing to accept a waiver; or

c) that the bank is returning the documents; or

d) that the bank is acting in accordance with instructions previously received from the presenter.

d. The notice required in sub-article 16 (c) must be given by telecommunication or, if that is not possible, by other expeditious means no later than the close of the fifth banking day following the day of presentation.

e. A nominated bank acting on its nomination, a confirming bank, if any, or the issuing bank may, after providing notice required by sub-article 16 (c) (iii) (a) or (b), return the documents to the presenter at any time.

f. If an issuing bank or a confirming bank fails to act in accordance with the provisions of this article, it shall be precluded from claiming that the documents do not constitute a complying presentation.

g. When an issuing bank refuses to honour or a confirming bank refuses to honour or negotiate and has given notice to that effect in accordance with this article, it shall then be entitled to claim a refund, with interest, of any reimbursement made.

Article 17

Original documents and copies

a. At least one original of each document stipulated in the credit must be presented.

b. A bank shall treat as an original any document bearing an apparently original signature, mark, stamp, or label of the issuer of the document, unless the document itself indicates that it is not an original.

c. Unless a document indicates otherwise, a bank will also accept a document as original if it:
   i. appears to be written, typed, perforated or stamped by the document issuer's hand; or
   ii. appears to be on the document issuer's original stationery; or
   iii. states that it is original, unless the statement appears not to apply to the document presented.

d. If a credit requires presentation of copies of documents, presentation of either originals or copies is permitted.

e. If a credit requires presentation of multiple documents by using terms such as "in duplicate", "in two fold" or "in two copies", this will be satisfied by the presentation of at least one original and the remaining number in copies, except when the document itself indicates otherwise.

Article 18

Commercial invoice

a. A commercial invoice:
   i. must appear to have been issued by the beneficiary (except as provided in article 38);
   ii. must be made out in the name of the applicant (except as provided in sub-article 38 (g));
   iii. must be made out in the same currency as the credit; and
   iv. need not be signed.

b. A nominated bank acting on its nomination, a confirming bank, if any, or the issuing bank may accept a commercial invoice issued for an amount in excess of the amount permitted by the credit, and its decision will be binding upon all parties, provided the bank in question has not honoured or negotiated for an amount in excess of that permitted by the credit.

c. The description of the goods, services or performance in a commercial invoice must correspond with that appearing in the credit.

Article 19

Transport document covering at least two different modes of transport

a. A transport document covering at least two different modes of transport (multi-modal or combined transport document), however named, must appear to:
   i. indicate the name of the carrier and be signed by:
      - the carrier or a named agent for or on behalf of the carrier, or
      - the master or a named agent for or on behalf of the master.

      Any signature by the carrier, master or agent must be identified as that of the carrier, master or agent.

      Any signature by an agent must indicate whether the agent has signed for or on behalf of the carrier or for or on behalf of the master.
   ii. indicate that the goods have been dispatched, taken in charge or shipped on board at the place stated in the credit, by:
      - pre-printed wording, or
      - a stamp or notation indicating the date on which the goods have been dispatched, taken in charge or shipped on board.

      The date of issuance of the transport document will be deemed to be the date of dispatch, taking in charge or shipped on board, and the date of shipment. However, if the transport document indicates, by stamp or notation, a date of dispatch, taking in charge or shipped on board, this date will be deemed to be the date of shipment.
   iii. indicate the place of dispatch, taking in charge or shipment, and the place of final destination stated in the credit, even if:
      a) the transport document states, in addition, a different place of dispatch, taking in charge or shipment or place of final destination, or
      b) the transport document contains the indication "intended" or similar qualification in relation to the vessel, port of loading or port of discharge.
   iv. be the sole original transport document or, if issued in more than one original, be the full set as indicated on the transport document.
   v. contain terms and conditions of carriage or make reference to another source containing the terms and conditions of carriage (short form or blank back transport document). Contents of terms and conditions of carriage will not be examined.
   vi. contain no indication that it is subject to a charter party.

b. For the purpose of this article, transhipment means unloading from one means of conveyance and reloading to another means of conveyance (whether or not in different modes of transport) during the carriage from the place of dispatch, taking in charge or shipment to the place of final destination stated in the credit.

c. i. A transport document may indicate that the goods will or may be transhipped provided that the entire carriage is covered by one and the same transport document.
   ii. A transport document indicating that transhipment will or may take place is acceptable, even if the credit prohibits transhipment.

Article 20

Bill of lading

a. A bill of lading, however named, must appear to:

i. indicate the name of the carrier and be signed by:
   - the carrier or a named agent for or on behalf of the carrier, or
   - the master or a named agent for or on behalf of the master.

   Any signature by the carrier, master or agent must be identified as that of the carrier, master or agent.

   Any signature by an agent must indicate whether the agent has signed for or on behalf of the carrier or for or on behalf of the master.

ii. indicate that the goods have been shipped on board a named vessel at the port of loading stated in the credit by:
   - pre-printed wording, or
   - an on board notation indicating the date on which the goods have been shipped on board.

   The date of issuance of the bill of lading will be deemed to be the date of shipment unless the bill of lading contains an on board notation indicating the date of shipment, in which case the date stated in the on board notation will be deemed to be the date of shipment.

   If the bill of lading contains the indication "intended vessel" or similar qualification in relation to the name of the vessel, an on board notation indicating the date of shipment and the name of the actual vessel is required.

iii. indicate shipment from the port of loading to the port of discharge stated in the credit.

   If the bill of lading does not indicate the port of loading stated in the credit as the port of loading, or if it contains the indication "intended" or similar qualification in relation to the port of loading, an on board notation indicating the port of loading as stated in the credit, the date of shipment and the name of the vessel is required. This provision applies even when loading on board or shipment on a named vessel is indicated by pre-printed wording on the bill of lading.

iv. be the sole original bill of lading or, if issued in more than one original, be the full set as indicated on the bill of lading.

v. contain terms and conditions of carriage or make reference to another source containing the terms and conditions of carriage (short form or blank back bill of lading). Contents of terms and conditions of carriage will not be examined.

vi. contain no indication that it is subject to a charter party.

b. For the purpose of this article, transhipment means unloading from one vessel and reloading to another vessel during the carriage from the port of loading to the port of discharge stated in the credit.

c. i. A bill of lading may indicate that the goods will or may be transhipped provided that the entire carriage is covered by one and the same bill of lading.

   ii. A bill of lading indicating that transhipment will or may take place is acceptable, even if the credit prohibits transhipment, if the goods have been shipped in a container, trailer or LASH barge as evidenced by the bill of lading.

d. Clauses in a bill of lading stating that the carrier reserves the right to tranship will be disregarded.

Article 21

Non-negotiable sea waybill

a. A non-negotiable sea waybill, however named, must appear to:

i. indicate the name of the carrier and be signed by:
   - the carrier or a named agent for or on behalf of the carrier, or
   - the master or a named agent for or on behalf of the master.

   Any signature by the carrier, master or agent must be identified as that of the carrier, master or agent.

   Any signature by an agent must indicate whether the agent has signed for or on behalf of the carrier or for or on behalf of the master.

ii. indicate that the goods have been shipped on board a named vessel at the port of loading stated in the credit by:
   - pre-printed wording, or
   - an on board notation indicating the date on which the goods have been shipped on board.

   The date of issuance of the non-negotiable sea waybill will be deemed to be the date of shipment unless the non-negotiable sea waybill contains an on board notation indicating the date of shipment, in which case the date stated in the on board notation will be deemed to be the date of shipment.

   If the non-negotiable sea waybill contains the indication "intended vessel" or similar qualification in relation to the name of the vessel, an on board notation indicating the date of shipment and the name of the actual vessel is required.

iii. indicate shipment from the port of loading to the port of discharge stated in the credit.

   If the non-negotiable sea waybill does not indicate the port of loading stated in the credit as the port of loading, or if it contains the indication "intended" or similar qualification in relation to the port of loading, an on board notation indicating the port of loading as stated in the credit, the date of shipment and the name of the vessel is required. This provision applies even when loading on board or shipment on a named vessel is indicated by pre-printed wording on the non-negotiable sea waybill.

iv. be the sole original non-negotiable sea waybill or, if issued in more than one original, be the full set as indicated on the non-negotiable sea waybill.

v. contain terms and conditions of carriage or make reference to another source containing the terms and conditions of carriage (short form or blank back non-negotiable sea waybill). Contents of terms and conditions of carriage will not be examined.

vi. contain no indication that it is subject to a charter party.

b. For the purpose of this article, transhipment means unloading from one vessel and reloading to another vessel during the carriage from the port of loading to the port of discharge stated in the credit.

c. i. A non-negotiable sea waybill may indicate that the goods will or may be transhipped provided that the entire carriage is covered by one and the same non-negotiable sea waybill.

   ii. A non-negotiable sea waybill indicating that transhipment will or may take place is acceptable, even if the credit prohibits transhipment, if the goods have been shipped in a container, trailer or LASH barge as evidenced by the non-negotiable sea waybill.

d. Clauses in a non-negotiable sea waybill stating that the carrier reserves the right to tranship will be disregarded.

Article 22

Charter party bill of lading

a. A bill of lading, however named, containing an indication that it is subject to a charter party (charter party bill of lading), must appear to:
   i. be signed by:
      - the master or a named agent for or on behalf of the master, or
      - the owner or a named agent for or on behalf of the owner, or
      - the charterer or a named agent for or on behalf of the charterer.

      Any signature by the master, owner, charterer or agent must be identified as that of the master, owner, charterer or agent.

      Any signature by an agent must indicate whether the agent has signed for or on behalf of the master, owner or charterer.

      An agent signing for or on behalf of the owner or charterer must indicate the name of the owner or charterer.
   ii. indicate that the goods have been shipped on board a named vessel at the port of loading stated in the credit by:
      - pre-printed wording, or
      - an on board notation indicating the date on which the goods have been shipped on board.

      The date of issuance of the charter party bill of lading will be deemed to be the date of shipment unless the charter party bill of lading contains an on board notation indicating the date of shipment, in which case the date stated in the on board notation will be deemed to be the date of shipment.
   iii. indicate shipment from the port of loading to the port of discharge stated in the credit. The port of discharge may also be shown as a range of ports or a geographical area, as stated in the credit.
   iv. be the sole original charter party bill of lading or, if issued in more than one original, be the full set as indicated on the charter party bill of lading.

b. A bank will not examine charter party contracts, even if they are required to be presented by the terms of the credit.

Article 23

Air transport document

a. An air transport document, however named, must appear to:
   i. indicate the name of the carrier and be signed by:
      - the carrier, or
      - a named agent for or on behalf of the carrier.

      Any signature by the carrier or agent must be identified as that of the carrier or agent.

      Any signature by an agent must indicate that the agent has signed for or on behalf of the carrier.
   ii. indicate that the goods have been accepted for carriage.
   iii. indicate the date of issuance. This date will be deemed to be the date of shipment unless the air transport document contains a specific notation of the actual date of shipment, in which case the date stated in the notation will be deemed to be the date of shipment.

Any other information appearing on the air transport document relative to the flight number and date will not be considered in determining the date of shipment.

iv. indicate the airport of departure and the airport of destination stated in the credit.

v. be the original for consignor or shipper, even if the credit stipulates a full set of originals.

vi. contain terms and conditions of carriage or make reference to another source containing the terms and conditions of carriage. Contents of terms and conditions of carriage will not be examined.

b. For the purpose of this article, transhipment means unloading from one aircraft and reloading to another aircraft during the carriage from the airport of departure to the airport of destination stated in the credit.

c. i. An air transport document may indicate that the goods will or may be transhipped, provided that the entire carriage is covered by one and the same air transport document.

ii. An air transport document indicating that transhipment will or may take place is acceptable, even if the credit prohibits transhipment.

Article 24

Road, rail or inland waterway transport documents

a. A road, rail or inland waterway transport document, however named, must appear to:

i. indicate the name of the carrier and:

- be signed by the carrier or a named agent for or on behalf of the carrier, or
- indicate receipt of the goods by signature, stamp or notation by the carrier or a named agent for or on behalf of the carrier.

Any signature, stamp or notation of receipt of the goods by the carrier or agent must be identified as that of the carrier or agent.

Any signature, stamp or notation of receipt of the goods by the agent must indicate that the agent has signed or acted for or on behalf of the carrier.

If a rail transport document does not identify the carrier, any signature or stamp of the railway company will be accepted as evidence of the document being signed by the carrier.

ii. indicate the date of shipment or the date the goods have been received for shipment, dispatch or carriage at the place stated in the credit. Unless the transport document contains a dated reception stamp, an indication of the date of receipt or a date of shipment, the date of issuance of the transport document will be deemed to be the date of shipment.

iii. indicate the place of shipment and the place of destination stated in the credit.

b. i. A road transport document must appear to be the original for consignor or shipper or bear no marking indicating for whom the document has been prepared.

ii. A rail transport document marked "duplicate" will be accepted as an original.

iii. A rail or inland waterway transport document will be accepted as an original whether marked as an original or not.

c. In the absence of an indication on the transport document as to the number of originals issued, the number presented will be deemed to constitute a full set.

d. For the purpose of this article, transhipment means unloading from one means of conveyance and reloading to another means of conveyance, within the same mode of transport, during the carriage from the place of shipment, dispatch or carriage to the place of destination stated in the credit.

e. i. A road, rail or inland waterway transport document may indicate that the goods will or may be transhipped provided that the entire carriage is covered by one and the same transport document.

ii. A road, rail or inland waterway transport document indicating that transhipment will or may take place is acceptable, even if the credit prohibits transhipment.

Article 25

Courier receipt, post receipt or certificate of posting

a. A courier receipt, however named, evidencing receipt of goods for transport, must appear to:

i. indicate the name of the courier service and be stamped or signed by the named courier service at the place from which the credit states the goods are to be shipped; and

ii. indicate a date of pickup or of receipt or wording to this effect. This date will be deemed to be the date of shipment.

b. A requirement that courier charges are to be paid or prepaid may be satisfied by a transport document issued by a courier service evidencing that courier charges are for the account of a party other than the consignee.

c. A post receipt or certificate of posting, however named, evidencing receipt of goods for transport, must appear to be stamped or signed and dated at the place from which the credit states the goods are to be shipped. This date will be deemed to be the date of shipment.

Article 26

"On deck", "shipper's load and count", "said by shipper to contain" and charges additional to freight

a. A transport document must not indicate that the goods are or will be loaded on deck. A clause on a transport document stating that the goods may be loaded on deck is acceptable.

b. A transport document bearing a clause such as "shipper's load and count" and "said by shipper to contain" is acceptable.

c. A transport document may bear a reference, by stamp or otherwise, to charges additional to the freight.

Article 27

Clean transport document

A bank will only accept a clean transport document. A clean transport document is one bearing no clause or notation expressly declaring a defective condition of the goods or their packaging. The word "clean" need not appear on a transport document, even if a credit has a requirement for that transport document to be "clean on board".

Article 28

Insurance document and coverage

a. An insurance document, such as an insurance policy, an insurance certificate or a declaration under an open cover, must appear to be issued and signed by an insurance company, an underwriter or their agents or their proxies.

   Any signature by an agent or proxy must indicate whether the agent or proxy has signed for or on behalf of the insurance company or underwriter.

b. When the insurance document indicates that it has been issued in more than one original, all originals must be presented.

c. Cover notes will not be accepted.

d. An insurance policy is acceptable in lieu of an insurance certificate or a declaration under an open cover.

e. The date of the insurance document must be no later than the date of shipment, unless it appears from the insurance document that the cover is effective from a date not later than the date of shipment.

f. i. The insurance document must indicate the amount of insurance coverage and be in the same currency as the credit.

   ii. A requirement in the credit for insurance coverage to be for a percentage of the value of the goods, of the invoice value or similar is deemed to be the minimum amount of coverage required.

   If there is no indication in the credit of the insurance coverage required, the amount of insurance coverage must be at least 110% of the CIF or CIP value of the goods.

   When the CIF or CIP value cannot be determined from the documents, the amount of insurance coverage must be calculated on the basis of the amount for which honour or negotiation is requested or the gross value of the goods as shown on the invoice, whichever is greater.

   iii. The insurance document must indicate that risks are covered at least between the place of taking in charge or shipment and the place of discharge or final destination as stated in the credit.

g. A credit should state the type of insurance required and, if any, the additional risks to be covered. An insurance document will be accepted without regard to any risks that are not covered if the credit uses imprecise terms such as "usual risks" or "customary risks".

h. When a credit requires insurance against "all risks" and an insurance document is presented containing any "all risks" notation or clause, whether or not bearing the heading "all risks", the insurance document will be accepted without regard to any risks stated to be excluded.

i. An insurance document may contain reference to any exclusion clause.

j. An insurance document may indicate that the cover is subject to a franchise or excess (deductible).

Article 29

Extension of expiry date or last day for presentation

a. If the expiry date of a credit or the last day for presentation falls on a day when the bank to which presentation is to be made is closed for reasons other than those referred to in article 36, the expiry date or the last day for presentation, as the case may be, will be extended to the first following banking day.
b. If presentation is made on the first following banking day, a nominated bank must provide the issuing bank or confirming bank with a statement on its covering schedule that the presentation was made within the time limits extended in accordance with sub-article 29 (a).
c. The latest date for shipment will not be extended as a result of sub-article 29 (a).

Article 30

Tolerance in credit amount, quantity and unit prices

a. The words "about" or "approximately" used in connection with the amount of the credit or the quantity or the unit price stated in the credit are to be construed as allowing a tolerance not to exceed 10% more or 10% less than the amount, the quantity or the unit price to which they refer.
b. A tolerance not to exceed 5% more or 5% less than the quantity of the goods is allowed, provided the credit does not state the quantity in terms of a stipulated number of packing units or individual items and the total amount of the drawings does not exceed the amount of the credit.
c. Even when partial shipments are not allowed, a tolerance not to exceed 5% less than the amount of the credit is allowed, provided that the quantity of the goods, if stated in the credit, is shipped in full and a unit price, if stated in the credit, is not reduced or that sub-article 30 (b) is not applicable. This tolerance does not apply when the credit stipulates a specific tolerance or uses the expressions referred to in sub-article 30 (a).

Article 31

Partial drawings or shipments

a. Partial drawings or shipments are allowed.
b. A presentation consisting of more than one set of transport documents evidencing shipment commencing on the same means of conveyance and for the same journey, provided they indicate the same destination, will not be regarded as covering a partial shipment, even if they indicate different dates of shipment or different ports of loading, places of taking in charge or dispatch. If the presentation consists of more than one set of transport documents, the latest date of shipment as evidenced on any of the sets of transport documents will be regarded as the date of shipment.

   A presentation consisting of one or more sets of transport documents evidencing shipment on more than one means of conveyance within the same mode of transport will be regarded as covering a partial shipment, even if the means of conveyance leave on the same day for the same destination.
c. A presentation consisting of more than one courier receipt, post receipt or certificate of posting will not be regarded as a partial shipment if the courier receipts, post

receipts or certificates of posting appear to have been stamped or signed by the same courier or postal service at the same place and date and for the same destination.

Article 32

Instalment drawings or shipments

If a drawing or shipment by instalments within given periods is stipulated in the credit and any instalment is not drawn or shipped within the period allowed for that instalment, the credit ceases to be available for that and any subsequent instalment.

Article 33

Hours of presentation

A bank has no obligation to accept a presentation outside of its banking hours.

Article 34

Disclaimer on effectiveness of documents

A bank assumes no liability or responsibility for the form, sufficiency, accuracy, genuineness, falsification or legal effect of any document, or for the general or particular conditions stipulated in a document or superimposed thereon; nor does it assume any liability or responsibility for the description, quantity, weight, quality, condition, packing, delivery, value or existence of the goods, services or other performance represented by any document, or for the good faith or acts or omissions, solvency, performance or standing of the consignor, the carrier, the forwarder, the consignee or the insurer of the goods or any other person.

Article 35

Disclaimer on transmission and translation

A bank assumes no liability or responsibility for the consequences arising out of delay, loss in transit, mutilation or other errors arising in the transmission of any messages or delivery of letters or documents, when such messages, letters or documents are transmitted or sent according to the requirements stated in the credit, or when the bank may have taken the initiative in the choice of the delivery service in the absence of such instructions in the credit.

If a nominated bank determines that a presentation is complying and forwards the documents to the issuing bank or confirming bank, whether or not the nominated bank has honoured or negotiated, an issuing bank or confirming bank must honour or negotiate, or reimburse that nominated bank, even when the documents have been lost in transit between the nominated bank and the issuing bank or confirming bank, or between the confirming bank and the issuing bank.

A bank assumes no liability or responsibility for errors in translation or interpretation of technical terms and may transmit credit terms without translating them.

Article 36

Force majeure

A bank assumes no liability or responsibility for the consequences arising out of the interruption of its business by Acts of God, riots, civil commotions, insurrections, wars, acts of terrorism, or by any strikes or lockouts or any other causes beyond its control.

A bank will not, upon resumption of its business, honour or negotiate under a credit that expired during such interruption of its business.

Article 37

Disclaimer for acts of an instructed party

a. A bank utilizing the services of another bank for the purpose of giving effect to the instructions of the applicant does so for the account and at the risk of the applicant.

b. An issuing bank or advising bank assumes no liability or responsibility should the instructions it transmits to another bank not be carried out, even if it has taken the initiative in the choice of that other bank.

c. A bank instructing another bank to perform services is liable for any commissions, fees, costs or expenses ("charges") incurred by that bank in connection with its instructions.
If a credit states that charges are for the account of the beneficiary and charges cannot be collected or deducted from proceeds, the issuing bank remains liable for payment of charges.
A credit or amendment should not stipulate that the advising to a beneficiary is conditional upon the receipt by the advising bank or second advising bank of its charges.

d. The applicant shall be bound by and liable to indemnify a bank against all obligations and responsibilities imposed by foreign laws and usages.

Article 38

Transferable credits

a. A bank is under no obligation to transfer a credit except to the extent and in the manner expressly consented to by that bank.

b. For the purpose of this article:
Transferable credit means a credit that specifically states it is "transferable". A transferable credit may be made available in whole or in part to another beneficiary ("second beneficiary") at the request of the beneficiary ("first beneficiary").
Transferring bank means a nominated bank that transfers the credit or, in a credit available with any bank, a bank that is specifically authorized by the issuing bank to transfer and that transfers the credit. An issuing bank may be a transferring bank.
Transferred credit means a credit that has been made available by the transferring bank to a second beneficiary.

c. Unless otherwise agreed at the time of transfer, all charges (such as commissions, fees, costs or expenses) incurred in respect of a transfer must be paid by the first beneficiary.

d. A credit may be transferred in part to more than one second beneficiary provided partial drawings or shipments are allowed.
A transferred credit cannot be transferred at the request of a second beneficiary to any subsequent beneficiary. The first beneficiary is not considered to be a subsequent beneficiary.

e. Any request for transfer must indicate if and under what conditions amendments may be advised to the second beneficiary. The transferred credit must clearly indicate those conditions.

f. If a credit is transferred to more than one second beneficiary, rejection of an amendment by one or more second beneficiary does not invalidate the acceptance by any other second beneficiary, with respect to which the transferred credit will be amended accordingly. For any second beneficiary that rejected the amendment, the transferred credit will remain unamended.

g. The transferred credit must accurately reflect the terms and conditions of the credit, including confirmation, if any, with the exception of:
   - the amount of the credit,
   - any unit price stated therein,
   - the expiry date,
   - the period for presentation, or
   - the latest shipment date or given period for shipment,

   any or all of which may be reduced or curtailed.

   The percentage for which insurance cover must be effected may be increased to provide the amount of cover stipulated in the credit or these articles.

   The name of the first beneficiary may be substituted for that of the applicant in the credit.

   If the name of the applicant is specifically required by the credit to appear in any document other than the invoice, such requirement must be reflected in the transferred credit.

h. The first beneficiary has the right to substitute its own invoice and draft, if any, for those of a second beneficiary for an amount not in excess of that stipulated in the credit, and upon such substitution the first beneficiary can draw under the credit for the difference, if any, between its invoice and the invoice of a second beneficiary.

i. If the first beneficiary is to present its own invoice and draft, if any, but fails to do so on first demand, or if the invoices presented by the first beneficiary create discrepancies that did not exist in the presentation made by the second beneficiary and the first beneficiary fails to correct them on first demand, the transferring bank has the right to present the documents as received from the second beneficiary to the issuing bank, without further responsibility to the first beneficiary.

j. The first beneficiary may, in its request for transfer, indicate that honour or negotiation is to be effected to a second beneficiary at the place to which the credit has been transferred, up to and including the expiry date of the credit. This is without prejudice to the right of the first beneficiary in accordance with sub-article 38 (h).

k. Presentation of documents by or on behalf of a second beneficiary must be made to the transferring bank.

Article 39

Assignment of proceeds

The fact that a credit is not stated to be transferable shall not affect the right of the beneficiary to assign any proceeds to which it may be or may become entitled under the credit, in accordance with the provisions of applicable law. This article relates only to the assignment of proceeds and not to the assignment of the right to perform under the credit.

Supplement to the Uniform Customs and Practice for Documentary Credits for Electronic Presentation

Article e1

Scope of the eUCP 600

a. The Supplement to the Uniform Customs and Practice for Documentary Credits for Electronic Presentation ("eUCP 600") supplements the Uniform Customs and Practice for Documentary Credits (2007 Revision ICC Publication No. 600) ("UCP 600") in order to accommodate presentation of electronic records alone or in combination with paper documents.
b. The eUCP 600 shall apply as a supplement to the UCP 600 where the credit indicates that it is subject to eUCP 600.
c. This version is Version 1.1. A credit must indicate the applicable version of the eUCP 600. If it does not do so, it is subject to the version in effect on the date the credit is issued or, if made subject to eUCP 600 by an amendment accepted by the beneficiary, on the date of that amendment.

Article e2

Relationship of the eUCP 600 to the UCP 600

a. A credit subject to the eUCP 600 ("eUCP 600 credit") is also subject to the UCP 600 without express incorporation of the UCP 600.
b. Where the eUCP 600 applies, its provisions shall prevail to the extent that they would produce a result different from the application of the UCP 600.
c. If an eUCP 600 credit allows the beneficiary to choose between presentation of paper documents or electronic records and it chooses to present only paper documents, the UCP 600 alone shall apply to that presentation. If only paper documents are permitted under an eUCP 600 credit, the UCP 600 alone shall apply.

Article e3

Definitions

a. Where the following terms are used in the UCP 600, for the purposes of applying the UCP 600 to an electronic record presented under an eUCP 600 credit, the term:
    i. appear on their face and the like shall apply to examination of the data content of an electronic record.
    ii. document shall include an electronic record.
    iii. place for presentation of electronic records means an electronic address.
    iv. sign and the like shall include an electronic signature.
    v. superimposed, notation or stamped means data content whose supplementary character is apparent in an electronic record.
b. The following terms used in the eUCP 600 shall have the following meanings:
    i. electronic record means
        - data created, generated, sent, communicated, received or stored by electronic means

- that is capable of being authenticated as to the apparent identity of a sender and the apparent source of the data contained in it, and as to whether it has remained complete and unaltered, and
- is capable of being examined for compliance with the terms and conditions of the eUCP 600 credit.

ii. electronic signature means a data process attached to or logically associated with an electronic record and executed or adopted by a person in order to identify that person and to indicate that person's authentication of the electronic record.

iii. format means the data organization in which the electronic record is expressed or to which it refers.

iv. paper document means a document in a traditional paper form.

v. received means the time when an electronic record enters the information system of the applicable recipient in a form capable of being accepted by that system. Any acknowledgement of receipt does not imply acceptance or refusal of the electronic record under an eUCP 600 credit.

Article e4

Format

An eUCP 600 credit must specify the formats in which electronic records are to be presented. If the format of the electronic record is not so specified, it may be presented in any format.

Article e5

Presentation

a. An eUCP 600 credit allowing presentation of:
   i. electronic records must state a place for presentation of the electronic records.
   ii. both electronic records and paper documents must also state a place for presentation of the paper documents.

b. Electronic records may be presented separately and need not be presented at the same time.

c. If an eUCP 600 credit allows for presentation of one or more electronic records, the beneficiary is responsible for providing a notice to the bank to which presentation is made signifying when the presentation is complete. The notice of completeness may be given as an electronic record or paper document and must identify the eUCP 600 credit to which it relates. Presentation is deemed not to have been made if the beneficiary's notice is not received.

d. i. Each presentation of an electronic record and the presentation of paper documents under an eUCP 600 credit must identify the eUCP 600 credit under which it is presented.
   ii. A presentation not so identified may be treated as not received.

e. If the bank to which presentation is to be made is open but its system is unable to receive a transmitted electronic record on the stipulated expiry date and/or the last day of the period of time after the date of shipment for presentation, as the case may be, the bank will be deemed to be closed and the date for presentation and/or the expiry date shall be extended to the first following banking day on which such bank is able to receive an electronic record. If the only electronic record remaining to be presented is the notice of completeness, it may be given by telecommunications or by paper document and will be deemed timely, provided that it is sent before the bank is able to receive an electronic record.

f. An electronic record that cannot be authenticated is deemed not to have been presented.

Article e6

Examination

a. If an electronic record contains a hyperlink to an external system or a presentation indicates that the electronic record may be examined by reference to an external system, the electronic record at the hyperlink or the referenced system shall be deemed to be the electronic record to be examined. The failure of the indicated system to provide access to the required electronic record at the time of examination shall constitute a discrepancy.

b. The forwarding of electronic records by a nominated bank pursuant to its nomination signifies that it has satisfied itself as to the apparent authenticity of the electronic records.

c. The inability of the issuing bank, or confirming bank, if any, to examine an electronic record in a format required by the eUCP 600 credit or, if no format is required, to examine it in the format presented is not a basis for refusal.

Article e7

Notice of refusal

a. i. The time period for the examination of documents commences on the banking day following the banking day on which the beneficiary's notice of completeness is received.

ii. If the time for presentation of documents or the notice of completeness is extended, the time for the examination of documents commences on the first following banking day on which the bank to which presentation is to be made is able to receive the notice of completeness.

b. If an issuing bank, the confirming bank, if any, or a nominated bank acting on their behalf, provides a notice of refusal of a presentation which includes electronic records and does not receive instructions from the party to which notice of refusal is given within 30 calendar days from the date the notice of refusal is given for the disposition of the electronic records, the bank shall return any paper documents not previously returned to the presenter but may dispose of the electronic records in any manner deemed appropriate without any responsibility.

Article e8

Originals and copies

Any requirement of the UCP 600 or an eUCP 600 credit for presentation of one or more originals or copies of an electronic record is satisfied by the presentation of one electronic record.

Article e9

Date of issuance

Unless an electronic record contains a specific date of issuance, the date on which it appears to have been sent by the issuer is deemed to be the date of issuance. The date of receipt will be deemed to be the date it was sent if no other date is apparent.

Article e10

Transport

If an electronic record evidencing transport does not indicate a date of shipment or dispatch, the date of issuance of the electronic record will be deemed to be the date of shipment or dispatch. However, if the electronic record bears a notation that evidences the date of shipment or dispatch, the date of the notation will be deemed to be the date of shipment or dispatch. A notation showing additional data content need not be separately signed or otherwise authenticated.

Article e11

Corruption of an electronic record after presentation

a. If an electronic record that has been received by the issuing bank, confirming bank, or another nominated bank appears to have been corrupted, the bank may inform the presenter and may request that the electronic record be re-presented.
b. If the bank requests that an electronic record be re-presented:
    i. the time for examination is suspended and resumes when the presenter re-presents the electronic record; and
    ii. if the nominated bank is not the confirming bank, it must provide the issuing bank and any confirming bank with notice of the request for re-presentation and inform it of the suspension; but
    iii. if the same electronic record is not re-presented within thirty (30) calendar days, the bank may treat the electronic record as not presented, and
    iv. any deadlines are not extended.

Article e12

Additional disclaimer of liability for presentation of electronic records under eUCP 600

By satisfying itself as to the apparent authenticity of an electronic record, banks assume no liability for the identity of the sender, source of the information or its complete and unaltered character other than that which is apparent in the electronic record received by the use of a commercially acceptable data process for the receipt, authentication and identification of electronic records.

APPENDIX VII

Vienna Convention on sale of goods 1980

1. United Nations Convention on Contracts for the International Sale of Goods

PREAMBLE

The States Parties to this Convention,

Bearing in mind the broad objectives in the resolutions adopted by the sixth special session of the General Assembly of the United Nations on the establishment of a New International Economic Order,

Considering that the development of international trade on the basis of equality and mutual benefit is an important element in promoting friendly relations among States,

Being of the opinion that the adoption of uniform rules which govern contracts for the international sale of goods and take into account the different social, economic and legal systems would contribute to the removal of legal barriers in international trade and promote the development of international trade,

Have agreed as follows:

Part I. Sphere of application and general provisions

CHAPTER I. SPHERE OF APPLICATION

Article 1

(1) This Convention applies to contracts of sale of goods between parties whose places of business are in different States:

(a) when the States are Contracting States; or

(b) when the rules of private international law lead to the application of the law of a Contracting State.

(2) The fact that the parties have their places of business in different States is to be disregarded whenever this fact does not appear either from the contract or from any dealings between, or from information disclosed by, the parties at any time before or at the conclusion of the contract.

(3) Neither the nationality of the parties nor the civil or commercial character of the parties or of the contract is to be taken into consideration in determining the application of this Convention.

Article 2

This Convention does not apply to sales:

(a) of goods bought for personal, family or household use, unless the seller, at any time before or at the conclusion of the contract, neither knew nor ought to have known that the goods were bought for any such use;

(b) by auction;

(c) on execution or otherwise by authority of law;

(d) of stocks, shares, investment securities, negotiable instruments or money;

(e) of ships, vessels, hovercraft or aircraft;

(f) of electricity.

Article 3

(1) Contracts for the supply of goods to be manufactured or produced are to be considered sales unless the party who orders the goods undertakes to supply a substantial part of the materials necessary for such manufacture or production.

(2) This Convention does not apply to contracts in which the preponderant part of the obligations of the party who furnishes the goods consists in the supply of labour or other services.

Article 4

This Convention governs only the formation of the contract of sale and the rights and obligations of the seller and the buyer arising from such a contract. In particular, except as otherwise expressly provided in this Convention, it is not concerned with:

(a) the validity of the contract or of any of its provisions or of any usage;

(b) the effect which the contract may have on the property in the goods sold.

Article 5

This Convention does not apply to the liability of the seller for death or personal injury caused by the goods to any person.

Article 6

The parties may exclude the application of this Convention or, subject to article 12, derogate from or vary the effect of any of its provisions.

CHAPTER II. GENERAL PROVISIONS

Article 7

(1) In the interpretation of this Convention, regard is to be had to its international character and to the need to promote uniformity in its application and the observance of good faith in international trade.

(2) Questions concerning matters governed by this Convention which are not expressly settled in it are to be settled in conformity with the general principles on which it is based or, in the absence of such principles, in conformity with the law applicable by virtue of the rules of private international law.

Article 8

(1) For the purposes of this Convention statements made by and other conduct of a party are to be interpreted according to his intent where the other party knew or could not have been unaware what that intent was.

(2) If the preceding paragraph is not applicable, statements made by and other conduct of a party are to be interpreted according to the understanding that a reasonable person of the same kind as the other party would have had in the same circumstances.

(3) In determining the intent of a party or the understanding a reasonable person would have had, due consideration is to be given to all relevant circumstances of the case including the negotiations, any practices which the parties have established between themselves, usages and any subsequent conduct of the parties.

Article 9

(1) The parties are bound by any usage to which they have agreed and by any practices which they have established between themselves.

(2) The parties are considered, unless otherwise agreed, to have impliedly made applicable to their contract or its formation a usage of which the parties knew or ought to have known and which in international trade is widely known to, and regularly observed by, parties to contracts of the type involved in the particular trade concerned.

Article 10

For the purposes of this Convention:

(a) if a party has more than one place of business, the place of business is that which has the closest relationship to the contract and its performance, having regard to the circumstances known to or contemplated by the parties at any time before or at the conclusion of the contract;

(b) if a party does not have a place of business, reference is to be made to his habitual residence.

Article 11

A contract of sale need not be concluded in or evidenced by writing and is not subject to any other requirement as to form. It may be proved by any means, including witnesses.

Article 12

Any provision of article 11, article 29 or Part II of this Convention that allows a contract of sale or its modification or termination by agreement or any offer, acceptance or other indication of intention to be made in any form other than in writing does not apply where any party has his place of business in a Contracting State which has made a declaration under article 96 of this Convention. The parties may not derogate from or vary the effect of this article.

Article 13

For the purposes of this Convention "writing" includes telegram and telex.

Part II. Formation of the contract

Article 14

(1) A proposal for concluding a contract addressed to one or more specific persons constitutes an offer if it is sufficiently definite and indicates the intention of the offeror to be bound in case of acceptance. A proposal is sufficiently definite if it indicates the goods and expressly or implicitly fixes or makes provision for determining the quantity and the price.

(2) A proposal other than one addressed to one or more specific persons is to be considered merely as an invitation to make offers, unless the contrary is clearly indicated by the person making the proposal.

Article 15

(1) An offer becomes effective when it reaches the offeree.

(2) An offer, even if it is irrevocable, may be withdrawn if the withdrawal reaches the offeree before or at the same time as the offer.

Article 16

(1) Until a contract is concluded an offer may be revoked if the revocation reaches the offeree before he has dispatched an acceptance.

(2) However, an offer cannot be revoked:

(a) if it indicates, whether by stating a fixed time for acceptance or otherwise, that it is irrevocable; or

(b) if it was reasonable for the offeree to rely on the offer as being irrevocable and the offeree has acted in reliance on the offer.

Article 17

An offer, even if it is irrevocable, is terminated when a rejection reaches the offeror.

Article 18

(1) A statement made by or other conduct of the offeree indicating assent to an offer is an acceptance. Silence or inactivity does not in itself amount to acceptance.

(2) An acceptance of an offer becomes effective at the moment the indication of assent reaches the offeror. An acceptance is not effective if the indication of assent does not reach the offeror within the time he has fixed or, if no time is fixed, within a reasonable time, due account being taken of the circumstances of the transaction, including the rapidity of the means of communication employed by the offeror. An oral offer must be accepted immediately unless the circumstances indicate otherwise.

(3) However, if, by virtue of the offer or as a result of practices which the parties have established between themselves or of usage, the offeree may indicate assent by performing an act, such as one relating to the dispatch of the goods or payment of the price, without notice to the offeror, the acceptance is effective at the moment the act is performed, provided that the act is performed within the period of time laid down in the preceding paragraph.

Article 19

(1) A reply to an offer which purports to be an acceptance but contains additions, limitations or other modifications is a rejection of the offer and constitutes a counter-offer.

(2) However, a reply to an offer which purports to be an acceptance but contains additional or different terms which do not materially alter the terms of the offer constitutes an acceptance, unless the offeror, without undue delay, objects orally to the discrepancy or dispatches a notice to that effect. If he does not so object, the terms of the contract are the terms of the offer with the modifications contained in the acceptance.

(3) Additional or different terms relating, among other things, to the price, payment, quality and quantity of the goods, place and time of delivery, extent of one party's liability to the other or the settlement of disputes are considered to alter the terms of the offer materially.

Article 20

(1) A period of time for acceptance fixed by the offeror in a telegram or a letter begins to run from the moment the telegram is handed in for dispatch or from the date shown on the letter or, if no such date is shown, from the date shown on the envelope. A period of time for acceptance fixed by the offeror by telephone, telex or other means of instantaneous communication, begins to run from the moment that the offer reaches the offeree.

(2) Official holidays or non-business days occurring during the period for acceptance are included in calculating the period. However, if a notice of acceptance cannot be delivered at the address of the offeror on the last day of the period because that day falls on an official holiday or a non-business day at the place of business of the offeror, the period is extended until the first business day which follows.

Article 21

(1) A late acceptance is nevertheless effective as an acceptance if without delay the offeror orally so informs the offeree or dispatches a notice to that effect.

(2) If a letter or other writing containing a late acceptance shows that it has been sent in such circumstances that if its transmission had been normal it would have reached the offeror in due time, the late acceptance is effective as an acceptance unless, without delay, the offeror orally informs the offeree that he considers his offer as having lapsed or dispatches a notice to that effect.

Article 22

An acceptance may be withdrawn if the withdrawal reaches the offeror before or at the same time as the acceptance would have become effective.

Article 23

A contract is concluded at the moment when an acceptance of an offer becomes effective in accordance with the provisions of this Convention.

Article 24

For the purposes of this Part of the Convention, an offer, declaration of acceptance or any other indication of intention "reaches" the addressee when it is made orally to him or delivered by any other means to him personally, to his place of business or mailing address or, if he does not have a place of business or mailing address, to his habitual residence.

Part III. Sale of goods

CHAPTER I. GENERAL PROVISIONS

Article 25

A breach of contract committed by one of the parties is fundamental if it results in such detriment to the other party as substantially to deprive him of what he is entitled to expect under the contract, unless the party in breach did not foresee and a reasonable person of the same kind in the same circumstances would not have foreseen such a result.

Article 26

A declaration of avoidance of the contract is effective only if made by notice to the other party.

Article 27

Unless otherwise expressly provided in this Part of the Convention, if any notice, request or other communication is given or made by a party in accordance with this Part and by means appropriate in the circumstances, a delay or error in the transmission of the communication or its failure to arrive does not deprive that party of the right to rely on the communication.

Article 28

If, in accordance with the provisions of this Convention, one party is entitled to require performance of any obligation by the other party, a court is not bound to enter a judgement for specific performance unless the court would do so under its own law in respect of similar contracts of sale not governed by this Convention.

Article 29

(1) A contract may be modified or terminated by the mere agreement of the parties.

(2) A contract in writing which contains a provision requiring any modification or termination by agreement to be in writing may not be otherwise modified or terminated by agreement. However, a party may be precluded by his conduct from asserting such a provision to the extent that the other party has relied on that conduct.

CHAPTER II. OBLIGATIONS OF THE SELLER

Article 30

The seller must deliver the goods, hand over any documents relating to them and transfer the property in the goods, as required by the contract and this Convention.

Section I. Delivery of the goods and handing over of documents

Article 31

If the seller is not bound to deliver the goods at any other particular place, his obligation to deliver consists:

(a) if the contract of sale involves carriage of the goods – in handing the goods over to the first carrier for transmission to the buyer;

(b) if, in cases not within the preceding subparagraph, the contract relates to specific goods, or unidentified goods to be drawn from a specific stock or to be manufactured or produced, and at the time of the conclusion of the contract the parties knew that the goods were at, or were to be manufactured or produced at, a particular place – in placing the goods at the buyer's disposal at that place;

(c) in other cases – in placing the goods at the buyer's disposal at the place where the seller had his place of business at the time of the conclusion of the contract.

Article 32

(1) If the seller, in accordance with the contract or this Convention, hands the goods over to a carrier and if the goods are not clearly identified to the contract by markings on the goods, by shipping documents or otherwise, the seller must give the buyer notice of the consignment specifying the goods.

(2) If the seller is bound to arrange for carriage of the goods, he must make such contracts as are necessary for carriage to the place fixed by means of transportation appropriate in the circumstances and according to the usual terms for such transportation.

(3) If the seller is not bound to effect insurance in respect of the carriage of the goods, he must, at the buyer's request, provide him with all available information necessary to enable him to effect such insurance.

Article 33

The seller must deliver the goods:

(a) if a date is fixed by or determinable from the contract, on that date;

(b) if a period of time is fixed by or determinable from the contract, at any time within that period unless circumstances indicate that the buyer is to choose a date; or

(c) in any other case, within a reasonable time after the conclusion of the contract.

Article 34

If the seller is bound to hand over documents relating to the goods, he must hand them over at the time and place and in the form required by the contract. If the seller has handed over documents before that time, he may, up to that time, cure any lack of conformity in the documents, if the exercise of this right does not cause the buyer unreasonable inconvenience or unreasonable expense. However, the buyer retains any right to claim damages as provided for in this Convention.

Section II. Conformity of the goods and third-party claims

Article 35

(1) The seller must deliver goods which are of the quantity, quality and description required by the contract and which are contained or packaged in the manner required by the contract.

(2) Except where the parties have agreed otherwise, the goods do not conform with the contract unless they:

(a) are fit for the purposes for which goods of the same description would ordinarily be used;

(b) are fit for any particular purpose expressly or impliedly made known to the seller at the time of the conclusion of the contract, except where the circumstances show that the buyer did not rely, or that it was unreasonable for him to rely, on the seller's skill and judgement;

(c) possess the qualities of goods which the seller has held out to the buyer as a sample or model;

(d) are contained or packaged in the manner usual for such goods or, where there is no such manner, in a manner adequate to preserve and protect the goods.

(3) The seller is not liable under subparagraphs *(a)* to *(d)* of the preceding paragraph for any lack of conformity of the goods if, at the time of the conclusion of the contract, the buyer knew or could not have been unaware of such lack of conformity.

Article 36

(1) The seller is liable in accordance with the contract and this Convention for any lack of conformity which exists at the time when the risk passes to the buyer, even though the lack of conformity becomes apparent only after that time.

(2) The seller is also liable for any lack of conformity which occurs after the time indicated in the preceding paragraph and which is due to a breach of any of his obligations, including a breach of any guarantee that for a period of time the goods will remain fit for their ordinary purpose or for some particular purpose or will retain specified qualities or characteristics.

Article 37

If the seller has delivered goods before the date for delivery, he may, up to that date, deliver any missing part or make up any deficiency in the quantity of the goods delivered, or deliver goods in replacement of any non-conforming goods delivered or remedy any lack of conformity in the goods delivered, provided that the exercise of this right does not cause the buyer unreasonable inconvenience or unreasonable expense. However, the buyer retains any right to claim damages as provided for in this Convention.

Article 38

(1) The buyer must examine the goods, or cause them to be examined, within as short a period as is practicable in the circumstances.

(2) If the contract involves carriage of the goods, examination may be deferred until after the goods have arrived at their destination.

(3) If the goods are redirected in transit or redispatched by the buyer without a reasonable opportunity for examination by him and at the time of the conclusion of the contract the seller knew or ought to have known of the possibility of such redirection or redispatch, examination may be deferred until after the goods have arrived at the new destination.

Article 39

(1) The buyer loses the right to rely on a lack of conformity of the goods if he does not give notice to the seller specifying the nature of the lack of conformity within a reasonable time after he has discovered it or ought to have discovered it.

(2) In any event, the buyer loses the right to rely on a lack of conformity of the goods if he does not give the seller notice thereof at the latest within a period of two years from the date on which the goods were actually handed over to the buyer, unless this time limit is inconsistent with a contractual period of guarantee.

Article 40

The seller is not entitled to rely on the provisions of articles 38 and 39 if the lack of conformity relates to facts of which he knew or could not have been unaware and which he did not disclose to the buyer.

Article 41

The seller must deliver goods which are free from any right or claim of a third party, unless the buyer agreed to take the goods subject to that right or claim. However, if such right or claim is based on industrial property or other intellectual property, the seller's obligation is governed by article 42.

Article 42

(1) The seller must deliver goods which are free from any right or claim of a third party based on industrial property or other intellectual property, of which at the time of the conclusion of the contract the seller knew or could not have been unaware, provided that the right or claim is based on industrial property or other intellectual property:

(a) under the law of the State where the goods will be resold or otherwise used, if it was contemplated by the parties at the time of the conclusion of the contract that the goods would be resold or otherwise used in that State; or

(b) in any other case, under the law of the State where the buyer has his place of business.

(2) The obligation of the seller under the preceding paragraph does not extend to cases where:

(a) at the time of the conclusion of the contract the buyer knew or could not have been unaware of the right or claim; or

(b) the right or claim results from the seller's compliance with technical drawings, designs, formulae or other such specifications furnished by the buyer.

Article 43

(1) The buyer loses the right to rely on the provisions of article 41 or article 42 if he does not give notice to the seller specifying the nature of the right or claim of the third party within a reasonable time after he has become aware or ought to have become aware of the right or claim.

(2) The seller is not entitled to rely on the provisions of the preceding paragraph if he knew of the right or claim of the third party and the nature of it.

Article 44

Notwithstanding the provisions of paragraph (1) of article 39 and paragraph (1) of article 43, the buyer may reduce the price in accordance with article 50 or claim damages, except for loss of profit, if he has a reasonable excuse for his failure to give the required notice.

Section III. Remedies for breach of contract by the seller

Article 45

(1) If the seller fails to perform any of his obligations under the contract or this Convention, the buyer may:

(a) exercise the rights provided in articles 46 to 52;

(b) claim damages as provided in articles 74 to 77.

(2) The buyer is not deprived of any right he may have to claim damages by exercising his right to other remedies.

(3) No period of grace may be granted to the seller by a court or arbitral tribunal when the buyer resorts to a remedy for breach of contract.

Article 46

(1) The buyer may require performance by the seller of his obligations unless the buyer has resorted to a remedy which is inconsistent with this requirement.

(2) If the goods do not conform with the contract, the buyer may require delivery of substitute goods only if the lack of conformity constitutes a fundamental breach of contract and a request for substitute goods is made either in conjunction with notice given under article 39 or within a reasonable time thereafter.

(3) If the goods do not conform with the contract, the buyer may require the seller to remedy the lack of conformity by repair, unless this is unreasonable having regard to all the circumstances. A request for repair must be made either in conjunction with notice given under article 39 or within a reasonable time thereafter.

Article 47

(1) The buyer may fix an additional period of time of reasonable length for performance by the seller of his obligations.

(2) Unless the buyer has received notice from the seller that he will not perform within the period so fixed, the buyer may not, during that period, resort to any remedy for breach of contract. However, the buyer is not deprived thereby of any right he may have to claim damages for delay in performance.

Article 48

(1) Subject to article 49, the seller may, even after the date for delivery, remedy at his own expense any failure to perform his obligations, if he can do so without unreasonable delay and without causing the buyer unreasonable inconvenience or uncertainty of reimbursement by the seller of expenses

advanced by the buyer. However, the buyer retains any right to claim damages as provided for in this Convention.

(2) If the seller requests the buyer to make known whether he will accept performance and the buyer does not comply with the request within a reasonable time, the seller may perform within the time indicated in his request. The buyer may not, during that period of time, resort to any remedy which is inconsistent with performance by the seller.

(3) A notice by the seller that he will perform within a specified period of time is assumed to include a request, under the preceding paragraph, that the buyer make known his decision.

(4) A request or notice by the seller under paragraph (2) or (3) of this article is not effective unless received by the buyer.

Article 49

(1) The buyer may declare the contract avoided:

(a) if the failure by the seller to perform any of his obligations under the contract or this Convention amounts to a fundamental breach of contract; or

(b) in case of non-delivery, if the seller does not deliver the goods within the additional period of time fixed by the buyer in accordance with paragraph (1) of article 47 or declares that he will not deliver within the period so fixed.

(2) However, in cases where the seller has delivered the goods, the buyer loses the right to declare the contract avoided unless he does so:

(a) in respect of late delivery, within a reasonable time after he has become aware that delivery has been made;

(b) in respect of any breach other than late delivery, within a reasonable time:

(i) after he knew or ought to have known of the breach;

(ii) after the expiration of any additional period of time fixed by the buyer in accordance with paragraph (1) of article 47, or after the seller has declared that he will not perform his obligations within such an additional period; or

(iii) after the expiration of any additional period of time indicated by the seller in accordance with paragraph (2) of article 48, or after the buyer has declared that he will not accept performance.

Article 50

If the goods do not conform with the contract and whether or not the price has already been paid, the buyer may reduce the price in the same proportion as the value that the goods actually delivered had at the time of the delivery bears to the value that conforming goods would have had at that time. However, if the seller remedies any failure to perform his obligations in accordance with article 37 or article 48 or if the buyer refuses to accept performance by the seller in accordance with those articles, the buyer may not reduce the price.

Article 51

(1) If the seller delivers only a part of the goods or if only a part of the goods delivered is in conformity with the contract, articles 46 to 50 apply in respect of the part which is missing or which does not conform.

(2) The buyer may declare the contract avoided in its entirety only if the failure to make delivery completely or in conformity with the contract amounts to a fundamental breach of the contract.

Article 52

(1) If the seller delivers the goods before the date fixed, the buyer may take delivery or refuse to take delivery.

(2) If the seller delivers a quantity of goods greater than that provided for in the contract, the buyer may take delivery or refuse to take delivery of the excess quantity. If the buyer takes delivery of all or part of the excess quantity, he must pay for it at the contract rate.

CHAPTER III. OBLIGATIONS OF THE BUYER

Article 53

The buyer must pay the price for the goods and take delivery of them as required by the contract and this Convention.

Section I. Payment of the price

Article 54

The buyer's obligation to pay the price includes taking such steps and complying with such formalities as may be required under the contract or any laws and regulations to enable payment to be made.

Article 55

Where a contract has been validly concluded but does not expressly or implicitly fix or make provision for determining the price, the parties are considered, in the absence of any indication to the contrary, to have impliedly made reference to the price generally charged at the time of the conclusion of the contract for such goods sold under comparable circumstances in the trade concerned.

Article 56

If the price is fixed according to the weight of the goods, in case of doubt it is to be determined by the net weight.

Article 57

(1) If the buyer is not bound to pay the price at any other particular place, he must pay it to the seller:

(a) at the seller's place of business; or

(b) if the payment is to be made against the handing over of the goods or of documents, at the place where the handing over takes place.

(2) The seller must bear any increase in the expenses incidental to payment which is caused by a change in his place of business subsequent to the conclusion of the contract.

Article 58

(1) If the buyer is not bound to pay the price at any other specific time, he must pay it when the seller places either the goods or documents controlling their disposition at the buyer's disposal in accordance with the

contract and this Convention. The seller may make such payment a condition for handing over the goods or documents.

(2) If the contract involves carriage of the goods, the seller may dispatch the goods on terms whereby the goods, or documents controlling their disposition, will not be handed over to the buyer except against payment of the price.

(3) The buyer is not bound to pay the price until he has had an opportunity to examine the goods, unless the procedures for delivery or payment agreed upon by the parties are inconsistent with his having such an opportunity.

Article 59

The buyer must pay the price on the date fixed by or determinable from the contract and this Convention without the need for any request or compliance with any formality on the part of the seller.

Section II. Taking delivery

Article 60

The buyer's obligation to take delivery consists:

(a) in doing all the acts which could reasonably be expected of him in order to enable the seller to make delivery; and

(b) in taking over the goods.

Section III. Remedies for breach of contract by the buyer

Article 61

(1) If the buyer fails to perform any of his obligations under the contract or this Convention, the seller may:

(a) exercise the rights provided in articles 62 to 65;

(b) claim damages as provided in articles 74 to 77.

(2) The seller is not deprived of any right he may have to claim damages by exercising his right to other remedies.

(3) No period of grace may be granted to the buyer by a court or arbitral tribunal when the seller resorts to a remedy for breach of contract.

Article 62

The seller may require the buyer to pay the price, take delivery or perform his other obligations, unless the seller has resorted to a remedy which is inconsistent with this requirement.

Article 63

(1) The seller may fix an additional period of time of reasonable length for performance by the buyer of his obligations.

(2) Unless the seller has received notice from the buyer that he will not perform within the period so fixed, the seller may not, during that period, resort to any remedy for breach of contract. However, the seller is not deprived thereby of any right he may have to claim damages for delay in performance.

Article 64

(1) The seller may declare the contract avoided:

(a) if the failure by the buyer to perform any of his obligations under the contract or this Convention amounts to a fundamental breach of contract; or

(b) if the buyer does not, within the additional period of time fixed by the seller in accordance with paragraph (1) of article 63, perform his obligation to pay the price or take delivery of the goods, or if he declares that he will not do so within the period so fixed.

(2) However, in cases where the buyer has paid the price, the seller loses the right to declare the contract avoided unless he does so:

(a) in respect of late performance by the buyer, before the seller has become aware that performance has been rendered; or

(b) in respect of any breach other than late performance by the buyer, within a reasonable time:

(i) after the seller knew or ought to have known of the breach; or

(ii) after the expiration of any additional period of time fixed by the seller in accordance with paragraph (1) of article 63, or after the buyer has declared that he will not perform his obligations within such an additional period.

Article 65

(1) If under the contract the buyer is to specify the form, measurement or other features of the goods and he fails to make such specification either on the date agreed upon or within a reasonable time after receipt of a request from the seller, the seller may, without prejudice to any other rights he may have, make the specification himself in accordance with the requirements of the buyer that may be known to him.

(2) If the seller makes the specification himself, he must inform the buyer of the details thereof and must fix a reasonable time within which the buyer may make a different specification. If, after receipt of such a communication, the buyer fails to do so within the time so fixed, the specification made by the seller is binding.

CHAPTER IV. PASSING OF RISK

Article 66

Loss of or damage to the goods after the risk has passed to the buyer does not discharge him from his obligation to pay the price, unless the loss or damage is due to an act or omission of the seller.

Article 67

(1) If the contract of sale involves carriage of the goods and the seller is not bound to hand them over at a particular place, the risk passes to the buyer when the goods are handed over to the first carrier for transmission to the buyer in accordance with the contract of sale. If the seller is bound to hand the goods over to a carrier at a particular place, the risk does not pass to the buyer until the goods are handed over to the carrier at that place. The fact that the seller is authorized to retain documents controlling the disposition of the goods does not affect the passage of the risk.

(2) Nevertheless, the risk does not pass to the buyer until the goods are clearly identified to the contract, whether by markings on the goods, by shipping documents, by notice given to the buyer or otherwise.

Article 68

The risk in respect of goods sold in transit passes to the buyer from the time of the conclusion of the contract. However, if the circumstances so indicate, the risk is assumed by the buyer from the time the goods were handed over to the carrier who issued the documents embodying the contract of carriage. Nevertheless, if at the time of the conclusion of the contract of sale the seller knew or ought to have known that the goods had been lost or damaged and did not disclose this to the buyer, the loss or damage is at the risk of the seller.

Article 69

(1) In cases not within articles 67 and 68, the risk passes to the buyer when he takes over the goods or, if he does not do so in due time, from the time when the goods are placed at his disposal and he commits a breach of contract by failing to take delivery.

(2) However, if the buyer is bound to take over the goods at a place other than a place of business of the seller, the risk passes when delivery is due and the buyer is aware of the fact that the goods are placed at his disposal at that place.

(3) If the contract relates to goods not then identified, the goods are considered not to be placed at the disposal of the buyer until they are clearly identified to the contract.

Article 70

If the seller has committed a fundamental breach of contract, articles 67, 68 and 69 do not impair the remedies available to the buyer on account of the breach.

CHAPTER V. PROVISIONS COMMON TO THE OBLIGATIONS OF THE SELLER AND OF THE BUYER

Section I. Anticipatory breach and instalment contracts

Article 71

(1) A party may suspend the performance of his obligations if, after the conclusion of the contract, it becomes apparent that the other party will not perform a substantial part of his obligations as a result of:

(a) a serious deficiency in his ability to perform or in his creditworthiness; or

(b) his conduct in preparing to perform or in performing the contract.

(2) If the seller has already dispatched the goods before the grounds described in the preceding paragraph become evident, he may prevent the handing over of the goods to the buyer even though the buyer holds a document which entitles him to obtain them. The present paragraph relates only to the rights in the goods as between the buyer and the seller.

(3) A party suspending performance, whether before or after dispatch of the goods, must immediately give notice of the suspension to the other party and must continue with performance if the other party provides adequate assurance of his performance.

Article 72

(1) If prior to the date for performance of the contract it is clear that one of the parties will commit a fundamental breach of contract, the other party may declare the contract avoided.

(2) If time allows, the party intending to declare the contract avoided must give reasonable notice to the other party in order to permit him to provide adequate assurance of his performance.

(3) The requirements of the preceding paragraph do not apply if the other party has declared that he will not perform his obligations.

Article 73

(1) In the case of a contract for delivery of goods by instalments, if the failure of one party to perform any of his obligations in respect of any instalment constitutes a fundamental breach of contract with respect to that instalment, the other party may declare the contract avoided with respect to that instalment.

(2) If one party's failure to perform any of his obligations in respect of any instalment gives the other party good grounds to conclude that a fundamental breach of contract will occur with respect to future instalments, he may declare the contract avoided for the future, provided that he does so within a reasonable time.

(3) A buyer who declares the contract avoided in respect of any delivery may, at the same time, declare it avoided in respect of deliveries already made or of future deliveries if, by reason of their interdependence, those deliveries could not be used for the purpose contemplated by the parties at the time of the conclusion of the contract.

Section II. Damages

Article 74

Damages for breach of contract by one party consist of a sum equal to the loss, including loss of profit, suffered by the other party as a consequence of the breach. Such damages may not exceed the loss which the party in breach foresaw or ought to have foreseen at the time of the conclusion of the contract, in the light of the facts and matters of which he then knew or ought to have known, as a possible consequence of the breach of contract.

Article 75

If the contract is avoided and if, in a reasonable manner and within a reasonable time after avoidance, the buyer has bought goods in replacement or the seller has resold the goods, the party claiming damages may recover the difference between the contract price and the price in the substitute transaction as well as any further damages recoverable under article 74.

Article 76

(1) If the contract is avoided and there is a current price for the goods, the party claiming damages may, if he has not made a purchase or resale under article 75, recover the difference between the price fixed by the contract and the current price at the time of avoidance as well as any further damages recoverable under article 74. If, however, the party claiming damages has avoided the contract after taking over the goods, the current price at the time of such taking over shall be applied instead of the current price at the time of avoidance.

(2) For the purposes of the preceding paragraph, the current price is the price prevailing at the place where delivery of the goods should have been made or, if there is no current price at that place, the price at such other place as serves as a reasonable substitute, making due allowance for differences in the cost of transporting the goods.

Article 77

A party who relies on a breach of contract must take such measures as are reasonable in the circumstances to mitigate the loss, including loss of profit, resulting from the breach. If he fails to take such measures, the party in breach may claim a reduction in the damages in the amount by which the loss should have been mitigated.

Section III. Interest

Article 78

If a party fails to pay the price or any other sum that is in arrears, the other party is entitled to interest on it, without prejudice to any claim for damages recoverable under article 74.

Section IV. Exemptions

Article 79

(1) A party is not liable for a failure to perform any of his obligations if he proves that the failure was due to an impediment beyond his control and that he could not reasonably be expected to have taken the impediment into account at the time of the conclusion of the contract or to have avoided or overcome it, or its consequences.

(2) If the party's failure is due to the failure by a third person whom he has engaged to perform the whole or a part of the contract, that party is exempt from liability only if:

(a) he is exempt under the preceding paragraph; and

(b) the person whom he has so engaged would be so exempt if the provisions of that paragraph were applied to him.

(3) The exemption provided by this article has effect for the period during which the impediment exists.

(4) The party who fails to perform must give notice to the other party of the impediment and its effect on his ability to perform. If the notice is not received by the other party within a reasonable time after the party who fails to perform knew or ought to have known of the impediment, he is liable for damages resulting from such non-receipt.

(5) Nothing in this article prevents either party from exercising any right other than to claim damages under this Convention.

Article 80

A party may not rely on a failure of the other party to perform, to the extent that such failure was caused by the first party's act or omission.

Section V. Effects of avoidance

Article 81

(1) Avoidance of the contract releases both parties from their obligations under it, subject to any damages which may be due. Avoidance does not affect any provision of the contract for the settlement of disputes or any other provision of the contract governing the rights and obligations of the parties consequent upon the avoidance of the contract.

(2) A party who has performed the contract either wholly or in part may claim restitution from the other party of whatever the first party has supplied or paid under the contract. If both parties are bound to make restitution, they must do so concurrently.

Article 82

(1) The buyer loses the right to declare the contract avoided or to require the seller to deliver substitute goods if it is impossible for him to make restitution of the goods substantially in the condition in which he received them.

(2) The preceding paragraph does not apply:

(a) if the impossibility of making restitution of the goods or of making restitution of the goods substantially in the condition in which the buyer received them is not due to his act or omission;

(b) if the goods or part of the goods have perished or deteriorated as a result of the examination provided for in article 38; or

(c) if the goods or part of the goods have been sold in the normal course of business or have been consumed or transformed by the buyer in the course of normal use before he discovered or ought to have discovered the lack of conformity.

Article 83

A buyer who has lost the right to declare the contract avoided or to require the seller to deliver substitute goods in accordance with article 82 retains all other remedies under the contract and this Convention.

Article 84

(1) If the seller is bound to refund the price, he must also pay interest on it, from the date on which the price was paid.

(2) The buyer must account to the seller for all benefits which he has derived from the goods or part of them:

(a) if he must make restitution of the goods or part of them; or

(b) if it is impossible for him to make restitution of all or part of the goods or to make restitution of all or part of the goods substantially in the condition in which he received them, but he has nevertheless declared the contract avoided or required the seller to deliver substitute goods.

Section VI. Preservation of the goods

Article 85

If the buyer is in delay in taking delivery of the goods or, where payment of the price and delivery of the goods are to be made concurrently, if he fails to pay the price, and the seller is either in possession of the goods or otherwise able to control their disposition, the seller must take such steps as are reasonable in the circumstances to preserve them. He is entitled to retain them until he has been reimbursed his reasonable expenses by the buyer.

Article 86

(1) If the buyer has received the goods and intends to exercise any right under the contract or this Convention to reject them, he must take such steps to preserve them as are reasonable in the circumstances. He is entitled to retain them until he has been reimbursed his reasonable expenses by the seller.

(2) If goods dispatched to the buyer have been placed at his disposal at their destination and he exercises the right to reject them, he must take

possession of them on behalf of the seller, provided that this can be done without payment of the price and without unreasonable inconvenience or unreasonable expense. This provision does not apply if the seller or a person authorized to take charge of the goods on his behalf is present at the destination. If the buyer takes possession of the goods under this paragraph, his rights and obligations are governed by the preceding paragraph.

Article 87

A party who is bound to take steps to preserve the goods may deposit them in a warehouse of a third person at the expense of the other party provided that the expense incurred is not unreasonable.

Article 88

(1) A party who is bound to preserve the goods in accordance with article 85 or 86 may sell them by any appropriate means if there has been an unreasonable delay by the other party in taking possession of the goods or in taking them back or in paying the price or the cost of preservation, provided that reasonable notice of the intention to sell has been given to the other party.

(2) If the goods are subject to rapid deterioration or their preservation would involve unreasonable expense, a party who is bound to preserve the goods in accordance with article 85 or 86 must take reasonable measures to sell them. To the extent possible he must give notice to the other party of his intention to sell.

(3) A party selling the goods has the right to retain out of the proceeds of sale an amount equal to the reasonable expenses of preserving the goods and of selling them. He must account to the other party for the balance.

PART IV. FINAL PROVISIONS

Article 89

The Secretary-General of the United Nations is hereby designated as the depositary for this Convention.

Article 90

This Convention does not prevail over any international agreement which has already been or may be entered into and which contains provisions concerning the matters governed by this Convention, provided that the parties have their places of business in States parties to such agreement.

Article 91

(1) This Convention is open for signature at the concluding meeting of the United Nations Conference on Contracts for the International Sale of Goods and will remain open for signature by all States at the Headquarters of the United Nations, New York until 30 September 1981.

(2) This Convention is subject to ratification, acceptance or approval by the signatory States.

(3) This Convention is open for accession by all States which are not signatory States as from the date it is open for signature.

(4) Instruments of ratification, acceptance, approval and accession are to be deposited with the Secretary-General of the United Nations.

Article 92

(1) A Contracting State may declare at the time of signature, ratification, acceptance, approval or accession that it will not be bound by Part II of this Convention or that it will not be bound by Part III of this Convention.

(2) A Contracting State which makes a declaration in accordance with the preceding paragraph in respect of Part II or Part III of this Convention is not to be considered a Contracting State within paragraph (1) of article 1 of this Convention in respect of matters governed by the Part to which the declaration applies.

Article 93

(1) If a Contracting State has two or more territorial units in which, according to its constitution, different systems of law are applicable in relation to the matters dealt with in this Convention, it may, at the time of signature, ratification, acceptance, approval or accession, declare that this Convention is to extend to all its territorial units or only to one or more of them, and may amend its declaration by submitting another declaration at any time.

(2) These declarations are to be notified to the depositary and are to state expressly the territorial units to which the Convention extends.

(3) If, by virtue of a declaration under this article, this Convention extends to one or more but not all of the territorial units of a Contracting State, and if the place of business of a party is located in that State, this place of business, for the purposes of this Convention, is considered not to be in a Contracting State, unless it is in a territorial unit to which the Convention extends.

(4) If a Contracting State makes no declaration under paragraph (1) of this article, the Convention is to extend to all territorial units of that State.

Article 94

(1) Two or more Contracting States which have the same or closely related legal rules on matters governed by this Convention may at any time declare that the Convention is not to apply to contracts of sale or to their formation where the parties have their places of business in those States. Such declarations may be made jointly or by reciprocal unilateral declarations.

(2) A Contracting State which has the same or closely related legal rules on matters governed by this Convention as one or more non-Contracting States may at any time declare that the Convention is not to apply to contracts of sale or to their formation where the parties have their places of business in those States.

(3) If a State which is the object of a declaration under the preceding paragraph subsequently becomes a Contracting State, the declaration made will, as from the date on which the Convention enters into force in respect of the new Contracting State, have the effect of a declaration made under paragraph (1), provided that the new Contracting State joins in such declaration or makes a reciprocal unilateral declaration.

Article 95

Any State may declare at the time of the deposit of its instrument of ratification, acceptance, approval or accession that it will not be bound by subparagraph (1)*(b)* of article 1 of this Convention.

Article 96

A Contracting State whose legislation requires contracts of sale to be concluded in or evidenced by writing may at any time make a declaration in accordance with article 12 that any provision of article 11, article 29, or Part II of this Convention, that allows a contract of sale or its modification or termination by agreement or any offer, acceptance, or other indication of intention to be made in any form other than in writing, does not apply where any party has his place of business in that State.

Article 97

(1) Declarations made under this Convention at the time of signature are subject to confirmation upon ratification, acceptance or approval.

(2) Declarations and confirmations of declarations are to be in writing and be formally notified to the depositary.

(3) A declaration takes effect simultaneously with the entry into force of this Convention in respect of the State concerned. However, a declaration of which the depositary receives formal notification after such entry into force takes effect on the first day of the month following the expiration of six months after the date of its receipt by the depositary. Reciprocal unilateral declarations under article 94 take effect on the first day of the month following the expiration of six months after the receipt of the latest declaration by the depositary.

(4) Any State which makes a declaration under this Convention may withdraw it at any time by a formal notification in writing addressed to the depositary. Such withdrawal is to take effect on the first day of the month following the expiration of six months after the date of the receipt of the notification by the depositary.

(5) A withdrawal of a declaration made under article 94 renders inoperative, as from the date on which the withdrawal takes effect, any reciprocal declaration made by another State under that article.

Article 98

No reservations are permitted except those expressly authorized in this Convention.

Article 99

(1) This Convention enters into force, subject to the provisions of paragraph (6) of this article, on the first day of the month following the expiration of twelve months after the date of deposit of the tenth instrument of ratification, acceptance, approval or accession, including an instrument which contains a declaration made under article 92.

(2) When a State ratifies, accepts, approves or accedes to this Convention after the deposit of the tenth instrument of ratification, acceptance, approval or accession, this Convention, with the exception of the Part excluded, enters into force in respect of that State, subject to the provisions of paragraph (6) of this article, on the first day of the month following the expiration of twelve months after the date of the deposit of its instrument of ratification, acceptance, approval or accession.

(3) A State which ratifies, accepts, approves or accedes to this Convention and is a party to either or both the Convention relating to a Uniform Law on the Formation of Contracts for the International Sale of Goods done at The Hague on 1 July 1964 (1964 Hague Formation Convention) and the Convention relating to a Uniform Law on the International Sale of Goods done at The Hague on 1 July 1964 (1964 Hague Sales Convention) shall at the same time denounce, as the case may be, either or both the 1964 Hague Sales Convention and the 1964 Hague Formation Convention by notifying the Government of the Netherlands to that effect.

(4) A State party to the 1964 Hague Sales Convention which ratifies, accepts, approves or accedes to the present Convention and declares or has declared under article 92 that it will not be bound by Part II of this Convention shall at the time of ratification, acceptance, approval or accession denounce the 1964 Hague Sales Convention by notifying the Government of the Netherlands to that effect.

(5) A State party to the 1964 Hague Formation Convention which ratifies, accepts, approves or accedes to the present Convention and declares or has declared under article 92 that it will not be bound by Part III of this Convention shall at the time of ratification, acceptance, approval or accession denounce the 1964 Hague Formation Convention by notifying the Government of the Netherlands to that effect.

(6) For the purpose of this article, ratifications, acceptances, approvals and accessions in respect of this Convention by States parties to the 1964 Hague Formation Convention or to the 1964 Hague Sales Convention shall not be effective until such denunciations as may be required on the part

of those States in respect of the latter two Conventions have themselves become effective. The depositary of this Convention shall consult with the Government of the Netherlands, as the depositary of the 1964 Conventions, so as to ensure necessary coordination in this respect.

Article 100

(1) This Convention applies to the formation of a contract only when the proposal for concluding the contract is made on or after the date when the Convention enters into force in respect of the Contracting States referred to in subparagraph (1)*(a)* or the Contracting State referred to in subparagraph (1)*(b)* of article 1.

(2) This Convention applies only to contracts concluded on or after the date when the Convention enters into force in respect of the Contracting States referred to in subparagraph (1)*(a)* or the Contracting State referred to in subparagraph (1)*(b)* of article 1.

Article 101

(1) A Contracting State may denounce this Convention, or Part II or Part III of the Convention, by a formal notification in writing addressed to the depositary.

(2) The denunciation takes effect on the first day of the month following the expiration of twelve months after the notification is received by the depositary. Where a longer period for the denunciation to take effect is specified in the notification, the denunciation takes effect upon the expiration of such longer period after the notification is received by the depositary.

DONE at Vienna, this day of eleventh day of April, one thousand nine hundred and eighty, in a single original, of which the Arabic, Chinese, English, French, Russian and Spanish texts are equally authentic.

IN WITNESS WHEREOF the undersigned plenipotentiaries, being duly authorized by their respective Governments, have signed this Convention.

II. Explanatory Note by the UNCITRAL Secretariat on the United Nations Convention on Contracts for the International Sale of Goods

This note has been prepared by the Secretariat of the United Nations Commission on International Trade Law for informational purposes; it is not an official commentary on the Convention.

Introduction

1. The United Nations Convention on Contracts for the International Sale of Goods provides a uniform text of law for international sales of goods. The Convention was prepared by the United Nations Commission on International Trade Law (UNCITRAL) and adopted by a diplomatic conference on 11 April 1980.

2. Preparation of a uniform law for the international sale of goods began in 1930 at the International Institute for the Unification of Private Law (UNIDROIT) in Rome. After a long interruption in the work as a result of the Second World War, the draft was submitted to a diplomatic conference in The Hague in 1964, which adopted two conventions, one on the international sale of goods and the other on the formation of contracts for the international sale of goods.

3. Almost immediately upon the adoption of the two conventions there was widespread criticism of their provisions as reflecting primarily the legal traditions and economic realities of continental Western Europe, which was the region that had most actively contributed to their preparation. As a result, one of the first tasks undertaken by UNCITRAL on its organization in 1968 was to enquire of States whether or not they intended to adhere to those conventions and the reasons for their positions. In the light of the responses received, UNCITRAL decided to study the two conventions to ascertain which modifications might render them capable of wider acceptance by countries of different legal, social and economic systems. The result of this study was the adoption by diplomatic conference on 11 April 1980 of the

United Nations Convention on Contracts for the International Sale of Goods, which combines the subject matter of the two prior conventions.

4. UNCITRAL's success in preparing a Convention with wider acceptability is evidenced by the fact that the original eleven States for which the Convention came into force on 1 January 1988 included States from every geographical region, every stage of economic development and every major legal, social and economic system. The original eleven States were: Argentina, China, Egypt, France, Hungary, Italy, Lesotho, Syria, United States, Yugoslavia and Zambia.

5. As of 1 September 2010, 76 States are parties to the Convention. The current updated status of the Convention is available on the UNCITRAL website.[1] Authoritative information on the status of the Convention, as well as on related declarations, including with respect to territorial application and succession of States, may be found on the United Nations Treaty Collection on the Internet.[2]

6. The Convention is divided into four parts. Part One deals with the scope of application of the Convention and the general provisions. Part Two contains the rules governing the formation of contracts for the international sale of goods. Part Three deals with the substantive rights and obligations of buyer and seller arising from the contract. Part Four contains the final clauses of the Convention concerning such matters as how and when it comes into force, the reservations and declarations that are permitted and the application of the Convention to international sales where both States concerned have the same or similar law on the subject.

Part One. Scope of application and general provisions

A. Scope of application

7. The articles on scope of application indicate both what is covered by the Convention and what is not covered. The Convention applies to contracts of sale of goods between parties whose places of business are in different States and either both of those States are Contracting States or the rules of private international law lead to the law of a Contracting State. A few States have availed themselves of the authorization in article 95 to declare that they would apply the Convention only in the former and not in the latter of these two situations. As the Convention becomes more widely adopted, the

[1] www.uncitral.org/uncitral/en/uncitral_texts/sale_goods/1980CISG_status.html.
[2] http://treaties.un.org/.

practical significance of such a declaration will diminish. Finally, the Convention may also apply as the law applicable to the contract if so chosen by the parties. In that case, the operation of the Convention will be subject to any limits on contractual stipulations set by the otherwise applicable law.

8. The final clauses make two additional restrictions on the territorial scope of application that will be relevant to a few States. One applies only if a State is a party to another international agreement that contains provisions concerning matters governed by this Convention; the other permits States that have the same or similar domestic law of sales to declare that the Convention does not apply between them.

9. Contracts of sale are distinguished from contracts for services in two respects by article 3. A contract for the supply of goods to be manufactured or produced is considered to be a sale unless the party who orders the goods undertakes to supply a substantial part of the materials necessary for their manufacture or production. When the preponderant part of the obligations of the party who furnishes the goods consists in the supply of labour or other services, the Convention does not apply.

10. The Convention contains a list of types of sales that are excluded from the Convention, either because of the purpose of the sale (goods bought for personal, family or household use), the nature of the sale (sale by auction, on execution or otherwise by law) or the nature of the goods (stocks, shares, investment securities, negotiable instruments, money, ships, vessels, hovercraft, aircraft or electricity). In many States some or all of such sales are governed by special rules reflecting their special nature.

11. Several articles make clear that the subject matter of the Convention is restricted to formation of the contract and the rights and duties of the buyer and seller arising from such a contract. In particular, the Convention is not concerned with the validity of the contract, the effect which the contract may have on the property in the goods sold or the liability of the seller for death or personal injury caused by the goods to any person.

B. Party autonomy

12. The basic principle of contractual freedom in the international sale of goods is recognized by the provision that permits the parties to exclude the application of this Convention or derogate from or vary the effect of any of its provisions. This exclusion will occur, for example, if parties choose the law of a non-contracting State or the substantive domestic law of a contracting State as the law applicable to the contract. Derogation from the Convention

will occur whenever a provision in the contract provides a different rule from that found in the Convention.

C. Interpretation of the Convention

13. This Convention for the unification of the law governing the international sale of goods will better fulfil its purpose if it is interpreted in a consistent manner in all legal systems. Great care was taken in its preparation to make it as clear and easy to understand as possible. Nevertheless, disputes will arise as to its meaning and application. When this occurs, all parties, including domestic courts and arbitral tribunals, are admonished to observe its international character and to promote uniformity in its application and the observance of good faith in international trade. In particular, when a question concerning a matter governed by this Convention is not expressly settled in it, the question is to be settled in conformity with the general principles on which the Convention is based. Only in the absence of such principles should the matter be settled in conformity with the law applicable by virtue of the rules of private international law.

D. Interpretation of the contract; usages

14. The Convention contains provisions on the manner in which statements and conduct of a party are to be interpreted in the context of the formation of the contract or its implementation. Usages agreed to by the parties, practices they have established between themselves and usages of which the parties knew or ought to have known and which are widely known to, and regularly observed by, parties to contracts of the type involved in the particular trade concerned may all be binding on the parties to the contract of sale.

E. Form of the contract

15. The Convention does not subject the contract of sale to any requirement as to form. In particular, article 11 provides that no written agreement is necessary for the conclusion of the contract. However, if the contract is in writing and it contains a provision requiring any modification or termination by agreement to be in writing, article 29 provides that the contract may not be otherwise modified or terminated by agreement. The only exception is that a party may be precluded by his conduct from asserting such a provision to the extent that the other person has relied on that conduct.

16. In order to accommodate those States whose legislation requires contracts of sale to be concluded in or evidenced by writing, article 96 entitles those

States to declare that neither article 11 nor the exception to article 29 applies where any party to the contract has his place of business in that State.

Part Two. Formation of the contract

17. Part Two of the Convention deals with a number of questions that arise in the formation of the contract by the exchange of an offer and an acceptance. When the formation of the contract takes place in this manner, the contract is concluded when the acceptance of the offer becomes effective.

18. In order for a proposal for concluding a contract to constitute an offer, it must be addressed to one or more specific persons and it must be sufficiently definite. For the proposal to be sufficiently definite, it must indicate the goods and expressly or implicitly fix or make provisions for determining the quantity and the price.

19. The Convention takes a middle position between the doctrine of the revocability of the offer until acceptance and its general irrevocability for some period of time. The general rule is that an offer may be revoked. However, the revocation must reach the offeree before he has dispatched an acceptance. Moreover, an offer cannot be revoked if it indicates that it is irrevocable, which it may do by stating a fixed time for acceptance or otherwise. Furthermore, an offer may not be revoked if it was reasonable for the offeree to rely on the offer as being irrevocable and the offeree has acted in reliance on the offer.

20. Acceptance of an offer may be made by means of a statement or other conduct of the offeree indicating assent to the offer that is communicated to the offeror. However, in some cases the acceptance may consist of performing an act, such as dispatch of the goods or payment of the price. Such an act would normally be effective as an acceptance the moment the act was performed.

21. A frequent problem in contract formation, perhaps especially in regard to contracts of sale of goods, arises out of a reply to an offer that purports to be an acceptance but contains additional or different terms. Under the Convention, if the additional or different terms do not materially alter the terms of the offer, the reply constitutes an acceptance, unless the offeror without undue delay objects to those terms. If he does not object, the terms of the contract are the terms of the offer with the modifications contained in the acceptance.

22. If the additional or different terms do materially alter the terms of the contract, the reply constitutes a counter-offer that must in turn be accepted

for a contract to be concluded. Additional or different terms relating, among other things, to the price, payment, quality and quantity of the goods, place and time of delivery, extent of one party's liability to the other or settlement of disputes are considered to alter the terms of the offer materially.

Part Three. Sale of goods

A. Obligations of the seller

23. The general obligations of the seller are to deliver the goods, hand over any documents relating to them and transfer the property in the goods, as required by the contract and this Convention. The Convention provides supplementary rules for use in the absence of contractual agreement as to when, where and how the seller must perform these obligations.

24. The Convention provides a number of rules that implement the seller's obligations in respect of the quality of the goods. In general, the seller must deliver goods that are of the quantity, quality and description required by the contract and that are contained or packaged in the manner required by the contract. One set of rules of particular importance in international sales of goods involves the seller's obligation to deliver goods that are free from any right or claim of a third party, including rights based on industrial property or other intellectual property.

25. In connection with the seller's obligations in regard to the quality of the goods, the Convention contains provisions on the buyer's obligation to inspect the goods. He must give notice of any lack of conformity with the contract within a reasonable time after he has discovered it or ought to have discovered it, and at the latest two years from the date on which the goods were actually handed over to the buyer, unless this time limit is inconsistent with a contractual period of guarantee.

B. Obligations of the buyer

26. The general obligations of the buyer are to pay the price for the goods and take delivery of them as required by the contract and the Convention. The Convention provides supplementary rules for use in the absence of contractual agreement as to how the price is to be determined and where and when the buyer should perform his obligations to pay the price.

C. Remedies for breach of contract

27. The remedies of the buyer for breach of contract by the seller are set forth in connection with the obligations of the seller and the remedies of the seller are set forth in connection with the obligations of the buyer. This makes it easier to use and understand the Convention.

28. The general pattern of remedies is the same in both cases. If all the required conditions are fulfilled, the aggrieved party may require performance of the other party's obligations, claim damages or avoid the contract. The buyer also has the right to reduce the price where the goods delivered do not conform with the contract.

29. Among the more important limitations on the right of an aggrieved party to claim a remedy is the concept of fundamental breach. For a breach of contract to be fundamental, it must result in such detriment to the other party as substantially to deprive him of what he is entitled to expect under the contract, unless the result was neither foreseen by the party in breach nor foreseeable by a reasonable person of the same kind in the same circumstances. A buyer can require the delivery of substitute goods only if the goods delivered were not in conformity with the contract and the lack of conformity constituted a fundamental breach of contract. The existence of a fundamental breach is one of the two circumstances that justifies a declaration of avoidance of a contract by the aggrieved party; the other circumstance being that, in the case of non-delivery of the goods by the seller or non-payment of the price or failure to take delivery by the buyer, the party in breach fails to perform within a reasonable period of time fixed by the aggrieved party.

30. Other remedies may be restricted by special circumstances. For example, if the goods do not conform with the contract, the buyer may require the seller to remedy the lack of conformity by repair, unless this is unreasonable having regard to all the circumstances. A party cannot recover damages that he could have mitigated by taking the proper measures. A party may be exempted from paying damages by virtue of an impediment beyond his control.

D. Passing of risk

31. Determining the exact moment when the risk of loss or damage to the goods passes from the seller to the buyer is of great importance in contracts for the international sale of goods. Parties may regulate the issue in their contract either by an express provision or by the use of a trade term such as, for example, an INCOTERM. The effect of the choice of such a term

would be to amend the corresponding provisions of the CISG accordingly. However, for the frequent case where the contract does not contain such a provision, the Convention sets forth a complete set of rules.

32. The two special situations contemplated by the Convention are when the contract of sale involves carriage of the goods and when the goods are sold while in transit. In all other cases the risk passes to the buyer when he takes over the goods or from the time when the goods are placed at his disposal and he commits a breach of contract by failing to take delivery, whichever comes first. In the frequent case when the contract relates to goods that are not then identified, they must be identified to the contract before they can be considered to be placed at the disposal of the buyer and the risk of their loss can be considered to have passed to him.

E. Suspension of performance and anticipatory breach

33. The Convention contains special rules for the situation in which, prior to the date on which performance is due, it becomes apparent that one of the parties will not perform a substantial part of his obligations or will commit a fundamental breach of contract. A distinction is drawn between those cases in which the other party may suspend his own performance of the contract but the contract remains in existence awaiting future events and those cases in which he may declare the contract avoided.

F. Exemption from liability to pay damages

34. When a party fails to perform any of his obligations due to an impediment beyond his control that he could not reasonably have been expected to take into account at the time of the conclusion of the contract and that he could not have avoided or overcome, he is exempted from the consequences of his failure to perform, including the payment of damages. This exemption may also apply if the failure is due to the failure of a third person whom he has engaged to perform the whole or a part of the contract. However, he is subject to any other remedy, including reduction of the price, if the goods were defective in some way.

G. Preservation of the goods

35. The Convention imposes on both parties the duty to preserve any goods in their possession belonging to the other party. Such a duty is of even greater importance in an international sale of goods where the other party is from a

foreign country and may not have agents in the country where the goods are located. Under certain circumstances the party in possession of the goods may sell them, or may even be required to sell them. A party selling the goods has the right to retain out of the proceeds of sale an amount equal to the reasonable expenses of preserving the goods and of selling them and must account to the other party for the balance.

Part Four. Final clauses

36. The final clauses contain the usual provisions relating to the Secretary-General as depositary and providing that the Convention is subject to ratification, acceptance or approval by those States that signed it by 30 September 1981, that it is open to accession by all States that are not signatory States and that the text is equally authentic in Arabic, Chinese, English, French, Russian and Spanish.

37. The Convention permits a certain number of declarations. Those relative to scope of application and the requirement as to a written contract have been mentioned above. There is a special declaration for States that have different systems of law governing contracts of sale in different parts of their territory. Finally, a State may declare that it will not be bound by Part II on formation of contracts or Part III on the rights and obligations of the buyer and seller. This latter declaration was included as part of the decision to combine into one convention the subject matter of the two 1964 Hague Conventions.

Complementary texts

38. The United Nations Convention on Contracts for the International Sale of Goods is complemented by the United Nations Convention on the Limitation Period in the International Sale of Goods, 1974, as amended by a Protocol in 1980 (the Limitation Convention). The Limitation Convention establishes uniform rules governing the period of time within which a party under a contract for the international sale of goods must commence legal proceedings against another party to assert a claim arising from the contract or relating to its breach, termination or validity. The amending Protocol of 1980 ensures that the scope of application of the Limitation Convention is identical to the one of the United Nations Convention on Contracts for the International Sale of Goods.

39. The United Nations Convention on Contracts for the International Sale of Goods is also complemented, with respect to the use of electronic communications,

by the United Nations Convention on the Use of Electronic Communications in International Contracts, 2005 (the Electronic Communications Convention). The Electronic Communications Convention aims at facilitating the use of electronic communications in international trade by assuring that contracts concluded and other communications exchanged electronically are as valid and enforceable as their traditional paper-based equivalents. The Electronic Communications Convention may help to avoid misinterpretation of the CISG that might occur, for example, when a State has lodged a declaration mandating the use of the traditional written form for contracts for the international sale of goods. It may also promote the understanding that the "communication" and/or "writing" under the CISG should be construed so as to include electronic communications. The Electronic Communications Convention is an enabling treaty whose effect is to remove those formal obstacles by establishing the requirements for functional equivalence between electronic and traditional written form.

Further information can be obtained from:

UNCITRAL Secretariat
P.O. Box 500
Vienna International Centre
1400 Vienna
Austria
Telephone: (+43-1) 26060-4060
Telefax: (+43-1) 26060-5813
E-mail: uncitral@uncitral.org
Internet: www.uncitral.org

INDEX